LATE QUATERNARY LANDSCAPE EVOLUTION OF THE SWALE—URE WASHLANDS, NORTH YORKSHIRE

LATE QUATERNARY LANDSCAPE EVOLUTION OF THE SWALE–URE WASHLANDS, NORTH YORKSHIRE

edited by

David Bridgland, Jim Innes, Antony Long and Wishart Mitchell

Oxbow Books
Oxford and Oakville

Published by
Oxbow Books, Oxford, UK

© Oxbow Books and the individual authors, 2011

ISBN 978-1-84217-374-9

Cover image:
Aerial view of Marfield quarry from the north-east, with the River Ure meandering across the foreground.
The Marfield palaeochannel joins the river beyond the farm.

This book is available direct from:

Oxbow Books, Oxford, UK
(Phone: 01865-241249; Fax: 01865-794449)

and

The David Brown Book Company
PO Box 511, Oakville, CT 06779, USA
(Phone: 860-945-9329; Fax: 860-945-9468)

or from our website

www.oxbowbooks.com

A CIP record for this book is available from the British Library

Library of Congress Cataloging-in-Publication Data

Late Quaternary landscape evolution of the Swale-Ure washlands, North Yorkshire / edited by David Bridgland ... [et al.].
    p. cm.
  ISBN 978-1-84217-374-9 (hardback)
  1. Paleoecology--Holocene. 2. Paleoecology--England--North Yorkshire. 3. Paleogeography--Holocene. 4. Paleogeography--England--North Yorkshire. I. Bridgland, D. R.
  QE741.3.L38 2010
  551.7'93094284--dc22
                        2010050070

Printed and bound in Great Britain by
Short Run Press, Exeter

Contents

APPENDICES (on CD)

List of figures, tables and plates

Figures

Fig. 1.1. Aerial photograph (looking southwards) showing the quarry complex at Nosterfield with the three henges in the left middle distance. The northern henge, in the centre of the view, is under trees.

Fig. 1.2. Correlation diagram showing the Greenland ice-core record and the dated palaeo-climatic records from Britain and NW Europe. After Walker (2005). SMOW = Standard Mean Ocean Water.

Fig. 1.3. Distribution of erratics within the Washlands and adjacent areas. Data from Howarth (1908) and Harmer (1928).

Fig. 1.4. Summary distribution of moraine ridge fragments and meltwater channels in the project area (combining BGS data with mapping from this project). For the explanation of points labelled (in circles) K, L, M & W, see text (Section 4.3).

Fig. 1.5. Distribution of lake sediments cropping out in the Washlands (from BGS mapping).

Fig. 1.6. Idealized cross section through the terrace sequence of the Mosedale Beck, near Troutbeck, Cumbria (NE Lake District). Note that the highest (deglaciation) terrace was formed during the Loch Lomond Stadial (after Boardman, 1981).

Fig. 1.7. Idealized cross section through the terrace sequence in Upper Wharfedale (after Howard et al., 2000b).

Fig. 1.8. Flood data plotted against post-glacial time, showing timing of various anthropogenic impacts. Modified from Lewin et al. (2005).

Fig. 1.9. Distribution of palaeoenvironmental sites in the Yorkshire region mentioned in the text. 1. Hartlepool (Waughman, 2005) 2. Thorpe Bulmer (Bartley et al., 1976) 3. Hutton Henry (Bartley et al., 1976) 4. Bishop Middleham (Bartley et al., 1976) 5. Mordon Carr (Bartley et al., 1976) 6. Burtree Lane (Bellamy et al, 1966) 7. Neasham Fen (Bartley et al., 1976) 8. Seamer Carrs (Jones, 1976a) 9. Kildale Hall (Keen et al., 1984) 10. West House Moss (Jones, 1978) 11. Ewe Crag Slack (Jones, 1978) 12. White Gill (Dimbleby, 1962) 13. North Gill (Innes & Simmons, 2000) 14. Wheeldale Gill (Simmons & Cundill, 1974) 15. May Moss (Atherden, 1979; Chiverrell, 2001) 16. Harwood Dale Bog (Atherden, 1989) 17. Collier Gill (Simmons & Cundill, 1974) 18. Fen Bogs (Atherden, 1976) 19. Bonfield Gill Head (Simmons & Innes, 1988) 20. Botany Bay (Simmons & Innes, 1988) 21. Harold's Bog (Blackford & Chambers, 1999) 22. Star Carr (Day, 1996) 23. Seamer Carr (Cloutman & Smith, 1988) 24. Flixton Carr (Godwin & Willis, 1959) 25. Willow Garth (Bush, 1993) 26. Kilham Long Barrow (Manby, 1976) 27. Gransmoor Quarry (Lowe et al., 1995) 28. Skipsea Bail Mere (Flenley, 1984) and Skipsea Withow Mere (Hunt et al., 1984) 29. The Old Mere, Hornsea (Beckett, 1981) 30. Gilderson Marr (Tweddle, 2001) 31. The Bog, Roos (Beckett, 1981) 32. Routh Quarry (Lillie & Gearey, 2000) 33. Thorne Moors (Smith, 2002) 34. Hatfield Moors (Smith, 2002) 35. Burton Salmon (Norris et al., 1971) 36. Cawood (Jones & Gaunt, 1976) 37. Tadcaster (Bartley, 1962) 38. Askham Bog (Gearey & Lillie, 1999) 39. St. George's Field (Lillie & Gearey, 1999) 40. Gormire Lake (Blackham et al., 1981; Oldfield et al., 2003) 41. Dishforth Bog (Giles, 1992) 42. Fountains Earth (Tinsley, 1975) 43. Fortress Dike (Tinsley, 1976b) 44. Skell Gill (Tinsley, 1975) 45. Red Sike Moss (Turner et al., 1973) 46. Mire Holes (Squires, 1978) 47. Gate Gutter (Gear & Turner, 2001) 48. Whirly Gill (Honeyman, 1985) 49. Thornton Mires (Honeyman, 1985) 50. Fleet Moss (Honeyman, 1985) 51. Stump Cross (Walker, 1956) 52. Malham Tarn Moss (Pigott & Pigott, 1963) 53.Victoria Cave (Wymer, 1981) 54. Eshton Tarn (Bartley et al., 1990) 55. White Moss (Bartley et al., 1990) 56. Bingley Bog (Keen et al., 1988) 57. Soyland Moor (Williams, 1985) 58. Dunford Bridge (Radley et al., 1974).

Fig. 2.1. OSL sampling at Nosterfield Quarry. In order to extract sand grains from gravelly deposits, into which a tube could not be driven, it was necessary for Helen Roberts to undertake the sampling behind a black PVC sheet. See section 2.6.2.

Fig. 2.2. Selected sample from the main geomorphological map (Plate 2.1 and CD) for the area to the south-west of Ripon, showing major meltwater channels and moraine ridge fragments.

Fig. 2.3. How Hill (SE 278671); one of a series of lateral moraine ridge fragments to the south of Fountains Abbey; see geomorphological map (Plate 2.1 and CD).

Fig. 2.4. Clip'd Thorn (SE 261699) lateral moraine ridge between the Skell and Laver river valleys associated with a former Ure ice margin.

Fig. 2.5. Selected sample from the main geomorphological map (Plate 2.1 and CD) showing the Ure valley upstream from Hackfall Gorge towards Marfield. For key, see Fig. 2.2.

Fig. 2.6. Aerial view of the Ure valley north of Hackfall Gorge (middle distance left) around Aldburgh, south of Masham, showing mounds and associated meltwater channels (dashed lines). See Fig. 2.5.

Fig. 2.7. Moraine mounds near Swinton (SE 220790; see Fig. 2.5), looking north.

Fig. 2.8. Low Ellington (SE 204839), Ure valley north of Masham showing kettle holes and mounds associated with the ice limit at Marfield Quarry (to left).

Fig. 2.9. Low Ellington (SE 204839) kettle hole (see also Plate 2.1/CD; Figure 2.5).

Fig. 2.10. Selected sample from the main geomorphological map (Plate 2.1 and CD) showing interfluve area west of Leeming, with the drumlins around Thornton Watlass and the complex 'hummocky moraine' towards Newton-le-Willows (SE 215895). For key, see Fig. 2.2.

Fig. 2.11. Selected sample from the main geomorphological map (Plate 2.1 and CD) showing the area between Leeming and

Tables

Mires). Note: + indicates that fragments were recognized but no countable individuals were present.

Plates

Acknowledgements

Many people have helped us in the completion of this project. We wish to thank English Heritage for funding the work as part of the ALSF scheme and, in particular, Peter Wilson and James Leary who acted as project monitors. Alex Bayliss, Peter Marshall and John Meadows provided us with excellent support and advice regarding radiocarbon dating. We are also grateful to Simon Warwick and Siobhan Walker of the Swale Ure Washlands Trust for enthusiastic support on our many trips into the field area; indeed, Simon assisted with laborious field work on several occasions. The team also wishes to thank the owners and managers of the quarries, who provided us with valuable local advice and information and access to their workings at different times (see list of companies below). Many landowners – too many to be listed here – provided access for field mapping purposes; without their help this work would not have been possible. Those who kindly permitted the more intrusive activity of sample collection are as follows:

> Marfield (High Mains): The Swinton Estate
> Newby Wiske: Mr P. Richardson
> Sharow Mires: Mr T. Witworth
> Snape Mires: The Thorp Perrow Estate
> Langland's Farm: Mr L.M. Raine
> Thornton's Plantation: Mr A. Thornton

The following aggregates companies kindly provided access to their quarries, which have been key data sources within the project:

> Marfield: Lafarge Aggregates Ltd
> Nosterfield and Scorton: Tarmac
> Ripon North: Hanson Aggregates
> Ripon South: Brown & Potter Ltd
> Catterick: Pallett Hill Sand & Gravel Co Ltd

We are very grateful, in addition, to Dr. Richard Tipping (University of Stirling) for permitting use of an archived core from Nosterfield (F45), collected before the location was quarried, for palaeoecological analyses and radiocarbon dating.

Thanks are also due to Neville Tate, for taking Wishart Mitchell across the Washlands in his light aircraft, to Tom White, for assistance with differential GPS fieldwork, and Michael Alexander for accomodating a dGPS base station in his garden, to Rob Westaway, who assisted with the formatting of the CD appendices, and to Vicki Innes, who helped compile the index. Lastly, thanks must go to David Hume, Chris Orton and Steven Allan of the Durham Digital Design and Imaging Unit for their care and patience in the production of illustrative material for this publication and other project output. Photographs are by members of the project team unless otherwise attributed.

In addition to the authorship attributions documented below, Andy Howard kindly read and commented on parts of Chapters 1, 2 and 5 and Richard Chiverrell, acting as referee for English Heritage, provided valuable and constructive advice.

Authorship of Chapters and Appendices

Chapter 1: Wishart Mitchell, David Bridgland & Jim Innes
Chapter 2: Wishart Mitchell & David Bridgland
Chapter 3: Jim Innes & David Bridgland, plus Mairead Rutherford (palynology), Charlotte O'Brien (plant macrofossils, except Ripon South), Mike Field (plant macrofossils, Ripon South), David Keen (molluscs, except IL12, MH & TG2 at Snape), Russell Coope (insects, Ripon South), Emma Tetlow (insects, except Ripon South), Richard Preece & George Speller (molluscs at IL12, MH & TG2 at Snape) & Danielle Schreve (vertebrates).
Chapter 4: Blaise Vyner, Jim Innes, David Bridgland & Wishart Mitchell
Chapter 5: David Bridgland, Jim Innes & Wishart Mitchell
Appendix I: Peter Marshall, Alex Bayliss, John Meadows, C. Bronk Ramsey, Gordon Cook & J. (Hans) van der Plicht
Appendix II: Geoff Duller & Helen Roberts
Appendix III: Kirsty Penkman & Matthew Collins
Appendix IV: David Bridgland
Appendix V: David Bridgland
Appendix VI: Jim Innes
Appendix VII: Jim Innes

Affiliations

A. BAYLISS
English Heritage dating team

D.R. BRIDGLAND
Department of Geography, Durham University

M.J. COLLINS
BioArch, University of York

G. COOK
Scottish Universities Environmental Research Centre, East Kilbride

G.R. Coope
Department of Geography, Royal Holloway, University of London

G.A.T. Duller
Institute of Geography and Earth Sciences, Aberystwyth University

M.H. Field
Faculty of Archaeology, University of Leiden, The Netherlands

J.B. Innes
Department of Geography, Durham University

D.H. Keen
Institute of Archaeology & Antiquity, University of Birmingham †

A.J. Long
Department of Geography, Durham University

P.D. Marshall
English Heritage dating team

J. Meadows
English Heritage dating team

W.A. Mitchell
Department of Geography, Durham University

C.E. O'Brien
Durham Archaeological Services, Department of Archaeology, Durham University

H.M. Pedley
Department of Geography, University of Hull

K.E.H. Penkman
BioArch, University of York

R.C. Preece
Department of Zoology, University of Cambridge

C.Bronk Ramsey
Research Laboratory for Archaeology & the History of Art, University Of Oxford

H.M. Roberts
Institute of Geography and Earth Sciences, Aberystwyth University

M.M. Rutherford
Department of Geography, Durham University

D.C. Schreve
Department of Geography, Royal Holloway University of London

G.P. Speller
Department of Zoology, University of Cambridge

E. Tetlow
Headland Archaeology, 13 Jane Street, Edinburgh, EH6 5HE

J. van der Plicht
Archeologie, University of Leiden

B.E. Vyner
16 College Square, Stokesley, North Yorkshire TS9 5DL

Dedication

Sadly, our good friend and colleague David Keen died prematurely on 16th April, 2006. David was part of the project at the outset and participated in field work at Ripon South and Snape Mires, as well as receiving mollusc samples for analysis at his base in Coventry. He had worked previously in the area, being a member of the team who studied the early Holocene site in Ripon Racecourse quarry, work that was published in 2000 (*Proceedings of the Yorkshire Geological Society*; see Howard *et al.* 2000a in the reference list). David was an enthusiast for all types of natural history and had a particular love of birds, one of many and varied interests pursued in his spare time. As well as in Britain, David studied fossil molluscs on the Channel Islands and the European Continent, as well in North America and China. After joining Birmingham University he took on an important role as Coordinator of the 'National Ice Age Network', another initiative established with funding from the Aggregates Levy Sustainability Fund, jointly overseen in this case by English Heritage and English Nature (now Natural England). Amongst many distinguished positions, he was President (2002–2005) of the Quaternary Research Association and served for an extraordinarily long period as Editor (1991–2002) of the journal *Proceedings of the Geologists' Association*. He left Susan, his wife of 35 years, son Edmund and daughter Rosalind.

Professor David Henry Keen, born 26th January 1947, died 16th April 2006.

Preface

Emeritus Professor I.G. Simmons DSc FSA FBA

When I joined the University of Durham in 1962, as the first member of staff to have completed a PhD in Quaternary Ecology, the main emphasis of much of the work was in the uplands. The reasons for this are obvious: the north-east is rich in elevated terrain, some of it with a very diverse flora, and the uplands are rarely short of the kind of organic deposits which contain a well-preserved archive of macro- and micro-fossils. Thus an excursion into the palaeoecology of lower areas was seen as a diversion from the main task. That it could be an exciting track to follow was evident from the deposit at Burtree Lane near Darlington which was opened up by the improvement of the A68 and in which David Bellamy found a rich moss flora to complement the long pollen-analytical sequence that was recovered.

Yet such investigations were simplistic and isolated compared with the diversity and detail of the evidence present in the present volume. The early finds in the lower Tees were not followed up in any detail and the advances in techniques becoming available were not applied. Thus it is an enormous advance to have the very best of today's expertise put to such good use in the Washlands of two of the rivers – the Swale and the Ure – coming off the uplands of the Dales and North Pennines. This monograph takes us from the solid elements of the landscape in terms of its rocks and superficial mineral deposits through the natural biological colonisations of the land and waters to the effects of human activity, some of it subtle, much of it to a high degree transformational. The detail revealed by the authors is remarkable: the explanation of the way in which the Swale and Ure became incised into the landscape tells us a great deal about the latter stages of the great Ice Age, just as the microscope has yielded data about the colonization of the land thereafter. The analysis of sub-fossil pollen grains tells us that there was a time when climate was the supreme governor of the life of plants and animals. That this era was superseded by one in which climate vied for supremacy with human activities is well-known in general outline but in this work there is the particular facts of this locality. No need any more to apply general ideas and principles: we know how it was, and in particular there are data pertaining to the vegetation history of the central area of the Vale of York in post-Roman times, the provision of which is a notable advance.

One overall story does not alter: that change is permanent. There is no intellectual justification for hanging on to any particular slice of past time. Yet recent transformations have been of a scale and intensity never before experienced. Notably they can carry away the evidence for the past as well as making new landscapes. So with power (be it social, political or simply the use of a bulldozer) comes responsibility. Some of that belongs to the activists of change to make sure that they do not wipe away totally what and where we have been, leaving us rootless. Another part belongs to the members of the academic community whose task is to reveal the depth and diversity of place and habitat to which modern people are heirs. In this monograph, both are combined in a way which will enrich at many levels and to recommend it to a wide audience is a real pleasure.

Summary

This volume, reporting the findings of a multi-disciplinary project funded by English Heritage (Aggregates Levy Sustainability Fund), seeks to reconstruct the history since the last glaciation of an area encompassing the middle reaches of the Rivers Swale and Ure, in North Yorkshire, and the interfluve between them. Included in this history are both natural changes, determined from studies of landforms and sediments and documenting the evolution of the landscape following the melting of the last ice sheets, and human-induced changes, documented in archaeological and geo-archaeological records. The work is set in the context of previous research and pre-existing knowledge, outlined in the introductory chapter. Key methods include geomorphological mapping and the study of sediment exposures, both aimed at reconstructing the final phases of glaciation and then the melting of the ice and its replacement by the post-glacial rivers (Chapter 2), as well as the use of fossil materials to reconstruct the post-glacial record, both of natural change and increasing anthropogenic impacts (Chapter 3). Particular emphasis is given to pollen analyses, with supplementary data from plant macrofossils, molluscs, insects and vertebrates, the whole being constrained by some 57 new radiocarbon dates. The penultimate of the five chapters provides an overview of the archaeological record from the study area, while in the final chapter the work is synthesized and placed in a wider national and international context. The detailed geomorphological mapping has provided an improved understanding of the interactions of the various ice bodies during the Last Glacial, notably the Pennine ice from Wensleydale and its coalescence with the larger Vale of York ice-sheet. Also, by combining data from the various localities studied, the palaeoecological work provides an unusually complete record of environmental change from deglaciation to post-Medieval times. The accompanying CD provides a high-resolution electronic copy of the geomorphological map, as well as written reports on the radiocarbon dating and on attempted OSL and amino-acid dating, colour versions of some of the illustrations and other archival material (such as detailed gravel composition and the particle-size distribution of sampled sediments).

The research has been structured around representative sites, some of them aggregates quarries in which the sediments have been studied and interpreted, while others are repositories for fossil material, particularly pollen-bearing organic sequences; several sites fall into both categories, thus providing linkages between the clastic deposits and the palaeoecological archives. Thus a quarry at Marfield, which exposed the oldest gravels encountered, emplaced early during deglaciation, was juxtaposed with an abandoned channel of the Ure filled with organic sediments dating from the Lateglacial. At Nosterfield another gravel quarry exploits lower-level glacial gravels forming an outwash fan that spreads out downstream of Hackfall Gorge, an impressive landscape feature in the Ure valley. In the upper surface of these fan gravels are hollows infilled with organic sediments that provide records from the Lateglacial to the Roman period, providing a landscape context for the nearby triple-henge complex at Thornborough. Further downstream, two quarries at Ripon provide data on later parts of the post-glacial sequence. The first, Ripon North, exploits shelly terrace gravels dating from the mid–late Holocene that overlie glacial gravels and till, these representing a buried valley that underlies the modern river and is largely filled with glacial deposits. Organic sediments within the terrace gravels help pinpoint a Bronze Age–Iron Age date. At Ripon South the quarry extracts terrace gravels and sands that span the period from the Late Holocene to Medieval, with the latter represented by a highly fossiliferous channel-fill sequence from which rich molluscan and beetle faunas were obtained, as well as pollen. The quarry operators also recovered mammalian remains and archaeological material, including several Medieval shoes. On the other side of the river from the Ripon South quarry is another section of abandoned and partly infilled channel, at Sharow Mires, providing palaeoecological evidence from the latter half of the Holocene. There were also two quarry sites in the Swale, at Catterick and Scorton, neither yielding fossil material, although borehole sites provided palaeoecological records from that catchment. Thus at Newby Wiske, south of Northallerton, an early to mid-Holocene vegetation history points to substantial early Neolithic woodland clearance and cereal agriculture on favourable calcareous soils, in contrast to the minimal traces of early farming activity in other areas nearby. Further mid–late Holocene sequences were examined from boreholes at Morton-on-Swale and Pickhill. Finally a site on the interfluve between the Ure and Swale was also examined, this being Snape Mires, a partly infilled glacial lake basin in which several pockets of fossiliferous sediment were located and sampled, together providing a record from Lateglacial through to mid-Holocene (Late Mesolithic) times. High microscopic charcoal frequencies suggested that burning had influenced vegetation successions at Snape, perhaps encouraging the immigration of hazel in the early Holocene.

The geological and geomorphological findings point to a post-glacial history of punctuated but progressive incision by the Ure and Swale, which now flow as much as 30 m below the glaciated landscape, as also seen in a wider area of north-east England. Glacio-isostatic uplift is suggested as a cause of this phenomenon, which is not seen in valleys outside the limits of the last glaciation. The fluvial sedimentary archive shows the effects of climate change and human activity on river systems throughout the post-glacial, while the archaeological record indicates considerable human settlement and exploitation of this lowland area and its environs during that time. The palaeoenvironmental evidence records the development of a range of natural ecosystems, as well as the stages and means by which people, primarily through woodland clearance for increasingly intensive agriculture, changed the natural vegetation to the artificial and intensely managed rural landscape present today.

Résumé

Ce volume, qui rend compte des découvertes d'un projet multidisciplinaire financé par English Heritage (Aggregates Levy Sustainability Fund) cherche à reconstituer l'histoire d'une zone comprenant le bassin moyen des rivières Swale et Ure, dans le nord du Yorkshire, et leur domaine d'influence, depuis la dernière glaciation. Cette histoire inclut à la fois les changements naturels, définis à partir des études de la morphologie de la surface terrestre et des sédiments, que documente l'évolution du paysage à la suite de la fonte de la dernière nappe glaciaire, et ceux qui résultent de l'activité humaine, documentés dans les traces archéologiques et géoarchéologiques. L'ouvrage se situe dans le contexte de recherches antérieures et de connaissances pré-existantes dont les grandes lignes sont présentées dans le chapitre d'introduction. Les méthodes clés comprennent une cartographie géomorphologique et l'étude des affleurements sédimentaires, visant toutes deux à reconstruire les phases finales de glaciation puis la fonte des glaces et leur remplacement par des rivières post-glaciaires (chapitre 2), ainsi que l'utilisation de matériaux fossiles pour reconstruire les archives post-glaciaires à la fois des changements naturels et de l'impact anthropogénique grandissant (chapitre 3). On accorde une importance particulière aux analyses de pollen, avec des données supplémentaires provenant de macrofossiles de plantes, de mollusques, d'insectes et de vertébrés, le tout étant encadré par 57 nouvelles datations au C14. Le pénultième des 5 chapitres fournit une vue d'ensemble des trouvailles archéologiques de la zone étudiée tandis que nous présentons, dans le dernier chapitre, une synthèse de l'ouvrage et le replaçons dans un contexte national et international plus étendu. La cartographie géomorphologique détaillée a permis de mieux comprendre les interactions entre les divers corps glaciaires pendant la dernière glaciation, en particulier la glace des Pennines de Wensleydale et sa coalescence avec la nappe glaciaire, plus grande, de la Vale of York. De plus, en associant les données des diverses localités étudiées, le travail paléoécologique nous fournit un récit complet, ce qui est rare, des modifications de l'environnement depuis la fonte des glaces jusqu'à l'époque post-médiévale. Le CD qui accompagne l'ouvrage offre une copie électronique haute définition de la carte géomorphologique, ainsi que des comptes rendus écrits sur la datation au C14 et les tentatives de datation aux isotopes d'oxygène et aux amino-acides, des versions en couleurs de certaines des illustrations et d'autres matériaux d'archives (tels que la composition détaillée des graviers et la répartition, selon la taille des particules, d'échantillons de sédiments).

Les recherches s'organisent autour de sites représentatifs, certains sont des carrières d'agrégats dans lesquelles les sédiments ont été étudiés et interprétés, tandis que d'autres sont les reposoirs de matériaux fossiles, en particulier de séquences organiques porteuses de pollen; plusieurs sites appartiennent aux deux catégories, nous fournissant ainsi des dépôts clastiques et des vestiges paléoécologiques. Ainsi une carrière à Marfield, qui a révélé les plus vieux graviers jamais rencontrés, déposés tôt au début de la déglaciation, se trouvait juste à côté d'un chenal abandonné de l'Ure remblayé de sédiments organiques datant de la fin de la période glaciaire. A Nosterfield, une autre carrière de gravier exploite des graviers glaciaires d'un niveau inférieur qui forment un éventail d'eaux de fusion s'étalant en aval de Hackfall Gorge, un trait impressionnant du paysage de la vallée de l'Ure. Dans la couche supérieure de ces graviers de l'éventail se trouvent des creux comblés par des sédiments organiques qui fournissent des renseignements à partir de la fin de l'ère glaciaire jusqu'à l'époque romaine, offrant un contexte paysager pour le complexe à triple enceintes de Thornborough. Plus loin en aval, à Ripon, deux carrières apportent des données sur les périodes plus tardives de la séquence post-glaciaire. La première, Ripon North, exploite des graviers d'une terrasse coquillière, datant du milieu à la fin de l'holocène, qui recouvre des graviers et du terrain erratique glaciaire, ceux-ci représentent une vallée enterrée qui se trouve sous la rivière moderne et est en grande partie remblayée de dépôts glaciaires. Des sédiments organiques à l'intérieur des graviers de la terrasse permettent de fixer une datation de l'âge du bronze-âge du fer. A Ripon South, la carrière extrait des graviers et des sables de terrasse qui couvrent la période de l'holocène final au moyen-âge, ce dernier étant représenté par une séquence de chenal comblé extrèmement fossilifère d'où on a obtenu une faune riche en mollusques et coléoptères – ainsi que du pollen. Les exploitants de la carrière ont également recouvré des restes de mammifères et du matériel archéologique; y compris plusieurs chaussures médiévales. De l'autre côté de la rivière, par rapport à la carrière de Ripon South, à Sharow Mires, se trouve une autre section de chenal abandonnée et en partie comblée qui a fourni des témoignages paléoécologiques de la seconde moitié de l'holocène. Il y avait également deux sites de carrières dans la Swale, à Catterick et à Scorton, ni l'un ni l'autre n'a fourni de matériel fossile bien que des sites de trous de sondage aient révélé des renseignements paléoécologiques de ce captage. Ainsi à Newby Wiske, au sud de Northallerton, une histoire de la végétation du début au milieu de l'holocène atteste d'un défrichage substantiel de la forêt et de cultures céréalières sur des sols calcaires favorables au néolithique ancien, ce qui contraste avec le peu de témoignages d'un début d'activité agricole dans d'autres zones avoisinnantes. D'autres séquences de l'holocène moyen-final ont été examinées à partir des trous de sondages de Morton-on-Swale et de Pickhill. Finalement un site du domaine d'influence entre l'Ure et la Swale a également été examiné, il s'agissait de Snape Mires, le bassin d'un lac glaciaire en partie comblé dans lequel plusieurs poches de sédiments fossilifères ont été localisées et échantillonnées, ensemble elles offrent un témoignage des périodes allant de la fin de l'ère glaciaire jusqu'à l'holocène moyen (mésolithique final). La fréquente présence de charbons de bois microscopiques laisse supposer que le brûlage avait influencé l'évolution des essences végétales à Snape, encourageant peut-être l'immigration du noisetier au début de l'holocène.

Les trouvailles, géologiques et géomorphologiques font ressortir l'histoire post-glaciaire d'une incision intermittente mais progressive de l'Ure et de la Swale qui coulent maintenant jusqu'à 30 m en-dessous du paysage glaciaire, on a fait la même constatation dans une région plus étendue du nord-est de l'Angleterre. On suggère qu'un soulèvement glacio-isostatique est une des causes de ce phénomène qu'on ne trouve pas dans les vallées situées hors des limites de la dernière glaciation. Les vestiges sédimento-fluviaux mettent en évidence les effets des changements climatiques et des activités humaines sur les systèmes des cours d'eau tout au long de l'ère post-glaciaire tandis que les témoignages archéologiques indiquent une considérable implantation et exploitation humaine de cette zone de basses terres et de ses environs pendant cette période. Les témoignages paléo-environnementaux enregistrent le développement d'une gamme d'écosystèmes naturels ainsi que les étapes et les moyens par lesquels les hommes, essentiellement en défrichant la forêt pour faire place à une agriculture de plus en plus intensive, ont transformé la végétation naturelle en ce paysage rural artificiel et strictement contrôlé présent de nos jours.

Traduction: Annie Pritchard

Zusammenfassung

Mit dem hier vorliegenden Band wird der Versuch unternommen, die Geschichte der in North Yorkshire liegenden Region der mittleren Flussabschnitte von Swale und Ure sowie des zwischen diesen liegenden Höhenzuges seit der letzten Eiszeit zu rekonstruieren. Das interdisziplinäre Projekt wurde im Rahmen des Aggregates Levy Sustainability Fund von English Heritage gefördert. Berücksichtigt werden sowohl naturräumliche Veränderungen, die anhand von Studien zu Geländeformen und Sedimenten sowie zur Landschaftsentwicklung seit dem Abschmelzen der letzten Eisschilde untersucht wurden, als auch durch menschliches Handeln bewirkte und mittels archäologischer und geoarchäologischer Untersuchungen dokumentierte Veränderungen. Das einleitende Kapitel umreißt die Forschungsgeschichte und stellt die Arbeit in Bezug zu vorangegangenen Studien. Unter den zur Anwendung gekommenen Forschungsmethoden sind besonders geomorphologische Kartierung sowie Untersuchungen zu Sedimentexponierungen hervorzuheben. Mit deren Hilfe sollten zum einen die letzen Phasen der Vereisung, deren anschließender Schmelze und nachfolgende postglaziale Flüsse rekonstruiert (Kapitel 2), und zum anderen anhand der Nutzung fossiler Materialien der naturräumliche Wandel und zunehmende anthropogene Einflüsse während der Nacheiszeit aufgezeigt werden (Kapitel 3). Einen besonderen Schwerpunkt bilden Pollenanalysen, ergänzt durch Untersuchungen pflanzlicher Makroreste, Mollusken, Insekten und Wirbeltiere, deren chronologischer Rahmen durch 57 ^{14}C-Datierungen abgesichert ist. Während das vorletzte der fünf Kapitel einen Überblick über den archäologischen Bestand des Forschungsgebiets verschafft, werden im letzen Kapitel die Ergebnisse zusammengefasst und in ihren weiteren nationalen und internationalen Zusammenhang gestellt. Die detailierten geomorphologischen Kartierungen haben zu einem besseren Verständnis der Wechselbeziehungen zwischen den verschiedenen Eisschilden geführt, insbesondere des Pennine Eisschildes in Wensleydale und seines Zusammenflusses mit dem größeren Vale of York Eisschild. Durch die Kombination der Daten der verschiedenen Untersuchungsgebiete liefern die paläoökologischen Untersuchungen außerdem einen außergewöhnlich vollständigen Datensatz zum naturräumlichen Wandel vom Ende der Eiszeit bis in die frühe Neuzeit. Die beiliegende CD enthält eine hochauflösende elektronische Kopie der geomorphologischen Karte, Berichte zu den ^{14}C-Datierungen und den Versuchen zu OSL- und Aminosäuredatierungen, Farbversionen einiger Abbildungen sowie weiteres Archivmaterial (z.B. detaillierte Angaben zu Kieszusammensetzungen und Korngrößenverteilungen der untersuchten Sedimentproben).

Die Untersuchung wurde nach repräsentativen Fundstellen gegliedert, darunter einige Kiesgruben deren Sedimente analysiert und interpretiert wurden, während es sich bei anderen um Lagerstätten fossilen Materials, insbesondere mit pollenführenden organischen Schichtfolgen, handelt; mehrere Fundplätze gehören in beide Kategorien und bieten somit Verbindungen zwischen klastischen Ablagerungen und paläoökologischen Profilen. Auf diese Weise war es z.B. möglich, die Grube in Marfield, in der sich die ältesten der untersuchten Kiesschichten fanden, mit einem Altarm des Flusses Ure zu vergleichen, der organische Sedimente aus dem Spätglazial enthielt. In einer anderen Kiesgrube, in Nosterfield, werden tiefer liegende glaziale Kiese abgebaut, die einen Schwemmfächer bilden, der sich flussabwärts der Hackfall Gorge Schlucht erstreckt, eines eindrucksvollen Landschaftselements im Ure-Tal. In den oberflächennahen Schichten dieser Fächerkiese finden sich mit organischen Sedimenten von der Späteiszeit bis in die römische Kaiserzeit verfüllte Hohlformen, die es erlauben, das landschaftliche Umfeld des dreifachen Henge-Komplexes von Thornborough zu rekonstruieren. Weiter flußabwärts liefern zwei Kiesgruben bei Ripon Daten zu späteren Abschnitten der postglazialen Serie. In der ersten, Ripon North, werden muschelführende Terrassenschotter des mittleren bis späten Holozäns abgebaut, die über glazialen Schottern und Geschiebemergel liegen, welche zu einem reliktischen, hauptsächlich mit glazialen Sedimenten verfüllten Tal unterhalb des heutigen Flusses gehören. Organische Sedimente aus den Terrassenschottern lieferten eine Datierung in die Bronze- und Eisenzeit. In Ripon South werden Terassenschotter und Sande aus dem Zeitraum vom Spätholozän bis Mittelalter abgebaut, wobei letztere einer stark fossilienführenden Schichtenabfolge eines Kanals entstammen, die neben einer reichen Mollusken- und Käferfauna auch Pollen geliefert hat. Die Kiesgrubenbetreiber haben darüber hinaus auch Reste von Säugetieren sowie archäologisches Material geborgen, darunter mehrere mittelalterliche Schuhe. Auf der Ripon South gegenüberliegenden Flußseite befindet sich bei Sharow Mires ein weiterer Abschnitt eines teilweise verfüllten Altarms, der paläoökologische Daten zur zweiten Hälfte des Holozäns geliefert hat. Von zwei Gruben im Tal des Swale, bei Catterick und Scorton, liegen zwar keine fossilen Reste vor, aber mehrere Bohrungen haben paläoökologische Daten für diesen Bereich geliefert. So deutet eine früh- bis mittelholozäne Schichtenfolge bei Newby Wiske, südlich von Northallerton, auf ausgedehnte frühneolithische Rodungstätigkeit und Getreideanbau auf dafür günstigen kalkhaltigen Böden hin, was im Gegensatz zu den nur geringen Hinweisen auf frühe landwirtschaftliche Aktivitäten in der näheren Umgebung steht. Weitere mittel- bis spätholozäne Schichtfolgen wurden anhand von Bohrungen bei Morton-on-Swale und Pickhill untersucht. Abschließend wurde noch ein Fundplatz, Snape Mire, auf dem Höhenzug zwischen den Flüssen Ure und Swale untersucht, bei dem es sich um ein teilverfülltes Gletscherseebecken handelt, in dem mehrere Stellen mit fossilienführenden Sedimenten beprobt wurden, die zusammengenommen Untersuchungsmaterial für den Zeitraum vom Spätglazial bis zum Mittelholozän (Spätmesolithikum) lieferten. Für die Fundstelle Snape legt ein hoher Anteil mikoskopisch nachgewisener Holzkohle nahe, dass Brandrodung die Vegetationsabfolge beeinflußt hat, was vermutlich die Ausbreitung der Hasel im Früh-Holozän begünstigte.

Die geologischen und geomorphologischen Ergebnisse zur postglazialen Entwicklung weisen auf eine punktuelle aber fortschreitende Tiefenerosion der Flüsse Ure und Swale hin, die heute bis zu 30m unterhalb des Niveaus der vergletscherten Landschaft fliessen, wie dies auch in weiten Teilen Nord-Ost Englands zu beobachten ist. Als Ursache dieses Phänomens wird eine galzialisostatische Hebung angenommen, die in Tälern jenseits der Grenzen der letzten Vereisung nicht beobachtet wurde. Anhand des Bodenarchivs der fluvialen Sedimentschichten können die Auswirkungen von Klimawandel und menschlichem Handeln auf Flußsysteme während des Postglazials dargestellt werden, während für diesen Zeitraum die archäologischen Daten ein beträchtliches Maß menschlicher Siedlungstätigkeit und Nutzung dieser Flachlandregion und seiner Umgebung andeuten. Die umweltgeschichtlichen Ergebnisse beschreiben die Entwicklung einer Reihe natürlicher Ökosysteme, und darüber hinaus auch die Phasen sowie die Mittel mit deren Hilfe menschliche Gruppen, hauptsächlich durch Waldrodung für zunehmend intensivere Landwirtschaft, die Veränderung der natürlichen Vegetation in die künstliche und intensiv genutzte Landschaft von heute bewirkt haben.

Übersetzung: Jörn Schuster

1 Introduction and Background

The 'Swale–Ure Washlands' is the name given to the low-lying area between the eastern fringe of the Pennines and the North Yorkshire Moors, drained by the rivers Swale and Ure (Plate. 1.1). These are the northernmost two of the Pennine rivers that flow by way of the Vale of York to the Humber, their upper catchments fed by numerous smaller rivers, streams and becks. Along with the Rivers Swale and Ure, the Nidd, Wharfe and Aire all rise on the Carboniferous uplands of the central and eastern Yorkshire Dales and flow south and south-east through glacially modified valleys into the lowlands of the Vale of York. With the Derwent, which flows south from the North Yorkshire Moors, these are the main rivers of the Yorkshire Ouse system (Plate 1.1). With all these contributions, the Yorkshire Ouse basin drains the majority of North Yorkshire (*c.* 8000 km²).

Large amounts of sand and gravel were deposited in the Washlands in association with the melting, by around 15,000 years ago, of the last ice sheet to have covered northern Britain. These deposits were supplemented and redistributed, albeit on a smaller scale, by the post-glacial activities of the rivers that give their name to the field area. The surfaces of the gravels, particularly where they include basins and cut-off channels, have accumulated organic sediments such as peats, which represent rich sources of palaeoenvironmental evidence (encompassing records of vegetation, climate and human activity). Today, these various Washland sediments form a rich agricultural resource, support a wide range of wetland and terrestrial habitats and are extensively quarried by the aggregate industry (Fig. 1.1), providing geologists with the means for studying the sedimentary record as well as, following the cessation of quarrying, providing new wetland sites of potential nature conservation value.

The Washlands also preserve extensive archaeological evidence. There is a rich archive of human activity to be found both in prehistoric monuments, such as the henges at Thornborough (Fig. 1.1), the Devil's Arrows at Boroughbridge and more recent remains such as the Roman 'Dere Street' (forerunner of the current A1 road), as well as more mundane structures such as fish-weirs and artefacts that have been subsequently buried in various sediments, including those laid down by the rivers (cf. Chapter 4).

This monograph catalogues the findings of a major

Fig. 1.1. Aerial photograph (looking southwards) showing the quarry complex at Nosterfield with the three henges in the left middle distance. The northern henge, in the centre of the view, is under trees.

research project devoted to the Washlands that was resourced by English Heritage as part of the Aggregate Levy Sustainability Fund (ALSF). The work has been completed by a team in the Geography Department at Durham University, working closely with the following collaborators:

> The Lower Ure Conservation Trust
> North Yorkshire County Council
> Researchers at Durham Archaeological Services and from other universities (Aberystwyth, Birmingham, Cambridge, Leiden, Hull, London and York)
> Independent specialists.

In addition, radiocarbon dating was coordinated and undertaken by the English Heritage Dating Team (Chapter 3; Appendix I).

The project has been multi-faceted, involving studies of landscape evolution in the area since the last glaciation, including the post-glacial evolution of the rivers, vegetation and other aspects of the ecosystem and, with the onset of anthropogenic deforestation and farming in the later post-glacial (Holocene) period, the increasing impacts of human activity. The importance of chronological control is reflected in the generation, as part of this study, of 57 new radiocarbon dates (presented below: Chapter 3; Table 3.3), used to constrain important fluvial and environmental changes as demonstrated by the litho- and bio-stratigraphy. Dates are presented as conventional (uncalibrated) radiocarbon (^{14}C) dates, Before Present (BP = AD 1950) (cf. van der Plicht & Hogg, 2006), with calibrated estimate of age range (cal. BP, cal. AD or cal. BC) calculated using the calibration curve of Reimer *et al.* (1994) and the OxCal (v.3.10) program (Bronk Ramsey, 1995, 1998, 2001) following English Heritage Dating Team protocols (Section 1.9; Appendix I). The good practice of using multiple dating methods was achieved by applying the optically stimulated luminescence (OSL) and amino acid racemisation (AAR) techniques (see section 1.9; also Chapters 2 and 3).

It is hoped that this work has fulfilled one of the aims of the ALSF, by increasing awareness and appreciation of these landscapes at a number of scales, from the local community to national, and by exemplifying the changing relationship between people and their environment through time.

1.1 Introduction

The Vale of York and its northern continuation, the Vale of Mowbray, occupy a major tract of low-lying ground in eastern England between the Pennines and the North York Moors (Plate 1.2). The drainage of this area is predominantly from the Pennine uplands, with major east-flowing rivers converging in the lowlands to form the navigable River Ouse, which flows into the Humber Estuary. The area of present interest coincides with two of these rivers, the Ure and the Swale. The larger of these, the River Ure, flows through Wensleydale from a source in the western

part of the Pennines. The unusual mismatch between the names of the dale and the river in this particular system is perhaps relatively recent, as the alternative 'Yoredale' exists as a seemingly much older name appearing in early papers and in the former classification of part of the Carboniferous sequence in the Pennines ('Yoredale Beds'; Yoredale = Uredale; this division is now renamed 'Wensleydale Group'). From the same upland, the River Swale flows eastwards in a parallel valley to the north, Swaledale, before entering the Vale of York and flowing southwards to meet the Ure at Ellenthorpe Ings (SE 430660). Some 10 km further downstream the Ure is joined by the small left-bank tributary, the Ouse Gill Beck, from which point it becomes the River Ouse, which forms an important part of the Humber system (Plates 1.1 and 1.2).

The Swale–Ure Washlands combine the low-lying parts of the catchments of these two rivers, where they extend into the Vale of York, with the undulating relief that is characteristic of the transitional land between these lowlands and the uplands of the Yorkshire Dales (Plate. 1.2). The relief is moderate, with the main river valleys lying below 30 m O.D. and the intervening interfluves generally < 100 m O.D. Only to the west, as the Pennines are approached, does elevation begin to rise to >100 m O.D., relative relief increasing as a result of greater valley incision. Genuine upland is only encountered above Masham in the Ure valley and above Catterick in the Swale. The Washlands area has been described previously using the term 'piedmont' (e.g. Howard *et al.*, 2000a); however, such areas may best be regarded as a transitional zone with a distinctive geomorphological and stratigraphical record associated with glacial and Holocene landscape modifications.

The influence of bedrock characteristics on geomorphology and the impact of glaciation have combined to produce a landscape in which the major elements result from past geomorphological processes (Straw & Clayton, 1979). With modest relief, this is a subtle landscape, lacking in obvious landforms, that is often difficult to interpret. It is a gentle agricultural landscape of small villages and market towns, such as Ripon, Masham and Bedale (Plate 1.1). On the lower flat land of the Washlands, intense arable farming is practiced over much of the area, with permanent pasture on the wide floodplains of the major rivers. There is also increased pastoral farming on the higher ground in the western part of the area. The major routeway of the A1 road, originally established as Roman Dere Street, makes use of the minor interfluve between the Swale and Ure as it passes north–south through the Washlands.

The research area is within the limit of the last glaciation to have affected northern Britain, which has greatly affected the landscape. Early geologists attributed the deposits left behind by the ice sheets to the biblical flood, a view eventually overturned by the 'glacial theory' that is associated with the Swiss Louis Agassiz, who visited Britain and persuaded British workers that these islands had experienced widespread glaciation (Charlesworth, 1957; Imbrie & Imbrie, 1979; Ellis *et al.*, 1996; Oldroyd, 2002).

Almost as radical as the original theory of glaciation was the later realization that there had been many such glaciations, with intervening interglacials, leading to the adoption of a climato-stratigraphical scheme for interpreting the recent geological past, based on the cyclic fluctuation between these extremes of climate that has characterized this most recent geological period (cf. Bowen, 1999). However, terrestrial sequences are highly complex, with multiple depositional styles and a fragmentation of the evidence because of subsequent erosion (Gibbard & West, 2000). In comparison, deep marine sediments, deposited more or less continuously over the last few million years, have allowed the construction of a global timescale, based on the oxygen isotopic signal derived from the study of carbonate microfossils (Imbrie, 1984) and which forms the basis for a system of numbered Marine [oxygen] Isotope Stages (MIS) that is valid globally (Bowen, 1999; Shackleton, 2006). Only the most recent part of this record (MIS 2–1) will be represented by the deposits in the Swale–Ure Washlands.

Study of sedimentary and palaeoenvironmental evidence from this recent geological episode falls within the classification 'Quaternary' (= 1.8 to 0.01 Ma, an interval that encompassed >30 full climatic (glacial-interglacial) cycles; the Quaternary has been under review, with the lower boundary potentially changing to 2.6 Ma (Gibbard *et al.*, 2005; Walker, 2005; Bowen & Gibbard, 2007). The Quaternary is a period of geological time characterized by repeated glaciations of the temperate latitudes, culminating in the most recent of these 'Ice Ages', termed 'Devensian' in Britain, which started *c.* 116,000 years ago (Mitchell *et al.*, 1973; Lowe & Walker, 1997a; Bowen, 1999; Lowe, 2001) at the end of the Last (Ipswichian) Interglacial (= MIS 5e). The Devensian Stage was a lengthy period of generally cold climate interrupted by short warmer periods. These were neither as long nor generally as warm as interglacials and are termed 'interstadials', with the intensely cold periods separating them termed 'stadials'. The Devensian culminated in a major period of glaciation during the (Late Devensian) Dimlington Stadial (= MIS 2), formally defined as occurring between 26,000 and 13,000 ^{14}C years ago (Rose, 1985; Jones & Keen, 1993). This period incorporates the Last Glacial Maximum (LGM), when the global ice sheets reached their maximum volume and extent (Mix *et al.*, 2001), traditionally stated as occurring at 18,000 ^{14}C BP (Rose, 1985), although it now seems that it might have occurred earlier in the Dimlington Stadial (Section 1.4.5). This was a period when the global climate became extremely cold, with low mean annual air temperatures, reduced precipitation and greater annual temperature variability (e.g. Hubberten *et al.*, 2004; Kageyama *et al.*, 2006). The following Holocene (post-glacial) episode, in which we still live today, is generally regarded as the latest in the 100,000-year recurring interglacials.

Much of the geomorphological and sedimentological information found within the Washlands has been assigned to the most recent (Late Devensian, Dimlington Stadial)

glaciation, although there has been no direct dating evidence published from the Vale of York or the Washlands. Correlation of ice margins in these areas has been with the dated sequence at Holderness (cf. Huddart & Glasser, 2002a; Catt, 2007). Even after 150 years of research, the extent and timing of the Late Devensian British-Irish Ice Sheet (BIIS) is still controversial, as has been shown by the recent 'BRITICE' mapping project, which produced a spatial database of known geomorphological evidence of the last ice sheet (cf. Clark, *et al.*, 2004a; Evans *et al.*, 2005). Plate 1.2 shows the information in this database for the Washlands and adjoining regions and provides a useful summary of the available types of geomorphological evidence discussed in later sections of this chapter and thereafter.

In northern England, the Dimlington Stadial is represented by a complexity of tills (deposited directly by the ice sheets), glaciofluvial (meltwater) gravels and glaciolacustrine silts and clays. The end of this glaciation was marked by rapid climate change as the Earth moved out of glacial mode into the present interglacial. Climate change was not, however, unidirectional and there were marked climate fluctuations between periods of amelioration and deterioration that mark out the latter part of the Devensian Stage, termed the Lateglacial period (13,000–10,000 ^{14}C BP: Lowe & Walker, 1997a; Bell & Walker, 2005). A particularly warm interstadial period is identified between 13,000 and 11,000 ^{14}C BP; in the British sequence this has been termed the Lateglacial Interstadial or the Windermere Interstadial (see Fig. 1.2) and the short final episode of cold (glacial) conditions that separated it from the Holocene is called the 'Loch Lomond Stadial'. These episodes can be correlated with the stratigraphy developed for north-west Europe, in which they are called Allerød and Younger Dryas, respectively (Fig. 1.2), and with the higher resolution record from the Greenland ice cores, which identifies a number of interstadial–stadial fluctuations during the period 13,000 to 11,000 ^{14}C BP (Lowe & Walker, 1997a; Björk *et al.*, 1998; Mayle *et al.*, 1999; Walker, 2005; Fig. 1.2). Ice cores provide important evidence for enhancing the resolution of the climatic record, allowing correlation with the palaeoecological archive and improved understanding of Lateglacial environmental change (see Chapter 5).

The term Holocene, which has already been used several times (= Post-glacial; from 10,000 ^{14}C BP; calibration of this date indicates that this is 11,600 cal. BP), is now formally adopted for the geological episode that began with the end of the Late Pleistocene and continues to the present day (cf. Lowe & Walker, 1997a; Gibbard & van Kolfschoten, 2005). This name is suggestive of parity with the much longer Pleistocene. Although it is generally accepted that the Holocene is merely the latest in a long line of interglacials, it differs from all the earlier ones in that human activity became sufficient to have a noticeable effect within the geological record from *c.* 5000 years ago, with the advent of farming practices, beginning a trend that

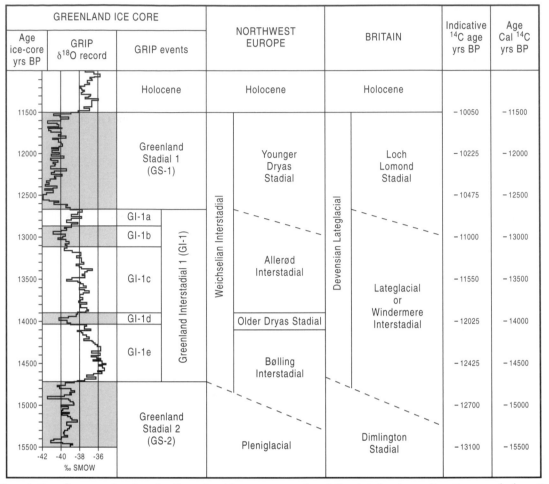

Fig. 1.2. Correlation diagram showing the Greenland ice-core record and the dated palaeo-climatic records from Britain and NW Europe. After Walker (2005). SMOW = Standard Mean Ocean Water.

has led inexorably towards present-day concerns about environmental modification and destruction (cf. Barber, 1993). The ability to date artefacts and develop a chronology is an important aspect of this archaeological research. As with any timescale, there are often subtle differences of boundary definition. Those in Table 1.1, currently employed by the English Heritage Dating Team, are taken as standard in this report.

Post-glacial sediments in the valleys, enclosed basins (lakes and bogs) and estuaries of northern England have played their part in establishing a definitive Holocene record. In the case of Yorkshire, Innes and Blackford (2003a) have reviewed the various types of Holocene sedimentary archives and their palaeoenvironmental potential, evaluating the importance of this type of record to the study of regional archaeology. Reconstructing palaeogeography and vegetation history provides a context within which the different strands of archaeological evidence can be positioned and human impacts on the landscape can be interpreted. Major processes and events in landscape history since deglaciation can be recognized and investigated using a wide range of scientific techniques. The changes in flora and fauna since deglaciation have taken

Period	Age range
Post-Medieval	after 1540 cal AD
Late Medieval	1066 – 1540 cal AD
Early Medieval	410 – 1066 cal AD
Roman	43 – 410 cal AD
Iron Age	cal BC 600 – 43 cal AD
Bronze Age	2,500 – 600 cal BC
Neolithic	4,000 – 2,500 cal BC
Mesolithic	c.10,000 – 4,000 cal BC
Palaeolithic	Until c.10,000 cal BC

Table 1.1. Dating of archaeological periods as defined by English Heritage.

place under the influence of many geographical factors, of which climate was perhaps the most fundamental. Analyses of the wide range of biological micro- and macrofossils preserved within the sediments reveal changes in past plant and animal communities and, therefore, in the wider ecosystem (e.g. Evans, 1991; Barber *et al.*, 1993; Gale & Cutler, 2000; Brown, 2002; Hall, 2003; Innes, 2005).

Many complementary techniques have been used in this project, with pollen, plant macrofossil, molluscan and beetle analyses to the fore (Chapter 3). Supported by the chronological control, provided primarily by radiocarbon dating, these techniques have allowed detailed investigation of over 15,000 years of environmental history in the Swale–Ure Washlands, including key stages such as the rapid environmental changes associated with climate amelioration and fluctuation in the Lateglacial followed by the general climatic stability and progression of the Holocene. Enigmatic events that might have had a mixture of human and natural causes, such as the mid-Holocene elm decline, are key to understanding the landscape within which major prehistoric cultural monuments such as the Thornborough Henges were constructed.

As a baseline for work undertaken during the project, the pre-existing knowledge of the past environment and archaeology of the Washlands will be summarized in this first chapter.

1.2 Bedrock geology

The bedrock geology of the Washlands is characterized by a series of eastward-dipping sedimentary rocks with a generally north–south strike, as seen from the pattern of outcrop (Plate 1.3). The area has been mapped at different times (on more than one occasion for most districts) by the British Geological Survey (BGS), recent memoirs having been published for the map sheets based on Thirsk (Sheet 52: Powell *et al.*, 1992), Harrogate (Sheet 62: Cooper & Burgess, 1993) and Northallerton (Sheet 42: Frost, 1998). No recent geological map is available for the southwest part of the study area (Sheet 61: Pateley Bridge). Updated maps are available for the areas around Masham (BGS Sheet 51) and Richmond (Sheet 41), but there are no published memoirs.

The oldest rocks within the Washlands occur in the west, where sandstones and shales of Carboniferous age (Namurian) are poorly exposed beneath superficial deposits, as well as forming the higher ground (Plate 1.3). They are unconformably overlain by Permian rocks, primarily dolomitic limestones and marls, which form the lower elevations of the Washlands, including the transitional zone leading to the main Vale of York, although they are mainly hidden by Quaternary sediments (Plate 1.3). The Permian rocks strike north–south across the area, with a gentle easterly dip (1–2°), and are locally displaced by a number of ENE-trending faults and monoclines (Cooper & Burgess, 1993). Apart from an intermittent basal breccia, the lowest division of the Permian is the Cadeby Formation (formerly Lower Magnesian Limestone: LML), which forms a north–south striking escarpment along the western margin of the Washlands. It is overlain by the Edlington Formation (Middle Marl), which includes significant anhydrite (gypsum) beds that underlie a narrow zone stretching north from Ripon towards Darlington. Thinly bedded dolomitic limestone of the Brotherton Formation (Upper Magnesian Limestone) underlies the Roxby Formation (Upper Marl). The Triassic Sherwood Sandstone Formation (formerly Bunter Sandstone) and overlying Mercia Mudstone Group (formerly Keuper Marl) cap the sequence in the eastern Washlands (Cooper, 1983; Morigi & James, 1984).

The Permian limestones and marls reflect cyclic deposition in the subtropical Zechstein Sea, with the limestones representing full marine inundation and the marls and anhydrite/gypsum layers recording increasing climatic aridity and sea-water evaporation (Cooper, 1986). The presence of the soluble anhydrite/gypsum layers has led to numerous solution collapse structures (subsidence hollows) associated with the transformation of anhydrite to gypsum and the solution of this by regional groundwater flow (Cooper, 1986). Such hollows are particularly well developed along the western edge of the present Ure valley around Ripon (Cooper, 1986, 2006; Thompson *et al.*, 1996), their infills representing important repositories of palaeoenvironmental evidence.

Topographic expression of the solid geology is ambiguous because of the generally thick drift cover (Straw & Clayton, 1979), but the high ground to the west and north of Ripon reflects the presence of the Cadeby Formation (LML), which has a subdued west-facing scarp, particularly north of the Ure valley. A second smaller escarpment is formed by the largely concealed outcrop of the Sherwood Sandstone, which runs roughly along the line of the A1 road through the Washlands. Few exposures of this bedrock are to be found, given the thick superficial cover, although small quarries are located near Kirklington. The lowest ground of the central Vale of York is underlain by the Mercia Mudstone (Plate 1.3).

1.3 Superficial (drift) deposits

The available geology maps (BGS 1: 50,000 series) are published either as combined solid (bedrock) and drift (superficial) editions (sheets 41 and 42) or as separate solid and drift versions (sheets 51, 52 and 62). The drift types mapped vary slightly between sheets but generally are divided between a variety of glacial (Devensian) and Holocene deposits. The glacial drift includes diamicton, designated as till (sometimes giving 'boulder clay', an older term, as an alternative) and sands and gravels associated with meltwater. On sheets 52 and 62 a separate 'sandy till' category has also been mapped. Glacial landform features (moraines) are separately identified on sheets 41 and 51 but not the others. Various deposits associated with glacial lakes have also been mapped, notably glacio-lacustrine silts and clays, fringing gravels (presumed to be lacustrine deltaic or beach deposits), laminated clays associated with glacial deposits and other, similar categories (these vary from map to map). Glaciofluvial deposits are variously mapped as 'Glacial Sand and Gravel', 'Fluvio-glacial Sand and Gravel', 'Fluvio-glacial Terrace Deposits' and 'Glaciofluvial Deposits', often with more than one such category per map. The rationale for these divisions and details of the mapping are provided in the various memoirs (Powell *et al.*, 1992; Cooper & Burgess, 1993; Frost, 1998) and other BGS reports. Amongst the latter, the BGS Mineral Assessment Reports (MAR) are prominent, assessing the aggregate resources of the areas around Boroughbridge (Abraham, 1981), Bedale (Giles, 1982), Catterick (Lovell, 1982), Tholthorpe (Stanczyszyn, 1982), Dalton (Benfield, 1983) and Ripon (Morigi & James, 1984) and including 1: 25,000 mineral assessment maps, with drift geology, for each area.

Holocene drift deposits vary considerably between the maps. River terrace deposits are recognized on each map but are only divided into first and second terraces of the Ure on sheet 51, between Wensley and Masham; elsewhere they are undivided. Floodplain alluvium is also recognized on all maps, with alluvial fan deposits distinguished on sheets 41, 42, 51 and 52. Post-glacial lacustrine deposits are recognized on sheets 41, 42 and 52. All the maps indicate peat as a Holocene deposit of valley-bottoms and other low and damp areas. Calcareous tufa appears on sheets 42, 51, 52 and 62, as well as in the Mineral Assessment Reports for Bedale and Boroughbridge (see above). Aeolian and slope deposits also appear on all the maps.

The distribution of the drift deposits, as mapped, reveals much about the drainage and landscape evolution of the area, with a plethora of former glacial lakes revealed as a significant feature of this lowland, the draining of which, with deglaciation, would have preceded the initiation of the present river systems. Much more can be learned from the subsurface distribution of these various late Quaternary deposits, information about which is less readily obtained from the maps but can be gleaned from the memoirs, other BGS publications and from borehole archives (e.g. in the various Mineral Assessment Reports cited above). The main rivers are seen to flow above deeply buried valleys (Plate. 1.4), typically up to 50 m below their modern floodplains, perhaps inherited from pre-Devensian courses that were buried and variously modified, if not obliterated, by Devensian glacial and glaciofluvial systems.

In the north of the area, buried valleys show little relation to the modern drainage and may hint at a different pre-Devensian drainage pattern (Plate 1.4). In particular, there is a northward-deepening buried valley beneath the lower River Wiske that would appear to have linked to the Tees north of Great Smeaton (Frost, 1998). This has previously been interpreted as a pre-Devensian proto-Swale route-way (Raistrick, 1931a; Radge, 1940). It is, however, separated from another buried valley that underlies the Swale valley west of Northallerton, which deepens northwards (upstream as far as the Swale is concerned) and then loops westwards and southwards beneath the modern Bedale Beck valley,

before ending in a closed basin, in which glacio-lacustrine deposits have been mapped, south of Snape. There is a connection between this obviously subglacial valley and the aforementioned northward-trending buried valley beneath the lower Wiske (Plate 1.4) through which a pre-Devensian River Swale might have flowed. Indeed, if this were not the case there is no obvious reason why the connection should exist. From borehole surveys, it has been shown that the present River Ure is flowing above an incised palaeo-valley extending to depths of 30 to 53 m below the present floodplain (Fig. 1.2; Plate 1.4), down to *c.* -30 m O.D. (Thompson *et al.*, 1996). This is filled by a complex drift sequence that has a major influence on groundwater flow, enhancing the solution of anhydrite in the Permian strata (Cooper, 1986; Cooper & Burgess, 1993; see above).

1.4 Previous research: Quaternary geology

The remainder of Chapter 1 is largely devoted to previous wisdom, beginning here with brief reviews of the major themes in Quaternary research that have a direct bearing on the Washlands, paying specific attention to the glacial inheritance that is such an important part of the present landscape and geomorphology. Background information on fluvial and palaeoecological topics is reviewed in later sections (Chapter 1.6 & 1.8).

1.4.1 The early contributions

The distribution of superficial deposits within the Wash-lands was remarked upon in the earliest reports of the geology of the area (Sedgwick, 1825; Phillips, 1829). Whilst observing that there were clear differences between the sediments that obscured most of the solid rock and that they could be readily distinguished from present fluvial deposits, the early geologists had great problems in trying to explain the deposits beyond recourse to the Biblical flood. Quaternary research in this part of the world thus began essentially with the recognition of past glaciation, a paradigm shift widely attributed to the promotion of 'glacial theory' by Louis Agassiz in the mid 19th Century (see Introduction; Imbrie & Imbrie, 1979; Ellis *et al.*, 1996). Subsequent contributions merged outmoded ideas of diluvialism, in which much of the superficial drift cover had been attributed to the Biblical flood, with a glacial scheme that envisaged marine submergence at the same time as glaciation, leading to the formation of sea ice and icebergs that were thought to have deposited the 'boulder clay' and erratics (see review in Oldroyd, 2002).

The Washlands played a small but important part in resolving these issues; any satisfactory glacial theory had to explain the distinctive boulders of Shap granite, found as a notable erratic throughout the Washlands, which had been observed to be widely distributed from a source outcrop in the Vale of Eden, a distribution now known to reflect a former ice stream that transported them through the Stainmore Gap (see Chapter 2). Although this erratic distribution was hard to reconcile with floating sea-ice, the debate continued until the early 1870s, by which time the role of land ice had finally been established from field evidence in the north of England (cf. Beaumont, 1968; Oldroyd, 2002) and, from the evidence of ice flow directions, it was realised that northern England had been completely enveloped by ice. These ideas involved ice both originating within the area, forming on the Pennines, and moving southwards from Scotland, establishing an explanation for the various glacial erratic sources that is still accepted in overall terms today (Goodchild, 1875; Trotter & Hollingworth, 1932; Evans *et al.*, 2005).

The 19th Century also saw the beginning of a national geological mapping programme. The southern area of interest, around Harrogate, was first mapped by the Geological Survey between 1869 and 1871, with an accompanying memoir (Fox-Strangways, 1873). The northern part of the Washlands, centred on Northallerton and Thirsk, was mapped during 1878–1880 but only a summary memoir was ever published to accompany the first maps (Fox-Strangways *et al.*, 1886). This research established the major divisions of superficial deposits including 'boulder clay' (till), which was found to be extensive across the area. Within the northern part of the area, this could be divided into at least two distinct units, with the recognition of a lower blue clay with many erratics (granite, other igneous rocks and flint) and an upper reddish clay with fewer stones (Fox-Strangways *et al.*, 1886). Other sedimentary units were noted to occur in association with the tills, including stratified sand and gravels and large areas of laminated fine-grained lake sediments. A number of terraces composed of gravel were also identified along the Ure and Swale valleys. However, only brief descriptions of these sedimentary units were included in the memoir and their significance to an understanding of landscape evolution would require more detailed fieldwork leading to a major synthesis in the following century (Kendall & Wroot, 1924).

1.4.2 The Yorkshire Boulder Committee

The acceptance, in the latter part of the 19th Century, that northern Britain had been glaciated brought with it a widespread interest in the related phenomena, one of which was the distribution of erratic boulders throughout the country. Thus were established, under the leadership of the British Association for the Advancement of Science, of a number of 'Boulder Committees' at county level; the Yorkshire committee was one of the more enthusiastic and produced a number of reports describing interesting erratics found across the county (summarized by Kendall & Howarth, 1902; Sheppard, 1902; Howarth, 1908). This was important research that identified the existence of Norwegian boulders along the east coast, indicating the former presence of Scandinavian ice, as well as recording the presence of rocks from southwest Scotland, the Lake District (including Shap granite) and from the Cheviot Hills within the tills of Yorkshire (Howarth, 1908; Harmer, 1928).

Figure 1.3 summarizes this information and indicates the different provenances recorded by erratics across the Washlands. Within the Vale of York, erratic distribution demonstrates that the ice which covered this area came from a number of sources (Raistrick, 1926; Harmer, 1928). On the basis of these erratics, Vale-of-York ice can be seen to have originated from accumulation centres in the Lake District and southern Scotland, entering eastern England through the Stainmore Gap and joining local ice from Teesdale. This met ice flowing southwards down the eastern coastal plain of Durham from sources in Scotland and Northumberland that was diverted around the North York Moors to coalesce with Stainmore ice in the Vale of Mowbray. In contrast, in studies of the glacial geology of the Pennine uplands the absence of such distinctive erratics was noted (Fig. 1.3), suggesting that the Yorkshire Dales had generated local ice that flowed eastwards to coalesce with the main southward-moving ice masses in the Vale of York (Kendall & Wroot, 1924; Raistrick, 1926). The presence of east-coast erratics within the lower valley of the Tees (Fig. 1.3) indicates an incursion of ice into the area from the North Sea at some time during the last glaciation.

1.4.3 Glacial inheritance

In addition to the information obtained from erratic studies, the Vale of York and the Washlands contain landforms and sediments associated with the passage of an ice sheet. Such a conclusion was established by the latter part of the 19th Century with the influential work of Carvill Lewis and Percy Kendall. Both these geologists provided detailed field observations of features associated with the last ice sheet in Yorkshire. Lewis's contribution was published posthumously in 1894; Kendall's appeared in a major book on the geology of Yorkshire published with H.E. Wroot in 1924. Further observations on the glaciation and landscape of the Yorkshire Dales were made by Arthur Raistrick in the early 20th Century and continue to influence research in this upland area that impinges on the Washlands (Raistrick, 1926, 1927, 1931b, 1931c, 1932, 1933).

Although the Washlands are covered by thick superficial deposits (generally > 10 m, with till reaching maximum thicknesses of 30 m: Powell *et al.*, 1992), there are few exposures. There are also few easily recognizable landforms in a broadly undulating landscape with little relief and broken by discrete ridges and mounds in just a few places. Overall, the terrain reflects the pattern of glacial sedimentation associated with combined flow down the Vale of York from ice masses entering the area from Stainmore, County Durham and the Pennines (Johnson, 1970; King, 1976; Teasdale & Hughes; Evans *et al.*, 2005; Catt, 2007). In terms of the overall sediment–landform assemblage, this can be interpreted as delimiting a former

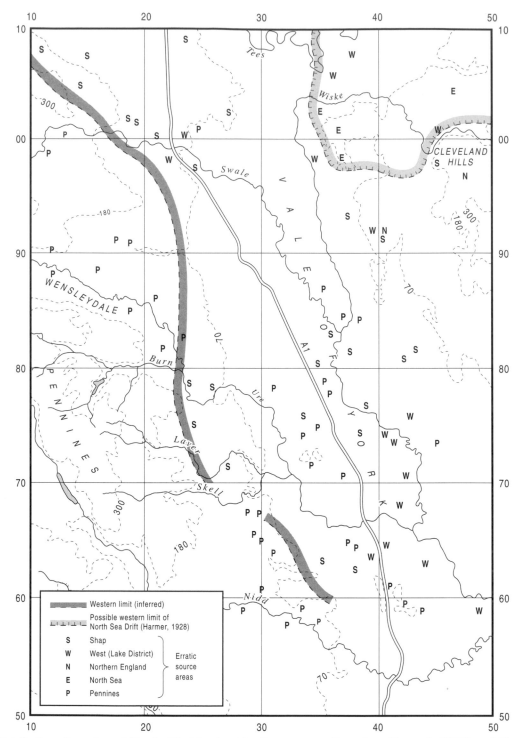

Fig. 1.3. Distribution of erratics within the Washlands and adjacent areas. Data from Howarth (1908) and Harmer (1928).

ice stream (cf. Stokes & Clark, 1999, 2001; Clark & Stokes, 2004) as is demonstrated by the occurrence of streamlined bedforms, including drumlins in certain areas, such as between Bedale and Masham (Johnson, 1969, 1974). Subsequent melting of this ice, leading to marginal retreat, is overprinted on the original subglacial landforms by the formation of a series of moraine ridges constructed by glacial depositional processes at former ice marginal positions. The presence of meltwater within this glacial system is marked by eskers (Plate 1.2), which are sinuous ridges formed by fluvial sedimentation within subglacial and englacial tunnels, and by the deposition of outwash sediments in the area beyond the former ice margins.

The most notable glacial landforms within the Vale of York are the impressive moraines at Escrick and York (Plate 1.2), which lie to the south of the present study area

(Lewis, 1887, 1894; Kendall & Wroot, 1924; Melmore, 1935; Gaunt, 1970). These terminal moraines can be traced across the vale and were originally interpreted as forming at an ice limit defining the maximum extent of the last ice sheet in the Vale of York (Lewis, 1894; Kendall & Wroot, 1924; Harrison, 1935; Melmore, 1935). An alternative interpretation has been proposed, however, that places the maximum extent of the Late Devensian ice sheet further south, near Doncaster (Gaunt, 1976, 1981), but the evidence remains equivocal (Straw, 2002; Evans *et al.*, 2005; Catt, 2007). This has important implications within the Washlands, as it questions the significance of the many moraine fragments that occur along the western flank of the Vale of York and, in particular, whether they mark the maximum lateral extent of the last ice sheet or are associated with recessional margins during deglaciation.

To the north of the York and Escrick moraines, a number of moraine fragments have been reported, particularly from the southern and western sectors of the Washlands (cf. Kendall & Wroot, 1924; see Chapter 2). There are few detailed published maps, although BGS drift maps for the area include possible moraines and eskers, information that is summarized in Figure 1.4. Many of the ridges appear to reflect former ice margins along the Pennine edge west of Ripon, from where they can be traced southwards and correlated with the western limits of the York and Escrick moraines around Knaresborough (Kendall & Wroot, 1924; Cooper & Burgess, 1993; A and B in Fig. 1.4). Some of these ridges may also be associated with a transverse moraine across the Vale of York defined as the Tollerton–Flaxby recessional ice limit (Cooper & Burgess, 1993; C in Fig. 1.4). Other moraines (including landforms constructed of sand and gravel) have been reported in the literature to the north-west of Ripon and interpreted as defining limits associated with Wensleydale ice (Kendall & Wroot, 1924; M in Fig. 1.4). Other such features have been identified along the edge of the Washlands from Kirklington to Catterick (K in Fig. 1.4), where they have been interpreted as marking either the western limit of Vale-of-York ice or as associated with Wensleydale ice after the two ice masses had pulled apart during deglaciation (Raistrick, 1926).

To the west of Catterick village, moraine ridges have also been described along the rising ground of on the northern side of Wensleydale (Raistrick, 1926) and are thought to be related to the northern limit of a glacier that occupied that valley at some stage during deglaciation (W in Fig. 1.4). These features can be correlated with the large moraine ridge at Leeming (L in Fig. 1.4) that reflects a readvance of Wensleydale ice during deglaciation (Frost, 1998; see Chapter 2). Recessional limits have also been proposed across the northern part of the Vale of York (Frost, 1998) but as no specific evidence was cited they are not recorded on Figure 1.4.

The presence of discrete topography associated with glacial and glaciofluvial sands and gravels has been used to identify anastomosing esker systems across the Vale of York (Plate 1.2; Fig. 1.4) that appear on the superficial geological maps of the area (Powell *et al.*, 1992; Cooper & Burgess, 1993; Frost, 1998). Two major systems have been mapped in the southern part of the Washlands (Aitkenhead *et al.*, 2002). The first of these, termed the Hunsingore esker (Cooper & Burgess, 1993), extends through the Tollerton–Flaxby recessional moraine just east of Flaxby (Fig. 1.4). To the east, a second esker system, the Helperby–Aldwark esker (Cooper & Burgess, 1993), extends northwards to continue as the Newby Wiske–Cundall esker (Powell *et al.*, 1992) along the western side of the River Swale towards the Wiske confluence (Fig. 1.4). Both of these eskers are thought to relate to former drainage lines within the Vale-of-York glacier that were maintained during deglaciation (Powell *et al.*, 1992; Cooper & Burgess, 1993).

The superficial deposits also contain information about the deglaciation of this area. It was during the ice retreat, with the associated generation of copious amounts of meltwater, that the main masses of sand and gravel were deposited. This has meant that the area has been the focus of aggregate resource evaluation (Abraham, 1981; Giles, 1982; Morigi & James, 1984). These Mineral Assessment Reports (see 1.3) have confirmed much of the earlier work but have also provided an assessment of the evidence with respect to the superficial deposits and associated landforms, including a number of borehole records across the Washlands.

1.4.4 Meltwater channels

Meltwater channels are found throughout the Washlands but are particularly well developed in certain areas (Plate 1.2; Fig. 1.4), reflecting a range of glaciofluvial influences in association with topography and former ice margins. It should be noted that there are variations associated with the presentation of channels on the BGS map sheets; for example, the high density of meltwater channels on Sheet 51 (Masham) results from a doctoral thesis (Wilson, 1957), but the same resolution of channels is not mapped southwards on Sheet 62 (Harrogate). This is clearly an artefact of intensive local study, as there is description of numerous channels in the literature on the Harrogate district (cf. Kendall & Wroot, 1924).

Along the Pennine slopes, there is a complex sequence of meltwater channels that have been previously interpreted as marginal to Vale-of-York ice (Kendall & Wroot, 1924; Melmore & Harrison, 1934; Melmore, 1935; Plate 1.2). However, the early papers record their origin as spillways of former lakes that were dammed between the slope and an ice margin (Kendall, 1902, 1903; Kendall & Wroot, 1924; Raistrick, 1926). Although it is likely that many of these channels are of ice marginal origin, they do not require the former presence of lakes for their formation (Gregory, 1962, 1965, 1967). This means that many of the earlier interpretations of landscape evolution in this area require modification in the light of later ideas of meltwater channel genesis, with a particular emphasis

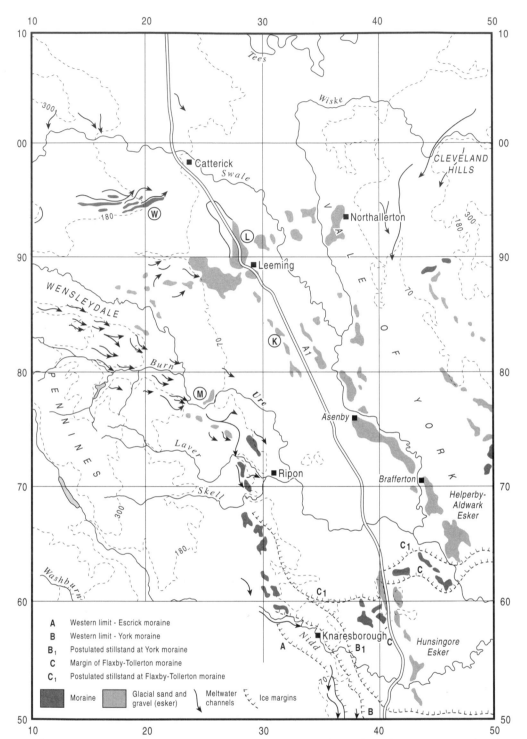

Fig. 1.4. Summary distribution of moraine ridge fragments and meltwater channels in the project area (combining BGS data with mapping from this project). For the explanation of points labelled (in circles) K, L, M & W, see text (Section 4.3).

on subglacial environments (cf. Sissons, 1960a, 1960b; Johnson, 1974). Present thinking is that there is a range of possible situations in which meltwater channels can form, including subglacial, marginal and proglacial types. Different geomorphological criteria for ascribing channels to specific environmental situations relate, for example, to the style of long profile, relationship to present day fluvial systems and anomalous dimensions in relation to present

streams (Huddart & Glasser, 2002a; Glasser *et al.*, 2004; McMillan *et al.*, 2005; Greenwood *et al.*, 2007).

The complex channel distribution along the Pennine flank reflects the retreat of an active ice margin northwards and westwards across the Washlands into the upland; this deglaciation sequence has had an important influence on the development of the present drainage pattern and the position of the major rivers, since there are a number of abandoned high-level channels that appear to be the precursors of the present rivers (Kendall & Wroot, 1924; Raistrick, 1926). Within the Washlands, the most impressive area for meltwater channels lies to the west, from Knaresborough north towards Ripon (Fig. 1.4), where the present river systems have a complex origin associated with changing ice limits (Kendall & Wroot, 1924; Johnson, 1969, 1974). Within the catchments of the Skell and Laver, two western tributaries that join the Ure at Ripon, there are numerous large incised abandoned channels indicative of formation against an ice margin that diverted lateral drainage south-eastwards along the Pennine flank towards the Vale of York. This can be seen to good effect in the present course of the Nidd and the abandoned channels that linked earlier versions of the Laver and Skell to this system (Kendall & Wroot, 1924; Raistrick, 1926; Melmore & Harrison, 1934; Johnson, 1974). Within the Ure valley between Ripon and Masham are abandoned channels that, although likely to have carried meltwater, are thought to represent former courses of the Ure. These include the Thieves Gill channel, which can be traced from the south side of Hackfall Gorge towards the Skell catchment at Ripon (Kendall & Wroot, 1924). Another abandoned channel of the Ure has been identified north of Masham, at Marfield (Kendall & Wroot, 1924; Raistrick, 1926). Two further abandoned channels are found downstream of Ripon at Sharow and Newby Hall.

A further complex set of large meltwater channels can be observed around Richmond, in Swaledale, associated with the northern margin of Wensleydale ice (Kendall & Wroot, 1924; Raistrick, 1926; Wells, 1955; Plate 1.2) and with an ice limit to the north thought to be the southern margin of Stainmore ice (Kendall & Wroot, 1924; Wells, 1955).

1.4.5 Glacial lakes

Widespread areas of fine-grained sediment, particularly clays, indicate the former presence within the Washlands of glacial lakes. These were generally associated with deglaciation, when meltwater was ponded in front of the remaining ice or dammed by glacial deposits (cf. Abraham, 1981; Giles, 1982; Morigi & James, 1984). The most extensive area of lake clay lies outside the Escrick moraine and extends southwards (Plate 1.2). These sediments reflect the former presence of a large proglacial lake, Lake Humber, which was formed by North Sea ice blocking drainage through the Humber (Lewis, 1894; Dalton, 1941; Gaunt, 1976; Gaunt et al., 1971; Straw & Clayton, 1979; Bateman & Buckland, 2001). This lake is thought to have continued in existence long after deglaciation, due to glacial sediments blocking the Humber Gap (Gaunt, 1981; Gaunt et al., 2006), and might have played an important role as a local base level for the river systems, including the Swale and Ure, which lay immediately upstream of the lake.

Extensive distribution of lacustrine clays and associated littoral sediments has allowed reconstruction of the extent and elevation of Lake Humber (Gaunt, 1974, 1976, 1981, 1994). The deposits have been interpreted as representing two phases of the lake; along the margins there are discontinuous sands and gravels between 27 and 33 m O.D. that are thought to indicate shorelines formed during an earlier high-level phase (Edwards, 1937; Gaunt, 1981, 1994). These extend northwards from Wroot, east of Doncaster (Gaunt, 1976), and generally rise in elevation northwards (due to isostatic recovery) terminating at the Escrick moraine, where they have been shown to onlap onto and nearly bury the ridge (Kendall & Wroot, 1924; Edwards, 1937; Gaunt, 1994). These deposits rest on an older 'lower periglacial surface' with cryoturbation structures and ventifacts (Gaunt, 1981; Gaunt et al., 2006) and are themselves disturbed to form the 'upper periglacial surface' which can be seen to be buried by lower littoral deposits. Evidence of desiccation of the clays at 4 m O.D. has been used to propose a draining of the high lake before it refilled to the second lower lake level at about 8 m O.D. (the 25' drift). This is marked by sands and widespread clays, in places > 20 m thick, over much of the southern Vale of York outside the Escrick moraine (Gaunt, 1981, 1994; Gaunt et al., 2006).

The high-level early Lake Humber is thought to have been in existence for about 4000 years (Bateman & Buckland, 2001); this is based on one radiocarbon date of 21,835 ± 1600 ^{14}C BP (>24,000 cal. BP; Bateman & Buckland, 2001), from a bone (unidentifiable) found within beach gravels (Older Littoral Sand and Gravel) interpreted as associated with the former lake (Gaunt, 1974). However, this pre-dates ice damming of the Humber Gap, which is thought to have occurred later, as demonstrated by the radiocarbon dates from Dimlington of 18,500 ± 400 ^{14}C BP (Penny et al., 1969; Rose, 1985) – c. 21,900 cal. BP (Bateman & Buckland, 2001; see Section 1.5.1). More recently, sediments thought to be from this high lake stage have given a thermoluminescence (TL) date of 22,670 ± 1400 BP (Bateman & Buckland, 2001). A further TL date of 17,670 ± 1200 BP from periglacially disturbed lake sands suggests that the high level of Lake Humber had receded by this time (Bateman et al., 2000); however OSL dates from littoral deposits at Ferrybridge have given slightly later ages of 16,500 ± 1,100 BP (Gaunt et al., 2006) and 16,600 ± 1200 BP (Bateman et al., 2008). It therefore appears that the first high-level stage of Lake Humber formed about 22,000 BP, dammed by an advance of ice along the east coast, and had drained by c. 16,000 years ago. However, there is still considerable ambiguity about the dating, given the standard errors of the TL/OSL dates (making them statistically indistinguishable) and uncertainty regarding radiocarbon calibration (cf. Walker, 2005).

The second stage, lower-level Lake Humber deposited an extensive and thick sequence of laminated lake clays and marginal sands (Gaunt, 1981, 1994). Little information is currently available about the time at which this lower lake was formed; indeed, there are problems in explaining the formation of a dam across the Humber Gap later in the

Dimlington Stadial, as the ice is supposed to have retreated by this time (Rose, 1985). An OSL date of 14,100 ± 2100 BP has been linked to the low-level lake; it comes from fluvial deposits filling a channel that is thought to have been feeding into this lake, which would thus have to have existed at that time (cf. Gaunt *et al.*, 2006). A minimum age for the final disappearance of the lake is derived from a date of 11,100 ± 200 ^{14}C BP from a buried soil developed on the lake clays (Bateman & Buckland, 2001). The lack of a series of shorelines, the similar elevation of the lake sediments to the adjacent sand units and the grading upwards of the lake sediments into sands are all thought to indicate that the lake ceased to exist by silting up rather than by draining (Gaunt, 1981), although this has been questioned by recent investigations of the till sequence at South Ferriby in the Humber Gap, from which have arisen suggestions of an earlier breaching of the glacial deposits impounding the lake (Frederick *et al.*, 2001). After the lake ceased to exist, there was incision through the lake sediments, perhaps resulting from adjustment by the rivers in response to isostatic uplift and/or the elimination of the intermediate base level that the lake represented.

During the time that Lake Humber was in existence, the land beyond the southern margin of the ice sheet was subjected to intense periglacial processes and the formation of a tundra environment of disturbed soils and limited vegetation (Jones & Keen, 1993; Bateman & Buckland, 2001). The climate at the LGM was arid and intensely cold (cf. Hubberten *et al.*, 2004). Much of lowland England consisted of bare ground associated with active glacial outwash systems, the floodplains of outwash-charged braided rivers and numerous dried-up lake beds. All of these areas supported thick continuous permafrost and were subjected to intense desiccation and erosion as a result of powerful winds blowing around the ice margin (Clarke *et al.*, 2007). These winds entrained silt and fine sand from the bare ground and deposited it downwind on the eastern side of the Vale of York as coversand and loess (e.g. Bateman *et al.*, 2000).

Lake Humber was not the only lake to come into existence during the last glaciation, although it was certainly one of the largest (Clark *et al.*, 2004a). There are extensive areas of lacustrine sediments in the Washlands (Plate 1.2; Fig. 1.5) deposited in numerous temporary lakes formed by meltwater impounded during northwards ice retreat in the Vale of York. The floors of these former lakes now form extensive areas of flat land within the present river system, particularly downstream of Ripon within the Ure catchment and in many parts of the present Swale floodplain between Boroughbridge and Catterick. One extensive area of lake sediments, Snape Mires, chosen as a site for detailed palaeoenvironmental investigation during this project has shown that the lake existed during the Lateglacial period but had disappeared by the early Holocene; it also revealed an interesting suite of tufa deposits that has provided important information on early Holocene conditions (Chapter 2.8.2).

1.5 Previous research: the last British–Irish Ice Sheet (BIIS)

The influence of former glaciation on the present Washlands landscape, described in the previous section, needs to be placed in the overall context of the last British–Irish Ice Sheet (BIIS), both in terms of regional and complete ice sheet reconstructions. This also necessitates a review of the ice sheet within the climate–ocean dynamics of the North Atlantic European margin to assess these reconstructions, based on the geological evidence, within models of climate and environmental change. This requires not only efforts to define the ice sheet but also to constrain it within a temporal framework.

Recent developments in dating techniques, particularly using cosmogenic radionuclides (CRN), together with new studies of the marine record from the Atlantic continental shelf and the North Sea, have required modifications to the accepted extent and established chronology for the BIIS (Bowen *et al.*, 2002; Wilson *et al.*, 2002; Hall *et al.*, 2003; Merritt *et al.*, 2003; Carr, 2004; Boulton & Hagdorn, 2006; Carr *et al.*, 2006). However, the data providing chronostratigraphical constraint on the development and extent of the ice sheet is still minimal. New Scottish sites at Sourlie (Ayrshire) and Balglass (Stirlingshire) have yielded important biostratigraphical evidence from organic sediments below till that has allowed the reconstruction and dating of environmental conditions and led to the conclusion that central lowland Scotland was ice-free during the Middle Devensian, around 30,000 ^{14}C ago (Bos *et al.*, 2004; Brown *et al.*, 2007a). However, palaeoclimate reconstructions from coleoptera at Balglass suggest that the mountain areas of the British Isles would have been glaciated at this time.

A comparison can be made with evidence from the North Sea, from which similar dates indicate ice-free conditions prior to advance of Scandinavian ice after 29,000 ^{14}C BP (Sejrup *et al.*, 1994, 2005). Recent investigations on the continental shelf west of the British Isles show a marked increase in ice rafted debris (IRD) associated with the BIIS at *c.* 26,500 BP, reflecting ice advance to the shelf edge at this time (Peck *et al.*, 2007). Thus, it appears that by the beginning of the Dimlington Stadial, the BIIS and Scandinavian ice sheets were in existence and advancing across lowland areas. No sites providing constraining evidence for the build up of the ice sheet are presently known from northern England.

1.5.1 Timing and extent

Recent research on the last glaciation in NW Europe indicates an early phase of ice advance, during which the British and Scandinavian ice sheets coalesced within the North Sea basin, beginning after 29,000 and reaching a maximum extent at around 23,000 ^{14}C BP (Sejrup *et al.*, 1994, 2000, 2005). This was followed at around 20,000 ^{14}C BP by a period of deglaciation, when large areas of the North Sea and possibly lowland areas of Britain became

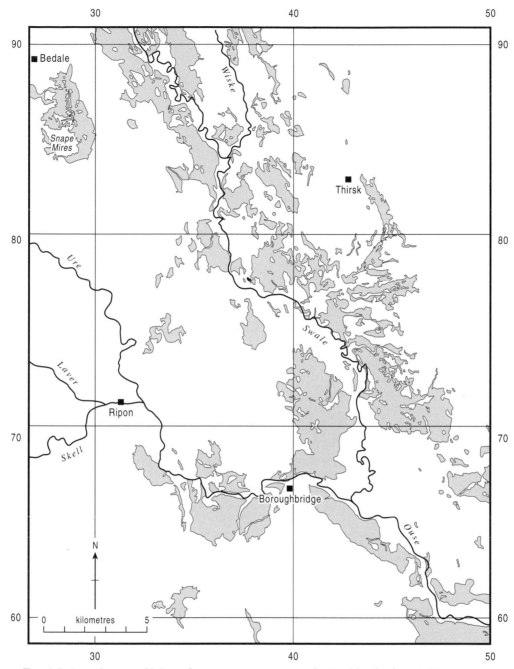

Fig. 1.5. Distribution of lake sediments cropping out in the Washlands (from BGS mapping).

ice-free. Based on the Dimlington dates (see 1.4.5), this 'interstadial' is thought to have lasted until around 18,500 [14]C (*c.* 22,000 cal. yrs) BP. This later advance of the BIIS has been traditionally accepted as the main advance, defining the LGM of the Dimlington Stadial (Rose, 1985; Clark *et al.*, 2004a, b). In the North Sea, the Scandinavian ice sheet also advanced at this time, but not to the same extent, so that the ice sheets no longer merged (Sejrup *et al.*, 2000; Carr, 2004). The precise extent of both ice masses in the North Sea and the position of sea level at this time continue to be debated. However, the geological record of ice-rafted debris (IRD) in the large submarine fans along

the western seaboard of the British Isles indicates that the ice had reached its maximal extent earlier in the Late Devensian, before 25,000 years ago (Wilson *et al.*, 2002; Peck *et al.*, 2007).

Studies of glacial landforms and sediments have shown that the BIIS was sourced from a number of upland areas of the British Isles, with major centres in the Grampians, Southern Uplands, northern England, Wales and Ireland (Clark *et al.*, 2004a; Knight, 2004; Evans *et al.*, 2005; Jansson & Glasser, 2005; Mitchell & Riley, 2006). There were also a number of smaller independent accumulation centres along the western seaboard, allowing local ice development over the Outer Hebrides and Shetland (Hall *et al.*, 2003; Stone & Ballantyne, 2006). A number of independent centres would seem to have operated in Ireland, with changes in their relative importance during the glaciation (Knight *et al.*, 2004; McCabe *et al.*, 2005; Clark *et al.*, 2006; Ballantyne *et al.*, 2007).

Along most of the western seaboard of Scotland and Ireland, the BIIS appears to have reached the shelf edge, where large submarine fans were formed, fed by ice streams within the BIIS (Sejrup *et al.*, 2005). Ice streams, which are dynamic fast moving components of ice sheets, are increasingly recognized from the pattern of streamlined subglacial landforms, such as drumlins, with superimposed former ice flow directions (Rose & Letzer, 1977; Mitchell, 1994; Stokes & Clark, 2001; Clark & Stokes, 2004; Mitchell & Riley, 2006). The evidence for these former ice streams shows that the BIIS was actively deforming its bed over many lowland areas (Boulton & Hagdorn, 2006; Plate 1.5). In the Irish Sea Basin, which was occupied by a very large ice stream between the British and Irish ice centres (and fed by both), the ice is now known to have reached as far south as the Isles of Scilly (Hiemstra *et al.*, 2006), where a recent CRN date of 19,800 BP shows that this occurred during the LGM (McCarroll *et al.*, 2006). By implication, this indicates that the ice sheet was more extensive in southern Ireland (O'Cofaigh & Evans, 2001, 2007; Evans & O'Cofaigh, 2003) and in the Celtic Sea (Sejrup *et al.*, 2005) than proposed in previous ice sheet reconstructions (for example, Boulton *et al.*, 1977; Boulton *et al.*, 1985; Bowen *et al.*, 2002; Knight, 2005).

Along the east coast of England, LGM ice is thought to have extended to north Norfolk, depositing the Hunstanton Till at the furthest edge of the ice sheet (Evans *et al.*, 2001, 2005). Offshore this till has been traced eastwards as an extensive lobe abutting against an older moraine complex that forms the Dogger Bank (Carr, 1999, 2004; Carr *et al.*, 2006). The limit of this ice, which blocked the Wash, can be traced northwards along the eastern side of the Lincolnshire Wolds towards the Humber (Straw & Clayton, 1979; Evans *et al.*, 2005), blocking the Humber Gap and leading to the formation of Lake Humber (Section 1.4.5). In coastal sections in east Yorkshire, two tills have been recorded above the dated Dimlington Silts. The lower of these, the Skipsea Till, is a dark greyish brown diamicton with erratics that include chalk and flint from the North Sea, Scandinavian metamorphic rocks, Cheviot porphyry and Southern Upland lithologies; it is overlain by the less extensively distributed Withernsea Till, which contains Carboniferous lithologies and igneous rocks from the Lake District (Rose, 1985; Catt, 1991b; Evans, 2002a; Evans *et al.*, 2005; Catt, 2007). The configuration of this part of the ice sheet has been interpreted as a southward surge along the east coast (Eyles *et al.*, 1994).

Further north, towards the Tees estuary, there is a more complex glacial sequence with further tills, together with sand and gravels (Elgee, 1908; Agar, 1954; Catt, 2007), allowing definition of an ice margin along the northern flank

of the North York Moors and the eastern side of the Vales of Mowbray and York (Melmore, 1935; Gayner & Melmore, 1936a, b; Radge, 1940; Catt, 1991a, b, 2007; Clark *et al.*, 2004a; Evans *et al.*, 2005). A similar suite of landforms on the western side of the Vale of York allows definition of a major ice lobe occupying the Vale and terminating at the York and Escrick moraines (Melmore & Harrison, 1934; Melmore, 1935; Peel & Palmer, 1955; Tolley, 1962; Penny, 1964; Gaunt, 1976; Gaunt *et al.*, 1971).

It is now also clear that the internal dynamics of an ice sheet are strongly controlled by the spatial organization of basal thermal regimes (Kleman & Glasser, 2007). Key elements of this pattern are the development of ice streams as the major means of ice flux through the system (Boulton & Hagdorn, 2006). Conversely, areas where there is no evidence of basal sliding and where non-glacial landforms and sediments are preserved covered by cold passive ice, frozen to the bed, which was incapable of erosion (Kleman & Glasser, 2007). These areas appear to be related to the main accumulation zones, where there were minimal values of basal stress; although they may also represent inter-ice stream areas where flow was slow and non-linear.

From on-shore geomorphological data and off-shore marine sediment sequences, the areal extent of the ice sheet can be reconstructed; however, the paucity of dates and the probable diachronous nature of a dynamic ice margin mean that, at present, there is still minimal temporal control on delimiting the BIIS. A conjectural impression of the ice sheet as presently understood is shown in Plate 1.5; because of the highly diachronous behaviour of the numerous ice centres, particularly during deglaciation, this does not represent any specific point in time (see 1.5.3).

1.5.2 Ice sheet dynamics: climate–ocean–ice sheet interactions

Recent research projects on marine cores from the North Atlantic and ice cores from the Greenland ice sheet have produced high-resolution proxy records for climate and oceanographic change that have been important in developing understanding of the dynamic behaviour of former ice sheets. Of particular importance is the complexity of the isotopic signal, indicating that within Milankovitch-driven 100,000 year glacial–interglacial climate cycles there are recurring events at shorter millennial and centennial timescales (Björk *et al.*, 1998; Johnsen *et al.*, 2001; Wilson *et al.*, 2002). These 'sub-Milankovitch' signals are poorly understood but appear to be important links between cryosphere, oceans and atmosphere, particularly during the last glacial cycle (Peck *et al.*, 2007). In the ice cores they are thought to equate with the Dansgaard–Oescher climatic cycles, which have a periodicity of around 2000–3000 years and are related to Heinrich events, which are maxima of ice rafted debris (IRD) identified in the North Atlantic marine cores (Björk *et al.*, 1998; Chapman *et al.*, 2000; Knutz *et al.*, 2001; Kageyama *et al.*, 2006; Peck *et al.*, 2007). Heinrich events indicate that vast armadas of icebergs formed at a *c.* 7000 year periodicity, perhaps triggered by warming in the north, although their southward drift within the North Atlantic gyre would have had a cooling effect on the ocean, either directly or by destabilizing the thermohaline circulation. The related millennial-scale cycles of climatic fluctuation (Chapman *et al.*, 2000; Scourse *et al.*, 2000) have been suggested as the driver of BIIS responses (McCabe *et al.*, 2005). In the ice cores, climatic warming events at the millennial scale are identified as interstadials (Björk *et al.*, 1998; Mayle *et al.*, 1999), typically beginning with rapid warming and then cooling over 1000–3000 years, culminating in a Heinrich event recorded in the marine record. Within the Late Devensian, four major Heinrich events have been noted at 26,700 (H3), 21,400 (H2), 14,200 (H1) and 10,000 (H0), all ^{14}C BP (Chapman *et al.*, 2000; Merritt *et al.*, 2003). There is, however, still a range of published dates for each Heinrich event, causing problems of correlation within glacial events such as ice sheet readvances (see, for example, McCabe *et al.*, 2005). New high-resolution multi-proxy records of IRD from west of Ireland question the above correlation and have led to the alternative proposal that the BIIS pulsed at a 2000 year periodicity, onto which are superimposed the Heinrich events, which were driven by the Laurentide ice sheet (Peck *et al.*, 2007).

1.5.3 Deglaciation

Deglaciation, by its nature, was strongly diachronous across the country with peripheral lowland areas of the ice sheet disappearing much earlier than in upland source areas. Rapid retreat would have first occurred in offshore areas, as the ice came into contact with rising marine water, which would have triggered glaciological changes such as ice-stream surges and rapid downwasting. On land, decay proceeded by both active marginal retreat of the ice and by melting of stagnant ice that had become separated from its source. The pattern of deglaciation can be clearly established by examination of the resultant landforms (cf. Evans, 2004). An important aspect of understanding deglaciation is establishing its timing in different areas, which has been traditionally achieved by radiocarbon dating the basal organic sediments deposited immediately following deglaciation, such as in kettle-hole lakes formed by the melting of ice within moraines or left as stagnant remnants. Such dates, however, only give minimum ages for deglaciation, there being uncertainty about any potential time lag between ice disappearance and the beginning of organic sedimentation. Most reported dates record Lateglacial ages of between 14,500 and 13,000 ^{14}C BP, with earlier dates in north-western England than in the lowlands of east Yorkshire, as noted by Innes (2002a).

For many years it was generally accepted that ice sheet retreat was a continuous process and that earlier ideas of major readvances during deglaciation were incompatible with the geomorphological evidence (cf. Sissons, 1976).

Detailed field mapping of landforms, as well as the results of stratigraphical analyses and improved dating (AMS radiocarbon, OSL and cosmogenic isotopes), have challenged this model in a number of areas of the British Isles. As well as the recognition of a more complex LGM glacial sequence, it is now considered that deglaciation was indeed marked by readvances in a number of different areas of Scotland and around the Irish Sea Basin (cf. Thomas *et al.*, 2004).

Cosmogenic dates from a number of different locations around the British Isles (Bowen *et al.*, 2002; Everest & Kubek, 2006; Everest *et al.*, 2006) combine to suggest a complex regional response that may relate to ocean–climate–ice sheet coupling around the North Atlantic. It has been proposed that these advances can be correlated with H1, but given that there are broad ranges of dates for both H1 and the BIIS advances, this remains speculative (Everest *et al.*, 2006). Indeed, it is becoming clear that the BIIS was a highly sensitive ice sheet with a number of different source areas that were responding independently to forcing mechanisms, leading to distinct regional-scale ice advances (McCabe *et al.*, 2005, 2007a, 2007b; Peck *et al.*, 2007).

In eastern England, there are relatively few sites with radiocarbon dates that constrain the timing of deglaciation within a regional pattern. These few sites may be correlated with others for which there is a Lateglacial palaeoenvironmental record, usually from pollen (e.g. Innes, 2002a), allowing the time of deglaciation to be estimated, albeit with limited resolution (see Section 1.8). Key pollen sites for deglaciation in eastern England include Kildale Hall, on the northern margin of the North York Moors (Jones, 1977a), where a date of 16,713 ± 340 ^{14}C BP was obtained from mosses within a shell marl. However, because of the calcareous nature of this deposit, it has been suggested that the date has been affected by hard-water error and is too old (Day, 1996a; Innes, 2002b). The basal date at Roos, Holderness, of 13,045 ± 270 ^{14}C BP (Beckett, 1981) is taken as marking the end of the Dimlington Stadial (Rose, 1985) and can be used as a minimum age for deglaciation. Recent investigations from sediments found within a kettle hole at Gransmoor, Holderness, has provided a wealth of high-resolution palaeoenvironmental data; the oldest date from here, 12,445 ± 90 ^{14}C BP, was not obtained from the basal sediments (Evans, 2002b). Other pollen sites in the area, such as Tadcaster (Bartley, 1962; Innes, 2002c), have Lateglacial sediments but have not been dated. Correlation with the few dated sites again suggests a minimum age for deglaciation and for the end of the Dimlington Stadial of 13,000 ^{14}C BP (Rose, 1985).

With the ice gone, the landscape began to adapt to new non-glacial environmental conditions during a period of 'paraglacial' adjustment (cf. Ballantyne, 2002). Although the climate remained severely cold during the main period of deglaciation, rapid climatic amelioration, which marked the early part of the Lateglacial, brought about geomorphological changes associated with more temperate conditions; at the same time there was dramatic ecological change, with the return to the Washlands of many temperate species including woodland trees (Chapter 1.8). The disappearance of the ice during deglaciation led to isostatic uplift, giving rivers an impetus for valley incision through the Lateglacial and into the Holocene (cf. Shennan & Andrews, 2000; Shennan *et al.*, 2006).

1.6 Previous research: post-glacial fluvial sequences

An important and fruitful avenue of research on fluvial sequences, and one with an international perspective, has been the documentation of changing fluvial regimes during the periods of differing climate since the LGM. Thus changes between braided and meandering regimes have been recognized, as well as more subtle changes in meander size, which is controlled by discharge (Dury, 1955, 1958; Leopold and Wolman, 1960; Bridge, 2003). Although the deposits of braided and meandering rivers can be distinguished from suites of sedimentary structures and from gross sediment architecture (Miall, 1977, 1978, 1985; Bridge, 1993), the best archives of this type are from broad floodplains on which rivers have migrated freely during the last climate cycle, leading to the preservation of numerous palaeochannels. Excellent records of this type come from the River Tisza in Hungary, the Warta in Poland and the Maas in the Netherlands (Gábris & Nagy, 2005; Vandenberghe *et al.*, 1994; Vandenberghe, 2003, 2007), in areas beyond the reach of the last ice sheets (and so with records for the LGM as well). From these optimal records a largely consistent pattern has emerged, one of braided systems during the colder episodes, such as the LGM and the stadials of the Lateglacial, changing to meanders during the warmer periods. There are also differences in meander wavelength and palaeochannel width that, in general, record declining discharge later in the Holocene.

In Britain, research on Lateglacial and Holocene fluvial sediments has primarily taken geomorphological and geoarchaeological approaches (see next section), with anthropogenic signatures, such as the onset of alluviation (caused by enhanced soil erosion as land was tilled for farming: Bell & Boardman, 1992; Brown, 1997; Edwards & Whittington, 2001) and pollution from early mining (Macklin *et al.*, 1997; Sedgewick, 1998; Macklin, 1999; Hudson-Edwards *et al.*, 1999a, b; Coulthard & Macklin, 2003; Dennis *et al.*, 2003), proving valuable as a means of reconstructing sedimentation histories and sediment movements within catchments. Fluvial sequences are complex, with subsequent deposition or erosion burying or removing previous alluvial units (Lewin & Macklin, 2003). Where suitable materials have been available, however, radiocarbon dating has been used successfully to constrain the ages of Late Devensian and Holocene fluvial sequences (e.g. Tipping, 1994; Howard *et al.*, 1999a, 2000a, b; Moores *et al.*, 1999; Passmore & Macklin, 2001;

Lewin *et al.*, 2005). The compilation of a database of >600 radiocarbon ages from appropriate fluvial contexts has provided important insights into flood periodicity and potential correlation with forcing mechanisms (Macklin & Lewin, 2003; Lewin *et al.*, 2005; Macklin *et al.*, 2005, 2006; Johnstone *et al.*, 2006). Early maps have provided means of tracking recent sedimentation, erosion, channel migration and other fluvial processes in considerable detail (e.g., Thorne & Lewin, 1979; Hooke *et al.*, 1990; Lewin *et al.*, 2005). Computer modelling of catchment response to such forcing mechanisms has allowed models of fluvial systems to be developed and evaluated against field data (Coulthard *et al.*, 2005).

Many of these fluvial studies relate specifically to Pennine catchments (Passmore *et al.*, 1992; Taylor & Macklin, 1997; Macklin *et al.*, 2000; Howard *et al.*, 2000a, b; Lewin *et al.*, 2005; Johnstone *et al.*, 2006). Some have studied linkages between hillslope and valley floor stability to ascertain the causes of periods of erosion and deposition within the Holocene (Foulds & Macklin, 2006), work that has demonstrated the importance of coupled hillslope and fluvial systems in understanding environmental change (Harvey, 2001, 2002; Chiverrell & Menuge, 2003; Chiverrell *et al.*, 2007a). Fluvial deposition may occur as bulk packages of sediment laid down during extreme events, such as flooding, rather than from the gradual sedimentation characteristic of environments like peat mires and lakes, leading most to conclude that rivers are poor sources of palaeoenvironmental data (Foulds & Macklin, 2006). Mixing of sediment during transport and the variability of transportation and sedimentation rates have been perceived as taphonomic problems that hamper interpretation of fluvial sequences. In places such as backwater areas or floodplain margins, however, regular processes such as seasonal over-bank flooding or slow accumulation within dense floodplain vegetation can preserve a detailed and relatively continuous time-series of both local- and catchment-scale events (Scaife & Burrin, 1992).

1.6.1 Post-glacial rivers are (re)established

By *c.* 13,000 ^{14}C BP (= *c.* 15,000 cal. BP), at the latest, climatic amelioration had resulted in removal of the Dimlington Stadial ice sheet from the whole of northern England. Fluvial records in the region generally commence with deglaciation, rivers having typically begun their role in modifying the landscape as meltwater streams related to the receding ice margins in the Vale of York and Wensleydale. Many valley sequences begin with thick, coarse gravel aggradations formed by meltwater from the degrading ice, which provided the new river systems with high discharge (enabling transport of coarse material) and large sediment loads. Many rivers were (re)established under periglacial conditions prior to Lateglacial climatic amelioration (Vandenberghe, 2001, 2007; Vandenberghe & Woo, 2002).

Fluvial records in northern England thus generally commence with late Devensian deglaciation, typically represented by a high-level 'outwash' terrace, following which the rivers have progressively incised their valleys. It has been suggested that low sea levels at the beginning of the Holocene permitted this incision, locally down to -20 m O.D. in the Vale of York (Gaunt, 1981), although Bridgland and Austin (1999) questioned whether rivers would cut down at a time when sea level was rising. Sea-level influences, often regarded as key in causing rivers to incise or aggrade (e.g., McCave, 1969; Törnqvist, 1998; Karner & Marra, 1998; Blum & Straffin, 2001), are probably less important than imagined, particularly upstream from coastal reaches (Bridgland, 2000; Maddy *et al.*, 2000; Bridgland & Westaway, 2007a, 2007b). In fact the progressive Holocene incision into their valley floors by piedmont river systems such as those flowing into the Vale of York was probably a response to declining sediment supply and ice sheet unloading (isostatic rebound); it gave rise to a series of river terraces above the contemporary channel (Howard *et al.*, 2000a).

Throughout much of the Holocene, prior to anthropogenic interference, the rivers traversing the lowlands of the Vale of York were probably stable multi-channelled (anastomosed) systems (Dinnin, 1997; Howard & Macklin, 2003). This would have reflected low rates of lateral movement and relatively high rates of fine-grained sedimentation and can be contrasted with the upland and piedmont rivers, which had greater vertical and lateral instability, as demonstrated by meander cut-offs and terrace incision (Macklin *et al.*, 2000; Taylor *et al.*, 2000). Documentary and cartographic evidence indicates that many of these channel systems survived in the Humber lowlands until large-scale drainage and land reclamation in the early 17th Century AD (Howard & Macklin, 2003). The advent of deforestation and farming in the Holocene brought soil erosion, enhancing sediment delivery to the valley floor (Taylor *et al.*, 2000; Chiverrell *et al.*, 2007a). This and the subsequent effects of metal mining, with its environmental contamination, are fruitful areas of geoarchaeological research (e.g. Hudson-Edwards *et al.*, 1999a; see below).

1.6.2 River terraces

Throughout northern England, the fluvial record from the period since deglaciation invariably takes the form of sporadic sedimentation within a regime of progressive incision (cf. Macklin, 1997). Given that sea level was rising for most of this period (see above), the most likely driver for the incision is glacio-isostatic uplift; i.e. rebound from the previous crustal depression beneath the weight of the last ice sheet. Rivers formed on the freshly deglaciated land surface often reoccupied pre-glacial drainage routes, many of which had been modified by subglacial and lateral meltwater; the River Wear and the coastal denes of County Durham are good examples (Woolacott, 1905;

Smith & Francis, 1967; Bridgland, 1999). Subsequent incision has left meltwater-deposited gravels as the highest, and frequently the most impressive, within the sequences of aggradational terraces that characterize many northern British valleys, recording progressive post-glacial downcutting by the rivers. In northern England, this type of record is seen both in the west, where Boardman (1981, 1994, 1997, 2002) instigated a detailed study of Mosedale Beck in the northeast Lake District (Fig. 1.6), and in the east, within the Pennine Dales, where Howard *et al.* (2000b) have established a definitive terrace sequence in upper Wharfedale (Fig. 1.7). This particular sequence represents a standard for comparison with the Washlands record.

Aggradational river terraces are much better known from areas beyond the reach of the last ice sheets, where they often represent long Pleistocene records, with glacial and interglacial environments recorded; this is the case even in systems just beyond the reach of the Devensian glaciation, such as the Trent (e.g. Brandon & Sumbler, 1988, 1991; White *et al.*, 2007) and the Fenland rivers (e.g. Gao *et al.*, 2007; Boreham *et al.*, in press). Thus areas in southern Britain provide exemplars for studying terrace deposits, albeit at different scales in both time and extent. The best such British record is undoubtedly that of the River Thames, the gravel terraces of which were originally mapped and given names by early Geological Survey researchers (Bromehead, 1912; Dewey & Bromehead, 1915, 1921; Dewey *et al.*, 1924), although later the classification of terraces by numbering was the favoured method of the British Geological Survey (BGS) for many years (1970s–'90s), including the mapping of the Ure upstream from Masham (see above, Section 1.3). The BGS has recently returned to using names for the Pleistocene terraces of the Thames and other major rivers, following the lead of the geological community in general, in which formal lithostratigraphy has been applied increasingly (cf. Bowen, 1999; Schreve *et al.*, 2002). Notwithstanding this trend with regard to Pleistocene terraces, each of which generally represents a whole 100,000 year Milankovitch cycle (or a large proportion of a cycle), there have been no attempts to apply this method of classification to Post-glacial (Holocene) terraces. Indeed, the above-mentioned recognition, on BGS sheet 51, of separate 1st and 2nd terraces of the Ure between Wensley and Masham is a rare example of such subdivision on published geological maps; generally BGS mapping has not distinguished separate terraces within Post-glacial fluvial deposits. The Holocene fluvial research community, in contrast, has recognized multiple terraces in many valleys, albeit small-scale and often localized features resulting from meander migration. These workers have generally numbered the terraces downwards, the reverse of BGS practice. In the Ure around Ripon, for example, Howard *et al.* (2000a) recognized four small-scale terraces, numbered downwards (see Chapter 2.6.4).

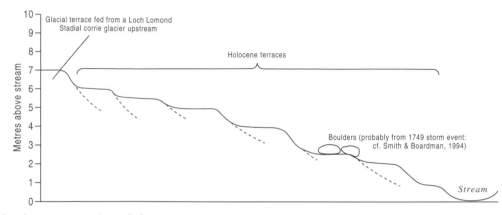

Fig. 1.6. Idealized cross section through the terrace sequence of the Mosedale Beck, near Troutbeck, Cumbria (NE Lake District). Note that the highest (deglaciation) terrace was formed during the Loch Lomond Stadial (after Boardman, 1981).

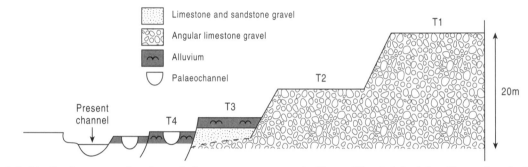

Fig. 1.7. Idealized cross section through the terrace sequence in Upper Wharfedale (after Howard et al., 2000b).

1.6.3 Holocene fluvial record: climatic and human influences

The use of the radiocarbon method to date episodes of river incision and sedimentation (by dating wood, bone and charcoal recovered from fluvial sediments) has shown that Holocene river activity can be correlated with climatic changes and, especially in the last 1000 years, with human impacts (Howard *et al.*, 2000a; Macklin *et al.*, 2000). In upland and piedmont regions, there was fluvial incision during phases of wetter and probably colder climate: 1850–900 BC, AD 775–1015, AD 1205–1450 and at *c.* AD 1800 (Howard & Macklin, 2003). Specific periods of sedimentation (alluviation) have been identified in the Yorkshire Ouse basin during the following intervals: 3700–3380 BC, 2320–1850 BC, 900–430 BC, AD 645–775, AD 1015–1290, AD 1420–1645 and AD 1750–1800 (Merrett & Macklin, 1999; Macklin *et al.*, 2000; Johnstone *et al.*, 2006).

The principal Holocene influence on fluvial activity appears to have been climate, through its influence on flood frequency and magnitude. Plotting of flood data (Fig. 1.8) shows a strong clustering of radiocarbon dated events in all catchments and also within upland and lowland floodplains. A number of correlations can be made to explain this, but it seems to be related to increased precursor rainfall or climatic cooling that raised water tables, thus leading to increased runoff (Macklin & Needham, 1992; Macklin *et al.*, 1992a, 2005; Merrett & Macklin, 1999; Macklin & Lewin, 2003). Human impact as a factor in fluvial activity has become increasingly important as the Holocene progressed (Chiverrell & Menuge, 2003; Foulds & Macklin, 2006; Chiverrell *et al.*, 2007a); since *c.* 3850 BP, progressive deforestation, associated with pastoral and arable farming, has enhanced both runoff and the supply of fine-grained sediment to valley floors (Fig. 1.8).

1.6.4 The Yorkshire Ouse catchment and the Rivers Swale and Ure

Relatively little was published on the Late Pleistocene–Holocene record in either Wensleydale or Swaledale until comparatively recently; indeed, Howard *et al.* (2000a) noted that the late Pleistocene and Holocene evolution of the River Ure and other rivers of the Ouse catchment was 'largely unknown'. Most previous work had been concentrated on the Vale of York (e.g. Melmore, 1940; Gaunt *et al.*, 1971; Gaunt, 1981; Cooper & Burgess, 1993), although Lateglacial deposits had been recorded at Lunds, in Upper Wensleydale (Walker, 1955), whereas Pounder (1979) and Rose (1980, 2006) had worked in

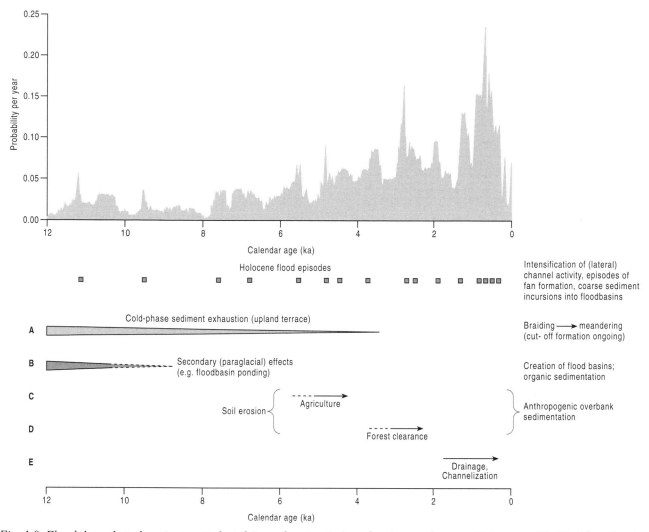

Fig. 1.8. Flood data plotted against post-glacial time, showing timing of various anthropogenic impacts. Modified from Lewin et al. (2005).

upper Swaledale. Pioneering work in the Washlands, during the 1980s and '90s, included the examination of earlier manifestations of some of the quarries studied as part of this project (compare with Chapters 2 and 3). These include the Marfield Quarry, described by Giles (1982), Ripon Racecourse Quarry in the Ure (Morigi & James, 1984) and quarries at Catterick (Lovell, 1982). Other studies of the Swale in the Catterick area have looked at small-scale terraces formed by channel deepening and meander migration (Taylor & Macklin, 1997, 1998) and the mapping of infilled and buried palaeochannels using ground-penetrating radar equipment (Jackson *et al.*, 1998). Some of this work formed part of the 'Land Ocean Interaction Study' (LOIS), funded by the Natural Environment Research Council (Shennan & Andrews, 2000), which led to considerable research in the Yorkshire Ouse catchment (Macklin *et al.*, 1997, 2000; Longfield & Macklin, 1999; Taylor *et al.*, 2000). The fluvial data-sets thus generated were correlated (with others) with proxy climate records from peat-bogs in the region (Macklin, 1999).

Much of the research conducted hitherto in the Swale and/or Ure catchments has been, at least in part, driven by interests in geomorphological processes and in modelling these. Thus Coulthard and Macklin used field-derived data from the Swale to test a cellular computer model designed to explain fluvial evolution in relation to changes in climate and land use. Using field data from earlier work (Taylor & Macklin, 1997), they developed high-resolution modelling of the River Swale over the past 9000 years and found a reasonable match between simulated discharge peaks and the dated sediment units known from earlier research (Coulthard *et al.*, 2005).

Extending this type of work into very recent times, historical climatic records and geomorphological evidence have been used in combination to show that the Yorkshire Ouse basin saw few significant flood events during the first four decades of the 20th Century (Longfield & Macklin, 1999; Merrett & Macklin, 1999). Since *c.* 1940, the number and severity of floods has increased, a trend that some have linked to climatic change (Longfield &

Macklin, 1999). However, the data show that there is no such simple relationship (Lane, 2003). It seems likely that there are issues of catchment management to be considered, particularly changing land use. The latter part of the last century was marked by increased drainage of moorland ('gripping'), as well as overgrazing of pasture and increased arable production; all are thought likely to have increased the speed of runoff of rainfall into river channels (Longfield & Macklin, 1999; Lane, 2003).

1.7 Archaeology

The area of North Yorkshire that includes the Swale–Ure Washlands has a rich and varied archaeological heritage. Distribution maps of cultural remains provide a partial record of past human settlement and activity, usually biased by differential preservation of non-organic material and by site destruction and concealment due to intensive agriculture in recent times (Chapter 4). Archaeological distributions inevitably form the basis for understanding past occupation and use of the land, although palaeoenvironmental evidence also makes an important contribution, particularly as prehistoric human activity and settlement in the lowlands seems to have had a strong association with wetlands and their diverse resources (Lillie, 2001). Previous publications (Butlin, 2003; Manby *et al*., 2003) have presented and discussed the regional archaeological evidence.

The Washlands boasts archaeological remains of national importance, particularly for the Neolithic and the Roman periods. The spectacular Thornborough Henges and their associated multi-period archaeological landscape, dating from the Neolithic, certainly belong in that category (Harding, 1997, 2000a, b), while Roman military and settlement sites between York and the river Tees are highly significant nationally and the Iron Age–Roman oppidum at Stanwick, just north of the Washlands, is also a key site for that period (cf. Chapter 4). The archaeology of the Washlands forms an important part of the present study, as it is the combination of anthropogenic and natural influences that have governed Holocene landscape changes.

1.7.1 Geoarchaeology of fluvial environments

Fluvial geoarchaeology has a lengthy pedigree in NW Europe, where stone artefacts representing early human activities were first recognized in the late 18th Century in East Anglia and were subsequently found in caves and rock shelters in France and southern England, as well as in fluvial deposits in the Somme valley in northern France and in the Thames (Prestwich, 1860; Evans, 1872; Wymer, 1968, 1999; Roe, 1981). Such artefacts became sought-after collectables, providing an additional source of income for gravel pit diggers prior to mechanization. Most such artefacts were of Lower or Middle Palaeolithic age, generally restricted to areas beyond the reach of the most recent ice sheets; in Britain that generally means no further

north than the Midlands (Wymer, 1999; Bridgland *et al*., in pressa). Indeed, no pre-Upper Palaeolithic archaeology has ever been proved in the present study area, although it cannot be stated unequivocally that pre-Devensian humans failed to penetrate this far north.

In Holocene geoarchaeology, there is a shift in emphasis from artefacts, which are still very important where present, to environmental evidence, within which an increasing human influence can be detected (Needham & Macklin, 1992; Brown, 1997a; Hosfield & Chambers, 2005). Finer-grained alluvial sedimentation during the Holocene has preserved biological material as well as artefacts; thus palynological studies, for example, have revealed a story of deforestation, the introduction of pastoralism and arable farming and eventual environmental degradation. Work on fossil insects has also been important, since these can provide precise indications of palaeoclimate (Coope & Brophy, 1972; Coope, 1977a, b, 1986; Atkinson *et al*., 1987; Lowe & Walker, 1997b; Elias, 2006) as well as ecological changes and floodplain evolution (Smith & Howard, 2004). Also, spatial expansion of alluvial cover across valley floodplains in the later Holocene will have preserved large areas of old ground surface with its associated archaeology, perhaps including entire settlements and agricultural landscapes. A wealth of environmental and cultural information is held in sequences of alluvial sediments in Britain but, despite its wide distribution and often considerable depth, this store of knowledge has thus far been exploited to a limited extent.

It is becoming apparent that both climatic and cultural high-resolution signals can be present in alluvial sequences (Macklin *et al*., 1992b) with complex interplay between the two factors influencing the environmental record. This has been demonstrated by several exemplary studies in northern England. Taylor *et al*. (2000) studied three reaches within Yorkshire Ouse tributaries, including two on the lower Swale, and were able to identify in detail records of agricultural and industrial activity, particularly in the last few millennia, and their effects on valley sedimentation. In the wider region, Passmore *et al*. (1992), in the Tyne valley, Tipping (1992) and Macklin *et al*. (1991), in Northumberland, and Brayshay and Dinnin (1999), in the lower Trent, have completed detailed analyses of alluvial deposits. Studies such as these are important for understanding individual river histories and linkage to archaeological study. It is likely that the great potential of alluvial geoarchaeology will make it one of the main research priorities in environmental and cultural archaeology in future (Macklin & Needham, 1992; Robinson 1992a). Geomorphological investigation has revealed considerable complexity in the evolution of these natural sedimentary systems and in the role of fluvial processes and channel dynamics in influencing archaeological site location and preservation quality (Lewin, 1992; Passmore & Macklin, 1997; Macklin, 1999).

Indeed, riverine landscapes, as attractive environments for human activity and settlement, have been the subject of intense world-wide archaeological and geoarchaeological research (e.g. Berendsen, 1993; Bettis, 1995; Brown, 1997a; Jing *et al.*, 1997; Joyce & Mueller, 1997; Martin-Consuegra *et al.*, 1998; Needham & Macklin, 1992; Howard & Macklin, 1999; Bettis & Mandel, 2002; Howard *et al.*, 2003; Hosfield & Chambers, 2005). Their modern utilization for aggregates extraction and as transport corridors ensures that continuing development leads to new data coming to light; in Britain this results from developer-funding assessment and rescue archaeology, through the planning system (Allen *et al.*, 1997; Darvill & Fulton, 1998). There is a down-side, however; there is considerable destruction of archaeological sites in river valleys as a result of these activities, in addition to which the drainage of valley floors, resulting in lower water-tables, causes oxidation of alluvium and progressive deterioration of subfossil remains (Howard & Macklin, 1999).

Geoarchaeological research on Holocene fluvial environments has concentrated on certain key themes. These include assessments of the potential attractiveness of river valley landscapes to human communities (Evans, 1991), analysis of the utilization of particular river zones (Robinson, 1978), and identifying causal mechanisms of changing catchment hydrology and sedimentation styles (Robinson & Lambrick 1984; Macklin & Lewin, 1993; Smith & Howard, 2004). Where water-tables are high, enhancing preservation of perishable materials, the potential resource of information can be extremely large (Bell & Neumann, 1997; Pryor *et al.*, 1986; Parker-Pearson & Sydes, 1997). Geomorphological investigation has revealed considerable complexity in the evolution of these natural sedimentary systems and in the role of fluvial processes and channel dynamics in influencing archaeological site location and preservation quality (Lewin, 1992; Passmore & Macklin, 1997; Macklin, 1999).

1.7.2 The post-industrial record: metal mining

During the last decade of the 20th Century considerable geoarchaeological research was undertaken on Pennine rivers, led by Mark Macklin (Macklin *et al.*, 1991, 1992a, 1992b, 1997, 2000; Macklin & Needham, 1992; Macklin & Lewin, 2003; Lewin *et al.*, 2005). This followed on from work on rivers in the North Pennines, particularly directed towards detecting sedimentary signals from metal mining in these catchments (Macklin *et al.*, 1997; Hudson-Edwards *et al.*, 1999a, b). Geoarchaeological work of this type has also been extended within the Humber catchment to the lower and middle Trent (Howard *et al.*, 1999a; Howard, 2005).

The metal mining industry that developed in the Yorkshire Dales during the last millennium (cf. White, 1997) was a further cause of sediment entering the rivers of the Ouse basin, as a result of the processing of mined materials as well as subsequent erosion of mine tailings (Macklin *et al.*, 1997; Hudson-Edwards *et al.*, 1999b). This sediment, often highly contaminated with heavy metals

such as lead, is still being redistributed downstream by the rivers and has proved to be a valuable geochemical time marker (Hudson-Edwards *et al.*, 1999a).

The fluvial sedimentological record indicates that there was a greater diversity of channel types and floodplain sedimentation styles prior to large-scale anthropogenic land drainage and channelization, activities that have greatly increased following industrialization (Macklin & Needham, 1992). The effects of temporal and spatial variability in fluvial activity on the preservation and visibility of the archaeological record in alluvial environments have been demonstrated by a number of papers (Brown & Keough, 1992; Lewin, 1992; Macklin *et al.*, 1992b; Macklin, 1999).

1.8 Palaeoenvironmental reconstructions

The remarkable global climatic changes that drove the last deglaciation and the transition into the present interglacial had a major impact on ecosystems. The geological record for the retreat of the ice sheet is complemented by a range of biological evidence illustrating these changes, from microscopic pollen grains to the bones of the animals that lived in the area, at first wild and later, in many cases, domesticated. One of the key areas of research employed in this project has been the reconstruction of vegetational evidence, using pollen and plant macrofossils, enhanced by data from Mollusca and insects as well as occasional vertebrate remains. Vegetation is a highly sensitive indicator of former environmental conditions. Internal successional change causes gradual alterations in plant associations, while changes in primary ecosystem factors, such as climate, soils and hydrology, will also elicit changes in plant communities. More dynamic changes, for example from external disturbance, can cause rapid change in the vegetation. Natural disturbances such as by storm, landslide or flood are also important but increasingly, during the course of the Holocene, it was human influence that became the most potent disturbing force on the vegetation. Indeed, in recent millennia the vegetation of the Washlands region, as for Britain as a whole, has become almost entirely an artificial construct, to a greater or lesser degree altered from its natural state (cf. Bell & Walker, 2005).

Climate change, associated with the global transition from glacial to interglacial regime, was often so rapid that flora and fauna had little time to adapt to the new environmental conditions. Thus the geological record for Lateglacial events is often dramatic, recording rapid temperature and environmental change (Innes, 2002a). It appears that the waning of the ice sheets had more to do with precipitation starvation than temperature change and conditions remained very cold even after the ice had left the lowland landscapes of northern England (e.g. Atkinson *et al.*, 1987). Tundra conditions prevailed, with sparse vegetation dominated by resilient pioneer species. Rapid warming marked the commencement of the temperate

Lateglacial Interstadial (Allerød/Windermere) at *c.* 13,000 ^{14}C BP, with the development of more thermophilous vegetation (Innes, 2002a). The sudden climatic deterioration that marked the dramatic return of cold glacial conditions during the Loch Lomond (Younger Dryas) Stadial and the associated vegetational response are also marked in Lateglacial sediment cores.

With the beginning of the Holocene the climate ameliorated rapidly, so that forests were able to develop and dominate the landscape. These interglacial woodland communities covered almost all the land surface of the Washlands during the early and mid-Holocene (Innes, 2002d). Disturbance to these forest ecosystems began in the mid-Holocene, when the first evidence of forest clearance appears in palaeoenvironmental records (Turner, 1965; Göransson, 1982; Simmons & Innes, 1987; Brown, 1997b). Woodland ecosystems were modified and displaced with increasing severity during the later Holocene through the advent of agriculture and the development of more complex human societies (Barber, 1993; Bell & Walker, 2005; Chiverrell, 2001; Innes, 2002d). Long-term human land-use, ranging from woodland management to eventual total forest clearance (Turner, 1965; Brown, 1997a), has resulted in the modern entirely-managed landscape, in which a very few areas, mainly small wetlands that survive despite several centuries of land drainage, resemble natural ecosystems.

1.8.1 Post-glacial vegetational records

The history of post-glacial vegetational change in the region has been reconstructed by the use of proxy data from the many sediment archives (Innes, 1999, 2002a, 2002d; Innes & Blackford, 2003a; Innes *et al.*, 2003), primarily by pollen analysis (Atherden, 1999; Lowe *et al.*, 1999) but also by the study of plant macrofossils (Birks, 2003). Together, these techniques provide both an on-site (macrofossils, being generally preserved where the plants lived) and an off-site (regional, in the case of wind-blown pollen) perspective to vegetation history. Figure 1.9 shows the key pollen sites of Lateglacial and Holocene age within the region, consideration of which allows the Washlands evidence to be placed in a wider context in the final chapter; indeed, it shows that there has been little previous palaeoecological work in the study area. In the south, pollen data were available previously only at Dishforth (Giles, 1992), but without radiocarbon support. The pollen record at this site spanned the Lateglacial and early Holocene, terminating at an estimated 8,000 ^{14}C BP, judging by the *Corylus-* and *Ulmus*-dominated assemblage, and so provided only a partial history. In the Washlands, three pollen levels only were analysed as part of a study of alluvial sequences at Ripon Racecourse (Howard *et al.*, 2000a; see Chapters 2.6.4 & 3.7). The transition from *Juniperus–Salix* to *Betula–Pinus* woodland in these levels indicated an early Holocene record, confirmed by radiocarbon dating. It is only in areas of North Yorkshire adjacent to the Washlands

that sufficient pollen records are available to reconstruct a full vegetation history for the study area (Innes, 2002d). To the south in the Vale of York (van de Noort & Ellis, 1999) considerable wetland potential exists, and at Tadcaster (Bartley, 1962) and Askham Bog (Gearey & Lillie, 1999), long pollen records with a Lateglacial signal have been recovered. Isolated records covering short periods of time also exist, such as the Loch Lomond Stadial pollen data from peat within coversand deposits at Cawood in the Vale of York (Jones & Gaunt, 1976).

To the east, on the fringes of the North York Moors, Blackham *et al.* (1981) have presented Lateglacial pollen data from Gormire Lake that might be associated with a former landslide. Jones (1976a) and Tooley *et al.* (1982) have published Lateglacial pollen diagrams from Seamer Carrs near Stokesley. Further Lateglacial and Holocene records are available from the North York Moors upland (Simmons *et al.*, 1993; Fig. 1.9), including some dedicated to the study of climate history rather than human impacts (Blackford & Chambers, 1991; Chiverrell & Atherden, 1999; Chiverrell, 2001). In the Tees valley, to the north, Bartley *et al.* (1976) have published a full Holocene record from Neasham Fen and Blackburn (1952) studied the Lateglacial vegetation there. Several pollen records are also available to the southwest of the Washlands. From Bingley Bog (Keen *et al.*, 1988), a Lateglacial pollen record includes sporadic thermophilous tree pollen, a feature that was also noted at Tadcaster (Bartley, 1962). Norris *et al.* (1971) have examined pollen data from marl deposits at Burton Salmon, while Tinsley (1975, 1976) contributed vegetation histories from the Pennine upland margins that extend into late Holocene times and show extensive human impact upon the forest. These and other more distal pollen sites provide a template against which the new data gained from the present project can be considered. Innes (2002a; 2002d) has reviewed the vegetation history for the Lateglacial and Holocene periods in northern England, providing a context for the further appraisal to follow in subsequent chapters.

1.8.2 Faunal records

Evidence from animal fossils can also assist greatly with palaeoenvironmental reconstruction, since many types can be identified to species level and have well-established habitat requirements (Sparks, 1961; Kerney, 1999; Currant & Jacobi, 2001). For example, molluscan records are known from several sites of value for comparison with the data recovered in the present study. At Bingley Bog (Keen *et al.*, 1988), Lateglacial temperature fluctuations are indicated by changes in molluscan assemblages. Giles (1992) also presented molluscan data to supplement the pollen record at Dishforth Bog, as did Keen *et al.* (1984) in their study of Lateglacial and early Holocene deposits at Kildale Hall, in the valley of the River Leven, on the north-western flank of the North York Moors.

Insect assemblages, particularly Coleoptera, have proved to be of great importance in interpreting environmental

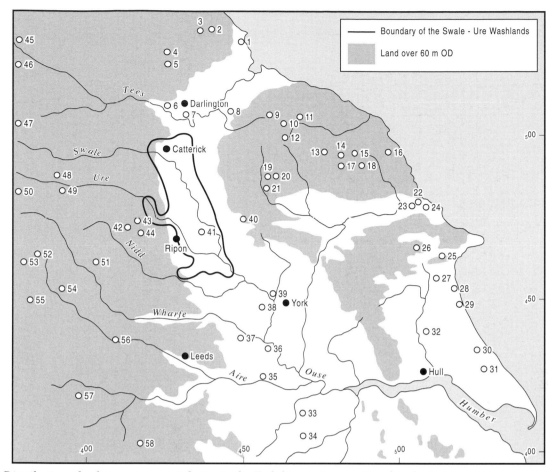

Fig. 1.9 Distribution of palaeoenvironmental sites in the Yorkshire region mentioned in the text.
1. Hartlepool (Waughman, 2005) 2. Thorpe Bulmer (Bartley et al., 1976) 3. Hutton Henry (Bartley et al., 1976) 4. Bishop Middleham (Bartley et al., 1976) 5. Mordon Carr (Bartley et al., 1976) 6. Burtree Lane (Bellamy et al, 1966) 7. Neasham Fen (Bartley et al., 1976) 8. Seamer Carrs (Jones, 1976a) 9. Kildale Hall (Keen et al., 1984) 10. West House Moss (Jones, 1978) 11. Ewe Crag Slack (Jones, 1978) 12. White Gill (Dimbleby, 1962) 13. North Gill (Innes & Simmons, 2000) 14. Wheeldale Gill (Simmons & Cundill, 1974) 15. May Moss (Atherden, 1979; Chiverrell, 2001) 16. Harwood Dale Bog (Atherden, 1989) 17. Collier Gill (Simmons & Cundill, 1974) 18. Fen Bogs (Atherden, 1976a) 19. Bonfield Gill Head (Simmons & Innes, 1988) 20. Botany Bay (Simmons & Innes, 1988) 21. Harold's Bog (Blackford & Chambers, 1999) 22. Star Carr (Day, 1996) 23. Seamer Carr (Cloutman & Smith, 1988) 24. Flixton Carr (Godwin & Willis, 1959) 25. Willow Garth (Bush, 1993) 26. Kilham Long Barrow (Manby, 1976) 27. Gransmoor Quarry (Lowe et al., 1995) 28. Skipsea Bail Mere (Flenley, 1984) and Skipsea Withow Mere (Hunt et al., 1984) 29. The Old Mere, Hornsea (Beckett, 1981) 30. Gilderson Marr (Tweddle, 2001) 31. The Bog, Roos (Beckett, 1981) 32. Routh Quarry (Lillie & Gearey, 2000) 33. Thorne Moors (Smith, 2002) 34. Hatfield Moors (Smith, 2002) 35. Burton Salmon (Norris et al., 1971) 36. Cawood (Jones & Gaunt, 1976) 37. Tadcaster (Bartley, 1962) 38. Askham Bog (Gearey & Lillie, 1999) 39. St. George's Field (Lillie & Gearey, 1999) 40. Gormire Lake (Blackham et al., 1981; Oldfield et al., 2003) 41. Dishforth Bog (Giles, 1992) 42. Fountains Earth (Tinsley, 1975) 43. Fortress Dike (Tinsley, 1976b) 44. Skell Gill (Tinsley, 1975) 45. Red Sike Moss (Turner et al., 1973) 46. Mire Holes (Squires, 1978) 47. Gate Gutter (Gear & Turner, 2001) 48. Whirly Gill (Honeyman, 1985) 49. Thornton Mires (Honeyman, 1985) 50. Fleet Moss (Honeyman, 1985) 51. Stump Cross (Walker, 1956) 52. Malham Tarn Moss (Pigott & Pigott, 1963) 53. Victoria Cave (Wymer, 1981) 54. Eshton Tarn (Bartley et al., 1990) 55. White Moss (Bartley et al., 1990) 56. Bingley Bog (Keen et al., 1988) 57. Soyland Moor (Williams, 1985) 58. Dunford Bridge (Radley et al., 1974).

change, because of their sensitivity and rapid response to climate change (Coope, 1977b, 1986; Atkinson *et al.*, 1987; Elias, 2006). There are few such sites within the region: a radiocarbon-dated Lateglacial insect record is available from Gransmoor, east Yorkshire (Walker *et al.*, 1993) and there have been coleopteran studies of sites within the Humberhead levels (Whitehouse, 2004). The

British entomofauna form an important fossil record in understanding the evolution and change that has affected ancient 'wildwoods' (*urwald*) (Robinson, 2000; Whitehouse, 2006) and alluvial systems (Smith & Howard, 2004) during the Holocene. Insect remains, predominantly Coleoptera, have been recovered from some of the Swale–Ure Washlands sites and provide valuable ecological information to enhance the palaeobotanical record (cf. Chapter 3).

Few vertebrate bones have been recovered during the present study, but recovery of mammalian skeletal remains from wetlands in the area has a long history (Cameron, 1878; Veitch, 1899). These are a reminder of the large herbivores that were present in both Lateglacial and Holocene times as part of the available resources for human exploitation. More recently, almost complete skeletons of *Alces alces* (elk), *Bos primigenius* (aurochs) and *Cervus elaphus* (red deer) have been reported, respectively by Blackburn (1952) at Neasham Fen, Jones (1976b) at Kildale Hall and Tooley *et al.* (1982) at Seamer Carrs, Stokesley. Although sinkage in soft deposits seems to have made the stratigraphic context of such large animal remains unreliable in these cases, they provide further valuable proxy evidence for past environmental conditions. Multi-proxy assemblages of faunal remains occur at sites close to the study area, as at Hartlepool, north of Teesside, where red and roe deer, aurochs, wild boar and various domestic stock bones, fish remains and molluscan assemblages have been recorded (Stalibrass, 2005). Bones of domesticated animals are often recovered from sediments associated with archaeological sites in the region (Huntley & Stallibras, 1995). In North Yorkshire, wetland sites in the Vale of Pickering have also preserved a wealth of early Holocene faunal material, mostly of game animals (Legge & Rowley-Conwy, 1988; Rowley-Conwy, 1998), but including dog bones (Day, 1996b), whereas finds from Late Devensian peat in the Flixton area include horse (Moore, 1954). Devensian mammalian faunal assemblages have also been recovered from several cave sites in Yorkshire, including Victoria Cave (Settle), Stump Cross (Grassington) and Kirkside Cave in the Vale of Pickering, adding to the comparative data available (Lord *et al.*, 2007).

The Holocene mammalian fauna differs from the Pleistocene interglacials in that large game animals were missing from European habitats. It is the first temperate period, since before the Pleistocene, in which no elephants or rhinoceroses lived in north-west Europe. The northern forms of such animals were, by the Holocene, extinct, a demise that has been attributed to the efficiency of hunting by *Homo sapiens*, although that view remains controversial (Stuart, 1999; Grayson, 2001). With no giant herbivores to create natural clearings during foraging by uprooting trees and trampling, and only the more solitary aurochs and elk present in Britain as very large forest mammals, the structure of the Holocene forest would have been different from that of previous interglacials, with little of the biological diversity that comes with the uprooting of trees (Falinski, 1978). The human populations of the Mesolithic in the early Holocene would probably have been confronted by forests denser than at any previous time. These were not favourable conditions for hunter-gatherers and were soon to be altered by humans learning to modify their environment.

1.9 Dating the sequence

An accurate dating framework is a fundamental requirement in Quaternary research and equally important to both the Earth science and the archaeological interests in this project. It is probably fair to say that archaeologists working on prehistoric periods have frequently looked to Earth scientists to provide dating evidence, whereas the Earth scientists are sometimes tempted to see artefact assemblages as means (akin to trace fossils) for determining age. There has been widespread agreement in recent years that multiple methods of dating should be employed (the jargon being 'multi-proxy') in the belief that agreement between these will provide a sound foundation and that disagreement will point to problems requiring further research. To many the term 'dating' points to 'high-tech' geochronological methods such as the various radiometric techniques (cf. Walker, 2005); in fact these should be integrated with a sound lithostratigraphical framework and, where possible, a detailed biostratigraphical interpretation of the record, the last providing a means for site correlation independent of the geochronology and a check on the reliability of numerical dates (see Chapter 3).

The Quaternary record in the Swale–Ure Washlands, being entirely post-LGM, falls fully within the age range of reliable radiocarbon dating (Walker *et al.*, 2001; Walker, 2005), although plateaux in the radiocarbon calibration curve that reduce the precision of dates during certain time periods need to be considered during interpretation. These are particularly problematic in the Lateglacial (Lowe & Walker, 2000), in the late Iron Age and in the first Holocene millennium, when early Mesolithic occupation of the region was well developed, as at the classic archaeological site of Star Carr in the Vale of Pickering (Day & Mellars, 1994; Mellars & Dark, 1998). Radiocarbon, nevertheless, has provided the principle basis for geochronology within the project (Appendix I). Pollen analysis has provided a detailed picture of regional vegetational history since Late Devensian deglaciation, building on published records that pre-dated the project. The combination of a detailed reconstruction of Lateglacial and Holocene vegetational development and radiocarbon dating of targeted horizons, a traditional approach to studies of this period, has been employed.

There have been endeavours to add a further dating 'proxy', to strengthen the temporal framework for the study (Chapter 3). In the first phase of research, the technique of optically stimulated luminescence (OSL) dating was employed in an attempt to apply geochronology directly to the minerogenic sediments within the project, the sands and gravels that provide the main basis for the fluvial record (and for the aggregates industry that led, via the government levy, to the initiation of the research project). This method measures a luminescence signal, stored in crystal lattices of sand grains, that has accumulated as a result of natural radiation within the sediment (and its surroundings) since the grain was last exposed to daylight.

It requires measurement of both the radiation dose within the sampled sediment and the dose susceptibility of the sand grain(s) being measured (Chapter 2.1.2; Appendix II). Unfortunately it was found that the vast majority of sand grains sampled from the Swale–Ure deposits were incapable of recording a meaningful luminescence signal; this method thus proved to be completely unsuccessful as a means of dating the sequences in the study area (Appendix II). As a result it was decided to try a further technique in the later phase of research, one that was undergoing development at the time, but had shown considerable promise: amino acid racemization (AAR) dating (Appendix III). No separate chapter on the dating is provided; instead the detailed methodology of each is explained in the appendices. Sampling for the unsuccessful OSL dating programme is described in Chapter 2 as part of section description; the radiocarbon dates are documented in Chapter 3, as are the AAR dates from selected mollusc shell samples.

1.10 Overview

The Swale–Ure Washlands form an important part of the river system linking the drainage of the Pennine uplands with the lower tidal reaches of the Ouse in the Humber estuary. They contain a geomorphological, sedimentological and stratigraphical signal that reflects changes within the river system, associated with extrinsic climatic and anthropogenic changes in the catchment, the impacts of which have been transferred downstream. As such, the long-term evolution of the rivers has played an important role in the development of this landscape connecting the upland and lowland areas. Understanding the Washlands will therefore allow better appreciation of the overall dynamics of the entire catchment, in terms of geomorphological evolution and sediment flux. Subsequent chapters will look in detail at various types of data collected from the Washlands as part of this project, starting with the geomorphology and regional stratigraphy (Chapter 2), followed by palaeoenvironmental evidence (Chapter 3) and then a review of the archaeology (Chapter 4), by way of context. Finally, in Chapter 5, the data is synthesized and discussed in the broader context of the history of northern Britain and areas further afield since the last glaciation, both in terms of natural and anthropogenic influences. There are a number of Appendices on the CD directed to specific dating techniques, details of the geomorphological map, sedimentological analyses and minor site details.

2 Geomorphology and Regional Stratigraphy

The aim of this chapter is to describe the geomorphology of the Washlands, placing emphasis on the landscape features that arose from the retreat of the last (Late Devensian) ice sheet and those that catalogue fluvial evolution from deglaciation to the systems that have developed under a more equable Holocene climate. Underpinned by geomorphological mapping, the reconstruction of the late Quaternary evolution of the Washlands also calls upon sedimentary evidence: the sedimentology of superficial deposits where these could be observed in exposure and their contents analysed (e.g. their gravel clasts). This research provides the physical background for more detailed reconstruction of environmental change, using data recorded from specific localities, and for understanding the post-glacial human occupation of the area.

The chapter is divided into sections introducing the different geomorphological methods that have been employed to determine landscape evolution and describing the different landforms that have been mapped across the Washlands. This is then synthesized into a number of sections that introduce the geomorphological character of specific parts of each river system and a section specifically on the river terraces. The latter part of the chapter is directed to descriptions of the studied exposures, including the results of sedimentological analyses. The latter includes the important technique of clast lithological analysis, which has been helpful in interpreting the sediments and the depositional processes and environments they represent.

2.1 Methods

A range of methods have been used to elucidate the geology and geomorphology of the Washlands, from geomorphological mapping to the recording (drawing, photographing and logging) and sampling of Quaternary geological exposures, the analyses of sediment samples (showing particle-size distribution and lithological content), together with related palaeontological studies and the application of dating methods. Where possible these various approaches have been integrated.

2.1.1 Geomorphological Mapping

A valuable approach in studies of landscape evolution is the preparation of a geomorphological map, which can allow the spatial distribution of landforms and sediments to be presented, thereby facilitating their interpretation, their relations to one to another and their role in landscape evolution. Such mapping can be achieved by a combination of fieldwork and imagery interpretation. Landforms are usually identified on a map using a set of symbols; examples of geomorphological maps developed by a number of workers can be found in publications by Sissons (1958, 1960b, 1974, 1980), Mitchell (1991a, b), Ballantyne and Harris (1994), Evans (2004), Mitchell and Riley (2006) and Smith et al. (2006).

Production of a geomorphological map, which represents a high-resolution spatial database, has formed an important part of fieldwork associated with this project (Plate 2.1). Better topographic maps and new technology have enabled increasingly accurate mapping in recent years; however, whereas much of the British landscape has been mapped with regard to bedrock geology and superficial deposits (McMillan & Powell, 1999; McMillan et al., 2005), less attention has been paid to the geomorphological features that form an important element of the Quaternary record in large areas of the British Isles, particularly those covered by the last British–Irish ice sheet (BIIS: see Chapter 1). This is unfortunate because numerical modelling of, for example, former ice sheets requires accurate field data about the landform distribution to validate increasingly sophisticated computer simulations.

Geomorphological maps combine an understanding of the morphology of a landscape with an interpretation of the processes that have been responsible for landform generation. This combination of geomorphology and sedimentology is necessary because there is a limited range of specific landform types within a landscape and many of these are ambiguous with respect to genesis; thus to understand them requires investigation of their internal composition. Mapping of the superficial deposits at available exposures will allow important information on landform genesis. In many areas, sedimentological analysis is limited or precluded by a lack of exposures. However, gravel extraction at a number of locations within the Washlands has provided access to important evidence from the sediments that characterize this area, which can then be linked to the geomorphology, allowing better understanding of the landforms.

The basic principle of geomorphological mapping is the demarcation of specific landforms with reference to breaks of slope, generally using basal concavities to define the shape of the landforms, in conjunction with a symbol to describe the upper extent. The main positive forms that can be observed, irrespective of genesis, are ridges and mounds. To these can be added negative forms such as hollows or depressions. Extensive flat areas of minimal slope, defined laterally by clear breaks of slopes to form 'terraces', may also be notable elements of a landscape. There are also many areas of more subtle undulating topography that are difficult to ascribe to specific process–response systems. Experience gained from present-day environments allows landforms associated with fossil landscapes to be explained with respect to active processes that can be seen to give rise to distinctive landforms and landsystems (cf. Evans, 2004).

Geomorphological mapping requires the ability to locate important breaks of slopes accurately on a 1:10,000 or 1:25,000 OS topographic map, using standard geological mapping procedures adapted to emphasize landforms (McMillan & Powell, 1999). It is usually the basal concavity that allows the planimetric shape of the landform to be expressed; this is most clearly observed in areas where there is a well-defined morphological expression, such as ridges or mounds that have clear basal breaks of slope. Such mapping can be enhanced by marking ridge crests or mound high points to give cartographic representation of the landform. More sophisticated classification schemes employ colours to enhance a classification. The availability of hand-held GPS has simplified this methodology in recent years; however, this does not reduce the requirement to be able to use large-scale maps.

Features are mapped by standing at important breaks of slope and then 'walking the ground' by traversing the landforms to allow them to be accurately marked on a map. This is necessary to avoid errors caused by perspective, which may lead to inaccuracies in definition and subsequent morphometric analysis. This also requires some operator experience of the different types of geomorphological environment to allow identification of important morphological elements and correct interpretation of landform genesis. Similarity of different basic forms also requires that mapping identifies associated landforms that can be linked within a specific landsystem or systems. These may become spatially discontinuous within the present landscape, with superimposed landsystems reflecting changes in geomorphological processes through time.

Recent availability of high resolution Digital Elevation (or Terrain) Models (DEM) for the British Isles has revealed a wealth of data about the former landsystems created by the last BIIS (Smith *et al.*, 2006). This has added another perspective to the mapping of terrain and allowed the creation of a summary interpretive map showing the main glacial features following established procedures (cf. Smith & Clark, 2005), particularly the well-defined streamlined trends across the Washlands derived from the NEXTMap© DEM (Plate 2.2). For copyright reasons this is presented as a layer on the lower resolution (50 m) OS Panorama™ DEM. However, most of the discussion below relates to the geomorphological map produced by field mapping;

the DEM has been helpful in allowing an overview to improve and sharpen interpretation of the field evidence and allow a better insight across the Washlands and the wider region.

2.1.2 Geological recording and sampling

The principal opportunities for making geological observations and records were at the various gravel quarries around which this project was based. Recording (cf. Jones *et al.*, 1999a) took the form of logging sediment stratigraphy, measuring and interpreting sedimentary structures, drawing and photographing more complex sections and recording the positions of various samples. Drawings and logs of the more important geological sections and cores will appear in this chapter and the next. Geological records were also made at natural exposures and coring localities, notably at a stream section near Snape Mill, part of the Snape Mires site, the most significant non-quarry locality studied.

Sediment type was generally identified in the field, with observations of the relative coarseness of gravel and sand. For finer-grained mineral sediments, particle-size assessments were routinely made by laboratory analysis of small samples using a laser analyser (see below). Larger samples were collected for clast analysis of gravels and for the recovery of fossils, particularly molluscs. Thick organic sequences present in exposures were sampled using monolith tins; most organic sediment was present below the surface, however, requiring the drilling of cores. During coring, sediments, organic and otherwise, were assessed and identified using the system of symbols and notation devised by Troels-Smith (1955) for the characterization of unconsolidated sediments (cf. Tooley, 1981; Long *et al.*, 1999).

The attempted OSL dating (Chapter 1.9) required a separate programme of sampling, during which the radiation dose within the sediment body was generally measured in the field. In all, nine samples were collected from four of the quarries studied, those at Marfield, Nosterfield, Ripon North and Ripon South (see below). The samples were extracted, where possible, by pushing an opaque plastic tube into the section and withdrawing it filled with the required sediment, quickly wrapping it to protect it from light. This requires discrete sand units into which the tubes can be inserted. Commonly, at the project sites, gravel-free sand beds were not present and it was necessary to sample from pebbly deposits, a procedure that required the sampler to work behind an opaque pvc sheet (Fig. 2.1); a trowel was used to dig sand from around the gravel clasts and place it into a black plastic bag. Many of the samples were collected in this way from gravel-rich sediments that could potentially have a heterogeneous radiation dose rate, making it essential to measure the dose rate *in situ* using a portable gamma spectrometer; this was undertaken for seven of the nine samples (Table 2.1). In addition, dose rates were assessed using laboratory-based measurements of thick-source alpha counting (TSAC) and GM-beta counting. These were undertaken on the samples after they were dried and finely milled to homogenize them (Appendix II). The best estimate of the dose rate to coarse quartz grains within the sample would come from combining the gamma dose rate measured using the portable gamma spectrometer and the GM-beta counting, since this would cope with heterogeneity in the dose rate. For the two samples where it was not possible to obtain field-based measurements using the gamma spectrometer, the gamma dose rate was calculated using a combination of the beta and alpha counting measurements (Appendix II).

Fig. 2.1. OSL sampling at Nosterfield Quarry. In order to extract sand grains from gravelly deposits, into which a tube could not be driven, it was necessary for Helen Roberts to undertake the sampling behind a black PVC sheet. See section 2.6.2.

Where regarded as important, sedimentary structures recorded from quarry sections will be described and discussed as part of the locality descriptions later in this chapter. They can be useful in distinguishing mode and energy of deposition, fluvial regime (meandering or braiding) and current direction (Jones *et al.*, 1999b; Lewis & Maddy, 1999). The last-mentioned can be determined by measuring foreset orientation in cross bedded or ripple laminated sediments, which was possible at a few Washlands localities, or clast imbrication in gravels with numerous flat shaped pebbles. Determining current direction was of low priority in this study, given that the identity of the river responsible for depositing the materials was rarely in question.

Heights (above sea level), which are of considerable importance in geomorphological mapping (especially of river terrace deposits), were determined by a variety of means. These included levelling, using a simple dumpy level, where several data-points existed in a small area and there was a known height conveniently located nearby. Leica System 300 differential GPS equipment, operated in static survey mode, was used to obtain accurate altitudes for scattered sites, measured relative to a base station (used to filter out the vagaries in GPS output). A combination of these was applied in some circumstances. It was necessary in some instances to estimate heights from large-scale maps, particularly where quarrying had removed original surface layers.

2.1.3 Geological analyses

A variety of analytical methods might have been applied in

Site	Sample	Grains measured	Grains with 'detectable' OSL signal	Grains passing IR OSL depletion ratio test and other criteria
Marfield	78/MA1	1000	16 (1.6%)	3 (0.3%)
	78/MA2	1000	12 (1.2%)	0 (0.0%)
Nosterfield	78/NO1	1000	9 (0.9%)	1 (0.1%)
	78/NO2	1200	26 (2.2%)	1 (0.1%)
	78/NO3	2000	24 (1.2%)	5 (0.3%)
	78/NO4	900	19 (2.1%)	2 (0.2%)
Ripon North	78/RN1	1000	16 (1.6%)	6 (0.6%)
Norton Mills	78/RN2	1000	17 (1.7%)	12 (1.2%)
Ripon South	78/RR1	2000	44 (2.2%)	20 (1.0%)

Table 2.1. – OSL results. The table shows (1) number of grains measured for each sample, (2) those from which a detectable OSL signal was observed and (3) the number of those grains that passed the IR OSL depletion ratio test and other criteria (primarily the recycling ratio). The numbers in brackets are the data expressed as a percentage of the total number of grains measured. For further details of the OSL dating see Appendix II.

the geological study of the Washlands deposits, from heavy-mineral analysis of sands to geochemical characterization (cf. Jones *et al.*, 1999a). Some of these would be appropriate in cases where the origin of the deposits was in doubt, while others are novel but of uncertain value. The decision was taken to use the available resources to apply two main methods: particle-size analysis (as mentioned above) was applied to fine-grained clastic sediments, for which the grain-size distribution could be more accurately determined by this means, and pebble lithology was determined for the main gravel deposits encountered, using clast lithological analysis or 'stone counting' (cf. Bridgland, 1986a).

2.1.3.1 Particle-size analysis

The analysis of particle-size distribution enhances the precision of sediment description, particularly in the case of clast sizes too small to be readily seen without optical aid, and can assist in the determination of mode and environment of deposition (Jones *et al.*, 1999b). In the latter case, differences in degree of sorting and other parameters of size distribution can be indicative of depositional agent. In this project, the depositional agent was rarely in doubt but particle-size analysis was applied to fine-grained sediments as an aid to description.

The analyses were undertaken using a Coulter Particle-size Analyser. This uses a method of sizing and counting particles based on measurable changes in electrical resistance produced by nonconductive particles suspended in an electrolyte. Suspended particles pass through a small opening (aperture) between electrodes, forming the 'sensing zone'. Here, each particle displaces its own volume of electrolyte. The volume displaced is measured as a voltage pulse, the height of each pulse being proportional to the volume of the particle. The quantity of suspension drawn through the aperture is precisely controlled, allowing the machine to count and size particles for an exact reproducible volume. Several thousand particles per second are individually counted and sized with great accuracy. The method is independent of particle shape and density.

The results of these analyses, presented in Appendix IV, have been used to enhance the sedimentological and stratigraphical descriptions in this chapter and the next.

2.1.3.2 Clast lithological analysis

Analysis of the clast content of Quaternary gravels is a technique that has proved extremely valuable in certain contexts, particularly in south-east England and East Anglia, where it has been used to reconstruct drainage history (including fluvial diversions and unspecified catchment changes) and to identify inputs of exotic material as a result of glaciation (e.g. Hey, 1965; Green & McGregor, 1978; Bridgland, 1986b, 1988, 1994, 1998, 2003; Bridgland *et al.*, 1995; Rose, 1994). Elsewhere in Britain the technique has been used less systematically. Allen and Gibbard (1993) found it to be of limited use

in categorizing and defining the terrace gravels of the erstwhile River Solent in Hampshire and Dorset, although it was used to good effect in the Severn and Avon catchments of the English Midlands (Maddy *et al.*, 1991, 1995).

In areas where there have been neither catchment changes nor periodic glacial inputs it is likely that gravels of different ages will comprise similar ranges of pebble types. Even under these circumstances, it is desirable that clast analysis be routinely applied in order to supply numerical data in support of (otherwise subjective) gravel description. It is always possible that analysis will reveal patterns in the data that could not have been casually observed and which can, for example, distinguish between tributary and main-stream deposits (Harding *et al.*, 1991).

Clast analysis was therefore undertaken for each of the gravel bodies seen in exposure. The methodology followed the Quaternary Research Association technical guide No. 3, which outlines recommended practice for sampling, size range selection and minimum count numbers (Bridgland, 1986a). In particular, gravel samples were split into the two size-fractions recommended: 16–32 mm and 11.2–16 mm. The larger fraction, clasts in which are more easily identified, was fully processed; the smaller fraction was archived in case its later analysis was deemed desirable. All 16–32 mm clasts in each sample were identified and counted, using a x 8–35 zoom reflected-light microscope, aided by a steel probe for testing hardness and 10% HCl for identifying calcareous rocks. Reference was made to comparative material from bedrock sources (see section 2.5). The data, calculated as % total, are presented in Table 2.2; see also Section 2.5; Appendix V (CD archive); reference will be made to these data in the site descriptions later in this chapter.

2.2 The Geomorphological Map

The geomorphological map that forms a major part of this project has been completed by fieldwork using topographic maps at a scale of 1:25,000. The choice of scale was determined by the areal extent of the Washlands (> 800 km^2) and the available time, entailing the mapping of 6–8 km^2 each day. The map provides the basis for a detailed explanation of the geomorphological evolution of the Washlands, as a background to the environmental changes that are recorded from biostratigraphical analysis of key sites. Because of its size, the full map (Plate. 2.1) is included on the CD, with segments of the map reproduced within this chapter.

Much of the text in this chapter relates specifically to the geomorphological map (Sections 2.2–2.4). There is an introductory section (2.2.1–2.2.2) that describes the main types of landforms found during the mapping and builds on previously described landforms from the literature (Chapter 1.4). This is followed by an interpretative synthesis of landscape evolution within the Swale and Ure river systems (Section 2.3) in which the individual river catchments are

Site	Ripon South				Ripon North				N.M.	Nosterfield		Marfield		Snape	Scorton		Catterick	
Sample	1A	1B	2A	2B	2.1	1.1	1.3	2.2	1	1	2	1	2	1	1A	1B	1A	1B
Carboniferous :																		
Carboniferous limestone	33.7	22.9	27.2	27.9	53.7	51.6	40.0	31.9	44.3	31.9	47.3	45.7	65.0	39.1	37.8	46.1	44.8	21.9
Carboniferous chert	6.1	17.7	16.5	17.4	4.3	7.4	10.4	7.8	11.5	9.3	9.9	16.1	1.2	4.7	6.4	2.7	4.5	15.0
Partial Chert (Silicified Limestone)	4.9	1.6	2.5	4.4	4.6	3.3	3.1	7.0	2.9	1.3	1.7	4.7	1.5	8.3	6.1	3.0	2.6	8.4
Orthoquartzite / quartzitic sandstone	19.7	40.6	27.6	30.7	13.1	20.9	26.8	23.0	20.1	20.6	17.3	13.8	11.5	17.7	14.7	10.3	14.5	25.3
Bedded / flaggy sandstone	3.4	4.7	6.6	5.0	3.4	1.2	1.7	0.8	1.6	3.3	3.7	0.6	1.5	1.6	3.4	2.0	2.3	2.7
Arkosic sandstone	8.1	2.1	7.8	5.8	9.1	4.1	6.2	14.3	8.3	7.6	7.4	10.0	7.3	4.7	10.6	8.9	7.7	14.8
Calcareous Sand(stone)	9.1	4.2	6.2	4.4	7.1	4.1	2.8	7.3	7.3	4.0	6.2	6.5	7.3	5.2	3.2	7.4	8.1	4.3
Sandstone with plant fossils	0.7			0.3	0.3					1.0	0.8	0.3		1.0		0.2	1.3	
Flaggy Limestone	0.5	0.5	0.8	0.8	0.9		2.3	2.2	1.0	0.3	0.8	0.3		1.0	2.9	3.0	1.9	2.3
Weathered Limestone (brash)	0.2							0.3	0.3		1.2	0.3	1.5	1.0	0.7	3.0	1.3	
Permian																		
Magnesian Limestone	9.8	3.1	1.2	1.4	1.1	4.5	6.5	3.9	0.3	18.6	1.7			15.6	3.9	4.4	2.3	
Igneous/metamorphic																		
Dolerite / trachyte	0.2		0.8	0.3														0.5
Granitic										0.3	0.4				0.6	0.6		
Weathered fine-grained											0.4				0.3			
Porphyry															1.0			
Metaquartzite / schist / gneiss															0.3			0.2
Others																		
Calcareous silt(stone)	1.7	0.5	1.2		0.9	0.4	0.3		2.5	0.3	1.2		0.3		0.5		0.6	0.5
Shale / slate / mudstone	0.5	0.5		0.6	0.6	1.2	0.8	0.8				0.3	1.5		3.9	0.2	0.6	2.5
Micaceous quartz sandstone			0.4														0.3	0.2
Vein (crystalline) calcite	0.2		0.4			0.4	0.3						0.3				1.0	
Bedded siltstone / mudstone						0.4	0.3										0.3	
Exotic limestone															0.2			
Cherty sandstone					0.3		0.3					0.3				0.2	0.3	
Breccia																0.2		
Ironstone	0.3	1.0		0.8	0.3		0.6	0.6				0.6	0.6		0.5	1.0	1.0	0.5
Greywacke sandstone	0.7	0.5		0.3						0.7					2.2	2.5	1.3	0.7
Various other sandstone						0.4				0.7		0.6	0.6				1.0	
Vein quartz															0.5	0.2	0.3	
Exotic quartzite			0.4														0.6	0.2
Total Count	593	192	243	362	350	244	355	357	314	301	243	341	331	192	407	407	310	439

Table 2.2. – Clast lithological data. N.M. = Norton Mills. Note that the lower glacial gravel at Ripon North, represented by Sample 2.1, is separated by a broken vertical line from the three samples from the Holocene terrace gravel at that site. More detailed clast data are provided on the CD in Appendix V.

subdivided into a number of manageable sectors in order to explain river history. A final section (2.4) introduces the river terrace sequences that have been identified by field mapping.

2.2.1 Glacial features

Glaciers and ice sheets are dynamic transportation systems that carry large amounts of debris, derived from erosion of underlying bedrock and pre-existing superficial sediments, that can be entrained and carried in the subglacial environment (Benn & Evans, 1998). Debris can also be carried in the more passive englacial environment, within the ice mass, and on the ice surface, termed the supraglacial environment. This latter environment receives sediment from two sources: first, debris transported from the subglacial and englacial environments along upward-directed thrust planes and, second, debris deposited on the ice surface from overlying rock and sediment slopes. The ice acts as a conveyor belt transporting this debris to the ice margin. If this margin is stable and stationary, the debris will accumulate continually and a ridge will be constructed, forming a terminal moraine at the ice front and lateral moraines along the margins; such landforms can be used to infer the position of former ice margins. If the ice stagnates (becomes stationary), material is dumped to form hummocky topography interspersed with kettle-hole lakes, the latter caused by the melting out of ice blocks.

Ice marginal environments are areas of complex interactions between sedimentological processes related both to ice and associated meltwater. The presence of eskers and large complex meltwater channel systems within the Washlands testifies to the role of water in this area during glaciation and deglaciation. Meltwater generated during the retreat of the ice margin has led to the formation of lateral drainage channels in association with lateral moraines, outwash sediments and the deposition of fine-grained sediment in temporary lakes within the proglacial environment.

2.2.1.1 Moraines

As noted in Chapter 1, moraine fragments have been reported in the literature on the Washlands, but often with minimal description. Within the mapping scheme of the Geological Survey, moraines are defined as being composed of glacial sediments (till or hummocky glacial deposits – cf. McMillan & Powell, 1999); this has meant that ridges associated with glacial sand and gravel have often been described as eskers in situations where, given that they have been formed at ice margins, they are more likely to be moraines. This suggests that areas of moraine defined by the Geological Survey may be more proscriptive than their actual distribution. Mapping within the present project has confirmed many of these features as moraines; it has also recognized many other ridges as additional moraines that are important in glacier reconstruction,

particularly in connection with the interaction between Vale of York and Wensleydale ice.

In the southern part of the mapped area, to the south-west of Ripon, there are a number of moraine ridge fragments and associated meltwater channels that can be used to reconstruct lateral ice limits. These limits can be traced northwards from South Stainley (SE 305632) as a belt, or as two distinct limits, towards the Skell Gorge at Fountains Abbey (Fig. 2.2). Prominent mounds and ridges can be seen, for example, at How Hill (144 m O.D.; SE 278671; Fig. 2.3), previously recognized as a moraine ridge (Cooper & Burgess, 1983). Other well-developed ridges are found to the west of Markenfield Hall (SE 295674). North of the major meltwater channel occupied by the Skell at Fountains and Studley Royal (SE 275683), a long well-defined ridge can be mapped for about 1 km at Low Lindrick (SE 275712) and towards High Birkby (SE 273723). This feature, well known from the literature (in which it is called 'Roman Ridge'), appears to be a lateral moraine (Kendall & Wroot, 1924). Morainic mounds from Aldfield (SE 264694) towards Clip'd Thorn (SE 261699; Fig. 2.4) can be traced northwards of another major meltwater channel (occupied by the River Laver) towards the village of Galphay (SE 255724) and possibly onwards towards Kirkby Malzeard (SE 235744).

A number of mounds have also been observed on the upstream northern side of Hackfall Gorge, where the River Ure has incised through the Magnesian Limestone (Fig. 2.5). These can be traced north-west towards Aldburgh Hall (SE 235791), where they are dissected by a set of meltwater channels (Fig. 2.6). On the interfluve area to the east of the Ure, at 140 m O.D. on the Magnesian Limestone escarpment, there is a series of mounds at Whitwell Hill (SE 248810), which can be linked to an arcuate ridge that descends downslope towards the mounds at Aldburgh (Fig. 2.5). Further ridges can be traced on the west side of the River Ure, to the south of Nutwith Cote (SE 230780) and westwards towards Low Swinton (SE 220790; Figs 2.5 & 2.7). All of this geomorphological evidence suggests a former limit to Wensleydale ice in this part of the Ure valley that may be associated with the formation of Hackfall Gorge.

West of Masham, the interfluve area between the Ure and the Burn is marked by a number of discrete ridges trending north-west–south-east (Fig. 2.5). At Micklebury Hill (SE 203812) and Low Sutton (SE 202825), mounds have been mapped in association with meltwater channels. Within the Ure valley, ridges and mounds can also be seen from High Mains Farm (SE 215836) westwards to Low Ellington (SE 204839) in an area called the Inner Hills (SE 214835), which lies just north of the present gravel quarry at Marfield (section 2.6.1). Associated with this area of mounds and ridges are several large depressions that appear to be kettle holes associated with ice stagnation (Figs 2.5, 2.8, 2.9). The ridges can be traced east across the River Ure, where there is a distinct ridge that crosses the slope just south-east of Clifton Castle (SE 225836). Although there

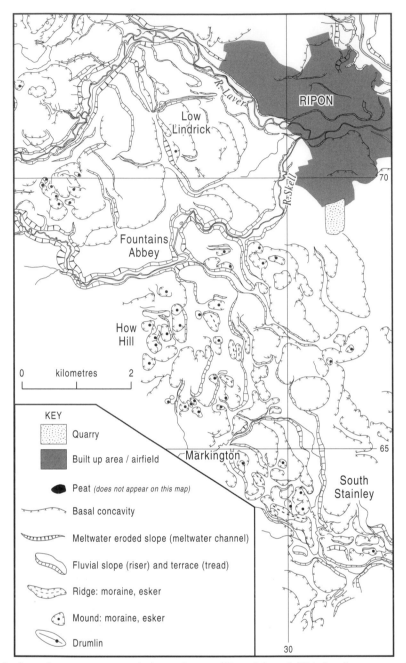

Fig. 2.2. Selected sample from the main geomorphological map (Plate 2.1 and CD) for the area to the south-west of Ripon, showing major meltwater channels and moraine ridge fragments.

are no obvious moraine ridges, the ground north of Clifton Castle towards Thornton Watlass (SE 238856) and Burrill (SE 204871), and westwards to the edge of the mapped area (easting 20) is covered by thick superficial deposits approaching the definition of hummocky moraine, with more distinct ridges evident towards Bedale (Fig. 2.10).

One of the largest moraine ridges in the Washlands occurs south of Catterick (Fig. 2.11), extending along the line of the A1 NW–SE for 7 km towards Killerby Farm (SE 251959). This ridge can be traced north-east as an arc from Aiskew (SE 270885), north-east of Bedale, towards Leases Hall (SE 280912) and then north towards St Ann's Cross

(SE 266934) and Holtby Grange (SE 269934), reaching a high point at Carr Hill (SE 274925) at 76 m O.D. (Fig. 2.11; see also below, Plate 2.4F). There are well-defined breaks of slope to both the east and west at 40 m O.D., making the ridge about 36–40 m in elevation. It continues northwards towards Goskins (SE 255942), where there is a well-marked slope to the west. Further north, there is a less defined ridge with smaller ridge fragments that are continued in the arc westwards towards East Appleton (SE 234957), where there is a more definite ridge. Around Killerby, there are other ridges associated with mounds and peat-filled hollows. The major ridge, here called the Leeming moraine, has

Fig. 2.3. How Hill (SE 278671); one of a series of lateral moraine ridge fragments to the south of Fountains Abbey; see geomorphological map (Plate 2.1 and CD).

Fig. 2.4. Clip'd Thorn (SE 261699) lateral moraine ridge between the Skell and Laver river valleys associated with a former Ure ice margin.

previously been interpreted as a lateral moraine of Vale-of-York ice (Lovell, 1982); an alternative explanation that it was associated with a local readvance of Wensleydale ice was proposed by Frost (1998, p. 69). Field mapping has confirmed the overall arcuate morphology of the Leeming moraine, showing that it was indeed formed by Wensleydale ice (Fig. 2.11). Geological investigations have found the ridge to be composed of sand and gravel overlying laminated lake sediments (Lovell, 1982). A former quarry at Leases (SE 275914) indicates that the sand and gravel has been disturbed, probably by glaciotectonism.

North of St Ann's Cross, the Leeming moraine is continued by a set of lower-elevation ridges that are arcuate towards the north-west, where they can be traced towards Tunstall (SE 218960), a village to the west of Catterick (Fig. 2.12). Here, they link into a suite of well-defined lateral moraine ridges and meltwater channels, first identified by Raistrick (1926) as marking the northern lateral limit of Wensleydale ice along the high ground south of Catterick Garrison (Fig. 2.11). Interestingly, north of these moraines around Tunstall, towards Brough Hall (SE 217979) and the Swale at Catterick, there is another suite of ridges composed of till but orientated north–south; these are interpreted as drumlins (see below for definition), associated with Vale-of-York ice, that are truncated by the west–east moraines at Tunstall (Fig. 2.11). This cross-cutting relationship clearly demonstrates that the Tunstall and Leeming moraines are younger than the north–south trending drumlins, indicating that Wensleydale ice readvanced to the Leeming moraine after Vale-of-York ice had retreated from the Catterick area.

There are a number of ridge fragments further south along the western margin of the Vale-of-York that have been interpreted as lateral moraines associated with ice in the main vale; this includes some of the ridges around Kirklington (Fig. 2.13). Along the ridge utilized by the A1 road south from Leeming there are several landforms that might be so defined. The situation is complicated by the fact that this ridge is lithologically controlled by the generally hidden outcrop of the Sherwood Sandstone. There is a series of small mounds between Ripon and Boroughbridge (Fig. 2.14), particularly well developed east of Copt Hewick (SE 340715), that are interpreted as hummocky moraine associated with a recessional ice limit. There is also a series of mounds extending from Boroughbridge (SE 397670) south-eastwards through the village of Grafton-cum-Marton (SE 416633), which have been interpreted as part of the Flaxby-Tollerton moraine, a retreat limit of the Vale of York lobe (Cooper & Burgess, 1993; Fig. 2.15).

In comparison with the large number of mounds and ridges along the Pennine margin of the Vale of York, there are fewer landforms within the vale itself and the well-reported cross-valley moraine limits of York and Escrick (Aitkenhead, *et al.*, 2002; Evans *et al.*, 2005) lie to the south of the study area. Possible moraines have been mapped near Newby Wiske (SE 364878), where there is a large ridge blocking a former meltwater channel. Another probable recessional margin can be found at Ainderby Steeple (SE 333923), just west of Northallerton, where there are ridges that reach 42 m O.D., standing above surrounding land at 30 m O.D. There are, however, reports that bedrock is near the surface in this area, which may be reflected in the relief; a former quarry at the eastern end of the ridge is reported to have exposed Sherwood Sandstone (Fox-Strangways *et al.*, 1886; Frost, 1998) but this cannot be confirmed.

2.2.1.2 Drumlins

Drumlins are streamlined hills with asymmetric long profiles that result from subglacial deformation and are aligned in the direction of ice flow (Benn & Evans, 1998). Within the Washlands, drumlins have been mapped by the Geological Survey in the Northallerton area, although no overall trend was identified (Frost, 1998). Drumlins have been reported by Johnson (1969, 1974) between Burrill (SE 240872) and around Thorp Perrow (SE 265855),

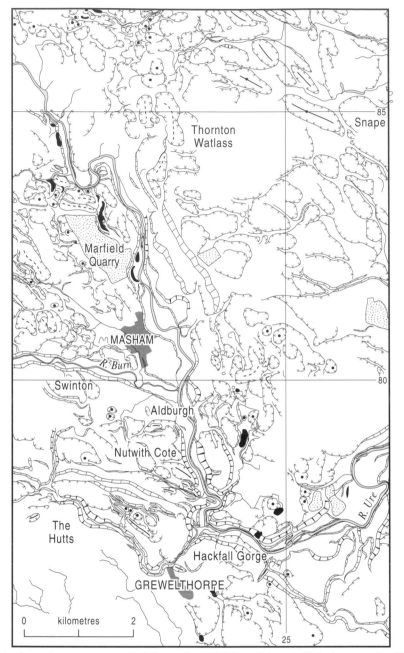

Fig. 2.5. Selected sample from the main geomorphological map (Plate 2.1 and CD) showing the Ure valley upstream from Hackfall Gorge towards Marfield. For key, see Fig. 2.2.

for example Oscar Hill (SE 247862; Fig. 2.16); mapping during this project has confirmed their existence. This small drumlin field indicates a general trend NW–SE associated with ice flowing out of Wensleydale across the interfluve area between Bedale and Masham towards Snape Mires (Fig. 2.10) converging with Vale-of-York ice. There are also numerous small drumlins around Kirklington (SE 319812) trending north–south, indicating ice flow along the Vale of York (Figs 2.13, 2.17), and around Brough Hall to the west of Catterick village, where they are terminated by moraine ridges at Tunstall associated with a readvance of Wensleydale ice (see 2.2.1.1).

2.2.2 Glaciofluvial Landforms

Most landscapes associated with former ice masses also bear clear witness to the former presence of large quantities of water released as the ice melted, forming impressive suites of meltwater channels in both subglacial and marginal locations, many of which are divorced from the present fluvial system. These meltwater rivers were also efficient transporters of sediment and this was deposited beyond the ice margins as proglacial sandur (outwash) plains.

Fig. 2.6. Aerial view of the Ure valley north of Hackfall Gorge (middle distance left) around Aldburgh, south of Masham, showing mounds and associated meltwater channels (dashed lines). See Fig. 2.5.

Fig. 2.7. Moraine mounds near Swinton (SE 220790; see Fig. 2.5), looking north.

Fig. 2.8. Low Ellington (SE 204839), Ure valley north of Masham showing kettle holes and mounds associated with the ice limit at Marfield Quarry (to left).

Fig. 2.9. Low Ellington (SE 204839) kettle hole (see also Plate 2.1/CD; Figure 2.5).

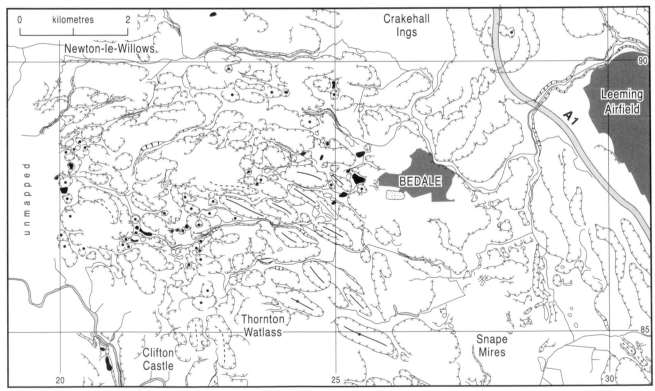

Fig. 2.10. Selected sample from the main geomorphological map (Plate 2.1 and CD) showing interfluve area west of Leeming, with the drumlins around Thornton Watlass and the complex 'hummocky moraine' towards Newton-le-Willows (SE 215895). For key, see Fig. 2.2.

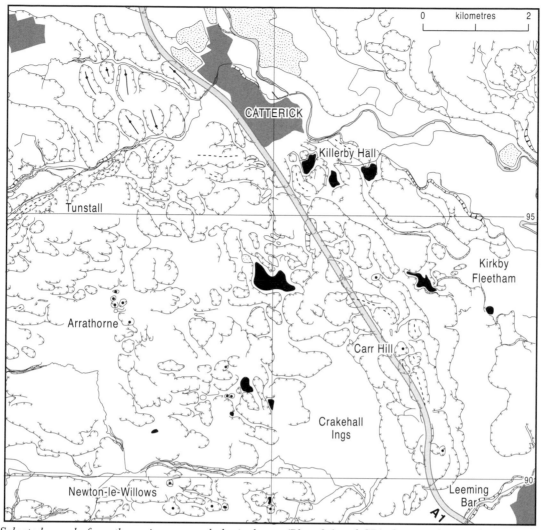

Fig. 2.11. Selected sample from the main geomorphological map (Plate 2.1 and CD) showing the area between Leeming and Catterick, particularly the Leeming Moraine (followed by the A1 between Catterick and Leeming Bar), the Kirkby Fleetham palaeochannels and the Tunstall moraines. For colour version, see CD.

Fig. 2.12. Tunstall moraine, marking the northern margin of Wensleydale ice to the south-west of Catterick village (SE 218960); see also Fig. 2.11.

2.2.2.1 Meltwater channels

Large meltwater channels, forming complex drainage patterns, are well developed along the Pennine foothills (Kendall & Wroot, 1924). Although such channels have traditionally been associated with lake overflow (see Chapter 1.5), it now seems more likely that they formed either along lateral ice margins or in the subglacial environment; however, it is often difficult to determine the environment of formation from channel morphology, since this may reflect utilization in a number of different ways over time. With respect to glacial reconstruction, it is important to be able to distinguish the formational environments of different channels (cf. Benn & Evans, 1998). Meltwater channels are most easily identified where they have no present stream and occur in locations that are not part of the present river system (e.g. Glasser et al., 2004). A meltwater origin for other channels can

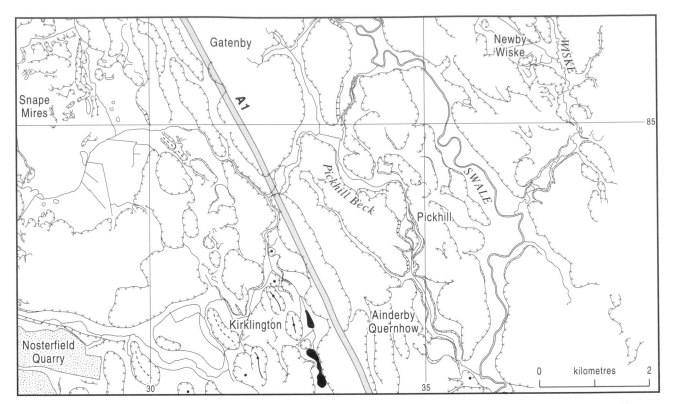

Fig. 2.13. Selected sample from the main geomorphological map (Plate 2.1 and CD) showing the Swale valley from Kirklington and Pickhill north-east towards Newby Wiske. For key, see Fig. 2.2.

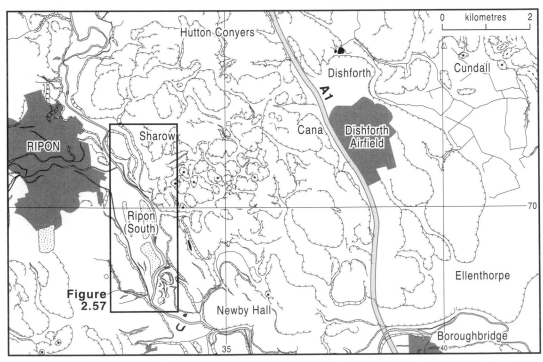

Fig. 2.14. Selected sample from the main geomorphological map (Plate 2.1 and CD) showing the Washlands from Ripon eastwards towards Dishforth. For key, see Fig. 2.2.

Fig. 2.15. (above) Moraine mounds at Grafton-cum-Marton, south of Boroughbridge (SE 416633).

Fig. 2.16. (left) Oscar Hill drumlin between Thornton Watlass and Bedale (SE 247862); see map (Fig. 2.10).

Fig. 2.17. Kirklington drumlin. This is one of a series of drumlins and associated mounds orientated NW–SE within the Vale of York (SE 319812; see Plate. 2.1).

Fig. 2.18. One of a series of meltwater channel near High Grantley (SE 235697), west of Ripon.

be indicated where they are occupied by a stream too small to have produced the channel (cf. Benn & Evans, 1998). Where the channels no longer form part of the present drainage system, their floors are often areas of peat accumulation. Subglacial channels can be distinguished by having a humped 'up and down' profile associated with erosion by water flowing under pressure.

In the Washlands, an intricate series of channels has

been mapped in the headwaters of the Skell and Laver, west of Ripon, for example near Grantley (SE 235 697; Fig. 2.18), which form part of a more extensive drainage system that can be traced southwards into the Nidd drainage and along the outer margin of the large York and Escrick moraine systems (Kendall & Wroot, 1924; Cooper & Burgess, 1993). It is also clear from the mapping of these features (Fig. 2.19) that they cross-cut each other and are

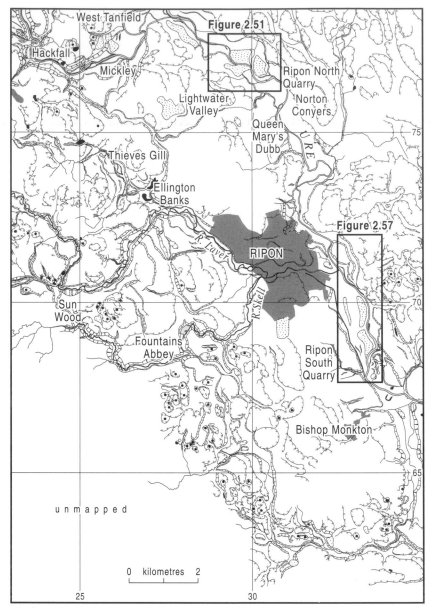

Fig. 2.19. Selected sample from the main geomorphological map (Plate 2.1 and CD) showing area along the ice fronts west of Ripon and the palaeochannels of the Ure (Thieves Gill) south of Hackfall. For key, see Fig. 2.2.

therefore diachronous, associated with changing positions of the ice margin during deglaciation.

Both the Laver and Skell occupy impressive gorges west of Ripon (Figs 2.2 & 2.19). The Skell becomes incised for much of its length from Grantley Hall (SE 234690) eastwards for 6 km to beyond Fountains–Studley Royal (SE 293690). Here, the river occupies a 50 m deep flat-floored valley cut in solid rock and with a maximum width of 400 m (Fig. 2.20), which is clearly too large to have been formed under present hydrological conditions. The Laver enters a similar large bedrock-incised channel east of Laverton at Winksley Banks (SE 245720) extending in a large loop to Ellington Banks (SE 276729). However, there is also a dry channel connecting the two rivers at Sun Wood (SE 245700; Fig. 2.19). South of the Skell there is also a meltwater

channel at Sawley Hall (SE 262668) that connects with the High Cayton channel and the Nidd drainage (Kendall & Wroot, 1924). Further channels extend south across the Skell, from Studley Royal towards Markenfield Hall and South Stainley (SE 305632), where there is another large channel now occupied by the main Ripon–Harrogate road (SE 305641; Plate 2.1). At South Stainley, this channel can be traced eastwards, where it is joined by further channels which commence abruptly within areas of mounds. This channel continues towards Copgrove, where there is an extensive area of sand and gravel in a wide shallow valley that extends northwards towards the River Ure, as well as a further channel extending towards a channel at Staveley (SE 366628).

The present interfluve between the Laver and the Ure

has a number of large meltwater channels occupied by small present-day streams (Plate 2.1). The Kex Beck, east of Kirkby Malzeard (SE 251743), occupies a meltwater channel system that joins the Laver at Ellington Banks. Another meltwater channel also joins the Laver system at this point; this is the Thieves Gill channel (Figs 2.19, 2.21 & 2.22), which is well reported as a former channel of the River Ure (Kendall & Wroot, 1924). This channel can be traced for >5 km from the eastern end of the Hackfall Gorge (SE 249763), in a south-easterly direction, falling in elevation from 120 m O.D. to *c.* 100 m O.D. before dropping rapidly to the peat-filled floor of the Laver at 60 m O.D. (Fig 2.19). Along its course, two channels deviate north-east from this channel towards Old Sleningford Hall (SE 265770) and the Lightwater Valley (SE 285752).

To the south-west of Hackfall Gorge, another former meltwater channel system is occupied by Hutts Beck, on the south side of Nutwith Common (Fig. 2.5; south of Nutwith Cote). This channel starts abruptly at 230 m O.D. near Hutts Cottage (SE 209778) and extends 4 km towards Grewelthorpe, where the channel turns north-east to Hackfall Gorge; this channel is >30 m deep and 250 m across at the widest point. On the upper slopes of Nutwith Common are a number of smaller channels associated with moraine ridges along the top of this ridge (Fig. 2.5).

East of the Magnesian Limestone ridge, between Ripon and Catterick, there are several meltwater channels. These are less-incised features that are relatively wide, shallow landforms eroded into superficial deposits. A meltwater origin is suggested by their large size relative to current stream activity, leaving abandoned poorly-drained peat-filled channels. An example of this is the large channel that drains the eastern side of the limestone outcrop from Snape (SE 262843) southwards towards Well (SE 268819) and Nosterfield (SE 279805) and beyond to a series of small channels incised into the till cover around Wath (SE 324770) and continuing towards the Ure upstream of Ripon.

Similar channel systems can be found within the Vale of York/Vale of Mowbray, associated with the River Swale. The present wide floodplain has been incised into thick superficial deposits with earlier river activity being recorded by a number of abandoned channels and erosional terrace levels (Fig. 2.13). The present river floodplain is, therefore, best regarded as only one of series of channel systems, at similar elevations, associated with a river that occupied a number of positions within the Washlands before the establishment of the present floodplain. Many of these meltwater channels probably have an origin associated with a northwards retreating ice front, given the occurrence of Lateglacial and full Holocene sediment sequences within the channels, such as at Newby Wiske (Chapter 3.3). Another good example of such a channel can be seen around Pickhill (SE 346837); Pickhill Beck occupies a much larger channel that can be mapped from Swainby (SE 335855) in the north to Howe (SE 358806; Fig. 2.13). There is also a rather indistinct interfluve with

a tributary stream that also flows south-west towards Kirklington, suggesting original drainage across the interfluve into the Ure drainage catchment.

2.2.2.2 *Eskers*

Eskers are formed subglacially in tunnels within ice sheets (cf. Benn & Evans, 1998). Linear ridges of this type within the Vale of York, composed of sand and gravel, have been traditionally interpreted as eskers (e.g. Cooper & Burgess, 1993). The use of this term has been thought appropriate to define irregular masses of sand and gravel that have a distinct morphology in the form of steep-sided ridges, up to 20 m in height, with sharp crests and orientated down valley. Within the Washlands, an esker has been identified between Helperby and Aldwark (Cooper & Burgess, 1993) which is continued northwards as the Newby Wiske–Cundall esker (Powell *et al.*, 1992; Fig. 2.23). Detailed mapping has not distinguished such a landform around Helperby (SE 440700). However, there is clear constructional topography north-west from Cundall (SE 425726) towards Asenby (SE 398755), where distinct ridges can be identified at Sheephills Farm (SE 409747) and Firtree Hill (SE 413743), which has been extensively quarried for sand and gravel.

Further ridges, with a similar trend, can also be mapped around Cundall for about 1 km; however, there are also ridges in the same area (SE 415735) that have their axes at right angles, which suggests that the origin of all these landforms might be more complex, particularly since exposures in the gravel quarries show a complicated stratigraphy suggestive of glaciotectonic disturbance (Powell *et al.*, 1992). North of Asenby, there is no evidence of a continuation of this ridge but there is a series of terraces between the Swale and a small tributary, which coincide with an area marked on the geological map as lake deposits (Powell *et al.*, 1992). Areas of glacial sand and gravel can be seen at Sandhutton and Kirby Wiske but, given the amount of fluvial erosion associated with the present channel of the Swale and the formation of river terraces, it is difficult to correlate these with the ridges at Cundall.

The interpretation of the above-mentioned landforms as eskers may require revision. A more likely explanation of these landforms and sediments is that they are associated with lateral margins of distinct ice streams from different sources that amalgamated in their passage down the Vale of York; that is, they are former 'medial moraines' (Plate 2.2) along which the ice 'unzipped' (i.e. the linear divide along which distinct ice streams parted) during retreat, allowing deposition of sand and gravel deposits (interlobate eskers: Plate 2.2).

2.2.2.3 *Depressions*

As well as the positive landform constructions found across the Washlands, there are also numerous areas marked by depressions. Whereas many of these are probably related

Fig. 2.20. (left) Aerial view of Fountains Abbey (SE 275683) and Studley Royal, in the former meltwater channel occupied by the River Skell; looking towards Ripon. Photo by permission of English Heritage.

Fig. 2.21. (above) Thieves Gill meltwater channel marking a course of the River Ure early during deglaciation when ice occupied the present valley. This photograph shows the main channel near Newfield Farm (SE 258755).

Fig. 2.22. Western end of Thieves Gill meltwater channel (SE 249761).

to deglaciation, having formed as kettle holes due to ice stagnation (for example at Low Ellington (Fig. 2.9), this area is also characterized by depressions reflecting special conditions in the underlying bedrock geology. The Permian rocks that occur under the thick drift cover of the Washlands are a sequence of limestones and marls with beds of anhydrite, which converts to gypsum in contact with groundwater. Gypsum is highly soluble, giving rise to underground karstic features (Waltham *et al.*, 1997) such as tubes and caverns, the formation rate of which greatly exceeds that of comparable features in limestone. The collapse of such features causes foundering of the overlying strata and is expressed at the surface as depressions. These are particularly well developed around Ripon, for example Queen Mary's Dubb (SE 304745; Fig. 2.24), where the anhydrite-bearing marls are well developed and exposed at the surface (Cooper, 1986, 1989, 1995, 1998). Many of

these depressions are now filled with peat, making them possible sites for palaeoenvironmental study.

2.3 Landscape Evolution

The present landscape clearly reflects former geomorphological activity associated with the last glaciation (Plates 2.1 and 2.2), which has modified the landscape in two main ways. First, through deposition, including the emplacement of thick till (>30 m) and other glacial deposits, which has buried the pre-Devensian topography and constructed moraine ridges at a number of locations associated with readvances or still-stands during ice retreat. Second, by the cutting of large complex meltwater channel systems (Plate 2.1), particularly within the western part of the district, which directed large amounts of water and sediment

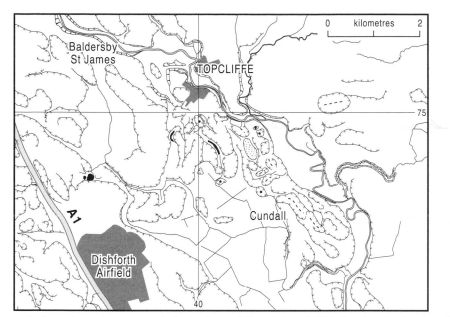

Fig. 2.23. Selected sample from the main geomorphological map (Plate 2.1 and CD) showing the Swale valley in the Topcliffe area, with detailed mapping of the Cundall esker system. For key, see Fig. 2.2.

towards the Washlands and resulted in the deposition of glaciofluvial and glacio-lacustrine sediments over much of the area. Both of these activities have had a major impact on the development and evolution of the river systems from deglaciation to the present day. This section aims to explain the development of particular parts of the Washlands on the basis of the present-day geomorphology so as to provide a regional context for the site descriptions later in this chapter and the site-specific palaeoenvironmental analysis that will appear in Chapter 3.

Thanks to its glacial history, much of the Washlands consists of an undulating or flat till plain with areas of lacustrine silts and clays, indicating the former existence of numerous lakes during deglaciation. The present rivers occupy only a limited proportion of the area. The river system has been subdivided into six sectors that reflect variations in the underlying geology, in the nature of the glacial record and in their Holocene evolution, as follows:

- The Ure valley upstream of the Magnesian Limestone escarpment at Hackfall Gorge.
- The Ure valley between Hackfall and Ripon
- The Ure valley south-east of Ripon, where it is joined by the Laver and Skell
- The Swale valley between Boroughbridge and Leeming
- The Swale valley from Leeming to Catterick
- The Swale valley from Catterick towards Richmond

Each of these has distinctive landscape elements that have determined the human occupation and land-use development of the area.

2.3.1 The River Ure

The Ure forms the major drainage flowing into the southern part of the Washlands through the impressive Hackfall Gorge (Fig. 2.25), cut in bedrock, which forms a major divide between the more topographically varied areas around Masham (Fig. 2.26) and the flatter areas of the Vale of York. Although not strictly part of the Washlands, the Ure valley upstream from Hackfall Gorge, including the area around Bedale and Newton-le-Willows, has been important in the determination of events within the lower part of the Ure catchment, particularly in connection with deglaciation and the evolution of the present fluvial system.

Between Hackfall Gorge and Ripon, the floodplain of the Ure widens across the lower relief of the Washlands formed on less resistant Permian marls. Extensive gravels have been deposited downstream of Hackfall, both as a major fan and within the Ure valley. There is a marked reduction in floodplain width towards Ripon, where there is further extensive gravel aggradation associated with the confluence of the Rivers Laver and Skell, eastward flowing tributaries from the Pennines. The presence of a large abandoned channel of the Ure at Sharow (see below and Chapter 3.5) attests to complex fluvial changes associated with this confluence.

Downstream of Ripon the floodplain again widens as the Ure flows across thick superficial deposits, mainly lake sediments. The presence of an enigmatic abandoned channel at Newby Hall again suggests an earlier drainage system, possibly associated with the large channel that extends southwards to Staveley and which the Ure avoids, having cut a smaller, more direct channel towards the gap in the Sherwood Sandstone at Boroughbridge (Plate 2.1).

Fig. 2.24. Aerial view of Queen Mary's Dubb, north of Ripon (see Fig. 2.19); these pools are solution hollows within Permian gypsum just north of Ripon. Also note the clear field markings showing meander cut off patterns on aggradational terraces on the east side of the River Ure.

Beyond that town, the floodplain again widens towards the confluence with the Swale.

2.3.1.1 Ure valley upstream of Hackfall Gorge

This area is characterized by moderate topography, with the highest ground (>200 m O.D.) in the western part of the mapped area, which is underlain by Carboniferous sandstones. The present Ure valley in this area is directed south-eastwards along the geological contact between the Carboniferous and Permian rocks. Higher ground to the east is associated with the west-facing Magnesian Limestone escarpment, which reaches a high point in this area of 148 m O.D. at Gebdykes (SE 234826), where there is an active limestone quarry (Fig. 2.27).

Over much of this area, the solid geology is obscured by glacial and glaciofluvial deposits that have created an undulating landscape of mounds, abandoned channels and enclosed hollows (Figs 2.5 & 2.10). West of Masham (SE 225808), the oldest meltwater channels appear to drain the high ground north of Fearby (SE 198812) on the interfluve area between the Ure and the Burn (Fig. 2.5). The present small stream of Swinney Beck (SE 200819) occupies a much larger discontinuous channel that trends south-east from a moraine ridge at High Sutton (SE 203826) towards Masham. Further ridges and mounds can also be observed south of the Fearby Road, occupying the ground towards the Burn channel, which appears to have acted as a meltwater conduit. The overall nature of these ridges and channels suggests that they are associated with a western margin of the Wensleydale glacier as it crossed the interfluve area.

North of Masham, the present River Ure has incised into a thick sequence (>20 m) of outwash gravels, which have been worked in a series of former quarries (Fig. 2.28) with the current extraction based at Marfield (SE 210830). Previous excavations have been in typical outwash gravels

but the present quarry sections (see below, section 2.6.1) show steeply dipping gravels and lake sediments, with evidence of folding and thrusting of these sediments, which are capped by till. The topography that has developed in this area is complex, with ridges such as the Inner Hills (SE 214833) reflecting the presence of thrust blocks (Fig. 2.5). Mounds and enclosed depressions at Low Ellington (SE 205839; Fig. 2.8) suggest ice stagnation after the advance that deformed the sedimentary sequence. These mounds can be traced eastwards across the river in a broad band that extends through Thornton Watlass (SE 235856) to Newton-le-Willows (SE 215895). In association with the lithostratigraphical sequence exposed at Marfield, these landforms are thought to define an ice margin associated with a readvance (possible surge?) of Wensleydale ice (see Chapter 5.2).

Immediately to the east of Marfield, a palaeochannel is observed at High Mains (SE 215834). This channel, which is filled with Lateglacial and Holocene sediments (see Chapter 3.4), occurs at elevations of *c.* 20 m above the present river and can be traced down valley for 1 km (Fig. 2.28), although its southward continuation towards Masham has been lost as a result of gravel extraction (Figs 2.5 & 2.28). This is interpreted as an early channel of the Ure; it is clear that it was abandoned when the present river began to incise into the glaciofluvial sediments to form the present large meander at Clifton Castle (SE 218844).

A complex suite of landforms can be observed between Thornton Watlass and Bedale (Fig. 2.10), where there are numerous mounds, moraine ridges and drumlins, for example Piney Moor Hill (SE 231874). The lack of simple plan-form in many instances may reflect erosion of the drumlins associated with two meltwater channel systems that intersect the mounds and ridges (Fig. 2.10). Both sets of channels begin in the west of the area near Hollin Hill (SE 201878), with one channel trending north-east towards the low ground occupied by the present valley

Fig. 2.25. Hackfall Gorge: the River Ure has cut this sinuous gorge through the Magnesian Limestone (looking downstream)

Fig. 2.26. Aerial view of the Ure valley looking downstream towards the town of Masham.

of the Bedale Beck. The other channel system has eroded through the moraine system north of Thirn (SE 207860), eventually becoming indistinct south east of Burrill (SE 240871), where it is lost in a number of wide flat areas that slope towards Snape (SE 270845). Here there are extensive laminated sediments (>16 m thick), indicating the former existence of a large glacial lake (Giles, 1982; Powell *et al.*, 1992; see below, Section 2.8.2).

To the west of Hackfall Gorge, along the crest of the ridge of Nutwith Common in the vicinity of Horsecourse Hill (SE 226774), there is a distinct moraine ridge with a number of mounds and smaller meltwater channels (Fig. 2.5). On the lower slopes to the north-west of this ridge, near Warthermarske (SE 208790), there are two large meltwater channels within Swinton Park (SE 209797). These indicate south-eastwards flow of meltwater in association with a possible ice margin, defined by mounds (Fig. 2.7) lying at the break of slope to the east between Low Swinton (SE 225796) and Nutwith Cote (SE 230790). The sudden

commencement of the large meltwater channel to the south of this ridge, as well as the other moraines and channels, suggests that an ice margin within the Burn valley lay along the north side of this ridge at a number of elevations.

These ice limits along Nutwith Common can be traced eastwards across the Ure to Aldburgh Hall (SE 234792) where mounds and enclosed depressions appear to indicate an ice margin (Fig. 2.5). They are associated with a large peat-filled meltwater channel, Black Robin Beck (SE 243790), which joins the Ure at the northern extent of the Hackfall Gorge (Fig. 2.29). This gorge extends for about 3 km and is deeply incised (>40 m) into the solid geology (Fig. 2.25), which changes here from Carboniferous to Permian through the gorge. Incision was not a single progressive event, as there are minor aggradational terraces within the gorge; it may even be reactivation of an older channel formed before the last glaciation. The land either side of the gorge is undulating but there are several peat-filled hollows and mounds, for example Neddy Brown

Fig. 2.27. Aerial view of the Permian limestone escarpment east of Masham, showing Gebdykes Quarry and the general profile of the western side of the escarpment down towards the present River Ure. The line shows the location of the Plate 2.4B transect.

Fig. 2.28. Aerial view of Marfield Quarry, north of Masham (SE 210830), showing current workings (July 2006) and the location of the High Mains palaeochannel (marked with dashed line). The Inner Hills marks one of the upstanding thrust blocks associated with a readvance of Wensleydale ice.

Fig. 2.29. Aerial view of Hackfall Gorge, west of West Tanfield, looking towards Grewelthorpe.

Fig. 2.30. (below) Aerial view across the Nosterfield fan surface, showing the Thornborough Henges in the foreground. Looking north-east towards Thornborough village and Sutton Howgrave (far distance, right).

Hill (SE 255778), near the southern end of the gorge near Tanfield Lodge (SE 250771), suggesting former ice marginal positions that can be correlated with the moraines at Nutwith Common.

The overall character of this part of the Ure valley is one of deposition related to subglacial processes and geomorphic activity along a number of ice marginal positions associated with retreat of a Wensleydale glacier. Related to this ice marginal retreat, numerous meltwater channels were formed, mainly in lateral situations or as proglacial valleys. However, the pattern of channel evolution is not easily determined from the geomorphological evidence. The higher and probably earlier channels grade to an elevated level of the river through the Hackfall Gorge and may in fact predate its incision.

Holocene activity appears limited within this sector of the Ure valley. Apart from extensive low terraces above the present river around Masham, particularly associated with the confluence of the Ure and the Burn, the river appears to have been confined within its valley since the occupation of Hackfall Gorge. Upstream of Masham, incision has been the dominant process, confining the river within the superficial deposits. Bedrock is exposed along the east bank of the Clifton Castle estate reach and on the west bank there is a terrace dominated by a peat-filled abandoned channel.

2.3.1.2 Ure valley from Hackfall to Ripon

As the Ure leaves the Hackfall Gorge between Mickley and West Tanfield, there is an overall change in landscape character. The terrain is much lower (<50 m O.D.), particularly to the north-east of the present river, where there is a large outwash fan associated with meltwater activity through the gorge and extending north-east towards Nosterfield (SE 278805). Beyond here, the fan terminates in a former meltwater channel that extends along the eastern side of the Magnesian Limestone ridge from near Snape

(SE 266843), past Well (SE 267819) towards Kirklington (SE 320812). Radiocarbon age estimates from peat-filled hollows on its surface suggest that the fan is of latest LGM age and was formed well before 11,140 ^{14}C years BP (about 13,000 calibrated years). The fan is composed of coarse gravels overlying glacio-lacustrine sediments and sand. Syngenetic ice-wedge casts are common within the gravels, indicating both a subaerial origin for the fan and the continued presence of permafrost during its formation. Extensive quarrying has destroyed much of this fan surface on which the henge complexes at Thornborough (SE 293797) were constructed in the late Neolithic (Fig. 2.30; see Chapter 4.5).

This fan can be traced eastwards towards a series of till ridges that extend southwards along the west side of the A1 from Exelby (SE 295870) through Carthorpe (SE 308838), Kirklington (SE 319813) to Sutton Howgrave (SE 318791). These ridges form drumlins, particularly around Kirklington (Johnson, 1969; Fig. 2.13). However, some may also be lateral moraine fragments of the Vale-of-York glacier deposited over a bedrock ridge of Sherwood Sandstone. This suggests that the Nosterfield fan was formed between two ice masses when the margin of Wensleydale ice lay across Hackfall Gorge from Tanfield towards Nutwith Common

Fig. 2.31. Aerial view looking east across Snape Mires towards the A1 (dashed line). The low-lying area is underlain by thick (>18 m) lacustrine silts and clays deposited in a former glacial lake. Two of the palaeoenvironmental sample locations (see Chapter 3) are indicated.

whilst the Vale of York ice lay to the east of Kirklington. Isolated hills between Sutton Howgrave and North Stainley, composed of till, appear to be erosional remnants of the former till surface and reflect incision by the distal channels that formed the Nosterfield fan.

North of the fan is large low lying area of Snape Mires (Figs 2.13 & 2.31), with geological evidence (Giles, 1982; Powell *et al.*, 1992) in the form of extensive laminated silts and clays (>18 m thick) to suggest the former existence of a large lake occupying ground between Snape and Burneston (SE 309850) and extending nearly to Bedale (SE 268880). This flat area is separated from the Nosterfield fan by a low ridge, composed of till, lying north of the Well channel (Fig. 2.13). Its exact significance is unclear but it is has been interpreted as a moraine, perhaps relating to an ice marginal position of either Wensleydale or Vale-of-York ice. The eastern extent of the lake can be determined from the distribution of lake sediments and associated lateral sand deposits, which abut against the higher till-covered land towards the A1. The western extent is less clear because the lake beds are overlain by sands and gravels that have prograded into the lake from channels draining the high ground between Bedale and Marfield, which marks a former ice limit (Fig. 2.5; see below).

South of Hackfall Gorge, the land is marked by a thin till cover with increased exposure of the Permian strata. Whilst lower terraces are clearly associated with fluvial deposition, there are possible upper terraces that appear to be erosional in origin and associated with gradual down-cutting of the river into the limestone (Fig. 2.19), perhaps marking the transition of the Ure from the level of the high abandoned Thieves Gill channel. This channel is associated with the ice margin at Mickley–Tanfield and pre-dates the incision of the Hackfall Gorge. Two major changes, or bifurcations, along the channel to the north-east can be discerned, indicating possible ice marginal retreat positions prior to a terminal position at Mickley, suggesting that the channel is composed

of a series of diachronous sections related to westward ice retreat. This channel may thus represent the first stage of post-glacial river evolution in this area. It was subsequently abandoned, after which Hackfall Gorge has been incised at least 40 m below the level of the Thieves Gill Channel. It was during the course of this incision that fluvial erosion is thought to have created the erosional terraces in the area between the channel and the modern river. The lower gravel terraces have been disturbed by aggregate extraction, particularly between West Tanfield (SE 270789) and North Stainley (SE 288770). The ground towards Ripon is covered by till with numerous depressions, such as Queen Mary's Dubb (Figs 2.1 & 2.24), that are clearly related to gypsum collapse (Cooper, 1986, 1995).

Holocene activity has been confined to a narrow floodplain either side of the present river. From West Tanfield downstream towards Norton Conyers, there are two small terrace levels just to the south of the Thornborough henge complex, suggesting that the southern henge was, when constructed, much closer to the river than at present. The floodplain widens towards Norton Conyers and Nunwick before it becomes confined again towards Ripon. Aerial photographs of the terraces towards Norton Conyers clearly show complex patterns of meander migration and cut offs (Fig. 2.24).

2.3.1.3 Ure valley south and west of Ripon, including the Laver and Skell

The ground to the west of Ripon is deeply dissected by a number of large rock-cut meltwater channels that formed along former ice margins (Kendall & Wroot, 1924). This area is dominated by the major west-bank tributaries of the Ure, the Laver and Skell, which occupy sections of these former large meltwater systems (Fig. 2.19). Eastwards towards Ripon, the ground declines in elevation from about 200 m O.D. to <100 m O.D. in association with

Fig. 2.32. Aerial views of the Ure valley at Ripon: A – View looking south, showing the Laver/Skell confluence and the abandoned channel at Sharow (dashed line); B – Close up of the southern end of the Sharow Channel.

the change in underlying geology from Carboniferous to Permian strata. The lower ground between Ripon and Boroughbridge (<30 m O.D.) is characterized by low flat areas reflecting the presence of former lakes and a number of channels which cut through substantial drift mounds that reflect changing ice margin positions. As already noted, a well-developed former channel of the Ure (Fig. 2.32) can be seen at Sharow (SE 325717), to the east of Ripon, its lower part filled with >10 m of sediments from the latter half of the Holocene, from which palaeoenvironmental evidence has been obtained (Chapter 3.5).

The most westerly of the channel systems mapped within this project is the headwaters of the Skell and Laver (Plate 2.1). Upstream of Winksley, the Laver occupies a broad open channel with an older abandoned channel immediately to the south, at Missies Farm (SE 230730). However, from Winksley Banks to the outskirts of Ripon,

the river occupies a deep rock-cut channel that swings through nearly 180 degrees. Near Low Grantley there are several meltwater channels that join from the west but there is also a further large channel at Sun Wood (SE 245699) that is no longer part of the present river system but originally joined the Laver to the Skell system (see above, section 2.2.2.1; Fig. 2.19). This was presumably when ice occupied the immediate area north of the Skell channel.

The Skell system can be traced from west of Grantley Hall towards Fountains Abbey (SE 275683) and then towards Ripon. There is also an abandoned channel system directed south from Mackershaw, near Fountains, towards Markenfield Hall (SE 295673), where there are several discontinuous interlinking channels. Lateral moraine ridges in this area, for example at How Hill (SE 276671) and Marlow Hill, near Markenfield Hall (SE 296674), indicate former ice margins. The complex pattern of channels is simplified into one large channel between Wormald Green (SE 304650) and South Stainley (SE 306642), where there are several channels and associated mounds (Plate 2.1). These again become a single channel, the Robert Beck, which can be traced eastwards towards Copgrove (SE 346633), where there are further mounds and peat-filled depressions. This channel can then be traced northwards, as the Holbeck, to the River Ure at Newby Hall (SE 348674). This complex suite of channels is interpreted as being formed by meltwater flowing along a receding ice margin.

Another channel system, which flowed parallel to the Robert Beck between South Stainley and Copgrove, can be found 1 km to the south, occupying the valley between Brearton (SE 323610) and Occaney (SE 351619), where the channel bifurcates to flow towards a large peat-filled depression near Loftus Hill (SE 371615), with a further secondary channel linking this system to Robert Beck at Copgrove. The main continuation of the channel is, however, to the north-east of Staveley, where there is a major input of sand and gravel into a former lake in the wetland area of Staveley Carrs (SE 370640), now drained by the River Tutt. All these channels are part of a much larger system that marks the diversion of much of the lateral drainage south-east along the ice margin, as discussed by Kendall and Wroot (1924).

A further ice marginal landscape can be observed from Aldborough, south of Boroughbridge, to Grafton. Here are several large irregular mounds and dissected terrace fragments that have been breached by the Ure at Boroughbridge, where there are extensive low terraces. These mounds form a ridge, which may also be rock-cored (Sherwood Sandstone), separating the low ground of the River Tutt from Staveley to Minskip. North of the Boroughbridge gap, there is a notable absence of mounds, although several terraces are recognized, extending to the interfluve area between the Ure and Swale. These are interpreted as having formed when ice stood at a further margin from Bridge Hewick towards Dishforth and before the Ure incised to its present level; they are regarded as quite early landforms in the sequence of deglaciation but are problematic in that they are not found to the south, around Roecliffe.

Holocene terrace sequences are well marked downstream of Ripon, resulting from the migration of numerous abandoned meanders associated with the present floodplain (Fig. 2.33); these can be best observed around the Ripon Sailing Club (SE 335680; cf. Howard, *et al.*, 2000a). A number of abandoned meander loops of the river can be seen around Newby Hall (SE 344673) and there is also a dry peat-filled meltwater channel that is parallel to the present river towards Givendale Grange (SE 344689), as well as a large abandoned channel between Newby Hall and the village of Skelton-upon-Ure (SE 360682). There is also a laterally extensive first terrace that can be traced downstream to beyond Boroughbridge.

Fig. 2.33. Small terrace fragments associated with meander migration, Ripon Sailing Club (see also Howard et al., *2000a).*

2.3.2 The River Swale

The second major Washland river is the Swale, with its important left-bank tributary, the Wiske. The Swale has been studied downstream from Richmond to its confluence with the Ure (Plate 2.1); in this reach the river generally flows across a thick sequence of superficial deposits that completely masks the underlying solid geology. Bedrock is prominent only upstream of Catterick, above which the Swale can be regarded as a Pennine river, flowing in a bedrock valley. Elsewhere there are isolated pockets where the solid is near the surface, particularly in the vicinity of the A1, which (as noted already) traverses the Washlands on a drift-covered bedrock ridge of Sherwood Sandstone. Downstream from Catterick, there is little topographic differentiation of the Swale catchment within the Vale of York/Vale of Mowbray. Taylor *et al.* (2000) considered the Swale reach at Catterick–Brompton-on-Swale to fall within the piedmont category, noting its coarse gravel bed and incision into the surrounding till plain by up to 17 m, in significant contrast to the situation near the confluence with the Ure, where they observed that the river has a somewhat sandier bed-load and is incised by only 1–2 m into Pleistocene lacustrine deposits.

Within the Washlands, the Swale meanders across a floodplain of variable width (Fig. 2.34), reaching a maximum of >2 km near Gatenby (SE 325880), at its confluence with the How Beck. This wide valley floor suggests that a larger and more energetic river existed earlier in its post-glacial history. The river has a very low gradient, falling from 50 m O.D. at Catterick to <11 m O.D. at its confluence with the Ure, over a horizontal distance of 35 km. Relief is minimal, with the interfluve areas of the small streams being only *c.* 20 m above the present river, the highest elevations being reached in the ridge between Bedale and Leeming, which reaches a height of 76 m O.D. at Carr Hill (SE 275925). The ground also

Fig. 2.34. Aerial view of the Swale valley looking northwards towards Catterick village from near Little Langton. In the conspicuous meander in the middle distance is the former quarry at Great Langton (SE 296963).

rises towards Catterick Garrison, where elevation ranges between 100 and 300 m O.D. To aid description of the Swale valley, it will be divided into three geographical areas in upstream sequence from its confluence with the Ure: Boroughbridge to Leeming, Leeming to Catterick, and Catterick to Richmond.

2.3.2.1 Boroughbridge to Leeming

The confluence of the Swale and Ure at Ellenthorpe Ings (SE 430660), Myton-on-Swale (east of Boroughbridge), occurs in an extensive area of Pleistocene lake sediments that extends northwards towards Brafferton (SE 439700) and the southern end of the Cundall esker system (Powell *et al.*, 1992). Along this part of the Swale upstream towards Leeming, there is minimal relief apart from the esker ridge between Asenby and Brafferton (Fig. 1.4; Plate 2.1). Large areas are extremely flat, particularly to the east of Thirsk, from Topcliffe (SE 400760) towards Breckenbrough (SE 370834). This appears to be associated with progradation by the Cod Beck (Fig. 2.23), which was a much larger, meltwater-charged river during deglaciation (when it acted as the major conduit draining the eastern side of the Vale-of-York ice lobe into a lake).

The present River Swale occupies a well-developed floodplain that is laterally defined throughout this reach by fluvially-cut features incised into a more general low-relief surface. This surface can be resolved into a series of low-relief 'terrace' levels, these being elevated flat surfaces above till. Whether these surfaces have been occupied by a river and therefore qualify as erosional fluvial terraces is an important issue that will be discussed below. There are also large flat areas that are composed of lake sediments, artificially drained within the last three centuries, over which the present stream network is poorly developed. There is increasing relief within the northern part of this area, upstream of the confluence with the River Wiske (SE

368833), where the interfluve area reaches 50 m O.D. north of Solberge Hall (SE 356893).

The River Wiske forms the second major drainage line along the axis of the Vale of York in the project area. Within the Washlands, the lower reach of this stream drains the central part of the vale in a poorly defined valley through thick superficial deposits. These parts of the Wiske, following the near right-angle bend in its course (Plate 1.1), follow the sub-drift valley that might represent the pre-Devensian Swale valley routed towards the Tees (Chapter 1.3; Plate 1.4). There are also a number of possible former channels that reveal abandoned drainage lines or short-lived drainage as the rivers re-established themselves across the area as the ice withdrew northwards.

2.3.2.2 Leeming to Catterick

Moving upstream, the section of the Swale valley between Leeming and Catterick is of similar landscape character, although to the west of this reach there are important geomorphological changes, in that the Leeming moraine creates a major topographic feature related to a readvance of Wensleydale ice (see above; Fig. 2.11). Between the moraine and the river there are fluvial gravels (Lovell, 1982) that define an abandoned channel of the Swale. This has been mapped from Killerby Hall south-eastwards towards Kirkby Fleetham and Leeming Bar (see above; Fig. 2.11) and appears to be confluent with widespread sand and gravel extending east from Bedale and southwards by way of the large 'terrace' feature on which Leeming airfield has been constructed.

Across the Vale of York there is also a notable increase in relief, east of Morton-upon-Swale and Ainderby Steeple towards the Wiske valley on the outskirts of Northallerton. This topography can be described as a series of mounds and ridges, up to 18 m in height, that are best expressed east of Ainderby Steeple (SE 335922). To the south a large

Fig. 2.35. Ainderby Steeple: the village is located on a moraine ridge marking a recessional limit across the Vale of York. The view was taken from the south, in a large channel (SE 333914) that terminates against the lower slopes of the moraine.

channel is suddenly terminated by the ridge (Fig. 2.35) and to the north there is extensive peat associated with lake sediments. As previously discussed, this topography is interpreted as a moraine that marks a recessional limit of Vale-of-York ice.

There is much evidence of former and present gravel extraction around Catterick village (see below), working a thick aggradation that has infilled the present valley (Lovell, 1982) and formed an extensive floodplain, particularly on the eastern side of the river. The largest operating quarry is to the north of the river at Scorton (see below, section 2.7.2), with a smaller working (section 2.7.1) just to the north-west of Catterick village. Both lithological sequences are complex, revealing a basal till, which forms the lowest unit, and a further 'upper' till interbedded with the gravels.

2.3.2.3 Catterick to Richmond

Upstream of Catterick, within the Pennine fringe, the Swale valley has a more directly west–east orientation. Its increasingly upland nature is reflected by the deep rock-cut channel from Brompton-on-Swale upstream towards Richmond. There is evidence of a drift-filled pre-Devensian valley of the Swale at Richmond that has been abandoned in favour of the present channel, cut into bedrock (Kendall & Wroot, 1924; Wells, 1955). Also, there are extensive sands and gravels associated with meltwater deposition, formed during deglaciation as the newly re-established outwash-charged river entered the lowlands (Lovell, 1982), and formerly worked at St. Trinians (NZ 194011), just to the east of Richmond. There is also a major meltwater channel, occupied by the Skeeby Beck (NZ 205015), that joins the Swale at Brompton-on-Swale (Plate 2.1).

There is a general rise in elevation westwards towards Catterick Garrison. As previously noted with respect to the Leeming moraine between Bedale and Catterick, this area appears to lie outside the extent of Wensleydale ice and is characterized by a number of north–south-directed drumlins around Brough Hall (SE 217979), associated with

the southerly flow of Vale-of-York ice from Stainmore across the present valley of the Swale. This is also seen in the distribution of erratics, with boulders of Shap granite being recorded from areas of the western Washlands (Fig. 1.3), such as Kirkby Malzeard (Raistrick, 1926).

There is no evidence of major ice flow out of Swaledale. Rather, it appears from the distribution of glacial landforms on the interfluve area north of the Swale, towards the Gilling Beck, that the lower Swale was formed as a major meltwater conduit from an important ice margin to the north of Richmond, marked by the Feldom moraine (Kendall & Wroot, 1924; Raistrick, 1926, 1932; Wells, 1955; Fig. 2.36). This moraine ridge, with its steep northern slope, can be clearly seen for 9 km from Barningham Moor (NZ 060085) south-east to Richmond Out Moor (NZ 132036), which lies 4 km north-west of the town (Wells, 1955). This is the southern limit of Shap granite erratics, from which it would appear that this moraine marks the position of a significant ice margin during the last glaciation (Wells, 1955). It is only one of a series of moraines and associated meltwater channels within this part of southern Stainmore.

This area has not been mapped in detail as part of the Washlands, but the meltwater channels here are of relevance because the drainage from the Feldom ice limit eroded large channels, such as the Marske Beck channel (NZ 095015), which can be traced from the moraine southwards, contributing a major input into the Swale drainage (Fig. 2.37). This channel, 120 m deep, is only one of a series that drained the ice margin. It would therefore appear that, at least around Richmond, the Swale was formed in association with meltwater, not from Swaledale, but from along the southern margin of the Stainmore ice stream and that the major gravel outwash sediments around Catterick are associated with this meltwater source (see below, section 2.5).

Just as Holocene river terraces are a feature of the Ure valley around Ripon, as it leaves the flanks of the Pennines and enters the Washlands (see above), similar features are well marked in the Swale around Catterick, as that river emerges from its upland bedrock valley. Well documented

Fig. 2.36. The Feldom moraine: this is an important moraine ridge (dashed line) along the southern edge of Stainmore, north of Richmond, defining an ice limit of the Stainmore ice stream.

Fig. 2.37. Aerial view of the Marske channel (NZ 095015), one of a set of large channels that drained the southern Stainmore ice (in association with the Feldom moraine) into the Swale valley just north-east of Richmond.

previously (Taylor & Macklin, 1997; Taylor *et al.*, 2000), these are similar to the terraces at Ripon, consisting largely of localized cut-and-fill features that record a progressive lowering of river level during meander migration (Fig. 2.38).

2.4 River Terraces

Over much of the Washlands, the re-establishment of the river system after deglaciation was across a surface formed of newly deposited glacial and glaciofluvial sediments. These unconsolidated deposits, predominantly diamictons, coarse-grained sands and gravels and finer-grained lake sediments, were easily eroded by the early rivers. This provided ample bed-load that was then deposited down-valley to form further sand and gravel bodies. The oldest deposits reflect early stages of deglaciation with ice still

in existence further upstream within the Vale of York and Wensleydale; these form the glacial and glaciofluvial sands and gravels described by the Geological Survey in the various Mineral Assessment Reports and the regional memoirs (see Chapter 1.3). The deposits at Marfield and Nosterfield, in the Ure, and at Scorton and Catterick, in the Swale, are good examples (see below). Isostatic readjustment of the land surface has led to uplift; the fluvial response has been incision into these sands and gravels, leaving abandoned floodplain surfaces to form river terraces (see below). Later, younger terrace surfaces, at lower elevations, reflect continued cycles of incision and aggradation through the Holocene, as the rivers reacted to climatic and anthropogenic changes within the catchments (Chapter 1.6).

Terraces are distinct landforms associated with fluvial processes, often forming composite staircases that can be mapped by identifying the main geomorphological

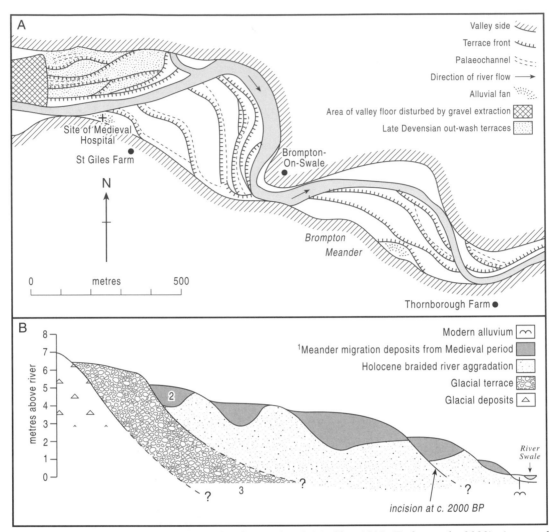

Fig. 2.38. Late Holocene river terraces at Catterick (after Taylor & Macklin, 1997; Taylor et al., 2000). A: map showing the two meander cores in which migration terraces are preserved (the St Giles and Brompton meanders); B: section, interpolated from logs in the original publications. Notes: [1] – Meander migration deposits on all terraces are capped, to various depths, by material contaminated from metal mining; [2] – [14]C date of 8950–8500 cal. BP from wood fragments near the base of a channel on the highest terrace, cut into this gravel (Brompton meander); [3] – this gravel is >18 m thick c. 2 km to the south-east (Lovell, 1982).

elements: the former valley floors (terrace 'treads') are preserved as flat areas with low down-valley and transverse gradients; the backs of such flat treads are defined by a break of slope at the base of a steeper 'bluff' (or riser), separating a particular terrace from others at higher levels within the landscape. Geomorphological mapping is used to delimit these distinct morphological features, particularly the breaks of slope between bluffs and terrace surfaces. The upper convex break of slope is also often observed, although in many situations this is less clearly preserved, having been degraded to form a more gentle inflection of slope.

The type of terrace described above is associated with alternations of sediment deposition and incision, giving rise to what are termed aggradational terraces. However, in a number of areas in the Washlands where

terrace surfaces have been identified during field mapping, consultation with the geological maps indicates that these have been formed across a range of superficial deposits and different bedrock types and do not coincide with gravel or other fluvial sediments (Plate 2.3). These are, therefore, seemingly of an erosional origin. However, in many areas, these terrace surfaces can be shown to be traced laterally into aggradational terraces. Such 'erosional terraces' suggest that the rivers have flowed across the area in erosional mode and left little depositional record (cf. McMillan *et al.*, 2005). Terraces of this sort have been termed 'straths' in the literature; their reported occurrence is usually in areas of rapid uplift, such as active orogens (Burbank & Anderson, 2001). Erosional terraces have not commonly been described in Britain, although they appear on the recently published BGS map of Leeds, where such features have been mapped across areas of till (Cooper & Gibson, 2003). Recognition and mapping of erosional terraces in areas where there are no exposures (i.e. on purely morphological grounds) is difficult, as landform expression may be a reflection of bedrock control rather than the pattern of fluvial erosion. It is also possible, in the absence of exposures, that thin veneers of fluvial sediment will have been overlooked by mappers.

The river terraces recorded in the Washlands reflect these two distinct types of fluvial terrace system (Plate 2.3). The rationale for delimiting both types of terrace is based on the geomorphological map, produced from field mapping across the area, in which areas of possible terrace are identified on morphological grounds (i.e. risers and treads). The aggradational terraces were defined in consultation with the published geological maps, memoirs and mineral reports for the area, which identify areas of 'glacial/glaciofluvial sands and gravels', 'terrace deposits' and 'alluvium'. Where these coincide with landform morphology, terraces of depositional origin can be confirmed. The problem of erosional terraces arose from the identification of areas with apparent terrace morphology, and at consistent elevations, but found from the geological maps to be formed on a range of non-fluvial superficial deposits. These are interpreted in two ways. First, the morphological information from the field map can be integrated with data on the superficial deposits to infer erosional terrace location by lateral interpolation from areas of aggradational terraces. Within the Washlands there are areas where gravel aggradational units with well-defined lower breaks of slope can be traced laterally into extensive flats at similar elevations; these are marked on the map as erosional terraces. Second, in areas where former channels were mapped, often at higher elevations above the present river system, interpretation takes into account how the channel system evolved in association with fluvial incision by identifying areas where the river must have been at some point during its progressive downcutting to the present level. This mapping has allowed the identification of a number of different aggradational and erosional terraces of variable extent and number through the Washlands (Plate 2.3).

Major areas of aggradation are limited to specific areas of the main river valleys; extensive gravel deposition is recorded at the confluence of the Laver and Skell systems on the west side of Ripon. Abandoned quarries around Ripon record former extraction of these gravels. Within the main Ure valley the area of most extensive aggradational terrace development occurs at the down-river side of Hackfall Gorge, where a major fan, fed by glacial outwash, was formed northwards from West Tanfield towards Nosterfield, with substantial down valley aggradation towards Ripon. These deposits have been extensively worked, with present quarry operations within the fan at Nosterfield (see below). Later terrace deposits and underlying glacial gravels are quarried east of North Stainley (Ripon North). Other areas of relatively well-defined terrace gravels occur around

Ripon Racecourse and towards Newby Hall. All these areas are described below in connection with quarry sites.

In the Swale system, the major areas of gravel aggradation and terrace development occur where the river emerges from its upland bedrock channel just east of Richmond and its valley widens over the lower ground from Catterick towards Ainderby Steeple. As noted above, there is much evidence of gravel extraction around Catterick, exploiting glaciofluvial deposits (see below, section 2.7). There is also an extensive terrace associated with a former channel that existed to the west of the present river along the outside edge of the Leeming moraine (north of Leeming Bar: Fig. 2.11; Plate 2.3). This also appears to be associated with an aggradational terrace within the small valley of the Bedale Beck east of Bedale. There is a further major terrace feature south of Bedale associated with gravel progradation into the former lake at Snape Mires (see below, Section 2.8.2).

Terrace staircases are not extensively developed in the Swale; four main levels have been mapped on morphological criteria at certain locations (Plate 2.3). Many of the terrace fragments appear to be of erosional origin, particularly in the upper part of the limited vertical range. Lower terraces are of an aggradational origin, found in association with the present river system and former meltwater channels. These include the flights of meander-migration terraces at Catterick and Brompton-on-Swale (Taylor & Macklin, 1997; Taylor *et al.*, 2000; Fig. 2.38). Like the similar terraces at Ripon (Howard *et al.*, 2000a), these fall within 'alluvium' on geological maps (cf. Plate 2.3).

According to geological survey reports, large-scale river terraces are not extensively developed across the area. There is no mention of any terraces within the Swale and Wiske valleys in the area covered by the Northallerton memoir (Frost, 1998). Further south, in the Thirsk area, the absence of terraces in the Swale has been attributed to the river flowing over and eroding extensive fine-grained silts and clays deposited in glacial lakes, sediments not considered conducive to the preservation of terraces, which are only found along Cod Beck within the Swale catchment (Powell *et al.*, 1992). In contrast, that memoir reports more extensive terraces within the Ure catchment, particularly within the Laver and Skell tributaries (Plate 2.3). Lack of terraces further south, within the area of the Harrogate memoir, is also associated with the existence of extensive lake sediments over which the rivers must have flowed before establishing their present courses (Cooper & Burgess, 1993). All of these observations appear to have been made with specific reference to aggradational terraces and there is no mention of possible erosional terraces.

An alternative explanation for the absence of terraces in the lowermost Swale is apparent from the work by Taylor *et al.* (2000) at Myton-on-Swale, near the confluence with the Ure. Both Washlands rivers here flow above narrow deep channels filled with sediments that would appear to represent a full Holocene aggradational record (albeit punctuated by erosion events), these channels having been incised into the glacial deposits at around the end of the Pleistocene (Fig. 2.39). Taylor and Macklin (1997, p. 324) envisaged three potential causes of incision at about this time: low sediment loads, low sea level and the breaching of the glacial barrier downstream that was responsible for the ponding of Lake Humber (see Chapter 1.4.5). The first two of these seem unlikely; deglaciation would have provided plentiful outwash sediment and, at the same time, sea level would have been rising (in response to global ice melting). The drainage of Lake Humber and its effects on the rivers of the Ouse system will be further considered below. Whatever caused the incision, it is clear that the rivers in their lowest Washlands reach have remained constrained within these narrow channels cut into the glacial deposits (for further discussion, see Chapter 5.6).

The terrace sequences identified within the Washlands will be demonstrated with reference to specific locations, chosen to illustrate the range of forms and sediments involved with the evolution of the present river system. Cross sections at these localities suggest terrace formation in both of the different styles outlined above, i.e. erosional and aggradational. These sections are cross-referenced to the superficial deposits recorded on the published maps of the Mineral Assessment Reports and the British Geological Survey (Chapter 1.3).

2.4.1 Section A – The Laver

The River Laver forms the northern of two major tributaries of the Ure west of Ripon (Plate 2.3) and occupies a large meltwater channel; present river level in this area is <60 m O.D. Cross cutting this channel is a higher (100 m O.D.) and by implication older channel and associated moraine ridge in the vicinity of Low Lindrick (Kendall & Wroot, 1924). North-east of this moraine, towards the river at the western edge of Ripon, the ground falls away in a series of terrace levels with well-defined risers. Cross referencing this profile to the published superficial geology maps indicates that the upper terraces, 2–4, are at approximately 100 m, 80 m and 70 m and eroded across till (Plate 2.4A). The lowest terrace (1) is formed of sands and gravels within both undifferentiated terrace deposits and 'fluvioglacial sand and gravel' (Strong & Giles, 1983).

2.4.2 Section B – Masham

Aggradation within the Ure valley upstream of Hackfall Gorge is concentrated around the town of Masham and northwards towards the present quarry at Marfield (see below). A section across the river just outside Masham (Fig. 2.27; Plate 2.4B) shows lower aggradational terraces on the eastern side of the river, rising to erosional terraces cut into till on the lower part of the main slope. The upper prominent breaks of slope on this hillslope are related to lithology associated with the geological boundary between Carboniferous and Permian rocks that are exposed in

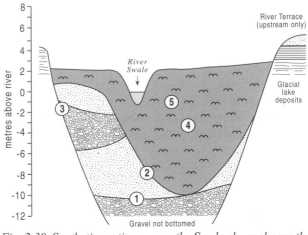

Fig. 2.39. Synthetic section across the Swale channel near the confluence with the Ure, Myton-on-Swale (after Taylor et al.*, 2000). Numbers in circles are the locations of radiocarbon dates obtained by Taylor* et al.*: 1 – 5650–5330 cal. BP; 2 – 5450–4990 cal. BP; 3 – 2750–2360 cal. BP; 4 – 930–730 cal. BP; 5 – 670–530 cal. BP. Taylor* et al. *also noted that alluvial deposits contaminated with metal mining residues, indicating deposition since c. 1750 AD, occurred up to 1 m below the floodplain surface.*

Gebdykes quarry on the upper dip slope (Fig. 2.27). On the western side of the river there is a main terrace cut in sand and gravel before becoming eroded across till. The lateral extent of the aggradation is limited to approximately 200 m either side of the present river channel and within a limited vertical range.

2.4.3 Section C – North Stainley

Hackfall Gorge, as already noted (Section 2.3.1), was cut through the Permian limestone escarpment by a meltwater-charged River Ure at some stage during deglaciation. It is not the oldest Ure channel; there is an extensive higher-level system, about 50 m above the present river (cf. Chapter 5.3). Often called Thieves Gill, this is thought to represent an earlier River Ure (Kendall & Wroot, 1924), extending from south-west of Mickley, near the eastern exit of the gorge towards the Laver at Ripon. Geomorphological mapping south of the present River Ure has revealed a series of breaks of slope that could define a suite of terraces associated with migration of this earlier river northwards prior to the cutting of the present gorge. Plate 2.4C indicates 'terraces' extending up to the interfluve at *c.* 100 m O.D. and cut across both till and bedrock (Permian limestone overlain by till is exposed in the active quarry at Potgate Wood (SE 276755)). Only at lower elevations, below 52 m O.D., are there aggradational terraces, the deposits of which have been extensively quarried for aggregate between North Stainley and West Tanfield. These lower terraces are associated with the large amount of glaciofluvial sediment brought through the gorge to form the extensive

Nosterfield gravel fan. Subsequent incision has formed two small terraces on the eastern side of the river towards the southernmost of the three Thornborough henges.

2.4.4 Section D – Newby Hall

Immediately south-east of Ripon Racecourse (Plate 2.1), there is a complex sequence of small terraces below 17 m O.D., associated with meander migration; these appear to be in a similar situation to those studied by Howard *et al.* (2000a) on the opposite side of the river. Higher terraces also exist towards Low Moor House at 30 m O.D. (Plate 2.4D). These upper terraces are difficult to define morphologically at the higher elevations, only becoming identifiable below 35 m O.D., where they are cut in till. However, there is a third terrace also cut in 'glacial sand and gravel' (Abraham, 1981), below which there is a well-defined abandoned peat-filled channel that cuts across the back of the second terrace extending from Morrell's Wood towards Givendale Grange at *c.* 27 m O.D. (SE 345690). The main break of slope to the present floodplain and lower smaller terraces, associated with meander migration, can be mapped from Newby Hall northwards towards Bridge Hewick. South-west of the river, an extensive flat between Littlethorpe and Bishop Monkton is explained as an erosional terrace cut across lake sediments (Plate 2.4D).

2.4.5 Section E – Catterick

One of the areas of large-scale gravel aggradation within the Swale valley occurs around Catterick, particularly on the east bank from Kiplin Hall to Scorton (Fig. 2.40B). A cross section drawn across the Swale valley north of Catterick village (Plate 2.4E) shows aggradational terrace deposits on both sides of the river, associated with an extensive gravel sequence (cf. Lovell, 1982) that appears to have a single surface level with an elevation at *c.* 52 m O. D. Lovell (1982), however, claimed that three terraces could be resolved within these gravels. There is a possible erosional terrace sequence at the eastern end of the transect, where three terraces have been mapped above till (Plate 2.4E), although Lovell (1982) reported blown sand on the interfluve here. The Late Holocene meander-migration terraces mapped by Taylor and Macklin (1997; Fig. 2.38) are from *c.* 300 m upstream and are largely coincident with alluvium on the geological maps (see above).

2.4.6 Section F – Scruton

This cross section has been drawn to include the Leeming moraine and the extensive terrace sequences associated with a former channel and the present channel of the Swale near the village of Scruton (Plate 2.4F). The Leeming moraine forms the largest ridge in the Washlands and was formed by a readvance of Wensleydale ice (see above, Section 2.2.1.1). The flatlands to the west and east are at similar elevations of *c.* 35 m O.D. To the west, inside the

moraine, are lake sediments and sand and gravel associated with a former lake at Crakehall Ings. Outside the moraine to the east there is an extensive area of river terrace deposits extending along the outer edge of the moraine (Lovell, 1982). These are not associated with the present Swale, but relate to a former channel, no longer occupied by a stream but artificially drained, that extended south-east from the present Swale towards Leeming Bar, where it forms the flat ground now occupied by Leeming Airfield (Fig. 2.40A). This forms an aggradational terrace (Plates 2.3 & 2.4F), with a back slope elevation of *c.* 50 m O.D., along the eastern side of the Leeming moraine and a more extensive erosional terrace defined by breaks of slope around the village of Scruton (Plate 2.4F); it should be noted that there is ambiguity about the deposits in this area, as they are described as till on the published Northallerton superficial deposits map and as undifferentiated river terrace gravels in the Mineral Assessment Report (Lovell, 1982).

2.4.7 Section G – Pickhill

In comparison with the River Ure, the Swale occupies a broad valley with minimal topographic relief. As demonstrated at Scruton, there are former abandoned channels indicating migration of the active fluvial system across this area of low relief. Around Pickhill is another area where there are channels of probable meltwater origin along the ill-defined watershed between Swale and Ure. The cross section here (Plate 2.4G) has been constructed from the A1 north-east to the present Swale just south of Pickhill. There is one dominant terrace level at 30 m O.D. crossing a number of different superficial deposits and into which are incised channels associated with the Pickhill Beck, which occupies a much larger channel than would be expected given the size of the present stream. Peat deposits have been recorded in an abandoned channel (Plate 2.4G). Although there is little change in elevation, the main terrace level is eroded across extensive lake sediments that have been mapped on both sides of the River Swale. On the eastern side of the river, terraces have been cut into these lacustrine sediments in the vicinity of the confluence of the Wiske and Swale, around Sion Hall (Plate 2.3). Only in the west, towards the higher ground, are till and gravels mapped (Powell *et al.*, 1988). There is no evidence of any aggradational terraces.

2.5 Gravel clast content

The rocks forming the gravel clasts (pebbles) in the various rudaceous deposits (aggregates) encountered during the project were identified as part of the clast lithological analysis procedure (see above, section 2.1.3.2). All of the rocks commonly represented in the various analysed samples (Table 2.2) can be found outcropping in the catchments of the two rivers (see Chapter 1.2; Plate 1.3). Exotic lithologies were primarily encountered in the

Fig. 2.40. Aerial views of the Swale: A – looking southwards across the former Swale channel (dashed line, yellow on CD) towards the line of the A1 and the Leeming moraine (solid line, blue on CD); B – view of the valley at Kiplin Hall, showing abandoned flooded gravel quarries within the present floodplain and former meander patterns around Kirkby Hall (looking north-west).

glacial gravels of the Lower Swale and in Swale terrace gravels, where they probably represent reworked glacial material. Although there are exceptions (see below), this serves to confirm the local derivation of even glacially derived material (associated with Pennine-generated Wensleydale ice) over much of the Washlands, with the influence of 'foreign' Stainmore ice confined to the main Vale of York.

2.5.1 Main local gravel-forming rocks

This section reports on the main rock types that form

clasts in the Swale and Ure gravels. Inevitably these will be the more resistant lithologies within the catchment areas, those that can readily survive abrasion and attrition in fluvial bed-load environments, with poorly consolidated materials such as shale absent or scarce, even if relatively abundant regionally.

2.5.1.1 Carboniferous limestones

Carboniferous limestone is a familiar Pennine rock-type, its relative hardness being reflected in the crags and other upland landscape features to which it gives rise.

Limestones, however, show relatively low durability when subjected to fluvial transport, being susceptible to chemical attack (including post-depositional weathering) as well as to mechanical breakdown. Nonetheless, Carboniferous limestone is a conspicuous component of all the gravels analysed, often being the modal clast type (Table 2.2). Specimens vary from typical homogeneous crystalline limestone to impure varieties, sometimes partly silicified. Highly fossiliferous examples are common, with crinoidal and sponge debris constituting the most common fossils, although coral also occurs. The fact that progressive variation between these end members can be observed means that subdivision during counting is of dubious value. No attempt was therefore made to distinguish fossiliferous and non-fossiliferous limestones, nor those with modest levels of silicification (those with significant silicification, however, have been counted as partial chert; see Table 2.2). Carboniferous limestone clasts are generally dark grey, often with a paler grey (weathered) surface. Paler, perhaps bleached specimens are also common. Highly iron-stained and weathered Carboniferous limestone 'brash' can also be distinguished.

Amongst the Carboniferous limestones, shaley varieties have been counted separately. These show clear evidence of shaley or flaggy bedding (lamination) and are argillaceous rather than crystalline. They originate from the cyclic ('Yoredale') sequences that characterize the Lower Carboniferous (Dinantian) in the North Pennines, in which limestones, sandstones and shales alternate (Edwards *et al.*, 1954; Aitkenhead *et al.*, 2002).

2.5.1.2 Sandstones and sedimentary quartzites

Cemented arenaceous rocks account for a significant proportion of all the gravels analysed. Only the most durable sandstones will survive as fluvial pebbles, so it is unsurprising that orthoquartzites and quartzitic sandstones are the most common (Table 2.2). Specimens with a significant feldspar component (arkosic), specifically where feldspar is estimated as >10%, were counted separately. Feldspar grains appear milky against a background of translucent quartz sand; they often show apparent weathering to kaolin. Clasts with pronounced bedding, such as might be termed 'flaggy' sandstones, were also counted separately. A significant subset of the sandstones has calcareous cement, as identified with HCl (it was necessary to break sandstone clasts open to carry out this test on fresh faces). Rare examples with ferruginous cement were also encountered and recorded separately, as were cherty specimens (again rare). Grain size varies from coarse to fine sand grade, although medium is predominant. No attempt has been made to distinguish amongst sandstones on grain size, although very occasional specimens were sufficiently fine-grained to be classified as siltstones.

All these different types of sandstone can be found in the Carboniferous strata of the Pennines, sandstones becoming more common above the limestone-dominated Lower Carboniferous. The Middle Carboniferous (Namurian) is characterized by hard arkosic sandstones (Millstone Grit), which pass upwards into the Coal Measures (Westphalian), also with prominent sandstones (interbedded with shale and coal seams). These Upper Carboniferous strata have been eroded from the Pennines sequence, although they occur to the east of the Pennines further north, in central County Durham, from where occasional examples might have been carried by glaciation into North Yorkshire. The transition into the Coal Measures is anticipated by minor coal occurrences in the Namurian of the Pennines. The occasional observation, during gravel analysis, of carbonaceous (coal) flecks within sandstone specimens (also separately counted; see Table 2.2) serves to confirm their Carboniferous (probably Namurian) source. Otherwise the distinction of sandstones from different sources is notoriously difficult; notwithstanding that occasional examples of apparent non-Carboniferous type have been counted (see Table 2.2), the presence of additional but unrecognizable exotic sandstones, introduced by glaciation from further afield, cannot easily be ruled out.

2.5.1.3 Carboniferous chert

This is one of the more distinctive clast types in the Swale–Ure gravels. Chert occurs in nodules and sheets within the Carboniferous Limestone series (Hey, 1956) and as partial chert (imperfectly silicified limestone). These cherts show similar varieties to the limestones, with fossiliferous specimens being particularly characteristic. Very often the fossils are displayed as empty moulds, giving the clasts a distinctive pock-marked appearance. The predominant fossil types are crinoidal and sponge debris. Such rocks probably once had calcareous fossils that have been preferentially weathered out; numerous fresher 'partial cherts' in which the fossils are calcitic were also observed. Indeed, the 'etching' of calcareous fossils in chert makes them much more distinctive than the same fossils in limestone. Some cherts are devoid of fossils, however, and are almost flint-like in their homogeneity and fineness of grain (cf. Hill, 1911). Others are shaley, being siliceous pseudomorphs of the shaley ('Yoredale') variety of limestone.

Chert and partial chert typically constitute up to 25% of the Swale–Ure gravels. This is likely to exaggerate their importance within the catchment, since they are the most durable of the various clast types encountered. Elsewhere cherts have been found to be important components of compositionally 'mature' gravels, the rigours of aqueous transport, together with mechanical and chemical weathering, serving to concentrate these highly durable rocks at the expense of more readily destructible types (Wells *et al.*, 1947; Bridgland, 1986b). Indeed, Carboniferous cherts from the Pennines are characteristic components of Quaternary gravels throughout eastern England and in the Thames valley (Bridgland, 1986b).

2.5.1.4 Magnesian Limestone (dolomite)

This is another hard limestone, of Permian age, that forms a subsidiary escarpment to the east of the main Pennine uplands, including outcrops within the study area. As its name implies, it is generally an impure dolomitized limestone, as is revealed by the occurrence of rhombohedral voids, pseudomorphing carbonate minerals, that formed during recrystallization and are best seen with a reflected-light microscope. Fossils are rarely observed. Other characteristics are a pale yellowish-buff colour and a typically weak reaction with HCl. This Permian limestone is generally softer, as well as paler, than those from the Carboniferous. Characteristic specimens are therefore readily distinguished from Carboniferous ones, but inevitably there are occasional clasts that are more difficult, given the occurrence of paler-than-normal and soft (weathered) Carboniferous specimens. The incidence of Magnesian Limestone in the clast analyses closely reflects the sample location with respect to the Permian outcrop. At Marfield, < 1 km upstream of the outcrop (in the Ure), it is absent (Table 2.2). In sample 1 from Nosterfield it reaches >18%, reflecting erosion by the River Ure of Hackfall Gorge through the Magnesian Limestone escarpment and the resultant progradation of a gravel fan at the downstream end of the gorge, which is the material exploited by the Nosterfield Quarry (see 2.6.2). At Catterick, where the Swale has just flowed onto the Permian outcrop (Plate 1.3), the lower glacial gravel contains *c.* 2% Magnesian Limestone but none was encountered in the upper fluvial gravel (Table 2.2).

2.5.1.5 Rare locally-derived clast types

There are several further lithologies originating within the Swale–Ure catchment that occur only sparingly in the gravels, either because they are rare or because they are of low durability (and therefore poorly suited to forming pebbles). The first of these is shale, of which only the harder varieties are likely to form pebbles and even these are likely to be rapidly broken down during transport. It is also difficult to be sure that individual specimens are hard examples of Carboniferous shale rather more exotic slate, hardened by mild metamorphism. Another locally-derived rarity is vein calcite, which is pure mineral calcite derived from veins of this common mineral within the Carboniferous or Permian limestones. Clasts of pure crystalline calcite can sometimes be seen to represent the infilling of fossils.

2.5.2 Exotic lithologies

Exotic rocks, from beyond the Swale–Ure catchment area, have been encountered only rarely in the gravel analyses. Even in the glacial gravels of the Lower Swale they constitute only a few percent of the total. The precise proportion is difficult to determine because of uncertainty over whether certain varieties of common rocks, such as sandstones, are truly exotic or aberrant local varieties. Many of the most characteristic 'exotics' are igneous rocks, prominent amongst which are medium- and fine-grained basic types: dolerites and trachytes. The obvious sources for such rocks occur relatively close by, since the well-known Permo-Carboniferous intrusions of the Whin Sill complex (including the Hett Dyke) consist of quartz-dolerite and related finer, more rapidly cooled varieties, the latter being practically indistinguishable (in hand specimen) from the much younger trachyte of the Tertiary Cleveland Dyke. The Whin Sill crops out widely in north-east England from Teesdale northwards, whereas the Cleveland Dyke passes under Teesside and extends westwards beneath the Tees valley, although downstream it is generally covered by increasing thicknesses of Pleistocene drift. In addition to the Swale samples, a few clasts of this type were encountered in counts from Ripon, although only in the low-level Ure terrace gravels at Ripon South. Given their likely glacial origin, these might indicate that the influence of Vale-of-York ice has reached here but not the Ripon North locality, further up Wensleydale. Granitic igneous rocks were much rarer but were found in some of the Swale counts, including examples of apparent Shap Granite. This is highly distinctive in large specimens, on account of its large phenocrysts of pink feldspar, but at the smaller pebble sizes it is more difficult to identify with certainty. One granitic clast was encountered in each of the two samples from the Nosterfield fan, a finding that is difficult to reconcile with Pennine derivation of the Wensleydale ice (see below, section 2.6.2) . Rarer igneous varieties include porphyries, the nearest source for which is the Cheviots (cf. Harmer, 1928).

Occasional poorly sorted sandstones of greywacke type were noted, particularly in the glacial gravels of the Lower Swale. Their preponderance in these deposits and general absence from the Wensleydale (fluvial) gravels suggests that they are exotic; they are probably from the widely distributed Palaeozoic greywacke outcrops of southern Scotland (Greig, 1971). Again a single specimen was encountered in the analyses of the Nosterfield fan deposits (Table 2.2).

Other exotics are generally unique occurrences that are only of additional value if a particular provenance can be determined. Otherwise they merely serve to confirm an input from outside the fluvial catchment. In this latter respect, however, it should be noted that occasional rarities might have been derived from pre-Devensian glacial deposits once covering the catchment (but now destroyed) or, unless they can be shown to be post-Triassic, from rare pre-existing clasts in the bedrock. Such may provide an explanation of the Nosterfield and Ripon South occurrences (see above).

Fig. 2.41. Aerial view of Marfield Quarry (July 2006), looking north.

2.6 Description of quarry sites: River Ure

The abundant sand and gravel in the Washlands is a natural resource that has been exploited as aggregate by a number of quarry companies. Exposures in these quarry workings have provided valuable information about the sedimentology and stratigraphy at a number of key locations. The following section reports on project work at these sites to record sections and collect samples.

2.6.1 Marfield Quarry

This working gravel pit lies in the Ure valley 5 km north of Masham (Fig. 2.41). Previous aggregate quarries nearby worked a thick sequence of stratified coarse gravels, associated with a former channel, southwards towards Masham (Giles, 1982). Current workings are located in an area of hummocky linear terrain that has been identified as a possible thrust moraine complex. Sections were visited in 2003 and 2004. The earlier visits ascertained the complexity of the sedimentary sequences and the potential for further visits. Although older faces in the southern area of the quarry (Plate 2.5) indicated a thick sequence of gravels with no evidence of disturbance, this was not the case for the working faces further north, studied during the project, where the presence of clay lenses and steeply dipping gravel units indicated a more complex sedimentary environment. It was also clear that there was till overlying the gravels (Plate 2.5).

In 2004, the northern face of the quarry (SE 214833) revealed a >25 m thick sedimentary sequence over a 400 m lateral section. This showed a stratified sequence of sands and gravels, tills and clays and silts, many with evidence of disturbance and deformation (Plate 2.5). The gravels are very coarse (>1 m), with numerous striated limestone boulders, and are locally cemented into conglomerate. In the southern part of the quarry they showed horizontal stratification but in the working face were steeply dipping, involving thinner layers and lenses of clay, and overlain by till. The report below describes sections in the active face logged in July 2004.

2.6.1.1 Sediment description

LOG 1

In the north-east corner of the quarry the base of the sequence showed a fining-upwards gravel and sand sequence between 0 and 7 m (Plate 2.5). The lower gravels had a sand/silt matrix and subrounded to rounded clasts up to 50 cm in diameter. There were areas that showed imbrication and there was subtle, crude planar stratification. The lower gravels also had discontinuous coarse sand units within them. The lower gravels showed fining upwards into crude horizontally stratified fine gravel and sands with occasional channel structures and planar cross bedding.

Between 7 and 11 m the sands and gravels were sharply overlain by a massive structureless till (Plate 2.5). This had a silt–sand matrix with occasional subhorizontal sand stringers. Clasts were subangular to rounded and up to 30 cm in diameter. At 9 m the colour changed from brown to brown/purple. The till was sharply overlain by horizontally stratified, slightly disturbed sands between 11 and 11.5 m, which were in turn overlain by a heavily (laterally) brecciated clay. In places this unit showed normal faulting but elsewhere it had a blocky, boudinaged structure. Above this, from 12 to 12.5 m, there was horizontally bedded silt–sand with signs of deformation (Plate 2.5).

LOG 2

Log 2 was located in the centre of the north section (Fig 2.42; Plate 2.5). From 0–3m the section was composed of coarse, poorly sorted, massive gravels (Plate 2.5). Gravel clasts were subrounded to angular and up to 40 cm in

Fig. 2.42. Marfield main section (SE 2122 8306) . This is the working north side of the quarry looking north towards Inner Hills (SE 214 835) along the strike of the different thrust planes (left of digger). The lighter brown uppermost unit above the thrust complex is till (see Plate 2.5). General location of log 2 (Plate 2.5) indicated by box.

diameter. There were occasional sand lenses and at 1.6 m there were shallow channel structures with internal planar cross stratification. The lower gravels were sharply overlain by stratified clays between 3 and 7 m. These were sheared and highly deformed, with slickenslided surfaces and occasional recumbent isoclinal folds, particularly towards the base of the unit (Figs 2.43 & 2.44).

The clays were sharply but conformably overlain by 5 m of massive, chaotically structured gravel. At 12 m there was another unit of highly deformed and sheared clays, which was in turn sharply overlain by massive, structureless gravels with occasional discontinuous sand lenses. Above this there was a discontinuous raft of sediment with partly stratified admixtures of gravel, clay and diamicton. Continuing upwards, between 22 and 34.5 m there was a series of poorly sorted, massive gravels, with contorted fine gravel and sand strata towards the base, although the upper gravels had a more chaotic and random structure, with variable matrix textures and inclined bedding. Within these upper gravels were two discontinuous rafts of deformed and sheared clays. The section was capped by a discontinuous upper brown diamicton (Fig. 2.42; Plate 2.5).

2.6.1.2 Lithofacies architecture and structural geology

The lithofacies architecture of the site is complicated by a series of sub-vertically orientated sediment units and variable degrees of deformation. The eastern side of the section showed little deformation, with lower crudely stratified gravels overlain by a till. The gravels showed no sign of deformation, while sand stringers in the till suggest lateral deformation and sediment attenuation. These units were truncated sub-vertically by the lowest sheared clay unit in the section, which ran from west to east. For 200 m laterally the unit was sub-horizontally orientated but dipped northwards. Slickenslided bedding surfaces and shears along the lower contact of the unit and within it dipped northwards at approximately 20 to 30° (Fig 2.43). From 200 to 300 m along the section the unit rose and cut across the whole section at approximately 45°. Between 250 and 300 m, a pod of gravel sat below the upturned sheared clay unit with an arcuate, diffuse lower boundary with the underlying till. Above the sheared clays, the orientation of sand and gravel beds mimicked that of the underlying clay and there was localized boudinage of strata.

The sheared clay unit is interpreted as a listric thrust (T1 – Plate 2.5; Fig. 2.43), one of three thrusts that crossed the section. The second, T2, sat above T1 between 0 and 200 m in the section. It dipped in a northwards direction at approximately 12° and, as with T1, had an upper unit of sand and gravel 'piggy backing' upon it. The two separate discontinuous rafts of partly stratified admixtures of gravel and clay and diamicton between 10 and 90 m formed part of this T2 complex.

Above T2 there was *c.* 1 m of crudely stratified gravel.

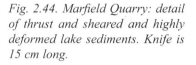

Fig. 2.43. Marfield Quarry: view of the main working face looking west along thrust complex (see log 2, Plate 2.5 for details).

Fig. 2.44. Marfield Quarry: detail of thrust and sheared and highly deformed lake sediments. Knife is 15 cm long.

Crude bedding within this unit appeared slightly inclined between 0 and 250 m along the section and there were discontinuous and contorted pods and rafts of clays, sand and gravels. Between 0 and 60 m this unit was overlain by another thrust structure composed of sheared clays (T3). Slickenslides and inclined bedding planes along and within the base of the sheared unit dipped steeply northwards at approximately 25 to 40° (Fig. 2.43). Occasional recumbent fold axes along the lower décollement surface trended east to west (Fig. 2.44). The upper reaches of the section were capped by discontinuous chaotically structured gravels

and a discontinuous massive brown diamicton (Fig. 2.42; Plate 2.5)

2.6.1.3 Interpretation

The lowest lithofacies in the section were clays (and clayey silts) attributable to lacustrine deposition. These underlie the site and point to the development of a large body of standing water. The fine-grained composition and planar-bedded character of the lake sediments suggest they were deposited by suspension in a distal setting. Indeed,

Fig. 2.45. Marfield Quarry – typical gravels exposed in the south-eastern part of the active quarry (July 2004). Till can be seen overlying the gravel sequence. See also Plate 2.5.

the lack of dropstones suggests that this was not an ice-contact lake.

The overlying sand and gravel sediments reflect a switch to glaciofluvial activity within the valley. The imbrication and crude planar stratification in the lower coarse gravels supports a proximal setting, probably related to an ice advance into the area, with high energy streams transporting sediment through basal traction and deposition on channel bars. The discontinuous coarse sand units within the lower gravels suggest switches in flow regime with periods of lower energy flow depositing sand lenses. The overall fining-upwards character of the gravels and switches in flow regime (horizontally stratified fine gravel and sands; small channel structures; planar cross bedding) suggest an overall decrease in flow energy with small bars and channels operating. Given that ice was advancing towards the site at this time, this switch in glaciofluvial regime can best be explained by channel migration, perhaps to the west and into the main axis of the valley.

The gravels and sands are overlain by a lower massive till, showing that ice overrode the location (Fig. 2.45). This till showed few diagnostic features other than occasional sub-horizontal sand stringers, indicative of lateral deformation, and without further work is best interpreted as a lodgement/deformation till. The recorded colour changes (from brown to brown/purple) are not associated with sediment structure or composition and may be a function of weathering.

After this till was deposited the ice retreated from the area. There are no clear outwash deposits associated with this phase, perhaps due to focussing of streams elsewhere in the valley; however, extensive proglacial glaciotectonism

of the site suggests that there was either a re-advance of the glacier into this area, or that retreat was punctuated by a series of ice marginal oscillations.

The western half of the section was truncated by a series of large thrust complexes (Fig. 2.43). Thrusts T1 and T2 were formed through proglacial bulldozing of the site and the development of compressive stresses, leading to listric thrusting through detachment of the lower lake clays and their subsequent over-riding of pre-existing sediments. T1 and T2 form a duplicate thrust, indicating two initial phases of ice pushing from the north. The steep 45° angle of T1 between 200 and 300 m suggests the sediments were thrust over differential topography as they developed. The pod of gravel beneath T1, between 250 and 330 m, indicates the mobilization of sandur sediments in front of the detached thrust.

The second thrust, T2, mimics T1 and also has an upper unit of sand and gravel 'piggy backing' upon it. The boudins within the sand and gravels overlying T1 are the result of the emplacement of T2 with lateral shear of sediment occurring beneath the thrust. The two separate discontinuous rafts of partly stratified admixtures of gravel, clay and diamicton between 10 m and 90 m formed part of this T2 complex, but may be related to earlier subglacial glaciotectonism during Phase 3.

Above T2 there was 10 m of crudely stratified gravel with inclined bedding and discontinuous and contorted pods and rafts of clays, sand and gravels (0 to 250 m). These were overlain by another thrust structure composed of sheared clays (T3), dipping steeply to the north and folded along an east to west trajectory (Fig 2.43). T3 was the final phase of proglacial glaciotectonic thrusting evident. The angle of T3 between 0 and 50 m (apparent dip east to west) again suggests that the sediments were thrust over pre-existing topography.

The upper reaches of the section were capped by discontinuous chaotically structured gravels and a discontinuous massive brown diamicton (Plate 2.5). The chaotic architecture of the poorly sorted gravel units and their mixture of random and slope-conformable unit-contact boundaries suggest that they are infill sediments deposited ice marginally in hollows adjacent to ridges and hummocks caused by bulldozing and thrusting. Coarse-grained and poorly sorted outwash and debris-flow deposits of this type are typical of modern glacier margins associated with ice thrusting.

The discontinuous upper brown diamicton capping the site was massive with few structures. It may represent a subglacial till deposited during later overriding of the site, after the T1–T3 proglacial thrusting.

2.6.1.4 Summary

The following is the overall interpretation of this sedimentary sequence:

> *Phase 1: Deposition in a lake (no glacial influence)*
> *Phase 2: Ice advance – sandur deposition*
> *Phase 3: Ice overrides the site – till deposition*
> *Phase 4: Ice retreat*
> *Phase 5: Ice marginal oscillation and thrusting*
> *Phase 6: Ice marginal deposition – inter-ridge fluvial infill*
> *Phase 7: Readvance of ice over site*

Marfield is therefore an important site recording a highly dynamic ice margin associated with Wensleydale ice. The marginal topography associated with this sedimentological and stratigraphical evidence can be traced towards Bedale and the Leeming moraine, indicating that these events are associated with a major advance of Wensleydale ice at some stage during deglaciation.

2.6.1.5 Clast lithologies

Samples for gravel clast analysis were taken at Marfield quarry from the southern face (SE 213831) in non-glaciotectonized deposits (Plate 2.5C). The upper gravel here (Marfield 2) proved to have the largest proportion of Carboniferous limestone of any deposit analysed within the project: 64% (Table 2.2). The Carboniferous limestone proportion was smaller in the lower gravel, at 46%, although this is within the high end of the typical range for this lithology elsewhere (Table 2.2). The two Marfield samples were correspondingly low in sandstone in comparison with the general trend. They differed from gravel counts from all other sites (Catterick 1B excepted) in that they contained no Magnesian Limestone, being from upstream of the Permian outcrop in the Ure system. A notable difference between the two samples is that the lower gravel contained 16% Carboniferous chert, one of the highest proportions of this rock recorded (Table 2.2), whereas the upper gravel contained just 1.2% chert, the lowest recorded anywhere in the Washlands. Amongst the rarer components were odd unprovenanced sedimentary lithologies, but nothing crystalline and nothing that could unequivocally be said to be foreign to Wensleydale. This fact is of interest; given their close interrelationship with the glacial deposits; it seems clear that the Marfield gravels are of glaciofluvial origin (this is particularly true of the lower gravel, which must have been emplaced before deglaciation), so their locally-derived composition supports the notion that the Wensleydale ice was generated within the catchment rather than spilling into it from further afield.

Attempts were made to date sand grains within the Marfield gravels by the OSL method but these proved unsuccessful (see Appendix II).

2.6.2 Nosterfield Quarry

There is evidence of a long history of gravel extraction in the vicinity of the village of Nosterfield (Figs 2.46 & 2.47), exploiting the extensive gravel fan that was deposited by the meltwater-charged River Ure at its exit from Hackfall Gorge (see above). This fan covers an area of *c.* 7 km^2 north of the present river, extending from an apex near West Tanfield (SE 258788) north-eastwards towards Nosterfield and Thornborough (SE 293798) and falling in elevation from *c.* 52 m O.D. to *c.* 43 m O.D. This surface has been abandoned by the river and now lies *c.* 15 m above the modern floodplain. There are small terrace risers, near the present river and opposite Sleningford Mill (SE 281783), that record later incision of the fan by the River Ure. It is on this surface that the Thornborough henges (Chapter 4.5; Fig. 2.47) were constructed during the mid-Holocene.

There are a number of abandoned quarries to the east of West Tanfield, as well as an extensive active quarry north of Nosterfield village, the object of the present study (Fig. 2.46). In 2003, exposures were limited to the western edge of the quarry, towards the village, where there were three north-facing sections at different levels within the upper part of the sequence. They were all in gravel, although in 2002 exposures of underlying clay and sand, over which the fan gravels had prograded, were observed but not recorded in detail. The clay appeared to be lacustrine but was obscured before it could be properly recorded and sampled.

The exposed gravels were poorly sorted, clast supported and had a sand matrix. The gravel clasts were subrounded to subangular and showed no obvious imbrication (Fig. 2.48). Odd vertical pockets of finer clast-supported gravel were observed. The dip of the beds is at a low angle towards the north, reinforcing their interpretation as part of a prograding fan with a series of distributaries. The gravels included a number of discontinuous sand lenses with high width-to-depth ratios. Sands were commonly cross bedded,

Fig. 2.46. Aerial view across Nosterfield Quarry (July 2006) looking south to Nosterfield village, former quarries and the northernmost henge (top left, wooded).

Fig. 2.47. Location of Nosterfield Quarry, showing investigated section and palaeoenvironmental sample sites (see Chapter 3.2). The northern end of the Thornborough henge complex is also shown. Inset shows palaeocurrent directions from the working section.

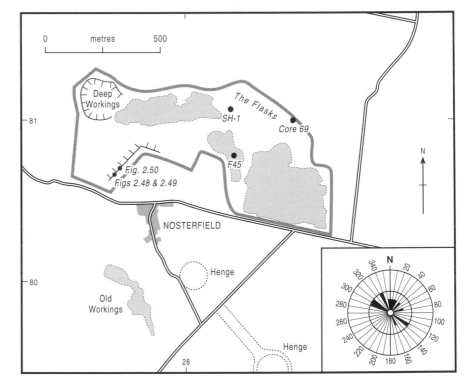

with foreset orientations revealing a range of palaeoflows in a wide arc to the north and east, presumably reflecting shifting channels within that part of the fan represented in the section (Fig. 2.47). Deeper workings in the northern part of the active quarry reached about 2–3 m below the previous sequence and showed better sorting with depth, suggesting a coarsening upwards prograding sequence.

Syn-depositional ice-wedge casts have been noted at a number of locations within the upper part of the gravel sequence (Figs 2.1, 2.48 & 2.49). These are filled with pale brown silt, which is also interbedded within the gravels (Fig. 2.48) and may mark wind-blown sediments

on a former fan surface. Radiocarbon assay of organic material infilling 'the Flasks 69', a peat-filled depression in the surface of the fan, gives an oldest date of $10,920 \pm 45$ [14]C BP (the dated material being slightly above the base of the organic sediments, which probably go back earlier than 11,000 ^{14}C BP), demonstrating fan formation during deglaciation and before the Lateglacial Interstadial (see Chapter 3.2.3). The ice-wedge casts are also interpreted as having formed before the interstadial.

An ephemeral working face, at SE 2767 8073, was recorded in detail and sampled for OSL dating and clast analysis (Figs 2.1, 2.49 & 2.50). The sequence here

Fig. 2.48. Nosterfield Quarry – syn-depositional ice wedge casts within gravel sequence (see also Fig. 2.1).

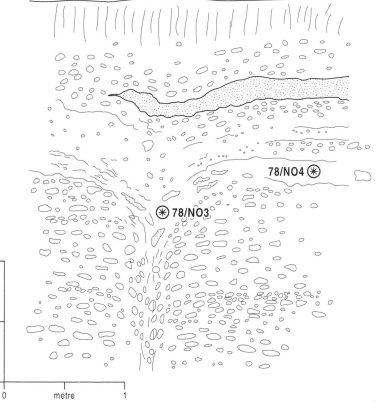

Fig. 2.49. Ice wedge cast exposed in the working face at Nosterfield Quarry (October 2003), looking east; OSL sample locations are marked by asterisks. Compare with Fig. 2.1, in which sample 78/NO4 is being collected and the dose reading is being taken for sample 78/NO3.

consisted of variable gravels and sands, showing evidence of channelling and with some units cross bedded. The two gravel clast samples proved to be somewhat different in composition, although both contained the full range of lithologies encountered in the Washlands deposits. The lower sample (Nosterfield 1) contained 18.6% Magnesian Limestone, a much larger proportion than most of the gravels analysed (Table 2.2). This undoubtedly results from localized erosion and entrainment of this rock from the

Hackfall Gorge, which is < 6 km upstream from the quarry (Plate 2.1). The other sample, from higher in the sequence, contained a relatively small Permian component (Table 2.2). This marked difference might result from variation in stream courses during the evolution of the fan or from burial of the local bedrock as the fan aggraded, which would have led to a decrease in Magnesian Limestone in higher gravel levels, as represented by Nosterfield sample 2. A larger-scale clast-lithological survey would be required

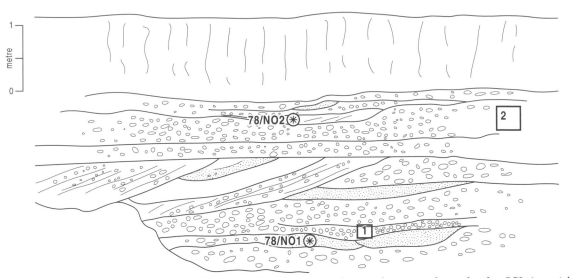

Fig. 2.50. Working face in gravels at Nosterfield Quarry (October 2003) showing location of samples for OSL (asterisks) and clast analysis (numbered boxes). Looking east.

to determine whether this was the case. Otherwise the two counts show compositions generally within the typical Washlands range; Sample 1 was poorer in Carboniferous limestone but richer in sandstone than sample 2. As already noted, both contained single examples of weathered granitic rocks, presumably glacially introduced; this is thought to confirm previous reports of Shap erratics as far west as Kirkby Malzeard (Raistrick, 1926). In addition, sample 1 contained a greywacke sandstone and sample 2 a weathered fine-grained crystalline rock, both presumably foreign to the catchment (Table 2.2; Appendix V).

2.6.3 Ripon North – North Stainley (Hanson's quarry)

This quarry complex is located on either side of the River Ure east of the village of North Stainley (Figs 2.51 & 2.52). It is <4 km downstream from Nosterfield Quarry, but working a different set of gravel deposits, which are located within the present river valley. The original gravel extraction site was on the south-west bank of the Ure; more recent workings (2004) have been concentrated on the east side of the river from Bellflask (SE 295774) downstream towards Norton Mills Farm (SE 300700). Aggregate has been extracted from two gravel units, an upper gravel that could be observed to overlie discontinuous thick (>5 m) till, which has complex stratigraphical relations with a lower glaciofluvial gravel, the second source of aggregate.

Sections were studied and recorded at three locations. Section 1 was in a temporary trench near Norton Mills Farm (SE 304768), which revealed 2.5 m of gravel between an underlying till and overlying alluvium (Figs 2.51, 2.53 & 2.54). Three samples (1.1; 1.2; 1.3) were taken for both clast and mollusc analysis (Chapter 3.6). Section 2 was from the upper part of a working face (SE 302772), which showed a complex gravel sequence underlying a till unit and also

banked against the till with a near vertical contact (Fig. 2.55). The lower gravel, seen only in Section 2 (Fig. 2.55; Sample 2.1), was well sorted and showed well-developed cross bedding in its finer-grained divisions, with a dip direction (indicating palaeo-flow) to the NW. The adjacent till was chocolate-brown in colour, with large (>1 m) striated Carboniferous limestone erratics. It appeared to be dipping steeply to the NW (into the present face; Fig. 2.55).

A single sample (Sample 2.1) of the lower gravel was analysed for clast content. Its composition proved generally similar to other Washlands gravels (Table 2.2), with no indication of its apparent glacial affinity; indeed, no samples from this locality contain unequivocally exotic material. Gravels also appear to have been deposited in a series of channels cut into this till. The upper gravel, clearly deposited during the Holocene (indicated by its conspicuous mollusc content; see Chapter 3.6.3), was exposed towards the southern end of operations and in the temporary trench (Section 1). Two samples from the trench and one from the main quarry (2.2) were analysed for clast composition. They revealed little variation except that sample 1.1 was significantly richer in Carboniferous limestone; indeed, it was the richest in this lithology of any Holocene gravel, although it has less than sample 2.1, from lower gravel at Ripon North (Table 2.2).

About 2 m of this upper gravel was observed in a general coarsening upwards sequence. Within it, an upper matrix-supported unit with cobbles of 20 cm long axis could be seen to overlie a finer, more clast-supported facies. Large tree trunks have been reported from the upper gravel but were never seen *in situ* during the present study. An alder trunk was, however, found *in situ* in section 3 by the quarry operators (Fig. 2.51) near the top of the gravel, which passed upwards at this point into a sandy organic sequence. Part of the alder trunk was radiocarbon dated and the associated sediments were studied for palaeoenvironmental

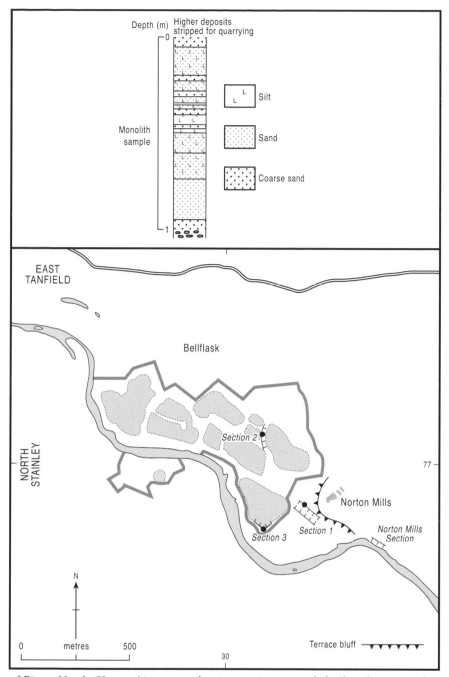

Fig. 2.51. Location of Ripon North (Hanson's) quarry, showing sections recorded. Also shown are the nearby section in the river cliff at Norton Mills and the terrace morphology in the vicinity. The inset shows the sediments recorded in Section 3, which was cleaned and sampled following the discovery there, during quarrying, of alder wood.

evidence (Chapter 3.6). Although a sample collected for OSL dating from Section 1 (Fig. 2.54) did not yield a successful age estimate (Appendix II), a second source of geochronology, AAR dating of shells from the gravel in Section 1, yielded meaningful results (Chapter 3.6.4; Appendix III).

As at Marfield, this is not a simple valley aggradation developed since deglaciation; rather the main gravel unit has been disturbed by an advance of ice across the area, causing glaciotectonic disturbance of the underlying

sediments as well as depositing till. Renewed aggradation within a forested (Holocene) landscape is indicated by the upper gravels, the palaeoenvironmental interpretation being derived from their contained molluscan fossils (cf. Chapter 3.6.3). There is clearly a significant hiatus between this Holocene upper (terrace) gravel and the underlying glacial tills and glaciofluvial gravels. The glacial deposits probably represent the infilled pre-glacial Ure valley previously reported (Chapter 1), this being a location where the Holocene and pre-glacial courses have coincided (as also

Fig. 2.52. Aerial view of Ripon North quarry looking from North Stainley eastwards towards Ripon. Investigated and sampled sections were near Norton Mills Farm.

Fig. 2.53. Ripon North: sampling for OSL and clast analysis from Section 1, in the temporary trench near Norton Mills Farm.

described by Howard *et al.* (2000a) at the Brown and Potter 'Ripon quarry', description of which (in its later form, as observed during the present project) will now follow.

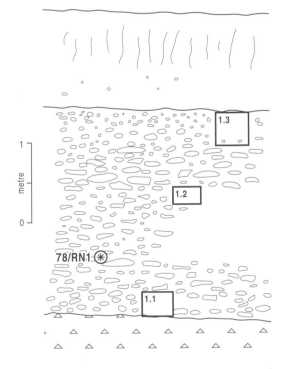

Fig. 2.54. Ripon North Section 1, showing stratigraphy and samples for OSL (asterisk) and clast/molluscan analyses (numbered boxes). For location, see Fig. 2.51.

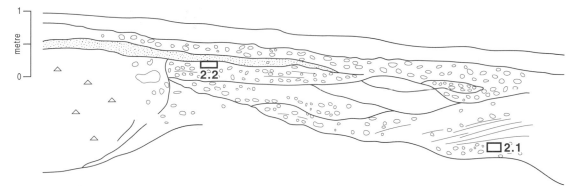

Fig. 2.55. Ripon North: Section 2, showing stratigraphical relations of the gravels and till, as well as the location of gravel samples (numbered boxes). For location, see Fig. 2.51.

Fig. 2.56. Ripon South: the quarry lies on the southern outskirts of Ripon (right of photograph). In the right foreground is the lower part of the Sharow palaeochannel.

2.6.4 Ripon South (Brown & Potter's quarry)

A gravel quarry immediately west of the River Ure south-east of Ripon, operated by the small local company 'Brown & Potter', provided important exposures in the low terrace deposits of the Ure, in the vicinity of the racecourse (Fig. 2.56; Plate 2.6). This working is a continuation of the quarrying activity that provided the exposures studied by Howard *et al.* (2000a) and published by them under the name 'Ripon Quarry'. In the five years between their research and 2003, when the work reported here commenced, the quarry faces moved *c.* 1 km south-eastwards, from a location to the west of the racecourse to one south-east of it (Fig. 2.57). Howard *et al.* (2000a) recorded four terraces

hereabouts, which they numbered downwards, attributing them to Holocene fluvial activity superimposed above Late Pleistocene glaciofluvial and glacio-lacustrine sediments occupying an earlier 'proto-Ure' valley (the last-mentioned as seen in the present project at Ripon North, described above). The separation of these four terraces records the shifting of the meandering course of the river, as well as (limited) progressive incision. Howard *et al.* (2000a) also reported on palaeoenvironmental analysis of channel infill deposits (at SE 326696) in their Terrace No. 2 (Fig. 2.57), shown by radiocarbon dating to be of early Holocene age (cf. Chapter 3.7).

The 2003 workings exploited the next lowest terrace

in the sequence, Terrace 3 of Howard *et al.* (2000a). This has an upper surface at *c.* 17.5m O.D., less than 2 m above the river (the lowest terrace, No. 4, is only just above river level) and little more than 1 m below Terrace 2, which was *c.* 18.5 m above O.D. in the area studied by Howard *et al.* (2000a). Sections on either side of the working pit were recorded and sampled (Plate 2.6). Section 1, on the west side of the working area (Plate 2.6a & b), abutted against a haul road and so exposed the full sequence of Terrace 3 sediments (including topsoil) above an artificially lowered water level. This showed *c.* 3 m of sandy gravel, horizontally bedded and fining upwards into sand, giving a total sand and gravel thickness of >4 m (Plate 2.6). The lowest exposed part of the gravel was conspicuously coarser than higher levels, reinforcing the impression of a fining-upwards sequence. The gravel was noticeably shelly, with the freshwater gastropod *Theodoxus fluviatilis* readily identified in the field from its conspicuous striped ornament (see Chapter 3.7; Table 3.30). Four gravel samples were collected for clast analysis, which revealed a typical River Ure composition, dominated by Pennine Carboniferous rocks (20–35% limestone, 8–20% chert, 35–46% quartzitic sandstones), with 3–6% Magnesian Limestone from the Permian (Table 2.2).

Into this sand and gravel, a steep-sided channel had been cut and then filled with a finer-grained sequence, variously organic, of sands, silts and clays. Molluscan and plant fossils were conspicuous within this channel-fill sequence, which was sampled (Plate 2.6a & b) for palaeoenvironmental analysis using four overlapping monolith tins and a series of bagged samples (for molluscs and other animal fossils). The monolith samples were subsampled for analysis of pollen and microscopic charcoal content (Chapter 3.7.2).

Section 2 was located on the eastern side of the active quarry and was an ephemeral working face (sampled early in 2003), the top several metres of which had been stripped prior to recording. The overburden was reported to be *c.* 2 m of organic floodplain sediment and was the source of collections of large vertebrate remains, including red deer antlers and domestic sheep, cattle and horse bones (Chapter 3.7.6). Despite this stripping, a sequence of *c.* 5 m of sands and gravels was recorded (Plate 2.6c). In contrast to Section 1, the sequence here showed thin sand bodies interbedded with medium-coarse gravels, although the uppermost cross-bedded sand unit pointed to an overall fining-upwards regime. In a deeper area in front of the main face (Fig. 2.58; Plate 2.6c) an organic lens was noted and sampled as monolith 2M. The organic sediments here occurred beneath cross-bedded sand. Two gravel samples were collected (Plate 2.6c) and revealed a clast content broadly within the range indicated by the Section 1 analyses, albeit with lower Magnesian Limestone counts in both cases (Table 2.2). The monolith sample was dominated by coarse sand with occasional organic layers. One thin (5 cm) horizon of organic-rich detrital sand proved to be the only productive sample for palynology from this monolith (Chapter 3.7.2).

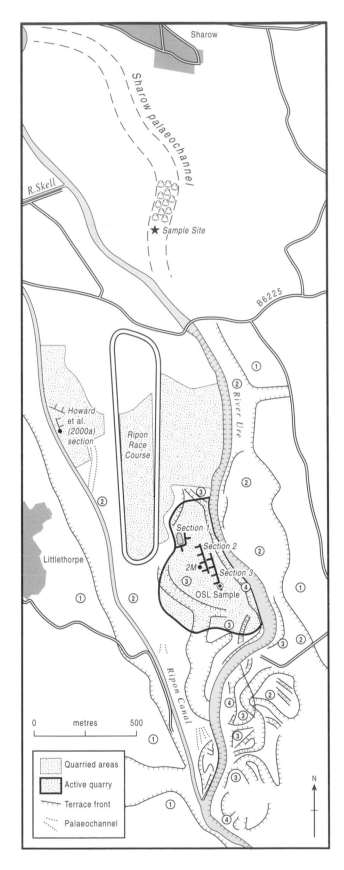

Fig. 2.57. Terraces (numbered in circles) in the vicinity of Ripon South Quarry (modified from Howard, et al., 2000a). This mapping is only available south of the B6225. North of that road, the Sharow palaeochannel is shown.

Fig. 2.58. Ripon South: view across the quarry from sample point 2M in the right foreground (see text) towards Section 1.

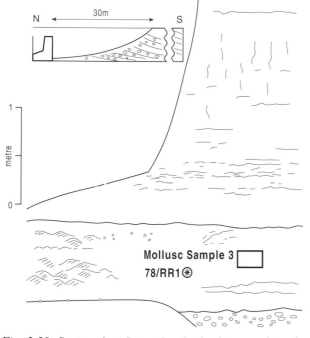

Fig. 2.59. Section 3 at Ripon South, the later working face from which an OSL sample (asterisk) and Mollusc Sample 3 were collected. The latter provided Bithynia *opercula for amino acid dating (see Chapter 3.7; Appendix III).*

In the upper part of Section 2 were found remains of a hand-made (Medieval) shoe; later, similar discoveries, together with a wooden object, constitute the only significant archaeological finds arising from project fieldwork (see Chapter 4.9.3; Figs 4.22–4.23; Plate 4.2).

In the deepest parts of the workings below Section 2, it was possible to dig down to a reddish silty sand. A spot sample of this material was collected and processed to determine whether it represented Permian bedrock material (cf. Cooper & Burgess, 1993). Pollen analysis of this sample yielded a species-poor assemblage of possibly reworked spores including *Lycospora pusilla,* a taxon that ranges from and is typical of sediments of Carboniferous age but which may occur within the Permian. Reworked taxa of Carboniferous and Permo-Triassic origin have been found in varying quantities throughout the studied Holocene sections. It was felt that this result, while somewhat equivocal, supported the visual supposition that this was bedrock. If so, the new sections must be beyond the limit of the above-mentioned 'proto-Ure' valley, with its glaciofluvial and glacio-lacustrine infill.

A later visit to the quarry was undertaken (October 2003) as part of the sampling programme for OSL dating, on which occasion a slightly different working-face exposure was recorded (Fig. 2.59), a few metres to the north-east of Section 2 (having been worked towards the river – see Fig. 2.57), and a single OSL sample was collected from this new face, Section 3. As noted previously (Chapter 1.9; Appendix II), attempts at OSL dating were almost entirely unsatisfactory, probably as a result of unsuitable quartz crystals. The Ripon South sample (Aber 78/RR1) was the least unsatisfactory of all those collected; 20 of the 2000 grains that were measured (1%) fulfilled the criteria used to determine suitability for dating (see Appendix II, in which Geoff Duller and Helen Roberts conclude that "statistical analysis of this small data set would be problematic, but the data are broadly consistent with a medieval age for this river terrace ... as deduced from the discovery of a leather shoe within the sediment nearby"). In Section 3 (Fig. 2.59) the upper sandy facies seen at the top of Section 2 (more organic upper material having been stripped off prior to extraction) has expanded to constitute the bulk of the section at its northern end. It clearly represents the edge of a fining-upwards channel fill, with ripple laminated sands at the base (the source of the OSL sample and of

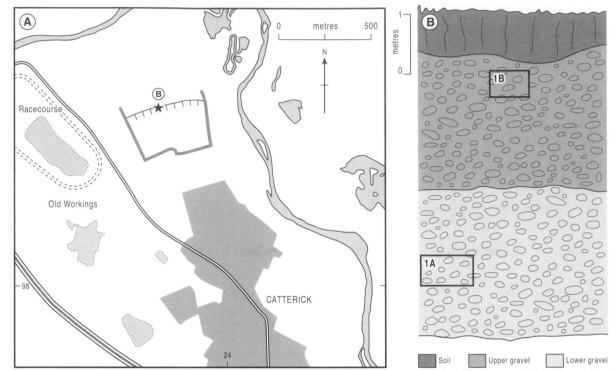

Fig. 2.60.Catterick Quarry: A – location of quarried area and working face as sampled; B – recorded section, showing stratigraphy and location of gravel samples.

molluscan material – see Chapter 3.7.4) passing up though rippled fine sands into silts.

The information from this site is important in reconstructing later Holocene fluvial activity, particularly since there is a previously published early Holocene record from nearby (Howard *et al.*, 2000a; see Chapter 3.7). An added complication, however, is that immediately upstream of the site the Ure appears to have occupied the now abandoned stretch of valley through Sharow (Fig. 2.57) until the mid-Holocene (Chapter 3.5).

2.7 Description of quarry sites: River Swale

2.7.1 Catterick

There are several former quarries around Catterick Village (SE 240980) and towards Brompton-on-Swale (SE 230995), particularly near the race-course. At the time of study there was a working quarry to the east of the road at the northern end of the village (Fig. 2.60A), with a south-facing working face. This showed >6 m of gravels overlying a till >1.5 m in thickness (Figs 2.60B & 2.61). Although not exposed, further gravels, stratigraphically lower in the sequence, were being worked below water level.

The till is a grey-brown over-consolidated diamicton with few large clasts but a scattering of smaller ones, including Cheviot erratics. The overlying stratified gravels (4 m) have a sandy matrix with occasional sand layers.

Fig. 2.61. Catterick quarry: view of working face, showing till overlain by the lower and upper gravels illustrated in Figure 2.60B.

They are overlain by a further 2 m of coarser poorly sorted boulder gravels with small channel fills of fine silts. Samples were taken from a section half-way along the working face (SE 2366 9898), where there was 5.5 m of coarse gravel exposed. This could be divided into a lower unit of coarse poorly sorted gravels (Sample 1A) overlain by much coarser cobble gravel (Sample 1B).

Clast analyses showed that the lower gravel is rich (in relative terms) in 'exotic' material of the sort seen only occasionally in the Ure; sample 1A had a full set of the five crystalline (igneous/metamorphic) lithologies distinguished

Fig. 2.62. Aerial view of Scorton quarry in July 2006, looking towards the studied faces (see Fig. 2.63), now flooded.

in Table 2.2, accounting for nearly 3% of the total count. It also yielded vein quartz and 'exotic' orthoquartzites as well as greywacke specimens, adding up to >5% material from outside the immediate area. This is in marked contrast to the composition of the various Ure gravels, even those thought to be of glacial origin, in which such material is only rarely present; indeed, it was completely absent in the unquestionably glacial gravel at Marfield (see above; Table 2.2).

The uppermost cobble-gravel, represented by sample 1B, contained elements of this 'exotic' suite, although in smaller quantities. Crystalline rocks were represented by a couple of dolerite clasts and a metaquartzite, with greywackes also present but at a reduced frequency compared with the lower sample. This diminution of the further-travelled, glacially-derived material may well indicate that this uppermost deposit is a post-glacial Swale terrace gravel, formed in part by reworking the earlier glacial sediment. This would account for the consistent separation of this upper deposit across the area of the quarry face, although there was no palaeontological evidence to support a Holocene age. If this interpretation is correct, Catterick sample 1B is the sole example of a post-glacial Swale gravel amongst the analyses. Further support for this interpretation might come from its richness in chert, the most durable locally-sourced rock, in keeping with selective destruction in fluvial bed-load of the softer lithologies. Indeed, this count has the lowest Carboniferous limestone fraction in Table 2.2, this lithology being less durable than the chert.

2.7.2 Scorton

Extensive gravels within the floodplain of the River Swale have been quarried at a number of locations, particularly on the east bank of the river between Kiplin Hall (SE 276976) and Scorton (NZ 246008; Figs 2.62 & 2.63A). The original quarries were associated with both the present floodplain and a low aggradational terrace. No exposures are currently accessible in the abandoned quarries, many of which are flooded. The main working quarry in the area at the time of study was located north-west of Scorton village, with a working face towards its north-eastern extremity (Fig. 2.63A).

Previous reports from the earlier workings within the Swale valley describe only coarse outwash sands and gravels associated with aggradation downstream of the confluence between the main Swale bedrock channel and a major meltwater channel that joins to the west of Brompton-on-Swale. However, the working quarry at the time of study had moved northwards away from the main axis of aggradation towards another south-directed meltwater channel. In contrast to the thick glaciofluvial and fluvial gravels of the main valley, the studied excavations encountered two distinct till layers at different levels within a sequence somewhat less satisfactory for aggregate extraction (Fig. 2.63B).

Site visits in 2004 showed that the lowest sedimentary unit in this area is a tough blue-grey till, extensively exposed in the quarry floor (Fig. 2.64), with a conspicuous erratic content that included granite. This was overlain by approximately 1.3 m of poorly sorted coarse gravel, with sub-angular to sub-rounded clasts and distinct better sorted clast-supported layers of cobble-sized clasts with sub-horizontal bedding (Figs 2.64 &. 2.65; Sample Scorton 1A). This in turn was overlain by a thick (3 m) red-brown till (Fig. 2.65) that showed a clean contact with the underlying gravels but was well 'laminated', showing evidence of faulting and deformation. Erratics were scarcer than in the lower till but included Cheviot porphyry and coal. This till was overlain by an upper gravel unit comprising about 5 m of open-framework coarse gravels (Fig. 2.66; Sample 1B) with some clasts of rotted rock and coal, although these did not survive into the analysed 16–32 mm sample (Table 2.2). Both samples showed significantly larger proportions

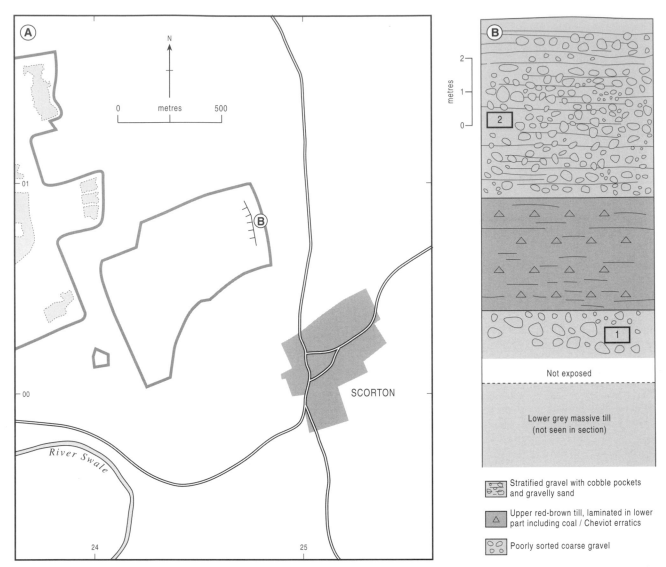

Fig. 2.63. Scorton Quarry: A – location of quarried area and working face as sampled; B – recorded section, showing stratigraphy and location of gravel samples.

of 'exotic' material than any of the Ure gravels; >5% in both cases (Table 2.2). These include both granitic and basic igneous rocks, porphyries, metaquartzite (only in 1B), vein quartz (never encountered in the Ure, despite being a ubiquitous and highly durable lithology) and, at over 2% in both counts, greywacke sandstone. Both Scorton counts were somewhat richer in this 'exotic' material than even the lower sample from Catterick (see above; Table 2.2).

2.8 Other Sites

Apart from the quarry sections, there are a very few natural exposures in the Washlands, two of which have provided study sites for the project. The first of these is a natural river-cliff section in the left bank of the Ure at Norton Mills, 0.5 km to the east of the Ripon North quarry

Fig. 2.64. Scorton Quarry. Section showing lower grey till exposed in quarry floor with overlying lower gravels.

Fig. 2.65. Scorton Quarry: lower gravels (sample 1A) and contact with upper till (see Fig. 2.63)

Fig. 2.66. Scorton Quarry: upper gravels (sample 1B – see Fig. 2.63).

workings. This type of exposure, formed and/or enhanced during high-flow events, can provide useful information, although usually restricted to deposits preserved close to river level. The second natural exposure occurs in the bank of a small stream that has, despite its size, cut into the local sedimentary sequence and provided valuable exposures in the deposits overlying the Snape Mires glacial lake deposits.

2.8.1 Norton Mills river-bank section

A short distance from Norton Mills Farm, 500 m downstream of the Hanson's (Ripon North) quarry, a natural river bank exposure cut by the River Ure (SE 3068 7665) reveals till and lake beds overlain by gravels (Figs 2.67–2.70). The till is a red-brown matrix-supported diamicton, more than 3 m thick, with large striated limestone clasts at the southern end of the section, where it is overlain by gravel. The till is replaced northwards by steeply dipping laminated silt and clay (Fig. 2.70), which appears to have been thrust over the till. Its emplacement could also relate to foundering of the strata associated with underlying Permian gypsum. The sequence is completed by two gravel units (Fig. 2.67), the lower of which is coarse, with both clast-supported and

Fig. 2.67 (above right). River-cliff section at Norton Mills Farm (SE 3068 7665), a short distance downstream (south) from Ripon North quarry. Shows locations of CLA sample (box) and OSL sample (asterisk). For location, see Fig. 2.51.

Fig. 2.68 (right). Norton Mills river-cliff section, showing lake deposits thrust over and against till, with overlying gravels

Fig. 2.69. Norton Mills section, showing till and overlying gravel sequence

Fig. 2.70. Norton Mills section: detail of lake deposits–till contact (scale: 20 cm, graduated in cm).

matrix-supported fabrics. The upper gravel unit shows a fining-upwards sequence with a number of sand lenses within the upper part of the stratigraphy. A gravel sample (Norton Mills 1) taken from the lower gravel unit (Fig.

2.67) proved to be composed of a typical Ure/Washlands suite of pebble lithologies, with nothing that is foreign to the catchment (Table 2.2). This gravel forms part of an aggradational terrace that sits *c.* 5.5 m above the river at

Fig. 2.71. Snape Mires: crop marks showing (1) former channels and (2) complex small ridges along the western edge of the former lake margin. Note also location 3 where there is a possible archaeological feature within the parkland of Thorp Perrow.

this point. It is a little more than 2 m higher than the terrace exposed in the Ripon North quarry (upper gravel), from which it is separated by a clear bluff (between 304769 and 307766). These two weakly separated terraces are presumed to be similar to those at Ripon South, mapped by Howard *et al.* (2000a), formed by minor migrations of the floodplain. OSL dating was attempted, based on a sample from a sandy lens in the upper gravel (Fig. 2.67); like other such attempts as part of the project, it proved unsuccessful (see above, Table 2.1; Appendix II).

2.8.2 Snape Mires

Snape Mires (Figs 2.31 & 2.71), a low-lying and formerly marshy area of *c.* 9 km² to the south of Bedale, constitutes a complex of separate sites rather than a single locality (Plate 2.7). Of geomorphological and geological interest, as well as a valuable source of palaeoenvironmental evidence (Chapter 3.8), these sites are united by a single genetic factor: all have formed in an area that was once a large glacial lake, as is indicated by thick underlying glacio-lacustrine sediments. Identified in BGS boreholes, these consist of consolidated heavy silt and clay, sometimes well laminated (perhaps even varved), in places >18 m thick. They were recorded at boreholes (Giles, 1982; Plate 2.7), such as at Lord's Moor Farm (SE 2828 8644) and Main Cut (SE 2858 8588).

The underlying bedrock at Snape Mires is Middle

Permian Edlington Formation marls, which dip gently eastwards, although there is no local outcrop, as the strata are buried by the thick glacial lake sediments. Boreholes to the west of the present basin have proved these lake deposits below glaciofluvial gravels (Giles, 1982). The lithological contact between these deposits is marked by a small terrace just east of Snape village and towards Thorp Perrow.

The surface of the Snape Mires lowland is far from the flat expanse that typifies many former lakes. It is marked in a number of places by micro-relief, with small (< 2 m) ridges in complex patterns (Figs 2.71); these are particularly well developed towards the western edge of the lake deposits, where there is a well-developed break of slope onto a gravel terrace. These have been attributed to the collapse of subterranean gypsum karst, a phenomenon well known in the Ripon area (Cooper, 1986), but have also been interpreted as moraines (Thompson *et al.*, 1996). It seems more likely that these are of permafrost origin, however, associated with the hydrological contrast between the lake sediments and the gravels, which has influenced the periglacial activity. Peat mounds such as Puddingpie Hill (SE 2784 8446) are evidence of continued high artesian water pressures within the basin (Giles, 1982). During the Lateglacial, when periglacial conditions prevailed, the lacustrine silts and clays would have provided ideal lithological context for the formation of segregated ice, allowing the formation of cryogenic mounds termed palsas,

Fig. 2.72. Snape Mires: general view of the Snape Mill tufa site, looking east. The stream section is in the trees to the right. The central part of the view shows the relief of the southern margin of the tufa lobe.

or alternatively lithalsas (cf. Pissart, 2002, 2003). These have left a geomorphological record in the form of small ramparts enclosing a range of circular to oval depressions that have a mutual interference pattern (Gurney, 2000). The high density of the ridges precludes an origin as pingos, which tend to be larger and more spatially separated (cf. Pissart, 2002). If this is correct, then these small ridges may indicate the former existence of discontinuous permafrost. Such conditions may have prevailed during the early part of deglaciation; this is the likely age of the ice wedges observed in the Nosterfield fan gravel (see above; Figs 2.48 & 2.49; see also Chapter 5.2.3) and is the period during which these features at Snape are likely to have formed. The lake may well have been very shallow, or even drained, by this time, leaving saturated sediments that would have been susceptible to frost heave under periglacial conditions.

Work within the project in this complex lowland was designed to assess its evolution since deglaciation. Previous mapping over the wider area of North Yorkshire had already thrown considerable light on the Devensian glacial history of the Snape district (Giles, 1982). The basin is enclosed to the south by a broad smooth ridge of till, with a more pronounced topographic ridge to the east, which is probably bedrock-controlled although covered by streamlined superficial deposits. The area to the west is a flat dissected terrace composed of gravels associated with progradation into the lake from meltwater systems draining the interfluve area between Thornton Watlass (SE 235855) and Bedale (SE 254880). A somewhat undersize sample (192 clasts) was obtained from gravel exposed in a stream section at Mill House (Plate 2.8) that is either the feather-edge of

this deposit or a slopewash-gravel derived from it. Its clast content proved to be similar to other Washlands deposits, entirely made up of material derived from the Swale–Ure fluvial catchment (Table 2.2). Its Magnesian Limestone component is the 2nd largest encountered, which is perhaps unsurprising, given the underlying Permian bedrock.

The present surface of the basin floor is formed on discontinuous thin peats and poorly drained silts and clays forming a natural wetland. Several ditches have been installed to improve drainage by directing water northwards to the Bedale Beck. Many glacial lakes persisted as lacustrine, or at least wetland areas, into the subsequent Lateglacial and early Holocene, leading to sedimentary sequences in which glacio-lacustrine deposits are overlain by limnic or organic sediments, often of substantial thickness and, classically, with a tripartite sequence that typifies what was long interpreted as a warm–cold–warm climatic fluctuation of the Devensian to Holocene transition (Innes, 2002a). A number of different sites have been investigated across the former lake basin to determine the palaeoenvironmental record (Plates 2.7 & 2.8; Chapter 3.8). It was clear from even a cursory investigation of the Snape lowlands that, even though the area has been wetland-dominated until recent drainage for agriculture, no significant lake persisted into the Holocene. Instead the outcrop of the glacio-lacustrine deposits is dotted with small basins of modest depth, containing mixtures of peats and organic sediments together with calcareous shell-marls.

The present morphology of the former glacial lake basin, its dissection by moderately incised post-glacial streams and the geometry of the localized bodies of Holocene sediment that overlie the glacio-lacustrine deposits together indicate considerable change since the area was deglaciated. It is presumed, from the considerable thickness of laminated sediments, that the lake existed for a significant period during the Late Devensian, impounded by ice against higher land to the west and south. The lake surface was probably several metres above the highest point now reached by the glacio-lacustrine sediments, which are a few metres above the modern base level in the Snape lowland (difficult to determine precisely because of drainage). It is thus clear that, without an ice dam, the lake would have drained rapidly, perhaps catastrophically. Such drainage might account for the incision of the modern streams into the lowland landscape and some of the complex morphology of the former lake surface; a similar mechanism has been invoked further north in explanation of the deeply incised 'denes' of the north-east coast, in connection with glacial lakes that once existed in the interior of County Durham. It is perhaps more likely, however, that post-glacial isostatic rebound has brought about much of the incision in both cases, with streams cutting down in response to uplift that occurred in the early Holocene, following crustal unloading.

The drainage exit of 'Glacial Lake Snape' is difficult to determine. There is a channel indicated on the high resolution DEM that is difficult to find in the field. It appears to be just to the south of Burneston (SE 305845), where there is evidence of sand and gravel that have been worked in a number of small quarries. A small outlet to the north of Carthorpe (SE 309840) would have allowed outflow into a small channel system, developed in the ill-defined interfluve between the Swale and Ure around the A1 Road, draining towards Kirklington, where there is a large peat-filled abandoned channel (Fig. 2.13).

2.8.2.1 The Snape Tufa

On the western side of the former lacustrine basin, at Mill House (SE 2740 8410) near Snape village, is a subaerial tufa, forming a lobate mound that has formed around a calcareous spring (Plates 2.7 & 2.8; Fig. 2.72). One of several streams draining the Snape basin dissects the Mill House tufa lobe, providing exposures through >2 m of this variably-lithified, porous calcareous precipitate, full of the empty moulds of vegetable material (plant fossils). The presence of tufa here was indicated by Geological Survey mapping (Giles, 1982). Detailed investigation using coring equipment revealed that the tufa overlies a basin infill consisting of >3 m of clayey silts (Plate 2.8). The deepest core (MH1) was stopped by impenetrable gravel, perhaps a continuation of material exposed and sampled in the stream bank further upstream (see above). Palaeoenvironmental investigations of the fossiliferous deposits, including the tufa, will be reported in Chapter 3.8.3.

The occurrence of tufa at Snape is of considerable interest, the deposits having never been described in detail. It is therefore worth reviewing briefly the existing knowledge of Quaternary/Holocene tufas in general and the occurrence of such deposits in northern England in particular. Tufas have generated considerable interest, as indicators of groundwater and stream chemistry and of palaeoclimate, as well as sources of fossil molluscs, ostracods and plant remains (e.g. Pentecost, 1993, 1995, 1998; Ford & Pedley, 1996; Preece & Bridgland, 1998). Stable isotopes of oxygen and carbon have been studied in thick tufa deposits, as potential sources of palaeoclimatic data (Dandurand *et al.*, 1982; Andrews *et al.*, 1994). Tufas are recorded from limestone areas worldwide and have attracted particular attention in Italy, France, Germany, Hungary and Turkey, as well as Britain (see Ford & Pedley, 1996). They can be classified according to different modes of formation (Pedley, 1990; Pedley & Hill, 2002). Some involve geothermal waters and should, according to Ford and Pedley (1996), be classified as travertine. Other authors have variously substituted the terms travertine and tufa; Ford and Pedley (1996) decried the tendency for tufa to be used for soft, unlithified precipitates and travertine for hard ones, preferring to classify according to water temperature and to define all cold/ambient-water concretions as tufa. There are two principal modes of tufa formation, by precipitation in calcareous springs or by encrustation of detritus barrages across stream courses in limestone areas, the latter phenomenon eventually leading to the development of separate pools or even lakes with tufa dams between them, sometimes forming a series of downstream-descending cascades. The pools in these circumstances become infilled with mixtures of calcareous and organic sediments and can be rich sources of fossils (Taylor *et al.*, 1994a; Ford & Pedley, 1996).

One of the best-known British Holocene tufas occurs at Caerwys, North Wales (Pedley, 1987; Campbell & Bowen, 1989; Preece & Turner, 1990), where a deposit of the barrage type, exceeding 10 m in thickness and extending down-slope for over 1 km, has been quarried for lime and, more recently, for horticultural uses. The site is now conserved as a Site of Special Scientific Interest (SSSI). Other Holocene tufa SSSIs include Blashenwell, Dorset, where the deposit incorporates Mesolithic artefacts (Preece, 1980) and Holywell Coombe, Folkestone, Kent, where the site was the object of a rescue excavation ahead of construction, through part of it, of the Channel Tunnel (Preece & Bridgland, 1998, 1999). The last two of these sites are calcareous spring deposits on Jurassic limestone and Chalk respectively; at Caerwys the source of the lime is Carboniferous Limestone. The latter bedrock type gives rise to several tufa occurrences in the Pennines, notably the barrage tufas of the Rivers Lathkill and Wye (tributaries of the Derwent–Trent) in the southern Peak District (Taylor *et al.*, 1994a). These have been the subject of considerable research, including investigation of pollen and ostracods, stable isotopes and radiocarbon dating.

Pennine tufas nearer to the present study area include cascades at Goredale Scar and Janets Foss, in the Aire system (Pentecost & Lord, 1988; Ford & Pedley, 1996), and another at nearby Lower Beck, Malham. From the last-mentioned a Holocene molluscan assemblage numbering 24 species was recovered (Keen, 1989): 22 snails together with the slugs *Milax* and *Limax*. The snails include the only Holocene record of *Vitrea subrimata*, an extant species that is confined to the Pennines. Tufa occurrence above Permian limestone, as at Snape, is relatively uncommon (cf. Ford & Pedley, 1996). Of 29 tufa localities in the Yorkshire Dales listed by Pentecost and Lord (1988), 17 were noted by them to be no longer active, a phenomenon that afflicts tufas throughout Europe and has been variously attributed to climatic and/or anthropogenic factors (cf. Preece, 1978; Willing 1985; Goudie *et al.*, 1993; Griffiths & Pedley, 1995; Preece & Bridgland, 1998). Tufas are also reported from non-Pennine sites in North Yorkshire on Jurassic limestone bedrock, Permian Magnesian Limestone and even calcareous glacial deposits (Ford & Pedley, 1996), the last being a possible reference to the Snape occurrence. Other minor tufa occurrences have been observed in the Washlands, above Permian limestone, by BGS surveyors (Abraham, 1981), notably north of Copgrove (SE 345644). Giles (1982), who has provided the only previous descrip-tion of the tufa at Snape Mills, reported a second outcrop, too small to appear on his map, forming mounds at the edge of Black Plantation (SE 2906 8589), near the northern outlet through which the Snape glacial lake might have drained. He also noted that tufa occurs within alluvial fan deposits at Well, north of Nosterfield.

The Snape tufa is localized within a small lobate area lying to the north-east of the Snape Mill farmhouse (SE 2740 8410; Fig. 2.72; Plates 2.7 & 2.8). At its maximum, the deposit is about 2.1 m thick and is seen to thin over a distance of about 20 m in a north-easterly direction, downstream of the main site at Mill House (MH1) to a feather-edge (Plate 2.8a). However, outcrops away from the stream are rare and the dimensions of the deposit are based mainly on feature mapping. Small unmeasured outcrops occur 20 m north of the main site along an apparent man-made low-relief scarp and within the field margin close to the stream section on its southern side but these contribute little to a better understanding of the depositional geometry of the tufa deposit. It is clear, however, that its aerial extent is small and that the stream effectively cuts a longitudinal section through the deposit. In addition to the tufa at Mill House, the farmer believes that another small localized tufa outcrop is developed close by to the east-south-east. Although not specifically seen in outcrop it is believed to underlie the east–west orientated ridge in the field immediately to the south of the farm.

2.8.2.2 Outcrop details

At MH1 the base of the tufa lies directly on a peaty sapropel (Plate 2.8a). The upper part of this sapropel is transitional, with wispy bands (laminae) of intraclast tufa. This transitional bed is considered to lie at the base of the tufa

Fig. 2.73. Snape Mires, Mill House MH1: detail of tufa section lithologies, with beds described in the text indicated (A – D).

deposit (Bed A, Fig. 2.73). It passes up into friable pale grey marly tufa with crude wavy bedding (Bed B, Fig. 2.73). The palest cream layering is caused by a greater abundance of tufa intraclasts. The tufa layers contain moulds of sedges or grasses, ostracods and diminutive gastropod shells. Above the marly tufa, lithified tufa classified as Bed C is overlain by strongly lithified tufa of Bed D (Plate 2.8a).

There is a correlation problem with respect to the better lithified tufa(s) (Beds C & D), which are represented in the topmost metre of the main site at MH1. Here there is a gradual transition between Beds B and C. In the adjacent MH3 site, however, a 10–20 cm composite peat and intraclast tufa bed separates two principal tufa units (Plate 2.8a). These interrelationships will be resolved below.

2.8.2.3 Petrological details

All of the tufa samples consisted of friable material with open to clayey textures. Consequently, samples were vacuum impregnated with low viscosity araldite prior to cutting thin sections. Five standard thin sections were cut and stained for carbonate recognition using the technique outlined by Dickson (1966). In addition, all samples were subjected to scanning electron microscopic analyses using a Cambridge Instruments S360 SEM. This machine is also equipped with a Link analytical energy dispersive

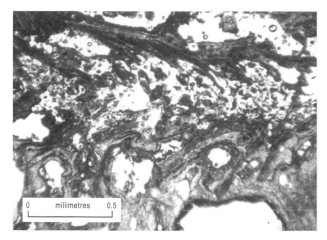

Fig. 2.74. Bryophyte frond coated in lime mud (opaque material from Bed C in Fig. 2.73. Spar cement fringes (translucent pinkish areas [see CD]) are also early cements contemporary with the later stages of moss growth.

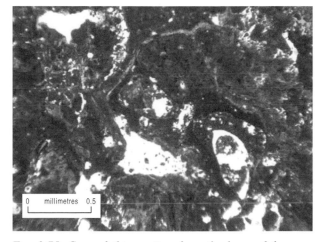

Fig. 2.75. General thin section from the base of the upper tufa (Bed C, Fig. 2.73). Note the abundance of lime mud interspersed with thin wispy micritic fringe cements.

spectrometer (microprobe) facility for major elemental analysis.

MH1
SAMPLE 1 (BED A, FIG. 2.73): INTRACLAST TUFA
This consists of thin, allochthonous tufa intraclast laminae interleaved with organic-rich laminae. Tufa within the tufa laminae consists of uncemented platy fragments, originally representing micritic calcite coatings on sedge or similar ribbed grasses and associated mosses. [*Note:* The sample is extremely friable and represents the earliest development of tufa at MH1, at a time when conditions were unfavourable, possibly due to low temperatures].

SAMPLE 2 (BED B, FIG. 2.73): MARLY INTRACLAST TUFA
This is a very open-textured and crumbly pale grey deposit taken from one of the tufa-rich horizons within this unit formed of irregularly bedded alternations of brown tufa-rich and grey clayey silt-rich layers. The sample shows evidence of extensive syndepositional interconnected cavity development. Individual tufa clasts are crumb-like rather than platy and are associated with abundant ostracod carapaces and small gastropod shells. [*Note:* The association of tufa and clay is unusual, as clay has a deleterious effect on tufa precipitation. It is possible that clay particles (20–30%, according to Coulter analyses of samples from the thicker divisions lower in the sequence: see Appendix IV) were introduced into the depositing waters intermittently. Nevertheless, this is the principal aquifer within the deposit and gives rise to small resurgences throughout its outcrop].

SAMPLE 3 (BED C, FIG. 2.73): GRASS AND BRYOPHYTE FRAMESTONE TUFA
This is a very open-textured, friable, pale brown tufa. Poorly cemented lime mud (now micrite) typically coats the bryophyte fronds in this bed. In thin section (Fig. 2.74)

a typical bryophyte frond is preserved. However, the outer edges of the fronds are buried in coarser sparite fringe cements. Away from the bryophyte cushions the deposit is predominantly poorly cemented lime mud with thin spar coatings and abundant contemporaneous infill of clay and detrital tufa within primary cavities (Fig. 2.75). [*Note:* The primary fabric appears to have precipitated onto a grass and bryophyte framestone developed where water seeped through grass and moss cushions. The clay appears to have been introduced later than the cement growth, although many of the original cavities once occupied by living plant tissues remain sediment free].

SAMPLE 4 (BED D, FIG. 2.73): GRASS RHIZOME AND BRYOPHYTE FRAMESTONE TUFA
This is an open-textured, pale greyish-brown grass rhizome and bryophyte framestone. The tufa cements are much thicker than in sample 3 but still contain considerable interstitial clay in this sample. Many grass stalks and bryophyte cavities remain open and preserve *in situ* plant orientations. The sample contains several small high-spired gastropods. Several platy cemented areas within the sample show speleothem fabrics.

In hand specimen and in thin section this tufa is seen to be composed of thin fringe cements surrounding conduit cavities (stained pink in Fig. 2.76 [see colour version on CD]). These cement skins originally coated the living aquatic mosses (possibly *Cratoneuron* sp.) but have subsequently become buried by later diagenetic clear calcite cement. Figure 2.77 shows a similar development of coarse sparite surrounding the bryophyte frond. Many primary cavities have now become partly or fully infilled by clay and detrital tufa clasts, which have been carried into the primary fabric (central area in Fig. 2.76; top right in Fig. 2.77). [*Note:* The coarse cement fringes (unstained in Fig. 2.76 and all the pale pink stained coarse spar in Fig. 2.77) coating the primary fringe cements are probably speleothem

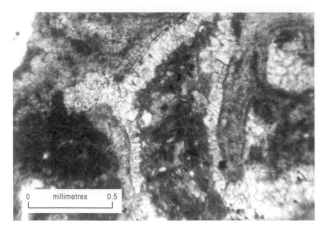

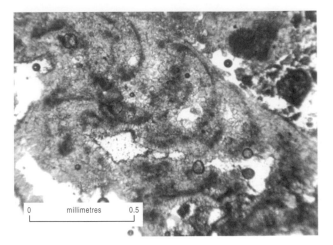

Fig. 2.76. Sample from Bed D (0.5 m above Bed C in Fig. 2.73) showing the extensive late stage clear calcite cement (speleothem fringe) coating the primary tufa fabric. Note the muddy detrital late stage infill within the primary cavity (centre of photomicrograph).

Fig. 2.77. Well-cemented tufa from Bed D. Note that the bryophyte frond (outlined by opaque peloidal micrite) is buried in thick sparite cement (cf. Fig. 2.73).

fabrics. Their presence strongly suggests that there has been a considerable through flow of water in the past].

MH3 (15 m upstream of MH1)
Sample 5 (base of site): Grass and bryophyte framestone tufa
This is a pale brownish-white, fairly well cemented grass and bryophyte framestone tufa with a well orientated vertical fabric of grass stalk tubes. This sample shows a very similar fabric to sample 3 but is less thickly cemented. There is some evidence of local penecontemporaneous collapse within the framestone fabric. In thin section it is clear that a large part of the deposit is composed of friable peloidal micrite (opaque patches coating the moss in Fig. 2.77) but that there is also a considerable amount of spar cement coating the plant remains. [*Note:* The sample is similar to Sample 4 except that there is considerably more clay infilling (best seen in hand specimen). Deposition was probably in a more sluggish flow than for Sample 4].

Sample 6 (top bed, MH3): Bryophyte framestone tufa
This is a pale brownish-grey, massive, well-cemented bryophyte framestone tufa, very similar in texture and hardness to Sample 4. There is considerable clay sediment infilling the inter-frond areas, although the bryophyte and grass stalk cavities remain unfilled. In thin section the vegetable material is coated in a thin peloidal micrite layer, later coated by a heavy sparite precipitate (Fig. 2.78). Nevertheless, considerable primary porosity still remains (Fig. 2.79), some being partly filled by peloidal micrite (Fig. 2.78). [*Note:* This is a well-cemented sample in all respects. The cements are typical of contemporaneous cementation associated with living bryophyte cushions in paludal and perched springline situations].

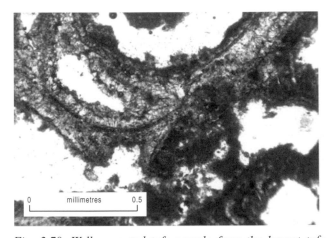

Fig. 2.78. Well-cemented tufa sample from the lowest tufa layer at MH3 (see Plate 2.8a). Note the development of spar on the moss pinnule surfaces and the later part-infilling of primary cavities by peloidal lime mud.

2.8.2.4 Calcareous deposits at other Snape localities

Exposures and cores elsewhere in the Snape lake basin revealed calcareous sediments within the various primarily organic sequences, including a number of shell marl deposits rich in molluscs, such as at Ings Lane 6 and the Gallop (Chapter 3.8.1 and 3.8.4). While these will be described in detail in Chapter 3, petrological examination of the Ings Lane 6 shell marl (Sample 7) will be reported here.

This was a pale grey to white uncemented lime mud with evidence of thrombolitic texture. Scattered tufa intraclast flakes within the deposit indicate the presence of grasses that provided a local substrate for precipitation. [*Note:* This is a typical lake chalk. It is principally a bacterial

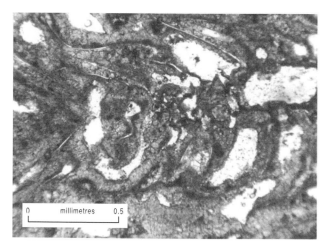

Fig. 2.79. Well-cemented bryophyte tufa from the topmost tufa layer at MH3. Note the dominant sparite cement coating the bryophyte frond and the unfilled primary porosity which originally occupied inter-pinnule areas surrounding the frond.

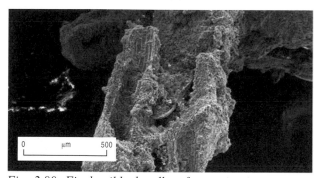

Fig. 2.80. Finely ribbed stalks of erect in situ vegetation (?Chara sp.) which provided a framework for micritic tufa precipitation. An ostracod carapace is visible in the centre field. Sample 2 (from Bed B in Fig. 2.73)

biomediated precipitate (see Pedley, 1992, 1994) deposited in clear shallow water without clay contamination].

2.8.2.5 Scanning Electron Microscopy (SEM) – Analyses and interpretations

Representative specimens from each of samples 1 to 6 were subjected to an SEM study. This has aided in the identification of the plant casts, helped to tighten up the palaeoenvironmental interpretations and has also shed light on the late stage diagenetic processes. Samples 2, 4 and 5 were most instructive in these respects:

Sample 2 (Bed B in Fig. 2.73) shows finely a ribbed stem, possibly from *Chara* sp., together with an ostracod valve (Fig. 2.80). [*Note:* When viewed together with the friable and clayey nature of this deposit, the association strongly suggests the associated development of small shallow pools of water within the earliest tufa deposits. In contrast, Figures 2.81 and 2.82, both from the upper

Fig. 2.81. Bryophyte frond and pinnule moulds in cemented lime mud in Sample 5 (base of MH3).

part of the deposit, show the typical development of bryophyte fronds associated with cushions of moss. These more typically develop on steeper slopes more proximal to resurgence points].

The clear spar fringe cements (Bed C, Fig. 2.73), which developed as a speleothem coating on the bryophyte framestones, are here seen as bladed sparite in the photomicrograph of Sample 4 (Fig. 2.82). [*Note:* This is common phreatic cement that develops where there has been an active through-flow of water several centimetres below the accreting living surface].

In contrast, Figure 2.83 shows a corrosion feature from a much later stage. Here, there is clear evidence of dissolution of the outer tufa surface, which has created smoothly rounded micro-topography to the original, irregular tufa fabric surrounding a bryophyte frond. [*Note:* Such an effect is common where acidified circulating groundwater has come into contact with the carbonates over a prolonged period].

2.8.2.6 Correlation between MH1 and MH3

Despite the close proximity of the two tufa sections, correlation between them is difficult. This is because similarities in petrology between tufa sites are not good guides to correlation, as bed characteristics and facies change significantly over very short distances. Inter-layered organic beds and laminites are generally useful for correlation and clay beds can be helpful. In muddy tufa deposits the purest carbonate accumulations usually develop very close to resurgence points and may be quite lenticular in profile. Thick, well-cemented, proximal bryophyte tufa in MH3 can reasonably be expected to pass transitionally in the down-flow direction into very thin, muddy, laminated and poorly cemented tufa in MH1. Consequently, it is considered that the organic beds found in the upstream site are very likely to be represented in MH1 by the basal tufa with wispy organic laminations (Bed A, Fig. 2.73).

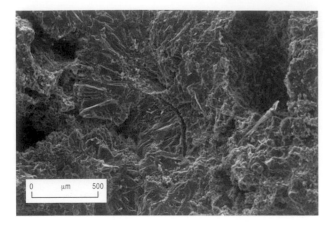

Fig. 2.82. Development of bladed sparite fringe cement surrounding a bryophyte pinnule (centre). Sample 4, taken about 0.5 m above Bed C in Fig. 2.73 (cf. Fig. 2.75)

Fig. 2.83. A Cratoneuron (bryophtye) frond enclosed in micrite precipitate. Note the smooth outer surface of the micrite caused by later phreatic dissolution of the fabric (from Sample 4, taken about 0.5 m above bed C in Fig. 2.73)

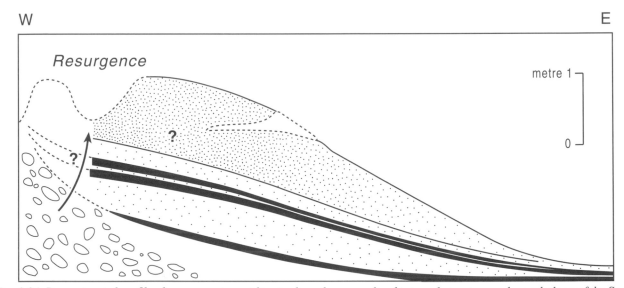

Fig. 2.84. Reconstructed profile along an east–west line to show the generalized internal structure and morphology of the Snape Mill paludal tufa deposit. Symbols: tufa deposits are stippled with denser stipple indicating better cementation; organic bands are black; clays are unshaded; glacial gravels are indicated bottom right.

Figure 2.84 represents a point in time when Bed A (transitional peaty sapropel at the base of the tufa) was being deposited at the main site (MH1; extreme right-hand side of diagram), before the tufa lobe grew forwards to engulf it. Note how the prominent organic and tufa-rich beds on the left-hand side of Figure 2.84 (representing the MH3 site, 15 m upstream of MH1) become thinner and converge into the basal laminated Bed A alternation on the right-hand side of the diagram. Note also in Figure 2.84 how the degree of cementation (indicated by density of stipple) is greatest in areas closest to the resurgence point.

2.8.2.7 Interpretation

This is a typical temperate-climate paludal tufa deposit (cf. Pedley, 1992; Ford & Pedley, 1996). The lime mud shedding from bryophyte stands is a feature typical of temperate deposits and is particularly well seen in the Belgian 'Cron' paludal deposits (Symoens *et al.*, 1951) and in many of the small active paludal sites in the eastern parts of the Yorkshire Dales (Pentecost & Lord, 1988; Pentecost, 1993). However, the Snape tufa developed into a broad slope-dominated spread much more closely related to the low gradient carbonate marsh deposits of El Jardin, Spain (Taylor & Pedley, 1998), and Ddol, North Wales (Pedley, unpublished). It is noteworthy, however, that the Snape tufa has a total absence of oncoid facies (cf. El Jardin and Ddol deposits). This indicates strongly that there was no actively flowing channel development within the tufa lobe. The low gradient lobate mound at Snape developed eastwards (down palaeoslope) from a single resurgence point and attained greatest thickness in close proximity to the spring. In all probability water escaped by slow seepage between grass tussocks in the vicinity of the resurgence and exited onto a very gently inclined surface.

Although small in extent, this tufa deposit is a valuable local palaeoenvironmental indicator (see Chapter 3.8.3). It appears to have commenced development from a single, large resurgence lying low on the valley side, close behind the new outbuilding immediately to the north of Snape Mill. The association of this resurgence with a 3.5 m deep sub-tufa depression infilled by gravel and sand deposits at MH1 may be significant (Fig. 2.84). The limited data suggests that this depression might serve as a conduit holding a perched local aquifer, fed directly from the adjacent glaciofluvial terrace deposits outcropping on the higher ground immediately west of the tufa outcrop (Plate 2.7). Water still issues from the main resurgence and from Bed B lithofacies wherever they outcrop, although active carbonate precipitation was not seen during this study.

Much of the Snape Mill deposit consists of allochthonous micritic tufa material that has been carried down-slope under sluggish flow conditions from a more proximal site close to the resurgence. Consequently, the distal deposits are typically thinly laminated and fine grained, often being inter-laminated with partly degraded organic detritus (sapropel). This scenario is especially typical of paludal tufa deposits, many of which accumulate locally on badly drained or impermeable surfaces where small-scale ponding occurs. The appearance of true peat beds within the tufa succession may indicate a temporary cessation of resurgence activity (e.g. the tufa interlaminated peats in MH3). More typically, however, they record intervals of outflow switching to another area of the tufa lobe.

Many paludal tufas can be identified by the presence of phytoherm cushion development. These represent former clumps of grass and bryophytes that stood in the water and helped to further impede surface drainage, thereby enhancing the swampy conditions. Evidence for these at the Snape site is patchy, although the petrological and SEM investigation have revealed that bryophytes and, to a lesser extent, grasses have been the principal macrophyte colonisers. Initial precipitation (peloidal micrite) occurred directly on the living leaf surfaces of this vegetation but much was subsequently shed and carried down-flow to distal facies (represented by beds A and B. The topmost massive tufas (beds C and D), however, contain abundant evidence of *in situ* phytoherm cushion development, both by grasses and by bryophytes. Clearly, conditions for growth were maximized as the mound increased in elevation, with the result that the deposit rapidly built up into a better drained mound in the immediate vicinity of the resurgence point. This upper part of the deposit is very

well cemented and has the typical framestone fabric of an active flow deposit.

The youngest diagenetic features of the deposit are all associated with corrosion of the tufa fabric. The implications here are that acidification of the groundwater occurred quite early in the Holocene, at a time when the resurgence was still actively providing a high volume discharge that was sufficient to infiltrate the entire deposit including the highest bryophyte mounds. It must be noted that the outflow today is insufficient to saturate Bed C (Fig. 2.73) and the highest beds in the upstream tufa site.

Finally, the Snape Mill tufa deposit has been partly encroached upon and buried by peat. Although this occurs in the depression that seems likely to represent a former water mill, and so is a recent feature, it further reinforces the conclusion that carbonate precipitation at Snape has ceased a considerable time ago.

There is a moderate probability that the tufa deposit is contemporaneous with the widespread 'shell marl' which generally is sandwiched between the underlying glacial-lake deposits and overlying peats at the Ings Lane sites and at the Gallop (see Chapter 3.8). This deduction is based on the fact that strongly alkaline conditions and abundant water supply would have been required for the various carbonate-rich deposits to have formed, yet throughout the Snape basin subsequent deposition has been of organic limnic muds (although the end of tufa deposition at Snape Mills cannot be dated, there being no later overlying deposits there). Although the trigger for this brief alkaline episode is unclear, it may correlate with early Holocene run-off, which rapidly leached out much of the glacially derived carbonate from the substrate, an interpretation that has been invoked in Holderness (R. Middleton, pers. comm.). Once removed, this material would not have been readily replenished. Hence, the tufa system would have shut down once the water supply had discharged the majority of available carbonate ions to the surface. If so, then the tufa deposit must date from the early part of the Holocene. At this time there was a brief window when rising ambient temperatures conspired with a plentiful supply of calcium carbonate in solution to generate an important, albeit brief, early tufa episode.

It is possible that the resurgence was directly fed from the underlying Permian marls, although this is less likely, since these lie at some depth beneath the Pleistocene sequence. The time of tufa development might, in this second scenario, have continued later into the Holocene, particularly around 6500 ^{14}C BP, when many of the larger British tufa deposits were formed (e.g. Preece & Bridgland, 1998). In this case it would be surprising that the tufa episode produced so little deposit. In North Derbyshire, for example, over 16 m of deposits resulted from similar later Holocene tufa development in the Lathkill valley (Pedley, 1993) and 12 m of tufa formed at this time is preserved at Caerwys, North Wales (Pedley, 1987).

3 Palaeoenvironmental reconstruction

The results of palaeoenvironmental analyses carried out during the Swale–Ure Washlands project are presented and interpreted in this chapter on a site-by-site basis (for site locations, see Fig. 1.1). Cores were taken at the following sites, which have been studied in detail: Nosterfield, Newby Wiske, Marfield, Sharow Mires, Ripon North (Hanson's Quarry), Ripon South (Brown & Potter's Quarry) and Snape Mires; multiple cores were analysed at Nosterfield and Snape Mires. Two further sites, at Langland's Farm and Thornton's Plantation, were specifically investigated with respect to fluvial sedimentation. Several other minor sites were also investigated, results from these being presented in Appendix VI, along with additional records from the major sites. A regional synthesis will be presented in the final chapter.

Within each site report, the following pattern has been adopted: a general introduction to the site leads into a brief description of lithostratigraphy. This is then succeeded by individual descriptions of the different proxy evidence, which may differ between sites depending on available material, and a report on any radiocarbon dates and other geochronology (see also Appendix I, Table 1, which presents all the radiocarbon dates from the project). There are specific sections on the chronology of each site, with a table evaluating the geochronology with respect to the litho- and biostratigraphy, particularly the pollen evidence. Each site report ends with a site-specific synthesis; an overall summary of the Washlands sites will form part of the final chapter.

3.1 Methods

Detailed records of Lateglacial and post-glacial environmental change can be established by multi-proxy analyses of stratigraphical sequences, such as have accumulated in lakes, abandoned river channels and other depressions in the landscape (cf. Lowe & Walker, 1997a; Brothwell & Pollard, 2001). An integrated suite of analytical methods has been employed in this study, designed to produce a range of complementary data sets that will enable palaeoenvironmental reconstruction. Lithostratigraphy, palynology, plant macrofossil analysis and molluscan analysis were the principal techniques used, with the main geochronology provided by AMS radiocarbon dating (Appendix I). In addition, studies of bones and insects, particle size analysis, loss on ignition and clast analysis

have been used where appropriate; some of these data, where useful, have already been presented in Chapter 2.

3.1.1 Recording of lithostratigraphy

The lithostratigraphy of each core extracted for palaeoenvironmental analysis was recorded in the field and/or laboratory using the systematic methodology, symbols and notation devised by Troels-Smith (1955) for the characterization of unconsolidated sediments, and further described by Tooley (1981) and Long et al. (1999). These symbols, which have been applied to the lithostratigraphy columns of microfossil and other figures, are explained on the diagrams. The Troels-Smith notation is defined in Table 3.1 and results of Troels-Smith sediment analysis are tabulated for each site, with conventions shown in Table 3.2.

3.1.2 Palynology

Laboratory preparation techniques for pollen analysis follow the standard methods outlined by Moore et al. (1991). Exotic marker grains of Lycopodium clavatum were introduced in tablet form (Stockmarr, 1971) to allow the calculation of microfossil and micro-charcoal concentrations, expressed as number per unit volume of wet sediment. As this study includes analyses of Lateglacial depositional environments that were poor in trees, pollen and other microfossil frequencies have been calculated throughout as percentages of a total land pollen sum including trees, shrubs and herbs but excluding aquatic pollen and all spores (Berglund & Ralska-Jasiewiczowa, 1986). Micro-charcoal frequencies have been calculated in the same way. A sum of 300 land pollen grains from each level was counted as the desired target; additional microfossils encountered were also recorded. Where there were very low concentrations or poor preservation, a lower sum was sometimes necessary.

Pollen and spores have been classified in life-form groups (trees, shrubs, herbs, etc.) on the pollen diagrams. Common names are shown at the first appearance of the taxon in the text. Local pollen assemblage zones (PAZ) have been delimited for each core and are presented on the pollen diagrams, which also show radiocarbon dates at their appropriate stratigraphical levels. Pollen nomenclature follows Moore et al. (1991) to allow comparison with previously published sites from the region. Correlation with

Name	Code	Sediment type	Field characteristics
Argilla steatodes	As	Clay (<0.002mm)	May be rolled into a thread ≤ 2mm diameter without breaking. Plastic when wet, hard when dry.
Argilla granosa	Ag	Silt (0.002–0.06mm)	Will not roll into thread without splitting. Will rub into dust on drying (such as on hands). Gritty on back of teeth, like carborundum.
Grana arenosa	Ga	Fine and medium sand (0.06–0.6mm)	Crunchy between teeth. Lacks cohesion when dry. Grains visible to naked eye.
Grana saburralia	Gs	Coarse sand (0.6–2mm)	Crunchy between teeth. Lacks cohesion when dry. Grains visible to naked eye.
Grana glareosa (minora)	Gg(min)	Fine gravel (2–6mm)	
Grana glareosa (majora)	Gg(maj)	Medium and coarse gravel (6–20mm)	
Testae molluscorum	test.(moll.)	Whole mollusc shells	
Particulae testarum molluscorum	part. test. (moll.)	Shell fragments	
Substantia humosa	Sh	Humified organics beyond identification	Fully disintegrated deposit lacking macroscopic structure, usually dark brown or black.
Turfa herbacea	Th^{0-4}	Roots, stems and rhizomes of herbaceous plants	Can be vertically aligned or matted within sediment in growth position.
Turfa bryophytica	Tb^{0-4}	The protonema, rhizods, stems, leaves etc. of mosses	Can be vertically aligned or matted within sediment in growth position.
Turfa lignosa	Tl^{0-4}	The roots and stumps of woody plants and their trunks, branches and twigs.	Can be vertically aligned or layered within sediment in growth position.
Detritus lignosus	Dl	Detrital fragments of wood and bark >2mm	Non-vertical or random alignment. May be laminated, not in growth position.
Detritus herbosus	Dh	Fragments of stems and leaves of herbaceous plants >2mm	Non-vertical or random alignment. May be laminated, not in growth position.
Detritus granosus	Dg	Woody and herbaceous humified plant remains <2mm >0.1mm that cannot be separated.	Non-vertical or random alignment. May be laminated, not in growth position.
Limus detrituosus	Ld^{0-4}	Fine detritus organic mud (particles <0.1mm).	Homogenous, non-plastic, often becomes darker on oxidation and will shrink on drying. Most colour shades.
Limus calcareus	Lc	Fine detritus calcium carbonate deposit, marl.	Homogenous, light, very easily crushed between the fingers.
Limus ferrugineus	Lf	Mineral and/or organic iron oxide	Forms mottled staining. Can be crushed between fingers. Often in root channels or surrounding Th.
Anthrax	anth.	Charcoal	Crunchy black fragments
Stratum confusum	Sc	Disturbed stratum	

Table 3.1 The notation for stratigraphical description according to Troels-Smith (1955) as used in this study.

the botanical terminology of Stace (1997), as suggested by Bennett *et al.* (1994), is shown in Appendix VII. Palaeobotanical diagrams have been constructed using the TILIA program of Grimm (1993).

3.1.3 Plant macrofossil analysis

Laboratory preparation of subsamples for macrofossil analysis involved disaggregation in cold water and washing through a nest of sieves ranging from 500–150 μm mesh

Degree of humification (superscript values applied to Th, Tb, Tl & Ld – see Table 3.1)	
0	Plant structure fresh. Yields colourless water on squeezing.
1	Plant structure well-preserved. Squeezing yields dark coloured water. 25% of deposit squeezes through fingers.
2	Plant structure partly decayed although distinct. Squeezing yields 50% deposit through fingers.
3	Plant structure decayed and indistinct. Squeezing yields 75% deposit through fingers.
4	Plant structure barely discernable or absent. 100% passes through fingers on squeezing.

		Nigror (degree of darkness)
	0	The shade of quartz sand
	1	The shade of calcareous clay
nig.	2	The shade of grey clay
	3	The shade of partly decomposed peat
	4	The shade of black, fully decomposed peat

		Stratificatio (degree of stratification)
	0	Complete heterogeneity: breaks equally in all directions
	1	Intermediate between 0 and 4
strf.	2	Intermediate between 0 and 4
	3	Intermediate between 0 and 4
	4	Very thin horizontal layers that split horizontally

		Elasticitas (degree of elasticity)
	0	Totally inelastic, plastic
	1	Intermediate between 0 and 4
elas.	2	Intermediate between 0 and 4
	3	Intermediate between 0 and 4
	4	Elastic

		Siccitas (degree of dryness)
	0	Clear water
	1	Thoroughly saturated, very wet
sicc.	2	Saturated
	3	Not saturated
	4	Air dry

		Limes superior (type of boundary)
	0	>1cm boundary area – *diffusus*
lim. sup.	1	<1cm and >2mm – *conspicuus*
	2	<2mm and >1mm – *manifestus*
	3	<1mm and >0.5mm – *acutus*
	4	<0.5mm

Table 3.2 Troels-Smith (1955) sediment characteristics, as used in stratigraphical description in this study.

size. Subsample volumes were consistent within each profile but varied from site to site, depending on the amount of material available in the cores and ranging from 50–150 ml. Analysis was at 10 cm intervals at Nosterfield SH1 and Newby Wiske, whereas intervals at Sharow ranged from 15 to 50 cm, as analysis was carried out on bulk samples collected in the field. The residues were scanned for plant macrofossils using a low-power binocular microscope and identification was made by comparison with modern reference material and manuals including Beijerinck (1947) and Katz *et al.* (1965). Taxonomic nomenclature follows Stace (1997). Additional wood remains, analysed by Rowena Gale, were prepared by standard methods (Gale & Cutler, 2000) and matched to reference slides of modern wood.

3.1.4 Malacology

Samples for molluscan analysis were dried at 40°C and washed through sieves to an aperture of 500 μm and then re-dried. The samples were sorted under a ×10–60 binocular microscope. The counting conventions follow Sparks (1961), with each bivalve shell counting as half an individual and each gastropod apex counting as a single individual. Opercula of *Bithynia tentaculata* are listed separately in the accompanying tables but are not included in the molluscan total. Shells of the late Holocene species *Cecilioides acicula*, which commonly burrows to 1.5 m depth (Evans, 1972; Kerney, 1999), are listed in the tables but not included in the molluscan totals. Taxonomic nomenclature follows Kerney (1999).

3.1.5 Entomology

Insect remains are abundant in sediments that have remained anoxic since their deposition, such as infillings of ancient ponds or wells, or in waterlogged archaeological contexts. Most of the identifiable remains are fragments of Coleoptera (beetles), which survive because of their robust exoskeletons. These can often be identified to species, even as far back in time as the early Quaternary. Because many individual species have precise ecological requirements, it is possible to use coleopteran fossils as indicators of past environments and particularly past climates. As well as the abundant beetles, remains of Trichoptera (caddis flies), Diptera (mostly Chironomidae) and Hymenoptera (including ants) were also recovered, but these have not been studied in detail. The reports in this chapter are generally concerned only with the Coleoptera.

Insect remains may easily be extracted from sediment samples using the now standard techniques (Coope, 1986). The extracted remains were then sorted from the paraffin flot and the sclerites identified under a low-power binocular microscope at x10 magnification. Where possible, the insect remains were identified by comparison with modern specimens from several collections, including the Gorham and Girling collections housed at the University of Birmingham. Taxonomy used for the Coleoptera (beetles) follows that of Lucht (1987); the habitats of the insects identified in this study are described in Table 3.3. Results are presented as tables within each appropriate site report, in most cases indicating presence/absence or frequency; for Ripon South, which has yielded by far the most detailed entomological evidence, actual counts are presented.

3.1.6 Geochronology

Dating control for the litho- and biostratigraphy was achieved primarily by AMS radiocarbon dating of small terrestrial macrofossils such as seeds, although some conventional radiometric analyses were made on large samples such as wood remains. Bulk sediment was never used for AMS dating. The methods for sampling and dating are explained in Appendix I, where tables and figures giving details of each dated sample are provided, including those few determinations that appear to be unacceptable on the grounds of incompatibility with the dated pollen zone stratigraphy established for northern England (e.g. Hibbert & West, 1976; Innes, 2002a, d). In these cases, contamination is assumed to be the cause, as discussed in Appendix I. Dates had to be obtained from levels where terrestrial macrofossils were available for dating, so their stratigraphical positions are not always optimal with respect to the palynology. Table 1 in Appendix I (see CD) presents all the dates completed as part of this project; both basic ^{14}C dates and calibrated dates, which are shown both as dates before present (BP) and, in some cases linked to archaeological data, as calendar years BC/AD (cf. Walker, 2005). The same protocol is used in the summary tables that are provided in this chapter for each dated site.

The use of the radiocarbon method to provide dating control for palaeoenvironmental reconstructions derived from pollen and plant macrofossil remains has a lengthy pedigree and is the established strategy in studies of past environmental change (e.g. Birks & Birks, 1980; Lowe & Walker, 1997a; Walker, 2005). Pollen analysis is also used as a relative dating technique to evaluate the accuracy of the radiocarbon dates. In northern England, the boundaries between major pollen assemblage zones have now been radiocarbon dated at considerable numbers of sites (Greig, 1996; Innes, 2002d). In the Lateglacial, early Holocene and the mid-Holocene up to the *Ulmus* decline (c. 5000 ^{14}C BP), when major changes in the dominant vegetation were caused primarily by climate, analogous features such as the immigration of particular trees were, although not fully synchronous, sufficiently similar in age to be regarded as biostratigraphical marker horizons in pollen diagrams on a regional or even national level (West, 1970; Hibbert & Switsur, 1976). Although local environmental factors such as soils, climate, topography and even human activity may cause differences in the timing and character of these changes, in broad terms such dated horizons allow correlation and comparison between sites (Smith & Pilcher, 1973). Events such as the *Corylus* pollen rise or the *Ulmus* pollen decline (elm decline) occurred at comparable times and so provide a good relative framework for regional chronological comparison. The radiocarbon dates have been used to assist correlation of these relative and absolute dating techniques.

Other dating methods employed in this research were optically stimulated luminescence (OSL), which was largely unsuccessful (see Chapter 2; Appendix II), and amino acid racemization (AAR) dating. The latter is a relative dating technique based on the alteration of amino acids within mollusc shell *post mortem*. It has been applied at four sites, using an enhanced methodology (Penkman, 2005; Penkman

Table 3.3 Habitats of the insects identified in this study (excepting the large assemblage from Ripon South).

Taxon	Habitat
Carabidae	
Dyschirius globosus	Moist ground in all types of country
Trechus spp.	Open semi-shaded country near water
?Bembidion varium (Olivier, 1795)	Sparsely vegetated clay substrates
Bembidion spp.	
Harpalus spp.	Dry, open country
Agonum thoreyi	Clay substrates with reeds and bulrushes
Agonum spp.	
Pterostichus spp.	
Gyrinidae	
Gyrinius spp.	Deep, open water
Dytiscidae	
Hydroporous spp.	Open ponds and pools
Graptodytes spp.	Swampy bogs and ponds
Illybius spp.	
Agabus spp.	
Colymbetes fuscus	Well vegetated standing waters
Hydraenidae	
Hydraena spp.	Muddy, ephemeral pools and water bodies
Octhebius spp.	Muddy, ephemeral pools and water bodies
Limnebius spp.	Muddy, ephemeral pools and water bodies
Helophorus spp.	Muddy, ephemeral pools and water bodies
Hydrophilidae	
Aquatic *Cercyon* spp.	Ponds and pools with rotting organic material
Cryptopleurum minutum (Fabricius)	In all kinds of decaying organic matter
Hydrobius fuscipes	Well vegetated standing waters
Cymbiodyta marginella (Fabricius)	Well vegetated standing waters
Staphylinidae	
Olophrum spp.	Swamps and bogs
Lesteva longelytrata (Goeze)	Damp watersides
Lesteva spp.	
Trogophloeus spp.	
Oxytelus rugosus (Fabricius)	In all kinds of decaying organic matter
Stenus spp.	
Philonthus spp.	
Lathrobium spp.	
Tachinus rufipes	In all kinds of decaying organic matter dung and carrion
Aleocharinae gen. & spp. Indet.	
Helodidae	
Helodidae gen & spp. indet	Muddy, ephemeral pools and water bodies
Dryopidae	
Dryops spp.	Muddy, ephemeral pools and water bodies
Esolus parallelepipedus (Müller)	Gravel and stones at the edges of lakes, pools and streams
Chrysomelidae	
Donacia versicolorea	*Potamogeton natans*
Plateumaris/Donacia spp.	Emergent aquatics, rushes, sedges and reeds.
Phylotreta spp.	
Curculionidae	
Apion spp.	Grassland
Sitona spp.	Grassland
Bagous spp.	Waterside plants
Tanysphyrus lemnae Payk.	Duckweed
Gymnetron spp.	Grassland
Baris spp.	Waterside plants
Ceutorhynchus spp.	Grassland

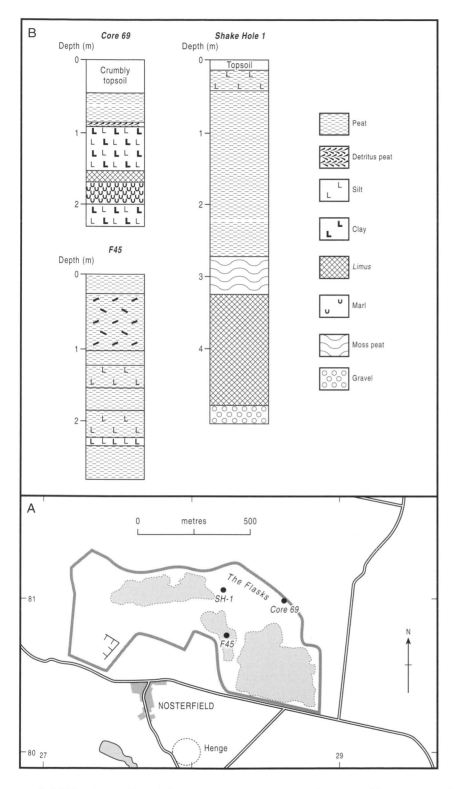

Fig. 3.1 Nosterfield: A – Location of the palaeoenvironmental sites F45, Flasks Shakehole SH1 and Flasks 69; B – Summary stratigraphical columns.

et al., 2008a; Appendix III) developed at the NEaar facility in York (see Chapter 1.1), which has provided particularly good data from samples of various ages (early Middle Pleistocene–Late Pleistocene) using the calcite opercula of the aquatic gastropod *Bithynia* (Penkman, 2005; Penkman *et al.*, in press). Although these common calcitic fossils have provided more consistent results than aragonite mollusc shells, they are not always present, so the technique has also been developed for dating shell (Penkman *et al.*, 2007);

shells were dated from just one of the Washlands sites, that at Sharow Mires (see below, section 3.5).

3.2 Nosterfield sites

Three sites have been investigated in the vicinity of Nosterfield village, in the central part of the Swale–Ure Washlands (Fig. 3.1). The area was chosen because it has

Unit	Depth (cm)	Description
10	0–14	Well-humified peat with small amounts of *detritus*, wood fragments, *turfa* and small stones Sh4, Dl+, Dh+, Th+, Gg(min)+, nig.4, strf.0, elas.0, sicc.3
9	14–50	Humified peat with Cyperaceae and vertical *Phragmites* stems Sh3, Dh1, Dl+, Th(*Phrag.*)+, nig.3, strf.0, elas.0, sicc.2, lim.sup.0
8	50–100	Well-humified amorphous and *detritus* peat with some wood fragments, small stones, silt and sand Sh3, Dh1, Ag+, Th(*Phrag.*)+, Dl+, Ga+, Gg(min)+, nig.4, strf.0, elas.0, sicc.2, lim.sup.0
7	100–119	Humified peat with wood fragments and some *detritus* and *turfa* Sh2, Dl2, Dh+, Th+, nig.3, strf.0, elas.0, sicc.2, lim.sup.0
6	119–129	Well-humified peat with some silt, *detritus*, wood fragments and *turfa* Sh4, Dl+, Dh+, Th+, Ag+, nig.3, strf.0, elas.0, sicc.2, lim.sup.0
5	129–166	Humified peat with silt lenses and some clay, sand, wood fragments, *detritus* and *turfa* Sh3, Ag1, As+, Dl+, Dh+, Th+, Ga+ nig.3, strf.1, elas.0, sicc.2, lim.sup.0
4	166–189	Well-humified peat with some *detritus*, *turfa*, wood fragments and small stones Sh4, Dh+, Th+, Ag+, Gg(min)+, nig.4, strf.0, elas.0, sicc.2, lim.sup.0
3	189–221	Peat with silt and some stones, sand, *detritus*, *turfa* and wood fragments Sh2, Ag2, Dl+, Dh+, Th+, Ga+, Gg(maj)+, nig.3, strf.0, elas.0, sicc.2, lim.sup.0
2	221–227	**Clayey** silt with sand and stones Ag3, As1, Ga+, Gg(maj)+, Dh+ (mica), nig.3, strf.0, elas.0, sicc.2, lim.sup.0
1	227–281	Well-humified peat with clayey silt bands, wood fragments, detrital reed stems, sand and stones. Wood fragments at 257-260 Sh4, Ag+, As+, Dl+, Dh+(*Phrag.*), Ga+, Gg(min+maj)+, nig.4, strf.0, elas.0, sicc.2, lim.sup.0

Table 3.4 Stratigraphy of Nosterfield Core F45 (after Long & Tipping, 1998)

been the location of large-scale sand and gravel extraction in recent years and lies close to the nationally important Neolithic Thornborough Henges and their associated archaeological landscape (Chapter 4). In addition to rescue work in advance of quarrying activity, the workings have provided sections yielding important information on the environmental context of the Thornborough archaeological complex. The three analysed sites lie to the north–east of Nosterfield village (Fig. 3.1). One of them, profile F45, was an archived sediment profile recovered as part of an earlier environmental assessment of the site by other workers (see below). At the other two sites, the Flasks Shakehole 1 and the Flasks Core 69, sediment profiles were recovered as part of the Swale–Ure Washlands project.

3.2.1 Nosterfield F45

Core F45 (SE 2850 8055) is from one of three deep infilled shafts discovered in 1998 in advance of aggregate extraction at Nosterfield (Fig. 3.1) that have had their sedimentary records examined previously (Long & Tipping, 1998). The deposits in the other two shafts, F44 and F46, were similar to F45 and so have not been studied as part of the current project. A third site, 'Find 14', also investigated by Long and Tipping and including peat above lake marl, was near to the Flasks Core 69 and so has not been studied further (although it was radiocarbon dated: see below). At first it

was thought that the shafts might be anthropogenic features but the dating of their sediments (Tipping, 2000) showed that they were natural, perhaps related to gypsum solution (see Chapter 1). Tipping (2000) obtained radiocarbon dates for all four sites (funded by Tarmac Ltd), including the top and base of the shaft sediments; details are included in Appendix I. The F45 sediment profile was collected during work by Field Archaeology Specialists of York University, as part of a programme of archaeological intervention under the overall direction of Dr. Mike Griffiths and sanctioned under a planning permission granted by North Yorkshire County Council. The stratigraphy of the core was discussed by Long and Tipping (1998), after which radiocarbon dates were obtained for the top and base of the sediments (Tipping, 2000), funded by Tarmac Ltd. The site was subsequently destroyed by quarrying.

3.2.1.1 Lithostratigraphy

The stratigraphy of this core (Table 3.4) indicates several phases of deposition under contrasting hydrological conditions. The various peat sediments that make up most of this sequence contain high proportions of detrital organic material, which probably indicate some standing water within the shaft or at least a very wet sediment surface. However, the consistent presence of *turfa* (which is peat composed of plant roots and stems: Table 3.1) within the sediment column suggests that any water covering the sediment was of minor, probably fluctuating depth. Minerogenic sediments, ranging in size from clay to gravel, occur at intervals and represent periodic flooding of varying intensity and the inwash of soil material, which may have included much organic detritus.

3.2.1.2 Pollen

Pollen subsamples were prepared from throughout the F45 core to its base at 280 cm, but pollen was not preserved below 136 cm. The pollen diagram (Fig. 3.2) has counts at four centimetre intervals from 136 to 4 cm below the ground surface. Despite the calcareous nature of the site, pollen was generally well preserved in the upper part of the core. The absence of pollen below 136 cm might result from a dry phase in the mid- to late Holocene, causing a fall in water table and the drying and oxidation of the sediments. The vegetation history for the lower part of the profile, shown by radiocarbon to have begun at the Lateglacial–Holocene transition, has therefore not been preserved (i.e. there is no pollen preservation, despite the survival of organic material for dating). From 136 cm upwards, however, there is a full pollen record from which to reconstruct vegetation history. The pollen diagram is subdivided into nine local pollen assemblage zones (F45a–F45i).

ZONE DESCRIPTIONS

Zone F45a (136–130 cm)
Pollen frequencies for *Betula* (birch), *Pinus* (pine) and *Alnus* (alder) are substantial in this basal zone, with lesser *Quercus* (oak) and negligible percentages for *Ulmus* and *Tilia* (lime). *Corylus* (hazel) shrub pollen is high at 30% of the total land sum, with *Salix* (willow) the only other significant shrub. Several open-ground herbs also appear in the pollen record; herbaceous pollen percentages are contributed mainly by Cyperaceae (sedges) and Poaceae (grasses), with significant lesser counts for *Filipendula* (meadowsweet), *Plantago lanceolata* (ribwort plantain) and *Taraxacum*-type (e.g. dandelion). Other herb types are represented only by very low counts. Filicales (undifferentiated Pteridophytes) frequencies are moderate and *Pteridium* (bracken) percentages rise at the end of the zone.

Zone F45b (130–122 cm)
Tree pollen frequencies are unchanged from the previous zone except for *Betula*, which falls markedly. A peak in *Corylus* percentages occurs late in the zone. Herbaceous types common in the previous zone change little, except for *Filipendula*, values of which are much reduced. A range of weed taxa appears, with *Artemisia* (mugwort), Chenopodiaceae (fat hen family) and Cruciferae

(charlock family) appearing, together with cereal-type pollen grains. Several other herb taxa also appear for the first time, such as *Silene*-type (e.g. campion) and *Potentilla*-type (e.g. cinquefoil), while there is a peak of *Plantago lanceolata*.

Zone F45c (122–102 cm)
Betula and *Corylus* percentages return to their F45a levels in this zone, as do those for most taxa. Cyperaceae and Poaceae values still dominate the herb pollen assemblage, but *Mentha*-type (mint) and Rosaceae (rose family) become prominent, with *P. lanceolata* and *Taraxacum*-type still consistently present. There are low levels of micro-charcoal.

Zone F45d (102–94 cm)
This zone sees a reduction in the frequency of *Alnus*, while *Corylus* also declines slightly, with little change otherwise. There are no peaks in herbaceous pollen except for a slight rise in *Taraxacum*-type. Cereal-type pollen is present throughout.

Zone F45e (94–74 cm)
Again there is modest change in this zone. *Betula* remains low and fluctuating and *Fraxinus* (ash) is significant for the first time. Several herbaceous taxa are present as before, but all in very low percentages. Umbelliferae (parsley family) show a slight increase. Cereal-type pollen is now absent

Zone F45f (74–66 cm)
Betula, *Pinus*, *Quercus* and *Corylus* percentages all fall sharply in this zone. Cereal-type pollen is recorded again and peaks occur in the frequencies of several weeds, mainly *Plantago lanceolata* and *Taraxacum*-type. *Plantago major-media* (great and hoary plantains) and *Silene*-type are significant. Extremely high frequencies of *Pteridium* (bracken) spores occur (this spore reaches almost 80% of total land pollen, although not counted in that total). Cyperaceae percentages are also greatly increased, reaching 50% of the total land sum. Low levels of micro-charcoal are also recorded.

Zone F45g (66–50 cm)
Woodland trees return to dominance in this zone, with *Alnus* particularly increased. The previously unimportant woody taxa *Tilia* and *Salix* also increase at this time. Herbaceous pollen frequencies are reduced to their lowest values on the diagram, with their diversity also reduced.

Zone F45h (50–38 cm)
Frequencies of most tree types decline through this zone; first *Betula* then *Pinus*, *Tilia* and *Alnus* falling in turn, although *Alnus* achieves its highest values on the diagram before its decline. *Fraxinus*

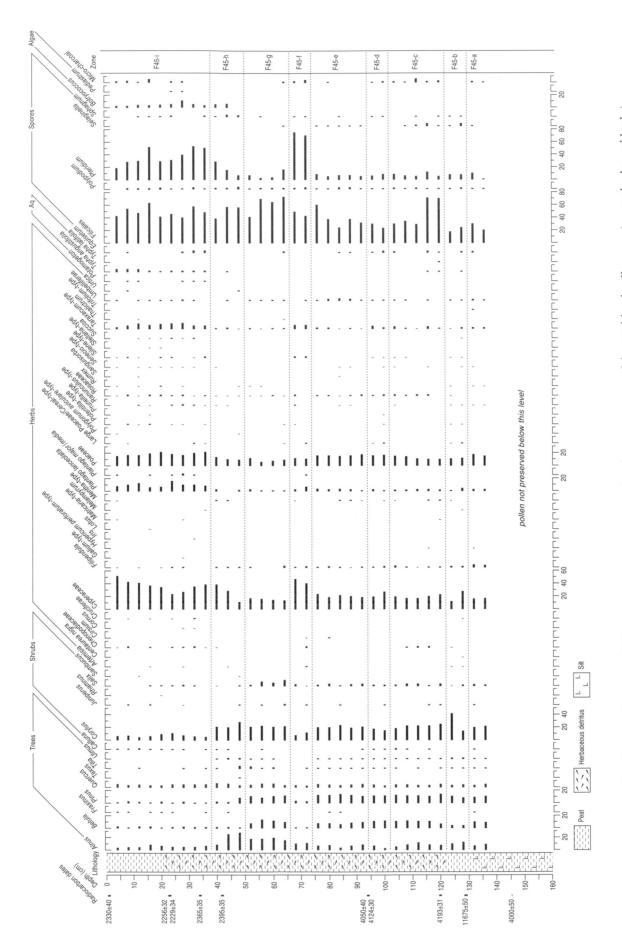

Fig. 3.2 Pollen diagram from Nosterfield F45. Frequencies are calculated as percentages of the total land pollen sum (trees, shrubs and herbs).

is present in just one level. *Corylus* maintains high percentages although *Salix* falls sharply. Cyperaceae and *Pteridium* frequencies gradually increase through the zone. Other herbaceous pollen types are sparsely represented, *Plantago lanceolata* even ceasing to be recorded at one level. *Sphagnum* (bog moss) spores and *Botryococcus* alga frequencies rise.

Zone F45i (38–4 cm)

In this uppermost zone values of woody taxa continue to decline as *Corylus*, the only tree or shrub type remaining at high frequencies, falls sharply. Cereal-type pollen is recorded at the start of the zone and major increases in the curves for *Plantago lanceolata* and *Taraxacum*-type occur. *Pteridium* frequencies are also greatly increased and sustained. Although cereal-type pollen is not present in most levels in the zone, a much greater range of weeds of open ground occurs throughout, including *Plantago major-media*, Chenopodiaceae, *Senecio* (ragwort)-type, *Succisa* (devil's-bit scabious) and *Polygonum aviculare* (knotgrass). The Cyperaceae and *Typha angustifolia* (lesser reedmace) curves rise. Micro-charcoal becomes common late in the zone.

3.2.1.3 Chronology

In addition to the two dates presented by Tipping (2000), nine AMS dates were obtained during the present project, thus totalling eleven dates providing a chronology for the environmental history (Table 3.5; Fig. 3.2). The dates from this profile form a broadly consistent chronological series, although there are age inversions between individual adjacent dates (although the dates in question overlap at the 95% confidence level; cf. Appendix I, Table 1). The exception is OxA-13530, from zone F45b, which gives a Lateglacial age of 11,675 ± 50 ^{14}C BP and is clearly in error by several thousand years; the charred wood that provided this date was probably reworked (see Appendix I). The other dates provide a chronology from mid-Neolithic to late Iron Age. The profile thus forms a valuable record of local prehistoric vegetation change near to the major Thornborough archaeological monuments and their hinterland. The very low *Ulmus* frequencies at 136 cm and the presence of cereal-type pollen just above this suggest, in combination, that all the countable levels post-date the elm decline (*c.* 5000 ^{14}C BP). This has been confirmed by the AMS dating at 140 and 125 cm, which shows the early part of the pollen profile to have formed around 4000 ^{14}C BP. Although there is a small reversal between these two dates, they constrain the vegetation disturbance at this level to the late Neolithic or early Bronze Age.

The end of the disturbance in zone F45d is also dated around 4000 ^{14}C BP, implying very rapid deposition in this part of the profile, unless the dates, which are on wood or

bark, are all from reworked material of similar age. The radiocarbon dates from 42 cm upwards are in sequence between *c.* 2400 ^{14}C BP and *c.* 2200 ^{14}C BP, except for the surface date, which shows a minor inversion (Fig. 3.2). These dates, however, support the age of the pollen changes in zone F45h as corresponding with the major mid-3rd Millennium BP climatic deterioration, which caused greatly increased wetness and mire growth across north-west Europe (van Geel *et al.*, 1996; van Geel & Renssen, 1998). The dates also allocate the agricultural activity and dominance of open habitat vegetation in zone F45i to the Iron Age. By interpolation the major but temporary clearance episode of zone F45f is likely to have occurred during the Bronze Age, before *c.* 3000 ^{14}C BP.

3.2.1.4 Synthesis: Nosterfield F45

The low *Ulmus* pollen frequencies from the base of the pollen stratigraphy onwards suggest a post-elm-decline, later Holocene date after *c.* 5000 ^{14}C BP for the whole of the profile. At the level above which pollen is preserved, the local landscape seems to have been well wooded, with a substantial cover of trees including *Alnus*, *Betula*, *Pinus* and *Quercus*, and shrubs including *Corylus*. The significant levels of Cyperaceae and Poaceae are probably associated with local wetland vegetation on or at the edge of the site. The low levels of grassland weeds, such as *Plantago lanceolata* and *Taraxacum*-type, are associated with open areas within the woodland. Zone F45b records a phase of human activity close to the site as cereal-type pollen grains occur together with cultivation weeds like *Artemisia*, Chenopodiaceae and Cruciferae. Several other open-ground herbs also appear in the pollen record, including a peak of *Plantago lanceolata*. A phase of arable farming, either at low intensity or not closely adjacent to the site, seems to be reflected here, as other tree taxa are unaffected. Zone F45c records an increase in woodland, with no indications of renewed disturbance, although the continuing presence of weed types *Plantago lanceolata* and Chenopodiaceae suggests that open areas remained around the site. In Zone F45d cereal-type pollen points to renewed agricultural activity; however, no major reduction of woodland cover occurred, suggesting that this activity was either small-scale or at some distance from the site. In zone F45e there are no indications of woodland disturbance. Some grassland areas persisted within the open woodland community, revealed by the persistent record of open-habitat weeds. Herbs such as *Mentha*-type and *Filipendula* will have been associated with the wetter areas on the site.

In Zone F45f there was a substantial reduction in woodland cover. The extremely high frequencies of *Pteridium* spores and the fall of all tree frequencies except *Alnus* point to a removal of trees on the dryland areas around the site. Forest clearance may have encouraged land drainage into the small wetland, increasing mire surface wetness and sedge growth. Micro-charcoal increases may indicate the use of fire in the land clearance, although the

Beta-143452 2330 ± 40 ^{14}C BP (2430–2310 cal. BP; 480–360 cal. BC)	

This date is from the top of the profile and provides an age for the most recent surviving sediments. It suggests a late Iron Age date for this infill and is indistinguishable from the dates below it in the profile, suggesting very rapid accumulation of sediment in this period and perhaps bulk influx of material rather than gradual accumulation.

OxA-13558 2256 ± 32 ^{14}C BP (2350–2150 cal. BP; 400–200 cal. BC)	

This date provides an age for the upper part of the upper peat profile in this basin. The date suggests a late Iron Age date for this infill. The very low tree pollen frequencies and high indicators of grassland conditions would be compatible with such a late prehistoric age. The date is similar to a date for the top of the profile obtained by Tipping (2000) of 2330 ± 40 BP. High Cyperaceae and other wetland herbs would conform to conditions of wet and cold climate in the later Iron Age.

OxA-13559 2229 ± 34 ^{14}C BP (2340–2140 cal. BP; 390–190 cal. BC)	

This date is from a level immediately below that of date OxA-13558 and is almost indistinguishable from it. It confirms that date as accurate and shows the local Cyperaceae, Poaceae and *Pteridium* vegetation to be late Iron Age in date. Human activity and climatic deterioration at this time are compatible with the pollen evidence.

GrA-25299 2365 ± 35 ^{14}C BP (2470–2330 cal. BP; 520–380 cal. BC)	

This date provides an age for the final fall of woodland pollen, represented by *Corylus*, and establishment of open wet grassland vegetation dominated by Cyperaceae, Poaceae, *Plantago lanceolata* and *Pteridium*. The date indicates that this change took place during the late Iron Age. The vegetation change is compatible with environmental conditions at that time.

GrA-25300 2395 ± 35 ^{14}C BP (2690–2340 cal. BP; 740–390 cal. BC)	

This date provides an age for the fall of most types of woodland pollen, particularly *Alnus* and the start of the establishment of open wet grassland vegetation dominated by Cyperaceae, Poaceae, *Plantago lanceolata* and *Pteridium*. The date indicates that this change took place during the late Iron Age. The vegetation change is compatible with environmental conditions at that time.

GrA-25301 4050 ± 40 ^{14}C BP (4790–4420 cal. BP; 2840–2470 cal. BC)	

This date provides an age for mid-profile dominance of woodland vegetation, particularly *Pinus*, *Betula* and *Corylus*. Non-arboreal pollen types are low and very few agricultural indicators are present. *Ulmus* frequencies are low and the pollen assemblage is compatible with this date in the late Neolithic.

OxA-13494 4124 ± 30 ^{14}C BP (4830–4520 cal. BP; 2880–2570 cal. BC)	

This date provides another age estimate from the same level as date OxA-25301 and confirms it as an accurate age for this post elm decline woodland phase. The pollen assemblage is compatible with this late Neolithic date.

OxA-13530 11,675 ± 50 ^{14}C BP (13,690–13,380 cal. BP; 11,740–11,430 cal. BC)	

This date was intended to provide an age for a decline in *Betula* frequencies and the first record of cereal-type pollen, near the base of the polleniferous profile. The Lateglacial date is clearly far too old to be acceptable for the pollen data and this date must therefore be considered unreliable.

OxA-13553 4193 ± 31 ^{14}C BP (4850–4570 cal. BP; 2900–2620 cal. BC)	

This date provides an age for levels soon after the decline in *Betula* pollen and the first presence of cereal-type pollen which sample OxA-13530 was intended to date. The small scale disturbance of the woodland for cultivation would appear to have taken place in mid-Neolithic times not long before the woodland regeneration phase at the level of this date. The pollen assemblage is compatible with such a date for this activity.

GrA-25355 4000 ± 50 ^{14}C BP (4780–4300 cal. BP; 2830–2350 cal. BC)	

This date provides an age for the upper part of the non-polleniferous profile. There are therefore no pollen data with which to test this date. It lies twenty-five centimetres below the level of OxA-13553, however, which at 4193 ± 31BP is similar in age. The ages are inverted, however, and it seems that this date of 4000 ± 50BP is too young, although not excessively so. It broadly confirms this section of the profile as Neolithic in age, but beyond that is unreliable.

Beta-143456 10,180 ± 60 14C BP (12,090–11,610 cal. BP; 10,140–9660 cal. BC)	

This date provides an age for the base of the profile, indicating that sediment accumulation started at the Lateglacial to Holocene transition. The lack of pollen preservation in the lower part of the profile prevents pollen stratigraphical confirmation of the date.

Table 3.5 Evaluation of radiocarbon dates from Nosterfield Core F45. The Beta dates were provided by Tipping (2000).

records are generally sporadic and not always associated with disturbance phases. In zone F45g, full regeneration of tree cover occurred, with peak *Salix* values indicating an extension of local wetland habitats and marshy ground after the previous phase of agricultural activity and clearance.

In the succeeding phase F45h, dryland trees were greatly reduced, although indicators of agriculture are not significantly increased. There are no cereal-type grains to indicate cultivation and the percentages of pasture or grassland herbs are reduced. The rise in Cyperaceae percentages, allied to increases in *Sphagnum* and *Botryococcus* algae, suggests increased wetness. This is supported by continued high frequencies of the wetland tree *Alnus* at a time when most dryland trees and shrubs suffered major reductions. In the absence of indicators of agricultural clearance, climatic change may have been responsible for the general forest decline. Hydrological changes on the mire surface may have increased the pollen representation of wetland plants, mainly Cyperaceae, and so suppressed tree pollen values further.

The final phase, F45i, represents a time of greatly increased forest clearance and agriculture. Cereal-type pollen is recorded at the start of the zone and major increases in *Plantago lanceolata* and *Taraxacum*-type occur, symptomatic of renewed human agriculture as the cause of this increased clearance. *Plantago major-media* and *Polygonum aviculare* (knotgrass) indicate more arable cultivation with increased areas supporting grassland/ pasture. The considerable diversity of weeds of open or cultivated ground, such as Chenopodiaceae, *Ranunculus* (buttercup-type), *Silene*-type (campion) and *Rumex* (dock), suggests a much higher scale and intensity of land use in this phase. The consistent curves for *Typha angustifolia* (lesser reedmace) and *Botryococcus* indicate that the trend towards increased wetness continued.

In conclusion, there are four phases in this sequence that are characterized by degrees of woodland disturbance. Zones a, c, e, g, and h represent periods during which human disturbance pressure on the vegetation was low or non-existent. Zones b, d, f, and i represent periods with higher levels of disturbance activity, with pollen records of agricultural indicators suggesting that anthropgenic land-use was instrumental in the opening and then eventual removal of woodland. The radiocarbon dating (Table 3.5) is inconclusive but suggests Bronze Age dates for the earlier phases of disturbance: b, d, and f. The radiocarbon date for the end of zone F45h suggests that the short-lived but major climatic deterioration of the early 3rd Millennium BP (van Geel *et al.*, 1996) may have been responsible for an expansion of wetland communities and any associated woodland recession. Zone F45i records major agricultural activity and forest clearance, the radiocarbon dates for this period indicating a correlation with the Iron Age.

3.2.2 The Flasks, Shakehole 1 (SH1)

The area known as the Flasks (Fig. 3.1), which lies in

Unit	Depth (cm)	Description
6	0–11	Topsoil *Stratum confusum*
5	11–40	Crumbly organic silty peat with occasional wood Sh3, Ag1, Dl+, nig.3, strf.0, elas.0, sicc.2, lim.sup.0
4	40–285	Well humified peat; increasingly woody at depth. Occasional iron staining Sh4, Dl+, Fe+, nig.3, strf.0, elas.0, sicc.2, lim.sup.0
3	285–330	Moss peat Tb4, nig.3, strf.0, elas.0, sicc.2, lim.sup.0
2	330–491	Grey brown *limus* Ld^{3}4, nig.2+, strf.0, elas.0, sicc.2, lim.sup.0
1	491–500	Gravel Gg(maj) 4, nig.2+, strf.0, elas.0, sicc.2, lim.sup.0

Table 3.6 Stratigraphy at Nosterfield, the Flasks, Shakehole SH1

the north-eastern part of the gravel quarry at Nosterfield, contains several deep, steep-sided shafts. These are analogous to those discovered elsewhere at the site, such as F45 (reported above), and are probably of the same origin, perhaps having formed as gypsum-karst features (see above, 3.2.1). One of these depressions, termed Shakehole 1 (SE 2815 8070), was chosen for detailed analysis after manual augering (Plate 3.1a) showed that it contained deep organic sediments.

3.2.2.1 Lithostratigraphy

Beneath a thin topsoil cover, the centre of the depression, which was <10 metres in diameter, was found to contain five metres of organic deposits overlying gravel. The lowest organic unit comprised limnic sediments, which graded upwards through moss peats into a well-humified peat that contained wood and occasional silty inclusions. The detailed stratigraphy of the sampled core is shown in Table 3.6.

3.2.2.2 Pollen

Samples for pollen analysis were prepared throughout the organic sequence at five centimetre intervals. Preservation was generally good, although some sections were poor and a few levels failed to yield countable pollen. The results of the analysis are shown in Figure 3.3, which is sub-divided into five local pollen assemblage zones.

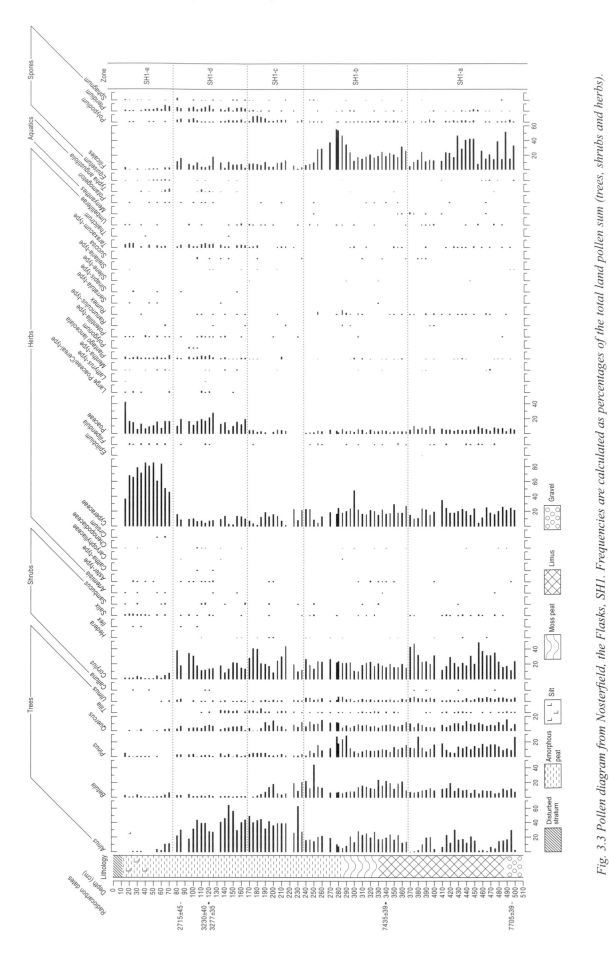

Fig. 3.3 Pollen diagram from Nosterfield, the Flasks, SH1. Frequencies are calculated as percentages of the total land pollen sum (trees, shrubs and herbs).

ZONE DESCRIPTIONS

Zone SH1-a (500–367.5 cm)

This basal zone is characterized by generally high but fluctuating percentages of *Corylus*. *Alnus* rises to replace *Corylus* at levels where frequencies of the latter decline. There are substantial frequencies of *Pinus*, *Betula* and *Quercus*, with lower but consistent percentages for *Ulmus*. The assemblage is dominated by tree and shrub pollen. Cyperaceae consistently account for 25% of total pollen and Poaceae are the only other significant contributor, although there are sporadic records of a wide range of herb types, of which *Rumex* and *Taraxacum*-type are most prominent.

Zone SH1-b (367.5–237.5 cm)

Corylus frequencies decline sharply from their peak at the end of the previous zone, while *Alnus* becomes consistently present at higher values. *Quercus*, *Pinus* and *Betula* are consistently recorded at moderate percentages. *Ulmus* values are low but recover towards the end of the zone. Little herb pollen occurs and, amongst this, only Cyperaceae at moderate percentages.

Zone SH1-c (237.5–182.5 cm)

In this zone *Alnus* rises from moderate to high frequencies and *Pinus* falls sharply to low values. *Ulmus* declines from about 5% of total pollen to very low percentages indeed. All other pollen types remain unchanged, with only Cyperaceae present at significant percentages.

Zone SH1-d (182.5–75 cm)

Alnus remains abundant but *Corylus* frequencies are much reduced from their previous peak and *Betula*, already declining in the previous zone, falls to very low values. *Quercus* also declines, whereas *Tilia* rises late in the zone. Poaceae frequencies rise sharply and consistent curves for *Plantago lanceolata*, *Taraxacum*-type and *Pteridium* begin. *Tilia* frequencies fall sharply in mid-zone, when *P. lanceolata* and *Taraxacum*-type frequencies rise and cereal-type pollen is consistently recorded.

Zone SH1-e (75–0 cm)

In this zone Cyperaceae frequencies rise very sharply to over 80% of total pollen. All tree and shrub pollen percentages fall to very low values indeed, with *Ulmus* hardly recorded, although there is some recovery of *Salix*. *Alnus* declines to very low values. A wide range of dryland herbs is recorded, with Poaceae, *P. lanceolata* and *Taraxacum*-type important. Cereal-type pollen is still recorded. *Pteridium* becomes less well represented after a peak early in the zone. Aquatic taxa, especially *Typha angustifolia*, rise in frequency.

3.2.2.3 Plant macrofossils

The plant remains recorded from the shake hole core SH1 are presented in Figure 3.4, which has been divided into four local plant macrofossil assemblage zones (SH1m-1 to SH1m-4). Macrofossils were poorly preserved in the top 1.5 metres of the core, particularly from *c.* 70 cm to the surface (Fig. 3.4).

ZONE DESCRIPTIONS

Zone 1 SH1m-1 (500–340 cm)

The macrofossil assemblage of SH1m-1 is dominated by *Juncus* spp. (rushes), Musci sp(p). (mosses) and *Menyanthes trifoliata* (bog-bean). Macrofossil remains of the aquatic taxa *Chara* sp(p). (stonewort) and *Potamogeton coloratus* (fen pondweed) are also frequent. Low numbers of woodland remains were recorded, including fruit of *Betula* sp(p). (birch) and *Alnus glutinosa*. A few wood and charcoal fragments are present, together with occasional sclerotia of the soil fungus *Cenococcum geophilum*.

Zone SH1m-2 (340–290 cm)

There are slight decreases in the number of aquatic remains in this zone, whereas macrofossils of *Menyanthes trifoliata*, *Carex* sp(p). and *Musci* sp(p). increase. *Betula* sp(p). fruits are present and an increase in the number of fragments of wood is recorded towards the end of the zone.

Zone SH1m-3 (290–155 cm)

Betula sp(p). fruits and wood fragments are abundant in SH1m-3. Fruits and a female cone of *Alnus glutinosa* were also encountered. Macrofossils of *Chara* sp(p). and *Potamogeton coloratus* form a significant part of the assemblage, which also includes remains of the waterside and damp ground taxa *Eupatorium cannabinum* (hemp-agrimony), *Lychnis flos-cuculi* (ragged-robin) and *Menyanthes trifoliata*. Pteridophyte sp(p). sporangia and nutlets of *Carex* sp(p). are frequent.

Zone SH1m-4 (155–0 cm; subdivided at 100 cm)

Fragments of wood are abundant in SH1m-4a but decline sharply in SH1m-4b. Macrofossils of waterside and aquatic taxa, recorded sporadically through the zone, include *Mentha* cf. *aquatica* (water mint), *Menyanthes trifoliata*, *Persicaria lapathifolia* (pale persicaria), *Chara* sp(p). and *Ranunculus* subgenus *Ranunculus*. Seeds of *Juncus* spp. and fruit stones of *Rubus idaeus* (raspberry) occur and achenes of *Urtica dioica* (common nettle) are abundant towards the top of the core. A few small fragments of charcoal were found in SH1m-4b.

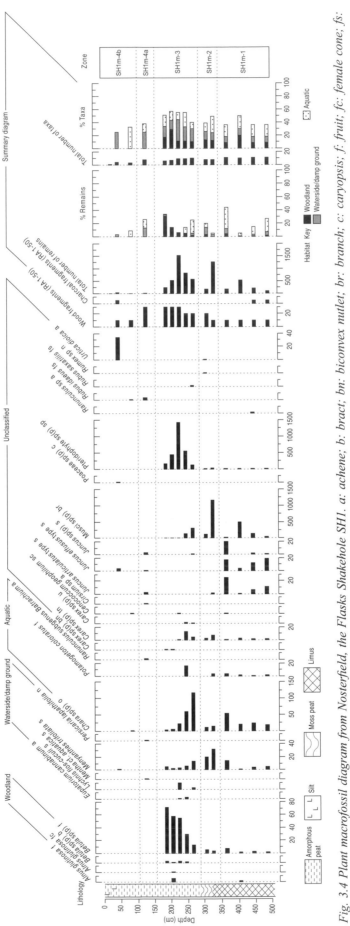

Fig. 3.4 Plant macrofossil diagram from Nosterfield, the Flasks Shakehole SH1. a: achene; b: bract; bn: biconvex nutlet; br: branch; c: caryopsis; f: fruit; fc: female cone; fs: fruitstone; n: nutlet; o: oosporangium; s: seed; sc: sclerotium; sp: sporangium; tn: triogonous nutlet; u: utricle.

Preservation Viable sclerites Comments	V. poor Yes Frag.	Poor Yes Frag.	Poor Yes	No	Poor Yes Frag.	Poor Yes Frag.	Poor Yes Frag.	Poor Yes Frag.	Poor Yes Frag.	Poor Yes Frag.	No	Poor Yes	Poor Yes
Sample depth (cm)	20–30	40–50	120–130	180–190	220–203	240–250	260–270	300–310	320–330	360–370	400–410	440–450	480–492
Carabidae													
Harpalus spp.			*										
Pterostichus spp.								*					
Dytiscidae													
Agabus spp.												*	
Hydraenidae													
Helophorus spp.						*							
Hydrophilidae													
Cymbiodyta marginella									*				
Staphylinidae													
Lathrobium spp.										*			
Helodidae													
Helodidae gen & spp. indet					*		*						
Chrysomelidae													
Plateumaris/Donacia spp.		*	*										
Curculionidae													
Sitona spp.	*												
Baris spp.							*						*

Table 3.7 Insects from Nosterfield, the Flasks, Shakehole SH1. Note: Frag = fragmentary

3.2.2.4 Insects

Sclerites (hardened body parts) from this core were consistently poorly preserved and highly fragmentary but, nevertheless, the majority of samples contained interpretable material (Table 3.7). At the base of the core (4.92–3.2 m), the taxa are indicative of relatively deep, open water; both the predatory dytiscid *Agabus* spp. and the hydrophilid *Cymbiodyta marginella* are found in permanent water bodies (Hansen, 1987; Nilsson & Holmen, 1995). These taxa are replaced in the upper part of the core by others associated with bogs and marshes, such as the Chyrsomelidae families, e.g. *Plateumaris* spp. and *Donacia* spp. (Menzies & Cox, 1996). Species associated with open water are absent, whereas further hygrophilous taxa, such as the hydraenid *Helophorus* spp., are associated with muddy, ephemeral, possibly seasonal pools (Hansen, 1987). Also worthy of note is the xerophilous family of Carabidae, represented by *Harpalus* spp., and the curculionid family, in the form of *Sitona* spp. The former is found on open, sandy substrates, whereas the latter is found on leguminous plants in dry meadows and grassland (Lindroth, 1974; Koch, 1992).

3.2.2.5 Chronology

The dates from the SH1 profile form a consistent series and may be accepted as providing a reliable chronology for the profile (Table 3.8). The lower dates seem rather old given their relation to the *Alnus* pollen curve, which usually increases around 7000 ^{14}C BP in Britain. However, there is considerable variation in the age of the '*Alnus* rise' in lowland northern England and the two lower dates are acceptable, as similar ages have been reported from North Yorkshire (Innes, 2002d). The two uppermost dates are highly compatible with their pollen stratigraphical context and can be readily accepted. The association of the upper date with evidence of a major climatic shift to increased wetness is supported by several similar dates for this change elsewhere in northern England.

3.2.2.6 Synthesis: the Flasks (Nosterfield), SH1

Organic sedimentation began in the SH1 shaft in a small calcareous pool <1 m in depth (cf. Preston, 1995), as is indicated by the occurrence of *Chara* sp(p). and *Potamogeton coloratus* macrofossils at the base of the profile. Macrofossil remains of *Juncus* species and *Menyanthes trifoliata* indicate that these plants would have grown in and around the edges of the water, an interpretation strongly supported by the insect evidence, which is suggestive of relatively deep, open pools fringed by a rich, emergent herbaceous community. Most insect taxa recorded from this profile are indicators of wetland habitats and so are associated with the peat-forming vegetation and environments at the site. The pollen data

GrA-24566	2715 ± 45 ^{14}C BP (2930–2750 cal. BP; 980–800 cal. BC)

This date provides an age for a major vegetation change from an at least partially wooded local landscape to one completely dominated by non-tree taxa. The date falls around the Bronze Age to Iron Age transition and there are enough pollen indicators of agricultural activity to suggest that farming contributed to the change. Cyperaceae provide most of the increase in herbaceous pollen, however, and a major climatic shift to wetter conditions which occurred throughout north- west Europe at this time was probably responsible. The date is typical for the age of this climatic change recorded in peat profiles in northern England and beyond.

GrA-25048	3230 ± 40 ^{14}C BP (3560–3370 cal. BP; 1610–1420 cal. BC)

This date provides an age for a phase of increased agricultural activity with peak pollen frequencies for cereal-type, *Plantago lanceolata* and other weeds of cultivation and pasture. A decline in woodland cover also occurs. The date shows these vegetation changes to have taken place in the later Bronze Age, an acceptable time for the agricultural activity recorded, and the date is considered reliable.

OxA-13225	3277 ± 35 ^{14}C BP (3830–3580 cal. BP; 1880–1630 cal. BC)

This date provides an age for the phase of increased agricultural activity with peaks in pollen indicators of cultivation and pasture. It is from the same level as date OxA-25048 and is almost the same age, providing confirmation of the Bronze Age date for the expansion in farming shown in the pollen data.

OxA-13104	7435 ± 39 ^{14}C BP (8370–8170 cal. BP; 6420–6220 cal. BC)

This date provides an age for the major lithological change from limnic mud to moss peat which occurred as part of the hydrological succession. *Ulmus* pollen frequencies are relatively low but there are no indicators of vegetation disturbance due to human activity and it is probable that a mid-Holocene age is correct. *Alnus* values are high and the date seems rather old but the date of the *Alnus* rise varies considerably due to local conditions and this date is not unacceptable.

OxA-13012	7705 ± 39 ^{14}C BP (8590–8410 cal. BP; 6640–6460 cal. BC)

This date provides an age for the start of peat formation within the depression. The mid-Holocene mixed deciduous forest trees dominate the pre-*Ulmus* decline pollen assemblage and so the date is acceptable in relation to the pollen data. Substantial *Alnus* frequencies at this level suggest an age younger than the rise of *Alnus* pollen which usually is dated to around 7000 ^{14}C BP in lowland northern England. This date seems therefore rather old, but there is considerable variation in the dating of the *Alnus* rise and so the date is likely to be reliable.

Table 3.8 Evaluation of radiocarbon dates from Nosterfield, the Flasks, Shakehole SH1

indicate a mid-Holocene age for the start of deposition, as the full suite of deciduous forest trees was present, with considerable frequencies of *Ulmus* indicating a date before the regional mid-Holocene elm decline at around 5000 ^{14}C BP. A few *Betula* macrofossils occur, showing that either birch woodland grew at some distance from the site or a few trees grew more locally. The presence of wood fragments in the sediment, unfortunately not identifiable, suggests the latter.

No *Alnus* macrofossils were recorded in the basal sediment, but substantial *Alnus* pollen frequencies indicate that alder grew nearby, suggesting an age after *c.* 7000 ^{14}C BP for the start of organic sediment accumulation, in accordance with the general post-glacial vegetation history for northern England (Innes, 2002d). Dates for the 'rational limit' of *Alnus* pollen (i.e., its rise to consistently high values) vary considerably, however, and the radiocarbon date for the base of the organic profile of 7705 ± 39 ^{14}C BP (Table 3.8), although very early, is not without precedent. Similar dates of around 7700 ^{14}C BP have been reported from lowland sites in north Yorkshire (Innes, 2002d; see Chapter 5.4.3), so this is an acceptable age for the early presence of alder at Nosterfield. The basal counted level

has very low *Alnus* and high *Pinus*, yet the next has the opposite. Given the basal radiocarbon date, it is conceivable that the transition between these two horizons represents the first rise of *Alnus* pollen to high values. *Alnus* percentages fluctuate considerably over the next metre of the profile, however, due to relative increases in the frequency of other tree and shrub taxa. It may well be that the basal rise of alder at this site is merely another such fluctuation, with the real early mid-Holocene alder rise having occurred before the start of the pollen record. The persistence of *Pinus* throughout the lower half of the profile also makes woodland evolution during this period difficult to interpret. Because of the radiocarbon date of 7435 ± 39 BP at 338cm, it appears that the bottom metre of sediment accumulated very rapidly over a short period of only a few hundred years, before the regional pine decline but while early alder populations were established near the site. Macrofossil wood of *Alnus* at 400 cm, midway between the two dated levels, proves its presence locally at an early date. Very rapid sedimentation within the water-filled shaft over a period of a few hundred years before 7000 ^{14}C BP could thus be an explanation of the behaviour of the pine and alder curves.

The fluctuations in the *Alnus* curve during this time, with temporary falls to virtual absence, could have been due to brief phases of drier climate or to periods of disturbance, with *Corylus* temporarily replacing *Alnus* in at least three phases. Human impact seems a likely cause, but there is no microfossil charcoal recorded here or in the rest of the diagram, although some of the levels in which alder wood fragments are common contain large pieces of charcoal. Similarly, there is no synchrony between the alder pollen troughs and herbaceous indicators of open conditions (like *Plantago lanceolata*, *Rumex* and *Taraxacum*-type), although these are present sporadically. Hazel must have been naturally very common on the calcareous soils around this site and the periodic rises in its pollen may be a relative effect, perhaps caused by declines in alder populations for edaphic or hydrological reasons. If the *Alnus* pollen was being contributed by a small population of very local trees, any recurring natural event such as individual tree senescence or storm damage could have caused such pollen fluctuations.

A real change seems to have occurred at the start of zone SH1-b, with the reduction of *Corylus* pollen frequencies to moderate values. When a further *Alnus* pollen trough occurs in mid zone, it is *Pinus* that replaces it, showing that populations of pine must have persisted near this shakehole at around 7000 ^{14}C BP, assuming that the dating is correct. Again, there is no clear evidence of anthropogenic or natural disturbance or of any increase in open ground locally. Hydrological changes may have been responsible and it is interesting that this temporary alder decline coincides with the end of the moss peat layer that signifies 'terrestrialization' of the wetland surface in the shaft itself, a process that started about 7435 ^{14}C BP. Some instability of the wetland system at this time may have temporarily disadvantaged *Alnus*. *Pinus* persisted as a significant member of the woodland community until about the 340 cm level, above which it declines to permanently low values that probably mean only a regional pollen signal. The same applies to *Ulmus* at the end of pollen zone SH1-b and it is likely that this slump in *Ulmus* representation is the regionally important elm decline of about 5000 ^{14}C BP. Unfortunately no appropriate macrofossils were present from which this level could be radiocarbon dated, but interpolation between the two dated levels at 340 and 120 cm produces a date for this *Ulmus* decline of *c*. 5200 ^{14}C BP. More regular sediment accumulation rates after terrestrialization of the wetland surface seems likely, which would make an age of around 5000 ^{14}C BP, the generally accepted mean date of the elm decline (Parker *et al.*, 2000), a reasonable estimate. The absence of any indications of woodland clearance and human activity at this time does not necessarily argue against this interpretation, as such indicators are not always present at securely dated elm decline horizons (Innes, 2002d). Plant macrofossils show that during this stage fen, dominated by *Menyanthes trifoliata* and *Carex* sp(p)., with abundant Musci sp(p). had developed at the site itself.

Above the probable elm-decline level there is some discrepancy between the pollen and macrofossil data, as *Betula* dominates the macrofossil assemblage and suggests that local woodland may have been largely birch (probably *B. pubescens* due to its tolerance of wet conditions), with *Alnus* present but confined to wetter locations. The pollen data, however, indicate that *Alnus* became the dominant tree, with *Corylus* the only other type present in quantity, *Betula* percentages being relatively low. The two types of botanical evidence are difficult to reconcile but presumably reflect the differences between on-site (macrofossils) and more distant (pollen) source areas. Unfortunately evidence of this area of local woodland is absent from the coleopteran record. The identification of alder woodland in the palaeoenvironmental record using entomological data is in any case problematic, as has been discussed by a number of authors, including Girling (1985), Robinson (1993), Smith *et al.* (2000) and Smith and Whitehouse (2005a, b). Plant macrofossil evidence shows that Pteridophyte sp(p)., *Carex* sp(p). and damp ground herbs formed the understorey of this local woodland. Calcareous pools supporting *Chara* sp(p). and *Potamogeton coloratus* were also present, with *Eupatorium cannabinum*, *Lychnis flos-cuculi* and *Menyanthes trifoliata* growing at their margins.

A lesser *Ulmus* pollen decline around 180 cm, with associated decreases of *Betula* and *Quercus*, coincides with the start of high and maintained curves for *Plantago lanceolata*, *Taraxacum*-type and *Pteridium*, thus reflecting disturbance, woodland removal and the creation of open ground. More open conditions persisted throughout zone SH1-d, caused by human activity but also by a general trend towards wetter environments. The presence of *Typha angustifolia* and *Potamogeton* pollen point to some standing water nearby, although the sediment type at the sampling point and the lack of aquatic macrofossils do not reflect that. Rising Poaceae levels could have been associated with increased wetness and marsh habitats around the site, but as the highest grass percentages occur at a horizon with a major peak in cereal-type pollen, dated to 3230 ± 40 ^{14}C BP, they could just as easily reflect woodland removal. The records of the open-habitat dryland insect taxa *Sitona* and *Harpalus*, which reflect the nearby presence of dry-grassland vegetation, further support the notion that open ground had been created. The record from this late Bronze Age phase of cultivation includes a range of likely agricultural indicators, such as Chenopodiaceae, *Lathyrus*-type and *Polygonum*, and peaks in *Plantago lanceolata*, *Taraxacum*-type and *Pteridium*. *Sambucus* occurs, which is typical of disturbed environments associated with humans. Overall, this record indicates a substantial phase of woodland clearance for agriculture at this time. Unfortunately plant macrofossils, which might have assisted the pollen data in reconstructing the local vegetation, were extremely sparse in the sediments above 170 cm in the profile. The sharp decline in wood fragments around 100 cm depth suggests a reduction in local woodland, possibly due to clearance. The sporadic occurrence of waterside, damp-ground and aquatic taxa

Unit	Depth (cm)	Description
10	0–45	Topsoil. *Stratum confusum*
9	45–75	Crumbly humified amorphous peat. Sh4, nig.4, strf.0, elas.0, sicc.3, lim.sup.0
8	75–86	Herbaceous *detritus* peat. Charcoal present from 80-85cm. Dh4, anth.+++, nig.3, strf.0, elas.0, sicc.2, lim.sup.0
7	86–96	Brown organic shelly silt with *limus*. Ag3, Ld^{3}1, Sh+, part.test.(moll.)+, nig.2+, strf.0, elas.0, sicc.2, lim.sup.0
6	96–110	Grey-yellow clayey silt. Ag3, As1, nig.2, strf.0, elas.0, sicc.2, lim.sup.2
5	110–153	Grey clayey silt with *limus*. Ag2, As1, Ld^{3}1, nig.2+, strf.0, elas.0, sicc.2, lim.sup.0
4	153–164	Brown *limus*. Ld^{3}4, nig.2+, strf.0, elas.1, sicc.2, lim.sup.0
3	164–166	Grey clayey silt. Ag3, As1, nig.2, strf.0, elas.0, sicc.2, lim.sup.1
2	166–200	Grey-yellow shell marl. Lc4, part.test.(moll.)+, nig.1, strf.0, elas.0, sicc.2, lim.sup.0
1	200–235	Grey-yellow clayey silt with sand. Ag3, As1, Ga++, nig.2, strf.0, elas.0, sicc.2, lim.sup.1

Table 3.9 Stratigraphy at Nosterfield, the Flasks 69. The particle-size distribution of units 5 and 6 was confirmed using a Coulter Particle-size Analyser (see Chapter 2.1.3.1; Appendix IV).

suggests the continued presence of some wetland habitats. *Urtica dioica* (stinging nettle) may have grown here in areas of open/disturbed ground. Insect evidence suggests a slightly more complex mosaic of boggy, open ground surrounding muddy, ephemeral pools. The Coleoptera also indicate much drier sand substrates and grassland in the upper parts of the profile, habitats not represented in the plant macrofossil record, although grass pollen is present in substantial quatities.

Pollen indicators of woodland clearance or open ground continue periodically to the top of the diagram, which, extrapolating from the radiocarbon date of 2715 ± 45 ^{14}C BP at the end of pollen zone SH1-d, must equate with the late Iron Age (or later). More significant, however, is the major environmental change recorded by the huge increase in Cyperaceae frequencies after 2715 ± 45 ^{14}C BP in zone SH1-e. A major hydrological shift must have occurred at this time to cause the occupation of the wetland surface by sedges and other marsh plants tolerant of extremely wet conditions. The virtual absence of tree and shrub pollen is probably a percentage effect of the superabundance of Cyperaceae pollen, although a real and significant reduction in woodland is likely to have occurred. *Alnus* in particular may have been expected to survive locally but the combination of clearance and hydrological change must have been inimical even to this water logging-tolerant tree.

A severe climatic shift towards wet conditions (van Geel *et al.*, 1996) is likely to have been the main cause of these changes, although forest clearance may also have been a factor. The presence of open, dry-grassland insects (see above; Table 3.7) near the top of the profile must reflect post-clearance open ground. The silty nature of the peat near the present surface of the shaft infill reflects inwash of soil material under these wet, unstable post-clearance conditions. Truncation of the record, probably in the late Iron Age or later (unless sedimentation in the upper half metre has been extremely slow indeed), was probably due to the shakehole being effectively filled by sediment at that stage.

3.2.3 The Flasks, Core 69

This site also lies in the area known as the Flasks (SE 2845 8080; Fig. 3.1). Previous survey by the West Yorkshire Archaeology Service (Berg & Bastow, 1992) had proved an extensive but thin peat deposit, with a maximum depth of less than a metre and becoming shallower to the north, extending in places to the surface and otherwise covered by clayey topsoil. A more intensive survey (by Mike Griffith Associates), during which hand boreholes were carried out grid-wise across the area of the Flasks, discovered deeper peat-filled hollows within the general area of organic sediments. At the point where the organic sediments were deepest and representative of the general site stratigraphy, a sample profile was obtained with a Russian corer: Core 69.

3.2.3.1 Lithostratigraphy

The sediment sequence below 75 cm at Core 69 is detrital in nature and signifies deposition within a water body, probably of small size; this sequence is not recognized in nearby cores (Table 3.9). Detrital peats, organic limnic muds, marls and silts/clays indicate changing environments in and around this small pond or channel. A completely inorganic clayey silt unit is notable in mid-profile, above which an upper peat unit represents the extensive near-surface peat traced across most of the Flasks during general survey of the site, oxidized in its surface horizons.

3.2.3.2 Pollen

Samples were prepared for pollen analysis at five centimetre intervals through the core, although a few in mid-profile did not preserve countable pollen. Preservation was generally only moderate and a degree of corrosion of pollen grains was common. Further intermediate samples were taken from the upper profile to establish pollen zone boundaries more closely and aid selection of levels for dating. The pollen diagram (Fig. 3.5) is subdivided into eight local pollen assemblage zones (F69-a to F69-h).

ZONE DESCRIPTIONS

Zone F69-a (180–177.5 cm)
Pollen values for *Betula*, *Juniperus* (juniper) and *Salix* are substantial in this zone but all other tree and shrub taxa are hardly recorded. Cyperaceae is the most abundant type at over 30% of total pollen. Poaceae and *Rumex* are the only other herbs present in quantity, although a range of additional herb types occurs. Low levels of *Pediastrum* algae are recorded. Micro-charcoal values are substantial.

Zone F69-b (177.5–167.5 cm)
Betula percentages are maintained but *Juniperus* and *Salix* are much reduced in this zone. There is little change in the other common taxa except that *Artemisia* percentages are greatly increased. There is a greater diversity of herb types, including *Helianthemum* (rockrose), *Plantago maritima* (sea plantain) and *Mentha*-type. *Rumex*, common at first, declines sharply. Micro-charcoal values remain high.

Zone F69-c (167.5–107.5 cm)
In this zone *Betula* frequencies fluctuate but are consistently over 20% of total pollen. All other tree and shrub percentages remain low, although *Pinus* is much better represented than in the previous zones. The assemblage is dominated by Cyperaceae, Poaceae being consistent but low. There is a low but significant curve for *Filipendula* early in the zone but this then fades from the record. All other herb pollen frequencies are very low and sporadic, including *Artemisia*. *Pediastrum* percentages are greatly reduced. Micro-charcoal is present throughout and reaches high values later in the zone.

Zone F69-d (107.5–97.5 cm)
Betula pollen frequencies fall sharply, while Cyperaceae values rise to dominate the assemblage at almost 80% of total pollen. All other taxa are very low and show little change, although Poaceae values, in particular, decline in this zone. Micro-charcoal frequencies reach peak values.

Zone F69-e (97.5–84.5 cm)
This zone sees Cyperaceae values falling to around 40% of total pollen with *Betula* frequencies recovering, although remaining low. Poaceae frequencies are high and curves for other herbs increase slightly, particularly *Filipendula*, *Ranunculus*, *Rumex* and *Thalictrum* (meadow rue). Trees and shrubs are represented mainly by *Quercus* and *Corylus*, which appear at very low values. *Typha angustifolia* and *T. latifolia* occur in high percentages and *Pediastrum* frequencies rise. Micro-charcoal frequencies remain high.

Zone F69-f (84.5–67.5 cm)
Betula frequencies increase to around 40% of total pollen, and Salix values increase; all other tree and shrub types are low in this zone, although *Juniperus* is consistently present and *Corylus* frequencies begin to rise. Sporadic *Quercus* and *Ulmus* records occur. Cyperaceae and Poaceae are at low values. Aquatic types *Menyanthes*, *Typha angustifolia* and *Equisetum* (horsetail) show consistent low curves. The micro-charcoal values decline through the zone.

Zone F69-g (67.5–53.5 cm)
In this zone *Betula* remains high, but *Pinus* and *Corylus* frequencies are increased. *Salix* is reduced and *Juniperus* fades from the record. Cyperaceae and Poaceae remain low and the diversity of the herb pollen assemblage is much decreased. Micro-charcoal frequencies are low.

Zone F69-h (53.5–45 cm)
Corylus dominates the assemblage in this final zone, at around 50% of total pollen, and *Betula* falls to low values. The Cyperaceae and Poaceae curves are very low and few other herb or spore types occur. Micro-charcoal records are almost absent.

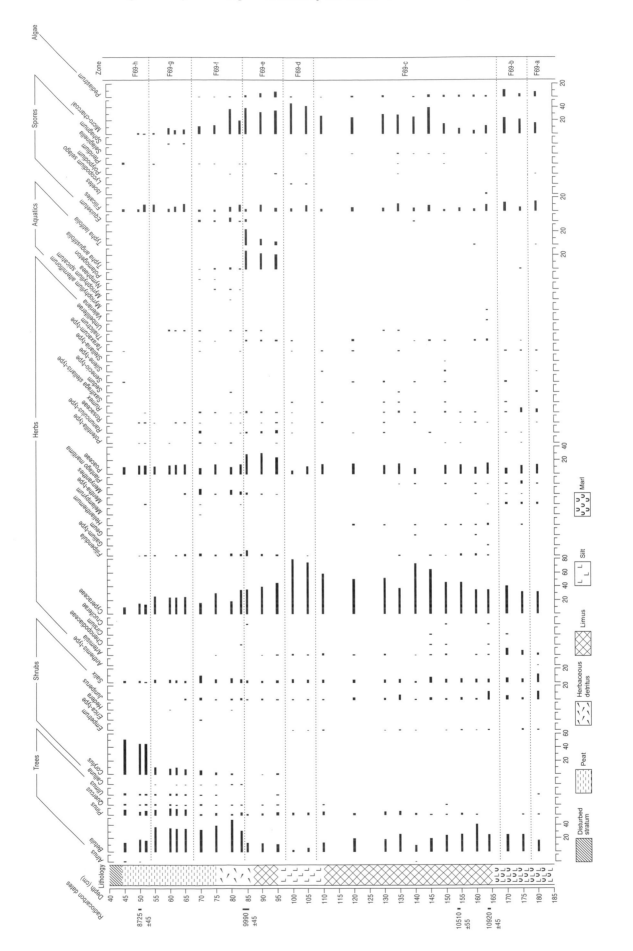

Fig. 3.5 Pollen diagram from Nosterfield, the Flasks core 69. Frequencies are calculated as percentages of the total land pollen sum (trees, shrubs and herbs).

Sample depth (cm)	55–85	88–94	95–135	135–140	140–165	165–170	170–175	175–180	180–185	185–190	190–195	195–200	200–205	205–210	210–220	220–225	225–230	230–235
Aquatic																		
Valvata piscinalis (Müller)		1					3	1	1	3	15	5	6	12				
Bithynia tentaculata (Linnaeus) opercula																	1	
Lymnaea peregra (Müller)		2					1	2	1	6	5	3	1	3		1		
Gyraulus laevis (Alder)										3	5		4				2	
Gyraulus crista (Linnaeus)										4	24	5						
Planorbidae										11	12	3	16	6		1	3	
Sphaerium corneum (Linnaeus)		1																
Pisidium personatum Malm																1		
Pisidium milium Held											1	1	1					
Pisidium spp.		1		1		1							1	2			1	
Terrestrial																		
Vertigo spp.											1							
Total	0	5	0	1	0	1	4	3	1	27	63	17	29	23	0	3	6	0

Table 3.10 Molluscs from Nosterfield, the Flasks 69

3.2.3.3 Molluscs

The subsamples for molluscan analysis were taken from the core at approximately 5 cm intervals. The succession was limited and included a number of significant gaps (see below), indicated in Table 3.10. Only the samples between 185 and 210 cm produced shell counts of over 20 individuals, with the rest yielding totals in single figures. The restricted fauna (9 species only) does not allow any detailed palaeoecological conclusions to be drawn, although tentative comments may be made about the most productive levels, the fauna from which is dominated by *Gyraulus crista* and *Gyraulus laevis*. The totals for the latter are probably on the low side, as many of the shells recorded as Planorbidae (undetermined) are almost certainly *G. laevis*, but were too fragmentary or juvenile for positive identification. These are pioneer species that can colonize new water bodies very rapidly, as they are tolerant of a variety of conditions, although both thrive in standing water with some macrophytic vegetation.

Only a single land shell was found (an apex of a *Vertigo* sp.) at 190–195 cm. Their paucity is a clear indication that the site of deposition was a closed pond, as land shells are not easily recruited to water bodies without the sweeping action of floods (Sparks, 1961; Jones *et al.*, 2000). The occurrence of the single shell of *Vertigo* suggests that the pond was fringed with reeds, the habitat of several of the species of this genus.

All of the species found are recorded in Lateglacial and early Holocene contexts in West Yorkshire (Keen *et al.*, 1988) and Northumberland (Jones *et al.*, 2000), so the assemblage is of little value for age determination.

3.2.3.4 Chronology

The four dates from the Flasks Core 69 form a good chronological series, with the upper three at least very close to expected ages for the lithostratigraphical and pollen zone changes they were selected to date (Table 3.11). The dates show a Lateglacial and early Holocene chronology for sediment accumulation, in good agreement with the pollen stratigraphy. This site adds to the pollen record recovered from the nearby Nosterfield Shakehole 1 locality and extends the local vegetation history to cover almost the entire Lateglacial and Holocene time period.

3.2.3.5 Synthesis: the Flasks (Nosterfield), Core 69

The lithostratigraphy at the Flasks Core 69 comprises an organic limnic sequence separated from surface muds and peat by a thick clayey silt layer. The completely inorganic clayey silt in mid profile indicates a period during which biological productivity in the water body ceased; its catchment was largely unvegetated and eroded fine-grained mineral material was washed into the depression. Such a tripartite sequence is typical of deposition during the Lateglacial period, with interstadial organic lake muds deposited under temperate climate conditions and covered by inorganic inwashed clayey silts associated with the

OxA-12960	8725 ± 45 ^{14}C BP (9910–9540 cal. BP; 7960–7590 cal. BC)

This date provides an age a little after the main rise of *Corylus* pollen and confirms that pollen zone boundary as the early Holocene rational limit of hazel. It also provides a date just below the top of the undisturbed peat in the profile. The date conforms to other dates for the *Corylus* rise in lowland northern England.

OxA-12932	9990 ± 45 ^{14}C BP (11,710–11,260 cal. BP; 9760–9310 cal. BC)

This date provides an age for the main rise in *Betula* pollen, and confirms that the rise represents its early Holocene rational limit, replacing more open habitat herbaceous plant cover. The date conforms to other dates for this pollen zone boundary in lowland northern England.

OxA-12972	10,510 ± 55 ^{14}C BP (12,730–12,230 cal. BP; 10,780–10,280 cal. BC)

This date provides an age for the start of an increasing silty clay fraction within the organic detrital lake mud of the profile and an increase in Cyperaceae pollen and gradual decline in *Betula*. It marks the start of the vegetation changes associated with the increasingly cold climatic conditions of the Lateglacial (Loch Lomond) stadial. The date conforms with other dates for this climatic and vegetation change in northern England.

OxA-12997	10,920 ± 45 ^{14}C BP (12,940–12,830 cal. BP; 10,990–10,880 cal. BC)

This date provides an age for sediment a little after the start of organic detrital lake mud accumulation above inorganic shell-rich clay. It is near the start of a phase of increased *Betula* frequencies and reduced herb values, and so probably warmer conditions. The underlying shell-rich clay contains a more open ground pollen assemblage and the date seems rather recent for the switch to warmer conditions during the Lateglacial Interstadial.

Table 3.11 Evaluation of radiocarbon dates from Nosterfield, the Flasks 69

severe cold conditions of the succeeding Loch Lomond Stadial (= GS-1; see Fig. 1.2), before the renewed deposition of organic muds and peats in the temperate Holocene This is supported by the pollen data, with open *Betula* woods established before and after the intercalated clayey silt layer, but with tree-*Betula* virtually absent during the period of clayey silt deposition, when a sedge-tundra type of open herbaceous vegetation was dominant in the intervening cold phase in pollen zone F69-d. The main mollusc-bearing levels were restricted to the lower, interstadial sediment body. The molluscan evidence points to a closed pond environment with pioneering species dominant in an assemblage of little biostratigraphical value, albeit fully in keeping with the Lateglacial interpretation proferred here.

The expansion of *Corylus* and other deciduous tree pollen in the peat of the upper profile indicates an early Holocene age for these later sediments. This Lateglacial and early Holocene age for the Flasks Core 69 pollen record is confirmed by the series of radiocarbon dates (Table 3.11). They show deposition starting a little before 11,000 ^{14}C BP during the final phase (GI-1a) of the Lateglacial (Windermere) Interstadial (Fig. 1.2) and terminating around 8500 ^{14}C BP, with a date during the centuries before 10,000 ^{14}C BP for cold-phase clastic deposition. This conforms very well with the pollen data. During the periods of Lateglacial and initial Holocene temperate climate, *Salix* and particularly *Juniperus* were important subsidiary members of the developing open *Betula* woodland, with herbs favoured by higher temperatures, particularly *Filipendula*, also common.

After the cold phase of zone 69-d, which equates with the Loch Lomond Stadial (GS1), increased biological productivity in the pond and stabilized soils around it led to typical transitional communities with aquatics, mainly *Typha,* and herbs like *Rumex* and *Thalictrum* prominent, before being shaded out by the woody taxa. Closed canopy woodland appears to have become established during zones 69-g and h, with herbs and low shrubs intolerant of shade becoming much less common. The fall in micro-charcoal in these later zones may be a further reflection of dense woodland developing, reducing transport of charcoal particles to the site, although a reduced incidence of fire is possible. Fires this early are likely to have been mainly natural, although human agency (Upper Palaeolithic – Mesolithic) cannot be ruled out. This Lateglacial and early Holocene pollen record at the Flasks Core 69 is comparable with other profiles in the area, notably those from Dishforth Bog (Giles, 1992), Bingley Bog (Keen *et al.*, 1988) and Tadcaster (Bartley, 1962).

3.2.4 Palaeoenvironmental Summary: Nosterfield sites

The archaeological evidence from the area of the Thornborough Henges and its environs (Harding, 1998, 2000a, b) shows a multi-period cultural landscape that extends well beyond the henge monuments to encompass the surrounding area. Access to gravel sections and organic sediment-bodies of Nosterfield quarry, to the north of the henge landscape, has provided geological and environmental evidence of value as a context for the various social, cultural, economic and ritual activities evidenced by archaeological data from the monuments.

The data recovered in this study provides an almost

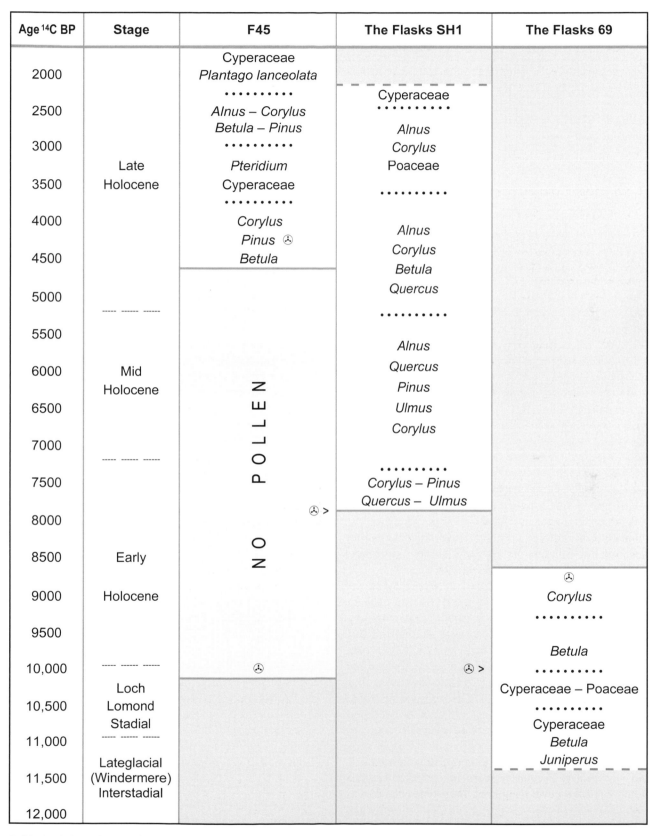

Age ¹⁴C BP	Stage	F45	The Flasks SH1	The Flasks 69
2000		Cyperaceae *Plantago lanceolata* · · · · · · · · · ·		
2500		*Alnus – Corylus* *Betula – Pinus*	Cyperaceae · · · · · · · · · · *Alnus*	
3000		· · · · · · · · · ·	*Corylus* Poaceae	
3500	Late Holocene	*Pteridium* Cyperaceae · · · · · · · · · ·	· · · · · · · · · ·	
4000		*Corylus*	*Alnus*	
4500		*Pinus* ☢ *Betula*	*Corylus* *Betula*	
5000	----- ------ ------		*Quercus*	
5500			· · · · · · · · · ·	
6000	Mid Holocene		*Alnus* *Quercus*	
6500		N O	*Pinus* *Ulmus*	
7000	----- ------ ------	P O L L E N	*Corylus*	
7500			· · · · · · · · · · *Corylus – Pinus* *Quercus – Ulmus*	
8000		☢ >		
8500	Early	N O		
9000	Holocene			☢ *Corylus*
9500				· · · · · · · · · ·
10,000	----- ------ ------	☢	☢ >	*Betula* · · · · · · · · · ·
10,500	Loch Lomond Stadial			Cyperaceae – Poaceae · · · · · · · · · ·
11,000	----- ------ ------			Cyperaceae *Betula*
11,500	Lateglacial (Windermere) Interstadial			*Juniperus* - - - - - - -
12,000				

Table 3.12 Correlation of pollen data from Nosterfield. Stratigraphical positions of key radiocarbon dates are indicated by the atomic symbol.

continuous record of the climate, geomorphology, biota and habitats of the area from about 12,000 ^{14}C BP to about 2000 ^{14}C BP. Only a period of about 1000 ^{14}C years is unrepresented, falling between the Flasks 69 and SH1 records; unfortunately this includes the important *Alnus* rise. The Nosterfield fan, upon which the henge landscape was established, was deposited during the deglaciation phase at the end of the Dimlington Stadial, so its surface features began to evolve from before *c.* 15,000 ^{14}C BP, rather than at the start of the Holocene. Meltwater and periglacial activities were therefore able, over the several thousand years of the Lateglacial, to create channels, gullies and depressions in the fan that contrast with the elevated sand and gravel ridges where much of the archaeology is situated. The negative topographic features have provided the long-term sediment traps within which the environmental record has been preserved.

The pollen record for the three Nosterfield sites is correlated in Table 3.12. The Core 69 depression at the Flasks formed a large area of peat that has now been destroyed by aggregate extraction, but other similar areas of peat may well exist in the area. Mollusc and pollen data show the existence of a shallow enclosed pond that persisted through the Lateglacial and into the early Holocene, when the record is truncated. The sediments and radiocarbon date from the nearby 'Find 14' profile (see above; Appendix I) support this. The pollen record of the terrestrial vegetation from the fan surface shows the same progression through herbaceous, shrub and then woodland vegetation that characterizes the Lateglacial flora regionally and throughout Britain, including the short-lived and severely cold Loch Lomond Stadial (c. 11,000–10,000 14C BP) that immediately preceded the Holocene. The radiocarbon dates from the basal sediments of the three shafts support this interpretation, indicating Lateglacial (F44) or early Holocene (F45 & F46) ages (Appendix I). The truncated Flasks 69 profile provides data on the early Holocene development of woodland but does not extend to the time of the full deciduous woodland.

The two solution-hollow infills at Nosterfield (F45 and SH1) provide a record from the mid-Holocene until the hollows became full of sediment about 2000 years ago. SH1 shows no indications of local woodland opening by hunter-gatherers. Even the records for micro-charcoal, which might have provided an indication of woodland disturbance over a wider area, remain extremely low, indicating that the forest around these sites remained stable while evolving towards the mid-Holocene deciduous maximum. The record at SH1 shows greater domination by local wetland vegetation, particularly alder, than F45 and so the two sites provide spatially contrasting information. Site F45, apparently less cloaked by fen–carr wetland scrub, should contain a clearer signal of human farming activity than SH1, and so may have received pollen from as far as the Thornborough landscape as well as from the local area at Nosterfield. Both profiles record phases of forest disturbance in the later Holocene that can be attributed to

agriculture from the Neolithic period to the Iron Age. Some of these records include cereal-type pollen, indicative of arable cultivation, although the grass and weed pollen ratios suggest that pasture was always an important element in the local agricultural economy. The mid-Bronze Age, around 3200 ^{14}C BP, appears to have been a period of substantial woodland opening for farming; both the plant macrofossils and the insects from SH1 agree with the pollen in recording a reduction in the number of trees around the site at this time, together with the expansion of grassland. The same mid-Bronze Age peak in clearance occurred at F45, by interpolation at the same date; woodland regeneration was successful at both sites.

The Iron Age record is masked somewhat by the expansion of wetland herbaceous vegetation, caused by severe climatic deterioration in the first half of the 3rd Millennium BP, that is recorded clearly at both sites. Major forest clearance certainly took place in the Iron Age, with extensive deforestation around Nosterfield in comparison with previous periods. Most relevant to the Thornborough henge landscape is the evidence from the late Neolithic to early Bronze Age period. While there are indications of forest opening around both sites during this period, these are not substantial and the Nosterfield area remained well wooded. The vegetation cover around Nosterfield cannot be extrapolated directly to the Thornborough landscape, where the situation cannot be known for certain, but it is clear that the wider area carried considerable woodland and, unless the higher and so presumably drier area at Thornborough had been selected for differential clearance, the henge monuments were probably constructed within a largely wooded landscape. Certainly, the combined Nosterfield record contains no evidence of substantial deforestation that could be attributed to Late Neolithic to early Bronze Age activities, either economic or cultural, within and beyond the landscape of the henges.

3.3 Newby Wiske

The Newby Wiske (NW) site is located at The Carrs (SE 3690 8650), south of the villages of Newby Wiske and South Otterington, within the Wiske valley, the major eastern tributary of the River Swale within the Washlands (Fig. 3.6). The Carrs is an extensive area of peat bog within a former meltwater channel (Chapter 2.2.1.1) that is artificially drained by the Spudling Dike. A series of reconnaissance cores were taken across the bog to determine the location of the deepest profile, which was found to occur in the centre of the channel and was sampled for analysis of pollen, macrofossils and Mollusca.

3.3.1 Lithostratigraphy

Over four metres of sediment was recovered from the centre of the channel (Fig. 3.6; Table 3.13), the stratigraphy showing stiff grey clayey silt at the base that included some

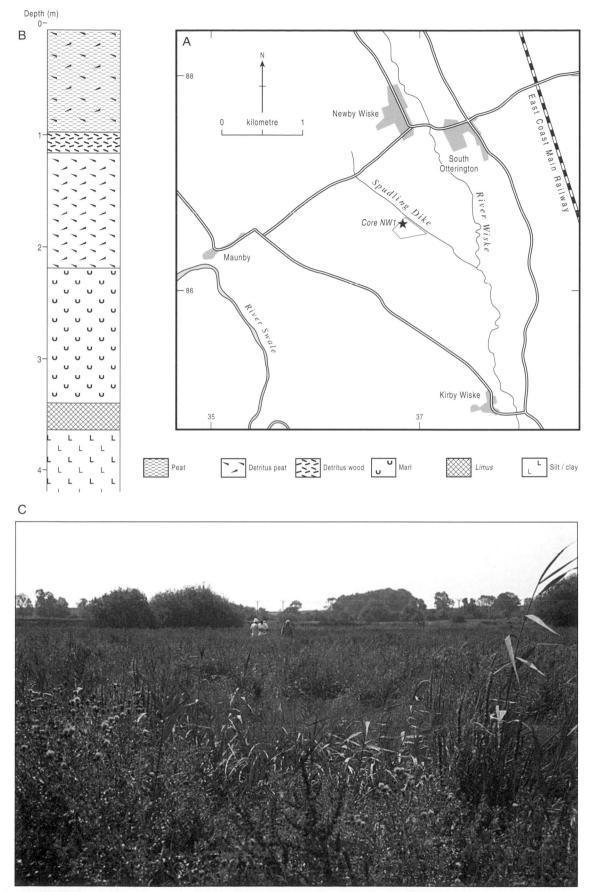

Fig. 3.6 Newby Wiske: A – location map, showing the coring site adjacent to the Spudling Dike; B – Stratigraphy of core NW1; C – View of the site, showing modern vegetation, with prominent Lythrum salicaria *(looking south).*

Unit	Depth (cm)	Description
15	0–98	Black herbaceous *detritus* and woody peat with amorphous organic material. Dh2, Dl1, Sh1, nig.4, strf.0, elas.1, sicc.3
14	98–118	Orange-brown wood. Dl4, nig.2, strf.0, elas.0, sicc.3, lim.sup.4
13	118–155	Black herbaceous *detritus* peat with many wood fragments. Dh3, Dl1, Sh++, nig.4, strf.0, elas.0, sicc.2, lim.sup.4
12	155–182	Black herbaceous *detritus* peat. Dh4, Sh++, nig.2, strf.0, elas.0, sicc.2, lim.sup.0
11	182–218	Fine black *detritus* peat with *limus*. Small shell fragments up to 210cm. Dh3, Ld³1, part. test. (moll.)+, nig.4, strf.0, elas.0, sicc.2, lim.sup.0
10	218–222	Fine black *detritus* peat with yellow-grey marl and many shell fragments. Dh3, Lc1, part. test. (moll)+++, nig.3++, strf.1, elas.0, sicc.2, lim.sup.0
9	222–340	Slightly organic yellow-grey marl with shell fragments throughout and occasional whole shells. More organic bands at 233, 258, 282, 303, 332 and 325 cm. Lc4, part. test. (moll.)+++, test. (moll.)+, Sh+, nig.1, strf.1., elas,0, sicc.2, lim.sup.0
8	340–349	Grey-green silty *limus* with small plant fragments. Ld³4, Ag+, Dh+, nig.3, strf.0, elas.0, sicc.2, lim.sup.0
7	349–354	Grey-yellow *limus*. Ld³4, nig.2, strf.0, elas.0, sicc.2, lim.sup.0
6	354–361	Organic brown *limus*. Ld³4, nig.3, strf.0, elas.0, sicc.2, lim.sup.0
5	361–362	Yellow-grey *limus*. Ld³4, nig.2, strf.0, elas.0, sicc.2, lim.sup.0
4	362–364	Grey-green *limus*. Ld³4, nig.3, strf.0, elas.0, sicc.2, lim.sup.0
3	364–386	Soft grey clayey silt. Ag3, As1, nig.2, strf.0, elas.0, sicc.2, lim.sup.1
2	386–412	Soft grey clayey silt with *Scorpidium scorpioides* moss stems. Most stems below 406cm. Ag3, As1, Tb+, nig.2, strf.0, elas.0, sicc.2, lim.sup.0
1	412–440	Pinky-grey stiff clayey silt. Ag3, As1, nig.2+, strf.0, elas.0, sicc.2, lim.sup.0

Table 3.13 Stratigraphy at Newby Wiske, Core NW1.

strands of plant material. A limnic mud overlies the clayey silt and is overlain in turn by shelly marl. Detrital peats seal the marl and are covered by a surficial deposit of humified *turfa* peat (cf. Plate 3.1c). The detrital peat sediments contain abundant wood remains that form discrete layers in many places. One such thin wood layer occurred in the sampled core at about one metre depth.

3.3.2 Pollen

The Newby Wiske profile was subsampled for pollen analysis at four centimetre intervals throughout the core, closing to 2 cm where major frequency changes occurred, allowing more precise definition of pollen zone boundaries. Pollen preservation was generally good, although some

oxidation and corrosion of pollen was noted in the upper metre and preservation was poor in the clayey silt near the base, where some of the sampled levels did not contain enough to count. The results of the analysis are presented in Figure 3.7, which is subdivided into nine local pollen assemblage zones (NW-a to NW-i).

ZONE DESCRIPTIONS
Zone NW-a (414–388 cm)
Cyperaceae and Poaceae are the main contributors to the pollen assemblage in this zone. Tree pollen frequencies are very low, at about 10% of total pollen, and are almost entirely *Betula*. *Juniperus* and *Salix* are present in consistently moderate values and there is some *Empetrum*. An extensive

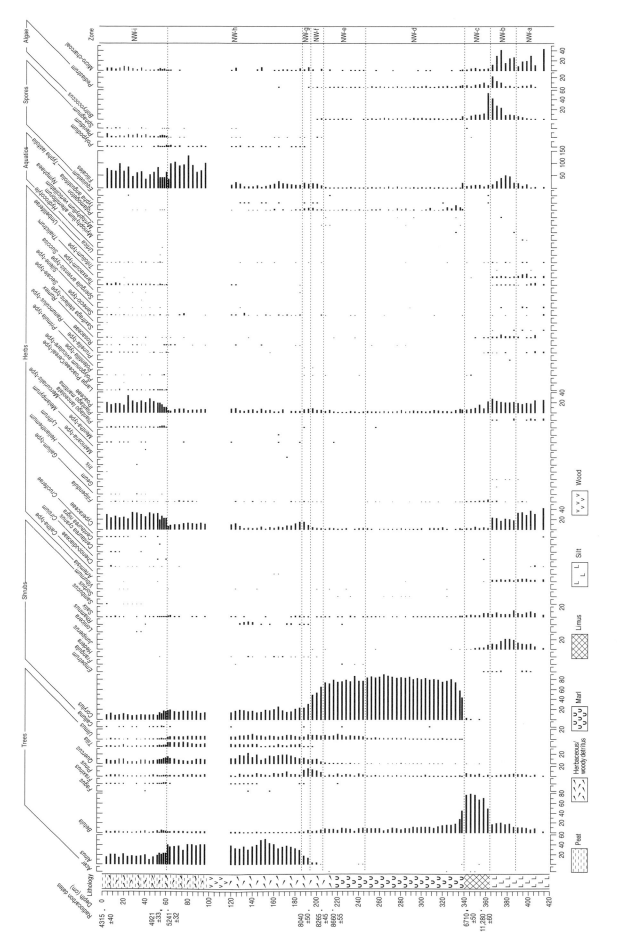

Fig. 3.7 Pollen diagram from Newby Wiske NW1. Frequencies are calculated as percentages of the total land pollen sum (trees, shrubs and herbs).

suite of open-habitat herbs occurs, with *Artemisia*, *Rumex*, *Plantago maritima*, *Taraxacum*-type, Chenopodiaceae and *Thalictrum* prominent. Few aquatic pollen grains or algal spores are present. There is abundant microscopic charcoal.

Zone NW-b (388–364 cm)

Betula and *Juniperus* frequencies are doubled in this zone, with Cyperaceae the most reduced taxon. Most other herbaceous taxa remain unchanged; *Helianthemum* is consistently present in very low values and there are small peaks in *Pediastrum* and *Botryococcus* algae. Micro-charcoal values remain high.

Zone NW-c (364–340 cm)

This zone is characterized by the increase in the *Betula* curve to almost 80% of total pollen, with all other previously present taxa severely reduced. *Juniperus*, *Salix* and Cyperaceae fall to very low frequencies, although they are consistently present; *Artemisia*, however, is virtually absent from the assemblage. The herbaceous pollen suite is greatly reduced, with only sporadic records of very few taxa. *Filipendula* increases and is consistently recorded. Algae and micro-charcoal frequencies fall from the peaks of the previous zone.

Zone NW-d (340–246 cm)

Corylus frequencies rise sharply to almost 80% of total pollen and replace *Betula*, which contributes about 20%, as the dominant taxon in this zone. All other taxa are very poorly represented, although *Salix*, Cyperaceae and Poaceae are almost always recorded. Very low curves for *Quercus* and *Ulmus* are maintained throughout. There are sporadic herb grains, with *Typha angustifolia*, which appears for the first time, present in most levels.

Zone NW-e (246–206 cm)

Corylus dominance is maintained in this zone, although the curve begins to decline gradually. Within a uniformly low range, *Ulmus* values show a significant increase through the zone. All other taxa are present in very low frequencies only.

Zone NW-f (206–194 cm)

Corylus percentages fall through this zone to about 40% of total pollen but it remains easily the most abundant pollen type. *Quercus* increases to match the *Ulmus* frequencies and *Alnus* pollen is consistently present for the first time. *Pinus* values increase to almost 20% as *Betula* declines. All other taxa are present at very low percentages only.

Zone NW-g (194–186 cm)

This zone is characterized by rising *Alnus*

frequencies and *Corylus* falling to about 20% of total pollen. Little change occurs in any other taxa, except that Cyperaceae increase and *Tilia* is consistently present for the first time, although only as single grain counts.

Zone NW-h (186–60 cm)

Alnus rises to contribute almost 40% of total pollen throughout this zone, while *Pinus* falls to very low values. *Quercus* rises and *Corylus* falls, so that each contributes about 20% of the assemblage. *Tilia* is present throughout at low frequencies.

Zone NW-i (60–4 cm)

At the base of this zone, *Ulmus* and *Tilia* percentages fall sharply to low values. *Alnus* also declines to only 20% of total pollen. *Fraxinus* and *Calluna* are consistently recorded. Cyperaceae and Poaceae frequencies increase and the representation of herbaceous taxa is greatly enhanced. Many weed types are intermittently recorded but cereal-type, *Plantago lanceolata*, *Taraxacum*-type, *Senecio*-type and *Ranunculus* are consistently present. *Pteridium* and micro-charcoal frequencies are increased.

3.3.3 Plant macrofossils

The plant macrofossil record from Newby Wiske (Fig. 3.8) has been divided into six assemblage zones, NWm-1 to NWm-6. Macrofossils were well preserved in the majority of the core, but preservation was poor in the top metre. Macrofossil analysis was carried out to a depth of 364 cm, below which was clayey silt in which the only macrofossil remains were stems of the moss *Scorpidium scorpioides*.

Zone descriptions

Zone NWm-1 (370–320 cm)

The number of remains and taxa are low in this basal zone; fruits of *Betula* sp(p). dominate the woodland assemblage and a few *Corylus avellana* (hazel) nut fragments occur towards the top of the zone. Small fragments of wood and charcoal were recorded. Nutlets of *Cladium mariscus* (great fen-sedge) and oogonia of *Chara* sp(p). are represented, in addition to remains of Poaceae sp(p)., Musci sp(p). and Pteridophyte sp(p). A seed of the aquatic plant *Nymphaea alba* (white water-lily) and fruits of *Typha* sp(p). were recorded towards the top of the zone.

Zone NWm-2 (320–220 cm)

The numbers of *Corylus* nut fragments increase, while *Betula* sp(p). fruits decrease slightly in this zone, which is dominated by aquatic remains, mainly those of *Chara* sp(p)., with *Nymphaea alba* and *Potamogeton* sp(p). also occurring. A

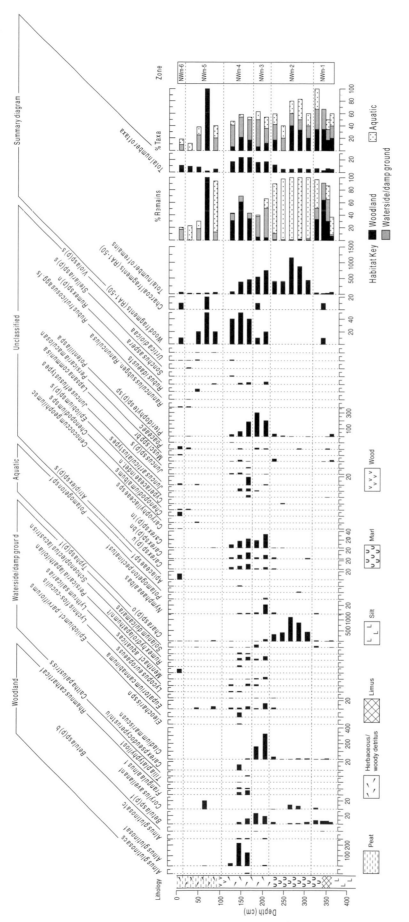

Fig. 3.8 Plant macrofossil diagram from Newby Wiske NW1. a: achene; b: bract; bn: biconvex nutlet; br: branch; c: caryopsis; cs: cone scale; f: fruit; fc: female cone; fs: fruitstone; n: nutlet; nf: nut fragment; n/t: nutlet and tepals; o: oosporangium; s: seed; sc: sclerotium; sp: sporangium; tn: triogonous nutlet; tn/u: triogonous nutlet and utricle; u: utricle.

few waterside taxa, including *Cladium mariscus*, *Eupatorium cannabinum* and *Lychnis flos-cuculi*, occur towards the top of the zone, together with nutlets of *Carex*.

Zone NWm-3 (220–175 cm)

This zone is characterized by an abundance and diversity of waterside and damp-ground taxa, including *Schoenoplectus lacustris* (common club-rush), *Mentha* cf. *aquatica* (aquatic mint) and *Lythrum salicaria* (purple loosestrife), in addition to increases in those that occurred in previous zones. There were also abundant remains of *Carex* and Pteridophyte species, with seeds and nutlets of *Juncus* sp(p). and *Rumex* sp(p). also present. A fruit and female cone of *Alnus glutinosa* is recorded and fruits of *Betula* sp(p). increase in number. Wood fragments are also recorded in this zone (Fig.3.8). Fruits of *Potamogeton pectinatus* (fennel pondweed) and numerous seeds of *Nymphaea alba* were encountered at the base of the zone, although the number of *Chara* sp(p). oogonia were greatly reduced.

Zone NWm-4 (175–105 cm)

This zone shows an increase in the number and diversity of woodland remains. Macrofossils of *Alnus glutinosa* dominate, although fruits of *Betula* sp(p)., *Frangula alnus* (alder buckthorn), *Rhamnus cathartica* (buckthorn) and a single fruit of *Tilia platyphyllos* ssp *cordifolia* (large leaved lime) also occur. Wood fragments are abundant. Although there is a reduction in the number of *Cladium mariscus* nutlets, the overall diversity of waterside and damp-ground herbs increases with the additions of *Carex pseudocyperus* (cyperus sedge). *Eleocharis* sp. (spike-rush), *Epilobium* cf. *parviflorum* (hoary willowherb) and *Rumex hydrolapathum* (water dock). Macrofossils of other *Carex* species also remain abundant, but the numbers of Pteridophyte sp(p). sporangia fall towards the end of the zone. Few aquatic remains are recorded.

Zone NWm-5 (105–15 cm)

Plant macrofossil remains are poorly preserved in this zone; wood and charcoal fragments were recorded and there were numerous *Corylus* nut fragments between 60 and 70 cm depth. Also recorded were fruit stones of *Rubus idaeus* (raspberry) and *R. fruticosus* agg. (blackberry), in addition to achenes of *Urtica dioica* and seeds of *Viola* sp. (pansy) and *Stellaria* sp(p). (stichwort). *Eupatorium cannabinum* and *Typha* sp(p). are the only waterside and damp ground taxa represented, with rare aquatic remains.

Sample depth (cm)	220–230	270–280	336–346	346–356	356–366
Aquatic					
Valvata cristata Müller	114	40	3		
Valvata piscinalis (Müller)	263	69	12	1	1
Bithynia tentaculata (Linnaeus)	43	10	3		
Opercula	36	4	1	2	
Physa fontinalis (Linnaeus)	23	1			
Lymnaea stagnalis (Linnaeus)	5				
Lymnaea peregra (Müller)	570	114	10	1	
Gyraulus laevis (Alder)	7				2
Gyraulus crista (Linnaeus)	44	6	1	1	
Hippeutis complanatus (Linnaeus)	29	11	1		
Acroloxus lacustris (Linnaeus)	3				
Sphaerium corneum (Linnaeus)	16				
Pisidium personatum Malm		1			
Pisidium milium Held	5	2			
Pisidium subtruncatum Malm	1				2
Pisidium nitidum Jenyns	20				3
Pisidium spp.	35	2			
Terrestrial					
Succineidae	2				
Vertigo spp.	1	1			
Total	1181	257	30	3	8

Table 3.14 Molluscs from Newby Wiske, Core NW1. Opercula of Bithynia tentaculata, listed in the accompanying table in bold grey type, are not included in the molluscan total.

Zone NWm-6 (15–0 cm)

Plant remains are again poorly preserved; the majority of the records in this zone are members of the Chenopodiaceae (goosefoot family), including seeds of *Atriplex* sp(p). (orache), *Chenopodium album* (fat-hen) and *Chenopodium* sp(p). Macrofossils of Poaceae sp(p)., *Ranunculus* subgenus *Ranunculus* (buttercups), *Persicaria maculosa* (redshank) and *Urtica dioica* were also encountered, as were nutlets of the waterside taxon *Persicaria lapathifolia* (pale persicaria).

3.3.4 Molluscs

The Newby Wiske molluscan samples were provided as discrete sieved residues (270–280 cm; 336–345 cm; 346–356 cm; 356–366 cm) and as a 10 cm section cut from a Russian core (220–230). The fauna consists of 17 species, 15 freshwater and two land snails; all remain part of the modern British fauna (Table 3.14). The state of preservation of the shells is good, allowing identification even of the smallest juveniles in almost all cases. Although five

Preservation Viable sclerites Comments	Exceptional Yes	Exceptional Yes	Exceptional Yes	Exceptional Yes	Exceptional Yes	Exceptional Yes
Sample depth (cm)	20–30	140–150	160–170	180–190	200–210	346–356
Carabidae						
Agonum thoreyi			*			
Dytiscidae						
Illybius spp.					*	
Hydraenidae						
Hydraena spp.					*	
Hydrophilidae						
Cercyon spp.	*					
Hydrobius fuscipes			*			
Staphylinidae						
Philonthus spp.	*					
Helodidae						
Helodidae gen & spp. indet					*	*
Chrysomelidae						
Plateumaris/Donacia spp.			**	*	***	
Curculionidae						
Sitona spp.		*	*			

Table 3.15 Insects from Newby Wiske, Core NW1.

samples were provided, only sample 220–230 cm yielded a large number of molluscs. This sample also had 16 of the 17 species recovered, so the observations and conclusions about the environment are largely based on this single sample. The samples below 336 cm had too few shells to draw firm conclusions, although there is little difference in the species present at any of the levels, suggesting little change in conditions through the sequence.

Sample 220–230 cm is dominated by the gastropods *Valvata cristata*, *Valvata piscinalis* and *Lymnaea peregra*. There are also high numbers of *Bithynia tentaculata* and lesser quantities of the planorbids *Gyraulus crista*, *Gyraulus laevis* and *Hippeutis complanatus*. *Physa fontinalis* is also moderately common. The sequence is generally poor in bivalves, with *Pisidium nitidum*, *Pisidium milium* and *Sphaerium corneum* the main species present. The two land taxa were a small juvenile of a succineid and the apex of a *Vertigo*.

3.3.5 Insects

Preservation of insect remains from this core was exceptional and, with the exception of the basal sample (356–366 cm), in sufficient quantities to be of interpretable value (Table 3.15). Hygrophilous taxa dominate the assemblage; phytophagous beetles, which can provide information on the the herbaceous composition of the wetland, are restricted to a singles species of Carabidae, *Agonum thoreyi* (in the 160–170 sample), which is found on a variety of tall, emergent reeds (Lindroth, 1974). The remaining taxa, with one exception (see below), could not be identified to species level but can be used as generic indicators of wetland environments, possibly tall herb fen. The aquatic environment was similar to that of Nosterfield SH1: pools of deeper, more permanent standing water with a muddy periphery, fringed by taller reeds. Particularly characteristic of this type of environment is the hydrophilid, *Hydrobius fuscipes* (Hansen 1987), the exception referred to above. A further similarity with the Nosterfield core is the presence of taxa associated with drier grassland.

3.3.6 Chronology

The radiocarbon dating results from Newby Wiske (Table 3.16) indicate that the pollen profile provides an almost complete stratigraphy from Lateglacial to mid-Neolithic times. The two lower dates are associated with the early Holocene rise and fall of *Betula* and the rise of *Corylus* pollen frequencies. Both dates are widely different to the ages for these events recorded at many other sites in the region (Innes, 2002d) and one is out of chronological sequence with dates higher in the profile. Therefore, both dates must be considered unreliable.

The three mid-profile dates form a good chronological

GrA-25031	4315 ± 40 ^{14}C BP (4980–4830 cal. BP; 3030–2880 cal. BC)

This date provides an age for the surface of the surviving peat in the Newby Wiske channel, presumably truncated by recent drainage and other activities, and so also for the end of the pollen record. The date is mid-Neolithic in age which is in accordance with the pollen data, with low *Ulmus* values, high non-tree pollen frequencies and the continuous presence of agricultural and open ground indicators including cereal-type, *Plantago lanceolata*, *Pteridium* and several others.

OxA-13321	4921 ± 33 ^{14}C BP (5730–5590 cal. BP; 3780–3640 cal. BC)

This date provides an age for the end of the main agricultural episode associated with the *Ulmus* decline in this profile. Agricultural indicators continue after this level but at lower frequencies than before. Cereal-type pollen and the main weeds of cultivation decline and are replaced by more general open ground indicators, mainly Poaceae and Cyperaceae. The date is very close to an expected age for the closing phases of the elm decline.

OxA-13322	5241 ± 32 ^{14}C BP (6180–5920 cal. BP; 4230–3970 cal. BC)

This date provides an age for the start of the main mid-Holocene *Ulmus* decline and is closely comparable with other dates for the start of this event in lowland northern England. As well as the fall in elm pollen frequencies, other trees including *Tilia* and *Alnus* also decline. Continuous pollen curves for agricultural indicators cereal-type, *Plantago lanceolata* and other open ground weeds begin at this level, supporting its identification as the early Neolithic elm decline.

GrA-25028	8040 ± 50 ^{14}C BP (9040–8720 cal. BP; 7090–6770 cal. BC)

This date was intended to provide an age for the main mid-Holocene rise in *Alnus* pollen to high frequencies, its rational limit. Although some considerable variation in age for this feature has been recorded, most dates fall around *c.* 7000 ^{14}C BP in lowland northern England. This date is therefore unusually old for this pollen zone boundary. Although not entirely unacceptable, the date must be considered suspect.

OxA-13226	8265 ± 45 ^{14}C BP (9430–9030 cal. BP; 7480–7080 cal. BC)

This date was intended to provide an age for the rise of *Pinus* and *Quercus* pollen percentages and the start of the pollen curve for *Alnus*. This date is not incompatible with the pollen data and compares with the range of dates for such a pollen assemblage elsewhere in lowland northern England. The date can be considered to be broadly acceptable.

OxA-13107	8660 ± 55 ^{14}C BP (9750–9530 cal. BP; 7800–7580 cal. BC)

This date was intended to date the transition from marl to organic mud deposition in the basin. The pollen data at this level show very high *Corylus* frequencies and moderate *Ulmus*. *Pinus* and *Quercus* are low, and *Alnus* is not yet recorded. The date is not incompatible with these pollen data although is perhaps a little old compared with dates from similar pollen assemblages elsewhere in lowland northern England.

OxA-13112	6710 ± 50 ^{14}C BP (7670–7490 cal. BP; 5720–5540 cal. BC)

This date was intended to provide an age for the pollen zone boundary defined by the main fall in *Betula* pollen and the main early Holocene rise in *Corylus* pollen, its rational limit. The pollen data show the expected complete sequence of pollen zone changes for the early Holocene, and so the age of the *Corylus* rise, by analogy with many other dated profiles, would be expected to be about 9000 ^{14}C BP or a little earlier. This date of *c.* 6710 ^{14}C BP is incompatible with the pollen stratigraphy and is clearly too young and must be assumed to be unacceptable for this level.

GrA-25030	11280 ± 60 ^{14}C BP (13,280–13,070 cal. BP; 11,330–11,120 cal. BC)

This date was intended to provide an age as close as possible to the main early Holocene rise in *Betula* pollen, its rational limit. The pollen data show the expected complete sequence of pollen zone changes for the early Holocene, and so the age of the rise of birch pollen would be expected to be a little after *c.* 10,000 ^{14}C BP. This date of *c.* 11,280 ^{14}C BP is incompatible with the pollen stratigraphy; it is clearly too old and must be assumed to be unacceptable as a true age for this level.

Table 3.16 Evaluation of radiocarbon dates from Newby Wiske, Core NW1.

series. They are acceptable as boundary dates for pollen zones, with the *Quercus* rise at *c.* 8265 ^{14}C BP closely matching that from nearby Neasham Fen (Bartley *et al.*, 1976). The date for the *Alnus* rise seems rather old, although similarly early dates are known elsewhere and perhaps there was early development of alder hereabouts. The three upper dates are associated with the mid-Holocene *Ulmus* decline and later. They form a good chronological series and fit

extremely well with the expected ages of the elm-decline event and subsequent Neolithic land-use activities.

Three opercula of *Bithynia tentaculata* from the richest molluscan sample, from 220–230 cm (see above; Table 3.14), were passed to the NEaar laboratory for amino acid racemization dating (Appendix III). The relative D/L values and concentrations from these specimens, when compared with values from Quaternary sites within the UK (Penkman *et al.*, 2008b), are consistent with a Holocene age (see also Appendix III). Overall the data suggest that this is the oldest of the Swale Washlands sites to have produced useful AAR data (see below and Appendix III).

3.3.7 Synthesis: Newby Wiske

The soft grey clayey silt at the base of the sequence contains pollen assemblages suggesting a time at the Lateglacial–Holocene Transition. Successions of non-tree pollen indicate the rapid development of plant cover from open grass–sedge tundra vegetation, with arctic–alpine and ruderal herbs like *Thalictrum,* Chenopodiaceae, *Plantago maritima* and *Saxifraga*, to a tall herb and low shrub association in which *Salix* and *Juniperus* began to form a shrub canopy. The prominence of *Artemisia* indicates dry, cold environments during the latter stages of the Loch Lomond Stadial, while the significant *Rumex* percentages are characteristic of this end-stadial tall herb community, until shaded by taller shrub cover with the establishment of widespread *Juniperus* and then *Betula*. The only plant macrofossil in this basal clayey silt, *Scorpidium scorpioides*, indicates a calcareous pool or fen (Watson, 1995). The high levels of micro-charcoal are a common feature of these open, dry Lateglacial stadial records (Edwards *et al.*, 2000; Innes 2002a).

The increased biological productivity and vegetation cover that led to the deposition of the organic limnic mud unit above the basal clayey silt coincided with the establishment of closed birch woodland around the site, shown by the near total dominance of *Betula* pollen in the assemblage. Birch trees everywhere supplanted *Juniperus* as canopy dominant and shaded out the many herbaceous taxa that had flourished during the transition from the Lateglacial. The plant macrofossil assemblage from immediately above the clayey silt confirms the presence of local *Betula* woodland as well as base-rich fen and pools in which *Cladium mariscus*, *Typha* sp(p). and *Chara* sp(p). were growing; Pteridophyte sp(p)., Poaceae sp(p)., Musci sp(p). and *Carex* sp(p). were also present in the fen or as components of the woodland understorey. All insect remains from this point onwards confirm the local presence of the fen and pool habitats. The development of birch woodland marked the establishment of the Holocene deciduous forest. However, the radiocarbon dates at this site for the start and end of the high *Betula* pollen phase are clearly in error, in each case by about 2000 radiocarbon years, when compared with the previous dates for these pollen zone boundaries at many sites in the north of England (Innes, 2002d). More typical dates for the rise and fall of *Betula* pollen in the early Holocene are *c.* 10,000 and *c.* 9000 ^{14}C BP (Smith & Pilcher, 1973; cf. Table 3.16).

The rapid replacement of *Betula* by *Corylus* began several centuries of hazel domination of terrestrial environments at the site, no doubt favoured by the calcareous local conditions indicated by the deposition of the thick marl unit above the limnic mud. *Corylus avellana* macrofossils occur for the first time just above the point at which the *Corylus* pollen curve rises sharply, confirming the local presence of hazel, almost certainly as canopy dominant. The macrofossil evidence shows that the local wetland vegetation changed to one dominated by fully aquatic plants, particularly *Chara* sp(p). This submerged alga is indicative of base-rich, mesotrophic, open-water conditions, either quite shallow (1 m or less) or relatively deep (>6 m) but not in between (Moore, 1986); given the morphology of the site, the former seems more likely. Macrofossils further suggest that *Cladium mariscus* and *Carex* sp(p). formed the marginal wetland vegetation. Insect taxa from these deposits also suggest relatively shallow, well-vegetated waters: both the hydrophilid, *H. fuscipes*, and the Dytiscidae family, represented by *Ilybius* spp., are found in vegetation at the margins of stagnant ponds and pools (Hansen, 1987; Nilsson & Holmen, 1995). This open aquatic phase was concurrent with the deposition of the shelly marl, reflecting the calcareous conditions that would have promoted hazel abundance. The recognition of *Betula* macrofossils in this phase shows that, despite the dominance of hazel, birch trees were still present around the site.

Although there are indications from the pollen that other deciduous trees, particularly *Ulmus*, had joined the local woodland, the intense shade cast by dense *Corylus* thickets must have made it difficult for other taxa to compete. At the time that hazel abundance began to decline, the macrofossil data show that major changes were occurring in the character of the site, with the local wetland transforming from open aquatic conditions to a base-rich fen. This is evident from a sharp decline in *Chara* sp(p). remains, coupled with a large increase in the number and diversity of waterside and damp ground taxa. The fen was dominated by tall sedges, with herbs such as *Cladium mariscus*, *Eupatorium cannabinum*, *Schoenoplectus lacustris*, *Typha* sp(p). and *Carex* sp(p). and Pteridophyte sp(p). also abundant. A change from marl to organic sediment deposition coincided with the transition from open water to fen. More can be said about this hydrological development from the molluscan and insect data, which, like the plant macrofossils, provide mainly on-site, local ecological information. These data confirm that the site persisted as a quiet-water, isolated calcareous pool, apparently without access to flowing water, that became infilled with rich fen vegetation from the start of the third Holocene millennium. The presence of *Pisidium pectinatus*, which favours eutrophic waters (Preston, 1995), suggests that this small water body became rather nutrient-enriched, as do the aquatic Coleoptera: both *H. fuscipes,* and *Ilybius* spp. are predominantly found in stagnant, eutrophic waters (Hansen, 1987; Nilsson & Holmen, 1995). An indication of water depth can be gained from the relative numbers of *Valvata* species; the two species, *V. cristata* and *V. piscinalis*, have contrasting depth preferences, with *V. cristata* preferring depths of less than 2 m, whereas *V. piscinalis* is most abundant between 2 and 5 m (Økland,

1990), although it will live in shallow water. In the sample from 220–230 cm the ratio of *V. piscinalis* to *V. cristata* is around 5:2, suggesting that the depth of water was more congenial for *V. cristata*, although not limiting for *V. piscinalis*. The high numbers of *V. cristata* suggest the shallow end of the *V. cristata* range, so a depth of less than 1.5 m is most likely. This agrees well with the interpretation made from the *Chara* data mentioned above, and so a pool depth of about 1 m can be confirmed. The presence of *P. fontinalis* suggests that the pond was well oxygenated. However, disturbance of the water-body must have been periodic or limited because the ratio of shells to opercula of *B. tentaculata* is close to parity, a situation found only in quiet conditions. There are no species of Mollusca that suggest the pool was prone to drying even at its margins, so a permanent water body is indicated, which agrees well with the plant macrofossil, insect and pollen evidence for the lower and middle part of the core.

The records for *B. tentaculata, G. crista, H. complanatus* and *Acroloxus lacustris* in the molluscan assemblage suggest increasing quantities of macrophytic vegetation in the water body, although the low numbers of these taxa in comparison with *L. peregra, V. piscinalis* and *V. cristata* suggest that the vegetation cover was not dense. Some of the plant species were probably emergent above the water surface, providing a habitat for *Vertigo* spp. The large numbers of *L. peregra* also suggest shallow water, as this species prefers areas of muddy substrate around pools and in their shallow margins. The low numbers of *Pisidium* spp. and *S. corneum* may indicate that the bed of the pond was rich in plant debris provided by the abundant remains of *Chara*. Such conditions are generally not suitable for small bivalves, but *S. corneum* avoids them by climbing on aquatic vegetation (Killeen *et al.*, 2004). The molluscan data from Newby Wiske are similar to the assemblage found in calcareous valley pools and fens elsewhere in North Yorkshire, such as at Linton Mires in Wharfedale (Blackburn, 1938).

There is plant macrofossil evidence for increased vegetation in the wetland in the mid-Holocene, after the switch from *Chara* to organic mud and detrital peat sediment, as fen habitats became established and the pool became infilled. Fragments of wood in the sediment, in addition to increased numbers of *Betula* sp(p). fruits and the occurrence of a fruit and female cone of *Alnus glutinosa*, combine to suggest that wetland trees were encroaching on the fen as terrestrialization of the site proceeded. The absence of lignacious Coleoptera suggests that this mixed woodland was still located some distance from the site. By 170 cm depth, in the mid-Holocene, wet fen–carr woodland dominated the local vegetation, with *Alnus glutinosa* the most abundant taxon. *Frangula alnus* and *Rhamnus cathartica* formed the shrub layer of this characteristic *Alnus* carr. A diverse range of damp ground taxa, such as *Carex pseudocyperus* and *Lychnis flos-cuculi*, formed the herb layer. Aquatic plants declined but a few pools of standing water remained, surrounded by waterside

taxa such as *Rumex hydrolapathum* and *Schoenoplectus lacustris*.

Reconstruction of mid-Holocene environmental history beyond the wetland itself relies heavily on the pollen evidence. When the dominance of *Corylus* was finally broken, at about 8000 ^{14}C BP, the woodland swiftly diversified, with the expansion of *Ulmus, Pinus, Quercus* and finally *Tilia* to become major components. In wetter parts of the woodland, as well as in the wetland habitats, *Alnus* became locally common, surprisingly early if the date of *c.* 8000 ^{14}C BP is correct, as significant expansion of this tree is normally seen at around 7000 ^{14}C BP. There are, however, earlier dates for alder expansion in the region (Innes, 2002d), which are discussed in chapter 5. With the exception of *Pinus*, which declined as *Alnus* increased, this mixed deciduous forest was maintained until *c.* 5000 ^{14}C BP, when a decline in *Ulmus* pollen frequencies took place that probably signified a real decline in elm populations within the woodland. In the period before this *Ulmus* decline, very few plants were able to increase their representation in the vegetation cover, being unable to find favourable niches within the generally closed canopy forest. Only calcicole shrubs like *Corylus* and, briefly, *Rhamnus* were able to maintain significant populations within the mixed oak forest. The macrofossil record for *Tilia platyphyllos* shows that it was growing nearby, probably on well-drained soils slightly further from the site. This species of *Tilia* favours base-rich soils (Stace, 1997) but is rare so far north today (Preston *et al.*, 2002) and may indicate a higher temperature than at present.

The start date for the *Ulmus* decline at Newby Wiske, at 5241 ± 32 ^{14}C BP, is typical for this feature in British lowland pollen diagrams. The pollen evidence indicates that the closed forest canopy was broken, allowing the expansion of a range of open-ground species, including some that are clearly associated with agricultural activity. A consistent cereal-pollen curve from this point must represent cultivation by Neolithic farmers, the range of weeds that accompany the cereal curve reinforcing that interpretation. *Plantago lanceolata, Taraxacum*-type and *Pteridium* are perhaps the clearest members of this association, but several others also occur. The more open nature of the woodland after this event is demonstrated by the enhanced frequencies of *Fraxinus*, a successional forest tree. *Ulmus, Tilia* and *Alnus* are the trees most affected by the disturbance at this time. The radiocarbon date for the top of the truncated profile is 4315 ± 40 ^{14}C BP, showing that the vegetation history of most of the Neolithic period is preserved in the Newby Wiske core. It consistently shows that small-scale mixed farming was carried on within more open woodland throughout this period, probably attributable to the fertile soils associated with the calcareous environments around the site.

Plant macrofossils have not been well preserved above 100 cm depth and it is therefore not possible to reconstruct the local wetland vegetation with any certainty after that level, which probably dates to about 6000 ^{14}C BP, interpolated from the radiocarbon dating series. Wood fragments continue to occur in the sediment and *Corylus* nut fragments are recorded between 60 and 70 cm, suggesting local stands or a small hazel copse. *Rubus idaeus, R. fruticosus* agg. and *Urtica dioica* could have formed components of the understorey, while the presence of *Eupatorium cannabinum, Typha* sp and the occasional oogonium of *Chara* sp(p). suggest the persistence of ponds at the site. Macrofossils in the top 10 cm of the core include *Persicaria lapathifolia*, an indicator of damp ground conditions, but the assemblage is dominated by taxa that are often found in areas of open and disturbed ground, such as *Urtica dioica*, Poaceae sp(p)., *Persicaria lapathifolia, Ranunculus* subgenus *Ranunculus* and *Chenopodium album*. Seeds of *Atriplex* sp(p). are abundant, which, considering the inland location of the site, are likely to belong to *Atriplex patula* (common orache). This taxon also grows in disturbed and waste ground environments (Stace, 1997).

In summary, the analysed profile at Newby Wiske contains an environmental record from the end of the Loch Lomond Stadial until well into the Neolithic, a period of about six thousand years. Although the lower radiocarbon samples have produced erroneous ages, the upper sequence of dates provides an acceptable chronology for the profile. The plant macrofossils and Mollusca provide a detailed record of the vegetation in and around this calcareous wetland but add little to the off-site environmental information from palynology. The record for *Tilia platyphyllos* is noteworthy for its northern location, reflecting the calcareous nature of the soils at this site. The environment indicated by the coleopteran evidence changes little throughout the profile: it indicates marshy ground with surrounding muddy ephemeral pools, a notable exception being the upper samples, which provide some evidence of drier, open grassland. Evidence of human activity is restricted to the *Ulmus* decline and, later, indications of extensive forest clearance for mixed farming during the Neolithic.

3.4 Marfield

Located to the east of Marfield Quarry (Chapter 2.6.1), just north of Masham, in a peat-filled palaeochannel at Marfield High Mains (SE 2175 8280; Chapter 2.3.1.1). Truncated southwards by aggregate extraction, this channel was probably an early course of the River Ure that was abandoned when the present river began to incise into the glaciofluvial sediments of the area. Its location is shown in Figure 3.9, together with a detailed lithological column of the sampled profile.

3.4.1 Lithostratigraphy

Most of the lithology (Table 3.17) consists of shell-rich marls and clayey silts, probably deposited in shallow open water, while the well-humified peat in the upper part

of the section may well have had a less aquatic origin. Gravel (unit 5) 2 m below the surface was penetrated with difficulty by the gouge corer and had to be removed by auger to allow the Russian corer to access the sediments beneath (Plate 3.1b). Coring ceased when very stiff clayey silt was encountered.

3.4.2 Pollen

Samples were prepared for pollen analysis at ten centimetre intervals through the core, with slightly wider intervals near the more disturbed surface layers. A few levels in the humified peat (units 10 and 11) did not preserve pollen and levels in the stiff clayey silt below 300 cm were also barren; otherwise preservation was variable but often poor. It was also not possible to recover pollen from the gravel layer of unit 5. The pollen diagram (Fig. 3.10) is subdivided into seven local pollen assemblage zones (MF-a to MF-g). Horizons from which pollen could not be recovered are excluded from the assemblage zones.

ZONE DESCRIPTIONS

Zone MF-a (300–250 cm)
  Betula percentages in this basal zone are moderate at around 30% of total pollen, while other tree and shrub pollen is represented almost entirely by *Juniperus*, which rises to a peak of almost 50% in mid zone; there is a consistent but modest record of *Corylus*. Poaceae is the most important of the herb types, with Cyperaceae generally low. There is a considerable diversity of herb pollen taxa, albeit all in very low frequencies, of which *Artemisia, Helianthemum* and *Thalictrum* are most prominent. Micro-charcoal is high throughout.

Zone MF-b (190–175 cm)
  Betula frequencies are low and *Juniperus* has almost ceased to be recorded in this zone. Poaceae and Cyperaceae values are very similar to the previous zone. There is a great diversity of herb taxa, with *Artemisia* high and *Saxifraga stellaris* (starry saxifrage) and *Thalictrum* also markedly increased. *Pediastrum* and micro-charcoal frequencies are high.

Zone MF-c (175–155 cm)
  This zone is characterized by high Poaceae and Cyperaceae frequencies, with herb pollen taxa still present in great diversity, amongst which *Rumex* is prominent. *Artemisia* values have fallen from the previous zone and *Betula* percentages are rising. *Botryococcus* and *Pediastrum* algae percentages are high. Micro-charcoal frequencies are still high, but declining.

Zone MF-d (155–135 cm)
  High *Betula* and *Juniperus* percentages dominate

the assemblage in this zone. *Salix* increases, Poaceae decline and Cyperaceae are almost absent. Herb taxa diversity is greatly reduced; *Botryococcus* values are maintained but *Pediastrum* ceases to be recorded. Micro-charcoal values are very low.

Zone MF-e (135–77.5 cm)

In this zone *Betula* frequencies rise to almost 80% of total pollen, while *Juniperus* declines sharply and then ceases to be recorded. All other taxa are very poorly represented. *Pinus* and micro-charcoal values rise near the top of the zone.

Zone MF-f (77.5 cm)

This zone is represented by a single level in which *Betula* falls sharply, while *Pinus* rises to above 20% of total pollen and *Corylus* shows a small peak. Cyperaceae rise to 50% of total pollen. All

other taxa are very low. Moderate frequencies of micro-charcoal occur.

77.5–50 cm – barren of palynomorphs

Zone MF-g (50–10 cm)

Pollen assemblages of the final zone are dominated by Cyperaceae, which reach over 80% of total pollen, with Poaceae and *Taraxacum*-type also prominent. *Pteridium* and *Plantago lanceolata* show low but consistent curves. All other pollen types are very low, including all tree and shrub taxa. There are moderate frequencies of micro-charcoal at this level.

3.4.3 Plant macrofossils

No terrestrial plant macrofossils suitable for dating were

Unit	Depth (cm)	Description
13	0–16	Amorphous, slightly silty organic material Sh4, Ag+, nig.4, strf.0, elas.0, sicc.2
12	16–39	Orange-brown shell marl with some organic inclusions and Turritellids (some whole) Lc4, Sh+, test. (moll)+, part. test. (moll)+, nig.1, strf.0, elas.0, sicc.2, lim.sup.0
11	39–66	Brown, silty humified peat with some clay Sh3, Ag1, As+, nig.3, strf.0, elas.0, sicc.2, lim.sup.0
10	66–79	Black, well humified peat Sh4, nig.4, strf.0, elas.0, sicc.2, lim.sup.0
9	79–166	Buff shell-marl with silt and organic material Lc3, Ag1, part. test. (moll)+, Sh+, nig.1, strf.0, elas.0, sicc.2, lim.sup.0
8	166–175	Green-grey, silty shell marl with organic inclusions Lc4, Ag+, part. test. (moll)+, Sh+, nig.1, strf.0, elas.0, sicc.2, lim.sup.0
7	175–190	Dark grey clayey silt with shells and some gravel Ag4, As+, part. test. (moll)+, Gg(min.)+, nig.2+, strf.0, elas.0, sicc.2, lim.sup.0
6	190–210	Grey clayey silt with shells and gravel. Ag3, As1, part. test. (moll)+, Gg(min.)+, nig.2+, strf.0, elas.0, sicc.2, lim.sup.0
5	210–225	Gravel Gg(min.)4, nig.2, strf.0, elas.0, sicc.2, lim.sup.0
4	225–246	Clayey silt with small gravel Ag2, As1, Gg(min.)1, nig.2+, strf.0, elas.0, sicc.2, lim.sup.0
3	246–276	Buff sandy shell-marl with occasional small gravel Lc2, Ga2, part. test. (moll)+, Gg(min).+, nig.1, strf.0, elas.0, sicc.2, lim.sup.0
2	276–308	Dark grey clayey silt with shells and organic inclusions Ag3, As1, part. test. (moll)+, Sh+, nig.2+, strf.0, elas.0, sicc.2, lim.sup.0
1	308–329	Dark grey clayey silt Ag3, As1, nig.3., strf.0, elas.0, sicc.2, lim.sup.0

Table 3.17 Stratigraphy at Marfield, Core MF1. The particle-size distribution of silt units was confirmed using a Coulter Particle-size Analyser (see Chapter 2.1.3.1; Appendix IV).

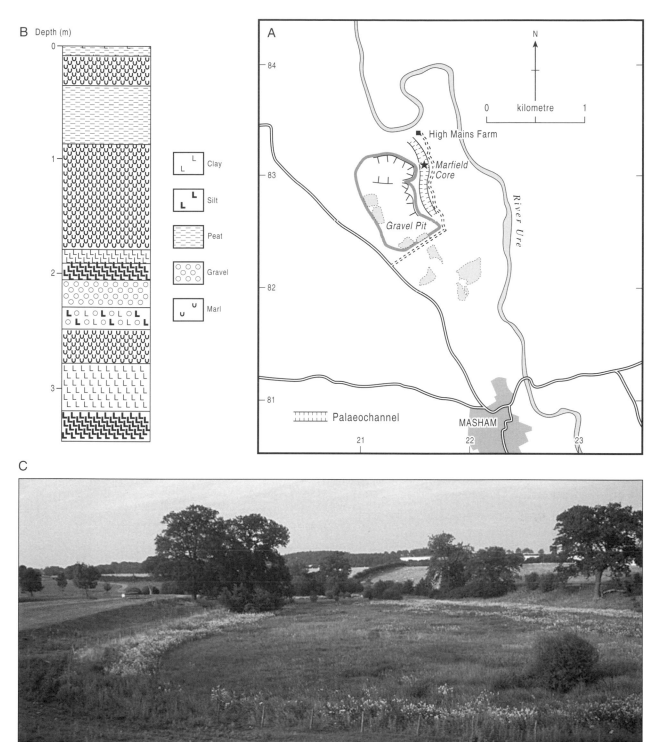

Fig. 3.9 The Marfield palaeoenvironmental site: A – Map showing the location of Core MF1 within the Marfield (High Mains) Channel (see also Plate 2.5); B – Stratigraphy of core MF1; C – View of the palaeochannel, looking north towards High Mains Farm.

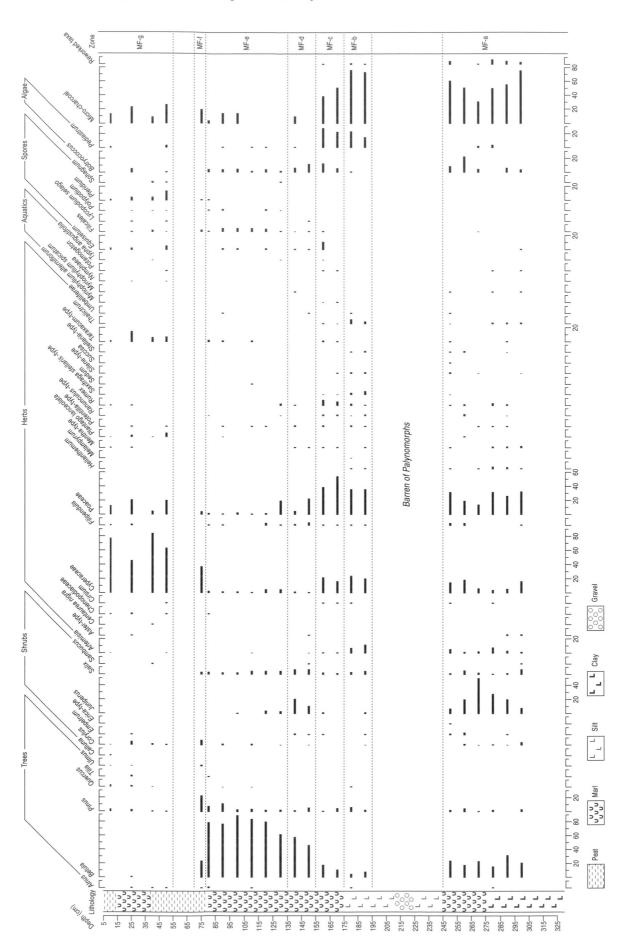

Fig. 3.10 Pollen diagram from Marfield MF1. Frequencies are calculated as percentages of the total land pollen sum (trees, shrubs and herbs).

Sample depth (cm)	16–20	20–25	25–30	30–35	35–39	85–90	90–95	95–100	100–105	105–110	110–115	115–120	120–125	125–130	130–135	135–140	140–145	145–150	150–155	155–160
Aquatic																				
Valvata cristata Müller	5	3	1	1	3	4						1								
Valvata piscinalis (Müller)						55	13	1	2	2	6	1								
Bithynia tentaculata (Linnaeus)																				
opercula																		1		
Lymnaea truncatula (Müller)	4			1															1	
Lymnaea stagnalis (Linnaeus)	2		2																	
Lymnaea peregra (Müller)	1					20	31	63	36	53	37	21	38	30	35	10	20	37	28	6
Planorbis planorbis (Linnaeus)			1																	
Anisus leucostoma (Millet)			1	1																
Gyraulus laevis (Alder)						3	9	24	16	13	20	9	15	16	6	13	18	30	21	13
Gyraulus crista (Linnaeus)		1	1	2	2	25	9	19	13	25	29	8	19	16	47	13	80	99	40	9
Hippeutis complanatus (Linnaeus)						1		1			1		1					3		
Planorbidae				2	2	9	22	38	16	32	24	11	11	30	21	11	42	56	99	22
Sphaerium corneum (Linnaeus)		1				2	1	3	1	5	5	3	1	2	3	6	4	5	5	4
Pisidium casertanum (Poli)																				
Pisidium personatum Malm			1																	
Pisidium milium Held						2		2	1	1	3		1	2	3	2	2			2
Pisidium hibernicum Westerlund									1		1		1	2	1					
Pisidium nitidum Jenyns						15	5	13	6	8	13	13	5	9	3	2	2	9	3	2
Pisidium spp.	1	3	1	1	2	11	4	8	4	8	7	10	7	7	4	1	8	10	2	1
Terrestrial																				
Carychium minimum Müller	1																			
Vallonia pulchella (Müller)	2																			
Cecilioides acicula (Müller)															[4]				[2]	
Total	17	8	8	8	9	147	94	172	96	147	146	79	99	114	123	58	176	249	199	60

Table 3.18 Molluscs from Marfield, Core MF1 (continued over the page).

Note: Numbers for Cecilioides acicula (Müller) are shown in brackets as this is a burrowing species and is often intrusive in association with fossil assemblages.

Sample depth (cm)	160–165	165–170	170–175	175–180	180–185	185–190	190–195	195–200	245–250	255–260	260–265	265–270	270–276	276–280	280–285	285–290	290–295	295–300	300–305	305–310
Aquatic																				
Valvata cristata Müller					7			1		4	1	78	246	13	6	14	64	48	50	70
Valvata piscinalis (Müller)					28															
Bithynia tentaculata (Linnaeus)																				
opercula											1					1				
Lymnaea truncatula (Müller)																				
Lymnaea stagnalis (Linnaeus)																				
Lymnaea peregra (Müller)	3		2		27				2	3	2	5	3	1	1		2	1	4	4
Planorbis planorbis (Linnaeus)																				
Anisus leucostoma (Millet)																				
Gyraulus laevis (Alder)	14				5						1	1				1		1	2	2
Gyraulus crista (Linnaeus)	11				20			2	1	7	2	22	30			3	29	32	50	26
Hippeutis complanatus (Linnaeus)	27	2		1	2			1	1		1		1				2	4	3	9
Planorbidae					13								10					1		12
Sphaerium corneum (Linnaeus)					1					2					1					
Pisidium casertanum (Poli)																				
Pisidium personatum Malm										2				2						
Pisidium milium Held					3											1				
Pisidium hibernicum Westerlund										3	4									
Pisidium nitidum Jenyns	1				12					5						1	2			2
Pisidium spp.	3			1	7		1		3		5	2		6	4		2	2	2	3
Terrestrial																				
Carychium minimum Müller																				
Vallonia pulchella (Müller)																				
Cecilioides acicula (Müller)																				
Total	59	2	2	2	125	0	1	4	7	26	16	108	290	22	12	20	101	89	111	128

Table 3.18 Molluscs from Marfield, Core MF1.

Note: Numbers for Cecilioides acicula (Müller) are shown in brackets as this is a burrowing species and is often intrusive in association with fossil assemblages.

recovered from the Marfield sediment profile, due probably to the preponderance of marl, which commonly lacks such remains. Factors of possible contamination by the modern sedge vegetation cover of the channel made macrofossil sampling from the near surface levels unwise, as any results that indicated a very recent origin for the sediment would therefore be open to question. Thus no macrofossil analysis of the Marfield core could be undertaken.

3.4.4 Molluscs

The samples from Marfield were provided as 5 cm sections cut from a Russian borer core. The fauna consists of 22 species, 18 from freshwater and 4 from land environments (Table 3.18). The state of preservation is mostly good, although levels with a high organic content have suffered some shell corrosion from the effects of organic acids. Although elements of the same 22 species are present almost throughout the succession, the variation in numbers of individuals of the species allows the identification of local mollusc assemblage biozones, which facilitate the description of the fauna and aid the evaluation of the palaeoenvironment.

ZONE DESCRIPTIONS

Biozone MFM-1 (310–265 cm) (Valvata piscinalis–Gyraulus crista)

This basal biozone contains abundant shells and is dominated by the gastropods *Valvata piscinalis* and *Gyraulus crista*. There is an almost continuous presence of *Lymnaea peregra* but the occurrence of *Gyraulus laevis* is sporadic. The only bivalve present in any numbers is *Sphaerium corneum*, although three species of *Pisidium* also occur at low frequencies. The environment indicated by the fauna is a pool without access to flowing water and with depths between 2 and 5 m, the water depth preferred by *V. piscinalis*. The continuous presence of *G. crista* suggests good quantities of macrophytic vegetation, although the low numbers of *L. peregra* suggests that areas of muddy sub-strate around the pool were limited.

Biozone MFM-2 (265–185 cm)

The sections sorted for Mollusca had only small totals, made up almost entirely of the species found in MFM-1. It is not possible to gain a clear idea of the environment from such small numbers, but the occurrence of fine gravel in some of the samples suggests disturbance and inwash. Whether this was due to natural causes, such as periglacial action, or anthropogenic activity such as agriculture is impossible to determine (but see below for discussion).

Biozone MFM-3 (185–180 cm) (Valvata piscinalis–Lymnaea peregra–Gyraulus crista)

This zone marks a return to the conditions of MFM-1, albeit with some slight differences. The high values for *V. piscinalis* and *G. crista* continue, as does the low representation of bivalves. The counts for *L. peregra* are high and *Valvata cristata* makes its first appearance. The occurrence of the latter species suggests a shallowing of the water from MFM-1, as *V. cristata* generally occurs in water less than 2 m in depth. The higher values for *L. peregra* in MFM-3 perhaps indicate infilling of the pool during MFM-2 and shallowing water with expansion of muddy substrate habitats as a consequence.

Biozone MFM-4 (180–165 cm)

This biozone has low molluscan totals and as such cannot be readily interpreted in terms of the palaeoenvironment, but the lack of Mollusca and the occurrence of gravel clasts up to 12 mm diameter together suggest a further phase of disturbance of the surface of the surrounding land (see MFM-2 and discussion below).

Biozone MFM-5 (165–120 cm) (Lymnaea peregra–Gyraulus laevis–Gyraulus crista)

MFM-5 is characterized by increasing numbers of Mollusca of a greater diversity of species, suggesting good conditions for ecosystem development. The absence of *V. piscinalis* suggests shallow water conditions, although the lack of *V. cristata* in what would otherwise seem a favourable habitat is difficult to explain, unless the harsh conditions of MFM-4 caused a local extinction of the species and its absence from MFM-5 is due to slow re-immigration into the water body. The abundance of *Gyraulus* indicates good quantities of macrophytic vegetation and probably areas of sandy substrate favoured by *Gyraulus laevis*. The consistent presence of the bivalves *S. corneum, Pisidium milium* and *Pisidium nitidum* indicates a stable substrate low in organic debris, as these shallow infaunal species are inhibited by disturbance of the bed of the pond and the presence of high amounts of organic material.

Biozone MFM-6 (120–85 cm) (Valvata piscinalis–Lymnaea peregra–Gyraulus laevis–Gyraulus crista)

MFM-6 marks a continuation of the conditions of MFM-5 but with the significant addition of rising numbers of *V. piscinalis*. The renewed presence of this species is either due to it being slow to re-colonize the water body after the local molluscan extinction of MFM-4, or due to an increase in the water depth in the pool. As *V. piscinalis* has good capacities of dispersal, as demonstrated by its occurrence in numbers in MFM-1 (see also Keen *et al.*, 1988), the most probable explanation of its re-appearance is that the water depth increased enough to allow a favourable habitat to develop. It is possible that a rise in water level was due to some climatic cause, either an increase in precipitation or decrease in evapo-transpiration, although the latter could also have been caused artificially by human-induced vegetation destruction.

Biozone MFM-7 (39–16 cm) (Valvata cristata–Lymnaea truncatula–Planorbis planorbis–Anisus leucostoma–Gyraulus crista)

The youngest biozone in the succession is separated from those below by a non-sampled level (39–85 cm) represented by a layer of peat. MFM-7 is low in molluscan numbers, but unmistakable in its environmental indications. The species of the relatively deep pool in MFM-6 are replaced by species of shallow water. The re-appearance of *V. cristata* at the expense of *V. piscinalis* clearly shows water depths considerably less than 2 m. The occurrence of *Lymnaea truncatula*, *Anisus leucostoma* and *Pisidium personatum* suggests stagnant conditions (the "slum" group in the terminology of Sparks (1961)), where water oxygen levels are low and pools are often only a few centimetres deep and prone to drying out. The presence in MFM-7 of a few land shells of wetland habitats (*Carychium minimum*, *Vallonia pulchella*) confirms that by the top of this biozone a fen or swamp had replaced the open water pool.

3.4.5 Chronology

Plant macrofossils suitable for AMS dating were not present within the Marfield sediments and so no radiocarbon chronology is available for this site. Relative dating from the pollen record suggests an age range for this profile from the Lateglacial Interstadial, about 11,000 ^{14}C BP, to the early Holocene, at about 9000 ^{14}C BP. Peat deposits of probable Late Holocene age cap the profile.

3.4.6 Synthesis: Marfield

The pollen spectra of zone MF-a, from beneath the gravel (unit 5), indicate sedge and grass vegetation growing at the site, with open *Betula* and *Juniperus* woodland and subsidiary *Pinus* and *Salix*, although the pine pollen may well have been transported from some distance away. The herb assemblage, particularly *Artemisia*, *Helianthemum* and *Thalictrum*, indicates pioneer taxa tolerant of the soil and climatic conditions that existed towards the end of the Lateglacial Interstadial. About half of the land pollen sum is contributed by *Juniperus* and *Betula*, however, suggesting that open park woodland remained important within the local vegetation in the later stages of this final part (GI-1a) of the Interstadial, although perhaps reduced from its interstadial

maximum. In that context, the gravels of unit 5 are likely to represent deposition of clastic material under the following severely cold conditions of the Loch Lomond Stadial (GS-1), within a virtually devegetated landscape. The reduction of Mollusca to very low levels in this part of the profile (MFM-2 & 4) supports this deduction and indicates radical changes in the local environment inimicable to biological production. The occurrence of near-extinction phases in the Molluscan record is similar to the sequence reported by Keen *et al.* (1988) at Bingley Bog, West Yorkshire, where Molluscan extinction levels are attributed to very cold climatic conditions during the Lateglacial. Under such sub-arctic conditions the ice-cover of the pond was prolonged into the summer and left only a short time for oxygen exchange between the atmosphere and the water, thus progressively de-oxygenating the water and making it unsuitable for life. Such a control is a major influence on the northern limits of many freshwater molluscan species in the present Arctic (Økland, 1990) and has been invoked by Jones *et al.* (2000) to explain similar extinction horizons in the Lateglacial deposits at Lilburn Steads, Northumberland. At Marfield the molluscan analyses have led to multiple zonation of the Lateglacial sediments and so agree well with the pollen data. The earliest biozone, MFM-1, already had a thriving population but the ecosystem received two setbacks to its development, in MFM-2 and MFM-4, separated by a more favourable time for molluscan growth in MFM-3. Biozones MFM-5 and 6 indicate good conditions for Mollusca, attributable by comparison with the palynology to the Holocene; MFM-7 marks the final infill of the pool and its replacement with a fen, probably at some stage in the later Holocene.

Pollen zones MF-b to MF-d represent transitional environments and a vegetation succession from open sedge-tundra conditions with *Artemisia* through more stable grassland and open *Juniperus-Betula* shrub woodland to fully developed closed *Betula* woodland. This must record improving climate and soil conditions at the start of the Holocene. The molluscan data from these levels also record increasingly genial environments and support this interpretation. Consistently high micro-charcoal percentages throughout the profile before the establishment of the birch forest point to the continuous presence of fire, as well as efficient particle transport across open herbaceous vegetation, during the Lateglacial period and the transition into the Holocene.

In the upper metre of the profile an important palynological change coincides with the major stratigraphical boundary between units 9 and 10, with the rise of sedges and the decline in birch dominance occurring at the same time as the switch from marl to peat deposition. The rise in sedges may represent the increase in available habitat on the wetland surface as the shallowing water body provided more local terrestrial environments, contributing a higher proportion of on-site pollen to the sediment. It is more likely, however, that a hiatus exists between units 9 and 10 that represents most of the Holocene. Zone MF-g is completely different to all previous pollen data, as the lack of virtually any tree and shrub pollen suggests an entirely cleared landscape of the kind produced by intensive human activity in recent, late Holocene times. As well as the local wetland sedge communities, pasture and waste ground types like *Plantago lanceolata, Taraxacum*-type and *Pteridium* indicate that the dryland areas also carried completely open, grassland vegetation. The lack of cereal-type pollen or any arable pollen indicators suggests any such activity near to the site was pastoral in nature. Peat cutting in the late Holocene could have been responsible, removing most of any existing mid- and late Holocene record, with regrowth of peat in recent times. The parallel molluscan analysis confirms a major change to the equivalent uppermost zone, MFM-7; the re-appearance of *V. cristata* at the expense of *V. piscinalis* points to a shallowing of water depths and there are species indicative of stagnant conditions (*L. truncatula, A. leucostoma, P. personatum*), with low oxygen levels and shallow pools that are prone to drying out. The presence in MFM-7 of a few land shells of wetland habitats (*C. minimum, V. pulchella*) confirms that by the top of this biozone a fen or swamp had replaced the former open-water pool, although the molluscan sequence across the boundary (and possible hiatus) is incomplete and thus cannot assist further with its interpretation.

In summary, although the Marfield profile has no radiocarbon dating control, the relative chronology of the pollen stratigraphy provides a satisfactory time frame for the bulk of the palaeoenvironmental record. The two thousand year record spanning the Lateglacial–Holocene transition includes typical vegetation changes from the shrub woodland of the Lateglacial temperate phase, through the tundra-type vegetation of the Loch Lomond Stadial, into the birch forest of the early Holocene. The climate inferences provided by the molluscan data support this analysis. The main value of the site is therefore its record of vegetation history for this transitional period. The upper half metre of the profile may be separated from the rest of the sediment column by a hiatus of several thousand years, as the almost complete absence of trees in this section suggests that it is very recent and may represent regrowth of the mire after peat cutting or some other form of disturbance. The vegetation away from the site itself seems to have been open grassland at this later stage in its history. The mollusc evidence agrees that the environment of deposition of this upper unit is quite different, being a fen rather than the quiet, isolated pool that existed here in the early Holocene.

3.5 Sharow Mires

Sharow Mires (SE 3250 7150) lies at the southern end of a well-marked linear feature that is a palaeochannel of the River Ure, the present course of which runs 300 metres to the west of the site (Fig. 2.32). This palaeochannel lies to the west and south of Sharow village, which itself is situated to the north-east of Ripon (Fig. 3.11). The sample site lies at the edge of cultivated farmland, adjacent to an area of mature woodland on wet and peaty soil.

3.5.1 Lithostratigraphy

The lithostratigraphy of the deposits at Sharow Mires is known only from the sample core (Fig. 3.11), which was difficult to recover and required repeated effort and the use of multiple types of coring equipment. The upper eight metres of generally very wet sediment was sampled using, in combination, a hand-held mechanical piston corer and, for material that was too soft to be retained in the piston tubes, a Russian corer. The remainder of the profile down to the underlying till (at *c.* 11 m) was sampled using a commercial percussion drilling rig. A coring transect that would have provided a three-dimensional reconstruction of the sediment body was therefore not a practical option. The composite core from the sample site comprises three different types of sedimentary facies. Most of the bottom metre is gravel and sand, the next five metres consist of various types of silty, organic material and the upper five metres are dominantly clastic material, mainly sands, silts and clays, with a low organic content (Table 3.19). This sequence is consistent with interpretation of the site as a fluvial channel infill, with the overlying sequence recording silting up of the channel following abandonment.

3.5.2 Pollen

Samples for pollen analysis were prepared at ten centimetre intervals through the core, with slightly closer intervals to establish some pollen zone boundaries (Fig. 3.12). Generally pollen preservation was moderate, although a few levels did not preserve pollen. It was also not possible to recover pollen from the occasional sand layers present in the sequence. The diagram (Fig. 3.12) is divided into six local pollen assemblage zones (SW-a to SW-f).

ZONE DESCRIPTIONS
Zone SW-a (1080–897.5 cm)
    This basal zone is dominated by high frequencies of *Corylus*, which reaches almost 60% of total pollen. *Alnus* percentages are also high, with *Quercus* present at moderate values. All other tree and shrub pollen types are low. Poaceae account for most herbaceous pollen, with peaks in *Plantago lanceolata*, Cyperaceae and the aquatic *Typha latifolia*. A substantial micro-charcoal curve is indicated.

Zone SW-b (897.5–665 cm)
    In this zone *Corylus* frequencies decline and *Alnus* increases to become the most important contributor to the assemblage. All other tree and shrub types are low, although *Betula* increases and *Fraxinus* shows a peak early in the zone. Other pollen curves are

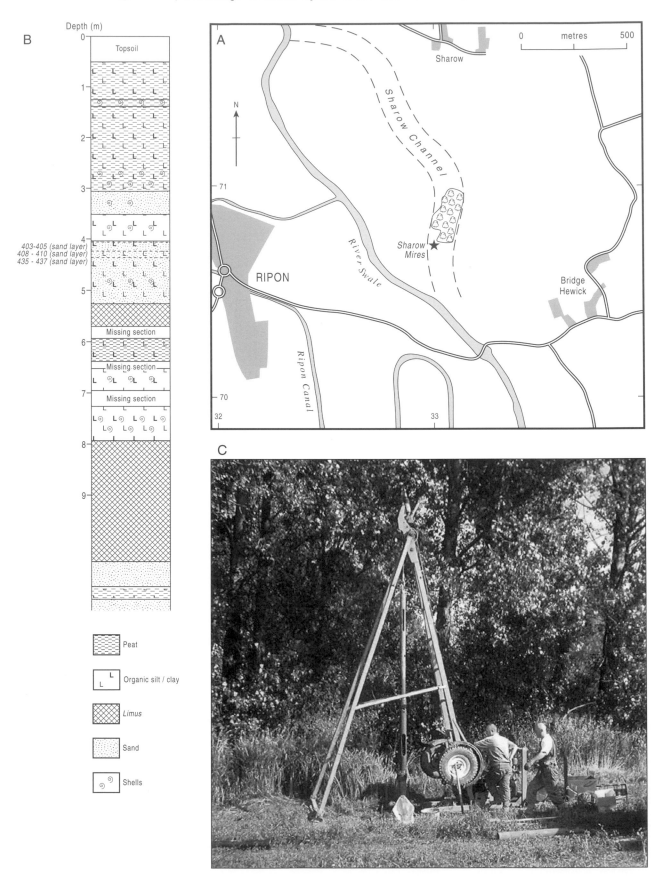

Depth (m)

B

Topsoil

403-405 (sand layer)
408 - 410 (sand layer)
435 - 437 (sand layer)

Missing section

Missing section

Missing section

A

N

71

RIPON

70

32   33

Sharow

Sharow Channel

River Swale

Sharow
Mires

Ripon Canal

Bridge
Hewick

0   metres   500

C

Peat

L L   Organic silt / clay
L

Limus

Sand

Shells

Fig. 3.11 Sharow Mires: A – Location of the coring site; B – Stratigraphy of core SW1; C – Coring for the deepest sediments using a percussion rig (the day England won the Ashes, 2005).

Unit	Depth (cm)	Description
19	0–61	Topsoil (*stratum confusum*): orange sand silt; occasional organic debris Sc4 (Ag2, Ga2, Dh+), nig.2, strf.0, elas.0, sicc.3,
18	61–138	Organic clayey silt with sand specks Ag2, As1, Sh1, Ga+, nig.2, strf.0, elas.0, sicc.3, lim.sup.0
17	138–144	Organic silty clayey peat with shells. Sh2, Ag1, As1, part. test. (moll.), nig.3, strf.0, elas.0, sicc.2, lim.sup.0
16	144–172	Organic silty peat Sh2, Ag1, As1, nig.3, strf.0, elas.0, sicc.2, lim.sup.0
15	172–173	Organic silty peat with shells Sh2, Ag1, As1, part. test. (moll.), nig.3, strf.0, elas.0, sicc.2, lim.sup.0
14	173–303	Organic silty peat with shells and plant debris Sh2, Ag1, As1, part. test. (moll.), Lf+, nig.3, strf.0, elas.0, sicc.2, lim.sup.0
13	303–309	Organic clayey silt with sand and shells Sh1, Ag1, As1, Ga1, part-test.(moll.), nig.2, strf.0, elas.0, sicc.2, lim.sup.0
12	309–345	Pale yellow silty clayey sand with shells Ga2, As1, Ag1, part. test. (moll.), nig.1+, strf.0, elas.0, sicc.2, lim.sup.0
11	345–395	Organic clayey silt with shells and occasional sand Sh2, Ag1, As1, Ga+, part. test. (moll.), nig.2, strf.0, elas.0, sicc.2, lim.sup.0
10	395–443	Organic clayey silt with discrete sand layers (403-5; 429-10; 435-7). Sh1, Ag1, As1, Ga1, part. test. (moll.), nig.2, strf.1, elas.0, sicc.2, lim.sup.0
9	443–533	Organic clayey silt with shells and occasional sand (esp. 451-462) Sh2+, Ag1, As1, Ga+, part. test. (moll.), nig.2, strf.0, elas.0, sicc.2, lim.sup.0
8	533–575	*Limus* with shells Ld^{3}4, part. test. (moll.), nig.3, strf.0, elas.0, sicc.2, lim.sup.0
	575–600	Section missing
7	600–650	Detrital silty peat with occasional shelly material. Dh1, Sh1, Ag1, As1, part. test. (moll.), nig.3, strf.0, elas.0, sicc.2, lim.sup.0
	650–660	Section missing
6	660–700	Black silty peat with shells Sh2, Ag1, As1, part. test. (moll), nig.4, strf.0, elas.0, sicc.2, lim.sup.0
	700–730	Section missing
5	730–800	Black silty peat with shells Sh2, Ag1, As1, part. test. (moll.), nig.4, strf.0, elas.0, sicc.2, lim.sup.0
4	800–1020	*Limus* with occasional shells Ld^{3}2, Ag1, As1, Ga+, part. test. (moll.), nig.3, strf.0, elas.0, sicc.2, lim.sup.0
3	1020–1055	Sand and coarse gravel Ga2, Gg2, nig.2, strf.0, elas.0, sicc.2, lim.sup.0
2	1055–1080	Organic clayey silt Sh2, Ag1, As1, nig.2, strf.0, elas.0, sicc.2, lim.sup.0
1	1080–1090	Coarse gravel Gg(maj)4, nig.2+, strf.0, elas.0, sicc.2, lim.sup.0

Table 3.19 Stratigraphy at Sharow Mires, Core SW1.

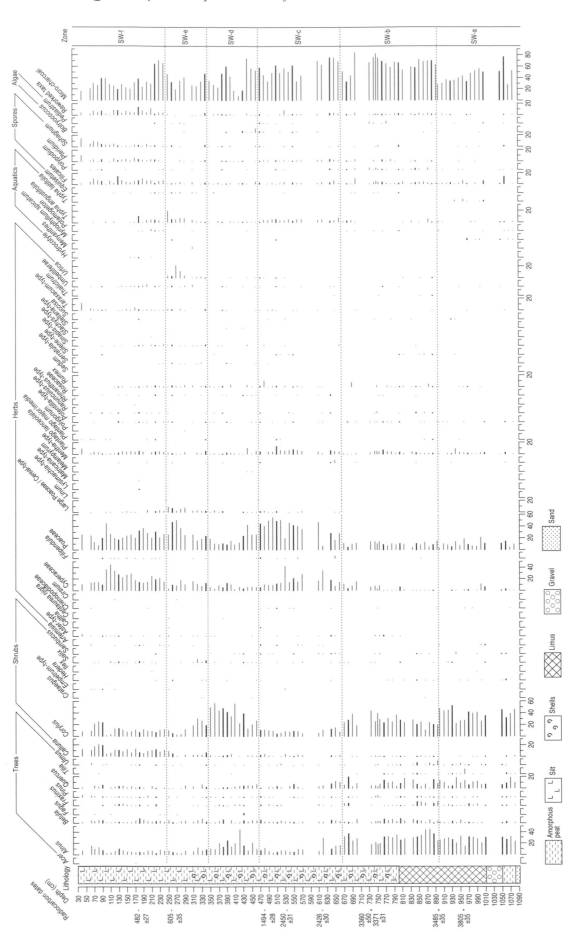

Fig. 3.12 Pollen diagram from Sharow Mires SW1. Frequencies are calculated as percentages of the total land pollen sum (trees, shrubs and herbs).

low, except for Poaceae, Cyperaceae and *Plantago lanceolata*, which achieve moderate values. Micro-charcoal percentages rise to high levels.

Zone SW-c (665–465 cm)

All tree and shrub pollen types are greatly reduced in frequency in this zone, while Poaceae and, to a lesser extent, Cyperaceae rise to high percentages. *Plantago lanceolata* is present throughout in substantial frequencies and there are low percentages of other open-ground indicator taxa like *Taraxacum*-type and *Pteridium*. Cereal-type pollen is consistently present, the aquatic *Typha angustifolia* occurs in substantial frequencies and micro-charcoal percentages remain high.

Zone SW-d (465–345 cm)

Corylus percentages rise sharply to almost 60% of total pollen in this zone, along with small rises in *Quercus* and *Betula*. *Alnus* also increases but all other tree and shrub types are low. Herbaceous pollen frequencies are very low, although with sporadic records for most types. Micro-charcoal frequencies are much reduced.

Zone SW-e (345–245 cm)

In this penultimate zone *Corylus* and *Alnus* percentages fall sharply and tree pollen frequencies are generally very low, while there are small increases in *Quercus* and *Betula*. Poaceae frequencies rise, herbaceous pollen in general is present in higher values and cereal-type and *Urtica* occur at peak frequencies. *Typha angustifolia* percentages increase markedly. Peak micro-charcoal frequencies were recorded.

Zone SW-f (245–40 cm)

Towards the top of the core, tree and shrub pollen frequencies remain low, except for *Calluna*, which rises to form a substantial curve at almost 20% of total pollen. Cyperaceae, *Plantago lanceolata* and *Pteridium* frequencies increase, as does the range and frequency of dryland weeds, with several types present at low but consistent values. The curve for reworked pre-Quaternary spores increases sharply, while *Sphagnum* also rises late in the zone. Micro-charcoal values are the lowest on the diagram.

3.5.3 Plant macrofossils

Plant macrofossils are well preserved throughout the Sharow core (Fig. 3.13), within which six plant macrofossil assemblage zones (SW-m1 to SW-m6) have been recognized.

ZONE DESCRIPTIONS

Zone SWm-1 (960–900 cm)

Aquatic taxa are abundant in the basal zone, including *Potamogeton natans* (broad-leaved pondweed), Characeae, *Myriophyllum verticillatum* (whorled water-milfoil) and *Ceratophyllum demersum*. Waterside and damp ground taxa, such as *Sium latifolium* (greater water-parsnip), *Persicaria lapathifolia* (pale persicaria), *Lycopus europaeus* (gypsywort) and *Alisma* cf. *plantago-aquatica* (water-plantain) are also present. Woodland remains are dominated by fruits of *Alnus glutinosa* but *Fraxinus excelsior* (ash) charcoal and wood and *Corylus avellana* nut-shell fragments were also recorded. *Stellaria media* (common chickweed), *Sonchus asper* (prickly sow-thistle) and *Persicaria maculosa* are amongst the disturbed ground indicators in SWm-1. Macrofossils of *Juncus* spp. and Musci sp(p). are abundant.

Zone SWm-2 (900–650 cm)

This zone yielded a high total number of plant macrofossil remains, with abundant wood fragments together with fruit, cone scales and female cones of *Alnus glutinosa* and fruitstones of *Sambucus nigra* (elder). Fruits of *A. glutinosa* are particularly abundant at 660–700 cm depth. A diverse range of waterside and damp ground taxa were also recorded, dominated by *Eupatorium cannabinum* and *Typha* sp(p). at the beginning of the zone, but the diversity increases upwards with the addition of a number of taxa including *Carex pseudocyparus*, *Cladium mariscus*, *Eleocharis* cf. *palustris* (common spike-rush) and *Menyanthes trifoliata*. Fruits of *Alisma* cf. *plantago-aquatica* (water-plantain) are present throughout the zone. Oogonia of *Chara* sp(p). and fruits of *Potamogeton natans* occur early in the zone, although the diversity of aquatic plant remains increases later, between 660–700 cm depth, where *Nuphar lutea* (yellow water-lily), *Ranunculus* subgenus *Batrachium* (crowfoots) and *Sparganium* subgenus *Xanthosparganium* (bur-reeds) also occur. Remains of Musci spp, *Carex* spp, *Juncus* spp, Pteridophyte sp(p). and *Urtica dioica* are also abundant.

Zone SWm-3 (650–488 cm)

In this zone, few wood fragments and no macrofossils of woodland taxa were recorded in an assemblage dominated by remains of *Carex* sp(p)., *Juncus* spp. and Pteridophyte sp(p). Waterside and damp ground taxa include *Alisma* cf. *plantago-aquatica*, *Apium* sp (marshwort), *Hydrocotyle vulgaris* (marsh pennywort) and *Sparganium erectum* (branched bur-reed). A few macrofossils of the aquatic taxa *Ceratophyllum demersum* (rigid hornwort), *Chara* sp(p). and *Potamogeton* sp were also encountered.

Zone SWm-4 (488–170 cm)

Number and diversity of aquatic remains increases. Initially these are dominated by *Ceratophyllum*

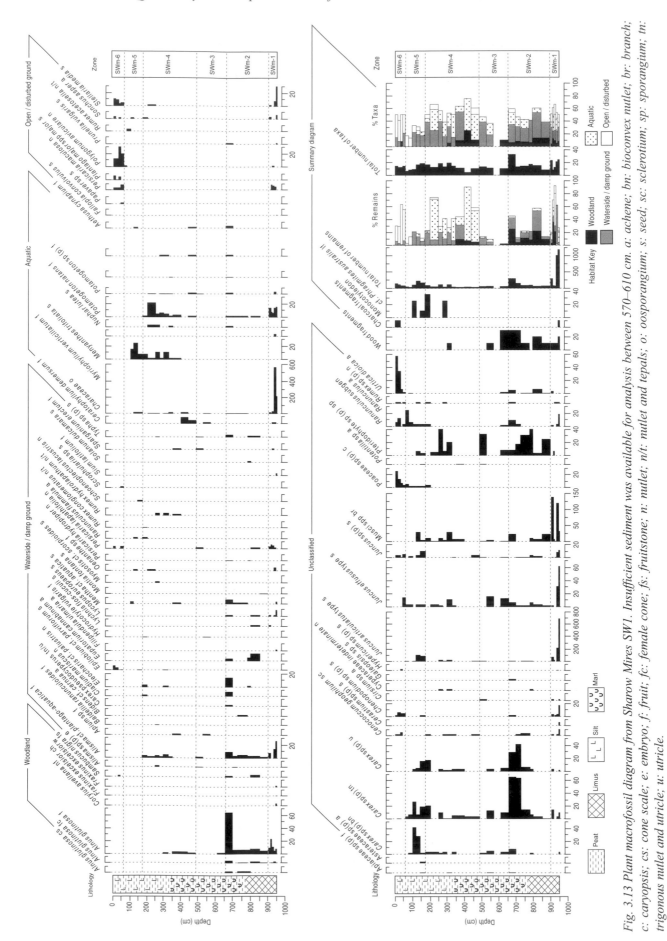

Fig. 3.13 Plant macrofossil diagram from Sharow Mires SW1. Insufficient sediment was available for analysis between 570–610 cm. a: achene; bn: bioconvex nutlet; br: branch; c: caryopsis; cs: cone scale; e: embryo; f: fruit; fc: female cone; fs: fruitstone; o: oosporangium; s: seed; sc: sclerotium; sp: sporangium; tn: trigonous nutlet and tepals; n: nutlet; n/t: nutlet and tepals; o: oosporangium; s: seed; sc: sclerotium; sp: sporangium; tn: trigonous nutlet and utricle; u: utricle.

demersum and *Chara* sp(p)., but *Nuphar lutea* and *Potamogeton natans* become more important towards the top of the zone. Waterside and damp-ground taxa include *Baldellia ranunculoides* (lesser water-plantain), *Menyanthes trifoliata*, *Myosotis* cf. *scorpioides* (water forget-me-not), *Oenanthe* sp (water-dropwort) and *Rumex hydrolapathum*. Pteridophyte sp(p)., Musci spp. and *Carex* spp. occur in slightly lower numbers than previous zones and few woodland remains were recorded.

Zone SWm-5 (170–60 cm)

This zone is dominated by macrofossils of *Carex* spp. and *Juncus* spp. Nutlets of *Menyanthes trifoliata* are also abundant and other waterside and damp ground taxa include *Cladium mariscus, Ranunculus flammula* (lesser spearwort), *Rumex conglomeratus* (clustered dock) and *Schoenoplectus lacustris*. The number and diversity of aquatic remains is reduced and no woodland taxa were recorded.

Zone SWm-6 (60–0 cm)

Taxa of open and disturbed ground habitats are abundant, including *Papaver* sp (poppy), *Persicaria maculosa, Plantago major* ssp *major* (greater plantain), *Polygonum aviculare* (knotgrass), *Rumex acetosella* (sheep's sorrel), *Sonchus asper* (prickly sow-thistle) and *Stellaria media* (common chickweed). Poaceae sp(p)., *Ranunculus* subgenus *Ranunculus* and *Urtica dioica* remains are also abundant. Few waterside and damp ground taxa occur and the only woodland macrofossil recorded was a *Sambucus nigra* fruit stone. Small fragments of charcoal are present in the uppermost sample.

3.5.4 Molluscs

Although Mollusca were present in most of the samples from Sharow (Table 3.20), and were analysed at approximately 20 cm intervals, only two levels (410–420 and 560–570 cm) produced over a hundred individuals and many samples had fewer than 30 shells. The high content of organic material at most levels in the core would have made for a hostile geochemical environment for the preservation of the aragonite shells of molluscs. Indeed, the leaching out of shell at a number of levels is indicated by the last, unidentifiable pieces of acid-damaged molluscan material. The calcite opercula of *Bithynia tentaculata* are more resistant to dissolution and some samples (620–630, 660–670, 680–690 cm) had these as the only molluscan remains, although some acid damage was apparent in most cases. The samples between 50 and 170 cm had no Mollusca.

The small numbers of shells recovered at most levels preclude the delineating of biozones and make ecological interpretation difficult. Overall, the Mollusca indicate that the site of deposition was a pond throughout its history. However, it is clear from the fauna (Table 3.20)

that, although the same general suite of species is present throughout the assemblage, detailed changes in numbers of individuals hint at environmental changes. In particular, the abundance of *Valvata piscinalis* between 440 and 610 cm, coupled with the low numbers for *Valvata cristata* (a real abundance, as indicated by the values in sample 560–570 cm, which has a total count of 129 shells) suggests water depths of 2–5 m, the preferred environment of *V. piscinalis,* in contrast to the <1 m depth preferred by *V. cristata* (Kerney, 1999). The replacement of *V. piscinalis* by *V. cristata* in level 410–420 cm (also a level with a significant molluscan count of 230 shells) indicates shallowing of the water body. The return to high values for *V. piscinalis,* in contrast to limited representation of *V. cristata,* at 300–310 cm is perhaps indicative of an increase of water depth, although total numbers in this sample (64) are marginal for firm palaeoecological reconstruction.

There is little evidence within the fauna for the 'slum' species of Sparks (1961), which would have suggested a stagnant marshy pool, prone to drying. The most abundant species present throughout the succession are Planorbidae, most notably *Gyraulus crista* (but also *Gyraulus albus*), which occupy quiet, weed-rich waters. The presence of *Acroloxus lacustris,* the lake limpet, suggests that the macrophytic vegetation was large enough to provide the thick stems or broad leaves required by this species. The occurrence of *Sphaerium corneum* in many of the samples and the general paucity of species of *Pisidium* may also suggest that the bottom of the pool was choked with organic debris hostile to the existence of most *Pisidium* spp.

The molluscan assemblage has only one fragment of a land shell, a piece of *Discus* sp. in the lowest sample (880–890 cm). The lack of land shells is typical of isolated pond environments, lacking flood inputs from rivers which would have incorporated land shells swept from the floodplain and into aquatic deposits.

3.5.5 Insects

A relatively large insect assemblage was recovered from the upper part of the Sharow Mires core, between 300 and 60 cm (Table 3.21). Preservation was exceptional and sufficient quantities were recovered to be of interpretable value, with the exception of a single sample, 300–275 cm, in which material was highly fragmentary and poorly preserved. Material sufficiently well preserved for analysis was also recovered from between 955 and 900 cm. Other parts of the core did not yield insects.

The assemblage from Sharow is predominantly composed of hygrophilous and aquatic species, found in marsh environments and open, standing bodies of relatively deep water. The lower part of this core (3–9 m) is dominated by representatives of the hygrophilous chrysomelid families, *Plateumaris* spp., and *Donacia* spp., impying a mixture of low-growing sedge fen and possibly taller reeds. The limited aquatic taxa, *Limnebius* spp. and Helodidae are associated with muddy, ephemeral pools; species directly

Sample depth (cm)	20–30	40–50	50–170	180–190	200–210	220–230	240–250	260–270	280–290	300–310	320–330	340–350	360–370	380–390	410–420	440–450	460–470	480–490	500–510	520–530	540–550
Aquatic																					
Theodoxus fluviatilis (Linnaeus)				1	1		2	1		3										1	
Valvata cristata Müller										25		1				6					
Valvata piscinalis (Müller)				1	3		2	9	4	19	2		4		35	4	3	4	11	10	2
Bithynia tentaculata (Linnaeus)						1					1		5	3	24	4		8	2	3	
Opercula				1	3	1	3		8	33		8	22	1	14	13	4	3	1	3	
Physa fontinalis (Linnaeus)										1											
Lymnaea truncatula (Müller)				1																	
Lymnaea stagnalis (Linnaeus)																					
Lymnaea peregra (Müller)				1	1		1			1	22		3		25	3				1	
Lymnaea spp.	1																				
Planorbis planorbis (Linnaeus)		1		1					1	6			1		4	1					
Anisus spp.																					
Bathyomphalus contortus (Linnaeus)				2						1					1						
Gyraulus albus (Müller)								1						6	2	1	2				
Gyraulus crista (Linnaeus)								2	2	2	1		1	13	127	10	5				
Hippeutis complanatus (Linnaeus)					3									5	3				1	7	
Planorbidae				1	1			7	1	1				4	9						
Acroloxus lacustris (Linnaeus)						1	2	3										1	1		
Sphaerium corneum (Linnaeus)		1			1			2		2							1	4	2		
Pisidium personatum Malm								1					3								
Pisidium obtusale (Lamarck)								1					1								
Pisidium subtruncatum Malm																					
Pisidium nitidum Jenyns									1							1	1	1		3	1
Pisidium spp.				1	1	1		2	1	3		1	1	1			1	3	1	2	1
Terrestrial																					
Discus spp.																					
Total	1	2	0	9	11	3	7	29	11	64	26	2	19	32	230	30	13	21	18	30	4

Sample depth (cm)	560–570	600–610	620–630	640–650	660–670	680–690	740–750	760–770	780–790	800–810	840–850	860–870	880–890	905–910	910–915	915–920	920–925	925–930	930–935	935–940	940–945	945–950	950–955
Aquatic																							
Theodoxus fluviatilis (Linnaeus)	1																						
Valvata cristata Müller	81	1		4				3			1	3	5			1	3	1	3				
Valvata piscinalis (Müller)	14	14		4				1	1	1	1	3				4	1	2	1	4	1		
Bithynia tentaculata (Linnaeus)	8	4						3	3	3	3				4	4	2	2		6			
Opercula	8	1	1	3	2	10		3	3	5	3			63	2	4	2	6	6	37	31	19	17
Physa fontinalis (Linnaeus)																				2			
Lymnaea truncatula (Müller)																							
Lymnaea stagnalis (Linnaeus)								1		1										1			
Lymnaea peregra (Müller)				2											1	1	1						
Lymnaea spp.	3																						
Planorbis planorbis (Linnaeus)				2																			
Anisus spp.								1															
Bathyomphalus contortus (Linnaeus)	1										1	1											
Gyraulus albus (Müller)	2			1				2							3	3	3	1	1				
Gyraulus crista (Linnaeus)												3					2	7		4			
Hippeutis complanatus (Linnaeus)								3	2														
Planorbidae				2									1										
Acroloxus lacustris (Linnaeus)	1			1																			
Sphaerium corneum (Linnaeus)	8	1								1							1						
Pisidium personatum Malm																							
Pisidium obtusale (Lamarck)																						1	
Pisidium subtruncatum Malm																	1						
Pisidium nitidum Jenyns	8	2		1							1									1	1		
Pisidium spp.	6	3		4					1	1	1				1								
Terrestrial																							
Discus spp.													1										
Total	129	26	0	20	0	0	0	12	7	8	5	10	7	0	9	8	12	14	5	18	2	2	0

Table 3.20 Molluscs from Sharow Mires, Core SW1.

Preservation Viable sclerites Comments	Good Yes	Excptnal Yes	Good Yes	Good Yes	Good Yes	Good Yes	Poor Yes	Good Yes	Good Yes
Sample depth (cm)	60–80	100–122	122–144	144–172	172–200	250–275	275–300	300–325	325–350
Dyschirius globosus									
Trechus spp.						*			
Bembidion spp.			*		*				
Pterostichus spp.									
Gyrinidae									
Gyrinius spp.	*	*			*		*		
Dytiscidae									
Graptodytes spp.						*			
Illybius spp.				*					
Agabus spp.			*						
Hydraenidae									
Hydraena spp.								*	
Octhebius spp.					*	*			
Limnebius spp.	*								
Helophorus spp.						*			
Hydrophilidae									
Cercyon spp.	*	*	*						
Crptopleurum minutum	*								
Hydrobius fuscipes						*			
Staphylinidae									
Olophrum spp.									
Oxytelus rugosus		*							
Aleocharinae gen. & spp. Indet.		*							
Helodidae									
Helodidae gen & spp. indet				*	*				
Dryopidae									
Esolus parallelepipedus					*				
Chrysomelidae									
Donacia versicolorea *Plateumaris/Donacia* spp.	*			*	*		*	*	*
Chrysomelidae									
Phylotreta spp.									
Curculionidae									
Apion spp.	*								*
Sitona spp.						*			
Bagous spp.									
Tanysphyrus lemnae									

Good Yes	Good Yes	Good Yes	Good Yes	Good Yes	Good Yes	Good Yes	Good No	Good Yes	Good Yes Frag.	Good Yes	Good Yes
660–700	700–730	730–780	800–850	850–900	905–910	910–915	915–920	925–930	935–940	945–950	950–955
											*
									*		
					*						
					*				*		*
*										*	
*						*					
											*
*											
*	***	*		*				*	*		
								*		*	
											*
			*								

Table 3.21 Insects from Sharow Mires, Core SW1.

OxA-12929   482 ± 27 ^{14}C BP (540–500 cal. BP; cal. AD 1410–1450)

This date provides an age for the switch from highly organic peat-rich sediments to domination of alluvial silts and clays. It indicates a late Medieval (early 15th century AD) age for this transition. Low tree pollen values, indicating only patchy scrub growth and high non-arboreal frequencies in this upper part of the profile are compatible with this date.

GrA-25050   605 ± 35 ^{14}C BP (670–530 cal. BP; cal. AD 1280–1420)

This date provides an age for a phase of increased agricultural indicator pollen within a highly organic part of the alluvial profile. Tree and shrub frequencies are particularly low and cereal-type pollen rises to a peak. Agricultural weeds including *Urtica* and *Plantago lanceolata* are also present in high values. *Linum* is present also. The date indicates a late Medieval, 14th century AD, age for this agricultural expansion, which fits well with the pollen evidence.

OxA-13105   1494 ± 28 ^{14}C BP (1420–1310 cal. BP; cal. AD 530–640)

This date provides an age for a switch from highly organic alluvial sediments to a minerogenic layer. This corresponds with an increase in tree pollen frequencies and reduction in probably local Poaceae percentages. Cereal-pollen peaks and *Plantago lanceolata* occur prior to this switch in increased frequencies. The date suggests that these vegetation changes occurred in the late 6th and early 7th centuries AD. The pollen data are quite compatible with such a date.

OxA-13141   1170 ± 100 ^{14}C BP (1300–920 cal. BP; cal. AD 650–1030)

This date is from a level only a few centimetres below date OxA-13105. It also provides an age for the mid-profile switch from highly organic alluvial sediments to a minerogenic layer, with high Poaceae, cereal-type and *Plantago lanceolata* pollen before the change, replaced by increased tree pollen frequencies above it. The date, with a greater standard deviation than date OxA-13105, indicates an age range between the 8th and 10th centuries AD. Again the pollen data are compatible with such an age.

OxA-12930   2450 ± 31 ^{14}C BP (2720–2350 cal. BP; 770–400 cal. BC)

This date provides an age near the replacement of *Alnus* and *Corylus* woodland by Poaceae and Cyperaceae dominated vegetation. Agricultural indicator pollen also increases during this change. This layer is more organic than those below and above it. The date suggests an age between the 4th and 7th centuries BC for this vegetation change. This is an acceptable date for the pollen data. Iron Age agriculture may be partly responsible for this reduction in tree cover and spread of cultivation and open ground. A climatic shift around this time towards wetter and colder conditions may also have caused such changes, increasing wetland communities.

OxA-12931   2426 ± 30 ^{14}C BP (2700–2350 cal. BP; 750–400 cal. BC)

This date provides another age estimate of the change from woodland to sedge grassland with increased agricultural indicators recorded by OxA-12930. The same environmental changes are beginning at this level and again are dated to between the 4th and 7th centuries BC. Iron Age agriculture and climate deterioration at this time could well have caused the pollen changes recorded. This date is very similar to OxA-12930 and conforms with the pollen data.

GrA-24645   3360 ± 50 ^{14}C BP (3710–3460 cal. BP: 1760–1510 cal. BC)

This date provides an age for sediment accumulation near the base of the pollen profile, just above a level with falls in *Quercus*, *Alnus* and *Betula* and increases in open ground weeds including *Plantago lanceolata*. This limited woodland opening is therefore dated to the middle Bronze Age. This is an acceptable date for the pollen changes recorded.

OxA-12928   3371 ± 31 ^{14}C BP (3700–3490 cal. BP; 1750–1540 cal. BC)

This date provides another age estimate from the same level as GrA-24645; being almost identical, it supports attribution of this small-scale clearance and spread of more open conditions (see above) as middle Bronze Age.

SUERC-8886   3485 ± 35 ^{14}C BP (3850–3640 cal. BP; 1900–1690 cal. BC)

This date provides an age for a significant change in woodland composition at the end of pollen zone SW-a, apparently caused by disturbance as levels of micro-charcoal and pollen indicators of disturbed conditions increase. The changes are of mid-Bronze Age date.

SUERC-8885   3805 ± 35 ^{14}C BP (4430–4230 cal. BP; 2480–2280 cal. BC)

This date provides an age for a minor phase of woodland disturbance near the base of the diagram, in which elevated frequencies of *Plantago lanceolata* occur with fluctuations in the main tree and shrub pollen types. This event can be assigned to the early Bronze Age. This lowermost date agrees with the low *Ulmus* percentages from the base of the diagram onwards in confirming the post elm decline age for the start of organic sediment accumulation at this site.

SUERC-8881   3905 ± 35 ^{14}C BP (4350–4080 cal. BP; 2400–2130 cal. BC)

This date provides another age estimate from the same level as date SUERC-8885 and while it differs from it, it is of the same order as the other date and confirms the age of this part of the diagram.

Table 3.22 Evaluation of radiocarbon dates from Sharow Mires, Core SW1.

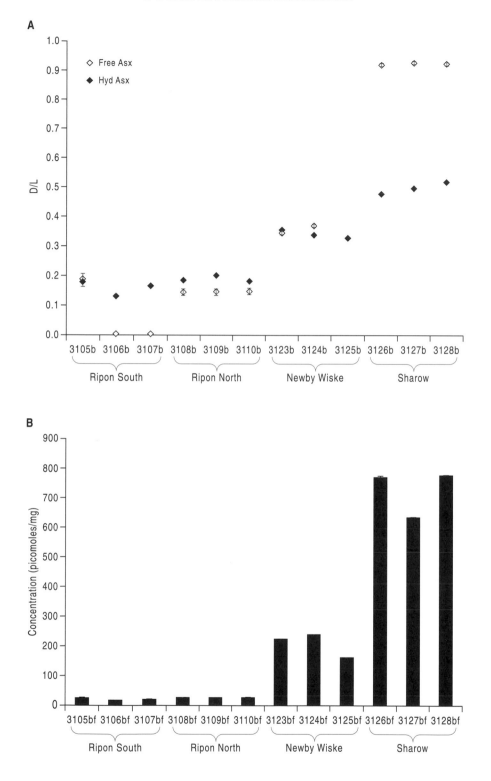

Fig. 3.14 Data from AAR analysis:

A – D/L values for Asx in Bithynia tentaculata *opercula from the four Washlands sites, with error bars representing one standard deviation about the mean for the duplicate analyses. An increase in the D/L value (the extent of racemization) signifies an increase in age of the sample. The AAR data for the Ripon and Newby Wiske sites are consistent with a Holocene age, with the Ripon sites being similar, significantly younger than Newby Wiske.*

B – Free Asx concentrations (in picomoles/mg) in B. tentaculata opercula. Error bars represent one standard deviation about the mean for the duplicate analyses. As the age of the sample increases, the protein breaks down, generating free amino acids, giving rise to the increase in free amino acid concentration from the Ripon samples to the older Newby Wiske samples. The Sharow samples are unreliable (see text and Appendix III.

associated with substantial bodies of permanent open, standing water are absent. The curcuilionid *Apion* spp. indicates that an area of drier grassland existed nearby, but in general the insect evidence suggests that quite dense wetland vegetation probably existed around an ephemeral, perhaps seasonal water body at Sharow during its early history.

In the upper section of the core, a similar assemblage persists, indicating marshland vegetation, although the aquatic assemblage is subtly different. Many of the species found in this deposit, such as *Gyrinius* and *Hydrobius fuscipes*, have been recovered from other cores in the Ure and Swale catchments and suggest permanent open water. A single indicator of flowing water, the elmid or 'riffle beetle' *Esolus parallelipepidus*, was recovered in the 2.0–1.72 m sample; its presence suggests periodic influxes of water from a more rapidly flowing source (Holland, 1972). Riffle beetles have been very badly affected in lowland river systems by the impact of alluviation (Smith, 2000). Also worthy of note are the species associated with damp, rotting, organic material in the upper three samples; the hydrophilids *Cryptopleurum minutum* and *Cercyon* sp., and the staphylinid *Oxytelus rugosus*, are all found amongst accumulations of this type of material and possibly indicate that the site was well vegetated, with open water persisting.

3.5.6 Chronology

The dating series from Sharow Mires has provided a detailed chronology for the alluvial sediments in this channel. The dates form a consistent chronological series and provide an age range for climatic change, human agricultural activity and changes in alluvial history from late Neolithic to recent times (Table 3.22). The relative dating provided by the pollen record, i.e. post-*Ulmus* decline, and other biostratigraphical indicators, such as the occurrence of the aquatic gastropod *T. fluviatilis*, does not conflict with this late Holocene age range. The Sharow sequence is clearly late Holocene in age, beginning after the immigration of the various forest trees, so there are no major pollen zone boundaries that could, with reference to regional pollen records, have provided relative ages. There is some supporting evidence, however, from the *Tilia* curve, as this tree is present in the Sharow record until about 3371 ^{14}C BP; that mid-Bronze Age date is very similar to age estimates from regional pollen diagrams at the point where *Tilia* pollen declines sharply or disappears completely (Innes, 2002d).

Molluscan specimens from Sharow were submitted to the NEaar facility (see above) for amino acid analysis, including both *Bithynia tentaculata* opercula (calcite), the usual three specimens, and three *Valvata piscinalis* shells (the only aragonite shells to be analysed from the Washlands). The resultant data, both from the *Valvata* shells and the *Bithynia* opercula, showed very high levels of racemization and protein degradation, to an extent

that is not consistent with the expectation from Holocene samples. However, there is significant evidence that the integrity of the closed system of intra-crystalline protein has been damaged during diagenesis. The clear divergence of these samples from the general trend in data from the NEaar laboratory (Fig. 3.14) is taken as an indication that *post-mortem* protein contamination or leaching has occurred, possibly as a result of corrosion (see Appendix III). Unfortunately, no age estimates are therefore possible from the data.

3.5.7 Synthesis: Sharow Mires

The very low frequencies of *Ulmus* at the base of the Sharow Mires pollen diagram (Fig. 3.12) indicate that organic sedimentation began after the elm decline, which occurred regionally at about 5000 ^{14}C BP. Mixed *Quercus*, *Corylus* and *Alnus* woodland dominated the local landscape, with alder occupying wetter areas in and around the channel. Wetland herb pollen representation is low, suggesting a dense cover of woodland taxa forming a closed canopy around the mire. Limnic sediments near the base show that the mire formed as a small pool, an interpretation supported by the presence of pollen of aquatic plants at low frequencies. The plant macrofossil and coleopteran assemblages in these basal sediments indicate that the pool was calcareous, with still water dominated by submerged and floating aquatic plants. The insects suggest that this water body, created following the abandonment of the former Ure channel, may have been relatively ephemeral and subject to seasonal drying. *Alisma* cf *plantago-aquatica* was growing in the shallow water at the edge of the pool, with *Alnus glutinosa*, *Filipendula ulmaria*, *Lycopus europaeus*, *Carex* spp. and *Juncus* spp. among the diverse range of vegetation occupying its damp margins. The presence of *Corylus avellana* and *Fraxinus excelsior* macrofossils agrees with the pollen data in demonstrating the presence of these taxa on the better-drained soils in the area, while a piece of *Fraxinus* charcoal suggests that some localized burning was taking place. The macrofossil records for open and disturbed ground taxa (Fig. 3.13) indicate the presence of these habitats around the site.

Above the basal horizons the increasingly soligenous nature of the mire is indicated by the high proportion of minerogenic material in the sediments. Increased levels of clastic deposition are most clearly manifested by layers of coarse-grained material such as the sand layer that interrupts the pollen record between 1010 and 1050 cm (Fig. 3.12). There are few indications of disturbance on the drier areas adjacent to the mire sufficient to have caused soil erosion and thus accounted for this greatly enhanced level of clastic input. Occasional *Plantago lanceolata* pollen occurs, suggesting some small localized areas of disturbed soils and damp grassland, perhaps associated with grazing of stock near the channel, but not at levels sufficient to account for the high-energy depositional event that caused the sand layer. A major flooding event that encroached on or utilised the channel might have been responsible, perhaps linked to the proximity of the river Ure following channel abandonment.

A real peak in *P. lanceolata* occurs at 950 cm, which might represent an episode of woodland clearance, although tree and shrub values are not reduced and so little opening of the woodland canopy can have occurred. There are no other weeds or other indicators of forest clearance or agricultural activity to support the *P. lanceolata* peak, although some increases are seen in the percentages of heliophyte trees and shrubs. Open ground weeds are present in the macrofossil assemblege, however, supporting the *P. lanceolata* record. Table 3.22 shows this minor disturbance to have occurred around 3805 ± 35 ^{14}C BP, in the early Bronze Age, although its impact on the local woodland appears to have been slight. The levels of micro-charcoal present in the sediment of the lowest assemblage zone, SW-a, are considerable, which is perhaps surprising given the unbroken nature of the woodland in this period. This evidence of burning may well have had a non-local source and was probably introduced in the same way as the high silt fraction in the sediment, either as a background extra-local atmospheric rain of particles, indicating extensive activity in the wider landscape, or by fluvial processes.

The next phase of the pollen record, in zone SW-b, records a substantial degree of woodland recession, probably attributable to forest clearance. Table 3.22 shows that this period encompasses the rest of the Bronze Age and it was during this time that human activity appears to have had a real impact on the vegetation. The levels of micro-charcoal are elevated to high values, broadly double those of the previous phase, and *P. lanceolata* is persistently present and regularly forms significant peaks. Other open-habitat herbs are present in low quantities too, including *Rumex*, *Ranunculus*-type, *Potentilla*-type, Chenopodiaceae and *Aster*-type, supporting the contention of some increase in disturbed habitats and a more broken forest cover. That Poaceae do not really increase in frequency suggests that this pollen curve is contributed mainly by wetland taxa associated with the mire itself, rather than grassy sward on the adjacent drier areas. Although *Corylus* and *Quercus* are reduced in this phase, they are replaced by other, secondary, tree types like *Betula* and *Fraxinus*, with *Tilia* also taking the opportunity to expand. A change in woodland composition rather than overall density seems likely.

In contrast to the pollen data, the plant macrofossil remains from this period of mire development do not include taxa of open or disturbed ground but are confined to wetland varieties. The macrofossils indicate that a local carr woodland, dominated by *Alnus glutinosa* with a lesser *Sambucus nigra* component, developed at the site. Locally produced *Alnus* pollen dominates the pollen assemblage in this phase. This dense woody vegetation, both on and around the mire, could well have screened the wetland from events on the surrounding drier areas where clearance would have occurred, preventing macrofossils of open

ground taxa being transported into the mire. Macrofossils of on-site wetland herbs are common, such as *Carex* spp., Pteridophyte sp(p). and *Urtica dioica*, suggesting that a wide range of damp-ground herbs formed the understorey vegetation of the carr. Evidence for particularly well-established wet woodland is seen at 660–700 cm depth, with peaks in the number of plant remains and the diversity of taxa recorded, although indicators of this on-site woodland are absent from the palaeoentomological record. Whereas all palaeobotanical indicators point to the development of carr woodland, the presence of aquatic taxa in the macrofossil record, including *Potamogeton natans*, *Nuphar lutea* and Characeae, as well as a few aquatic pollen types, points to the continued presence of areas of standing water. The major change in both the pollen and macrofossil assemblages that occurs around 670 cm suggests that there was a decline or retreat of the *Alnus* carr. Macrofossil remains indicate that it was replaced by a short-lived fen dominated by *Carex* and *Juncus* spp., in which *Typha* sp(p)., *Sparganium erectum*, *Alisma* cf. *plantago-aquatica* and *Baldellia ranunculoides* also occurred.

After this transitional fen phase, a more open, aquatic environment became established, shown by the initial domination of the macrofossil record by the submerged aquatic plants *Ceratophyllum demersum* and Characeae, the former indicating still, nutrient-enriched water, since it grows in eutrophic conditions and rarely produces seeds in flowing water (Preston *et al.*, 2002). *Nuphar lutea* and *Potamogeton natans* later became the dominant aquatic plants, probably as a result of out-competing the submerged plants for light, as both of the former have broad, floating leaves, and other macrofossil records show that *Alisma* cf *plantago-aquatica*, *Menyanthes trifoliata*, *Rumex hydrolapathum* and other damp-ground taxa grew at the edges of the water-body. The local pollen assemblage confirms this ecological interpretation, being dominated by swamp, fen and aquatic taxa. The occurrence of a few *Alnus* fruits suggests that this tree was growing around the damp margins.

The vegetational development in the middle part of the sequence confirms that a change to much wetter hydrological conditions had taken place. Table 3.16 shows that this occurred before 2426 ± 30 ^{14}C BP and so it is likely to have been prompted by the major climatic deterioration that took place about 2650 ^{14}C BP (van Geel *et al.*, 1996), which caused raised water levels and accelerated peat formation in mires and raised bogs throughout north–west Europe and beyond. Evidence of this process can be seen at Sharow Mires in the similarity of the two radiocarbon dates at 620 and 530 cm (Table 3.22), and the switch from slow silty peat formation to a rapidly forming detrital peat. The rise in aquatic macrofossils and *Typha angustifolia* pollen is symptomatic of this change and the very high Poaceae and enhanced Cyperaceae frequencies during this phase (the last in particular reprenting the mire surface vegetation) suggest the spatial expansion of the mire upslope, taking in higher areas of the channel previously above the wetland. Although short-lived, this wet shift caused major hydrological changes that persisted for centuries during the Iron Age. Forest clearance for agriculture may have contributed to environmental change at this time, as *P. lanceolata* values are consistently high, supported by peaks in *Rumex, Taraxacum*-type and other wet grassland weed taxa. *Calluna* increases also, signifying forest opening and perhaps some acidification of local soils or colonization of mire fringe areas due to paludification and thin peat formation.

Equally significant, however, is the low but persistent cereal-type pollen curve late in the phase. While its coincidence with the Poaceae peak warns that some of these large grains may originate from the greatly increased pollen production of wild wetland grasses, which are large enough to confuse with cereals (cf. Joly *et al.*, 2007), its symmetry with the *P. lanceolata* and other ruderal peaks suggests that Iron Age and Roman period cultivation was going on near the site. While the collapse of the tree and shrub pollen curves owes much to the relative rise of the Poaceae and Cyperaceae curves, some real deforestation seems certain, given the significant presence of the cultural indicators cereal-type, *P. lanceolata*, Chenopodiaceae and several other taxa. Iron Age forest clearance will have had a major environmental impact in this area and the pollen changes can be explained as easily by deforestation as by climate change. Tree removal could also have upset the mire hydrology though increased runoff from the cleared land surface. Even more intensive deforestation may have occurred during the warmer drier conditions of the Romano-British period when climatic conditions allowed the expansion of agriculture. Any tree and shrub removal would have added to the input of water and elevation of water tables in the mire. That micro-charcoal values remain very high during this period of wet climate suggests an anthropogenic cause for the fire and adds weight to the probability of human impact on the vegetation at this time.

The replacement of Poaceae by *Corylus* and *Alnus* in pollen zone SW-d reflects major changes in both climatic and anthropogenic factors that occurred at about 1494 ± 28 ^{14}C BP (Table 3.22), after the Roman period. This would place it culturally in the earliest Medieval (Anglian) in north Yorkshire. The warmer and drier climate of Roman times would have caused a change in mire hydrology that is represented by a gradual switch from detrital sediments to a more terrestrial peat, although the macrofossil remains of wetland plants are still common. Amongst the Mollusca, the switch from *Valvata piscinalis* to *V. cristata* confirms a shallowing of the water body at this point in the sequence. The great decline in Poaceae and Cyperaceae frequencies might also reflect the hydrologically-driven change in mire-surface vegetation, but indicators of agriculture, like *P. lanceolata* and cereal-type pollen, show similar sharp declines. Renewed climatic deterioration about 1500 ^{14}C BP (Blackford & Chambers, 1991; Chiverrell & Atherden, 1999, 2000) would have increased the presence of aquatic mire taxa, as shown by the plant macrofossil and molluscan

records, but would also have prompted some reduction in farming activity around the site, allowing the regeneration of hazel and alder as at least scrub woodland, suppressing the relative importance of dry ground herb pollen types. Both hazel and alder produce large amounts of pollen but also, if they were growing around the wetland, would physically screen out extra-local pollen from deposition upon the mire. Other woodland taxa like *Quercus* remain low, showing that the clearances of the previous Roman period could have brought about significant and long-term reductions in woodland cover in the wider area. Expansion of scrub woodland could also simply reflect the abandonment of much agricultural land at the time of the Roman withdrawal from Britain. Again the combination of human and climatic factors is probable. This local growth of scrub woodland was ended in the next pollen phase, SW-e.

Interpolation between the dates of 1494 ± 28 ^{14}C BP and 605 ± 35 ^{14}C BP (Table 3.16) suggests that, at about 1000 ^{14}C BP, a major episode of woodland clearance for agriculture began, lasting until about 605 ± 35 ^{14}C BP. It is logical to correlate this with the Medieval Warm Period of the centuries before *c.* 1300 AD, when environmental conditions permitted an expansion of agriculture into more marginal areas of the landscape. High cereal-type pollen percentages coincide with a major peak in *Urtica* and suggest arable cultivation as the main element of land use in this phase, supported by the records of arable weeds like *Sinapis*-type and *Artemisia*. Poaceae and other herb percentages also increase as the local hazel and alder woodland was removed, probably by human clearance. The end of this farming phase, at about 605 ± 35 ^{14}C BP, did not permit a regeneration of woodland cover around Sharow Mires. Renewed climatic deterioration, bringing colder, wetter conditions in the later Medieval and modern periods, was probably the cause of the agricultural recession, but much of the land remained as rough grassland while the spread of more acid heathland environments is shown by the greatly increased pollen frequencies for *Calluna* and *Pteridium*. The climate shift, added to probable overcultivation of soils, would have been responsible for the generally more acidic condition of the local soil and vegetation. This is reflected in the mire, with *Sphagnum* becoming important for the first time.

From this point the macrofossil record shows a return to fen and reedswamp conditions, dominated by *Carex* spp, *Juncus* spp. and *Menyanthes trifoliata* and with other damp-ground taxa such as *Cladium mariscus, Eleocharis* cf *palustris* and *Schoenoplectus lacustris* present in lower numbers. Caryopses of Poaceae sp(p)., which also occur, might belong to semi-aquatic grasses such as *Phragmites australis* (common reed), *Glyceria maxima* (reed sweet-grass) or *Phalaris arundinacea* (reed canary-grass); monocot leaves and stems resembling those of *P. australis* are present in the sediment from 172–100 cm depth. The insect remains also indicate low-growing, sedge-dominated wetlands but communities that would indicate taller reed vegetation were absent, despite the macrofossil records of *P. australis*.

With a radiocarbon date of 482 ± 27 ^{14}C BP at 174 cm, it is likely that the pollen record extends almost to the present-day at 40 cm, which may well be the base of the modern cultivated soil. It is possible to discern a small increase in the pollen of woody taxa, notably *Corylus*, *Calluna*, *Alnus* and *Betula*, at the top of the diagram, as well as macrofossil remains of *Sambucus nigra*, indicating some expansion of scrub woodland locally, followed by a reversion to grassland pasture with *P. lanceolata*, *Taraxacum*-type and *Pteridium*. The presence of these open habitats is supported by the macrofossil assemblage at the top of the core, which indicates open, waste and disturbed ground, dominated by taxa such as *Papaver* sp, *Plantago major* ssp. *major*, *Polygonum aviculare*, *Rumex acetosella* and *Sonchus asper*. Poaceae sp(p)., *Ranunculus* subgenus *Ranunculus* sp(p). and *Urtica dioica* were also abundant. Some evidence of this disturbance may also be identified in the insect assemblages; the presence of taxa associated with accumilations of rotting organic material may suggest a trash line at the periphery of this relict channel, perhaps a result of an increasingly active hydrological regime or a period of channel re-activation. The occurrence of *Epilobium* cf *parviflorum*, *Persicaria lapathifolia* and *Scrophularia* sp. (figwort) macrofossils suggests the presence of a few areas of damp ground. The present mature woodland adjacent to the site must have formed very recently, since it has no representation within the pollen record.

The changes in the local mire vegetation through this sequence would have resulted from fluctuations in the local hydrological conditions. Rises in the local water table could have come about by increased precipitation or by anthropogenic activity, such as increased runoff as a result of woodland clearance in the vicinity. Alternatively, a change in the flow of the River Ure may have flooded the abandoned channel, leading to the development of aquatic communities. Periodic flooding of this sort would have produced the sand/silt layers that are recorded in the stratigraphy. That open-water environments were consistently present at the site throughout almost all its history, however, is shown by the long-term stability of the wetland molluscan assemblage. Although assemblages of a similar type to that of Sharow Mires have not been widely reported from northern Britain (Jones *et al.*, 2000), such sites that have been published show a consistent fauna from the Early Holocene onwards. For example, most of the species from Sharow were recorded at Bingley Bog, West Yorkshire, in an early Holocene context (Keen *et al.*, 1988), although *Pisidium* species such as *P. casertanum* and *P. hibernicum*, relatively common at the latter site, were missing at Sharow, possibly for reasons of an unfavourable substrate (see above). The fauna from the pool at Lilburn South Steads, Northumberland, which has the *Pisidium* species lacking at Sharow but is otherwise similar in species composition, was dated by Jones *et al.* (2000) to 8710 ± 70 ^{14}C BP, again showing that the general fauna of the Sharow type immigrated into northern England early

in the Holocene. The later Holocene radiocarbon dates from Sharow Mires have shown that this fauna persisted relatively unchanged from then on.

The channel fill from Sharow Mires thus provides a continuous Late Holocene environmental record from some stage in the Neolithic period after 5000 ^{14}C BP, low *Ulmus* percentages from the base of the profile showing it to post-date the mid-Holocene *Ulmus* decline at about 5000 ^{14}C BP. The series of eight radiocarbon dates provides an excellent chronological framework that allows secure interpolation of events throughout the pollen stratigraphy. Although only the broadest relative dating is possible, based on the palynology, the post-*Ulmus*-decline character of the whole record and the Bronze Age disappearance of *Tilia* are in good agreement with the radiocarbon chronology. That the most significant evidence for woodland clearance for agriculture coincides with parts of the Iron Age, the Roman period and the later Medieval period, with lower-scale activity in the middle Bronze Age, accords with the regional picture (Innes, 2002d). The timings of the agricultural and woodland regeneration phases, again shown by the pollen, fit well with the wet and dry climatic periods recorded in the regional bog surface wetness records (e.g. Barber *et al.*, 1994a, b; Mauquoy & Barber, 1999; Hughes *et al.*, 2000). This lowland channel wetland has recorded what appear to have been sensitive responses of human populations to changes in climate, and thus also in soils and other environmental factors. The plant macrofossils, Mollusca and insect evidence all support the pollen in showing changes in water level in the Sharow pond at different times that correspond well with the regional climatic record. Such changes could have been stimulated by rainfall fluctuations and also by changes in land use around the site. Flooding from the nearby River Ure is an alternative cause, as that would have increased in frequency during the cold and wet climate phases.

In summary, the pollen, plant macrofossil and insect evidence concur in suggesting that the environment at Sharow was lush and well vegetated from the mid-Holocene to the late Medieval period, subsequent to which the site has been drained for agricultural use.

3.6 Ripon North (Hanson's quarry)

Hanson's quarry (SE 303767; Fig. 2.51) lies in the present floodplain of the Ure, near North Stainley, only a few kilometres south of the Nosterfield complex of sites but within a completely different sedimentological situation. At the time of study, exposures here showed a complex sediment sequence of glacial diamictons and gravels, capped by a mollusc-rich fluvial terrace gravel (Chapter 2.6.3). Organic material occurred within localized finer-grained sediments in the upper part of the terrace deposits, seen only in Section 3 (Fig. 2.51), perhaps representing a palaeochannel-fill.

3.6.1 Lithostratigraphy

The stratigraphy of the non-fossiliferous lower sequence is described in Chapter 2 (part 6). The shelly terrace deposits cap the earlier sequence over a wide area (Figs 2.51–2.55). The lithostratigraphy of the fine-grained channel-fill sequence comprises mainly silts with varying degrees of organic content and interbedded sandy horizons, resting upon the terrace gravel (Table 3.23). The palaeo-environmental investigation of this section was instigated following the recovery from it, by the quarry operator, of part of the trunk of an alder tree near the top of the gravel, which was sampled for radiocarbon dating.

3.6.2 Pollen

Two half-metre monolith samples were recovered from organic silts exposed at the top of Section 3 (Fig. 2.51). Samples were prepared for pollen analysis at four to five centimetre intervals through the sequence, according to the distribution of the more promising finer-grained sediments. Many levels did not preserve pollen, particularly in the upper part of the section. Where pollen was present the preservation was generally poor. The pollen diagram is subdivided into two local pollen assemblage zones, RN-a and RN-b (Fig. 3.15).

Z ONE DESCRIPTIONS

Zone RN-a (80–72 cm)

This lower zone is characterized by Poaceae, which contribute up to 40% of total pollen. Of the tree and shrub taxa, only *Alnus* and *Corylus* are present in significant percentages. *Taraxacum*-type, Cyperaceae and *Plantago lanceolata* are the other main herbaceous contributors, although several additional herbs occur in low frequencies. *Pediastrum* algae percentages are high.

Zone RN-b (72–52 cm)

This zone is similar to the previous one, albeit with some important differences. *Pediastrum* values are much reduced, *Calluna* percentages rise strongly and cereal-type pollen is recognized for the first time, persisting through the zone. *Alnus* values show a peak in mid-zone, but otherwise there is little change in the assemblage.

3.6.3 Molluscs

The molluscan samples (Table 3.24) were obtained from the sieved residues from samples 1.1, 1.2 and 1.3 from the trench section (Chapter 2.6.3, see Fig. 2.53 & 2.54); these had dry weights of over 10 kg. Samples 1.1, 1.2 and 1.3 proved to be similar in fossil content, although only 1.1 has a well-developed molluscan assemblage. Altogether 657 shells were counted from Sample 1.1, although the vast majority were *Theodoxus fluviatilis* (Plate 3.2f) and only *Lymnaea peregra* and *Ancylus fluviatilis* also occurred in any numbers.

Unit	Depth (cm)	Description
16	0–5	Orange coarse sand Gs4, nig.2, strf.0, elas.0, sicc.3
15	5–19	Sandy silt Ag2, Ga2, nig.2, strf.0, elas.0, sicc.3, lim.sup.0
14	19–22	Orange coarse sand Gs4, nig.2, strf.0, elas.0, sicc.3, lim.sup.0
13	22–27	Sandy silt Ag2, Ga2, nig.2, strf.0, elas.0, sicc.3, lim.sup.0
12	27–30	Coarse sand Gs4, nig.2, strf.0, elas.0, sicc.3
11	30–33	Silty sand Ga2, Ag2, nig.2, strf.0, elas.0, sicc.3, lim.sup.0
10	33–34	Coarse sand Gs4, nig.2, strf.0, elas.0, sicc.3
9	34–36	Sandy silt Ag2, Ga2, nig.2, strf.0, elas.0, sicc.3, lim.sup.0
8	36–39	Coarse sand Gs4, nig.2, strf.0, elas.0, sicc.3, lim. sup.0
7	39–44	Grey silt Ag4, nig.2, strf.0, elas.0, sicc.3
6	44–46	Orange, iron stained coarse sand Gs4, Lf+, nig.2, strf.0, elas.0, sicc.3, lim.sup.0
5	46–48	Grey silt Ag4, nig.2, strf.0, elas.0, sicc.3, lim.sup.0
4	48–58	Yellow orange silty sand Ga3, Ag1, nig.2, strf.0, elas.0, sicc.3, lim.sup.0
3	58–71	Grey sandy silt Ag2, Ga2, nig.2, strf.0, elas.0, sicc.3, lim.sup.0
2	71–91	Grey black sand, orange at the top Ga4, nig.3, strf.0, elas.0, sicc.3, lim.sup.0
1	91–95	Coarse orange sand Gs4, nig.2, strf.0, elas.0, sicc.3, lim.sup.0

Table 3.23 Stratigraphy at Ripon North (Hanson's Quarry), Section 3 (RN1).

The richest sample (1.1) contained eight freshwater and four land taxa. The occurrence of *T. fluviatilis* and *A. fluviatilis* clearly indicates flowing water, as do the bivalves *P. amnicum* and *P. henslowanum*. The coarse gravel sampled would, in any case, clearly require this;

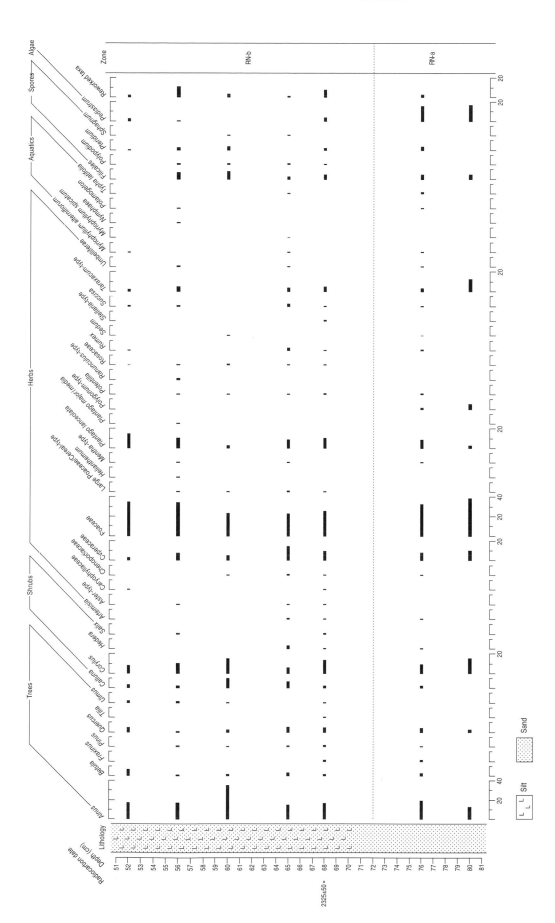

Fig. 3.15 Pollen diagram from Hanson's Quarry (Ripon North), Section 3 (RN1). Frequencies are calculated as percentages of the total land pollen sum (trees, shrubs and herbs).

the consistency suggests that the deposits and fauna are contemporaneous, however. The predominance of *A. fluviatilis* over *T. fluviatilis* in sample 1.2 may indicate that the riverbed was less gravelly than during deposition of the basal material sampled in 1.1 (Table 3.24), as the latter species prefers hard material such as stones as the substrate. Although *A. fluviatilis* also lives in such conditions, it can use wood or plant stems as an anchor point. The presence of a number of species of Planorbidae and *L. peregra* suggests that aquatic plants were present in the water body.

The small numbers of land shells, probably recruited into the assemblage by floods, included none that could be determined to species. The Succineidae indicate exposed mud or wetland environments close to the channel, a habitat which would also be suitable for slugs of the genus *Limax*.

Many of the molluscs were battered by transport within moving gravel, but the robust shells of *T. fluviatilis* and *A. fluviatilis* remained identifiable even when heavily damaged. The shells from 1.2 and especially 1.3 also showed evidence of damage by post-depositional decalcification, such that 1.3 contained only 5 identifiable shells.

The presence of 121 shells of *Lymnaea peregra* in Sample 1.1 is somewhat difficult to reconcile with an assemblage so dominated by Mollusca indicative of a stream sufficiently fast flowing to move fine gravel, as this species is usually found living in organic mud fringing channels or pools, not in moving water. However, the occurrence of this species may be due to its buoyant shell, which is capable of some *post mortem* transport by floating from its preferred habitat. Floating may also account for the presence of shells of *B. tentaculata*, as this gastropod (Plate 3.2e) is also usually found in slow-flowing, plant-rich water, unlike the conditions preferred by the moving-water species.

It is notable that the assemblage contains no *Valvata piscinalis*, which might be expected in a river assemblage living in pools over 2 m in depth and with stands of macrophytic vegetation. The absence of this taxon might suggest that the river was very shallow and flowing over a gravel bed. Under such conditions mud-drapes over point

bars, exposed at low stage flows, would have provided a habitat for *L. peregra* close to the channel and ensured that the shells of this species were incorporated in the gravel during floods.

The presence of *T. fluviatilis*, which may be a mid-Holocene immigrant into Britain (Holyoak, 1983; Chambers *et al.*, 1996; see below, section 3.7.8), could provide a maximum age for the sample, although there is some doubt as to its status in this respect. Nevertheless, a late Holocene age would fit well with the radiocarbon and pollen evidence.

3.6.4 Chronology

Two radiocarbon dates are available for the sequence at Ripon North (Table 3.25), providing an age estimate for the change from gravel deposition to fine-grained sedimentation. This occurred at or after *c.* 3900 ^{14}C BP,

Sample	1.1	1.2	1.3
Aquatic			
Theodoxus fluviatilis (Linnaeus)	451	11	3
Bithynia tentaculata (Linnaeus)	17		
Opercula	13	6	
Lymnaea truncatula (Müller)	1		
Lymnaea peregra (Müller)	121	6	
Ancylus fluviatilis Müller	56	19	2
Pisidium amnicum (Müller)	2	1	
Pisidium henslowanum (Sheppard)	1		
Pisidium nitidum Jenyns	1		
Pisidium spp.	1	1	
Terrestrial			
Succineidae	1		
Limax spp.	3	1	
Trichia spp.	1		
Cepaea/Arianta spp.	1	1	
Total	657	40	5

Table 3.24 Molluscs from Ripon North (Hanson's Quarry), Section 3 (RN1).

GrA-25377	2325 ± 50 ^{14}C BP (2460–2180 cal. BP; 510–230 cal. BC)
This date provides an age late in the Iron Age for the start of evidence of cereal cultivation not long after the start of an increase in finer grained silt deposition within the sediment column. As some levels below this horizon do not preserve pollen, cultivation could have started earlier than this limiting date. The low levels of tree pollen in the assemblage support a date in the later prehistoric period for this pollen record.	
GU-5998	**3900 ± 50 ^{14}C BP (4510–4150 cal. BP; 2560–2200 cal. BC)**
This date provides a limiting age in the early Bronze Age for the end of deposition of the gravel unit that underlies the sand and silt alluvial units. It suggests that no great hiatus exists between the stabilisation of the gravel deposit and the accumulation of the finer grained alluvial sediments above it. The age is on tree trunk wood included in the upper level of the gravel and so the date of gravel deposition could postdate the radiocarbon date if the wood is older and incorporated within the gravel unit.	

Table 3.25 Evaluation of radiocarbon dates from Ripon North (Hanson's Quarry), Section 3 (RN1).

based on the earlier date, whereas the later date of *c.* 2325 ^{14}C BP for the first appearance of cereal-type pollen higher in the section supports the late Holocene age for the sequence suggested by the pollen data. The wood that provided the earlier radiocarbon date came from the top of the gravel and so might be somewhat older than the fine-grained sediments, thus providing only a maximum age for the change in depositional regime. Lewin *et al.* (2005) noted that old tree trunks may be reworked from catchment sediment archives during flood events, carried downstream and deposited on the surface of gravel bars, providing an age consistent with neither the underlying gravel nor the finer-grained sediment that accumulates above it. The upper date, which was from small plant macrofossils, is much less likely to be based on reworked material.

Three opercula of *Bithynia tentaculata* from Sample 1.1 (see above) were passed to the NEaar laboratory for amino acid racemization dating. The relative D/L values and concentrations from these specimens (Appendix III), when compared with values from Quaternary sites within the UK (Penkman *et al.*, 2008b), are consistent with an age assignment within the Holocene. The data obtained from Asx, Glx, serine, alanine and valine are discussed in detail in Appendix III. Overall the data suggest that the Ripon North opercula are significantly younger than those from Newby Wiske (Fig. 3.14).

3.6.5 Synthesis: Ripon North

The earliest palaeoenvironmental evidence from Ripon North comes from the molluscan assemblages from the body of the upper (terrace) gravel. As well as the dominant species indigenous to the fast-flowing river channel represented by this deposit, together with inwashed aquatic molluscs from gentler environments, there were occasional terrestrial taxa. These provide an indirect record of a mosaic of nearby habitats, including marsh, grassland, disturbed ground and shaded areas, all of them earlier than the directly recorded palaeobotanical evidence from the fine-grained channel sediments. The occurrence of *T. fluviatilis* throughout the sequence might imply an age later than the early Holocene (see above).

As few of the sampled levels contained enough preserved pollen to count, the palynological record from Ripon North is fragmentary and no detailed interpretation is possible. There is little change between the pollen spectra through the sequence, even though the radiocarbon dates suggest that it may represent a considerable period of time. It is possible that the base of the fine-grained section may be more recent than the radiocarbon date suggests, as the dated alder log might have been reworked, which would allow the palynological sequence to represent a shorter period of deposition. The high *Pediastrum* frequencies of the lower part of the section imply deposition within a water body surrounded by grassland, with a variety of open-ground and marsh herbs. Such wet marshland agrees well with the interpretation of the sparse assemblage of terrestrial

Mollusca that has been recovered from the earlier terrace deposits, suggesting persistence of these environments. Some local alder–hazel scrubby woodland also existed, presumably with the alder in the damper areas. Generally, however, the pollen data record a non-wooded landscape on the drier areas away from the alluvial system.

The presence of *Plantago lanceolata* might imply human activity, although damp, disturbed grassland might well have existed through natural processes in an alluvial environment such as this. More certain evidence of human land use occurs in the upper part of the profile, in which cereal-type pollen is consistently recorded, although not in abundance. The range of weeds, such as Chenopodiaceae and *Artemisia*, supports the interpretation of at least a low-scale human agricultural influence. As several levels below the dated horizon at 69 cm proved to be barren, there remains the possibility that cultivation could have been introduced earlier, but the evidence has not been preserved. The major decline in the curve for *Pediastrum* in the upper part of the profile indicates a hydrological change from flowing water, although perhaps shallow, to a drier depositional regime, possibly due to a reduced incidence of flooding. Alternatively, sedimentation might have generally reduced the level of standing water at the sampling point. The sporadic aquatic pollen grains that are still recorded suggest nearby water bodies but the silts and sands of the upper profile are more likely to have been laid down within a marshy alluvial environment. The presence of reworked spores of pre-Quaternary type increases in the upper part of the sequence, indicating erosion and transport of old material. It is possible, therefore, that some of the other palynomorphs recorded in this sequence might also be derived and so interpretation must allow for this being a partly mixed assemblage. The poor condition of many pollen grains supports that view.

Although a short sediment sequence, this site preserves a valuable environmental record that shows some low-scale arable agricultural activity around a valley-floor alluvial wetland after 2325 ^{14}C BP. Although the top of the sampled profile is undated and the lower date on stratified wood provides only a maximum age for the start of fine-grained sediment deposition, the record appears to span at least part of the Bronze Age, the Iron Age and subsequent periods. The end of gravel accumulation appears to have occurred at the start of the Bronze Age, about 3900 ^{14}C BP, if the dated incorporated wood is in context.

3.7 Ripon South (Brown & Potter's quarry; Ripon Racecourse)

The Brown & Potter gravel quarry (SE 333691), extracting low terrace deposits to the west of the River Ure at Ripon (Fig. 2.57; see Chapter 2.6.4), provided palaeoenvironmental data from mid- to late Holocene sediments. This working is a continuation of the quarrying activity that provided the exposures studied by Howard *et al.* (2000a) and published by them under the name 'Ripon Racecourse' (see below).

The location of the sections studied as part of the present project has already been described, along with the fluvial stratigraphy (Chapter 2.6.4). A *c.* 4 m thick channel infill, cutting into the main Terrace 3 gravel and sand deposits of Section 1, provided the principal palaeoenvironmental evidence (Fig. 2.57; Plate 2.6). This channel was filled with variously organic sands, silts and clays containing conspicuous molluscan and plant fossils. The sequence was sampled using four overlapping monolith tins and a series of small bag samples (used for molluscan and other animal fossil analysis). The monolith samples were analysed for pollen and microscopic charcoal content.

3.7.1 Lithostratigraphy

3.7.1.1 Section 1 (Bulk Samples 1A and 1B; Monoliths 1–4, continuous sequence)

The sequence in the main investigated face, at the NW edge of the working, comprised sands and gravels overlain by a richly fossiliferous and organic sequence, the latter apparently confined to a channel infill. The sequence as a whole, including its sedimentology, was described in Chapter 2.6.4. The sands and gravels were conspicuously shelly and were therefore sampled for molluscan analyses: Samples 1A and 1B (Plate 2.6).

The channel-fill sequence was sampled by Monoliths 1–4 and a series of 16 contiguous samples for molluscs and other animal fossils. The monoliths and series samples covered a total sediment thickness of 179 cm, within which three coarsening-upwards units and three fining-upwards units were recognized (Table 3.26; see Chapter 2; Plate 2.6). The interval from 179 cm to 117 cm represents a fining-upwards sequence, grading from sand and gravels through sand, sandy clay/silt to clay/silt. At 117 cm there is a discontinuity or erosional base after which the sequence coarsens upwards from sand/silt to coarse sand to 84 cm. From 84 to 68 cm, a dominantly sandy interval grades from coarser sediments to finer sediments and is succeeded from 68 cm to 44 cm by a coarsening up sequence. From 44 cm to 15 cm, the sediments again fine upwards to a clayey silt unit, which is finally overlain by coarse yellow silt sand (Table 3.20).

3.7.1.2. Section 2

This section was located on the eastern side of the active quarry and was an ephemeral working face, the top several metres of which had been stripped prior to recording (Table 3.27; Plate 2.6c). The overburden was reported to be *c.* 2 m of organic peaty sediment and was the source of collections of large vertebrate remains, including red deer antlers and domestic cattle and pig bones. Despite this stripping, a sequence of *c.* 5 m of sands and gravels was recorded here (Table 3.27; Plate 2.6c). In contrast to Section 1, the sequence here showed thin sand bodies interbedded with medium-coarse gravels, although the uppermost cross-bedded sand unit pointed to an overall fining upwards situation (Chapter 2.6.4). In a deeper area in front of the main face (Fig. 2.58; Plate 2.6c), an organic lens was noted and sampled as monolith 2M (see Chapter 2.6.4). The organic sediments here underlay cross-bedded sand; the monolith sample was dominated by coarse sand with occasional organic layers.

3.7.2 Pollen

The monolith sample from Section 2 represents the oldest Quaternary palaeoenvironmental evidence from this site. It was dominated by coarse sand with occasional organic layers, amongst which a thin (5 cm) horizon of organic-rich detrital sand proved to be the only productive sample for palynology (Fig. 3.16). In addition, a single sample was analysed from the basal calcareous marl deposit, exposed beneath Section 2 to test the assumption that it was of Permian age. It yielded a species-poor assemblage of possibly reworked spores including *Lycospora pusilla*, a taxon that is typical of sediments of Carboniferous age but which may occur within the Permian. Reworked taxa of Carboniferous-Permo/Trias origin have been found in varying quantities throughout the Holocene sections.

The samples from Section 1, all of them from the upper organic channel-fill sequence, were prepared for pollen analysis at four centimetre intervals, except within the coarse sand layers. Although the monoliths from Section 1 proved productive, there were barren parts of the sequence that are excluded from the pollen zones. Where pollen was recorded, preservation was generally poor and grains were frequently corroded. The pollen diagram (Fig. 3.16) is subdivided into five local pollen assemblage zones (RS-a to RS-e).

Zone descriptions

Zone RS-a (Monolith 2M)

    This zone comprises the single productive sample from the lower sandy facies, which was dominated by *Corylus* pollen and a variety of tree pollen including, in order of abundance, *Alnus, Ulmus, Quercus* and *Tilia*. Low values for *Betula, Pinus, Carpinus* and *Fraxinus* were also recorded. Hardly any herbaceous pollen grains were present and spores were also rare, except for reworked pre-Quaternary types.

Zone RS-b (168–118 cm)

    This zone is the first from section 1 and contains a very wide variety of pollen types. *Alnus, Corylus, Calluna* and *Betula* are all present in moderate frequencies but Poaceae is the most abundant type. Subsidiary taxa like *Plantago lanceolata, Taraxacum*-type and Cyperaceae are present in low but consistent curves, while some herb taxa show

Unit	Depth (cm)	Description
17	0–15	Loose yellow silty sand Ga3, Ag1, part. test. (moll.)+, nig.3, strf.0, elas.0, sicc.2
16	15–23	Soft dark grey silty fine sand with black streaks. Irregular upper contact. Ga2, Ag2, Dl+, Sh++, nig.3+, strf.0, elas.0, sicc.2, lim.sup.4
15	23–44	Brown grey sand with silt, 2 fining upwards cycles. Some detrital wood. Ga3, Ag1, Dl+, nig.3, strf.0, elas.0, sicc.2, lim. sup.0
14	44–54	Well sorted yellow-brown sand, some iron staining Ga4, Ag+, Lf+, nig.3, strf.0, elas.0, sicc.2, lim. sup.3
13	54–57	Grey-brown, iron-stained thin silty sand with clay. Ga2, Ag2, As+, Lf+, nig.2, strf.0, clas.0, sicc.2, lim.sup.3
12	57–68	Well sorted grey-brown silty sand with iron staining. Ga3, Ag1, Lf+, nig.2, strf.0, elas.0, sicc.2, lim.sup.0
11	68–79	Soft, dark grey sandy silt. Occasional shells and thin black laminae (1.2 mm) towards top of unit. Ag3, Ga1, As+, Lf+, Dl+, Sh+, Ptm+, nig.2+, strf.0+, elas.0, sicc.2, lim. sup.4
10	79–84	Brown-yellow sandy silt with some wood and iron staining. Fining upwards. Ag2, Ga2, Dl+, Lf+, nig.3, strf.0, elas.0, sicc.2, lim.sup.0
9	84–89	Soft, well sorted yellow fine sand containing occasional silt balls. Erosional base with rip-up structures. Irregular lower contact. Ga4, Ag+, nig.2, strf.0, elas.0, sicc.2, lim.sup.1
8	89–99	Brown-orange laminated silty sand with occasional thin (2mm) organic lenses. Some iron staining. Ga3, Ag1, Dh+, Lf+, nig.3, strf.1, elas.0, sicc.2, lim.sup.4
7	99–117	Dark grey silty sand with rare detrital wood. Ga3, Ag1, Lf+, Dl+, nig.3, strf.0, elas.0, sicc.2, lim.sup.0
6	117–147	Soft dark grey sand, fining upwards to silt, with shells and black oxidized organics. Ag2, Ga2, Sh++, part. test. (moll.)+, nig.3+, strf.0, elas.0, sicc.2, lim.sup.0
5	147–153	Soft dark grey fine sand with shells and black oxidized organics. Occasional sand laminae. Ga4, Ag+, Sh+, nig.3+, strf.0, elas.1, sicc.2, lim.sup.0
4	153–163	Soft, moist, dark grey sandy silt with black mottles. Ag3, Ga1, Sh+, nig.3+, strf.0, elas.0, sicc.2, lim.sup.0
3	163–168	Dark grey sandy silt. More cohesive than above. Ag2, Ga2, nig.3, strf.0, elas.0, sicc.2, lim. sup.0
2	168–175	Dark grey silty sand with rounded gravel. Occasional shells and iron staining Ga3, Ag1, Gg(maj)+, part. test. (moll)+, Lf+, nig.3, strf.0, elas.0, sicc.2, lim. sup.0
1	175–179	Dry, crumbly, loose yellow brown sand with rounded gravel up to 3cm length Ga2, Gg(maj)1, Gs1, Ag+, Lf+, nig.2, strf.0, elas.0, sicc.3, lim. sup.3

Table 3.26 Lithostratigraphy at Ripon South (Brown & Potter's Quarry) – Section 1 (upper channel fill). The particle-size distribution was determined at 5 cm intervals using a Coulter Particle-size Analyser (see Chapter 2.1.3.1; Appendix IV), assisting in interpretation of all units and emphasizing alternating and fining upwards characteristics of some.

sporadic but occasionally peak values, *Artemisia* being an example. A wide range of marsh herb taxa occurs and the wet indicators *Sphagnum* and *Pediastrum* are common.

Zone RS-c (94–70 cm)
This zone incorporates the first half of the next polleniferous part of the sequence. Cyperaceae frequencies rise to rival Poaceae, whereas

Pediastrum is hardly recorded. Tree and shrub pollen values are similar to the previous zone, although *Betula* percentages are reduced. The wide variety of herbaceous pollen is maintained.

Zone RS-d (70–57 cm)
This zone is characterized by very high percentages of cereal-type pollen. Tree and shrub frequencies are much reduced, as are Cyperaceae. A peak of

Unit	Depth (cm)	Description
7	0–9	Yellow coarse sand Gs3, Ga1, Gg(min)+, nig.2, strf.0, elas.0, sicc.2
6	9–15	Yellow brown sand with occasional organic material. Faintly laminated. Gs3, Ga1, Ag+, Sh+, nig.2+, strf.0, elas.0, sicc.2, lim.sup.1
5	15–25	Yellow brown coarse sand Ga2, Gs2, Gg(min)+, nig.2, strf.0, elas.0, sicc.2, lim.sup.1
4	25–29	Grey silty sand with occasional organic matter. Ga3, Ag1, Sh+, nig.2, strf.1, elas.0, sicc.2, lim.sup.2
3	29–34	Dry, dark grey organic rich silty sand with twiggy debris. Faintly banded, fining upwards. Ga2, Ag1, Dg1, Dl+, nig.3, strf.1, elas.0, sicc.2, lim.sup.4
2	34–42	Brown grey sand with occasional organic matter, fining upwards. Faintly banded. Ga3, Gs1, Sh+, nig.2+, strf.1, elas.0, sicc.2, lim.sup.2
1	42–50	Brown grey medium wet sand with fine gravel Gs3, Ga1, Gg(min)+, nig.2, strf.0, elas.0, sicc.2, lim.sup.0

Table 3.27 Lithostratigraphy at Ripon South (Brown & Potter's Quarry) – Section 2M monolith. The particle-size distribution was determined at 5 cm intervals using a Coulter Particle-size Analyser (see Chapter 2.1.3.1; Appendix IV), confirming the siltier nature of the more organic units.

Woodland or scrubland	
Ericaceous	leaf fragment
Sambucus nigra or *racemosa*	seed

Grassland and/or open and/or disturbed ground	
Cerastium sp(p).	seed
Fumaria sp(p).	seed
Papaver rhoeas	seed
Polygonum arenastrum	nutlet
Polygonum lapathifolium	nutlet
Prunella vulgaris	nutlet
Sonchus asper	achene

Waterside and damp ground	
Hippuris vulgaris	fruit

Aquatic	
Potamogeton natans	fruit

Unclassified	
Atriplex sp(p).	seed
Carduus sp(p).	achene
Carex sp(p).	trigonous nutlet
Caryophyllaceae sp(p).	fragment of seed
Cenococcum geophilum	sclerotium
Chenopodium sp(p).	seed
Compositae sp(p).	achene
Musci sp(p).	piece of stem
Ranunculus subgenus *Ranunculus* sp(p).	achene
Rumex sp(p).	nutlet
	perianth
Urtica dioica	achene
Viola sp(p).	fragment of seed
Unidentified bud	
Unidentified leaf fragment	
Unidentified piece of twig	

Table 3.28 Plant macrofossils from Ripon South (Brown & Potter's Quarry) – Section 1, upper channel-fill (organic) facies. Amalgamation of residues from mollusc samples 2, 3, 4, 13, 14, and 15 (see Plate 2.6). The chosen categories were deliberately broad to reduce the possibility of taxa falling into a number of the habitat classifications. The aquatic group contains taxa that can only be described as obligate aquatic plants.

Lotus (bird's-foot-trefoil) pollen occurs but most herbaceous types show little change.

Zone RS-e (57–10 cm)

Cereal-type pollen percentages are much reduced in this uppermost zone, although a consistent presence is maintained. Tree and shrub values do not recover from the previous zone, but Poaceae, *Plantago lanceolata* and *Taraxacum*-type are all increased. A wide variety of herb pollen still occurs, with elevated levels for *Rumex, Sinapis*-type and *Plantago major-media*.

3.7.3 Plant macrofossils

Only limited plant macrofossil data are available for this site, all of it from the organic channel-fill sequence in the upper part of Section 1 (see Plate 2.6). The material

was identified by M. Field using residues from molluscan samples processed by D. Keen (Table 3.28) and correspond with the upper and lower sections of the channel infill that provided the palaeoenvironmental sequence, equivalent to pollen zones RS-b and RS-e. Only presence or absence was noted.

The residues yielded relatively diverse assemblages, with 23 plant taxa recorded. No major differences could be identified in the composition of the resultant assemblages but a variety of habitats is indicated. Only two taxa suggest that woodland or scrub existed at the time of deposition. The Ericaceous leaf fragment was too badly preserved

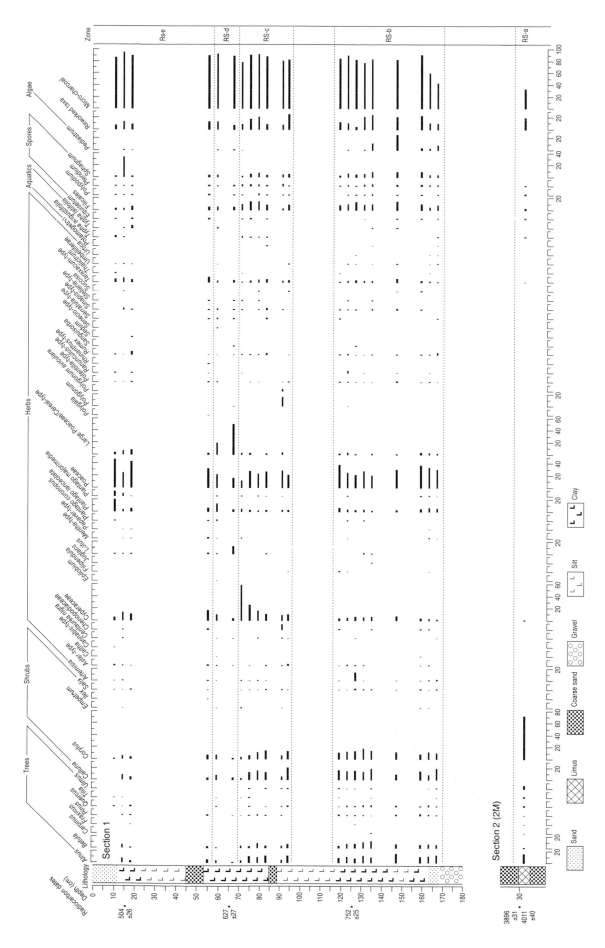
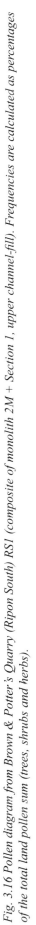

Fig. 3.16 Pollen diagram from Brown & Potter's Quarry (Ripon South) RS1 (composite of monolith 2M + Section 1, upper channel-fill). Frequencies are calculated as percentages of the total land pollen sum (trees, shrubs and herbs).

Sample	2M	1A	1B	2A	2B	3
Aquatic						
Theodoxus fluviatilis (Linnaeus)	135	1	1	6	3	4
Opercula	3					
Valvata cristata Müller	8					
Valvata piscinalis (Müller)	1					
Bithynia tentaculata (Linnaeus)	184			1	1	4
Opercula	36	1	1	2	1	6
Physa fontinalis (Linnaeus)	2					
Lymnaea truncatula (Müller)	34				1	2
Lymnaea peregra (Müller)	110	1	7	20	13	234
Bathyomphalus contortus (Linnaeus)	18					2
Gyraulus laevis (Alder)	1					
Gyraulus crista (Linnaeus)	1					
Gyraulus albus (Müller)				1	1	2
Hippeutis complanatus (Linnaeus)	1					1
Planorbarius corneus (Linnaeus)						1
Planorbidae						3
Ancylus fluviatilis Müller	121		11	16	12	123
Unio pictorum (Linnaeus)	1					
Unionidae	1					
Sphaerium corneum (Linnaeus)	6			1		4
Pisidium amnicum (Müller)	10	1	1		2	5
Pisidium personatum Malm	1					
Pisidium subtruncatum Malm	7					3
Pisidium henslowanum (Sheppard)	33		3	1	1	13
Pisidium nitidum Jenyns	31		1	1	2	19
Pisidium moitessierianum Paladilhe	1					7
Pisidium tenuilineatum Stelfox	1					
Pisidium spp.	21		2	1		14
Terrestrial						
Carychium minimum Müller	2					2
Carychium tridentatum (Risso)	6					
Carychium spp.	9					
Oxyloma pfeifferi (Rossmässler)	6					
Succineidae.	3		1			2
Azeca goodalli (Férussac)	2					
Cochlicopa lubrica (Müller)	2					1
Cochlicopidae	8		1	1		
Columella aspera / edentula	1					
Vertigo moulinsiana (Dupuy)	1					
Vertigo angustior Jeffreys	1					
Vertigo alpestris Alder						1
Vertigo spp.	2					
Pupilla muscorum (Linnaeus)	1		1			
Vallonia costata (Müller)	4					
Vallonia pulchella (Müller)	2					3
Vallonia spp.	13				2	5
Acanthinula aculeata (Müller)	1					
Ena obscura (Müller)	1					
Punctum pygmaeum (Draparnaud)	1					
Discus rotundatus (Müller)	13					1
Vitrea crystallina (Müller)	6					1
Oxychilus spp.						1
Aegopinella nitidula (Draparnaud)	1					
Nesovitrea hammonis (Ström)	1					
Zonitoides nitidus (Müller)	1					
Zonitidae	3					
Limax spp.	1		1	2	1	1
Cecilioides acicula (Müller)						1
Cochlodina laminata (Montagu)	1					
Clausilia bidentata (Ström)	2					
Balea perversa (Linnaeus)	1					
Clausiliidae	3					
Trichia hispida (Linnaeus)	8			2		6
Cepaea spp.	2				2	
Total	838	4	29	53	41	466

Table 3.29 Molluscs from Ripon South (Brown & Potter's Quarry), lower (sandy) facies, sections 1 & 2.

to make a more precise identification. The only plant recorded that would have cast any appreciable shade is *Sambucus nigra/racemosa.* An open or disturbed grassland community is well represented by seven taxa. It is probable that a number of the taxa listed in the unclassified habitat group also would have occurred in a similar setting (e.g. *Carduus* and *Ranunculus* subgenus *Ranunculus*). *Hippuris vulgaris* is the only waterside or damp-ground taxon recorded. This indicates that the margins of the water body in which deposition occurred lacked any sort of reed swamp or tall vegetation. The plant macrofossil assemblages provide little information about the nature of the water body, as there was just one aquatic, *Potamogeton natans,* which Preston (1995) noted to be ecologically perhaps the most tolerant *Potamogeton* species. The assemblages are undiagnostic of age.

3.7.4 Molluscs

Mollusca were analysed from the lower sand and gravel facies, which were conspicuously shelly, and from the organic channel-fill deposits, which also contained well-preserved shell material. These analyses were based on bulk samples with weights up to 15 kg (samples 1A and 1B from Section 1, plus 2M, the basal monolith, 2A and 2B from Section 2 and sample 3, from the later (October 2003) working face recorded at the time of OSL sampling), taken as representative of the moving-water facies at the site (see Plate 2.6; Fig. 2.59). The assemblages from the sandy facies collectively contained 23 freshwater and 27 land species (Table 3.29). Most of the shells from the coarse gravel samples (1A, 1B, 2A, 2B, 3) were heavily abraded, suggesting that the low counts are due to considerable destruction of specimens. Shells from the finer gravel of 2M were well preserved. This fauna is dominated by *Theodoxus fluviatilis, Bithynia tentaculata* (mostly represented by opercula rather than shells), *Lymnaea peregra, Ancylus fluviatilis* and the bivalve species *Pisidium amnicum* and *Pisidium henslowanum.* Although Sample 2M contained more land taxa (25) than those from the upper channel-fill in Section 1 (see below), only *Vallonia* spp. and *Discus rotundatus* were represented by more than 10 individuals.

From the Section 1 channel-fill facies, 16 serial samples were taken at 10 cm intervals through the full thickness of the fossiliferous muddy sediments described above. Each sample weighed *c.* 5 kg in field conditions (see Plate 2.6a). A further sample, weight 15 kg, was taken from the most fossiliferous part of the top of the section equating to serial samples 14–16. This sample, 17 in Table 3.30, was collected to obtain any rare taxa which might not have been found in the smaller serial samples. The assemblage from the channel-fill consisted of 30 freshwater and 20 land species (Table 3.30). Mollusca were reasonably abundant in the lower third of the channel-fill succession (samples 1–6) and at the top (15–16). Preservation was generally good or very good, except in Samples 10–14, in which organic acids

had damaged many of the shells. Samples 7–14 had only a rather sparse fauna, with the total counts in sample 12–14 being in single figures. The most numerous species present were *Lymnaea* spp. and the Planorbids *Planorbis planorbis* and *Bathyomphalus contortus.* The most abundant small bivalve was *Pisidium personatum,* present in 10 of the 17 samples. The list of land taxa is dominated by *Carychium minimum,* Succineidae and *Vallonica pulchella.*

The two types of sample (sandy samples and muddy channel-fill) are complementary in their environmental indications because of the contrasting taphonomic conditions under which they formed. Almost all of the 63 molluscan species recorded in these two facies at Ripon may be found in North Yorkshire today, although some, such as *T. fluviatilis,* are at their northern limit in the county (Kerney, 1999). Four species are not found in the area today. *Vertigo moulinsiana* has a few Holocene records in Yorkshire (Kerney, 1999) but is generally a southern species, with its main British distribution in south-east England. *Vertigo angustior* is also a southern species but found north to southern Sweden (Kerney & Cameron, 1979), and *P. moitessierianum* and *Pisidium tenuilineatum* have no records, living or from the Holocene, as far north as North Yorkshire, although these tiny bivalve species might have been overlooked by malacologists.

3.7.5 Insects

Insects were recovered from the organic lens from near the base of Section 2 (2M; Fig. 2.69) and, predominantly, from the upper organic channel-fill deposits in Section 1. Plentiful beetle remains were recovered from the residues of the same vertical series of contiguous 16 samples, collectively spanning the whole channel sequence, that had been processed for molluscs (see above; Plate 2.6a; Table 3.31). The use of a sieve aperture of 500 μm, coarser than that usually employed for the recovery of insect remains, apparently led to the loss of several smaller beetle species. Two additional bulk samples were collected; the first, numbered 17, was from the same levels as samples 14–16 combined and also processed for molluscs in the same way as samples 1–16. The second bulk sample, numbered 18, was a large volume of sediment from the combined thickness of the channel-fill and was processed specifically for insect remains using a finer (i.e. 300 μm) sieve mesh. The beetles from this last sample included numbers of very small species (e.g. *Hydraena riparia* and *Ochthebius minimus*) that had probably been missed in the other samples as a result of using the 500 μm mesh sieve. Otherwise there was no significant difference in beetle faunas from any of these samples, including that from the stratigraphically older sample 2M, and they will thus be considered here as if they were all part of a single assemblage.

Altogether 138 beetle taxa were recognized, of which 100 could be identified to the level of species or species group (Table 3.31). All the recorded species are living today in the British Isles, with the single exception of

Sample	1	2	3	4	5	6	7	8	9	10	11	12	13	14	15	16	17
Aquatic																	
Theodoxus fluviatilis (Linnaeus)	7				1			1									
Opercula				1													
Valvata cristata Müller		1														1	25
Valvata piscinalis (Müller)		1									1	1					
Bithynia tentaculata (Linnaeus)	3	3	9	6	5	1		1							2	1	41
Opercula			2	1											2	3	27
Physa fontinalis (Linnaeus)				1	1	1		1	1								3
Lymnaea truncatula (Müller)	19	5	21	80	56	48				7	2					2	7
Lymnaea palustris (Müller) agg.						2											4
Lymnaea stagnalis (Linnaeus)				20	29										1		28
Lymnaea peregra (Müller)	22	51	151	230	22	26		2	1								4
Lymnaea spp.	7	2	3	6	21	8		3		4					2		5
Planorbis planorbis (Linnaeus)			1	4	5	8					1				4	3	106
Planorbis carinatus Müller																	1
Anisus vortex (Linnaeus, 1758)	1	3	1														2
Bathyomphalus contortus (Linnaeus)	1		1	1		2	3	2							3	2	151
Gyraulus albus (Müller)																	7
Gyraulus crista (Linnaeus)	1	1	2		1												4
Hippeutis complanatus (Linnaeus)														1	3		32
Planorbarius corneus (Linnaeus)															1	2	27
Planorbidae undet.	1			1	1				1	1					11	3	111
Ancylus fluviatilis Müller	1	18	24	33	3	9				1	1						
Acroloxus lacustris (Linnaeus)		1	1												1	1	1
Sphaerium corneum (Linnaeus)	1			1													16
Pisidium amnicum (Müller)	1																
Pisidium casertanum (Poli)					3	5			1		2		1				8
Pisidium personatum Malm				2	3	96	1			1	2	2					40
Pisidium milium Held						1											21
Pisidium subtruncatum Malm	1	2	2			6			1								35
Pisidium henslowanum (Sheppard)	2	2	2	5													
Pisidium nitidum Jenyns			4	8								1					3
Pisidium pulchellum Jenyns		1		1													
Pisidium moitessierianum Paladilhe	1	1	1	2	1	1											
Pisidium tenuilineatum Stelfox	1	1		1	7										2		
Pisidium spp.	2	2	8	8		89		2	1	1	7					1	107

Sample	1	2	3	4	5	6	7	8	9	10	11	12	13	14	15	16	17
Terrestrial																	
Carychium minimum Müller			5	8	23	12				41	5			2	37	11	20
Carychium tridentatum (Risso)					2												
Carychium spp.		1	2		5	4				3					6		3
Oxyloma pfeifferi (Rossmässler)		1		3	7	7					1				1	7	3
Succineidae	1	1	11	8	20			6			2	1			1	2	15
Cochlicopa lubrica (Müller)				1					1	3							1
Cochlicopa spp.		1	3		6	3			1	1					4		
Vertigo antivertigo (Draparnaud)			1			1	1	1			5			1	7	1	30
Vertigo pygmaea (Draparnaud)								1								1	1
Vertigo spp.							1	1							4		10
Vallonia pulchella (Müller)		2	4	4	2	1	1	8	1	6	1	1		1	12	4	4
Vallonia spp.		2	6	6	3	14	8	12	2	7	1			1	18	5	9
Ena spp.	1									6							1
Vitrina pellucida (Müller)				1													1
Vitrea crystallina (Müller)			3	1	1			1		1			1				
Vitrea spp.							1										
Nesovitrea hammonis (Ström)						3	1										
Aegopinella pura (Alder)											5					1	
Zonitidae						2		1									
Limax spp.		1	1	2	1									1	2		1
Euconulus fulvus (Müller)				2						1	1				1		4
Cecilioides acicula (Müller)		2	2	2	1	1					2						
Balea perversa (Linnaeus) agg.																	1
Clausiliidae			1		1												
Helicella itala (Linnaeus)																	
Trichia hispida (Linnaeus)	1		2	2	4			4									
Cepaea spp.																	1
Total (aquatic & terrestrial)	67	100	273	471	236	351	17	47	10	83	39	6	2	7	124	48	894

Table 3.30 Molluscs from Ripon South (Brown & Potter's Quarry) – Section 1, upper channel-fill (organic) facies.

Airaphilus elongatus. This is a distinctive species that is widespread elsewhere in Europe at the present day (see below) and has been found as a fossil in such a variety of British Holocene deposits, including a Roman context (Osborne, 1974), that it seems only a matter of time before it is discovered living in these islands.

3.7.5.1 Local environmental indications from the beetle fauna

The relatively large number of species represented in this assemblage by just a single individual indicates that it is only a small sample of the beetle fauna of the times. Nevertheless, the assemblage as a whole provides a consistent picture of the local environment. From the ecological diversity of this fauna it is apparent that many of the species must have been brought together from a wide variety of habitats, either by being blown in or washed in accidentally from the surrounding landscape. For convenience, in this environmental analysis, the different habitats will be grouped together and the inhabitants of each group will be dealt with separately.

AQUATIC HABITATS

This fossil assemblage is largely made up of aquatic or semi-aquatic species. Of particular significance is the presence of a group of Dryopidae, which inhabit stony or mossy substrates in rapidly moving water. These include *Esolus parallelepipedus*, *Oulimnius troglodytes*, *Limnius volckmari* and *Riolus cupreus*, which occur in the lowest eight samples of the contiguous stratigraphical sequence (*Limnius volckmari* also occurred in the higher bulk sample 17). The gyrinid species *Orectochilus villosus* is also one of the few members of this group that regularly hunts on the surface of running water; its occurrence in sample 2 suggests that running water must have been present during the initial phase of channel filling.

The Dytiscidae are fast-swimming predatory water beetles, living in all manner of aquatic habitats (Balfour-Browne, 1950). However the Dystiscid species in this assemblage are characteristic of standing water, particularly where there is much submerged vegetation. Species of *Gyrinus*, the familiar 'whirligig beetles', are predators hunting for stranded insects on the water surface. The larvae of most of the Hydraenidae and Hydrophilidae are aquatic or semi-aquatic and are voracious predators feeding on snails, worms and insect larvae (those of some Hydraenids feed on algae). The adults are slow moving animals compared with the Dytiscidae and feed almost exclusively on plants and decaying vegetable debris (Hansen, 1987). In this assemblage these two families are represented by species that would be expected in stagnant, largely eutrophic water, much overgrown with emergent and submerged vegetation.

Some beetle species are phytophagous and their food preferences give an indication of the local flora. Thus *Macroplea appendiculata* is a subaquatic species that feeds principally on species of *Myriophyllum* and *Potamogeton*. *Donacia versicolorea* feeds predominantly on *Potamogeton natans*. *Notaris acridulus* is found almost exclusively on the sweet grass *Glyceria*. *Bagous* is an aquatic weevil that feeds on a variety of pond weeds in slowly moving or stationary water. *Haliplus obliquus* prefers clear base-rich bodies of stagnant water, in which it lives at depths of more than one metre, usually amongst characeans, upon which its larvae feed (Holmen, 1987). *Chaetarthria seminulum* inhabits the wet mud at the edges of stagnant, normally eutrophic, well-vegetated, fresh water, being also occasionally found on muddy banks along the slower reaches of streams (Hansen, 1987). The Helodidae have aquatic larvae but the adult beetles are terrestrial, living amongst the waterside vegetation. *Georissus crenulatus* lives beside water on sparsely vegetated banks of silt, clay or clayey sand (Hansen, 1987).

MARGINAL HABITATS

In this category are included those species that live in wet habitats, often adjacent to water. Many of the Carabidae, which are carnivorous or general scavenging beetles, prefer swampy conditions; such species include *Elaphrus cupreus*, *Bembidion biguttatum*, *Patrobus atrorufus*, *Pterostichus gracilis*, *Agonum moestum*, *Agonum gracile* and *Chlaenius nigricornis*. Certain carabid species are particularly informative. For example, *Bembidion doris* is a very hygrophilous species, usually found in marshes with *Carex* and *Eriophorum*. It is predominantly found in shaded habitats e.g. in deciduous forest swamps (Lindroth, 1992, p.184). *Bembidion gilvipes* is found under moss and fallen leaves in damp places under deciduous trees or bushes, e.g. *Salix* (Lindroth, 1974). *Loricera pilicornis* is typically found beside ponds and ditches where the water may be dirty and foul smelling and where the vegetation is rich but where the soil is bare in patches. *Bembidion schueppeli* is an exclusively riparian species, living where the substrate is composed of damp sand with a mixture of clay, frequently forming a muddy layer on the surface, usually where there is fairly rich vegetation of *Carex,* grasses and similar plants (Lindroth, 1992, p. 244). *Pterostichus diligens* is a very eurytopic species, being found in a wide variety of moderately wet marshy habitats.

Many of the hydrophilid species, such as *Cercyon analis, Megasternum boletophagum* and *Cryptopleurum minutum,* live in accumulations of rotting vegetation, often near to the edge of water (Hansen, 1987). Most of the staphylinid species in this assemblage also inhabit damp plant debris, where they are predators on other small invertebrates.

In places this swampy environment graded into damp meadow-like habitats with an abundant vegetation cover and a humus rich soil, as indicated by such carabid species as *Trechus obtusus, Pterostichus nigrita, Pterostichus melanarius* and *Calathus fuscipes. Bembidion bipunctatum* is found in relatively moist habitats where there is some cover of *Carex* or grasses. *Clivina fossor* is a subterranean predator that burrows in any type of soil that is damp

Sample	2M	1	2	3	4	5	6	7	8	9	10	11	12	13	14	15	16	18	17
Carabidae																			
Carabus violaceus L.	1																		
Nebria brevicollis (F.)												1							1
Elaphrus cupreus Duft.															1				
Loricera pilicornis (F.)									1										1
Clivina fossor (L.)					1	1													1
Dyschirius globosus (Hbst.)															1				
Trechus obtusus Er.	1				2				1				1	1			1	1	2
Bembidion lampros (Hbst.)				1						1	1	1		1	1				1
Bembidion bipunctatum (L.)																	1		
Bembidion schueppeli Dej.																		1	
Bembidion gilvipes Sturm,																		1	
Bembidion doris (Panz.)																		1	
Bembidion biguttatum (F.)																	1		1
Bembidion unicolor Chaud.													1						
Bembidion (Peryphus) sp	1	1		1	1														
Patobus atrorufus (Ström,)									1									1	
Poecilus sp.																			1
Pterostichus diligens (Sturm,)																		2	1
Pterostichus nigrita (Payk.)			1														2		
Pterostichus gracilis (Dej.)																			1
Pterostichus niger (Schall.)	1																		
Pterostichus melanarius (Illiger,)					1				1								1		1
Calathus fuscipes (Goeze,)									1										
Calathus micropterus (Duft.)											1	1							
Agonum muelleri (Hbst.)									1										
Agonum moestum (Duft.)															1				1
Agonum gracile (Gyll.)	1																		1
Amara aenea (Geer,)																		1	
Chlaenius nigricornis (F.)																			1
Haliplidae																			
Haliplus obliquus F.																		6	
Haliplus ruficollis(Geer,) group																		2	
Haliplus sp.	1				1														
Dytiscidae																			
Coelambus impressopunctatus (Schall.)																		1	
Hygrotus inaequalis (F.)																		3	
Hydroporus spp.																		2	1
Ilybius sp.														1					
Rhantus bistriatus (Bergstr.)																		1	
Colymbetes fuscus (L.)																		1	
Gyrinidae																			
Gyrinus sp.																		1	
Orectochilus villosus (Müll.)			1																
Hydraenidae																			
Hydraena riparia Kug. type.							1		1								1	11	
Ochthebius minimus (F.)												1						20	1
Limnebius sp																		1	1
Helophorus nubilus F.			1														1		2
Helophorus grandis Illiger																			2
Helophorus misc. small spp.																	1	2	1
Hydrophilidae																			
Coelostoma orbiculare (F.)																			1
Sphaeridium lunatum F.																	1		
Cercyon ustulatus (Preyssl.)				1							1				1	1	2		5
Cercyon melanocephalus (L.)																			3
Cercyon marinus Thoms.																	1		
Cercyon tristis (Illiger,)																		1	2

Sample	2M	1	2	3	4	5	6	7	8	9	10	11	12	13	14	15	16	18	17
Hydrophilidae (continued)																			
Cercyon sternalis Shp.												1				1	1		2
Cercyon analis (Payk.)					1														3
Megasternum boletophagum (Marsh.)	1							1		1					1	1		1	1
Cryptopleurum minutum (F.)																	1		2
Hydrobius fuscipes (L.)																	1	1	1
Laccobius sp.																		2	
Helochares obscurus (Müll.)																		1	
Enochrus testaceus (F.)																		2	
Enochrus sp.																		2	
Chaetarthria seminulum (Hbst.)								1										3	
Silphidae																			
Phosphuga atrata (L.)								1	1	1									
Catopidae																			
Choleva sp.							1	1		1									1
Clambidae																			
Clambus armadillo Geer,																		2	
Staphylinidae																			
Olophrum assimile (Payk.)																		1	
Acidota crenata (F.)													1						
Lesteva longelytrata (Goeze,)					1	1			1										
Oxytelus rugosus (F.)		1			1		1	1		1	1				1		1		1
Oxytelus laqueatus (Marsh.)																			1
Stenus spp				1						1						1	1	4	1
Trogophloeus sp.																		2	
Stilicus sp.															1				
Lathrobium terminatum Grav.																			1
Lathrobius spp.				1	1														1
Cryptobium fracticorne (Payk.)																		1	
Gyrohypnus punctulatus (Payk.)					1			1											1
Xantholinus glabratus (Grav.)																			1
Xantholinus linearis (Ol.)																		1	2
Xantholinus sp.				1	1				1				1						1
Philonthus sp.					1			1	1									1	4
Boletobiinae *Gen.et sp. indet.*																		1	
Tachyporus chrysomelinus (L.)																			1
Tachinus corticinus Grav.																		1	
Tachinus sp.																	1		1
Alaeocharinae *Gen. et sp. indet.*					1		1											4	
Pselaphidae																			
Pselaphus heisei Hbst.																		1	
Elateridae																			
Agriotes obscurus (L.)		1															1		
Ctenicera pectinicornis (L.)																		1	
Denticollis linearis (L.)																		1	
Buprestidae																			
Agrilus sp.																		1	
Helodidae																			
Gen.et sp. indet.																		7	1
Dryopidae																			
Dryops sp.					1												1	1	3
Esolus parallelepipedus (Müll.)				1	2		1												
Oulimnius troglodytes (Müll.)		1																	
Limnius volckmari (Panz.)	1	1		1					1									1	
Riolus cupreus (Müll.)									1										
Georissidae																			
Georissus crenulatus (Rossi,)					1														

Sample	2M	1	2	3	4	5	6	7	8	9	10	11	12	13	14	15	16	18	17
Cucujiidae																			
Airaphilus elongatus (Gyll.)																		1	
Cryptophagidae																			
Atomaria sp.																		1	
Lathridiidae																			
Corticarina sp.																		3	
Byrrhidae																			
Cytilus sericeus (Forst.)									1										
Coccinellidae																			
Coccinella sp.				1															
Anobiidae																			
Anobium punctatum (Geer,)																			1
Scarabaeidae																			
Geotrupes sp.	1																		
Aegialia sabuleti (Panz.)										1									
Aphodius. sp.	2		1	1	1		1	1	2	1	1				1	1	1		1
Melolontha melolontha (L.)																		1	
Phyllopertha horticola (L.)	1																		
Chrysomelidae																			
Macroplea appendiculata (Panz.)																		2	
Donacia versicolorea (Brahm.)							1												
Donacia thalassina Germ.		1													1	1			1
Plateumaris sericea (L.)																			4
Lema sp.																			1
Phaedon tumidulus Germ.					1														
Phaedon sp.																	1		
Hydrothassa glabra Hbst.					1	1	1	1	1								1		1
Galeruca taneceti (L.)							1												
Phyllotreta flexuosa (Illiger,)																		1	
Haltica sp.															1			1	1
Chaetocnema concinna (Marsh.)	1				1	1											1		1
Scolytidae																			
Hylastes angustatus (Hbst.)							2												1
Curculionidae																			
Apion spp				1	1	1		2	1	1				1		2	1		6
Otiorhynchus raucus (F.)								1											
Otiorhynchus ligneus (Ol.)					1	1													
Otiorhynchus ovatus (L.)																		1	
Trachyphloeus sp.																		1	
Phyllobius spp.							3											3	
Sitona flavescens (Marsh.)			1																
Sitona spp.		1			3		1	1	2	1		2	1	1					2
Tropiphorus obtusus Bon.																	1		
Bagous sp.															1	1			4
Notaris acridulus (L.)															1				2
Notaris aethiops (F.)																		1	
Thryogenes sp.																		5	1
Alophus triguttatus (F.)					1				1	1									
Hypera sp.																		1	
Mecinus pyraster (Hbst.)	1																		1
Rhynchaenus foliorum (Mull.)			1																

Table 3.31 Insects from Ripon South (Brown & Potter's Quarry) – Section 1, upper channel-fill (organic) facies.
Note: the figures opposite each species indicates the minimum numbers of individuals present in each sample. Nomenclature and taxonomic order follow the list employed by Lucht (1987). Although not all of these are the most up-to-date names, this list has been used extensively in the past for sub-fossil beetle assemblages and its use makes comparisons of past records simpler for the non-specialist. Specialists in any particular group of species can easily make the necessary adjustments of the names if desired.

enough to prevent its tunnels from collapsing. Many of these species are today favoured by cultivated soils, being found in gardens, parks and agricultural fields.

Amongst the phytophagous beetle species, *Plateumaris sericea* feeds on a variety of reedy plants, whereas *Donacia thalassina* feeds chiefly on *Scirpus lacustris* and also on *Glyceria. Thryogenes* feeds on the stems of various Poaceae and Cyperaceae, *Notaris aethiops* feeds principally on *Sparganium ramosum* but also on various species of Cyperaceae and *Hydrothassa glabra* eats various species of buttercup and marsh Ranunculaceae, whereas *Phaedon tumidulus* eats various species of Umbelliferae. Both larvae and adults of *Cytilus sericeus* feed exclusively on moss.

DRY HABITATS

Not unexpectedly only a few species in this assemblage come from truly dry habitats. *Bembidion lampros* is not very specific about its habitat requirements but often occurs in more or less dry open, sun-exposed situations where the vegetation is not too dense. *Amara aenea* is also found in open dry places where the vegetation is short but dense, frequently on heaths and grassland. *Aegialia sabuleti* lives in sandy places where it feeds on roots. *Helophorus nubilus*, unlike other members of this genus, is a terrestrial species associated with open grassland and can be a pest on sprouting grain (Angus, 1992). There are further indications of grassland from two of the species of Elateridae, *Agriotes obscurus* and *Ctenicera pectinicornis,* whose larvae are the familiar wireworms that feed on grass roots. Many of the weevils also have larvae that feed underground on the roots of various plants. Thus the larvae of *Sitona*, one of the most abundant species in this assemblage, feed on the roots of various Fabaceae, the youngest stages eating the bacterial nodules. The adults of *Mecinus pyraster* feed on *Plantago lanceolata*, whereas the larvae attack the roots of the same plant. The small weevil *Apion* eats a wide variety of weedy herbs. Species of *Otiorhynchus, Tropiphorus obtusus* and *Alophus triguttatus* are also polyphagous on a variety of low plants but, again, their larvae feed on roots. *Galeruca tanaceti* feeds on various species of Compositae, in particular on *Tanacetum vulgare* and *Achilea millifolium*.

WOODLAND INDICATORS

The presence of deciduous trees is indicated by *Melolontha melolontha*, the familiar cockchafer, whose larvae feed on the roots of various plants in open treeless areas but whose adults feed on leaves of trees, particularly oaks (Jessop, 1986). Similarly the adults of the chafer, *Phyllopertha horticola*, feed on the leaves of various deciduous trees and have larvae that develop underground. *Phyllobius* also has subterranean larvae that feed on various roots but the adults feed on the leaves of trees and shrubs as well as herbaceous plants. The larvae of many species of *Agrilus* develop under the bark or in the wood of a wide variety of trees. *Hylastes angustatus* attacks the trunk and exposed roots of sickly pine trees (Balachowsky, 1949).

Rhynchaenus foliorum is a minute weevil that mines the leaves of various species of willows. *Anobium punctatum*, the familiar woodworm beetle, attacks any dead wood, in particular if it has already been infested with fungus (Hickin, 1963). The larvae of *Denticollis linearis* are predators living in rotten wood.

Other species are not directly dependent on the presence of trees, but are shade-loving forest species. These include carabid species such as *Nebria brevicollis* and *Calathus micropterus*, which are absent from open habitats. They prefer deciduous and mixed forests where the soil must contain a rich layer of humus and be at least moderately moist (Lindroth, 1992).

THE DUNG BEETLE COMMUNITY

The common occurrence of *Aphodius* and the single occurrence of *Geotrupes* suggest the presence of dung, perhaps of large herbivorous mammals, in the neighbourhood. The larvae of many of the Hydrophilidae, such as *Sphaeridium lunatum* and *Cercyon melanocephalus*, are predators that feed on small invertebrates, usually in the dung of cow, horse and sheep; they are only rarely found in heaps of decaying vegetable matter (Hansen, 1987). Similarly the staphylinid *Oxytelus laqueatus* is a predatory species living in the dung of many mammal species but it also can inhabit heaps of decaying vegetable debris. *Oxytelus rugosus*, on the other hand, is more usually associated with rotting vegetation and only rarely found in dung.

SPECIALIST PREDATORS

A few of the species in this assemblage are predators of other animal groups; the larvae of the ladybird *Coccinella* (Majerus, 1994) feeds principally on species of aphid (greenfly), while the silphid species *Phosphuga atrata* has specialist jaws adapted to feeding on terrestrial snails.

SUMMARY OF LOCAL ENVIRONMENTAL EVIDENCE FROM THE BEETLE FAUNA

The Ripon South coleopteran assemblage represents two main beetle communities: (a) those that inhabit aquatic habitats and (b) those that live in terrestrial environments. Most of the latter must have been washed or blown into the deposit from the neighbouring landscape. Minor changes in the available aquatic habitats took place during the course of the sedimentary infilling of the channel, shown chiefly by the relative abundance of running-water species in the lowest part of the section. The upper part of the sequence is dominated by inhabitants of stagnant eutrophic water. This suggests that the channel started as a conduit for water but was later abandoned, leading to its gradual silting up. Notwithstanding the paucity of plant macrofossil data (see above), the coleopteran assemblages reveal that, towards the later stages of this infilling, various aquatic plants colonized the pond and the surroundings became dominated by a reedy swamp. Away from the water this marshy ground gradually gave way to meadow-like habitats that further afield became drier grassland with a sandy soil, on which were growing various weedy plants. Not far away was mixed woodland with both deciduous and coniferous trees, although this may not have grown in the immediate vicinity, since tree-dependent beetle species were rather uncommon in the assemblages. The relative abundance of dung beetles suggests the presence of large herbivorous mammals.

An interesting finding of this investigation is the presence, early in the Holocene, of so many beetles that subsequently have become characteristic of cultural environments; some have even become agricultural pests. It is evident that insect species required no new adaptations to equip them to take advantage of recent human activities.

3.7.5.2 Climatic implications of the Coleoptera

Almost all the species in this coleopteran assemblage can be found living today in northern England, with only *Airaphilus elongatus* absent from the area today. This grain beetle has a patchy distribution in central Europe, extending as far north as latitude 60°N in Sweden and latitude 62°N in Finland. *Bembidion schueppeli* has a boreo-montane distribution at the present day, with Yorkshire at the southern extreme of its range in the British Isles. *Notaris aethiops* is also a boreo-montane species and is very rare in Britain today, occurring only as far south as the north Pennines. The presence of these northern beetles, and the complete absence of any exclusively southern English species, suggests that the climate was at least as warm, or as cold, as that of North Yorkshire at the present day.

It has been possible, by using the Mutual Climatic Range (MCR) method (Atkinson *et al.*, 1987), to quantify the mean temperature of the warmest month (Tmax) and the mean temperature of the coldest month (Tmin), these being July and January–February, respectively. On the basis of 45 carnivorous and scavenging species in this assemblage that are also on the MCR data base, the following figures were obtained:

Tmax between 15°C and 17°C
Tmin between -7°C and 3°C

It should be emphasized that these figures mean that the actual mean temperatures lay somewhere between these limits and not that the mean temperatures ranged between these figures. They suggest that the thermal climate at the time when the Ripon channel was being filled was not significantly different from that of present-day North Yorkshire.

It is not possible at the moment to quantify the amount of precipitation from the evidence of the Coleoptera, but they show that it must have been adequate to support a pond with an elaborate floral and faunal ecosystem. Furthermore, the basal samples contained dryopid species that live in running water, spending almost their entire life history submerged (Holland, 1972) This indicates that sufficient precipitation must have been available throughout the year

to maintain a continuous flow in the channel at least in the early stages of its development.

3.7.6 Vertebrates

The organic alluvial overburden stripped from above Section 2 was the source of large vertebrate remains, generally collected by the quarry operators during stripping and not recorded *in situ*. This material was supplied in field damp and unwashed condition. After making observations on any sediment adhering to the material and any other superficial features likely to disappear during surface cleaning, the specimens were washed using warm water and gentle abrasion with an old toothbrush. The material was identified using modern comparative collections and measurements made according to von den Driesch (1976). The condition and adhering sediment suggest that these specimens were probably preserved in similar upper facies to the Section 1 channel sediments described above.

The following material was identified:

1. Virtually complete right scapula of horse (*Equus caballus*). This was supplied in the same bag as the cow mandible (see below) marked "Bone from Ripon City Quarry – found a few days earlier by the digger driver, 1/4/03". The specimen is very well preserved and stained dark brown, with small chunks of dark grey peaty clayey silt adhering to the surface. There is no evidence of abrasion although the surface of the bone shows signs of extensive root damage, thereby indicating that the material was exposed on the surface for some time prior to incorporation in the deposits. The distal end of the scapula is recently damaged, possibly the result of exposure during machining.

   Length of the glenoid cavity (LG): 58.90 mm
   Breadth of the glenoid cavity (BG): 49.62 mm

2. Virtually complete left mandible of adult domestic cow (*Bos taurus*) with m_1–m_3 *in situ*, in bag marked "Bone from Ripon City Quarry – found a few days earlier by the digger driver, 1/4/03". The specimen is mid brown in colour and is moderately abraded with the majority of the dental cement eroded. The teeth are in mid-wear. Measurements were taken at the occlusal (biting) surface:

   m_1 Length (L): 23.96 mm, Breadth (B): 11.48 mm
   m_2 L: 26.48 mm, B: 11.60 mm
   m_3 L: 33.34 mm, B: 10.90 mm

3. Bag containing two virtually complete articulating thoracic vertebrae, 4 vertebral fragments and 15 rib/rib fragments of domestic cow (*Bos taurus*), all probably from a single individual, marked "Base of upper organic", Ripon City Pit, 14/2/03". The specimens are mid brown in colour and well preserved although fragmentary.

4. Diaphysis of right humerus of juvenile artiodactyl of cf. sheep (*Ovis aries*), found in the same bag as the

above (Ripon City Pit). The specimen is missing both articular ends. It is mid brown with moderate abrasion and heavy root damage.

5. Left frontal bone and horn core of adult sheep (*Ovis aries*). The specimen is well preserved and stained mid brown in colour. No details of provenance were supplied.

6. Left cheek tooth of horse (*Equus caballus*), mid row p3–m2. The tooth is of an adult individual but in an early stage of wear. No details of provenance were supplied.
    L: 31.18 mm
    B: 18 mm

7. Pair of red deer antlers, shed. These were in clean condition when seen but were not available for inspection by DCS.

3.7.7 Chronology

The dates from this site form a good chronological series (Table 3.32). The lowest pair of dates, from Monolith 2M, provides a limiting age for the establishment of the Ure here in its present location (the modern channel is only *c.* 0.1 km from the dating locality), as well as valuable constraining data for the rate of incision of the river in the Holocene (i.e. it had incised to this level by *c.* 4000 BP. The other dates, from the organic channel-fill in Section 1, demonstrate rapid accumulation during Medieval times of alternating fine and coarse sediment units related to flooding episodes. These may reflect agricultural history as well as climatic shifts.

Three *B. tentaculata* opercula from Ripon South, from the sample collected from the sand and gravel facies exposed in the later working face (Section 3, sample 3; Fig. 2.59) during a visit to obtain OSL dates (see Chapter 2.6.4), were submitted for amino acid analysis at the NEaar facility in York. These specimens, considered to be representative of the fauna from the sandy facies (as exemplified by sample 2M: Table 3.29), provided good data that confirm this as the youngest of those Washlands sites to have produced Mollusca suitable for the use of this technique. Indeed, comparison of the three sets of operculum analyses from Newby Wiske, Ripon North and Ripon South suggest ages in the same sequence as the sites are listed here (Fig. 3.17), although the ages of the two Ripon sites are similar and confirmation of their separate ages would require further analyses (see Appendix III).

The OSL sampling programme in the Washlands was largely unsuccessful, but the single sample from Ripon South, from the sandy facies in Section 3 and close by the mollusc sample from which the above amino acid data were obtained (Fig. 2.59) gave a tentative indication of a late Holocene age (Appendix II).

3.7.8 Synthesis: Ripon South

The earliest environmental evidence at this site comes from the lens of organic sediment from below the quarry floor near the foot of Section 2, sampled by monolith 2M. This provides the earliest evidence from within the lower Terrace 3 sediments exploited by the modern quarry. Earlier workings, a little over a kilometre to the NNW (Fig. 2.57), were in Terrace 2 deposits, the greater antiquity of which was confirmed by analyses and radiocarbon dating (Howard *et al.*, 2000a, p.33), the latter giving an early Holocene age of 9710 ± 60 ^{14}C BP (Table 3.32).

From the 2003 workings, the pollen spectra from basal sample 2M were dominated by hazel (zone RS-a). The pollen data from this apparent palaeochannel deposit reflect habitats from a variety of depositional environments. Traditional palynological analysis from upland bog sites yield fluctuations in woodland trees that can be interpreted quite clearly both in terms of age and clearance due to human activity. The current dataset is derived from more complex eutrophic floodplain communities and contains low levels of tree pollen. The radiocarbon date for the lowermost pollen level, 4011 ± 40 ^{14}C BP, agrees with the pollen spectra of low *Ulmus* and *Alnus*, post-dating both the mid-Holocene rise of *Alnus* and the following decline of *Ulmus*. The abundance of *Corylus* pollen must indicate dense local stands of that shrub.

The sands and gravels that formed the lower part of the sequence here, in the basal part of which the above-mentioned organic lens occurred, contained mollusc shells in both recorded sections; however, as only the muddy fine gravel of Sample 2M (the organic lens) yielded a large fauna, the environmental interpretation based on the Mollusca is largely derived from this sample. The remaining samples from the sands and gravels (1A, 1B, 2A, 2B & 3; Table 3.29) were dominated by small numbers of aquatic Mollusca of types representative of strongly flowing water: *T. fluviatilis*, *A. fluviatilis* and *P. henslowanum*. Other significant remains were restricted to the resistant calcite opercula of *B. tentaculata* and the similarly resistant plates of limacid slugs, and to very broken, but still recognizable shells of *L. peregra*. The radiocarbon dating of monolith 2M, *c.* 4000 BP (see above), indicates deposition in the latest Neolithic period. The large 2M fauna is dominated by the same moving water species as the other samples from sands and gravels. *T. fluviatilis* and *A. fluviatilis* are the most numerous of the gastropods, along with the more catholic *B. tentaculata* and *L. peregra*. The most numerous bivalves are the moving-water species *P. henslowanum* and *Pisidium amnicum*, together with the catholic *Pisidium nitidum*. In contrast to the later organic channel-fill, in which the most numerous bivalve is *P. personatum*, this species is only represented by a single valve in 2M, illustrating the contrast between the bivalve content of moving water and pond faunas, with the implication being that the Section 1 organic channel-fill represents a cut-off meander channel (oxbow lake). Also

OxA-12553	504 ± 26 ^{14}C BP (550–500 cal. BP; cal. AD 1400–1450)

This date gives an age for the end of organic sedimentation and the start of minerogenic deposition. A late Medieval age of the first half of the 15th century AD is acceptable for the almost completely open agricultural landscape shown by the pollen data.

OxA-12552	627 ± 27 ^{14}C BP (670–540 cal. BP; cal. AD 1280–1410)

This date gives an age for a phase of arable expansion with major local cereal growing and the almost complete removal of even scrub woodland. The date of the 14th century AD would not be inconsistent with this. A coarsening of sediment grain size after this point may again reflect the result of this Medieval activity.

OxA-12551	752 ± 25 ^{14}C BP (730–660 cal. BP; cal. AD 1220–1290)

This date gives an age for the start of the infilling, by organic sediments, of an abandoned river channel. A Medieval date in the late 13th century AD is not contradicted by the pollen data which indicate an open agricultural landscape and little woodland other than heath scrubland. Agricultural improvement and expansion occurring at that time would seem to correspond with the vegetation record in this profile. The coarsening grain size in the sediment column at this point may reflect increased farming activity and local erosion of mineral soils.

OxA-12748	3896 ± 31 ^{14}C BP (4430–4230 cal. BP; 2480–2280 cal. BC)

This date (from an organic lens – Sample 2M – at the base of Section 2) gives a minimum age for the incision of the Ure in its present floodplain position and shows this to have taken place by late Neolithic to early Bronze Age times. This date significantly constrains the period during which this important change took place. The substantial elm pollen frequencies at this level suggested an earlier age for this sample, probably before the elm decline around 5000BP. The date is considerably younger however, and local surviving elm populations must have been responsible for the high elm percentages.

OxA-12636	4011 ± 40 ^{14}C BP (4580–4410 cal. BP; 2630–2460 cal. BC)

This second date on the same level as date OxA-12748 gives a similar result at the time of the Neolithic to Bronze Age transition. Although not strictly consistent with the other date, it confirms the general age of this thin detrital plant macrofossil layer and confirms this minimum value for the establishment of the Ure in its modern location.

Beta-116457	9710 ± 60 ^{14}C BP (11,240–10,810 cal. BP; 9290–8860 cal. BC)

This previously published date is from the site studied by Howard *et al.* (2000a) and published under the name 'Ripon Racecourse', although actually a forerunner of the Brown and Potter quarry described in this volume. The Ripon Racecourse sections were in deposits of the higher Terrace 3 of Howard *et al.* (2000a). The date was obtained from an organic lens in the alluvial sequence and places the higher terrace in the early Holocene.

Table 3.32 Evaluation of radiocarbon dates from Ripon South (Brown & Potter's Quarry) monolith 2M + Section 1, upper channel-fill. The Beta Analytic date is from the nearby Early Holocene site (Howard et al., 2000a; Fig. 2.57).

restricted in numbers and species in the sand samples are the Planorbidae, which are again more diverse and abundant in the oxbow fill, probably because of the presence of vegetated still water, which is the preferred habitat of many of the species of this family. The land assemblage in Sample 2M, because of the number of woodland species and lack of grassland ones, indicates that the banks of the river had not undergone much woodland clearance at the time the sediments were deposited.

By the time the pollen record resumes, in the form of the organic oxbow infill (which accumulated in Medieval times), the local vegetation has become much more diverse. Although most herb types recorded are of marsh taxa and can be attributed to rich alluvial floodplain plant communities, several weeds of disturbed ground or pasture are present. These suggest some human activity, although disturbance caused by flooding and other natural processes in the river valley may have provided the habitat. The low frequencies of *Alnus*, surprising for a eutrophic lowland floodplain environment (Brown, 1988), support the

hypothesis of a landscape previously subject to clearance of the major natural vegetation. The high *Calluna* frequencies, unlikely to orginate in dry bog surfaces fringing the floodplain, would also indicate post-clearance conditions and heathland. Some drainage of fertile floodplain areas for agriculture is possible by the late Medieval times indicated by the date of 752 ± 25 ^{14}C BP late in zone RS-b.

The molluscan data show that the lower sediments of the oxbow infill were deposited in a shallow, muddy pool rich in plant debris and often poorly oxygenated, as suggested by the presence of large numbers of *Lymnaea truncatula*, *Pisidium personatum*, *Carychium minimum*, Succineidae and *Vallonia pulchella*. The pollen of marsh and aquatic plants in these levels support this. The pool was sometimes a reed swamp, the habitat of *Vertigo antivertigo*, and water depths were at no time greater than 1–2 m and mostly much less than these values. Despite the clear indications that the general environment of deposition was a pool, there is a clear change in the fauna from bottom to top of the sequence. At levels below sample 5, numbers of the

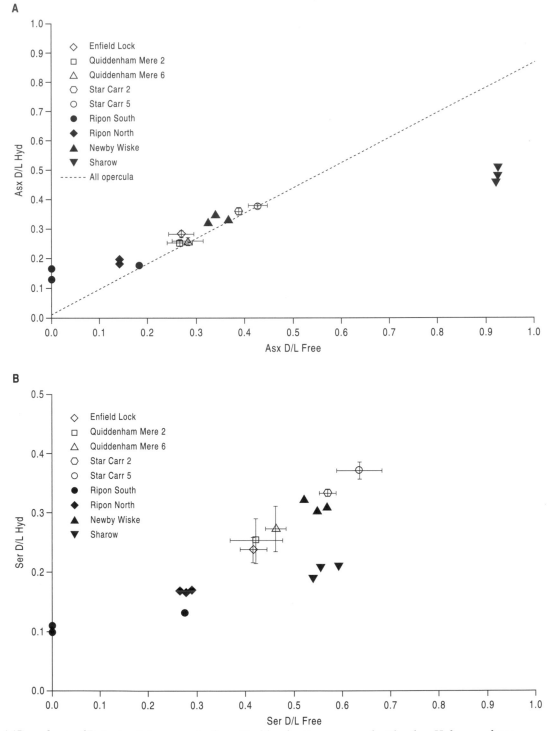

Fig. 3.17 AAR analyses of B. tentaculata *opercula from Washlands sites compared with other Holocene data:*
A – D/L Hyd vs D/L Free for Asx and the trendline observed for fossil. The data from the two subsamples (Free and Hyd) should be highly correlated: note the abnormal D/L ratios for Sharow, clearly indicating compromised samples. The error bars for the comparison sites represent two standard deviations about the mean for multiple samples. Two of three samples from Ripon South had levels of free amino acids so low that it was not possible to determine D/L Asx.
B – D/L Hyd vs D/L Free for Ser. Note the abnormal DL ratios for Sharow. The error bars represent two standard deviations about the mean for multiple samples.

obligate flowing water species *T. fluviatilis, A. fluviatilis, P. henslowanum* and *P. moitessierianum* are present in most samples. In the upper levels of the succession these species are absent. It is clear that the lower levels of the

channel infill could be accessed by water from the main channel of the river, probably in times of flood (in total corroboration of the beetle evidence – see above).

By the top of pollen zone RS-b, at 752 ± 25 BP, there

is persuasive evidence for anthropogenic activity from the occurrence of herbaceous taxa indicative of clearance weeds or heathland expansion associated with woodland reduction (cf. Edwards, 1999), and especially from the low but consistent curve for cereal-type pollen (Fig. 3.16). Local farming is confirmed by the occurrence of a phase of intensive cereal cultivation dated 627 ± 27 ^{14}C BP, with associated further reductions in the tree cover of the floodplain. Arable agriculture continued in a less intense form, or further from the sampled section, as cereal pollen remains important, together with several arable weeds or crops like *Centaurea nigra, Plantago major-media, Sinapis*-type, *Papaver*-type and *Cannabis*-type. Regeneration of tree and shrub vegetation was very slight and agriculture appears to have remained locally practised, at least until the diagram is truncated at 504 ± 26 ^{14}C BP. The discovery of Medieval shoes from the upper part of Section 2 (see Chapter 2.6.4) supports the radiocarbon dating of this upper facies and confirms human presence in the floodplain area.

Molluscan data show hydrological changes in the channel during deposition of the later profile. The major fluvial influence was ended after sample 4, although separate floods may have reached the oxbow in samples 7, 8 and 10. The highest parts of the succession after level 11–13, which have too small a fauna to be evaluated, have none of the above-mentioned moving-water species, even amongst the 894 molluscs counted in the bulk sample (17). This indicates that by this time the old channel was virtually cut off from the main river even at the highest floods. The large number of earthworm granules in samples between levels 6 and 14 suggests that at times the pool almost dried out, although the recurrence of species such as *B. tentaculata, P. planorbis* and *B. contortus* in samples 15 and 16 indicates a deepening of the water to a true pond with a moving water component, rather than a swamp. The scarcity of moving water species at these levels shows that renewed flooding from the river was not the prime cause of this water level change, but a more regional cause (water table rise due to climatic or anthropogenic reasons) was more probably responsible. All of this conforms with the interpretation of the uppermost (organic) facies in Section 1 as the infill of an abandoned section of channel, probably an oxbow. This agrees well with the vegetation history shown by the plant macrofossil and pollen results. In these higher levels the molluscan evidence shows that access to the channel by flood water became restricted (*P. henslowanum* and *P. moitessierianum* are only found up to sample 4, *T. fluviatilis* to sample 8 and *A. fluviatilis* to sample 11). This interpretation agrees well with the lithostratigraphy, with dominant fine-grained silts in the lower profile being replaced in the upper profile by sands.

The reasons for the contrasts in species make-up between the lower sandy facies and the upper (channel-fill) sequence in Sections 1 are probably that the pool faunas of the latter, especially in the top half of the section, recruited shells only from the water-body itself and the immediately

surrounding reed beds and swamp. The moving water assemblages of Section 2a and the lower parts of Section 1 incorporate Mollusca from all possible environments within the river, whether from the main, flowing channel or quiet backwaters, and also from a variety of land habitats reached by the river in times of flood. Such assemblages provide a more regional view of the mollusc fauna than that from a floodplain pond or oxbow. This is emphasized by the land fauna from the 2M monolith, from which, in total, 25 land species were recorded. These are indicative of marsh close to the river channel (*Carychium minimum, Oxyloma pfeifferi, Vertigo moulinsiana, Vertigo angustior*), drier grassland probably on the floodplain (*Pupilla muscorum, Vallonia costata*), shaded habitats (*Azeca goodalli*) and woodland (*Acanthinula aculeata, Ena obscura, Discus rotundatus, Cochlodina laminata, Clausilia bidentata* and *Balea perversa*). A number of the other species are catholic and may be found in shaded, damp or even open conditions (*Vitrea crystallina, Aegopinella nitidula,* and *Nesovitrea hammonis*).

There is nothing in the molluscan fauna from Ripon to suggest climatic conditions any different from those of the present. The modern mollusc fauna of the British Isles was largely established by Middle Holocene times (Holyoak, 1983; Kerney, 1999). A few species in the English fauna are later immigrants than the majority. A significant one of these occurs at Ripon: *T. fluviatilis* (Plate 3.2f). This species has been radiocarbon dated at two sites in the Thames catchment: at Staines, Surrey, to 6650 ^{14}C BP (Preece & Robinson, 1982) and at Enfield Lock, Middlesex, to 6620 ^{14}C BP (Chambers *et al.*, 1996). These dates suggest that it is unlikely that the Ripon deposits are much older than 6650 ^{14}C BP. The deposits at Ripon need not be much younger than this date, even given the need for the species to migrate the 300+ km from the Thames to North Yorkshire across catchment boundaries, as aquatic Mollusca are rapid colonisers if conditions are suitable (see review by Keen (2001) for some 20th Century examples). The age indications from the molluscan data therefore do not conflict with the Medieval age for the sediments of Section 1, or with the mid-Holocene (Neolithic) age for the thin lens sampled at Section 2M, as shown by the radiocarbon dates. They cannot assist with the question of of how much time elapsed between deposition of the sandy facies and the oxbow-infill deposits, although the tentative OSL age estimation from Section 3 (Fig. 2.59) of Medieval (Appendix II) suggests that the interval was short.

The coleopteran assemblage from the oxbow infill represents two main types of beetle communities: those from aquatic habitats and those living in terrestrial environments. The assemblage is made up of species that probably lived in the pool in which the sediment accumulated, together with extraneous species that had been washed or blown together into the deposit, more or less by accident, from the neighbouring landscape. Only minor changes appear to have taken place in this assemblage during the course of sedimentation, chiefly shown by the relative abundance of running water species that are commonest in the lower part of the succession, whereas the upper part is dominated by species typical of stagnant eutrophic water; in full agreement with the similar change in molluscan species (see above), this would be an expected consequence of the increasing separation of the oxbow from even the highest flow events of the river, leading to its eventual infilling. The beetle fauna shows that various species of pondweed lived in this water at this time. Also apparent is that, adjacent to the pool, the ground was marshy, with reedy vegetation that gave place to widespread damp meadow-like areas, which in turn gradually became drier further away from the water's edge, giving rise to rather sandy grassland with abundant ruderal vegetation. Both deciduous and coniferous trees were growing nearby but probably only sparsely. There is abundant evidence from the dung beetles for the presence of large herbivorous mammals, possibly representing domesticated livestock, as indicated by the sparse vertebrate assemblage (see below).

The material stripped from above Section 2 (before it could be recorded) was perhaps the youngest at the site, although it could well have been similar in age to the upper channel-fill in Section 1. It yielded the vertebrate faunal material, none of which is considered to be of any great antiquity and is plausibly late Holocene in age. Apart from the red deer antlers, all species represented are domestic animals, with a minimum of one individual of horse and cow present and two of sheep. The material varies in preservation type, with bones from the organic sediment being notably dark-stained. Root damage is present on several specimens, indicating a period of exposure of the material near the land surface.

In summary, the most important feature of the Ripon South site is the recovery of a fossiliferous alluvial section that covers most of the 1st Millennium BP, when Medieval land-use was causing great changes, essentially leading to the creation of the modern, mostly agricultural, landscape. This is a period that is generally poorly represented in the palaeoenvironmental archive. A successful series of radiocarbon dates and a high-resolution pollen diagram have allowed the reconstruction of environmental changes at this lowland site and in its local catchment. A major conclusion is that the intensity of Medieval farming correlates well with the changing climatic regime. Thus flooding events at times of poor climate deposited coarse-grained alluvium but during periods of milder climate, like the 'Late Medieval Warm Period', fine-grained alluvium accumulated in which a record of intensive cereal agriculture was preserved. The other proxy data, from plant macrofossils, Mollusca and insects, generally confirm this interpretation. Modern domestic animal remains confirm the very recent nature of the fill capping the sections.

3.8 Snape Mires

Snape Mires (SE 283 846), the extensive, low-lying and formerly marshy area to the south-west of Bedale (Fig. 3.18; see Chapter 2.8.2), was selected for investigation because of the presence within the basin of post-glacial limnic deposits and outcrops of calcareous tufa. Thin organic sediments have accumulated in the depressions within the undulating topography of the dissected and periglaciated lake floor. Although Snape Mires may have remained wetland-dominated through most of the Holocene, any surface organic deposits will have been greatly reduced in depth and distribution by extensive drainage for agriculture in recent centuries (cf. Butlin, 2003). The early map (1775) of the district published by Thomas Jeffery (www.digital archives.co.uk) shows what appears to be a wetland, bordered to the west by a northward-flowing stream that continues to the northern exit of the basin.

A thorough survey of Snape Mires was conducted by fieldwalking, inspection of drainage ditch sections and hand coring. The results show the basin to be characterized by higher areas of glacio-lacustrine clay dotted with small, shallow depressions infilled with mixtures of peats and organic limnic sediments, together with calcareous shell marls (Plates 2.7 & 2.8). Rather than a single depositional basin, Snape Mires consists of several small independent centres of sediment accumulation. Four of these centres (Fig. 3.18) have been investigated and representative profiles have been analysed in detail. These profiles are identified by their site name and by a core code number. Figure 3.18 also shows the location and details of a coring transect running east–west along Ings Lane with a side transect to the north at Ings Plantation. Two profiles were analysed; both have the prefix IL: IL6 (Ings Lane) and IL12 (Ings Plantation). Sediments revealed in a stream section in the western part of Snape Mires, around Snape Mill farmhouse, were analysed at two profile locations, termed Mill House (with the code MH); this is the location of the Snape Tufa (see Chapter 2.8, Plate 2.7). The fourth area analysed lies in the centre of Snape Mires, at the Gallop (Fig. 3.18), with the code TG. Despite detailed investigation of the whole of the southern and eastern parts of the Snape Mires basin, only very shallow and disturbed deposits were found there, not considered worthy of analysis. The investigated sites at Ings Plantation (IL 12) and the Gallop fall within the area of wetland depicted on the 1775 Jeffrey map (Fig. 3.18).

3.8.1 – Ings Lane IL6

Ings Lane IL6 lies midway along the Ings Lane transect in the northern part of Snape Mires (SE 2475 8475; Fig. 3.18).

3.8.1.1 Lithostratigraphy

The sampled core was selected because it contains a thick deposit of pale grey to white calcareous shell marl, mostly exposed in a ditch section, capped by a deeper layer of

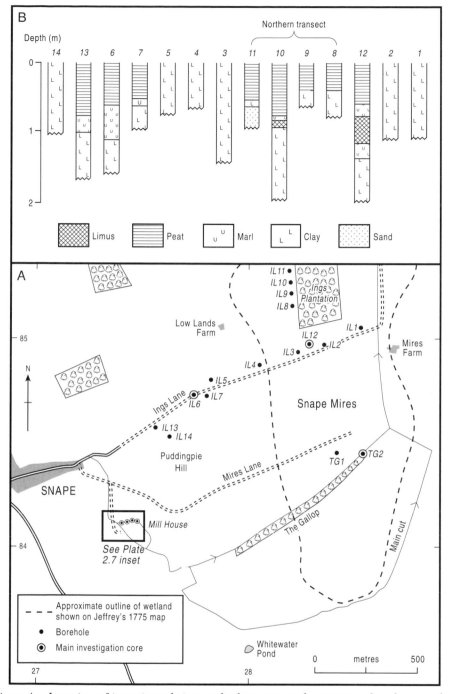

Fig. 3.18 Snape Mires: A – Location of investigated sites and other cores and transects, also showing drainage channels; B – Details of the Ings Lane transect, from which cores 6 and 12 were investigated fully.

surface peat than exists at most points on this transect (Table 3.33). The sediments above water-level were recovered using monolith tins, whereas the deeper part of the section was sampled by Russian corer. The marl was found to overly sticky blue-grey clayey silt of the type that underlies the entire Snape Basin and is attributed to glacio-lacustrine deposition (see Chapter 2.8.2). A bulk sample of the marl, taken from the stream section for analysis, forms sample 7 in the general series of tufa and marl samples analysed from Snape Mires. The marl is more properly

classified as uncemented lime mud. There is evidence of a thrombolitic texture and scattered tufa intraclast flakes within the deposit indicate the presence of grasses as a local substrate for precipitation. The sediment is a typical 'lake chalk' and is principally a bacterial biomediated precipitate (see Pedley, 1992, 1994) deposited in clear shallow water without clay contamination. It therefore records a period during the Holocene when clean standing water covered this part of the basin.

3.8.1.2 Pollen

Samples for pollen analysis have been prepared throughout the IL6 profile at two centimetre intervals. Pollen was not recovered from the grey clayey silt of unit 1. The results are shown on Figure 3.19, which is sub-divided into the following three local pollen assemblage zones (IL6-a to IL6-c).

ZONE DESCRIPTIONS

Il6-a (106–93 cm)

This lowest zone is dominated by *Betula*, which rises from moderate values to over 70% of total land pollen. *Juniperus* and *Salix* are significant but decline through the zone. There is some *Empetrum* and a continuous curve for *Filipendula* but Cyperaceae and Poaceae are low. *Pediastrum* algae values are very high and aquatic herb pollen is important, contributed mainly by *Myriophyllum spicatum* and *Typha latifolia*. Some reworked pollen occurs at the base of the zone.

IL6-b (93–69.5 cm)

Betula dominates this zone, at consistently over 70% of total land pollen. All other taxa are much reduced except Poaceae, which maintains its previous values. *Juniperus* is only intermittently recorded; *Pediastrum* is almost absent and all other aquatic types decline sharply except *Isoetes* (quillwort), which shows peak values late in the zone.

IL6-c (69.5–40 cm)

From peak frequencies of over 80% of total land pollen, *Betula* falls sharply until it maintains a curve of less than 20%, to be replaced mainly by *Pinus* and *Corylus*, the latter gradually rising through the zone. Other deciduous woodland trees also occur, notably *Alnus* and *Ulmus*. Cyperaceae and Poaceae both increase, while there is a low but consistent curve for *Taraxacum*-type. *Sphagnum* appears in low frequencies and for the first time micro-charcoal values become significant, rising to over 40% of total land pollen.

3.8.1.3 Plant macrofossils

The plant remains recorded from Ings Lane IL6 (Table 3.34) have been divided into two assemblage zones (IL6m-1 and IL6m-2). The analyses, which were carried out on 5 samples from the marl (between 140 & 65 cm) and two from the overlying peat (65–55 cm), revealed a low number and diversity of macrofossils.

ZONE DESCRIPTIONS

IL6m-1 (140–65 cm)

Characeae oogonia are abundant in this basal zone and are the only macrofossils recorded in several

Unit	Depth (cm)	Description
5	0–40	Organic topsoil with some tufa *stratum confusum*
4	40–66	Well humified silty peat Sh4, Ag+, nig.4, strf.0, elas.0, sicc.3, lim.sup.0
3	66–110	Shell marl Lc4, nig.1, strf.0, elas.0, sicc.2, lim.sup.0
2	110–116	Brown transitional silty marl deposit, root layer to base Lc3, Ag1, Th¹++, nig.2, strf.0, elas.0, sicc.2, lim.sup.0
1	116–167	Soft grey homogenous clayey silt Ag3, As1, nig.2+, strf.0, elas.0, sicc.2, lim.sup.0

Table 3.33 Stratigraphy at Ings Lane IL6 (Snape Mires). The particle-size distribution of Unit 1 (the glacial lake deposits that underlie the Snape basin) was confirmed using a Coulter Particle-size Analyser (see Chapter 2.1.3.1; Appendix IV).

of the contributing samples. The few other taxa present include *Betula pendula/pubescens*, *Carex* sp. and Pteridophytes.

IL6m-2 (65–55 cm)

A few charcoal and wood fragments occur in this upper zone, in which the number of Characeae oogonia declines sharply. A few macrofossils of *Sambucus nigra*, *Cladium mariscus*, *Menyanthes trifoliata*, *Chenopodium* sp. (goosefoot) and *Urtica dioica* were recorded.

3.8.1.4 Molluscs

The molluscan fauna from the Ings Lane IL6 shell marl consists of 23 species, 18 from freshwater and 5 from land environments (Table 3.35). The state of preservation of the shells is very good, allowing identification to the smallest juveniles in almost all cases. Most samples yielded good numbers of Mollusca, with only those from 125–120 cm, 110–105 cm and 65–60 cm producing fewer than 50 individuals. Apart from the topmost samples (65–55 cm), there were only slight differences in the species composition at any of the levels, suggesting that there was little change in conditions during the period of marl deposition.

Sample 230–220 cm was dominated by the gastropods *Valvata cristata*, *Valvata piscinalis* and *Lymnaea peregra*, with lesser quantities of the Planorbids *Gyraulus crista*, *Gyraulus laevis* and *Hippeutis complanatus*. *Physa fontinalis* was also moderately common. The sequence was found to be generally poor in bivalves, with *Pisidium obtusale*, *Pisidium nitidum*, *Pisidium milium* and *Sphaerium corneum* the main species present. Land taxa became

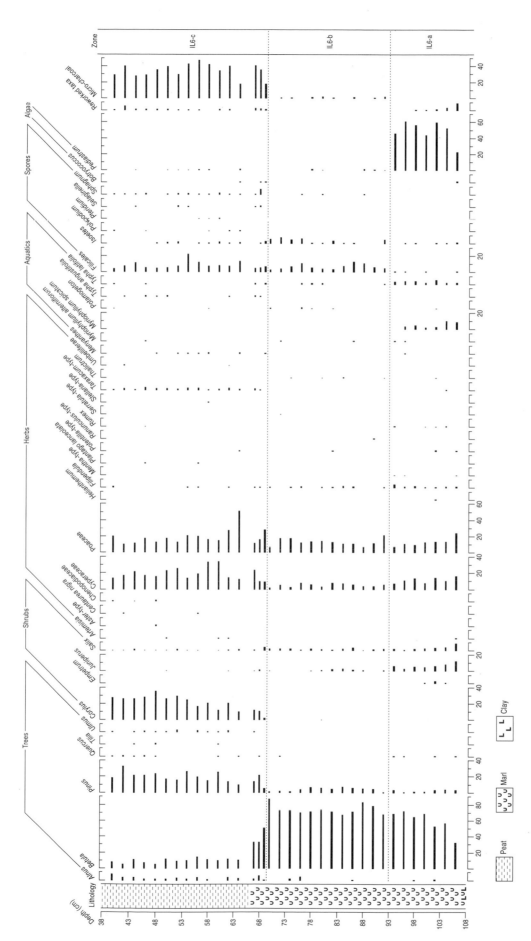

Fig. 3.19 Pollen diagram from Ings Lane IL-6. Frequencies are calculated as percentages of the total land pollen sum (trees, shrubs and herbs).

Sample depth (cm)		55–60	60–65	65–70	85–90	105–110	125–130	135–140
Woodland								
Betula pendula/pubescens	Cone scale						1	
Betula pendula/pubescens	Fruit			1				
Sambucus nigra	Fruitstone		1					
Charcoal	Fragment	1	1					
Wood	Fragment	+	+					
Waterside and damp ground								
Cladium mariscus	Nutlet	1						
Aquatic								
Characeae	Oogonia	16	14	>300	>300	>300	>300	>300
Menyanthes trifoliata	Seed	1	1					
Unclassified								
Carex sp	Trigonous nutlet							1
Chenopodium sp.	Seed	3						
Pteridophyte sp(p).	Sporangium			1				
Urtica dioica	Achene	2						
Assemblage zones		**MSm-2**		**MSm-1**				

Table 3.34 Plant macrofossils from Ings Lane, Section IL6 (Snape Mires).

numerous in the topmost samples, with a total of five species present in sample 65–60 cm.

3.8.1.5 Insects

Few insect remains were recovered from this profile and only from the upper part of the marl (Table 3.36). All were of Helodidae type, representing taxa from open, pond conditions, in good agreement with the depositional environment reconstructed from other evidence.

3.8.1.6 Chronology

Although several samples from IL6 were submitted for AMS dating, none was found to contain sufficient carbon to produce a date, as a result of which this core has no chronological control. Dating of the vegetational changes revealed in this profile therefore depends on the interpretation of the pollen stratigraphy. The base of the profile is interpreted as dating from the earliest Holocene, as the *Betula* curve rises to very high and sustained values and shrub and tall herb taxa like *Juniperus, Salix* and *Filipendula* are declining steadily in frequency. A date towards the end of the transition from cold Loch Lomond Stadial conditions to the temperate conditions of the Holocene seems certain, allowing a relative age of about 9800 ^{14}C BP to be inferred for the start of the pollen record here.

The other main palynological change, the fall of *Betula* and the rise of *Pinus* and *Corylus*, can be dated to *c.* 9400 ^{14}C BP by analogy with other dated pollen diagrams from the region (Innes, 2002d). By the top of this pollen diagram *Corylus* has not yet risen to abundant frequencies, which in dated sequences is a feature generally seen at about 9200 ^{14}C BP, suggesting that the pollen record from IL6 terminates before that date.

3.8.1.7 Synthesis: Ings Lane (IL6)

The rising *Betula*, declining *Juniperus* and *Salix*, and consistent *Filipendula* curves at the start of the pollen stratigraphy indicate a succession from open vegetation, dominated by shrubs and tall herbs with some birch copses, towards dense, closed-canopy woodland. This is typical of the closing stages of the transition from Loch Lomond Stadial cold environments to the temperate conditions at the start of the Holocene, when rapidly changing low stature vegetation communities were replaced by closed birch forest. The diversity and abundance of algal spores and aquatic pollen indicate open water conditions with gradual shallowing and increased organic content through time. Major diversification of the local woodland took place from the start of zone IL6-c (broadly coinciding with the change from marl to peat deposition), with the immigration and spread of *Corylus*, *Pinus* and other trees. The high micro-charcoal frequencies that accompany this

Sample depth (cm)	135–140	130–135	125–130	120–125	115–120	110–115	105–110	100–105	95–100	90–95	85–90	80–85	75–80	70–75	65–70	60–65	55–60
Aquatic																	
Valvata cristata Müller	35	4	9	15	5	15	9	42	46	66	11	24	42	64	104	9	2
Valvata piscinalis (Müller)	15	2		1	2	1	4	8	7	16	5	6	14	10	49	1	
Physa fontinalis (Linnaeus)	1						2		4	4			3	5	9		1
Lymnaea truncatula (Müller)													1			1	1
Lymnaea stagnalis (Linnaeus)											1		1	3			
Lymnaea peregra (Müller)	19	23	7	2	27	15	4	19	21	16	23	8	21	26	21	1	
Anisus leucostoma (Millet)																	
Gyraulus laevis (Alder)	6	8	14	2		4			1	3	1				5		
Gyraulus crista (Linnaeus)		2	8	3	2	20		3	6	7	14	6	10	10	31		
Hippeutis complanatus (Linnaeus)	2			2						2	1				3		
Planorbidae	8		10		2	2			1	3	1			2	17		
Acroloxus lacustris (Linnaeus)							1								1		
Sphaerium corneum (Linnaeus)	6	9	7	3	14	8	1	4	3	7	5	3		4	13	1	
Musculium lacustre (Müller)										1							
Pisidium personatum Malm													1	2			
Pisidium obtusale (Lamarck)			1			1	3	9	8	2	2	3	7	10	11	2	1
Pisidium milium Held			2	2	3			2	2	2	2		7	8	2		
Pisidium subtruncatum Malm							1							2			
Pisidium nitidum Jenyns	2		1		2			1	7	6	1	2	2	15	14		
Pisidium spp.	4		1		4	2	3	5	15	10	4	4	18	38	26		2
Terrestrial																	
Cochlicopa sp.																2	
Vallonia pulchella (Müller)																1	1
Vitrea crystallina (Müller)																1	1
Nesovitrea hammonis (Ström)																1	
Trichia hispida (Linnaeus)																1	
Total	110	48	60	30	61	68	28	93	121	145	71	56	127	199	306	21	9

Table 3.35 Molluscs from Ings Lane, Section IL6 (Snape Mires).

Preservation	Good
Viable sclerites	Yes
Comments	
Sample depth (cm	65–70
Helodidae	
Helodidae gen & spp. indet	*

Table 3.36 Insects from Ings Lane, Section IL6 (Snape Mires).

change suggest that fire was responsible for opening the *Betula* forest and allowing other taxa to colonize the area. Although the association of pine and hazel with fire might be coincidental, both are favoured by burning. The source of the fire, natural or human, remains conjectural. The recurring presence, although at very low values, of several open-ground weed pollen types, notably *Taraxacum*-type, suggests that some open areas were being created throughout the period after the *Betula* decline, presumably by fire.

The plant macrofossil data, although lacking in diversity and numbers of specimens, complement those from the palynology, with a close correlation with sediment type. The shell marl (zone IL6m-1) yielded little else but Characeae oogonia, suggesting a local environment dominated by a shallow, calcareous water body. *Betula pendula/pubescens* and ferns growing in the vicinity gave rise to the only other records (Table 3.34). The change to peat deposition at 65 cm coincides with a sharp reduction in Characeae oogonia, pointing to a lowering of the local water table. Fragments of wood in IL6m-2 may indicate that wet woodland had become established at the site, while the presence of *Cladium mariscus* would suggest this was an open fen–carr. Low numbers of *Menyanthes trifoliata* and Characeae indicate the persistence of small pools, whereas *Sambucus nigra*, *Chenopodium* sp. and *Urtica dioica* would have grown on areas of drier soil. Small fragments of charcoal indicate local burning, resulting either from natural or anthropogenic causes.

Both the pollen and the plant macrofossils point to palaeoenvironments fully in keeping with the sediment types. For the shell marl these are reinforced by the molluscan evidence, which goes further in indicating a pool without access to flowing water. As at Newby Wiske, the mollusc assemblages can also provide clues regarding palaeo-water depths, as indicated by the contrasting numbers of the species of *Valvata* present (see section 3.3.7). In all of the IL6 samples, the ratio of *V. cristata* to *V. piscinalis* is 6:1 to 2:1, suggesting that the water depth was closest to the preference of *V. cristata*, although within the limits for *V. piscinalis*; this suggests a likely depth of c. 1.5 m. The presence of *G. crista*, *H. complanatus* and *Acroloxus lacustris* suggests quantities of macrophytic vegetation in the water body, although the low numbers of these taxa compared to *L. peregra*, *V. piscinalis* and *V. cristata* might indicate that the vegetation cover was not dense. The *L. peregra* presence indicates a pool with muddy shallow margins, while the various records for *Pisidium* suggest significant plant debris within it but without full macrophyte surface cover. There were no species amongst the Mollusca that suggest that the pool was prone to drying, even at its margins, so a permanent water body is indicated until the topmost samples (65–55 cm) are reached. Towards the top of the sequence there are clear indications from the Mollusca of the transformation of the pond into a muddy vegetated swamp, in which the fen peat was deposited. The occurrence of the 'slum' (Sparks, 1961) species *Musculium lacustre*, *Pisidium personatum* and *Anisus leucostoma* show that the site was becoming shallow, swampy and probably lacking in open water. The topmost samples (65–55 cm) are low in numbers of freshwater Mollusca and have species of swamp/wet meadow conditions, such as *Vallonia pulchella* and *Vitrea crystallina*. This implies that the molluscan record continues into the early period of fen peat deposition, coinciding here with plant macrofossil biozone IL6m-2 and the lower part of pollen biozone IL6-c.

All of the molluscan species present at Ings Lane IL6 can be regarded as being part of the British fauna from the Lateglacial (Kerney, 1999). Holyoak (1983) suggested that all except *A. lacustris* were part of the fauna of Berkshire during that time, although he regarded the occurrence of significant frequencies of species such as *P. fontinalis* as indicative of an age no older than the Early Holocene. The age of the IL6 fauna therefore is within the Holocene, although no closer estimate can be made from the Mollusca alone. This conclusion does not disagree with the early Holocene age suggested by the other palaeoenviornmental evidence.

3.8.2 Ings Plantation IL12

Ings Plantation core IL12 was taken at the eastern end of the Ings Lane (IL) transect (SE 2830 8495; Fig. 3.18) in the north-eastern part of Snape Mires, at a location that remains waterlogged throughout the year.

3.8.2.1 Lithostratigraphy

The stratigraphy of the core (Table 3.37) comprised a surface layer of crumbly herbaceous peat overlying organic shell marl that contained an organic limus unit, which rests upon grey clayey silt. This lower clayey silt, being much softer than the stiff grey glacial lake clay in other cores at Snape Mires, is interpreted as a younger, limnic deposit. This was the deepest core at this end of the Ings Lane transect to contain peat, marl and limnic units. Several cores from this end of the transect contained similar sedimentary successions, although considerable variability occurs over small distances; the shell marl, in particular, appears to be highly localized. Nonetheless, core IL12 appears to be representative of this part of Snape Mires as a whole.

3.8.2.2 Pollen

Samples for pollen analysis were prepared throughout the IL12 profile at five centimetre intervals, with finer resolution sampling around the main lithostratigraphical boundaries (Fig. 3.20). Pollen was not preserved in the crumbly oxidized peat above 15 cm depth, or in the grey clayey silt below 144 cm. The sequence is subdivided into the following seven local pollen assemblage zones (IL12-a – IL12-g).

ZONE DESCRIPTIONS

Zone IL12-a (144–140 cm)

The basal zone is dominated by *Betula*, Cyperaceae and Poaceae, each of which accounts for about 30% of total pollen. Low frequencies of *Pinus*, *Salix* and *Filipendula* complete the assemblage. Some aquatic pollen and algae occur and there are considerable frequencies of reworked pre-Quaternary spores.

Zone IL12-b (140–127.5 cm)

In this zone *Betula* percentages fluctuate but generally increase to about 40% of total pollen. Poaceae frequencies rise to very high values, replacing those of Cyperaceae and almost all other taxa. A peak of *Pediastrum* algal colonies is recorded.

Zone IL12-c (127.5–108 cm)

Pollen frequencies for woody taxa increase in this zone, with *Betula* averaging over 60% and *Salix* increasing significantly. Poaceae fall from their abundance in the previous zone to very low values, whereas *Filipendula* shows a slight increase.

Zone IL12-d (108–77.5 cm)

Betula is the most abundant pollen type in this zone, at about 50% of total pollen, while Cyperaceae increase until they match Poaceae at about 20%. *Salix* shows a low but consistent curve. All other taxa are very poorly represented indeed.

Zone IL12-e (77.5–46 cm)

Corylus rises throughout this zone at the expense of *Betula*, reaching peak values of over 70% of total pollen. *Ulmus* appears in the assemblage with low values and *Salix* declines throughout. Cyperaceae and Poaceae are present in moderate frequencies. There is a small peak in micro-charcoal late in the zone.

Zone IL12-f (46–32.5 cm)

In this zone *Corylus* declines but still dominates the assemblage, at about 40% of total pollen, while *Pinus* rises to about 20%. There are low continuous counts for *Ulmus* and *Alnus*. Cyperaceae are present at moderate frequencies but all other pollen types are very low indeed.

Unit	Depth (cm)	Description
5	0–58	Crumbly black herbaceous peat Th²2, Sh2, nig.4, strf.0, elas.0, sicc.2
4	58–77	Peaty shell marl Lc4, part. test. (moll)+, Sh++, nig.1+, strf.0, elas.0, sicc.2, lim.sup.0
3	77–117	Brown *limus* Ld³4, nig.3, strf.0, elas.0, sicc.2, lim.sup. 0
2	117–144	Silty shell-marl Lc3, Ag1, part. test. (moll)+, nig.1+, strf.0, elas.0, sicc.2, lim.sup.0
1	144–200	Grey laminated clayey silt Ag3, As1, nig.2+, strf.2, elas.0, sicc.2, lim.sup.0

Table 3.37 Stratigraphy at Ings Plantation, Core IL12 (Snape Mires). The particle-size distribution of Unit 2 (the shell marl) was confirmed using a Coulter Particle-size Analyser, which revealed > 55% silt (see Chapter 2.1.3.1; Appendix IV).

Zone IL12-g (32.5–15 cm)

Alnus rises to about 25% of the assemblage while *Corylus* declines gradually through this final zone. *Pinus* values are maintained and there is a low but continuous *Tilia* curve. Cyperaceae frequencies gradually rise and there are sporadic counts for *Taraxacum*-type and *Pteridium* near the top of the zone.

3.8.2.3 Plant macrofossils

The plant remains recorded from Ings Plantation IL12 (Fig. 3.21) have been divided into five plant macrofossil assemblage zones (IL12m-1–5). In most of the samples, the macrofossils were well preserved but there were low numbers from the peat and the lowest section of the clayey silt.

ZONE DESCRIPTIONS

Zone IL12m-1 (185–165 cm)

The limited numbers of plant remains in this zone represent herbaceous taxa that occupy a range of habitats. These include Apiaceae (umbellifers), *Carex* sp(p)., *Juncus articulatus* type, Poaceae, *Ranunculus* subgenus *Ranunculus*, *Rumex* sp., *Sonchus arvensis* (perennial sow-thistle) and *Viola* sp. (violet).

Zone IL12m-2 (165–140 cm)

Aquatic plants dominate the assemblage; *Potamogeton berchtoldii* (small pondweed) is abundant at the start of the zone but is later replaced by *Potamogeton natans*. A diversity of waterside

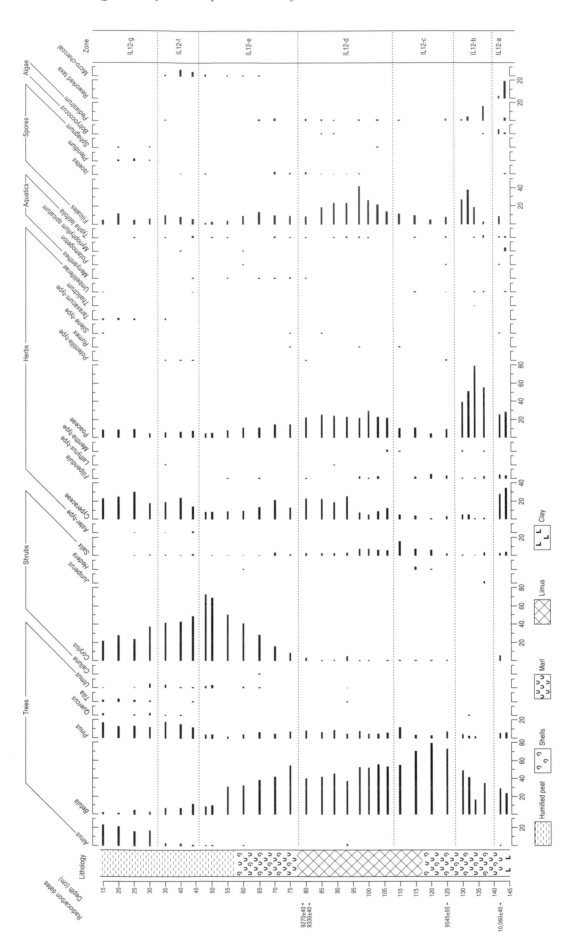

Fig. 3.20 Pollen diagram from Ings Plantation IL12. Frequencies are calculated as percentages of the total land pollen sum (trees, shrubs and herbs).

and damp ground taxa includes *Typha* sp(p)., *Schoenoplectus lacustris*, *Cladium mariscus* and *Carex* cf. *rostrata* (cf. bottle sedge).

Zone IL12m-3 (140–95 cm)

Macrofossils of woodland taxa are abundant, particularly those of *Betula*. The fruits and cone scales that could be identified to species are mainly of *Betula pubescens* (downy birch), although a few *Betula pendula* (silver birch) fruits also occur. Low numbers of *Populus tremula* (aspen) catkin bracts and *Populus* sp(p). bud scales are present. Characeae dominate the aquatic flora, whereas *Potamogeton* species are absent. Pteridophyte sporangia are abundant, particularly at the beginning and end of the zone.

Zone IL12m-4 (95–45 cm)

The number of woodland remains declines slightly, whereas Characeae oogonia increase in number. *Menyanthes trifoliata* and *Cladium mariscus* are recorded; the latter is particularly abundant towards the end of the zone. *Carex* sp(p). nutlets increase in number, while there is a decline in Pteridophyte sporangia. A few charcoal fragments were recorded between 60 and 50 cm.

Zone IL12m-5 (45–15 cm)

Macrofossils are poorly preserved; they include a few remains of *Betula pendula/pubescens*, *Cladium mariscus*, Characeae, *Menyanthes trifoliata*, *Juncus* sp(p)., Poaceae and *Ranunculus* subgenus *Ranunculus*. A few wood and charcoal fragments were recorded between 40 and 30 cm.

3.8.2.4 Molluscs

Molluscan analyses were undertaken from the localized marl horizons found in some of the cores; the difficulty experienced in following these laterally for significant distances probably points either to deposition in small hollows or to post-depositional disturbance and/or erosion. Nevertheless, it was possible to obtain molluscan residues from eleven different levels (derived from the plant macro-fossil samples). An aquatic fauna was clearly present throughout the period represented (Table 3.38).

The occurrence of two Red Data Book species, *Myxas glutinosa* (RDB category: Endangered) and *Pisidium pseudosphaerium* (RDB category: Rare), is especially noteworthy. Although *M. glutinosa* has been reported over the past 150 years from about 35 localities in England and Wales, it is now a rare species, found at only three sites in Britain since 1965 (Kerney, 1999). This species prefers very clean and quiet waters in lakes and slow-moving rivers, avoiding turbid or weed-choked habitats (Kerney, 1999). The occurrence of *P. pseudosphaerium* (Plate 3.2c) in the upper levels (above 106 cm) is especially important,

representing only its second Holocene record from Britain. The only other fossil record is from mid-Holocene shell marl at Burton Salmon (SE 4866 2811) in the Vale of York (Norris *et al.*, 1971). This uncommon species is today confined to lowland marsh drains and ponds with very clean, clear water, such as in the East Anglian broadland and the Pevensey and Lewes Levels, Sussex (Kerney, 1999).

3.8.2.5 Insects

The taxa recovered from the grey clayey silt in the lower part of the profile, *Helophorus*, *Hydraena* spp. and Helodidae (Table 3.39), are all species associated with muddy seasonal pools, a variety of more permanent water bodies and boggy ground (Hansen, 1987; Koch, 1989). The overlying marl layer yielded only remains of *Plateumaris/Donacia* type, which suggests an open environment, vegetated by a variety of lower growing wetland plants such as sedges and taller reeds. Throughout the core, the Coleoptera suggest that an open water environment persisted, since the assemblage is dominated by aquatic taxa, characteristic of open pools and more permanent water bodies: the Dytiscidae, *Hydroporus* spp., *Ilybius* spp. and *Agabus* spp., are all predatory species found in a variety of water bodies. A further dytiscid, *Colymbetes fuscus*, is found in well-vegetated marshland and fens and is typical of clay ponds (Nilsson & Holmen, 1995). A single carabid taxon, *Bembidion* spp., is a hygrophilous genus found in a variety of wetland habitat (Lindroth, 1974, 1985, 1986). Overall, the Coleoptera indicate conditions becoming increasingly damp with the establishment of a much more substantial, permanent pool in the upper samples.

3.8.2.6. Vertebrates

The 116–106 cm macrofossil sample yielded a mandible of *Esox lucius* (pike) and a trunk vertebra of *Bufo bufo* (common toad). The former, which provides clear evidence for the existence of a water body, was identified by Ms Deborah Jaques of Palaeoecology Research Services (Shildon, County Durham). The toad vertebra was identified by Dr Chris Gleed-Owen of the Herpetological Conservation Trust.

3.8.2.7. Chronology

Four radiocarbon dates are available from Ings Plantation IL12 (Table 3.40). The base of the analysed section, the point on the *Betula* curve where non-tree pollen finally falls to low values and the start of the rise of the *Corylus* curve have all been successfully dated. The date for the *Betula* peak seems late, but can be explained by local factors of abundant wetland grass pollen production delaying the expansion of the curve to dominance. All the dates are therefore acceptable. The absence of terrestrial macrofossils higher in the profile precluded dating after the start of the *Corylus* rise. The rise in *Alnus* pollen is likely

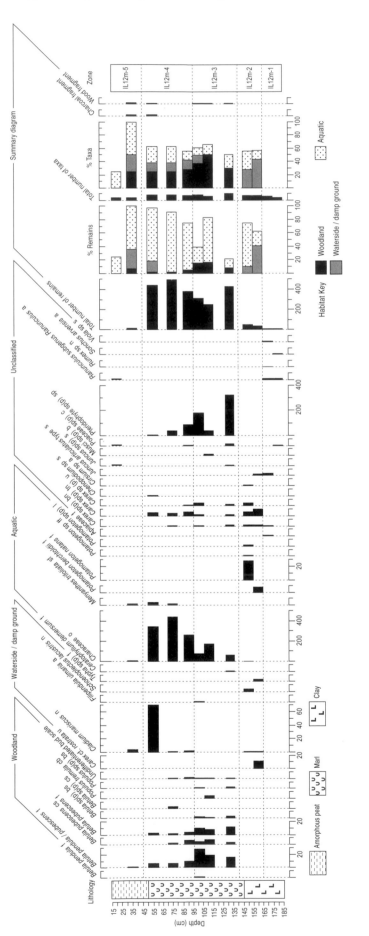

Fig. 3.21 Plant macrofossil diagram from Ings Plantation IL12. a: achene; b: branch; bn: biconvex nutlet; bs: bud scale; cb: catkin bract; cs: cone scale; c: caryopsis; f: fruit; ff: fruit fragment; l: lid; n: nutlet; o: oogonium; s: seed; sf: seed fragment; sp: sporangium; tn: trigonous nutlet; u: utricle.

Sample depth (cm)	48–50	50–60	70–80	79–81	86–96	96–106	106–116	125	128–136	140–142	145–155
Aquatic											
Valvata cristata Müller		7	13	1		5	6				
Valvata piscinalis (Müller)	3		15		40	8	5		3		9
Physa fontinalis (Linnaeus)	-		5		10	1	16				
Lymnaea palustris (Müller)				1							
Lymnaea peregra (Müller)	2	38	52	15	45	8	82	2	3	7	
Myxas glutinosa (Müller)											1
Bathyomphalus contortus (Linnaeus)					1	1					
Gyraulus laevis (Alder)				1					10	2	26
Gyraulus crista (Linnaeus)	1	9		2	6	4	8	5	1	2	3
Hippeutis complanatus (Linnaeus)		26	23	4	16	12	1	2	1		10
Acroloxus lacustris (Linnaeus)		4									1
Sphaerium corneum (Linnaeus)		7	3		4						
Pisidium obtusale (Lamarck)		6		1?							
Pisidium milium Held		3	1		2						
Pisidium pseudosphaerium Favre	1	17	55	2	10	7	2				
Pisidium subtruncatum Malm		1		1							
Pisidium nitidum Jenyns	1	11	3		6				2		5
Pisidium pulchellum Jenyns		1?									
Terrestrial											
Vertigo antivertigo (Draparnaud)				1							1
Total	8	130	170	28	141	45	120	9	20	11	56

Table 3.38 Molluscs from Ings Plantation, Core IL12 (Snape Mires).

to have occurred in the centuries before *c.* 7000 ^{14}C BP, judging from the regional range of dates for this feature (Innes, 2002d), so that the top of the analysed profile at IL12 is likely to date from *c.* 7000 ^{14}C BP or a little later.

3.8.2.8 Synthesis: Ings Plantation (IL12)

The pollen diagram from Ings Plantation IL12 provides a record of vegetation change from the beginning of the Holocene until a point after the rise in *Alnus* pollen, which typically occurs *c.* 7000 ^{14}C BP, albeit with considerable chronological variability (Innes, 2002d). In lowland areas in Yorkshire, the date of the alder rise can be several centuries earlier than this average figure, particularly in lowland eutrophic wetlands where conditions would have been very suitable for alder. Unfortunately no suitable plant macrofossils were present in the upper part of the profile to provide a date for this feature, but an age somewhat before 7000 ^{14}C BP for the IL12-f–g zonal boundary seems likely. Dates are available for the earlier part of the record and these fit well with the pollen stratigraphy.

The basal date of 10,060 ± 40 ^{14}C BP coincides with transitional plant communities that would be expected in the later stages of the change from the Lateglacial to the Holocene. The absence of arboreal macrofossil remains at and beneath the level of this date may indicate a predominantly unwooded local environment, in agreement with a Lateglacial age. At this early stage, before the pollen record becomes available, macrofossils of many herbaceous plants occur, including *Rumex* sp., Apiaceae, *Carex* sp(p)., *Juncus articulatus* type, Poaceae, *Ranunculus* subgenus *Ranunculus* and *Viola* sp., supportive of the existence of disturbed, bare and damp ground habitats, consistent with tundra-type Lateglacial conditions. The record for *Sonchus arvensis*, which prefers disturbed, nutrient-enriched habitats (Preston *et al.*, 2002) is indicative of the local open, calcareous soils around this site at the time. The abundance of macrofossil remains of aquatic plants in these levels indicates that sedimentation was occurring within a pond or small lake. This was initially dominated by the submerged pondweed *Potamogeton berchtoldii* but this was succeeded by the floating, broad-leaved species, *Potamogeton natans*. As both species have very wide ecological tolerances (Preston, 1995), the succession probably resulted from a competition for light. *Schoenoplectus lacustris* and *Typha* sp(p). also grew in the water body, which is likely to have been of moderate to shallow depth, as *S. lacustris* usually occurs in water

Sample depth (cm)	50–60	70–80	86–96	96–106	128–136	145–155	165–175	175–185
Preservation	Good	Good	Good	Good	Good	Good	Good	Good
Viable sclerites	Yes	Yes	Yes	Yes	Yes	No	Yes	Yes
Comments								
Carabidae								
Bembidion spp.	*							
Dytiscidae								
Hydroporous spp.		*	*					
Agabus spp.	*							
Illybius spp.		*						
Colymbetes fuscus	*							
Hydraenidae								
Hydraena spp.				*			*	
Octhebius spp.								
Helophorus spp.								
Hydrophilidae								
Cercyon spp.				*				
Helodidae								
Helodidae gen & spp. indet	*							*
Chrysomelidae								
Plateumaris/Donacia spp.		*		*	*			
Phylotreta spp.								

Table 3.39 Insects from Ings Plantation, Core IL12 (Snape Mires).

SUERC-8568   9270 ± 40 ^{14}C BP (10,660–10,420 cal. BP; 8710–8470 cal. BC)
This date provides an age for the start of the rise of the *Corylus* curve and is compatible with dates on this palyno-stratigraphical feature at other sites in the region. The date is therefore acceptable.
SUERC-8569   9330 ± 40 ^{14}C BP (10,580–10,280 cal. BP; 8630–8330 cal. BC)
This date is from the same level as SUERC-8568 and although different is of the same order of age. It is acceptable for the timing of the start of the *Corylus* rise in this region.
SUERC-8573   9545 ± 55[14]C BP (11,140–10,670 cal. BP; 9190–8720 cal. BC)
This date provides an age for the culmination of the early Holocene *Betula* pollen rise and the fall in local grass pollen frequencies. Although acceptable the date is rather late and the dominance of *Betula* pollen at this site may have been delayed by persistent high frequencies of grass pollen from local wetland sources.
SUERC-8574   10,060 ± 40 ^{14}C BP (11,820–11,350 cal. BP; 9870–9400 cal. BC)
This date provides an age for organic sedimentation at the base of the profile. It agrees with the pollen data in suggesting a time around the transition from the Lateglacial to the Holocene.

Table 3.40 Evaluation of radiocarbon dates from Ings Plantation, Core IL12 (Snape Mires).

between 0.3 and 1.5 m and *Potamogeton natans* favours depths of 1–2 m (Preston *et al.*, 2002). *Juncus articulatus* type, *Cladium mariscus*, *Carex* cf. *rostrata* and other sedges were present at the damp margins of the water body. There are also limited insect remains from these lowermost samples, consisting of hygrophilous, rather than distinctly aquatic taxa, less clearly indicative of a water body than those from higher-level samples in the core.

The disappearance of *S. lacustris*, *C. mariscus*, *Typha* sp. and *Potamogeton* from the macrofossil record by the beginning of the pollen sequence (at *c*. 140 cm depth) indicates a significant change in the local aquatic conditions. The sediments change from minerogenic clayey silt to *Chara* marl and the presence of macrofossils of the submerged aquatics Characeae and *Ceratophyllum demersum* shows that open water was still present at the site. This change in plant community is likely to have resulted from an increase in water depth and an expansion of the water body, resulting in its margin moving further from the coring site. The record of *E. lucius* from the lower part of the palynological sequence (see above) also points to a large water body, as might that of *B. bufo* from the same level; toads tend to breed in large, permanent ponds or lakes and often occur in fishponds, as the unpalatability of the tadpoles provides protection from fish predation (Beebee & Griffiths, 2000). Both taxa have occurred in Britain since the early Holocene. The insect evidence supports the idea of a large, open permanent pool or small lake; the Coleoptera present in these samples are types associated with larger water bodies, with distinctly terrestrial taxa virtually absent (restricted to a single taxon). The abundance of arboreal macrofossil remains in this part of the profile indicates that local birch woodland developed at the site. This agrees well with the pollen data, as slowly increasing *Betula* percentages across the clayey silt–marl transition indicate the spread of tree birches, while the still open nature of the vegetation canopy permitted sedge and grass associations

to survive. High but slowly reducing pollen values for the thermophilous *Filipendula* are typical of this warm early post-glacial stage, when damp open areas supported a tall herb flora among the expanding birch cover. The virtual absence of *Juniperus* from this record is surprising, deviating from the early post-glacial successional model, but there is a similar lack of juniper at other sites in mid-Yorkshire, such as Tadcaster (Bartley, 1962); in this area a swift transition to birch woodland may have precluded a juniper phase. High grass percentages before birch assumes dominance may well derive from wetland fringe vegetation. Dense *Betula* woodland became established by 9545 ± 55 ^{14}C BP and must have shaded out most other land taxa. Only marsh herbs bring diversity to the pollen assemblage at this time and increasingly organic sediments reflect the increase in marsh vegetation and aquatic plant diversity. The damp conditions would have favoured *Betula pubescens*, but *Betula pendula* was also growing on areas of lighter, well-drained soils. Both are represented in the macrofossil record, which also shows that Pteridophytes flourished in the moist, shaded conditions (Fig. 3.21). The presence in this woodland of *Populus tremula* is recorded by its catkin bracts, in addition to the presence of *Populus* sp(p). bud scales. As *Populus* pollen is very fragile and generally not preserved, these macrofossil records are a rare and valuable clue to its presence in these early Holocene woodlands. The occurrence of aspen in the British Isles extends back to the Lateglacial (Godwin, 1975).

By the latter stages of the first Holocene millennium the presence of *Menyanthes trifoliata* and *C. mariscus* in the macrofossil assemblage suggests a transition to a shallower water body. The large increase in *Cladium mariscus* at the end of the zone points to an encroachment of fen vegetation and the few small charcoal fragments indicate local burning either by natural or anthropogenic causes. This depositional change and evidence of fire coincides with the appearance and steady rise of *Corylus* pollen after about 9300 ^{14}C BP. The immigration of hazel at around this time is typical of post-glacial woodland development, as is the later penetration of *Ulmus*; interpolation from the other dated horizons suggests that this occurred at about 8500 ^{14}C BP. The replacement before 9000 BP of *Betula* by *Corylus* (as the most abundant arborial taxon) is again part of the expected norm, although it is perhaps more gradual here than elsewhere in the region (cf. Innes, 2002d). That hazel dominance was short lived at this site may be due to diversification brought about by fires, which are indicated by the appearance of both macroscopic and microscopic charcoal. Increased *Pinus* and *Alnus* populations locally coincide with this burning, with more *Taraxacum*-type and *Pteridium* also a symptom of disturbance. A surprising feature of this pollen record is the evident inability of *Quercus*, and less obviously *Ulmus*, to become established in the forest. There is no clear reason for this, and it may be a taphonomic artefact, with dense pine, hazel and alder stands around this small wetland area preventing the pollen of the main deciduous forest trees from reaching the coring location from more edaphically suitable areas. The sedimentary change to a more terrestrial peat above *c.* 50 cm coincides with a sharp fall in the number of macrofossils recovered from the profile. Those that are present in these upper levels after the rise of hazel indicate some woodland cover with areas of damp ground and open water. A mosaic of fen and small pools within dense mixed woodland is indicated by the palaeobotanical data, before the record is terminated soon after the rise of *Alnus* pollen.

The molluscan evidence broadly supports the palaeo-botanical interpretation outlined above. The assemblages throughout the sequence (Table 3.38) were dominated by aquatic taxa, with *Lymnaea peregra*, *Gyraulus crista* and *Hippeutis complanatus* present in relatively large numbers. The basal levels (155–128 cm) were dominated by *Gyraulus laevis* and, to a lesser extent, *Valvata piscinalis*. The former species typically occurs in lakes and ponds with clean and quiet waters, whereas *V. piscinalis* is more common in larger and deeper bodies of slowly flowing or still water. In the upper levels (above 116 cm), the records of *Valvata cristata* suggest that the water remained well oxygenated and slowly flowing or still, but became somewhat shallower, as was indicated by the *M. trifoliata* and *C. mariscus* macrofossils.

The entomological evidence further reinforces these interpretations. The beetle taxa recovered from the grey clayey silt in the lower part of the profile, *Helophorus, Hydraena* spp. and Helodidae, are all representative of open water environments, as might be anticipated from their position within the limnic sediments. The overlying marl layer yielded only remains of *Plateumaris/Donacia* type, which conforms with deposition within a small pond. The overlying *limus* unit contains a greater variety of insect taxa, all of which have habitat preferences for ponds and pools but some, like *Cercyon* spp., indicating the presence of detrital organic material. In this unit and the overlying thin marl layer, all the insect data reflect local taxa from aquatic

environments of various types, varying water depths and quality influencing the faunal changes. The upper unit of more terrestrial peat sediment contains mostly different taxa from the limnic layers below, although the environment was clearly still extremely wet. *Colymbetes fuscus* indicates very well-vegetated marsh and fen conditions, while *Bembidion* spp. often prefer more terrestrial habitats.

In summary, the landscape around IL12 was initially open and dominated by a moderately deep lake or pond with diverse marginal vegetation. Birch woodland developed locally and was dominated by downy birch, with silver birch and aspen also present in the vicinity. Mixed deciduous forest developed, while fluctuations in the water level occurred, the open water phase developing into a more complex wetland mosaic with the later encroachment of fen vegetation and the resulting onset of peat formation. The insect evidence is at a slight variance with this picture in suggesting that a larger, more permanent body of open water developed much later than is suggested by the palaeobotanical evidence for progressive drying of the site. Succession towards shallower waters is, however, implicit in the changes in insects through the profile, with a transition to marshland in the upper organic layers.

3.8.3 Snape Mill (Mill House)

On the western side of the Snape Mires basin, at Snape Mill farm house, is a deposit of subaerial tufa that has formed a lobate mound around a calcareous spring (SE 2745 8410; see Chapter 2, 2.8.2.1–3). One of the streams that drain the current basin dissects the main tufa lobe, providing exposures in section through more than two metres of this variably lithified, porous calcareous precipitate that is full of the empty moulds of vegetable material. Layers of highly organic clayey silt, marl and grey clayey silt were observed beneath the capping tufa. Four profiles were examined in the stream section (Chapter 2.8.2.1, Plate 2.8a), the site as a whole being termed Mill House (MH). At profile MH1 (Table 3.41) the exposed section was extended by mechanically-assisted hand coring through a further two metres of clayey silt (below stream level) that contained organic lenses, until gravel was reached. The section above the stream level was collected in monolith tins and the rest of the sequence was recovered using a wide-chamber piston corer. Profiles MH2 and 4 provided further stratigraphical details of what is clearly a small infilled depression beneath the tufa (Plate 2.8a) and, in MH4, a gravel sample, but MH3 was the only other profile examined for palaeoenvironmental evidence; it was used to investigate in detail at the highly organic clayey silt and marl intercalations in the upper part of the sequence.

3.8.3.1 Lithostratigraphy

The lithological succession at Snape Mill was constructed from the combination of stream sections and cores at the Mill House site (Plate 2.8a; Table 3.41). The basal gravel at MH1, which was not penetrated, may be an extension of the extensive gravel sheet mapped close to the study site to the west (Chapter 2.8.2, Plate 2.7). More likely it is a basal deposit within the depression here that has perhaps been reworked from that higher-level deposit. More than three metres of sticky blue-grey clayey silt overlies the gravel and forms the main stratigraphical unit in the infilled depression, although it was missing in the feather-edge section, MH4 (Plate 2.8a). Its particle-size distribution was confirmed using the Coulter Particle-size Analyser (see Chapter 2.1.3.1), which revealed, from various samples, a consistent dominance of silt (60–80%: see Appendix IV). This is likely to be a lake deposit formed under conditions of low biological productivity, as it contains virtually no organic material. Exceptions are a thin peat that rests beneath the clayey silt upon the basal gravel, a layer in the middle of the clayey silt that includes a high organic *limus* fraction and some peaty intervals in the upper part of the clayey silt. Overlying the clayey silt is a complex succession that includes two main clayey/silty peats (Plate 3.3), although these highly organic beds contain thin pure inorganic laminae composed of either grey clayey silt or calcareous marl. These thin intercalations suggest rapidly changing environmental conditions and depositional regimes, with an increased representation of marl layers in the upper profile. The clayey silty peats are thicker and higher in the section at MH3 (Plate 2.8a; Table 3.42). The sequence is sealed by variously soft and hard tufa, the product of a nearby calcareous spring, and then by modern disturbed soil horizons.

3.8.3.2 Pollen

The Mill House 1 (MH1) profile was subsampled for pollen analysis at varying intervals throughout the sequence, ten centimetre intervals in the lower, largely inorganic grey clayey silt and closing to 2 cm intervals in the highly organic layers in the uppermost part of the core (below stream level: Fig. 3.22). Preservation was generally poor and oxidation and corrosion of pollen were common. Preservation was particularly poor in the lower clayey silt, in which several of the sampled levels did not contain enough pollen to count and in others a lower pollen counting sum was necessary. Reworked pre-Quaternary spores were common throughout the profile. No countable pollen was found in the higher organic layers, including all those interbedded with the tufa (Table 3.42). The sequence (Fig. 3.22) has been subdivided into eight local pollen assemblage zones (MH1-a to MH1-h).

ZONE DESCRIPTIONS

Zone MH1-a (465–430 cm)

The assemblages in the basal zone contain only a few pollen types, with *Pinus* the only tree pollen recorded in assemblages dominated by Cyperaceae and Poaceae. *Rumex* occurs in very low frequencies. Notably, *Betula* and *Juniperus* are almost absent. There is some micro-charcoal.

Zone MH1-b (430–365 cm)

Cyperaceae and Poaceae remain important but this zone is characterized by increasing percentages of *Betula* and *Juniperus*, with some *Salix*, which dominate the assemblage by the end of the zone. Other herb pollen is very sparse, with *Filipendula*, *Helianthemum* and *Artemisia* present at the start of the zone and *Thalictrum* appearing later. *Selaginella* (lesser clubmoss) spores occur. Micro-charcoal percentages increase.

Zone MH1-c (365–345 cm)

This zone is characterized by a sharp reduction in *Betula* and, latterly, *Juniperus* frequencies. *Artemisia* and *Helianthemum* are recorded and Cyperaceae increases sharply late in the zone. Micro-charcoal frequencies remain high.

Zone MH1-d (345–325 cm)

Betula and *Juniperus* percentages recover to again dominate the assemblage in this zone. *Artemisia* disappears and Poaceae frequencies are reduced; *Filipendula* (last seen in zone MH1-b) reappears.

Zone MH1-e (325–285 cm)

In this zone *Betula* and *Juniperus* frequencies are reduced, although the latter only moderately so. *Artemisia* reappears and Poaceae increases. Micro-charcoal frequencies remain high. At the top of this zone is a level that is barren of pollen.

Zone MH1-f (285–255 cm)

Betula increases sharply, with *Juniperus* steadily declining; *Empetrum* is recorded late in this zone. *Artemisia* is present at first but is replaced by *Filipendula*. Micro-charcoal frequencies decline late in the zone.

Zone MH1-g (255–185 cm)

Tree and shrub frequencies are considerably reduced in this zone, although *Betula* and *Juniperus* are still the main types. *Empetrum* forms a low but consistent curve. Several open-ground herbs are recorded, with *Artemisia, Filipendula, Thalictrum* and *Helianthemum* important. *Isoetes* and *Selaginella* are prominent in the spore assemblage. Micro-charcoal frequencies recover to near maximum counts.

Zone MH1-h (140–125 cm)

Betula, Pinus and *Salix* frequencies rise in this zone but *Juniperus* remains very poorly represented. Cyperaceae and Poaceae frequencies remain high. No other taxa are important but micro-charcoal is still significant.

Unit	Depth (cm)	Description
19	0–35	Hard tufa
18	35–98	Rubbly tufa with clay pockets
17	98–103	Grey clay with tufa
16	103–109	Tufa
15	109–119	Tufa with organic bands
14	119–127	Alternating clayey peat and calcareous layers Sh2, As1, Lc1, nig.2+, strf.3, elas,0, sicc.3, lim.sup.4
13	127–131	Amorphous clayey peat Sh3, As1, nig.3, strf.0, elas.0, sicc.3, lim.sup.4
12	131–137	Grey clay As4, nig,2, strf.0, elas.0, sicc.2, lim.sup.0
11	138–145	Amorphous clayey peat Sh3, As1, nig.3, strf.0, elas.0, sicc.3, lim.sup.4
10	145–185	Soft grey blue clay As4, nig.2, strf.0, elas.0, sicc.2, lim.sup.4
9	185–250	Soft grey blue clay with gritty and organic layers (peaty at 195-201, pebbles at 225, molluscs at 230, medium sand parting at 239) As4, Sh+, Ga+, Gg(min)+, test. (moll.)+, nig.2, strf.0, elas.0, sicc.2, lim.sup.0
8	250–261	Gravelly clay As3, Gg(min)1, nig.2, strf.0, elas.0, sicc,2, lim.sup.0
7	261–266	Calcareous laminated clay As3, Ls1, nig.2, strf.1, elas.0, sicc.2, lim. sup.0
6	266–275	Organic clayey *limus* Ld^{3}2, As2, nig.2+, strf.0, elas.l,, sicc.2, lim.sup.0
5	275–283	Laminated grey clay As4, nig.2, strf.2, elas.0, sicc.2, lim.sup.1
4	283–305	Homogeneous clay (molluscs at 160) As4, test. (moll.)+
3	305–350	Stiff blue grey clay As4, nig.2, strf.0, elas.0, sicc.2, lim.sup.0
2	350–463	Poorly laminated grey clay with organic streaks (gastropods at 353, 373, 380) As4, Sh+, test. (moll.)+, nig.2, strf.1, elas.0, sicc.2, lim.sup.0
1	463–480	Gritty laminated clayey peat Sh3, As1, Gs+, nig.3, strf.1, elas.0, sicc.2, lim.sup.1
	480	Stopped on gravel

Table 3.41 Stratigraphy at Mill House MH1 (Snape Mires). The particle-size distribution of Units 2, 4, 9 and 10 was confirmed using a Coulter Particle-size Analyser (see Chapter 2.1.3.1; Appendix IV).

Profile MH3 was sub-sampled at two centimetre intervals in the organic layers. Unlike most of MH1, preservation was generally good, although countable pollen was not recovered from the marl and clayey silts between the peats. Four local pollen assemblage zones are recognized (Fig. 3.23).

ZONE DESCRIPTIONS

Zone MH3-a (235–227 cm)

This zone is dominated by Cyperaceae pollen with lesser frequencies of Poaceae and *Pinus*. *Juniperus* and *Salix* are present, *Betula* increases late in the zone and there are sporadic occurrences

Unit	Depth (cm)	Description
14	0–160	Rubbly tufa
13	160–167	Yellow marl Lc4, nig.1, strf.0, elas.0, sicc.3, lim.sup.0
12	167–173	Compact dark brown peat Sh4, nig.3+, strf.0, elas.0, sicc.3, lim. sup.4
11	173–174	Yellow marl Lc4, nig.1, strf.0, elas.0, sicc.3, lim.sup.4
10	174–177	Compact dark brown peat Sh4, nig.3+, strf.0, elas.0, sicc.3, lim. sup.4
9	177–181	Yellow marl Lc4, nig.1, strf.0, elas.0, sicc.3, lim.sup.4
8	181–186	Compact dark brown silty peat Sh3, Ag1, nig.3, strf.0, elas.0, sicc.3, lim. sup.4
7	186–210	Yellow marl Lc4, nig.1, strf.0, elas.0, sicc.3, lim.sup.4
6	210–216	Organic grey clayey silt Ag2, As1, Sh1, nig.2, strf.0, elas.0, sicc.3, lim.sup.2
5	216–224	Compact silty peat with clay blebs Sh3, Ag1, nig.3, strf.1, elas.0, sicc.3, lim.sup.2
4	224–231	Grey clayey silt with organic lenses Ag2, As1, Sh1, nig.2, strf.2, elas.0, sicc.3, lim.sup.1
3	231–233	Brown silty peat Sh3, Ag1, nig.3, strf.0, elas.0, sicc.3, lim.sup.0
2	233–234	Grey clayey silt Ag3, As1, nig.2, strf.0, elas.0, sicc.3, lim.sup.4
1	234–237	Grey organic clayey silt Ag2, As1, Sh1, nig.2, strf.0, elas.0, sicc.3, lim.sup.2

Table 3.42 Stratigraphy at Mill House MH3 (Snape Mires).

of thermophilous tree pollen. Micro-charcoal percentages are high.

Zone MH3-b (227–219 cm)
Cyperaceae continue to dominate the assemblage in this zone. *Betula* percentages increase to match *Pinus* and Poaceae, while shrub pollen frequencies

increase. Micro-charcoal percentages are reduced but are still significant.

219–186 cm barren of pollen

Zone MH3-c (186–183 cm)
The assemblage in this zone is mixed, with several types contributing significant percentages. *Salix*, *Corylus* and *Betula* are prominent, with Poaceae and Cyperaceae the main herbaceous types. Micro-charcoal frequencies are very low.

Zone MH3-d (183–164 cm)
Corylus pollen frequencies rise through the uppermost zone to dominate the assemblage, at up to 80% of total land pollen. *Pinus* percentages are high and *Ulmus* rises late in the zone. Poaceae and Cyperaceae remain the only important herb pollen types. Micro-charcoal frequencies are greatly increased.

3.8.3.3 Plant macrofossils

The plant remains recorded from Mill House MH1 (Fig. 3.24) have been divided into six plant macrofossil assemblage zones (MH1m-1 to MH1m-6). Macrofossils were poorly preserved in the core except between 340 and 195 cm.

ZONE DESCRIPTIONS

Zone MH1m-1 (475–430 cm)
The plant macrofossil assemblage in MH1m-1 is dominated by oogonia of Characeae, with fruits of *Potamogeton* cf. *filiformis* (cf. slender-leaved pondweed) also present. In the lower half of the zone, a few *Salix* sp(p). (willow) buds are recorded, and towards the top of the zone macrofossils of *Eleocharis* sp(p)., *Typha* sp(p)., *Juncus* sp(p). and Musci sp(p). appear.

Zone MH1m-2 (430–280 cm)
Characeae oogonia are abundant in this zone, but there are few other taxa. *Carex* spp. and *Valeriana dioica* (marsh valerian) appear towards the top.

Zone MH1m-3 (280–210 cm)
Betula pendula/pubescens (silver or downy birch) fruit and *Betula pubescens* cone scales are frequent and a few fruits of *Betula nana* (dwarf birch) are recorded at the top of the zone. Characeae oogonia are present in very low numbers compared with previous zones, while *Menyanthes trifoliata* seeds are common. Remains of *Carex* spp. and Musci sp(p). are abundant.

Zone MH1m-4 (210–190 cm)
In this zone, tree birch remains disappear while

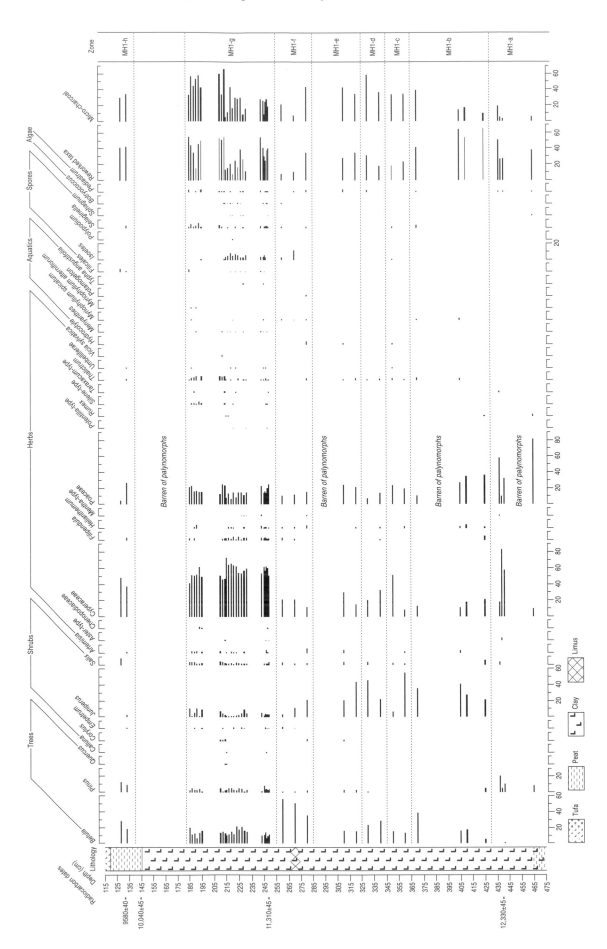

Fig. 3.22 Pollen diagram from Mill House MH1. Frequencies are calculated as percentages of the total land pollen sum (trees, shrubs and herbs).

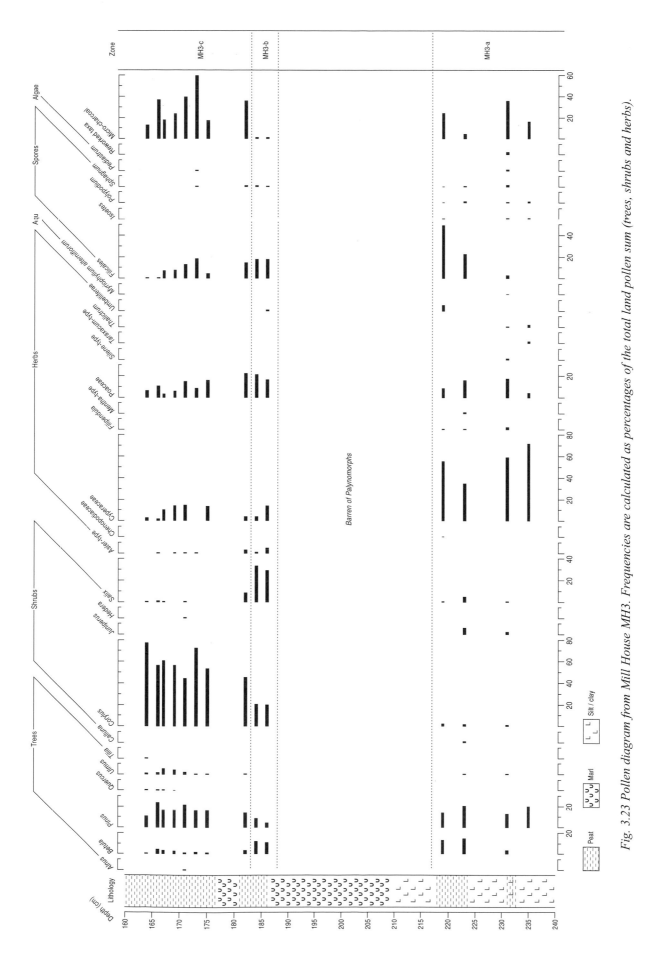

Fig. 3.23 Pollen diagram from Mill House MH3. Frequencies are calculated as percentages of the total land pollen sum (trees, shrubs and herbs).

fruits of *Betula nana* increase in number. Waterside and damp ground taxa include *Schoenoplectus tabernaemontani* (grey club-rush), *Selaginella selaginoides* (lesser club-moss) and *Thalictrum alpinum* (alpine meadow-rue). Macrofossils of *Carex* spp. and Musci sp(p). are abundant and *Rumex acetosella* and *Armeria maritima* (thrift) also occur in this zone. Characeae oogonia are present in large numbers.

Zone MH1m-5 (190–150 cm)

Tree birch macrofossils re-appear in this zone in low numbers, while *Betula nana* fruits decrease. Characeae, *Menyanthes trifoliata* and *Carex* spp. occur in moderate numbers.

Zone MH1m-6 (150–120 cm)

Tree birch fruits and cone scales are abundant, although macrofossils are poorly preserved in this zone. Low numbers of *Sphagnum* sp(p)., *Typha* sp(p)., *Menyanthes trifoliata*, *Carex* spp., *Epilobium* sp., Musci sp(p). and Pteridophytes are present. Fruitstones of *Arctostaphylos uva-ursi* (bearberry) are recorded between 145 and 139 cm.

Very few plant macrofossils were preserved in the samples from Mill House 3. They are presented in Table 3.43. The column samples consisted of dry, compacted peats and clayey silts. Plant macrofossil preservation was particularly poor in the peats, perhaps as a result of post-depositional dehydration of the deposits. Local woodland cover is suggested by the presence of fruits of *Betula pendula/pubescens* between 231 and 216 cm and low numbers of wood fragments throughout the section. Small charcoal fragments between 186 and 167 cm (and particularly abundant between 186 & 181 cm) indicate localized fires. Most of the fragments were too small (< 3 mm) to identify, but two pieces of larger charcoal were attributable to the Salicaceae (*Salix* or *Populus*). *Eupatorium cannabinum* and *Typha* sp(p). indicate waterside habitats, which may also have been occupied by *Carex* sp(p). and Musci sp(p).

Additional palaeoenvironmental information can be obtained from the plant fossils found in the tufa. It proved difficult to extract fossils from the tufa by conventional means, due to its varying degrees of lithification. Some observations are possible, however, based on the petrological examinations recorded in Chapter 2.8.2. The tufa layers contain sedge and/or grass moulds, as well as ostracods and diminutive gastropod shells. The basal material in MH1, as represented by Sample 1 (Bed A, Fig. 2.73), consisted of thin, allochthonous tufa intraclast laminae interleaved with organic-rich laminae. Uncemented platy fragments within the structure originally represented the micritic calcite coatings on sedge or similar ribbed grasses and associated mosses. This friable material, representing the earliest development of tufa at the site,

may record conditions that were generally unfavourable for tufa formation, possibly due to low temperatures (Chapter 2.8.2). The primary fabric of the overlying tufa of Bed C (Fig. 2.73–2.74) appears to have precipitated onto a grass and bryophyte framestone, developed where water seeped through grass and moss cushions. This is followed (0.5 m above Bed C; Fig. 2.75) by a grass rhizome and bryophyte framestone tufa in which grass stalks and bryophyte cavities remain open and preserve *in situ* plant orientations. Several platy cemented areas in this deposit show speleothem fabrics. The tufa is seen to be composed of thin fringe cement skins (stained pink in Fig. 2.75 [see colour version on CD]) that originally coated living aquatic mosses (possibly *Cratoneuron* sp.) but have subsequently become buried by later diagenetic clear calcite cement.

Grass and bryophyte framestone tufa again occurs in MH3, in which a well-orientated vertical fabric of grass stalk tubes was noted. It is overlain by bryophyte framestone tufa, as in MH1 (see Chapter 2.8.2.1; Figs 2.76–77). SEM study helped in the identification of the plant casts and with the palaeoenvironmental interpretations, as well as shedding light on late-stage diagenetic processes. Samples 2, 4 and 5 were most instructive in these respects: Sample 2 (Bed B in Fig. 2.73) shows a finely ribbed stem, possibly from *Chara* sp., together with an ostracod valve (Fig. 2.80).

3.8.3.4 Molluscs

There were only two productive basal MH1 samples, at 365–375 and 415–425 cm, which yielded freshwater mollusc species, *Lymnaea truncatula* being recorded in both (Table 3.44). There is then a gap in the record of over a metre before a very different assemblage appears in the calcareous sediments. Similar faunas are recorded from both the studied tufa profiles (MH1 & MH3), this being a somewhat restricted assemblage of land snails indicative of a marshy, rather open habitat.

The presence of *Vertigo genesii* (Plate 3.2b) throughout these samples (occasionally in large numbers) is noteworthy. Fossil occurrences show that this arctic–alpine species was relatively common in lowland England during the Lateglacial, before becoming extinct in many areas in the early Holocene, as a result of increasing warmth and woodland development. The Mill House occurrences clearly demonstrate persistence into the Holocene, since they are associated with a number of species unknown from the Lateglacial, such as *Vertigo substriata* and *Vitrea* sp. (cf. Preece & Bridgland, 1998, 1999). Today, *V. genesii* is known at very few English sites (Killeen, 2005) following its first discovery at Widdybank Fell, Teesdale, which is famous for its arctic–alpine flora (Coles & Colville, 1980). There, *V. genesii* lives in a calcareous flush amongst mosses and low-growing sedges within a north-facing hillside depression at 495 m O.D. This and the other extant British colonies have probably all persisted from the Lateglacial. The species is found more widely on the Continent, where its range is distinctly northern and

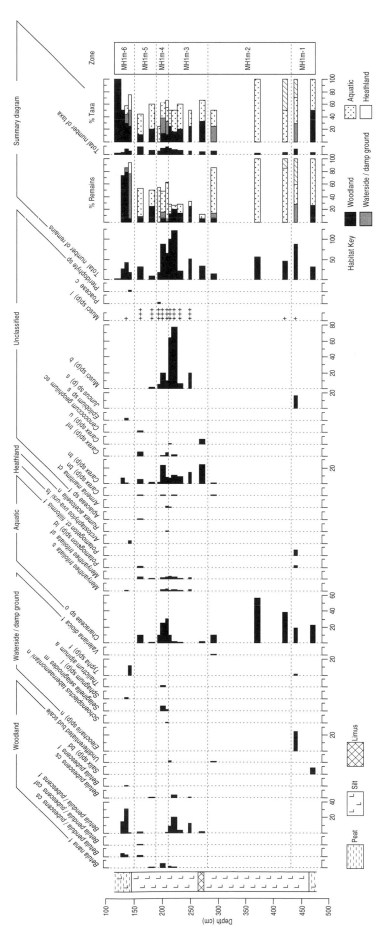

Fig. 3.24 Plant macrofossil diagram from Mill House MH1. Plus signs were used for the occurrence of Musci sp(p). leaves, where +: rare (<10); ++: common (10–300); +++: abundant (>300). a: achene; b: branch; bn: biconvex nutlet; bd: bud; c: caryopsis; ct: calyx tube; cf: cone scale fragment; csf: cone scale; cs: cone scale; cf: cone scale; f: fruit; fs: fruit stone; fs: fruit stone; l: leaf; ld: lid; m: megasporangium; n: nutlet; o: oogonium; s: seed; sc: sclerotium; sf: seed fragment; sp: sporangium; tn: trigonous nutlet; tnf: trigonous nutlet fragment; u: utricle.

Sample depth (cm)		167–173	174–177	181–186	216–224	224–231	234–237
Woodland							
Betula pendula/pubescens	Fruit				3	16	
Betula sp.	Cone scale fragment				1		
Salix/Populus charcoal	Fragment			2			
Unidentified charcoal	Fragment	5	10	177			
Wood	Fragment	+	+	+	+	+	+
Waterside							
Eupatorium cannabinum	Achene fragment	2	4	31			
Typha sp(p)	Fruit						2
Unclassified							
Carex sp(p)	Trigonous nutlet	1			1	5	
Musci sp(p)	Branch	2				1	

Table 3.43 Plant macrofossils from Mill House MH3 (Snape Mires).

alpine, occurring in Switzerland, Germany and Scandinavia (Kerney *et al*., 1983).

Another notable member of the same genus, *V. geyeri* (Plate 3.2a), was found in a single level (186–203) in MH3. This today is a rare snail found in unshaded calcareous fens in northern Britain and Ireland, often in the company of *V. genesii*, although it is more common as an early Holocene fossil, which is exactly its context at Mill House. It was, for example, recorded in an early Holocene context at Ripon Racecourse (Howard *et al*., 2000a), in an earlier exposure within the quarry complex referred to here as Ripon South (Chapter 2.6.4; Chapter 3.7).

3.8.3.5 Insects

The preservation of sclerites in samples 70–65 and 80–70 cm was exceptional. The majority of the Coleoptera from this site (Table 3.45) are species of wetland (swamp and bog) and pond habitats. At the base of the core, the assemblage is restricted to the hygrophilous Carabidae taxon, *Bembidion* spp. A single thorax of *Bembidion varium* was also recovered; this species is associated with sparsely vegetated clay substrates, which suggests a relatively open environment (Lindroth, 1974, 1985). The assemblage from the upper samples is dominated by hygrophilous species of swamps, bogs and marshy ground, with aquatic species notably absent. A large component of this assemblage is associated with damp, tussocky vegetation such as sedge-fen and mossy floodplains. These species include the staphylinid, *Lesteva longelytrata*, and the chrysomelid genus, *Donacia* spp. (Tottenham, 1954; Menzies & Cox, 1996).

Further remains were recovered in MH3 (Table 3.46); the taxa, being diagnostic of swamp and boggy conditions, add little to the interpretation of the site.

3.8.3.6 Chronology

Four radiocarbon dates were obtained from the MH1 profile (Table 3.47). Appropriate macrofossils were scarce in the sequence but were recovered from near the top, the base and in mid-section. The four dates form a good series and show the sub-tufa profile to cover a period of about three thousand years in the Lateglacial and early Holocene. This agrees well with the palaeoenvironmental data. Terrestrial macrofossils were not recovered from the MH3 section, so that profile remains undated. Relative dating, based on the pollen stratigraphy, indicates that the MH3 diagram covers a period from the latter stages of the Loch Lomond Stadial, before 10,000 ^{14}C BP, to a time before the arrival of the main mixed oak forest trees, like *Ulmus* and *Quercus*, at around 8500 ^{14}C BP (cf. Innes, 2002d).

3.8.3.7 Synthesis: Mill House

The abundance of macrofossil remains of aquatic plants throughout the MH3 core suggests that the local environment was dominated by an open water body such as a pond or lake for a lengthy period, shown by the radiocarbon record to equate to the Lateglacial. The presence of *Potamogeton* cf. *filiformis*, *Typha* sp(p)., *Eleocharis* sp(p). and *Juncus* sp(p). near the base of the core (between 436 & 442 cm) indicates that it was not particularly deep initially (not > 2 m), or that the sampling site was close to the water's edge. Insect evidence may also suggest that this is the case, as the single taxon recovered from the lower part of this core is found in open environments on silty substrates, generally close to water margins. Molluscan data confirm the palaeobotany in recording open-water environments and so the presence of a least a small lake. Macrofossils of *Salix*, which may have been a tree or a dwarf species, show that willow was growing around the water body in this early phase,

Sample depth (cm)	MH1						MH3	
	164–180	180–205	205–225	225–248	365–375	415–425	186–203	203–213
Aquatic								
Valvata piscinalis (Müller)					3	4		
Lymnaea truncatula (Müller)			25	4				
Lymnaea peregra (Müller)					9	9		
Musculium lacustre (Müller)					1			
Pisidium obtusale (Lamarck)					1			
Pisidium spp.			2					
Terrestrial								
Carychium minimum Müller	6	4	19	20				12
Carychium tridentatum (Risso)	1		2	1				
Carychium spp.	1		16	13				14
Succinea/Oxyloma	4	11	6	6			1	3
Cochlicopa sp.	22	22	32	61			2	15
Columella sp.								1
Vertigo antivertigo (Draparnaud)	1							
Vertigo substriata (Jeffreys)	8		4	3				21
Vertigo genesii (Gredler)		26	34	10			9	3
Vertigo geyeri Lindholm							2	
Vertigo pygmaea (Draparnaud)?	1							
Vertigo spp.	11	102	148	51			29	17
Pupilla muscorum (Linnaeus)		3	6				1	2
Leiostyla anglica (Wood)				1				
Vallonia pulchella (Müller)	54	22	42	4				4
Punctum pygmaeum (Draparnaud)	7	5	11	6			2	5
Vitrina pellucida (Müller)	3	1						
Vitrea spp.	1	1	9	42				
Nesovitrea hammonis (Ström)	21	16	45	24			4	23
Oxychilus spp.				2				
Deroceras/Limax				1				
Euconulus fulvus (Müller) agg.	14	7	16	6			3	18
Trichia hispida (Linnaeus)		1						
Cepaea spp.	4			+				2
Total	159	221	417	255	14	13	53	140

Table 3.44 Molluscs from Mill House MH1 and MH3 (Snape Mires).
Note: + indicates that fragments were recognized but no countable individuals were present

although perhaps not abundantly, as *Salix* pollen frequencies remain low. The abundance of Characeae higher in the core, in MH1m-2, and the absence of macrofossils of other aquatic and waterside taxa may indicate the transition to a deeper water level than represented by the previous zone. Characeae have been identified as an important pioneering taxon in Lateglacial aquatic systems, particularly as they are a source of carbonate.

The pollen evidence preserved in the limnic sediments from this shallow pond at Mill House provides a record of vegetation change over three millennia of the Lateglacial and early Holocene, although punctuated, since poor preservation and low concentrations of pollen in parts of the grey clayey silt unit made achieving an adequate pollen counting sum throughout the sequence impractical. The high *Corylus* frequencies of the higher pollen zones at MH3 mean that those sediments formed later than the top of the MH1 sequence, where *Corylus*-dominated assemblages are absent. The upper peat unit at MH3 is not represented at MH1, which agrees with the lithological

Preservation Viable sclerites Comments	Good Yes	Good Yes	Good Yes	Good Yes	Good Yes	Exceptional Yes	Exceptional Yes	Good Yes	Good Yes	Good Yes	Good Yes
Sample depth (cm)	0–6	6–12	12–19	30–45	45–50	65–70	70–80	100–106	140–150	291–297	320–330
Carabidae											
?*Bembidion varium*(Ol.)											*
Bembidion spp.					*						**
Agonum spp.							*				
Pterostichus spp.	*						*				
Dytiscidae											
Hydroporous spp.						*					
Hydraenidae											
Octhebius spp.										*	
Staphylinidae											
Olophrum spp.	*							*			
Lesteva longelytrata (Goeze)				**							
Lesteva spp.	**			*							
Trogophloeus spp.							*				
Stenus spp.						**					
Philonthus spp.		*					*				
Tachinus rufipes		*									
Chrysomelidae											
Donacia spp.		*									
Plateumaris/Donacia spp.											
Phylotreta			*								
Curculionidae											
Ceutorhynchus spp.									*		

Table 3.45 Insects from Mill House MH1 (Snape Mires).

Preservation Viable sclerites Comments	Good Yes	Good Yes
Sample depth (cm)	224–231	234–237
Carabidae		
Pterostichus spp.		**
Staphylinidae		
Olophrum spp.	*	

Table 3.46 Insects from Mill House MH3 (Snape Mires).

record, as the organic units at MH1 are highly organic clayey silts and not true peats. Tufa formation must have begun at MH1 several hundred years earlier than at MH3, where Holocene peats are not present, unless the MH1 section was truncated in antiquity. Some overlap between the two diagrams is apparent, however, with zone MH1-d resembling zone MH3-b closely, both having a very early Holocene assemblage. The MH3 diagram may therefore be dated relative to the radiocarbon dated MH1 profile. Although terrestrial plant macrofossils are not preserved at MH3, the sediments there clearly accumulated in the same shallow water body as the closely adjacent MH1.

The radiocarbon ages for pollen assemblage zones a and g at MH1 agree well with the pollen evidence that sediment formation started during the Lateglacial Interstadial temperate climatic phase. During the early part of this pollen record the high Cyperaceae and Poaceae frequencies indicate pioneer sedge–tundra biota with an absence of shrubs and trees. Thus during the first several centuries of the Interstadial, ending with the radiocarbon date of about 12,300 ^{14}C BP at the top of zone MH1-a, there was apparently no development of vegetation beyond low-stature steppe-tundra communities. During the rest of the Interstadial, zones MH1-b to MH1-f, open *Juniperus-Betula* park woodland developed within which the former was usually the more significant, although *Betula* periodically increased. There are zones (MH1-c and MH1-e) during which grass and other herb pollen values show expansion at the expence of the two woody taxa, probably reflecting colder climate events. As phase MH1-c can be dated broadly to 12,000 BP by interpolation between the two radiocarbon dated horizons, this zone probably corresponds with the distinct climatic deterioration that occurred in Britain at *c*. 12,000 ^{14}C BP and which can be correlated with the Greenland GRIP ice core (Björk *et al.*, 1998; Lowe *et al.*, 1999; Mayle *et al.*, 1999; Innes, 2002a).

SUERC-8879	9580 ± 40 ^{14}C BP (11,130–10,720 cal. BP; 9190–8770 cal. BC)

This date provides an age for the highest pollen level at this profile and is in series with the preceding date. Rising birch frequencies suggest the succession towards birch woodland in the early Holocene, although high local sedge percentages suppress the birch rise. The date is therefore acceptable.

SUERC-8880	10,040 ± 45 ^{14}C BP (11,770–11,310 cal. BP; 9820–9360 cal. BC)

This date provides an age for the return of the pollen record after a period during which pollen was not preserved in the profile. The pollen data suggest a time at the transition from the Lateglacial to the Holocene period. This date is similar to several dates for this change regionally and beyond, and so is acceptable.

SUERC-8566	11,310 ± 45 ^{14}C BP (13,280–13,100 cal. BP; 11,330–11,150 cal. BC)

This date provides an age for a switch from birch woodland to much more open tundra-type environments, presumably under severe cold climate. Although slightly early, the date corresponds with such a switch at the start of the Lateglacial (Loch Lomond) Stadial and is therefore acceptable.

SUERC-8567	12,330 ± 45 ^{14}C BP (14,600–14,050 cal. BP; 12,650–12,110 cal. BC)

This date provides an age for a phase near the base of the diagram that the sedge and grass pollen data suggest was a time of very severe cold climate. The age corresponds with such a cold period in the middle of the Lateglacial Interstadial that has been dated elsewhere in northern England to a little before 12,000 BP, and so is acceptable.

Table 3.47 Evaluation of radiocarbon dates from Mill House MH1 (Snape Mires).

This event is well represented in lowland Yorkshire, as at Tadcaster (Bartley, 1962), Seamer Carrs (Jones, 1976a), Dishforth Bog (Giles, 1992) and Gransmoor (Walker *et al.*, 1993). During the rest of the Interstadial the abundance of *Betula* and *Juniperus* in the dryland vegetation record indicates well-developed open woodland, with tree birch copses and juniper scrub, after climatic amelioration from *c.* 12,000 ^{14}C BP onwards. Zones MH1-c and MH1-e record phases of reduced *Betula* percentages and expansion of open herbaceous vegetation, representing reversals in the expansion of birch woodland probably caused by brief interludes of colder climate. Fully closed birch forest seems not to have developed locally until near the end of the Interstadial, in zone MH1-f, and woodland may have been absent altogether from the Mill House area. The absence of *Betula* macrofossils, as well as those of any other taxon except Characeae, in these purely clayey silt limnic sediments confirms that local vegetation was not well developed. The non-organic nature of the limnic sediments and the virtual absence of aquatic pollen at these levels support the macrofossil evidence of a deeper, clear water body with almost no aquatic vegetation and extremely low biological productivity. Although their macrofossils do not occur, high levels of sedge and grass pollen during the interstadial may well reflect local marsh populations in damp open areas around the site. This is supported both by the Molluscan data and by the record of the insect *Bembidion varium*, associated with sparsely vegetated clay surfaces during this phase in the earlier Lateglacial Interstadial, suggesting an incomplete vegetation cover immediately around the water body at this time. The high levels of micro-charcoal suggest that fire may have provided a mechanism whereby such open areas were maintained and the high levels of reworked palynomorphs in the sediments indicates considerable erosion into the pond from nearby bare ground.

The latter part of the Interstadial shows a change in the character of the wetland. The low numbers of Characeae in macrofossil zone MH1m-3, in addition to the presence of *Menyanthes trifoliata* and abundance of *Carex* nutlets, point to a drop in water levels and an encroachment of marginal vegetation. Tree birch macrofossils are frequent, indicating the development of local birch woodland and mean July temperatures of >10°C (Birks, 2003). All of the tree birch remains that could be identified to species were *Betula pubescens*. A few *Betula nana* fruits also occurred towards the top of the zone, suggesting that woodland cover became more open as the Interstadial ended. The pollen record supports this interpretation, with a corresponding increase in the density of local tundra-type communities. An increase in sedges, in particular, but also of a diagnostic open ground and tall herb flora comprising *Artemisia, Thalictrum, Helianthemum, Filipendula* and *Selaginella*, indicates the spread of herbaceous communities tolerant of disturbed soils and more severe climatic conditions. Locally, this tundra and tall herb vegetation may well have been quite rich in comparison with the vegetation around Mill House in the earlier parts of the Interstadial. A switch between *Filipendula* and *Thalictrum* pollen towards the end of this period indicates that colder conditions occurred in its later stages, as the Loch Lomond Stadial approached, a contention confirmed by the radiocarbon dates and also supported by the sharp decline in the presence of tree birch macrofossils and their replacement by remains of cold adapted *Betula nana*. In the British Isles *Betula nana*, a low-growing boreo-arctic montane shrub, presently inhabits upland heaths and blanket bogs in Scotland, with an English population on Widdybank Fell, County Durham (Godwin,

1975; Preston *et al.*, 2002). Pollen and plant macrofossil records show that during the Devensian Late-glacial it was much more widely distributed; it is believed to have been restricted to its present range during the early Holocene as a result of either increasing temperatures or growing competition from closed woodland (Godwin, 1975).

The replacement of tree birch with the dwarf species suggests a period of particularly cold climatic conditions (mean July temperatures <10°C). This is substantiated by the occurrence of macrofossils of a number of open-habitat, cold-adapted herbaceous taxa, including megasporangia of *Selaginella selaginoides*, achenes of *Thalictrum alpinum*, calyx tubes of *Armeria maritima* and a nutlet of *Schoenoplectus tabernaemontani. Selaginella selaginoides*, a moss-like, boreo-montane plant, is characteristic of damp, base-rich sites where there is little competition (Preston *et al.*, 2002). It is also associated with disturbed-ground habitats (Jones *et al.*, 2002) and may reflect instability within the lake catchment as a result of increased periglacial activity. Coarse-grained material and gravel increase in concentration in the core at this level. *Thalictrum alpinum* is also a small herb of damp, base-rich mountain habitats with a markedly northern range (Preston *et al.*, 2002). Both appear to have retreated northwards during the early Holocene in a very similar manner to *Betula nana. Armeria maritima* and *Schoenoplectus tabernaemontani* are currently most frequent at coastal locations, although they also occur in some inland areas (Preston *et al.*, 2002). At Mill House MH1 they may have formed part of halophilous vegetation that is considered characteristic of some periglacial and sub-arctic landscapes (Godwin, 1975). *Carex* sp(p). and *Rumex acetosella* also formed part of the open, herb-dominated flora. Evidence of this period of severe cold at Mill House was not recorded in the insect assemblages, with the possible exception of the grassland indicator *Ceutorhynchus, which* corresponds with a hiatus in the pollen record that the radiocarbon dates show occurred during the very cold climate of the Loch Lomond Stadial. Most insect taxa from MH1 (Table 3.45) are associated with wetland, generally swamp and pond habitats.

The severity of the Stadial climate (cf. Innes, 2002a) probably explains the absence of pollen from the sediments in the upper part of the MH1 sequence, during the extreme cold phase between about 10,500 ^{14}C BP and 10,000 ^{14}C BP, and perhaps also the analogous hiatus in the pollen record in adjacent core MH3. The few plant macrofossils, including tree birch, that occur in these levels at MH1 are perhaps reworked. At Gransmoor, in East Yorkshire, a thinning of *Betula* woodland was recorded during the cold episodes of the Interstadial (Walker *et al.*, 1993) but the absence of plant-macrofossil evidence there makes it unclear whether there was local birch woodland present during the Loch Lomond Stadial. The low numbers of *Betula* pollen grains recorded may have derived from long-distance transport or may be of *Betula nana. Betula* macrofossils from the coastal site of Skipsea Withow Mere, East Yorkshire,

suggest that at least some tree birch was present in northern England during the Loch Lomond Stadial (Hunt *et al.*, 1984) but *Betula* macrofossils disappear from the sediments from Hawes Water in north Lancashire at this time (Jones *et al.*, 2002).

In the uppermost levels of the limnic sediments, before their burial by tufa, the frequencies of *Betula nana* macrofossils decline and those of tree birch rise, suggesting an improvement in temperatures and the start of the spread of open birch woodland. Distinctly aquatic Coleoptera in this sample are scanty and taxa associated with birch woodland are absent, suggesting dominant vegetation composed of low-growing species such as grasses and sedges, possibly interspersed by muddy, ephemeral, probably seasonally dry ponds and pools. This is supported by evidence from the tufa itself, which contains abundant remains of ostracods and gastropods as well as probable *Chara*, signifying the aquatic nature of the local depositional environment. Grass and moss remains associated with the tufa are less environmentally diagnostic.

The radiocarbon date shows that this reflects warming at the onset of the early Holocene. The reduced number of preserved plant remains limits palaeoenvironmental reconstruction but *Typha* sp., *Sphagnum* sp(p)., *Menyanthes trifoliata* and *Carex* spp. macrofossils indicate shallow waterside conditions. This is further supported by the Coleoptera, which are species of low growing, relatively open environments with mosses, sedges and tussocky grasses. *Arctostaphylos uva-ursi* fruitstones occur in the increasingly organic limnic sediment at the start of this warmer phase. This boreo-montane, procumbent shrub is found today on upland heaths and moorlands, predominantly in Scotland (Preston *et al.*, 2002). Its presence at Mill House would have been facilitated by the occurrence of areas of open, bare ground and the continuation of cooler summer temperatures (Godwin, 1975) as the Holocene began. The limited pollen data from these levels at MH1 agree with this ecological interpretation. The pollen from MH3 extends the record into the earlier Holocene, as burial by tufa took place later there. The establishment of *Corylus*-dominated woodland and the immigration of other deciduous trees like *Ulmus* suggest at least an additional millennium of deposition at MH3, perhaps indicating a slow expansion rate of tufa deposition at Mill House. The significant *Pinus* pollen representation in the early Holocene at MH3 may well be linked to the considerable micro-charcoal evidence for burning in the locality.

3.8.4 The Gallop

The centre of the Snape Mires basin, the lowest lying part of the depression (Fig. 3.18), appears to have been the most severely affected by land drainage, as the surface peat here is very thin and oxidized, as shown in cores taken at the Gallop (TG). A modern drainage stream at the Gallop has exposed a sequence of surficial deposits (at SE 2855 8445); a profile for analysis, TG2, was recovered in monolith tins from this stream section (TG1 was a shallow core in the field to the west of TG2: Fig. 3.18).

3.8.4.1. Lithostratigraphy

The two profiles recorded, TG1 and TG2, contained very similar sequences of deposits in which a thin surface organic layer overlies thin shell marl and then thick laminated blue-grey clayey silt, which is the ubiquitous glacio-lacustrine clay that underlies the entire Snape basin (Table 3.48). Away from the drainage ditch, in the drained fields, the surface organic layer is very dry and oxidized. In the ditch section, however, the sediments have been sealed and protected by weathered loamy topsoil, perhaps mixed with spoil from the digging of the ditch, and the sedimentary succession is wetter and much better preserved. The organic layer can be seen to be a limnic mud peat containing many gastropod shells, as does the underlying thin marl.

3.8.4.2 Pollen

Sub-samples were prepared for analysis from the organic section of the TG2 profile at intervals of one centimetre. Pollen preservation was poor but counts could be made from all prepared levels. Three local pollen assemblage zones are recognized (Fig. 3.25): TG2-a to TG2-c.

ZONE DESCRIPTIONS

Zone TG2-a (94–89.5 cm)
> Dominated by high *Betula* percentages at about 70% of total pollen, this zone also has substantial *Pinus* frequencies and consistent but low percentages of *Juniperus*. *Pediastrum* and *Typha latifolia* are significant and there are moderate Poaceae values. All other taxa are very poorly represented.

Zone TG2-b (89.5–78.5 cm)
> In this zone *Juniperus* and *Pediastrum* cease to form consistent curves although *Betula* continues to dominate the assemblage. Poaceae frequencies remain significant at about 20% of total pollen, while all other taxa are very low indeed.

Zone TG2-c (78.5–70 cm)
> *Betula* frequencies fall sharply in this zone to only 20% of total pollen and are replaced by Poaceae and then Cyperaceae, which rise to high percentages. *Pinus* increases and a low *Corylus* curve begins and then increases sharply at the end of the zone. Pollen of the deciduous woodland trees *Ulmus, Quercus* and *Alnus* are recorded sporadically. *Typha latifolia* percentages rise and micro-charcoal frequencies increase to over 20%.

Unit	Depth (cm)	Description
4	0–70	Loamy disturbed topsoil *Stratum confusum*
3	70–83	Black silty amorphous peat with some shells Sh4, Ag+, part. test. (moll.)+, nig.4, strf.0, elas.0, sicc.3, lim.sup.0
2	83–110	Brown very shelly, silty marl Lc2, Ag2, part. test. (moll.) +++, test. (moll.)+, nig.1+, strf.0, elas.0, sicc.2, lim.sup.0
1	110–130	Laminated blue-grey clayey silt Ag3, As1, nig.2+, strf.2, elas.0, sicc.2, lim.sup.2

Table 3.48 Stratigraphy at the Gallop, Section TG2 (Snape Mires). The particle-size distribution of Unit 2 (shelly silty marl) was confirmed using a Coulter Particle-size Analyser (see Chapter 2.1.3.1; Appendix IV).

3.8.4.3 Plant macrofossils

The plant remains recorded from the stream section at the Gallop (Fig. 3.26) have been divided into two plant macrofossil assemblage zones (TG2m-1 & 2). A low number and diversity of macrofossils was recorded from most of the samples. Analysis was carried out between 110 and 90 cm.

ZONE DESCRIPTIONS

Zone TG2m-1 (110–93 cm)
> The plant macrofossil assemblage between 110 cm and 93 cm is relatively uniform and the samples fall into a single zone. The remains are dominated by the aquatic plants Characeae (stoneworts) and *Potamogeton* subgenus *Coleogeton* (pondweeds). Low numbers of Pteridophytes (ferns), *Urtica dioica* and Poaceae were also recorded, with fruit and cone scales of *Betula pubescens* also present in the upper half of the zone. A few nutlets of *Cladium mariscus* and *Carex* sp(p). appear in the final part of the zone between 94 and 93 cm.

Zone TG2m-2 (93–90 cm)
> Total number of remains increases sharply in this zone and are dominated by nutlets of *Cladium mariscus* and *Carex* sp(p). Pteridophyte sporangia increase in number while aquatic remains are very few. *Juncus effusus* type (rushes) and Musci sp. are present.

3.8.4.4 Molluscs

An aquatic molluscan fauna is present in the shell marl at the Gallop, persisting into the base of the overlying

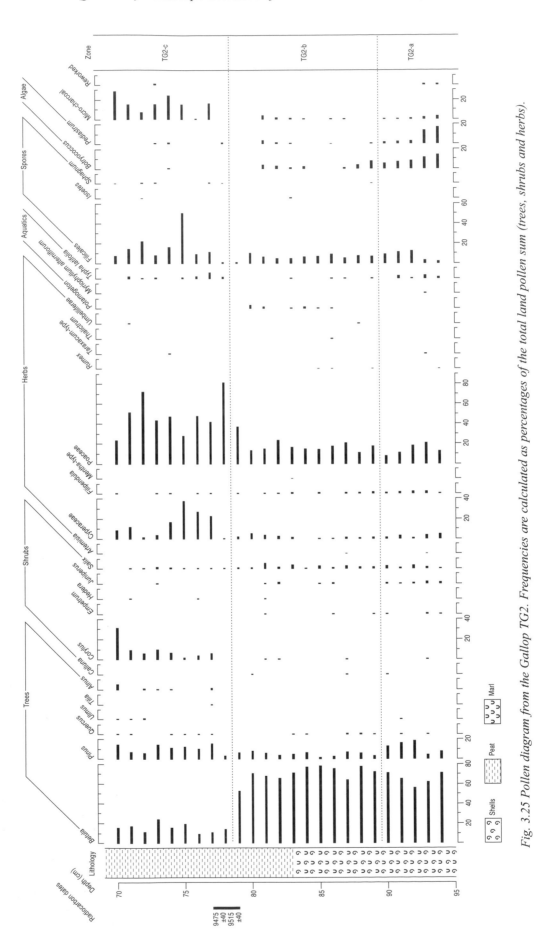

Fig. 3.25 Pollen diagram from the Gallop TG2. Frequencies are calculated as percentages of the total land pollen sum (trees, shrubs and herbs).

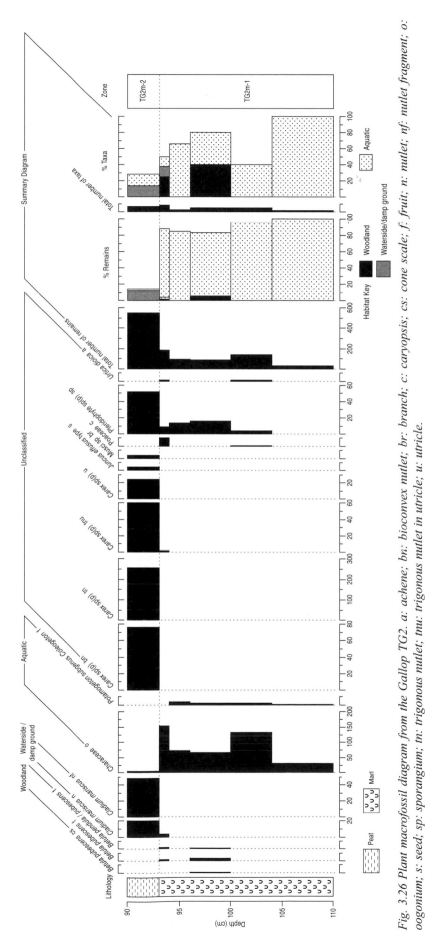

Fig. 3.26 Plant macrofossil diagram from the Gallop TG2. a: achene; bn: bioconvex nutlet; br: branch; c: caryopsis; cs: cone scale; f: fruit; n: nutlet; nf: nutlet fragment; o: oogonium; s: seed; sp: sporangium; tn: trigonous nutlet; tmu: trigonous nutlet in utricle; u: utricle.

peat, this upper sample proving somewhat richer in terms of species diversity (Table 3.49). As at IL6 and IL12, the assemblage is characterized by *Lymnaea peregra*, *Gyraulus crista* and *Gyraulus leavis*, these being the only taxa identified to species level within the shell marl. In the overlying basal peat they are supplemented by *Valvata piscinalis*, *Planorbis planorbis* and *Pisidium nitidum* as well as numerous undetermined planorbids.

3.8.4.5 Insects

Insect remains were sparse, comprising individual taxa from three of the marl samples (Table 3.50), all indicative of open water environments. *Gyrinius* spp. suggests quite deep water, while the presence of aquatic vegetation within the water body is indicated by *Plateumaris/Donacia* spp.

3.8.4.6 Chronology

The two radiocarbon dates from the Gallop come from the same level, 77 cm, and are so similar as to be statistically indistinguishable (Table 3.51). The dates, at *c.* 9500 ^{14}C BP, provide an age for the transition from *Betula* forest to a more mixed woodland, with increasing *Pinus*, with the rise in *Corylus* pollen beginning immediately after the dated level. The *Corylus* rise is dated at several sites elsewhere in northern England to about 9300–9200 ^{14}C BP, although some variation occurs depending on soils and other factors (Innes, 2002d). The date from the Gallop is therefore slightly early but well within the range of variation for the region. It is possible that local factors, such as the calcareous soils and the presence of fire in the area (shown by the micro-charcoal curve), encouraged an early *Corylus* rise. The dates are therefore acceptable and are supported by the pollen stratigraphy.

3.8.4.7 Synthesis: the Gallop

The sequence at the Gallop represents an early Holocene succession in which early *Betula*-dominated forest was replaced by more diverse mixed woodland, firstly by *Corylus* but also with sporadic indications of low populations of deciduous forest trees, particularly *Quercus*, *Ulmus* and *Alnus*. The radiocarbon dates from just before the start of a substantial *Corylus* curve average about 9500 ^{14}C BP, which is compatible for this feature in many regional pollen diagrams (Innes, 2002d), prior to its rise to regional high values at around 9200 ^{14}C BP. That a great increase in micro-charcoal frequencies closely matches the *Corylus* increase in the upper profile might not be coincidental, as will be discussed in Chapter 5.

The macrofossil record begins a little earlier than the pollen, with dominance of aquatic plant remains in TG2m-1, in combination with the sediment type (marl), pointing to the earliest deposition occurring under open water conditions. Characeae and *Potamogeton* subgenus

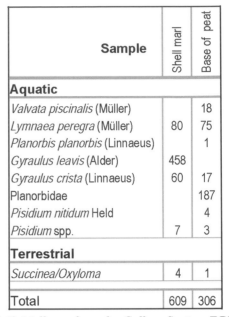

Sample	Shell marl	Base of peat
Aquatic		
Valvata piscinalis (Müller)		18
Lymnaea peregra (Müller)	80	75
Planorbis planorbis (Linnaeus)		1
Gyraulus leavis (Alder)	458	
Gyraulus crista (Linnaeus)	60	17
Planorbidae		187
Pisidium nitidum Held		4
Pisidium spp.	7	3
Terrestrial		
Succinea/Oxyloma	4	1
Total	609	306

Table 3.49 Molluscs from the Gallop, Section TG2 (Snape Mires).

Coleogeton indicate a relatively shallow, still, calcareous water body (cf. Moore, 1986; Preston, 1995). *Betula pubescens* was growing locally at least towards the second half of this earliest macrofossil zone, and may have grown around the damp margins of the water body. Pteridophytes would have favoured damp wooded areas and Poaceae (which may represent semi-aquatic taxa) were also present. The appearance of sedges at the end of the zone marks a transition from the open water body to a tall-herb fen, which is represented in TG2m-2. *Cladium mariscus* and *Carex* sp(p). dominate this environment, with Pteridophytes, Musci sp. and *Juncus effusus* type also important components. The establishment of the fen is marked by a change in the stratigraphy from marl to peat. The plant macrofossils thus indicate that birch woodland grew locally at the Gallop and that there was a change in the aquatic environment from a shallow calcareous pool to a tall-herb fen.

The marl also yielded data from molluscs and insects. Insect diversity was very low; all recorded taxa are indicative of open water environments, with *Gyrinius* spp. suggesting quite deep water, while the presence of aquatic vegetation within the water body is indicated by *Plateumaris/Donacia* spp. The molluscs presumably lived in the shallow calcareous pool identified from the plant macrofossils, an interpretation fully in keeping with the limited fauna in both samples, stongly dominated by planorbids.

An earliest Holocene date for the base of the pollen profile is shown by the presence, in low but continuous frequencies, of shrubs and tall herbs indicative of the successional vegetation communities of the Lateglacial to Holocene transition, such as *Juniperus, Salix* and

Preservation	Good	Good	Good	Good
Viable sclerites	No	Yes	Yes	Yes
Comments		Fragmentary		
Sample depth (cm)	90–93	93–94	94–96	100–104
Gyrinidae				
Gyrinius spp.			*	
Staphylinidae				
Aleocharinae gen. & spp. Indet.				*
Chrysomelidae				
Plateumaris/Donacia spp.		*		

Table 3.50 Insects from the Gallop, Section TG2 (Snape Mires).

SUERC-8887   9515 ± 40 ^{14}C BP (11,080–10,670 cal. BP; 9130–8720 cal. BC)
This date provides an age for the start of the pollen curve for *Corylus* after birch frequencies have fallen from dominance. The date in the mid first millennium of the Holocene is similar to several dates for this feature in northern England and so is acceptable.
SUERC-8888   9475 ± 40 ^{14}C BP (11,140–10,710 cal. BP; 9190–8760 cal. BC)
This date is from the same level as date SUERC-8887 and is indistinguishable from it. It is therefore also acceptable for the start of the *Corylus* rise in this profile.

Table 3.51 Evaluation of radiocarbon dates from the Gallop, Section TG2 (Snape Mires).

Filipendula. These faded from the record as full dense *Betula* forest cover became established. A date of about 9800 ^{14}C BP for the base of the diagram can therefore be inferred. The gradual reduction in the pollen of aquatic taxa and algal spores through the lower half of the profile and the increase in Cyperaceae and Poaceae thereafter trace the shallowing of the water body by infilling with organic sediment.

3.8.5 Palaeoenvironmental Summary: Snape Mires

The sedimentary records from various parts of Snape Mires suggest shallow and perhaps isolated areas of deposition in the millennia following the drainage of the glacial lake that formerly occupied the basin and in which were deposited the grey laminated clays that underlie the whole site. Now severely truncated, the thin sediments that remain record Lateglacial and early Holocene lacustrine sedimentation, presumably in shallow pools that remained in lower areas following the emptying of the deeper glacial lake. The shell marls found beneath and within the various organic layers suggest that these pools often contained clear, calcareous water, although perhaps the highly calcareous phase was restricted to the first two millennia of the Holocene (see Chapter 2.8.2). In addition to a large central shallow post-glacial depression at Snape, a more complex surface topography in the northern part of the site has allowed the formation of small sedimentary basins where later deposits have survived, probably because of the wetter nature of the land there due to water draining off the northern hillslope. Thus the isolated depressions at IL6 and IL12 are explained, although the deepest basin studied was on the western edge of the Snape depression, at Mill House (although IL 12 was not bottomed).

Rich molluscan faunas recovered from the Snape profiles have added significantly to the known distribution of rare species and helped to explain the environments of deposition existing in different parts of the site, as have the insect and macrofossil records. This wetter character of the land is exemplified by the existence in early modern times of a large mere in the north-eastern corner of the Snape depression (see above). It appears to have filled the channel by which the original glacial lake waters probably drained.

The Mill House tufa is an important addition to the small number of such deposits that have been investigated in detail by palaeoecological techniques in northern England (Taylor *et al.*, 1994a). The formation of this tufa may well have been restricted to the early part of the Holocene, when leaching of calcareous material from glacial deposits occurred. The deposit might merit further attention, perhaps using geochemical analytical techniques such as stable isotope analysis. It may also be possible to date the deposit, as has been achieved elsewhere in North Yorkshire (Black *et al.*, 1988).

The five pollen diagrams from the four palaeoenvironmental sampling sites at Snape Mires provide a composite record of vegetation history spanning the interval from the early part of the Lateglacial Interstadial to beyond the mid-Holocene rise of *Alnus* pollen frequencies (Table 3.52), i.e. approximately between 12,500 and 7000 ^{14}C BP. Mid- to late Holocene sediments have not been found at Snape Mires. While it is possible that an exhaustive survey might yet reveal such deposits, it is likely that any such sediments that existed have been removed by recent activities such as land drainage for modern agriculture. The very thin nature of the surface organic layer across most of the centre of the basin, as exemplified at the Gallop, suggests that it is a remnant of rather deeper organic deposits that existed in the past.

Overlap between some of these pollen profiles, covering a period of about 2000 years from the end of the Lateglacial and into the early Holocene, enables three-dimensional spatial correlation of vegetation patterns across about a kilometre of the Snape basin. The development of *Betula* forest at the start of the Holocene is recorded at all four sites, although only its initial stages are preserved at Snape Mill, in profile MH1 (this phase is entirely absent in MH3). The data indicate a generally homogeneous Early Holocene birch forest surrounding the Snape wetland, with little differentiation in terrestrial ecosystems, as birch pollen frequencies are consistently around 70%, except where very high frequencies of local wetland vegetation types dilute the woodland pollen signal. More diversity is associated with the rise of hazel pollen at around 9400 ^{14}C BP (although there is a later date for this change at Ings Plantation (IL12), where it was delayed until about 9200 ^{14}C BP). Four profiles record the *Corylus* rise: IL6, IL12, TG2 and MH3. It is notable that the *Corylus* pollen curves in the diagrams from TG2 and IL6 start abruptly at levels rich in micro-charcoal particles; MH3 is similar but less clear. In contrast, at IL12, where micro-charcoal particles are uncommon, the *Corylus* pollen curve rises gradually. It is tempting to interpret these data in terms of the immigration of hazel into the dense birch forest around the Snape wetland being assisted by fire, whereas this was slow to occur in that part of the site (IL12) where fire was absent or very slight. That the *Corylus* rise was assisted by burning has long been suspected (Simmons & Innes, 1987) and the three-dimensional data from Snape tend to agree with this hypothesis. Whether the fires were initiated by Mesolithic hunters or natural causes can only be a matter for speculation. It might be worth noting that there are early Mesolithic archaeological records from the Washlands area, as at Topcliffe near Ripon (Cowling & Stickland, 1947), while the hills to the west contain several early Mesolithic flint sites of this age (Laurie, 2003).

Only profile IL12 continues the pollen record into the mid-Holocene, beyond the rise of *Alnus* pollen. This record is notable, however, for its low *Quercus* and continuing high *Pinus* percentages, which is unusual in comparison with the regional forest history; it might well be a function of soil conditions around Snape, with a preponderance of calcareous strata being unsuitable for oak. It is a reminder that vegetation communities would have been very sensitive to soils and other environmental factors, as they still are today (Laurie, 2004), a point worthy of close consideration when reconstructing prehistoric landscapes.

3.9 Other sites

As part of the overall reconnaissance of the Washlands, a number of sites in the Swale were investigated to establish the timing of floodloam deposition above peat, a change that is seen in Holocene lowland valley sequences throughout Britain and more widely (see Chapter 1.6.3). Of the various sites inspected two were selected for analysis, the aim being to date the onset of such deposition (alluviation) and explore its possible link with early farming and/or with changes in climate. The sites are both within the Swale catchment, at Langlands Farm and Thornton's Plantation. Cores were taken for pollen analysis and radiocarbon dating only; no further palaeoenvironmental analyses were completed at these locations.

3.9.1 Langland's Farm, Morton-on-Swale

A coring transect undertaken on land known as The Bottoms (SE 3325 9100), at Langland's Farm (LF), near Morton-on-Swale, led to the discovery of a small area of *limus* and peat channelled into the top of a predominantly silty sand deposit (Fig. 3.27).

3.9.1.1 Lithostratigraphy

Seven cores were taken at Langland's Farm, on an east–west transect (Fig 3.27). Although the stratigraphical units showed considerable internal homogeneity, their distribution along the transect was more variable. The channel feature is entrenched within a basal grey clayey silt with sand partings, which is stiff in its lower parts but contains some rare detrital plant material in its upper layers, indicating a degree of weathering and reworking. The presence of detrital plant remains demonstrates the fluvial origin of this lowest recorded stratigraphical unit, which could not be penetrated with the hand-coring equipment used. The lowest channel deposit, a silty sand with occasional plant remains, occupies the eastern part of the channel and is draped over the basal clayey silt. Above this silty sand, organic sedimentation is represented first by a limnic deposit, which is confined to the channel, and then by a silty peat that fills the channel and extends beyond it to the west. The site is capped by a sticky surface clayey silt, presumably of alluvial origin. The detailed stratigraphy at the core chosen for analysis, LF1, is shown in Table 3.53.

Age ¹⁴C BP	Stage	Ings Lane	Ings Plantation	Mill House		The Gallop
		IL6	IL12	MH1	MH3	TG2
7000	Mid Holocene		*Alnus* • • • • • • •			
7500						
8000						
8500	Early		*Corylus*	TUFA	TUFA	
9000	Holocene	*Corylus* • • • • • •	• • • • • • • ☢		*Corylus*	*Corylus* • • • • • •
9500		*Betula*		*Betula*	MARL	☢
10,000			*Betula* ☢	☢		*Betula*
10,500	Loch Lomond Stadial			NO POLLEN	Cyperaceae	
11,000				Cyperaceae • • • • • • •		
11,500	Lateglacial (Windermere) Interstadial		☢ >	*Betula Juniperus* • • • • • • •	NOT STUDIED	
12,000				Cyperaceae		
12,500	Cold Phase		☢ >	Poaceae		

Table 3.52 Correlation of pollen data from Snape Mires. Stratigraphical positions of key radiocarbon dates are indicated by the atomic symbol.

3.9.1.2 Pollen

Samples were prepared for pollen analysis at five centimetre intervals through the organic part of core LF1, closing to two centimetres near the upper contact with the surficial clayey silt. Pollen preservation was variable but generally good in the upper peat, although a few levels in the lower part of this deposit lacked pollen. The pollen diagram (Fig. 3.28) is subdivided into seven local pollen assemblage zones (LF-a – LF-g).

ZONE DESCRIPTION
Zone LF-a (120–102.5 cm)
Cyperaceae percentages account for 60% of total pollen in this zone, while most of the rest of the assemblage is contributed by Poaceae; *Betula* is present in low frequencies. Pollen diversity is very low. There are high levels of aquatic pollen, initially *Myriophyllum alterniflorum* and *M. spicatum*, but then *Typha angustifolia*. *Equisetum* percentages are high, as is *Pediastrum* at first, although declining sharply. Some reworked pre-Quaternary spores occur.

Zone LF-b (102.5–87.5 cm)
Betula and *Corylus* percentages increase through this zone, whereas *Salix* is important at its base. Cyperaceae and Poaceae values fall through the zone and aquatic pollen frequencies are very low throughout.

Zone LF-c (87.5–82.5 cm)
Betula dominates the assemblage at over 80% of total pollen; percentages for all other taxa are very low in this zone.

Zone LF-d (82.5–77.5 cm)
Betula declines to very low values while *Pinus* and *Corylus* are the main tree and shrub types of this zone. *Quercus* and *Ulmus* are recorded significantly for the first time, while Poaceae values show a peak.

Zone LF-e (77.5–70.5 cm)
Tree and shrub pollen taxa dominate the assemblage in this zone. *Alnus*, *Pinus* and *Corylus* all contribute about 30% of total pollen and *Ulmus* occurs in

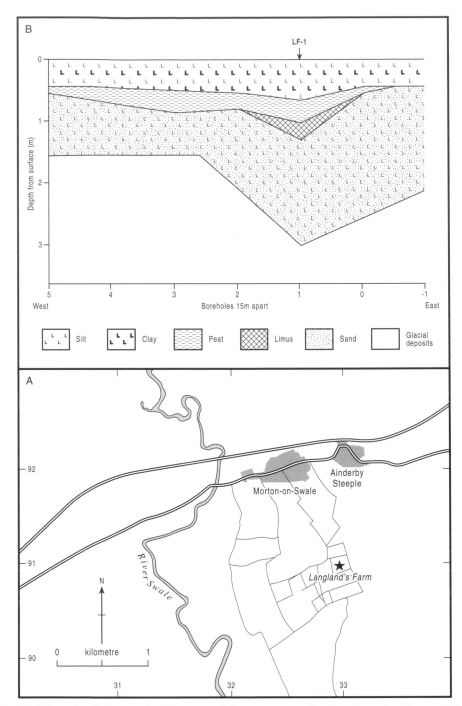

Fig. 3.27 Langland's Farm: A – Location of the coring site; B – Stratigraphy of core LF1.

substantial values, whereas *Betula* is very low. Herbaceous pollen types are hardly represented.

Zone LF-f (70.5–68.0 cm)

Alnus is the main contributor in this zone, which comprises a single counted level, at over 40% of total pollen. *Corylus* and *Pinus* fall markedly, the latter to very low values. *Tilia*, *Quercus* and *Ulmus* are all present in substantial frequencies but *Betula* and *Pinus* are very low.

Zone LF-g (68.0–57.0 cm)

In this final zone *Ulmus* declines to low frequencies. Other tree and shrub types remain unchanged initially, then *Corylus* increases as *Quercus* and *Tilia* decline. *Alnus* dominates the assemblage. Poaceae percentages increase steadily and herb taxa, including *Plantago lanceolata* and *Taraxacum*-type, appear. *Pteridium* also occurs. Cyperaceae replaces Poaceae late in the zone, where a single large Poaceae pollen grain of > 40 μm that could be of cereal type was also recorded.

Unit	Depth (cm)	Description
6	0–64	Sticky clay topsoil *Stratum confusum*
5	64–100	Silty well humified peat with rootlets Sh3, Ag1, Th2+, Dl+, nig.3, strf.0, elas.0, sicc.2, lim.sup.0
4	100–124	Silty brown *limus* with detrital herbaceous material Ld³3, Ag1, Dh++, nig.2+, strf.0, elas.0, sicc.2, lim.sup.0
3	124–131	Soft grey sandy silt with some clay and detrital material Ag2, Ga2, As+, Dh+, nig.2, strf.0, elas.0, sicc.2, lim.sup.0
2	131–138	Grey silty sand with detrital organic material Ga3, Ag1, Dh++, nig.2, strf.0, elas.0, sicc.2, lim.sup.0
1	138–310	Grey clayey silt with occasional sandy partings and rare detrital organic material. Denser towards the base. Ag2, As1, Ga1, Dh+, nig.2, strf.1, elas.0, sicc.2, lim.sup.0

Table 3.53 Stratigraphy at Langland's Farm, Core LF1.

3.9.1.3 Chronology

The single date from this site (Table 3.54) accomplished its objective of providing an age for the change from terrestrial peat accumulation to riverine alluvial sedimentation. The dating sample (5520 ± 50 BP) was located below a significant decrease in *Ulmus* pollen, taken to be the well-known elm decline that occurred in the centuries before 5,000 BP, and so agrees well with that biostratigraphical marker. It also generally confirms the mid-Holocene age of the upper part of the profile and is in agreement with the successive rises in tree pollen taxa recorded in the lower part of the sequence. Organic sedimentation appears to have begun in the earliest Holocene and continued until arrested by alluvial deposition after *c.* 5000 ¹⁴C BP.

3.9.1.4 Synthesis: Langland's Farm

It appears that organic sedimentation began at Langland's Farm in the very early Holocene, as the pollen data are dominated by local wetland marsh taxa, primarily grasses and sedges. The very low tree pollen count may even point to the end of the Lateglacial, given the high *Myriophyllum alterniflorum* counts, often a feature of the aquatic plant succession at the Lateglacial to Holocene transition. It is unfortunate that a radiocarbon date is not available to constrain the base of the organic sequence, but appropriate macrofossil remains were not available. Also unfortunate is the lack of good pollen preservation in the lower levels of the organic sequence, as data from this part of the profile would have provided biostratigraphically diagnostic pollen assemblages that would have constrained the age by

comparison with other pollen diagrams from Yorkshire. Nevertheless, the sequential rise of *Corylus*, *Pinus* and *Alnus* in mid-profile suggests that the sequence contains most if not all of the early and mid-Holocene vegetation history. The limnic sediments and high levels of pollen of floating aquatic plants in the lower part of the organic profile show that the depression contained a small lake at that time.

The land around the early Holocene water body was heavily wooded, with *Betula* and *Corylus* the dominant constituents for a long period, until first *Pinus* then *Alnus* and *Ulmus* became important. Unusually, evidence for *Quercus* expansion is muted and it did not really occur until the time of the *Ulmus* decline, when *Tilia* also increased. Pine and hazel seem to have remained important in this area, delaying the expansion of some of the deciduous taxa. Support for the interpretation that the fall of *Ulmus* pollen frequencies at the zonal boundary LF-f to LF-g is the main mid-Holocene elm decline is provided by the radiocarbon date and the absence of any indications of woodland opening and agriculture until after that point. Even then clearance indicators like *Plantago lanceolata* and other ruderal weeds are sparse, with a single very large grass grain that could represent cereal pollen from the top of the upper silty peat hinting at arable cultivation near this wet valley bottom location. There are no indications of significant environmental change accompanying the switch to alluvial clastic material deposition.

3.9.2 Thornton's Plantation, Pickhill

This site lies to the east of the village of Pickhill, in a linear depression not far from the present course of the river Swale (SE 3555 8320; Fig. 3.29). An extensive area of shallow peat sediments was found within a generally clayey silt deposit in the depression.

3.9.2.1 Lithostratigraphy

Seven cores were taken at Thornton's Plantation on an east to west transect (Fig. 3.29). The lithological units showed general internal homogeneity, with little variability along the transect. A shallow channel feature is present, cut into laminated grey clayey silt with sand partings, which in places is organic and contains some rare detrital plant material. As at Langland's Farm, this might suggest some degree of weathering and reworking. This lower clayey silt becomes much softer in its upper layers and grades within the channel feature into a well-humified, crumbly silty peat that contains some fragments of charred wood. This peat is confined within the channel feature. Resting upon this organic unit is an amorphous peat with a high silt fraction and herbaceous rootlets that extends beyond the channel to the west. This lower sediment sequence is sealed by a surficial sandy silt, presumably of alluvial origin. The detailed stratigraphy at the core chosen for analysis, TP2, is shown in Table 3.55.

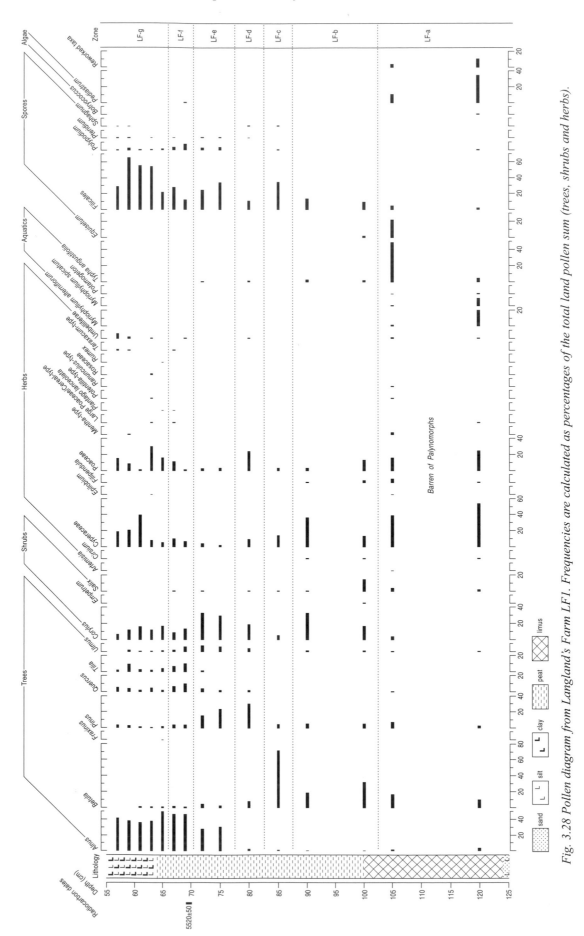

Fig. 3.28 Pollen diagram from Langland's Farm LF1. Frequencies are calculated as percentages of the total land pollen sum (trees, shrubs and herbs).

GrA-24660	5520 ± 50 ^{14}C BP (6410–6210 cal. BP; 4460–4260 cal. BC)

The sample for dating was taken at a point in the profile where elm pollen frequencies were high but about to decline sharply to very low values. The date shows this elm pollen reduction to equate with the main mid-Holocene *Ulmus* decline, supported by the start of a *Plantago lanceolata* curve and then other agricultural indicators. The date confirms that peat formation ended and riverine alluvial sedimentation began around 5000 [14]C.

Table 3.54 Evaluation of radiocarbon dates from Langland's Farm, Core LF1.

3.9.2.2 Pollen

Samples were prepared for pollen analysis at five centimetre intervals through the organic part of the core, closing to two centimetres within the surficial silt. Pollen preservation was variable but generally good in the upper peat. A few levels in the lower part of the peat did not preserve pollen and are not considered in the pollen zones. The pollen diagram (Fig. 3.30) is subdivided into five local pollen assemblage zones (TP-a – TP-e).

ZONE DESCRIPTION

Zone TP-a (110 cm)

The assemblage from the basal counted level is mixed, with several taxa contributing moderate counts. *Betula*, *Corylus* and *Alnus* are the main woody taxa with Cyperaceae and Poaceae constituting most of the rest of the assemblage, although *Equisetum* and *Pediastrum* are also prominent and sporadic specimens of various herbaceous types occur, including a large grass pollen grain. Reworked pre-Quaternary spores are common.

Zone TP-b (90–77.5 cm)

Pollen is preserved again at and above 90 cm and in this zone *Betula* rises to almost 40% of total pollen. Several other tree and shrub types occur, generally at low values; *Corylus*, *Salix* and *Alnus* are the most prominent. Cyperaceae and Poaceae are the main herbaceous pollen taxa, although several other types are recorded at low frequencies. *Equisetum* declines through the zone and *Pediastrum* occurs only occasionally. Aquatic pollen types are well represented but only *Typha angustifolia* shows high values.

Zone TP-c (77.5–72.5 cm)

The main change in this zone is that Cyperaceae and *Typha angustifolia* fall sharply and Poaceae frequencies increase. Most other taxa are unchanged from the previous zone.

Zone TP-d (72.5–57.5 cm)

Tree and shrub frequencies rise at the expense of herbaceous pollen types in this zone. *Betula* and then *Corylus* percentages are high, at about 40%

Unit	Depth (cm)	Description
6	0–74	Brown-grey mottled sandy silt Ga2, Ag2, Lf+, nig.2, strf.0, elas.0, sicc.2
5	74–81	Light brown amorphous silty peat with herbaceous rootlets Sh2, Ag2, Th2+, nig.3, strf.0, elas.0, sicc.2, lim.sup.0
4	81–110	Dark brown well humified crumbly peat with charred wood. Occasional silt inclusions near the base Sh4, Ag+, Dl+, nig.3+, strf.0, elas.0, sicc.2, lim.sup.0
3	110–169	Soft grey clayey silt Ag3, As1, nig.2, strf.0, elas.0, sicc.2, lim.sup.0
2	169–174	Highly organic soft clayey silt with detrital woody material Ag2, As1, Dh1, Sh+, Th2+, nig.2+, strf.0, elas.0, sicc.2, lim.sup.1
1	174–234	Laminated grey clayey silt with sand partings and occasional detrital organic material. Stiff at the base Ag3, As1, Dh+, nig.2, strf.1, elas.0, sicc.2, lim.sup.0

Table 3.55 Stratigraphy at Thornton's Plantation, Core TP1.

of total pollen. *Quercus* and *Alnus* percentages increase throughout, with *Ulmus* more prominent late in the zone. There are sporadic occurrences of *Plantago lanceolata* and other open-ground weeds.

Zone TP-e (57.5–52 cm)

Although tree and shrub percentages are still generally high, this zone sees diminution in some tree curves like *Quercus* and *Ulmus*. Herbaceous frequencies increase, particularly Cyperaceae and Poaceae, but this is also true for lesser curves like *Plantago lanceolata*, cereal/wild grass-type and *Taraxacum*-type.

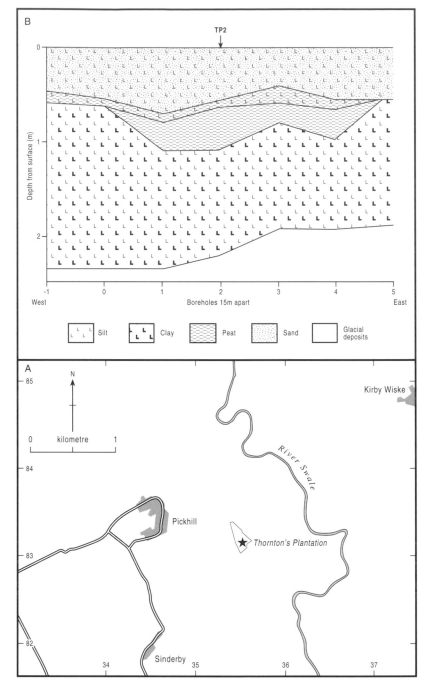

Fig. 3.29 Thornton's Plantation: A – Location of the coring site; B – Stratigraphy of core TP2.

GrA-24656	9060 ± 60 ¹⁴C BP (10,290–10,170 cal. BP; 8240–8220 cal. BC)
This date provides an age for the change from purely peat deposition to organic sedimentation with a high alluvial silt fraction. The age agrees with the pollen data as at this level high *Corylus* frequencies replace *Betula* as the main pollen type, a feature dated elsewhere in northern England to around 9000 ¹⁴C BP. Significant deciduous tree pollen frequencies below this level, however, seem anomalous and some disturbance of the peat profile seems possible. This date for the start of the transition to alluvial deposition seems early.	
GrA-25290	8850 ± 50 ¹⁴C BP (10,180–9690 cal. BP; 8230–7740 cal. BC)
This date from the same level as date GrA-24656 provides confirmation of the early Holocene age of the upper part of the organic unit at this site. Although the two dates are not identical, this later age is still within the range limits of the pollen changes observed at this level.	

Table 3.56 Evaluation of radiocarbon dates from Thornton's Plantation, Core TP1.

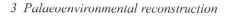

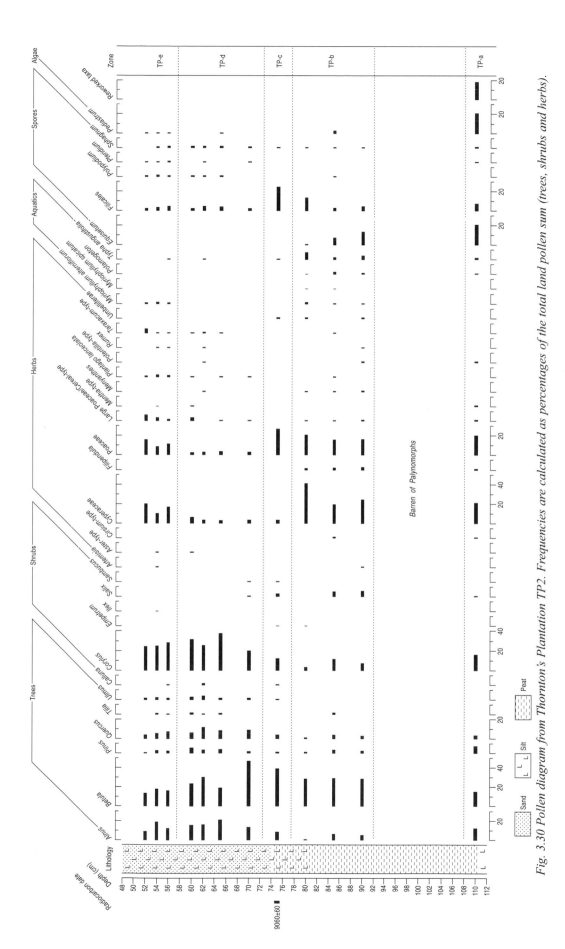

Fig. 3.30 Pollen diagram from Thornton's Plantation TP2. Frequencies are calculated as percentages of the total land pollen sum (trees, shrubs and herbs).

3.9.2.3 Chronology

The dates (Table 3.56) provide an age within the early stages of alluviation at this site. The two dates from the same level are sufficiently similar to be accepted as a reliable estimate of the start of riverine silt deposition within the peat unit some time between 9060 ± 60 ^{14}C BP and 8850 ± 50 ^{14}C BP. They are broadly supported by the pollen data, although some anomalies exist; for instance, this is very early for the appearance of *Alnus* and *Corylus*. This early Holocene age for the start of alluviation is older than expected. The poorly developed fall in *Ulmus* at the zone d–e boundary, possibly the well-known elm decline at around 5000 BP, provides a tentative indication of relative age; this is well above the radiocarbon dated level and conformable with it chronologically.

3.9.2.4 Synthesis: Thornton's Plantation

The aquatic pollen data suggest deposition in a small water body at the time organic sediment began to accumulate, with water depth decreasing up through the profile and taxa like *T. angustifolia* and *Equisetum* replacing *Pediastrum*. The upper part of this sequence provides a mid-Holocene record of vegetation change, with a general fall in *Betula* corresponding with a rise in *Corylus* and then in *Quercus* and *Alnus*. The signal is blurred, however, with substantial frequencies for all of these taxa present before their rise to higher values. Moderate frequencies for *Corylus* and *Alnus*, for example, are present from the start of the diagram. The vegetation successions in the lower part of the core do not follow the usual early Holocene sequence, suggesting that some mixing of the sediment may have occurred to produce somewhat homogenized results.

Evidence from the upper profile is clearer, with a possible *Ulmus* decline at the zone d–e boundary, supported by increases in *P. lanceolata* and other possible disturbance type pollen. The large grass pollen grains from this core are mostly borderline, in terms of morphology, between large grains of wild grass and those of cereal-type. The occurrence of sporadic large grass pollen from the start of the record suggests that wild grasses are the source. However, the occurrence of increased numbers of such grains above the possible *Ulmus* decline, with some of clear cereal-type, suggests that those at the top of the diagram may well indicate agricultural activity, which would support the identification of the fall in *Ulmus* as the true elm decline. If this is so, then the d–e zone boundary would have a date of *c.* 5000 ^{14}C BP, based on other *Ulmus*-decline ages from the region. A further repercussion would be that the switch to alluvial deposition, signified by the increasing silt proportion in the peat, occurred before the *Ulmus* decline at this site.

4 The Archaeology of the Washlands – A review

4.1 Introduction

This chapter reviews the archaeological resource of the Swale–Ure Washlands and adjoining areas. Published accounts are referred to where possible but, since the archaeology of this area has seldom been the focus of investigation, reference has perforce to rely on 'grey literature' to be found with other distributional information in the Historic Environment Record (HER) of North Yorkshire County Council. The paucity of publications on Washlands archaeology means that there is little detailed chronological information on traditionally observed archaeological periods from the Mesolithic through to the end of the pre-Roman Iron Age. Rather than use the scheme adopted recently for Yorkshire as whole (Manby *et al.*, 2003a), which would have input a spurious precision to the chronology of many sites for which dating evidence has yet to be provided (as well as, somewhat pointlessly, identifying a number of divisions for which the Washlands at present offer little information), the record is divided in a way that suits the data. Thus the chapter sections do not always match the simple divisions between Neolithic, Bronze Age and Iron Age, as distinctions between some of these are simply not present in the Washlands dataset and to use them would mean masking a number of potentially interesting continuities and discontinuities.

The human settlement of the area has clearly been a major factor in influencing the development of its landscape, particularly in terms of vegetation, although other natural and anthropogenic factors, such as land drainage and river regimes, sediment flux and mineral extraction, have also played a role. The geomorphological background, the legacy of its glacial past (see Chapter 2), will have had a major influence on settlement location, on subsistence choices regarding types of land use and on the placement of cultural structures within the landscape. In turn, the human imprint on the land will have modified the evolution of natural systems, producing an increasingly artificial landscape with time. The link between culture and environment cannot be disengaged and any appraisal of the history of the area must fully address both strands. Although the earlier cultural periods (Palaeolithic and Mesolithic) are poorly represented in the project area, there is a substantial Mesolithic record in adjacent uplands (Young, 1990; Spratt, 1993; Manby, 2003a); further research may well improve our knowledge of these cultures and their environmental relations within the Washlands. Archaeological remains become more visible from Neolithic times onwards and the cultural record is sufficiently substantial in the later prehistoric and historic periods to encourage a more detailed interpretation of the archaeological distributions and the place of people within the Washlands landscape.

4.2 Upper Palaeolithic (25,000–10,000 BP)

The Upper Palaeolithic archaeological record in North Yorkshire is slight, as it is for the whole of northern England. There is enough, however, to show that North Yorkshire was exploited by humans during the Lateglacial period and it is likely that Palaeolithic sites remain to be found within the Washlands. The elk skeleton from Lateglacial Interstadial sediments at Neasham Fen in the Tees valley (Blackburn, 1952) confirms that the lowlands of the area carried game animals that could be exploited by Palaeolithic hunters. In North Yorkshire, there are several lowland sites with Upper Palaeolithic tools, such as Flixton in the Vale of Pickering (Schadla-Hall, 1987), where they are associated with *Equus* bones within organic muds dated to 10,413 ± 210 ^{14}C BP (Godwin & Willis, 1959) with a Lateglacial pollen assemblage. The nearby site of Seamer Carr contains several Upper Palaeolithic flint artefacts within a Lateglacial peat, with radiocarbon dates ranging between 10,200 and 11,300 ^{14}C BP, that was separated from Mesolithic finds at the site by layers of wind-blown sand deposited during the later part of the Loch Lomond Stadial (Schadla-Hall 1989; Conneller & Schadla-Hall, 2003). These dates conform well with those from Lateglacial sites elsewhere in northern England (Innes, 2002a; Chapter 1). The only instance, so far, of late Upper Palaeolithic material from the Washlands is a shouldered point (Fig. 4.1), recently recovered with later material from Nosterfield (Rowe, 2006). A large flint blade of Upper Palaeolithic type with a compatible flake assemblage has also been identified from Nab End in middle Wensleydale (Jacobi, 1991; Laurie, 2003), not far up the Ure valley from the Washlands. These finds support the suggestion of an Upper Palaeolithic presence in the vicinity of the Washlands and, taken together with the Vale of Pickering evidence (Manby, 2003a), show that a cultural presence, if only occasional, must be taken into account during consideration of Lateglacial environmental change in North Yorkshire. There are also indications that this Upper Palaeolithic blade technology persisted into the early part of the Holocene, as

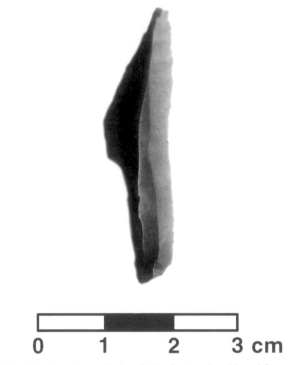

0   1   2   3 cm

Fig. 4.1. Late Upper Palaeolithic flint: a shouldered flint point from Nosterfield, one of the oldest artefacts from the Washlands area (photo: Peter Rowe)

at Flixton 2 in the Vale of Pickering, before being replaced by the Mesolithic microlithic industries (Manby, 2003a; Barton & Roberts, 2004).

4.3 Mesolithic (8000–4000 BC) [= 10,000–6000 BP]

North Yorkshire is one of the most prolific areas of Britain in terms of Mesolithic archaeological sites (Wymer, 1977; Manby, 2003a; Vyner, 2003a) but the great majority are in the Pennine and North York Moors uplands and there are few in the Washlands. It remains to be seen to what degree this imbalance in site distribution reflects the reality of Holocene hunter-gatherer occupation of the area. The paucity of sites in the lowlands, with the exception of the area around Star Carr in the eastern Vale of Pickering, may well reflect the effectiveness of environmental processes in reducing the visibility and preservation of archaeological material. Lowland Mesolithic sites may well have been concealed by later accumulations of alluvium and other sediments during the several millennia since their occupation. This is particularly the case in the Washlands, which has been an area of high intensity farming and alluviation.

That the known Mesolithic record is to some extent artificially sparse is illustrated by the recent discovery in the Washlands of an early Mesolithic site at Little Holtby, between Leeming and Catterick (Oxford Archaeology North, 1995). This location, on the western side of a moraine

ridge and near the former lake of Crakehall Ings (Chapter 2.4.4), is of particular interest because of the complete absence of evidence for subsequent prehistoric activity in the surrounding area. Cardwell and Speed (1996) have also reported flints of Mesolithic type from excavations at Brough St. Giles, near Catterick. Like most of the lowland sites, these are attributed to the early Mesolithic on the basis of flint typology. Study of the early Mesolithic in lowland North Yorkshire is inevitably conditioned by investigations at the classic early Holocene wetland site of Star Carr in the Vale of Pickering (Mellars & Dark, 1998), where half a century of integrated archaeological and palaeoenvironmental research has taken place (summarized by Gonzalez & Huddart, 2002). Early Mesolithic material also occurs in the Washlands, however. At Seamer Carrs, near Stokesley in the Vale of Mowbray (not to be confused with the Vale of Pickering site, Seamer Carr, mentioned above) and therefore on the northern fringe of the Washlands (Fig. 1.9), blunted triangle shapes were found in association with an early Mesolithic pick along the shoreline of a former lake (Spratt & Simmons, 1976). An early Mesolithic site has also been recorded in the south of the washlands at Topcliffe-on-Swale, where broad-blade microliths were recovered from eroding river-side alluvium (Cowling & Stickland, 1947). A pebble macehead and flints of similar age were also reported nearby from Melmerby by Wymer (1977), who also recorded an early Mesolithic tranchet axe from Raskelf, on the eastern fringes of the Vale of York.

There are few indications of settlement and exploitation of the Swale–Ure Washlands lowland during the Later Mesolithic, although sites with diagnostic geometrically shaped microliths are common on the uplands fringing the study area (Manby, 2003a). Several finds were made during the recent survey of the Thornborough–Nosterfield area (e.g., Harding & Johnson, 2003a), while recent excavations at Marne Barracks, Catterick have recovered a Late Mesolithic flint assemblage (Young, 2006). Older records of likely Late Mesolithic flint scatters come from the Tees valley at Yarm and Ingleby Barwick (NZ 447124; Wymer, 1977). Late Mesolithic flints also occur at Seamer Carrs (Spratt, 1993), clearly a long-lived focus of activity in that part of the lowland.

The end of Mesolithic culture in the Washlands is difficult to date, although radiocarbon dating of archaeological material from the North Yorkshire region suggests that the transition between the final Mesolithic and the earliest Neolithic occurred about 5000 ^{14}C BP (Spratt, 1993). A period of overlap between the two cultures is possible, but at present there is no securely dated archaeological evidence for co-existence. An early date for the Neolithic of 5040 ± 90 ^{14}C BP has been reported from East Ayton long barrow, at the south-eastern foot of the North York Moors (Spratt, 1993) but the known Neolithic features in the Washlands, such as cursus monuments, are considerably younger (Barclay & Bayliss, 2002). Neolithic flints, albeit unstratified, have been found on several Mesolithic sites on the North York Moors (Spratt, 1993). On the upland

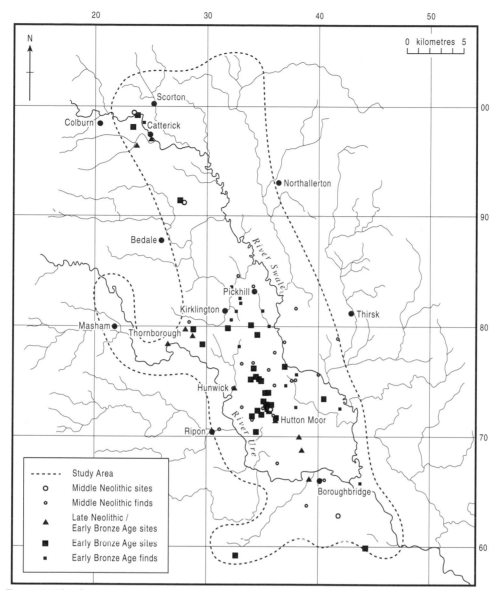

Fig. 4.2. The distribution of Middle Neolithic and Bronze age archaeology from the Washlands

Mesolithic sites, the diagnostic Neolithic flints are almost exclusively of arrowhead type, mainly leaf-shaped (Young, 1990), but the assemblages from the lowland sites include axes. Some of the sites mentioned above also have Neolithic and later flints as well as Mesolithic ones, but no clear association can be made other than the continued or repeated use of favourable locations. In summary, settlement has occurred in the Washlands since at least the early Mesolithic period, perhaps from the 6th Millennium BC, although the density and extent of settlement during the Mesolithic remains unclear.

4.4 Earlier and middle Neolithic (4000–3000 BC)

Discussion of the early part of the Neolithic period within the Washlands is restricted by the limited number of monuments and the doubtful attribution of many finds to this chronological horizon (Fig. 4.2). The archetypal monuments of the earlier Neolithic are causewayed enclosures and chambered cairns (megalithic and non-megalithic), neither of which is present in the Washlands; indeed, they are found only occasionally elsewhere in the region. Whether or not there were ever monuments of these kinds in the Washlands is debatable. While the earthworks of enclosures may have been removed by agriculture, it is difficult to explain why there is no crop-mark evidence for them here or elsewhere in the region. Harding (2000a) has noted the segmented nature of the outer enclosing ditches at the Thornborough henges (see below), suggesting that this may be evidence for earlier enclosures at the later henge sites. Further south, this is apparent in the crop-mark evidence at Newton Kyme (SE 459450) in the lower Wharfe valley

(Harding & Lee, 1987). However, significant though the succession of monuments at Thornborough and nearby locations may be, it is not immediately clear that the early enclosing phases are directly comparable with early Neolithic causewayed enclosures, nor, as discussed further below, is there archaeological evidence to deny the primacy of the cursus in the Thornborough monument sequence.

In Yorkshire as a whole, early funerary monuments are restricted to a thin scattering on the uplands of the north-eastern moors and the Wolds of eastern Yorkshire (Vyner, 2000), while causewayed and other enclosures of this period have yet to be confirmed as present anywhere in the region. In the Washlands, it may be not a question of population absence in the earliest part of the Neolithic, but merely that the people who were there did not construct monuments.

4.4.1 Range of monument and finds type

The earliest monuments in the Washlands date from the mid-Neolithic; linear embanked monuments from this period, termed cursuses, have been recorded at Thornborough (where a cursus underlies the central enclosure and henge), Copt Hewick, near Ripon, and Scorton (Topping, 1992). A recent review of the chronology of the cursuses suggests that the likely period of their establishment was around 2800 to 2700 BC (Barclay & Bayliss, 2002), with the evidence from Thornborough suggesting that the cursus there may have been constructed earlier. These monuments do not necessarily represent the arrival of new communities in the area; instead it is possible that here, as elsewhere in the north of England, ways of life that were essentially Mesolithic continued later than in some other areas of the country. There is also ceramic evidence for activity of probable early to middle Neolithic date in the vicinity of the potentially later monument complexes at Nosterfield, where sherds of Grimston Ware have been recovered from pits (Vyner, 1998, 1999), and more widespread evidence of Neolithic activity is recorded by the presence of Peterborough Ware pottery at Marton-le-Moor, Nosterfield, Catterick and Scorton (Manby, 2006).

4.4.2 Location and nature of activity

There are three confirmed cursuses from this period, as established above, all of them on river valley slopes. The sites comprise parallel ditches, originally with upcast banks (or a single central bank), extending over considerable distances and now only known through crop marks that fail to reveal their full extent. The Copt Hewick cursus is located between the henge sites of Cana Barn and Hutton Moor (Fig. 4.3). At Thornborough, the cursus was joined by a linear arrangement of circular enclosures and henges (Harding, 2003), as well as pit alignments and, later, round barrows. The Scorton cursus, which was set on the north bank of the Swale, does not appear to have become the location of later Neolithic monuments, although a continuing interest in the ritual nature of the site is demonstrated by the establishment of several probable round barrows or other circular monuments at its south-east end.

The function of cursus monuments has long been debated, with the long-standing explanation as ceremonial pathways having received further emphasis in the past decade (Tilley, 1994; Harding & Barclay, 1999). Their status as early (in the Washlands apparently the earliest) constructions in the landscape may well have imbued them with a number of functions. Community and ritual focus is likely to have been chief amongst these; while their extended linear character may have attracted processional use along them, it would also have provided a boundary that may have marked early territorial aspirations.

Although the extent of fieldwork has been limited, the sparse stray finds of the earlier Neolithic in the Washlands tend to support the notion of thinly scattered communities persisting with Mesolithic lifestyles. For the purposes of this discussion, unpolished and polished stone axes are put forward as evidence of activity in the middle Neolithic (together with a single arrowhead described as Neolithic), although it may well be that their currency extends throughout the Neolithic. The total number of finds recorded in this review is only 25, although a more detailed appraisal of the context of the Thornborough monuments suggests that there are over 40 axe finds from the area (Harding & Johnson, 2003b). Since the distribution of axes closely mirrors later Neolithic and early Bronze Age activity, their precise chronology is not an issue. However, they are of potential value not just for gauging the level of such activity but also for determining the beginning of the Neolithic in the area. There are few recorded instances of leaf-shaped arrowheads and relatively few axes when compared with the lower Tees area. However, within the Washlands there may be some factors that have combined to reduce the record of stray finds, among which may be adduced the absence of a strong museum presence (to which finds might have been taken) and the limited extent of archaeological fieldwork undertaken.

Assuming that these factors apply equally across the area, the pattern of distribution of sites and finds is remarkably similar to that seen for the succeeding later Neolithic and early Bronze Age period. With the exception of occasional outlying finds and the cursus at Scorton, activity in the earlier part of the Neolithic appears to have been concentrated in the lower part of the Ure–Swale interfluve, with a north-easterly trend to the finds distribution that suggests an extension of activity onto the ridge above the Swale which was not reflected in the construction of middle or later Neolithic monuments.

4.5 The later Neolithic/Early Bronze Age (3000–1600 BC)

The later Neolithic/Early Bronze Age sees a significant increase in the number of finds and sites in the Washlands

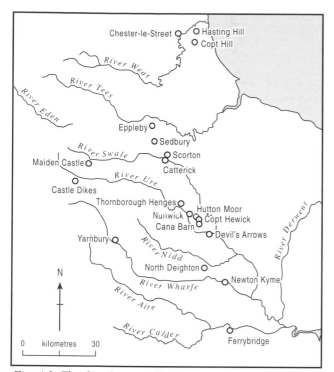

Fig. 4.3. The distribution of henge sites in the wider region

Fig. 4.4. The three Thornborough henges from the air pictured, looking north-west, with the Nosterfield Quarry in the background (photo: English Heritage)

Fig. 4.5 Henge bank at Thornborough: view through the entrance into the interior of the central henge earthwork, looking north (photo: Blaise Vyner)

(Fig. 4.2) in comparison with earlier periods. Perceptions of activity in this area during the later Neolithic, perhaps from around 2700 BC, are dominated by the great henge monuments clustered on the Ure–Swale interfluve (Figs 4.3 and 4.4). These massive circular-plan earthwork enclosures (Fig. 4.5) are thought to have been important ceremonial and ritual centres (Harding, 1998, 2000a, 2003). The major henges at Cana Barn (SE 360718), Hutton Moor (SE 352735), Nunwick (SE 322648) and Thornborough (SE 285 795; Fig. 4.3) are likely to have been constructed around 2800 BC (Harding, 2003). At Thornborough, three large henges occur in linear sequence (Fig. 4.4) with the central henge overlying the earlier cursus. The fact that the underlying cursus ditches had become silted up and grassed-over (Thomas, 1955) suggests that some considerable period, to be measured in decades at least, intervened between the abandonment of the cursus and the construction of the henge.

The concentration of major monuments from this period at specific focal points in the Washlands is remarkable; sites that are likely to be contemporaneous include the standing stones of the Devil's Arrows (SE 389663; Burl, 1991; Fig. 4.6) and a nearby pit alignment on the south bank of the Ure at Boroughbridge, as well as another pit alignment at Dishforth (Tavener, 1996). There is increasing evidence, however, for a further concentration of similar monuments on the Swale margins to the north of the study area, in the vicinity of Catterick (G. Speed, pers. comm.). During the early Bronze Age, from around 2000 BC, some of the earlier monument complexes continued to be a focus for ritual and funerary activity, as is reflected in concentrations

Fig. 4.6. The Devil's Arrows: aligned Neolithic standing stones at Boroughbridge. For location see Fig. 4.3

Component	Cursus	Henge	Pit alignment	Other	Associations
Devil's Arrows			Pit alignment	Stone row	
Dishforth			Pit alignment		
Cana		Henge			Round barrows ?
Hutton Moor		Henge			Round barrows
Nunwick		Henge			
Thornborough	Cursus	3 Henges	Pit alignment	Pits	Round barrows
Catterick (Colburn)		Henge		Pits Enclosure	Cairn
Scorton	Cursus	Henge			Round barrows
Ferrybridge		Henge		Timber circles	Round barrows
Hasting Hill	Cursus			Enclosure	Round barrows

Table 4.1. Component monuments of the Washlands Neolithic complexes

of round barrows, whereas other sites appear to have been abandoned. While the overall pattern of early Bronze Age activity in the Washlands appears to have remained little changed from that of the later Neolithic, a number of significant changes may be observed.

4.5.1 Range of monument and finds type

Enclosures, henges, pit alignments and stone alignments may at first sight appear to be a somewhat disparate group of monuments, but all form part of a suite that is a recurrent feature of the later Neolithic and these monuments may well have had broadly similar social functions. Table 4.1 summarizes information on the later Neolithic complexes of the Washlands, including the cursus monuments of the preceding mid-Neolithic and comparable information for the recently examined complex on the River Aire at Ferrybridge, West Yorkshire (Roberts, 2005), and the crop-mark complex at Hasting Hill, County Durham. Contemporary monument types that appear to be missing from the Washlands thus far include early round barrows. The general absence of monuments of earlier Neolithic date has already been noted, the cursuses at Thornborough, Copt Hewick and Scorton being notable exceptions. After them, the enclosures surrounding the henges, and perhaps closely followed by the henges themselves, may represent the first substantial constructions in the landscape.

In making the suggestion that the enclosure at Thornborough central henge is successive to the adjacent cursus monument, it is necessary to summarize briefly the evidence for the construction sequence at this site. The earlier excavations confirmed that the cursus monument underlies the henge monument and that the earlier monument had been significantly eroded by the time the henge was built (Thomas, 1955). No evidence was obtained for the chronology of the concentric circular ditch, although it was assumed that it was contemporary with the enclosed henge. Recent excavation at Thornborough has shown that the southern ditch of the cursus diminishes and terminates just short of the outer concentric ditch, prompting the suggestion that the cursus was respecting a pre-existing monument (Harding, 2000a). The excavations of 1952 showed the cursus northern ditch similarly diminished in Cutting IV beneath the henge bank (Thomas, 1955), so the more recent observation suggests that the construction of the cursus ditches mirrored each other. So, while the cursus south and north ditches are tangential to the entrances to the circular enclosure and the henge respectively, they do not throw any light on the sequence of circular enclosure and henge construction. While the spatial relations between cursus ditches and the entrances to both circular enclosure and henge are surely significant, it seems reasonable to suggest that both enclosures succeeded the cursus, which had perhaps included some feature that survived to provide a focus for the later constructions.

The recent discovery and excavation of a massive timber enclosure at Catterick (Plate 4.1), which has a radiocarbon date range of 2580–2480 cal. BC (Hale & Platell, 2007), emphasizes the range of monuments constructed in the Neolithic. Although henges are now dominant amongst the Washlands monuments complexes, the Catterick enclosure and the Devil's Arrows at Boroughbridge (Fig. 4.6) are indicators of other, less enduring, possibilities.

For the later Neolithic, the absence of round barrows might well be more apparent than real; indeed, it has been suggested that a round barrow near the southern Thornborough henge is Neolithic rather than Bronze Age (Harding & Johnson, 2003a). Neolithic round barrows tend to be larger than is normal for early Bronze Age burial mounds but agricultural attrition can make this

Fig. 4.7. Pallet Hill, Catterick, a possible Neolithic round barrow adjacent to the 15th Century church, which was built some distance to the west of the River Ure, where Paulinus had baptised King Edwin around AD 627 (photo: Blaise Vyner)

distinction unreliable. In any case, the excavation record for Washland round barrows is as scanty as elsewhere in North Yorkshire. There is also a tendency to assume that all large circular mounds in this region are Medieval earthwork mottes, although a Neolithic origin has been suggested for several (Vyner, 2000). In addition, the 1st edition Ordnance Survey map shows a now-vanished isolated mound, 'The Mount', north of Leeming (SE 278919) and there is another enigmatic mound adjacent to the churchyard at Catterick (Fig. 4.7). In contrast to the variety of the later Neolithic monuments, those from the early Bronze Age are virtually restricted to the smaller round barrows, now surviving as simple earth mounds or revealed by crop marks showing ditches formerly surrounding mounds.

Chronologically diagnostic lithic finds comprise flint axes, flint arrowheads (assumed from the limited records to be barbed-and-tanged), stone battle axes, maceheads, and shaft-hole adzes and hammers, all of which may be assigned to the early Bronze Age, together with flanged bronze axes and two gold arm rings. Some Neolithic leaf-shaped arrowheads may be included amongst occasional misidentified items, such are the limitations of the finds record. Grooved Ware, which is the distinctive pottery of the later Neolithic and is often associated with henge monuments, has been recovered in the Washlands from pits at Nosterfield (Vyner, 1998), close to the Thornborough henges, and at Scorton (Manby, 2006), as well as from beneath a Bronze Age barrow at North Deighton (Wood, 1971), *c.* 15 km south of Boroughbridge.

4.5.2 Location and nature of activity

Further investigation of this under-researched area may well extend the number and range of monuments (Figs 4.2 and 4.3), as demonstrated by M. Bastow's (pers comm.) recent discovery of documentary evidence for a stone alignment on Hutton Moor, as well as the Catterick timber

enclosure. Given the increasing evidence for significant Neolithic monument complexes in the valleys of all the other major rivers in northern England (including both Washlands rivers), it seems highly likely that another will be found in association with the River Nidd, perhaps in the vicinity of Little Ribston/North Deighton (Vyner, 2007). Otherwise, there is little to suggest that the pattern of distribution of monuments (Fig. 4.3) would be substantially changed by new discoveries. Agriculture has certainly destroyed some sites, but the distribution of stray finds of this period tends to mirror that of the known monuments. The distribution of 'howe' place names is also very much in accordance with the pattern of early Bronze Age burial mound distribution; these are commonly found in the area north-east of Ripon, are largely absent in the central and eastern part of the study area, and have been noted in the north only on the north bank of the Swale, east of Catterick Bridge.

As is usual in the English archaeological record, the location of domestic activity is hardly visible. For the later Neolithic, pits containing pottery suggest activity that might reflect domestic occupation in the vicinity of Marton (Tavener, 1996) and Catterick Racecourse (Moloney *et al.*, 2003), as well as the previously mentioned Nosterfield, Scorton and North Deighton. The coincidence of this pottery with ritual monuments, however, should prompt caution in assuming domestic activity, which may well have taken place elsewhere (but which is perhaps more likely to have been interwoven with ritual activity). It is highly likely that the monuments tell only part of the story; that domestic and other activity was more widespread than suggested by the ritual monuments is indicated by the distribution of stray finds of Neolithic affinity across the interfluve ridge eastwards towards the Swale, over the area later occupied by the early Bronze Age burial mounds (Harding & Johnson, 2003a). Evidence for the location of early Bronze Age settlement is completely lacking but, despite this, to sustain such a prolonged programme of monument construction and use (from around 3000 until at least 1800 BC) the continuing presence of a local population must be assumed.

The very strong correlation between monument construction and river valley landscapes in Yorkshire and the north-east has been emphasized previously (Vyner, 2000). Consideration of evidence from the Washlands further illuminates the strong relationships between topography, monuments, and the mobility of people (Vyner, 2007). The Devil's Arrows and the nearby pit alignment on the south bank of the Ure are mirrored by the Scorton cursus on the north bank of the Swale at Catterick (Fig. 4.3), potentially relating to former river crossing points. The major later Neolithic monuments are restricted to the narrow area that lies between the two rivers in the Washlands. Within the Ure valley, the monuments are found on the east bank downstream from Hackfall Gorge and the Magnesian Limestone escarpment. The Thornborough complex occupies a former outwash fan deposited by the river during deglaciation (Chapter 2.6.2). Small river terraces near the southern henge indicate that at some stage the Ure flowed much closer to the now-destroyed cursus and the henges. The more easterly collection of henges at Cana Barn and Hutton Moor occupy the higher ground towards the drift-covered ridge, associated with the Sherwood Sandstone, that is followed by Dere Street. Nunwick henge is an exception, since it lies on low ground near a former meander of the Ure, now marked by Hall Garth Ponds.

Northwards from Nosterfield, there is an absence of monuments until the Swale crossing at Catterick. On the banks of the River Swale, the ring ditches associated with the cursus at Scorton, on the north bank of the river, are now joined by a nearby henge and pit alignment (Northern Archaeological Associates, 2002, 2006) and a henge-like feature on the south bank at Colburn, near Catterick, upriver to the west (RCHME, 1977). Mention has already been made of the enormous timber enclosure at Catterick (Moloney *et al.*, 2003), also on the south bank. The excavations at Scorton also produced a panel of rock art, in the form of a stone decorated with cup-and-ring markings (Fig. 4.8), that is unique in the study area and likely to be broadly contemporary with the later Neolithic monuments (information courtesy of NAA).

Some consideration must now be given to the evidence for a north–south route through the Washlands, ultimately consolidated by Dere Street, which the prehistoric monument complexes suggest is likely to have been used by travellers, if only episodically, from earliest times. The evidence from the Washlands and the wider region has recently been discussed in detail by Vyner (2007). During the later Neolithic, travellers moving northwards may well have had a variety of route options. The Washlands monuments suggest that favoured routes crossed the Ure at Boroughbridge, adjacent to the Devil's Arrows, and then progressed north along the bank of the Ure or its eastern valley-side past the Cana, Hutton Moor, Nunwick and Thornborough henges. The Thornborough complex may well have marked the eastern end of a favoured route across the Pennines, but the monuments also suggest that the route continued northwards. North of the Thornborough complex, the route had to divert around the area of Snape Mires (see Chapters 2.8.2 and 3.8), which may still have existed as a lake and was certainly a wetland until recently. Thus it reached Bedale, from where high ground associated with the moraine ridge that extends eastwards towards Leeming then north to Catterick (Chapter 2.2.1.1) would have formed an obvious route around another lake or wetland, Crakehall Ings, towards a suitable crossing point over the Swale at Catterick.

Seen in this context, the incidence of the mid- and later Neolithic monuments is a product of the combination of route and river. All the monument complexes are sited at or close to the lowest fording places convenient for overland south–north travel, a feature reflected in the remarkable coincidence of monument complexes and the bridging points of Roman Dere Street, seen in the Washlands at

Fig. 4.8. Early Bronze Age decorated stone, or 'rock art', from Scorton, showing cup-and-ring markings (photo: Northern Archaeological Associates)

Boroughbridge and Catterick. It has to be remembered that in the Neolithic period the Washlands was heavily wooded and that the rivers were wide and sluggish, with multiple channels and attendant large areas of waterlogged carr (Innes & Blackford, 2003a; Long *et al.*, 2004). Riparian vegetation may have made water transport extremely difficult, while overland routes would have had to be chosen carefully (Vyner, 2007). The coincidence of route and river is also marked south of the Washlands by the major henges at Newton Kyme, on the River Wharfe (Harding & Lee, 1987), and at Ferrybridge (Roberts, 2005), where a north–south route may have crossed the River Aire (Fig. 4.3). The pattern appears to be repeated to the north, with indications of a possible henge at Eppleby, to the south of the River Tees. Evidence of a crossing of the River Wear at Chester-le-Street, County Durham, is similarly marked by a substantial Neolithic enclosure (Fig. 4.3).

The monument complexes suggest that large numbers of people travelled to and between the river valley complexes. The implication is that the Washlands and the wider Vale of York supported a considerable population, augmented at times by incursion from elsewhere. The monument evidence suggests that the population concentrations of the later Neolithic lay in eastern Yorkshire and on the Solway Plain (Bradley & Edmonds, 1993). Connections between them, indicated by axes and lithic items, may have been articulated around the Washlands monument complexes (Manby *et al.*, 2003b), amongst which Thornborough may have been pre-eminent (Harding, 2000b, c, 2003). However, as has been pointed out with respect to whether the Stainmore Pass was part of a route linking the Tees and Eden valleys, there is often little supporting evidence in the way of monuments or artefacts (Vyner, 2001a).

Fig. 4.9. The excavation of a low stone cairn within the henge monument at Catterick, probably early Bronze Age (photo: Paul Gwiliam, courtesy of Archaeological Services WYAS)

Fig. 4.10. Late Bronze Age burial mound at Blois Hall Farm, near Ripon. For location see Fig. 4.11

Conversely, the presence of smaller hengiform enclosures at Maiden Castle in the middle Ure and Yarnbury in the middle Wharfe may be indicators that these two valleys were preferred to others for a Pennine crossing.

Whatever the status of later Neolithic east–west routes, it may be argued that the Washlands monuments constitute evidence for a south–north route that can be identified as extending from Ferrybridge, on the River Aire, north to Chester-le-Street on the River Wear. The route across the Washlands study area, having crossed the Ure at Boroughbridge, stayed close to the east bank of the river and avoided the carr lands of the Swale margins, returning to cross that river in the Catterick area. In the early Bronze Age, the distribution of burial mounds suggests a shift eastwards, perhaps associated with the development of more localized communications. Seen in this context, Roman Dere Street appears to have marked the eventual consolidation of an alignment that had existed, however informally and episodically, since the early Bronze Age.

In contrast with some areas of southern England, there are suggestions from the North Yorkshire archaeological record that the Neolithic and Bronze Age interface was not a period of significant cultural change. Within the Washlands, the combined evidence for Neolithic and early Bronze Age activity is more extensive than in most other areas of Yorkshire, even if the detailed evidence from excavation is still largely absent. The Beaker horizon is poorly represented in the Washlands record, with only two records of Beaker cremations at West Tanfield and Scorton, although there are a few Beaker sherds from the Little Ouseburn barrow (Rahtz, 1989) in the south and from the later phases of the Catterick henge site to the north (Vyner, 2003b). Notwithstanding the limited excavation evidence, the sparsity of Beaker finds underlines the seeming lack of interest in the study area in cultural items. On the northern part of the North York Moors it can be suggested that the use of monuments in combination with landscape features, in particular the construction of boundaries and the establishment of ritual monuments, was taking place

during the period from the later Neolithic and into the early Bronze Age, giving an impression of continuity of activity and land use (Vyner, 1995).

That there were some changes during the later Neolithic and early Bronze Age period in the Washlands is clearly demonstrated by review of the data. This suggests that the later Neolithic monument complexes may have influenced the siting of the early Bronze Age burial mounds to a lesser extent than might be expected. Some of the early sites, however, became the focus for the construction of early Bronze Age burial mounds: at Catterick, an early Bronze Age collared urn was placed (perhaps in a burial mound) just north of the river crossing (Wilson, 2002) and a flat cairn was built within the henge to the south (Moloncy et al., 2003; Fig. 4.9). Ring ditches of former burial mounds cluster around the east end of the Scorton cursus and to south of the henge, while the henge at Hutton Moor is surrounded by numerous barrows. The Thornborough henges attracted rather fewer burial mounds, however, and there are no barrows known around the Nunwick henge and few that can be associated with the Cana monument.

It should be noted that other early Bronze Age barrows were constructed around three focal points to the east of the later Neolithic sites: at Grafton, in the southern part of the Washlands, in the central sector of the Washlands south of Melmerby, and at Kirklington. Thomas (1955) long ago suggested that the concentration of early Bronze Age monuments at Melmerby points to the former presence there of earlier monuments. However, the evidence from Nunwick and Cana rather weakens this argument in that, if some earlier sites did not attract later activity, there seems little reason to disallow the development of new focuses, as suggested in the Washlands by an eastward distribution of early Bronze Age burial mounds.

It is instructive to examine the distribution of barrows across the study area as whole. Setting aside the Thornborough and Hutton Moor concentrations, the distribution is almost entirely restricted to the interfluve ridge from Kirklington in the north southwards to Boroughbridge, and along the extension of the ridge south-east to Little Ouseburn. The landscape settings of these monuments are reminiscent of those observed in the distribution of round barrows on the North York Moors (Vyner, 2000). A preference for ridge-top location for some of the more substantial mounds is evident: e.g., the barrow near Blois Hall Farm (SE 347724; Fig. 4.10). Hutton Moor also has an extensive group of mounds, with settings of single, paired, or triple mounds present, some of them named: e.g., Three Hills (SE 286801), Quernhowe (SE 338805) and Howgrave (SE 319794).

What appears to be visible in the distribution pattern of the early Bronze Age burial mounds is the diminution of interest in the earlier monument complexes of the River Ure. Instead, the dominant theme of the round barrow setting is emphasis of the north–south ridge route, in the same way that some of the monuments on the North York Moors appear to mark the route of ancient tracks (Vyner, 2000, 2007). Although the excavated evidence from this area is very limited, and almost entirely antiquarian (Dennison, 1993), the change of focus may be reflected in the fact that the excavation of the Ure barrows group has produced a single timber coffin from Thornborough, while two coffins have been recovered from less well recorded excavations of the north–south ridge monuments at Marton and Low Ouseburn. In landscape terms, the contrast between the siting of the Ure Neolithic monument complexes and those of the early Bronze Age is quite clear, with the early monuments looking towards the River Ure on its eastern valley side. But while some of the later round barrows can be seen to cluster around these earlier monument sites, the majority do not. Instead, an extended distribution of round barrows can be observed, principally focused in a north–south linear arrangement set slightly to the east, along the Ure–Swale interfluve ridge and its south-eastern extension.

A general north–south linearity within the landscape is brought about by the course of the rivers Ure and Swale, which themselves mirror the flanking Pennines and the North York Moors; all of which is accentuated by the interfluve ridge. The importance of the north–south route is underlined not only by the Washlands Neolithic monuments, on and adjacent to the crossings of the rivers Ure and Swale, but also by the linear arrangement of the early Bronze Age burial mounds. It would be unwise, for the early Bronze Age, to make too much of the north–south route at the expense of any east–west communications. The limited information from the excavated barrows suggests that regional linkages existed, predominantly with the North Yorkshire Moors, the western fringes of which are only 18 km away across the Vale of Mowbray. The similarity in landscape setting of the burial mounds in the two areas has been commented on above. Attention is here drawn to the common practice of urned cremation in Food Vessels and, especially on the North York Moors, Collared Urns (Smith, 1994). The artefact record for the moorland burial mounds is more complete than for the Washlands and the

palaeoenvironmental record for the Bronze Age is also much better in the uplands (Innes, 2002d). The record shows occasional forest clearance from the 6th Millennium BC gaining momentum during the Neolithic and Bronze Age, as is well seen in the North Yorkshire Moors (Simmons, 1995; Innes, 1999, 2002d). The likelihood that groups of barrows represent the accrual of monuments over fairly lengthy periods is suggested by the pollen evidence from the Burton Howes, where Barrow 4d was built in thick woodland that had been considerably reduced by the time Barrow 1A was constructed (Dimbleby, 1962).

Northwards from Nosterfield, a thin scattering of early Bronze Age burial mounds suggests an extension of activity into the Bedale area and the consolidation of settlement along the interfluve ridge above the Swale. The high distribution of burial mounds along this ridge contrasts with the apparent absence of such sites on the glacial deposits to the east (Radley, 1974). It has been suggested that the scattered isolated mounds here indicate low density settlement based on forest clearance and shifting agriculture (Crawford, 1980). To the east, if the large numbers of burial mounds are any guide, lighter soils on the upland margins of the North York Moors encouraged agricultural activity and sedentary settlement, activity that may have been mirrored on a smaller scale on the lighter Washlands soils.

In conclusion, there are significant concentrations of later Neolithic and earlier Bronze Age monuments in the Washlands, reflecting the strategic importance of the area in conjunction with an important north–south route and the crossing point of the local rivers. In the later Neolithic, from around 2800 BC, major monument complexes were developed at a series of focal points along the route corridor: around the river crossing at Boroughbridge, along the interfluve area of the Rivers Ure and Swale and again at the Catterick Swale crossing. The monuments include linear earthwork cursuses, pit alignments and standing stones, as well as the better known major (henge) earthwork enclosures. This pattern of monument complexes at the conjunction of routes and rivers is repeated elsewhere in north-east England.

Despite the scale of the later Neolithic monument complexes, which rival contemporary sites elsewhere in the British Isles, the location of burial mounds suggests that interest in the earlier sites was not fully sustained in the early Bronze Age. From perhaps 1900 BC onwards, the distribution of round barrows and other early Bronze Age monuments shows a markedly eastern bias, such that they are much more fully on the interfluve ridge than on its western slope. If the barrows reflect continued communication, in the same way as the earlier monuments, their distribution suggests that this was more localized, while maintaining the same crossings of the Ure and Swale. Communications from early in the Bronze Age followed a more direct north–south alignment along the interfluve ridge. Thus it may be claimed that the Dere Street alignment was initially established during the early Bronze Age.

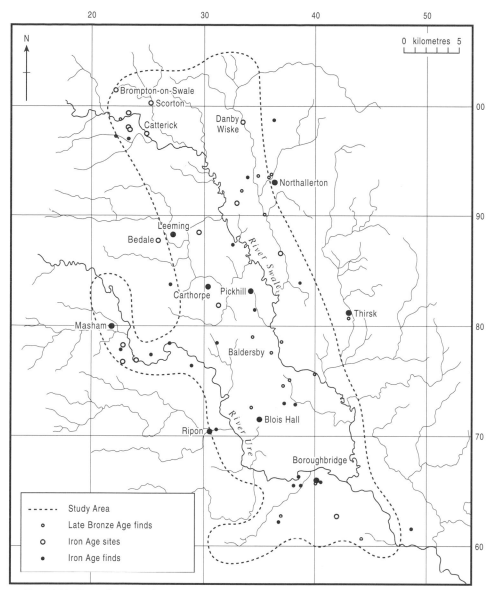

Fig. 4.11. Distribution of Late Bronze Age and Iron Age archaeology in the Washlands

4.6 Later Bronze Age and pre-Roman Iron Age (1600 BC–70 AD)

As in many lowland areas of England, the later Bronze Age is scarcely visible in the Washlands (Fig. 4.11), since the transition within the Bronze Age is marked by a decline in the visibility of funerary and other ritual practices. Although chronological information is poor, it is generally assumed that the development of an agriculturally bounded landscape first occurred, on soils that were then favourable, during the middle Bronze Age. On the uplands of the North York Moors, extensive field systems, sometimes associated with groups of small clearance cairns, are thought to date to this time (Spratt, 1978, 1993), and may extend into the later Bronze Age. Evidence for contemporary agriculture on the lowland areas, however, remains elusive. During the pre-Roman Iron Age, pastoralism appears to have been intensified on the Pennine uplands, while a regime

of successful mixed agriculture developed in the lowlands of the Tees valley and the Vale of York (Vyner, 2001a). Within the region it seems that it was only on the uplands of the North York Moors that agriculture was scaled back in the face of deteriorating soils and encroaching heather, bracken and peat.

Hillforts, strongly defended earthwork enclosures that were built on well-defined topographic defendable locations (Manby *et al.*, 2003b), are sparsely distributed across North Yorkshire and there is little evidence that they formed the focuses of occupation. Instead, pre-Roman Iron Age settlement in lowland North Yorkshire is typified by farmsteads of round houses and other buildings set within sub-rectangular enclosures, visible as crop marks; there is also growing evidence for unenclosed individual and clustered settlements. While it might be unwise to overstate the continuum between later Bronze Age and pre-Roman Iron Age in the study area, the combined

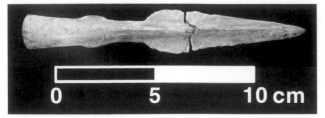

Fig. 4.12. Bronze Age bronze spearhead, a stray find from Baldersby (photo: Northern Archaeological Associates). For location, see Fig. 4.11.

Fig. 4.13. The upper stone of an Iron Age beehive quern from Scorton (photo: David Heslop)

data are suggestive of some common preferences for locations that were marginal to those chosen during the later Neolithic and early Bronze Age, and which suggest an intensification of activity in the valley of the River Swale. A similar disjuncture can be observed with the onset of Romanization. Many successful pre-Roman Iron Age settlements appear to have been abandoned early in the Roman period, suggesting in that instance that preferences for settlement location may have been altered by cultural and tenurial changes accompanying Romanization.

4.6.1 Range of monument and finds type

Within the Washlands study area there is a very limited range of site types for the mid- and later Bronze Age, with no surviving monuments or excavated evidence for this period and only a thin scatter of bronze implements and weapons (e.g. Fig. 4.12). The recent discovery of a late Bronze Age metal founder's hoard at Ainderby Steeple is of interest, since it is clearly not a stray find and occurs in an area of apparently limited early activity. There are few records of any field monuments that might be ascribed to the pre-Roman Iron Age, although notable among these are surviving earthworks on the low rolling hills south-west of Masham, in the western part of the study area. Here, a small cairn adjacent to the enclosure on Roomer Common may be a rare example of an Iron Age burial mound, such as are found elsewhere in the region (Wainwright & Longworth, 1969).

Since almost all the site-based information for Iron Age settlement in the Vale of Mowbray and the lower Tees valley derives from aerial survey, the restricted flying zones around Catterick and Leeming airfields may go a long way towards explaining the lack of aerial evidence in the arable parts of the Washlands. The area has not yet had the linear intrusion of pipelines and road development that has provided increasing information on the extent of Iron Age settlement and enclosure in the Vale of York and the A1 corridor in West Yorkshire, although field survey programmes in advance of the A1 upgrade between Dishforth and Scotch Corner (Pell Frischmann, 1999) have produced information on potential Iron Age settlements near Leeming and at Brompton-on-Swale (as yet unpublished). The site record within the Washlands

hardly extends beyond recently noted sub-rectangular settlement enclosures near Bedale, one known from excavation at Catterick, another at Danby Wiske, and an unenclosed settlement at Scorton: all in the central and northern part of the area (Fig. 4.11).

There is very little evidence as yet for field systems such as are known to have developed during the pre-Roman Iron Age on the limestone hills of West Yorkshire to the south, although ditches excavated at Yafforth may be of this kind, as may be some of the linear features found by the recent geophysical survey noted above. Neither is there any information on the extent of tracks in this period, although in the Tees valley, immediately to the north, crop marks suggest the existence by this time of a network of local and regional tracks, their courses marked by flanking ditches. The palaeoenvironmental record from the Tees valley and south-east Durham, to the north of the Washlands, suggests that woodland clearance to allow mixed agriculture took place on the lowland areas from the earlier pre-Roman Iron Age (Bartley *et al.*, 1976; Fenton-Thomas, 1992), intensifying from the mid-Iron Age (Heslop, 1987). Excavated evidence from the Washlands is still lacking, but analysis of carbonized plant macrofossils from the lower Tees valley suggests that settlements in the productive lowlands switched from emmer to spelt wheat as part of the intensification of agricultural production, perhaps during the 3rd Century BC (van der Veen, 1992). The limited finds-and-sites dataset from the Washlands suggests that this may well have been the case here as well.

Information for the Iron Age in the Washlands is greatly augmented by the data derived from the Yorkshire quern survey, which records beehive querns, or millstones, from 23 locations within the Washlands (e.g. Fig. 4.13). This strongly suggests that the crop-mark and earthwork record is indeed artificially low. The querns are chronologically diagnostic, being introduced during the middle Iron Age, perhaps from the 3rd Century BC, to be supplanted by rotary querns at the beginning of the Roman period. Additionally, the querns are especially valuable as a dataset because they are too heavy to be readily portable. Although they may have been re-used in walling or track metalling, their weight makes them a very reliable indicator of nearby occupation. The lithology of the stones is also illuminating in that it can reveal patterns of social contact and trade (Gwilt & Heslop, 1995).

4.6.2 Location and nature of activity

Elsewhere in Yorkshire, later Bronze Age activity is marked by early phases of hillforts and occasional other defended 'Thwing-type' sites (Manby, 1980) or by early phases in the life of hillforts, as at Scarborough Castle. No such sites are known from the Washlands, nor is the short record of stray finds of middle and later Bronze Age implements and weapons especially illuminating, although the small Thirsk hoard of bronze and goldwork appears to represent the property of a wealthy individual living in the Washlands (Manby *et al.*, 2003b). Rivers attracted votive depositions in this period, but there is only a limited relationship between the two in this area, with swords from river terraces at Ripon and Brompton-on-Swale now joined by the rapier excavated from the Swale bank at Catterick Bridge (Burgess, 1995).

As has already been noted, crop-mark information from this area is very limited, although it is highly likely that the beehive-shaped querns (Fig. 4.13) indicate the presence of enclosed and unenclosed roundhouse settlements of the kinds known from the Tees valley. Similarity of settlement types with those to the north and east would be supported by the pattern of the stray-find distribution, which is very much an eastward one and related more to the Swale than the Ure, with a group of finds around Northallerton at the eastern end of the 'Bedale gap'.

The Washlands show little evidence of having been divided by linear earthwork territorial boundaries during the pre-Roman Iron Age, although there is increasing evidence for such organization on the northern fringes of the North York Moors and on the Tabular Hills to the south (Spratt, 1989). It may be that the numerous watercourses made boundary earthworks redundant in the Washlands, but the record on the Ordnance Survey 1st edition map of a sinuous linear earthwork extending 1 km north from Camp Hill (SE 312825) to How Hill (both significant names), Carthorpe, is of note in that it is likely to belong either to the pre-Roman Iron Age period or to post-Roman times. Assuming that this is, or was, an artificial feature, it might be explained as a fragment of a formerly longer boundary or part of an enclosure that was once as extensive as Stanwick. While it is tempting to speculate that it may be here that the location of Cartimandua's capital settlement should be sought (Hartley & Fitts, 1988), not so very far from the eventual site of the Roman tribal capital, the evidence of the querns tends to argue against this.

The picture of pre-Roman Iron Age activity, provided largely by the querns, is one of increasingly widespread settlement, a trend comparable with that shown by site distributions in the southern Vale of York (Howard *et al.*, 2008), although there remain some areas with little obvious activity. The querns suggest two focuses for pre-Roman Iron Age occupation, at Boroughbridge and Catterick, with elsewhere a thin scatter of sites that falls short of the more intensive pattern now known from the northern part of the Vale of Mowbray and the lower Tees valley (Still *et al.*, 1989). For the Iron Age, there continues to be an absence of visible settlement activity around Ripon, although the discovery from aerial photographs of a sub-rectangular enclosure east of Bedale is now confirmed by geophysical survey (Dennison, 2006). Within the Washlands it may be anticipated that two pre-Roman Iron Age economic traditions merge: the increasingly well-evidenced arable agriculture of the Tees Valley and the northern Vale of Mowbray, and the still poorly known pastoral farming of the Pennine foothills. There is a suggestion that the former predominated, since the quern finds suggest growing activity along the Swale margins to the east and north-east, and along the western Ure margins to the west. The success of the Roman town of *Isurium Brigantium*, established in the early 2nd Century AD at Aldborough, near Boroughbridge, also confirms the developed social and economic nature of the local pre-Roman Iron Age people.

It is not clear to what extent the quern finds from the vicinity of Catterick and Boroughbridge relate to pre-Roman settlement. Since these were the locations of Roman forts, it may be assumed that there was early access to Romanized quern styles and that settlement developing after the establishment of the forts was more immediately Romanized than elsewhere. The beehive querns, then, might be taken to be evidence for settlement clustered at these locations before the arrival of the military, reflecting the attraction of the combination of high-quality agricultural land and the north–south river crossing, as is even clearer in evidence around Piercebridge on the River Tees (Still & Vyner, 1986). It may be noted that occupation of the excavated settlement at Scorton, beside the Swale north of Catterick, appears to have been abandoned before the Roman period (Vyner, 2001b), while settlement adjacent to Catterick racecourse and the more vestigial evidence for Iron Age activity at St. Giles by Brompton Bridge also appear not to have persisted into the Roman period (Cardwell & Speed, 1996, 29–32; Moloney *et al.*, 2003; Fig. 4.14). It may well be that the construction of the fort and associated structures here brought about changes in the established pattern of local settlement, drawing some of it into the new community.

From the middle Bronze Age the tradition of barrow burial appears to have been abandoned and interest in the earlier monuments is no longer evident. It may be assumed that within the Washlands, as was the case elsewhere in lowland North Yorkshire, successful farming settlements persisted. The widespread discovery of beehive-shaped

Fig. 4.14. Wall slot and encircling drainage gullies of an Iron Age round house, Catterick Racecourse (photo: Paul Gwiliam, courtesy of Archaeological Services WYAS)

querns for grinding corn certainly suggests that when the area became the subject of Roman administration in the later part of the 1st Century AD it was well able to contribute to Imperial taxation.

4.7 Roman period (AD 70–410)

The military imposition of Roman administration in northern England around AD 70 only slightly accelerated cultural changes that had already begun and which are intermittently visible in the archaeological record, in the form of pottery and metalwork, from around the 2nd Century BC. Gradual change is also seen in the palaeoenvironmental record from the same interval, which points to successful mixed agriculture supporting increasingly ambitious lifestyles. The artefact record (Fig. 4.15) from the region as a whole suggests that the initial acceptance of pottery and coinage

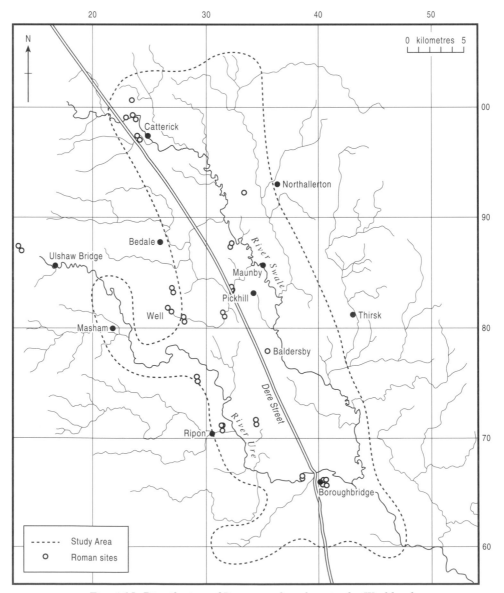

Fig. 4.15. Distribution of Roman archaeology in the Washlands

was slow and, although Romanized sub-rectangular building styles were taken up, many houses remained unambitious by the standards of southern England at that time. Despite the evidence for Roman activity in the area, a recent review reveals that, with the exception of Catterick, there has been little modern investigation of Roman period sites in the Washlands (Ottoway, 2003).

The Washlands contrasts with much of the Yorkshire region in that it contains significant Roman military installations and successful towns, as well as the largest concentration of opulent town and country houses in the north of England (Burroughs, 2001; Ottoway, 2003). Within the region, a network of roads and tracks had been developing since at least the Iron Age (Vyner, forthcoming). The north–south route was consolidated during the Roman occupation as the well-engineered Dere Street, while other communication routes, both land and river, were also exploited. While the rivers had previously been a constraining influence on land travel, in the Roman period they might have offered important opportunities for the transport of heavy cargoes, such as lead from the Yorkshire Dales (White, 1997), building stone and timber. It is not beyond the bounds of probability that, within the River Ouse system north of York, the Ure was navigable to shallow draught vessels at least as far upstream as Ulshaw Bridge (*c.* 10 km north-west of Masham), and the Swale as far as Catterick.

4.7.1 Range of monuments and finds type

Monuments in this area that began life with a Roman military purpose quickly assumed a civilian importance. In the Washlands, the northward campaigns of Agricola around AD 70 are marked by forts at Roecliffe (west of Boroughbridge), Healam Bridge (on the Swale–Ure interfluve between Boroughbridge and Catterick), and Catterick Bridge (Fig. 4.15). There is limited evidence for the initial stages of the Roman advance towards Scotland; the aerial photographic evidence for a suggested temporary camp on the eastern edge of Catterick (MacLeod, 2002) is not especially convincing compared with the clear plan of such an earthwork, now established by geophysical survey, at Bainesse Farm, 2 km to the south of Catterick (Archaeological Services, 2005).

As elsewhere, civilian settlement (vicus) was soon attracted to the forts (Hartley & Fitts, 1988), and these continued to develop after the military had been moved north. Outside the Washlands, the evidence shows that existing rural farmsteads continued in use into the Roman period (Heslop, 1987), which was no doubt the case here also. In contrast to the situation in the southern Vale of York, where recent survey has revealed a high Romano-British site density (Howard *et al.*, 2008), the paucity of survey and excavation data in the Washlands is perhaps compounded by the evidently minimal use of pottery by the rural communities. At Aldborough the developing town was accorded the status of a tribal capital, *Isurium Brigantium*,

the continuing success of which is demonstrated by the existence of a series of sumptuous buildings with mosaic floors. Rural establishments with Roman pretensions are known from no fewer than six locations in this small town (Burroughs, 2001).

4.7.2 Location and nature of activity

Dere Street appears to have followed a course not far removed from, but probably slightly east of, a route that had been first marked out in the early Bronze Age (Fig. 4.15). Attention given to the Roman road system here has been focused on the north–south alignment of Dere Street (Margary, 1967) but, as discussed above, the military advance into the north of England necessitated the construction of forts at regular intervals and strategic locations, which would have entailed considerable attention to the communications infrastructure.

The development of significant east–west land routes was constrained by the rivers, although a route westwards into Wensleydale across the interfluve from Dere Street, leaving the latter at Healam Bridge and reaching the River Ure at Ulshaw Bridge, was suggested following the discovery of the fort at Wensley (Hartley & Fitts, 1988). The suggested route runs west from the Healam Bridge fort, passing Carthorpe and avoiding the wetland of Snape Mires, and then along the northern side of the River Ure. From here a road is likely to have extended westwards along Wensleydale, with a north-west branch to the lead mines at Marrick Moor (Fleming, 1996, 1998).

Leading east from Healam Bridge, a potential extension of this route crossed the Swale at Maunby, extending to Crosby to meet the cartographically well-attested north–south route running up the western side of the Vale of Mowbray. This eastwards extension, which would have linked the two north–south routes at their closest point, may be evidenced today in tracks and footpaths. The fact that it is no longer part of the modern road system may reflect the difficulty of maintaining a crossing of the River Swale, combined with limited strategic and economic significance. The suggested early demise of this road mirrors the postulated early decline of the Vale of Mowbray route (Vyner, 2007).

Before the end of the 1st Century AD, however, the area was effectively demilitarized and the pace of Romanization increased. The latter was reflected in the development of the money economy, the adoption of new building styles and the acquisition of pottery, metalwork and other items (e.g. Fig. 4.16), although it was based on an underlying agricultural economy that remained fundamentally unchanged (Jones, 1991). Despite this, however, there is evidence that the structure of the rural landscape in the region was changing during the period, although it is difficult to establish a chronology. Change may not have been widespread, but was a response to the specific land requirements of the military, the need to apportion land for administrators and officials adjacent to urban settlement, or to establish officials in

Fig. 4.16. Roman jet finger ring from Baldersby (photo: Northern Archaeological Associates). For location, see Fig. 4.15.

Fig. 4.17. Fragment of mosaic from the Roman villa at Well (see Fig. 4.15), re-set in the Church of St Michael, Well (photo: Blaise Vyner)

rural residences. Something of the process may be visible at Ingleby Barwick, on the lower reaches of the River Tees, where a system of large fields with curvilinear boundaries was replaced or extended by one of small geometrically shaped land-holdings (Heslop, 1984), and where further excavations have recently revealed a substantial stone building of Roman construction, perhaps a depot.

The military advance had left an infrastructure of engineered and graded main roads with bridge crossings to the major rivers. The presence of the army had generated a series of sizeable towns capable of sustaining themselves through the remaining period of Roman administration. The establishment of the Brigantian tribal capital of *Isurium Brigantium*, already mentioned, may reflect the earlier construction of a fort nearby at Roecliffe and its associated vicus. However, the quern evidence from this area (Section 4.6.1) implies a large number of pre-Roman settlements, suggesting that it was well populated, which may also have influenced the location of the capital. It may also be noted that the eventual success of the Roman town, marked by a notable concentration of buildings with mosaic floors, was part of a trend that suggests that Roman impact in the area had been a reinforcing one (Millett, 1992).

Catterick also became established as the focus of extensive settlement that appears to have developed from the location of a Roman fort. The core of the settlement around the fort lay on the south bank of the Swale, but at Bainesse Farm, only slightly further south, a self-contained roadside settlement appears to have included at least one substantial building, which may have had an administrative function (Wilson, 2002), and survey in that area revealed much military and other material (Brickstock *et al.*, 2007). The fort and vicus at Healam Bridge is much less well known even than these other two sites; the existence of a vicus settlement to its south is now confirmed by evaluation in advance of the proposed A1 upgrade (Jones, 1994; Dennison, 1993).

By analogy with the extensive and more fully invest-igated evidence from the lower Tees valley, it may be suggested that the majority of pre-Roman Iron Age settlements continued to prosper and develop during the Roman period. The presence of urban settlements would

have encouraged and supported the development of the existing rural settlements and the adoption by the elite of Roman styles of rectangular buildings (Millett, 1992). Rural establishments that might merit the title 'villa' are present at Middleham, Well, Langwith House, Snape and Castle Dikes, North Stainley (Burroughs, 2001; Fig. 4.17), although none has been examined on the scale of Dalton Parlours, in the Dere Street corridor further south, or Dalton in the Tees valley to the north. The Washlands villas, such as at Castle Dikes, North Stainley, deserve further consideration in that they are somewhat anomalous even in a northern-England context. These villas indicate a sophisticated and Romanized element of society living in high-status rural estates set in the western part of the Washlands, sharing a preference for locations close to water, such as the natural spring at Well.

During the 2nd and 3rd Centuries AD, this rural area appears to have been one of the most prosperous in northern England, although it suffered a decline that seems to have set in well before the end of the Roman period. From the 3rd Century onwards, settlement may have become less urban-based and more dispersed, in a similar pattern to that of the pre-Roman Iron Age. How long these settlements continued is not readily demonstrable from the Washlands, but it has been recently argued that Romanized settlement, both urban and rural, was in decline from the 4th Century if not before and that it did not survive into the 5th Century (Faulkner, 2003). The lack of correlation between the evidence for Roman activity in the Washlands and the somewhat limited information on early Medieval settlement goes some way to support this argument.

4.8 The early Medieval period (AD 410–1066)

As elsewhere, evidence for settlement during the post-Roman centuries is thinly and variably represented

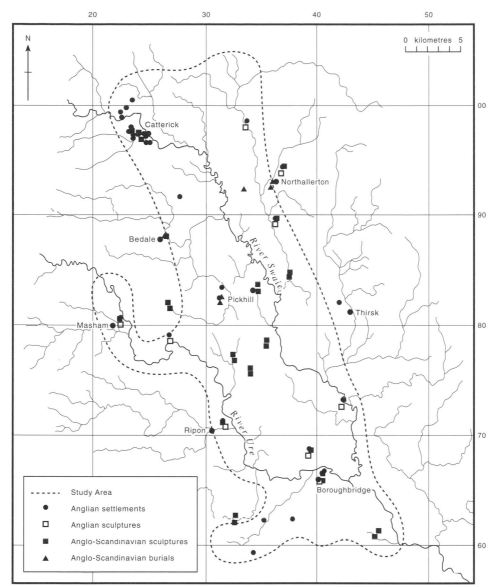

Fig. 4.18. Distribution of Anglian and Anglo-Scandinavian period archaeology in the Washlands

within the Washlands (Fig. 4.18). The sparse evidence that is available suggests that Romanized urban and rural settlements continued unchanged into the 5th Century (Faulkner, 2003; Ottoway, 2003); indeed, there can be little doubt that the majority of the local population, having few alternative options, continued to live in the area after the collapse of Roman administration, albeit adopting new and much less archaeologically visible lifestyles. New economic and political structures accompanied a cashless society. The development of post-Roman petty kingdoms in the region is most clearly seen in the Kingdom of Elmet (Loveluck, 2003), its northern boundary approximately contiguous with the southern boundary of the Washlands. The southern Washlands would appear to have constituted the eastern part of a kingdom of Craven (Mashamshire), whereas the northern part of the study area coincides with an early form of Richmondshire.

While many aspects of material culture may have changed little over the centuries prior to the Norman Conquest, a distinction may be made between the period of Anglian settlement and influence from the 5th to the 8th Century and the Anglo-Scandinavian or Viking-Age period of the 9th and 10th Centuries. In the Washlands the distinction is primarily visible in the evidence for burial and ritual, but is sufficiently strong to allow the beginnings of a model against which further evidence may be set.

4.8.1 Range of monument and finds type

It is likely that the farming and economic exploitation of this productive landscape continued during the post-Roman period and that the framework of settlements, boundaries, tracks and fields changed only slowly, if, in the case of many boundaries, fields and tracks, it did at all. Change may have come fastest to the larger settlements and craft centres, those that had been dependent on a Romanized economy, although it is increasingly suspected that these had in any case been in decline during much of the preceding two centuries (Faulkner, 2003). Evidence for houses of the Anglian period in the Washlands is known only from Catterick, although there is sufficient indirect evidence to be confident that the population level of the Washlands was at least of the level obtaining elsewhere in rural North Yorkshire. As elsewhere, the funerary evidence for this area is also sparse, with two chronological focuses, pagan Anglian burials of the 6th Century and Anglo-Scandinavian burials of the 9th or 10th Centuries.

4.8.2 Location and nature of activity

It was during the post-Roman centuries that the settlement of the Washlands (Fig. 4.18) became established in its present pattern, although the extent to which settlement before the Norman Conquest was focused within cores rather than spread thinly across the countryside remains unclear. The chronology and the mechanisms of change remain to be elucidated, but a simplistic interpretation is that during the 5th, 6th, and 7th Centuries settlement retained a pattern that most closely resembled that of the pre-Roman Iron Age. While the essential network of tracks and fields in use during the Romano-British period may have been maintained, there is evidence from elsewhere that discrete settlement was re-established on new sites in the countryside. In the Vale of Pickering and the southern part of the Vale of York, ladder pattern settlement (of conjoined farmstead and house enclosures that could extend over a kilometre or more) appears to have become the norm (Loveluck, 2003). Similar settlement may be present at Street House, Loftus, on the coast of north-east Yorkshire, where a 7th Century burial ground set within a pre-Roman Iron Age enclosure included an aristocratic burial with goldwork (Sherlock, 2008), although whether this pattern was replicated in the Washlands area remains at present unknown. Although the Washlands evidence remains sparse, the presence of extensive cemeteries at Saltburn and Norton-on-Tees (Sherlock & Welch, 1992), and now Street House, all on the coastal fringe of north-east Yorkshire, suggests the presence in the region of a substantial and prosperous population in the post-Roman centuries.

There is no reason to suppose that this area was any less densely populated than anywhere else in North Yorkshire in the post-Roman centuries. Direct evidence for settlement is known only from Catterick, where isolated sunken-floored buildings of probable 6th Century date have been excavated at various locations, including north of the Swale crossing near Dere Street, west of Catterick village, and on the airfield south of Catterick village (Wilson *et al.*, 1996). Larger buildings of timber, which frequently accompanied such structures, have so far not been discovered, and it is not clear whether these attenuated finds represent individual settlements or are part of an extended linear settlement.

Fig. 4.19. 6th Century AD Anglian burial at Scorton, furnished with a bronze brooch and glass bead necklace (photo: Northern Archaeological Associates)

Although direct evidence has yet to be discovered, the burial data rather support a model of settlement being set apart from the centres of activity in the Romano-British period, and in locations that did not sustain settlement in the post-Conquest period. By comparison with the preceding economic and administrative situation, such settlements may have been much more introverted, operating within a smaller range of social contacts, and within a more restricted economic context.

The burial evidence is much more extensive, although mostly found serendipitously. This suggests widespread settlement across the Washlands, although the pattern appears to be random in relation to the present parish and village structure. Burials of 6th Century date are recorded from Scorton (Fig. 4.19), north of Catterick airfield, and from Bainesse Farm, south of Catterick village, while other burials of similar date are also known from the area to the south of Catterick Bridge (Wilson *et al.*, 1996), including sites adjacent to Catterick Racecourse (Moloney *et al.*, 2003). Later Anglian burials are distributed quite widely across the Washlands, including Scorton (Northern Archaeological Associates, 2002), Ailcy Hill (Ripon), and Cloven Hill (Leeming). While it has been suggested that Anglians had an interest in re-using earlier burial sites, it seems more likely that they were interested in prominent landscape features, which might on occasion have been earlier burial mounds. Thus Catterick churchyard is adjacent to the prominent mound of Pallet Hill, Ailcy Hill at Ripon is a distinct natural mound, and Cloven Hill lies close to another natural mound, 'The Mount'. The Stadium at Aldborough, an elongated mound of unknown character, may also have been a focus for Anglian burial.

Fig. 4.20. Masham Cross: a late 8th or early 9th Century columnar monument in Masham churchyard (photo: Blaise Vyner)

It would be dangerous to generalize from the limited evidence, but it may be possible to distinguish an earlier post-Roman settlement pattern in the Washlands from those of the preceding Romano-British period and the ensuing Anglo-Scandinavian period by dint of a greater willingness to occupy the Dere Street corridor. Romano-British settlement adjacent to Dere Street appears to have been restricted to the nucleated settlements that grew up around the Roman forts and towns, while later settlement, as reflected by modern villages, shows a similar lack of interest in the north–south road. The explanation no doubt lay in the existence of the road itself, which, while it allowed social and economic access, also afforded an easy route for robbers and other miscreants. Then, as now, an isolated roadside house was not desirable and what settlement existed was along the road clustered around locations where traders and other services became established. During the earlier post-Roman centuries, the situation appears to have been slightly different and perhaps reflected a smaller and less mobile population combined with the presence of strong social codes; here maybe lies one of the origins of the myth of Merrie England (Hutton, 1994).

From the 8th Century onwards settlement seems to have eschewed the road corridor, although the likelihood that the Roman road remained a significant landscape feature is suggested by the fact that it marks a parish boundary over a distance of 12 km from Norton-le-Clay to Burneston, and intermittently elsewhere. There are differences in settlement and burial patterns that reflect significant social and economic changes. Burials show evidence for a more deeply stratified society under the increasing authority of the Northumbrian kings; Yorkshire constituted the southern part of the kingdom, known as Deira. Viking influence is unusually visible in the Washlands: among the very few burials from this period in England as a whole are a male burial at Wensley, to the north–west of the study area, a burial with a Viking-style sword and spearhead at Camp Hill, Burneston, and a 9th Century female burial with a tortoise brooch at Bedale (Hall, 2003). These burials (and a group of significant Anglo-Scandinavian style sculptured stones noted below), however, represent the only physical evidence for Viking settlers in the Washlands, despite the development of the Viking trading town at York, which would almost certainly have influenced the economic development and the material culture of the Washlands.

The Washlands have had considerable significance in the ecclesiastical development of the region. It was in the River Swale, near Catterick, in around AD 627 that Paulinus baptised the Deirans, probably in the presence of King Edwin (Lang, 2001). The early development of Catterick as a religious centre, however, was halted by Edwin's death in 653. The influence of the Northumbrian royal house is today seen most clearly in the remains of the monastic church established at Ripon around 670, which developed under Bishop Wilfred to become an influential centre for the region. The earliest evidence for activity at Ripon comprises a number of burials at Ailcy Hill that are suggested to date from the 6th Century and occupation activity is very loosely associated with the findspot of the later 7th Century 'Ripon jewel' (Hall & Whyman, 1996). A second phase of cemetery use at Ailcy Hill is dated to the 8th Century, by which time the monastery had been established nearby, although the relationship between the two is unclear. There may also have been early ecclesiastical activity at Ladykirk/St Marygate in Ripon, where an 11th Century pre-Conquest establishment certainly existed (Hall & Whyman, 1996).

The combination of archaeological evidence and topography has led to the suggestion that in the 8th Century a polyfocal ecclesiastical establishment developed within a well-defined area adjacent to the west bank of the Ure at Ripon (Hall & Whyman, 1996). The lack of evidence for earlier activity at Ripon suggests that the settlement was relocated here during the 8th Century. To the east of Ripon, at Kirby Hill, a decorative impost of late 8th or early 9th Century date suggests the existence of an important church (Lang, 2001). At Masham, there is a further significant columnar monument of similar date (Fig. 4.20), perhaps indicating another important ecclesiastical site, while at West Tanfield an early 9th Century decorated shaft combines with a landscape location to suggest a monastic site and at Cundall another significant 9th Century cross shaft is present; none of these sites, however, appears to have been the focus of earlier Anglian activity. Although Ripon's fortunes fluctuated, the influence of the early church across the Washlands was clearly extensive, and Ripon has been suggested as the base for the master craftsman, 'the Uredale Master' (Lang, 2001), who created the more significant sculptures found at Cundall, Masham, and West Tanfield.

A renewed interest in the Christian church is demonstrated in the establishment of sculptured stone monuments of later 9th and 10th Century date, usually in the form of crosses and hogback tombstones, at sites that were later to be occupied by churches. Fragments of sculpture with Sigurd tale motifs from Ripon and Kirby Hill (Bailey, 1980) demonstrate the continuing cohesion of motifs and craftsmen. These monuments are significant in that their locations are those of surviving villages. Whether or not there was nucleated settlement in the Anglo-Scandinavian period, the fact that the church sites were the focus for ritual activity from the 9th Century suggests that settlement was also re-focusing within the framework that is recognizable today.

Scattered pagan Anglian-period rural settlement is suggested by a thin general distribution of burials, the few house sites discovered at Catterick perhaps reflecting the concentration of 20th Century archaeological endeavour rather than the urban aspirations of the Washlands population of the period. In many places in rural North Yorkshire there is evidence for Viking influence in the 9th and 10th Centuries, in the form of occasional burials and in sculptured stone monuments. In summary, Ripon was the base for the early church, but its influence across the Washlands is reflected in a number of high quality stone monuments that indicate an early ecclesiastical focus in many of the settlements. These suggest that it was in these last two centuries before the Norman conquest that most of the familiar settlement pattern was first established.

4.9 The later Medieval period (AD 1066–1540)

The settlement pattern of Medieval and later times appears to have been established during the later pre-Conquest period, with an early ecclesiastical focus in many places that, at some stage, became nucleated settlements. The nature of settlement and land use in the Washlands from the Norman Conquest through to the period of the Dissolution of the Monasteries is less well known than for many other areas of North Yorkshire, for a variety of reasons. The Washlands area is lacking in significant religious institutions, although it is fringed by the great Cistercian abbeys of Fountains and Jervaulx to the west and Byland to the east. The influence of the monasteries was most clearly felt through the pattern of grange farms that extend along the valleys of both the Ure and the Swale (Burton, 2003). One Medieval establishment of note was the Hospital of St Giles by Brompton Bridge (Fig. 4.21), which was established beside a crossing of the River Swale some 2 km upstream of Catterick (despite the place name it is uncertain whether there was a bridge; if so it was later superseded by the bridge at Catterick). This appears to have been an Augustinian establishment that was in existence before the end of the 12th Century and continued until around 1440, its importance perhaps diminished by the establishment of a new bridge over the Swale at Catterick in 1421–22 (Cardwell, 1995).

Similarly, none of the more important manorial centres was located in this area and thus the documentary evidence is less extensive, and less investigated, than elsewhere. Whereas the absence of major castles and religious institutions restricted early antiquarian interest, in recent times there has been minimal archaeological investigation of Medieval rural and urban settlement because of the limited development that has taken place in the historic cores of towns and villages. The landscape archaeology of the Washlands has been similarly neglected, perhaps because of the absence of any local urban population and also because aerial photography has been discouraged in the corridor extending from Dishforth through Leeming to Catterick due to the presence of military airfields. The importance of a holistic review of the landscape has recently been underlined with respect to Yorkshire in general (Moorhouse, 2003). So far as archaeological investigation is concerned, therefore, the story is one of potential rather than of achievement.

4.9.1 Range of monuments and finds type

The settlements that have survived to become the major towns of the Washlands, Ripon, Thirsk, Northallerton, Boroughbridge and Bedale, remain largely uninvestigated archaeologically, although it may be anticipated that a wide range of archaeological information remains to be recovered concerning the detail of urban development, the range of buildings present during the Medieval period and the nature of the local economy. Within the wider region only the City of York has been the subject of archaeological investigation on any significant scale, although a number of excavations have thrown light on the small Medieval town of Yarm on the River Tees (Heslop, 1983). Only extended investigation can piece together the picture of development at any urban centre; in future the examination of small areas may allow an aggregate picture to be obtained.

While rural Medieval settlement in the Vale of Mowbray has not been the subject of concerted archaeological investigation (cf. Fig. 4.21), a body of information has been obtained from the lower Tees valley immediately to the north (Vyner, 1990). Various domestic Medieval building types are known from that area, with the suggestion that early construction, chiefly utilizing timber, was superseded by a wider range of building methods and materials (Daniels, 1988). There is a need for archaeological investigation to establish whether similar patterns of construction are visible in the Washlands, and the extent to which they support the suggestion of an early decline in the availability of wood in this area. Notably, the two project palaeoenvironmental sites with significant records of the period, at Sharow (Chapter 3.5) and Ripon South (Chapter 3.7), suggest minimal woodland in the region by late Medieval times. Deserted

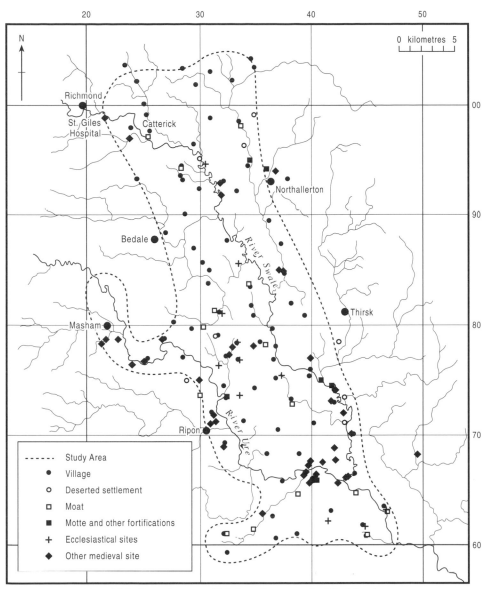

Fig. 4.21. Distribution of Medieval sites in the Washlands area

or shrunken settlements are present in the Washlands in roughly the same proportion as elsewhere in the Vale of Mowbray and the lower Tees valley; they represent untapped reservoirs of information on the use of space in, and development of, village communities. Although continuing arable farming has reduced Medieval earthworks, it is notable that extensive areas of ridge and furrow, earthwork boundaries, lynchets, and other features have been mapped from aerial photographs in and around Nidderdale and in the Yorkshire Dales National Park. Earthworks survive in many areas of the Washlands, especially in the pasture areas to the west, in low-lying parts of the Swale and Ure valleys, and in the many areas of parkland that have not been subject to agriculture. These have the capacity to delineate the Medieval landscape and to provide information on vegetation and crops through pollen sealed in buried soil horizons, as with farmstead buildings at Elton, Stockton-

on-Tees (Innes, 1992) and earthwork enclosure walls on Ravock Moor, Stainmore (Innes, 2001a).

4.9.2 Location and nature of activity

Place-names and documentary evidence suggest that the Washlands in the Medieval period contained less woodland than adjoining areas of North Yorkshire. In this it appears to have shared some of the characteristics of the Vale of Mowbray as a whole, as well as the Cleveland Plain further to the north. On the Pennine foothills to the west and in the Vale of York to the south, woodland appears to have remained much more extensive than in the Washlands (Gledhill, 2003). It was noted in Chapter 3.5 (Sharow Mires) and 3.7 (Ripon South) that widespread late Medieval clearance for arable agriculture took place in the Washlands, possibly in association with a low regard for the conservation of woodland resources. This was a time of political uncertainties surrounding the Crown, which had a physical manifestation in King William's 'Harrying of the North' in 1069–77, and the long-term history of incursion from the Scots that bedevilled northern England until near the end of the 15th Century. The Washlands were particularly affected, since the north–south corridor afforded ready access for invading forces from either of these directions, but evidence for political and any resulting economic and social uncertainty has yet to be recognized in the archaeological record and it is not clear to what extent the visible shrinkage or desertion of Medieval settlements was the result of warfare, plague or tenurial change.

In the Washlands, from the late 12th Century, a dispersed rural population may have increasingly coalesced in nucleated villages and the developing market towns, a trend that may have increased during the 13th Century. There is evidence from this period for the development of planned villages, such as Catterick (Daniels, 2002; Fig. 4.22). Market towns developed at the same time: Boroughbridge received a charter in 1165 and Thirsk was another early establishment, although across the Washlands as a whole, including at Topcliffe, Pickhill, Burneston, Masham, Bedale and Northallerton, market status was acquired mostly during the 13th Century. North of Bedale there is a conspicuous gap in the development of market settlements, while a number of those in the central area may never have been sustainable (Britnell, 2003).

Communications during the Medieval period appear to have been more constrained than previously, with silting and course variations affecting the larger rivers and little apparent interest in the use of water transport in this inland area of North Yorkshire. While it has been suggested that the Roman road system continued to provide a backbone for transport, within the Washlands there is perhaps more evidence that a renewed system of roads developed in relation to changing distribution of settlement (Daniell, 2003). It is not clear that the direct routes (later resurrected by the Turnpike trusts) were maintained. Instead (by way of examples), diversions of the Dere Street route through Ripon are suspected, a route between Leeming and Catterick (Low Street) became important and another, from the south towards Richmond, crossed the River Swale *c.* 2 km upstream from Catterick, near the above-mentioned Medieval hospital at St Giles (Cardwell, 1995). Furthermore, only the general alignment of the route from Healam Bridge up Wensleydale was preserved by later roads and it is at least probable that the Roman road up the eastern side of the Vale of Mowbray was completely lost before the end of the Roman period.

Rural industries are also not well evidenced in the Medieval archaeology of the Washlands. The area is poor in extractive resources, although there was iron to the east and lead in the Yorkshire Dales to the west. Timber, clay and surface stone and rubble from the river bottoms provided the staple building materials until the advent of fired clay products. Judging by the evidence from north-

Fig. 4.22. Planned village at Catterick: a Washland village set around a green, distinct from the linear arrangement of 18th century inns and other service buildings that were established alongside the Great North Road, nearby to the east (photo: Blaise Vyner)

east Yorkshire and the east coast, fired clay roof tiles and the use of bricks and tiles for fireplaces and chimneys was promoted by the Medieval religious houses, creating a prodigious demand for such products. The more general use of brick and tile as construction materials, however, did not develop until the 17th Century. One industry that was locally important in the Medieval period was the production of pottery. There were pottery kilns in the Hambleton Hills area, east of Thirsk, while kilns of 13th Century date have been excavated at Winksley, to the west of Ripon (McCarthy & Brooks, 1988), and clay deposits have been worked since the 1830s at nearby Littlethorpe (Brears, 1971). Wood for charcoal and timber crafts may have been in limited supply in the Swale valley, but more plentiful along the Ure and to the west. Mixed farming is likely to have been the mainstay of the agricultural economy since at least the pre-Roman Iron Age; mapping of the earthwork evidence east of the Yorkshire Dales National Park area would be a valuable exercise that could elucidate the Medieval agricultural processes of the area as well as its settlement history.

In conclusion, the Medieval landscape and below-ground archaeology of the Washlands remains a neglected resource, with the spectacular castles and monasteries lying outside the area. The mostly modest villages, however, have origins in the immediate post-Conquest period, if not before, and are set in a landscape that, away from the arable core of the Washlands, retains the earthwork remains of the agricultural systems that sustained them during the Medieval period. The history of the individual village components, not least the church centres, remains to be examined in detail and related to the surrounding countryside.

4.9.3 Finds from the project

The Swale–Ure ALSF project has made a small contribution

to the archaeological record of the late Medieval period in the Washlands. Discoveries were made in the uppermost sediments at Ripon South Quarry (Chapter 2.6.4), which have also provided a wealth of palaeoenvironmental evidence, reinforced by radiocarbon dates showing sedimentation between the 13th and 15th Centuries AD (Chapter 3.7). The finds included the sole and heel-part of the upper of a hand-made shoe, found in 2003 while recording the sections (Chapter 2.6.4); the Brown and Potter quarry staff subsequently found a further half dozen shoes in this deposit (Plate 4.2; Fig. 4.23). Rebecca Shawcross (Northampton Museum and Art Gallery) was able to determine, from the narrow waist of the sole, the pointed toe and the slightly asymmetrical sole, that the original shoe dates from the late 14th Century. It is quite large and so probably belonged to a man. Also found in the uppermost deposit at Ripon South, but of unknown date, were two attached pieces of wood of uncertain purpose (Fig. 4.24). Together, these finds illustrate the potential survival of organic material in riverine locations, in recent years more commonly instanced in the more extensive Trent gravels (Knight & Vyner, 2006).

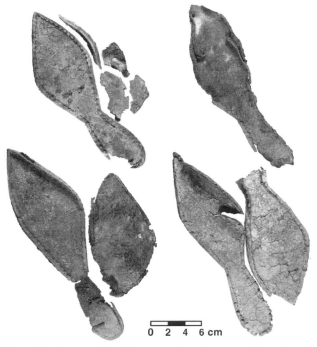

Fig. 4.23. Some of the Medieval shoes found at Ripon South (see also Plate 4.2)

Fig. 4.24. Wooden object from Ripon South, found in association with the shoes (dismantled in second view)

5   Synthesis

5.1 Introduction

This chapter provides an overview of the diverse findings that have arisen from the Swale–Ure Washlands ALSF project, synthesizing them and placing them into a wider context. As the wealth of information in Chapter 3 indicates, the principal thrust has been the study of palaeoenvironmental evidence, building on what was previously known about post-glacial ecological evolution in northern England east of the Pennines. An important part of that prior knowledge came from palaeobotanical studies of the North Yorkshire Moors (Simmons *et al.*, 1993; Atherden, 1999; Innes, 1999), which lie to the east of the Washlands, preventing the Swale and Ure from flowing directly to the North Sea. Comparison of the abundant new palaeobotanical data from the Washlands (see Chapter 3) with that area is valuable, although the upland nature of the latter means that differences would be expected. Previous pollen data from the central Yorkshire lowlands and the eastern flanks of the Pennines have also been used for comparative analysis. The age ranges and major components of the pollen data recovered in this project, which provide a template for much of the interpretation of landscape history presented in this chapter, are shown in Table 5.1. The systematic analyses of molluscan and insect faunas have provided useful supplementary information of a type applied comparatively rarely in this region hitherto. Indeed, some notable new molluscan records have been established, particularly from the former glacial lake basin at Snape Mires (Chapter 3.8).

Another important strand of the research undertaken has been the geomorphological mapping of landscape features resulting from the last glaciation and, more especially, its demise, as well as the record from the post-glacial rivers. These have left sediments and geomorphological features that can be used to reconstruct their evolution as they adapted to the newly exposed post-glacial terrain, the ensuing development of interglacial forest and then the advent of agriculture and ever increasing human impacts. This type of data has been presented and discussed in Chapter 2, along with analyses of gravel content and other aspects of the sedimentary record, generally available for study only as a result of aggregate extraction. In this chapter such information will be used to reconstruct the physical context for the ecological evolution of the region since deglaciation, within which an increasingly influential human presence can be recognized. The last-mentioned must be reconciled with the archaeological evidence

reviewed in Chapter 4, to which modest additions have been made during the life of the project, both directly and as a result of the allied ALSF project on the Thornborough Henges and their cultural environment and significance (http://thornborough.ncl.ac.uk/; cf. Harding, 2000b).

This synthesis will be organized in approximate chronological sequence, charting what can be determined about the Late Quaternary evolution of the research area and the formation of the Washlands as they exist today. This is underpinned by new dating evidence, principally using the well-established radiocarbon method, there being 57 new dates instigated by the project (Chapter 3.1.6; Table 3.3; Appendix I). The desire to use a second dating proxy led to attempts, by the optically stimulated luminescence (OSL) method, to obtain age estimates for the last exposure to daylight of quartz grains in Washlands sand and gravel deposits. This proved largely abortive, since the vast majority of the sand grains sampled proved to have inadequate electron trapping qualities for retention of the necessary signal (see Chapter 2.1.2; Appendix II). Subsequent attempts to use the same technique to date sand grains in other Pennine rivers have met with the same outcome (Yorke, 2008) A further successful dating method utilized was amino acid racemization (AAR) geochronology of molluscan fossils, a pioneering technique based on a novel methodology being developed at the University of York (Appendix III). While the results generally reinforce ideas of age derived from radiocarbon and biostratigraphy, the greatest value of this exercise is probably the impetus it has given to developing the methodology, these being some of the first Holocene results to be obtained. When further AAR dating has been carried out on other sites, providing a larger pool of comparative material, the value of the results from this project (Chapter 3.7.7; Appendix III) should be reassessed.

The pre-Quaternary geological evolution of the Washlands, while of considerable importance, is a topic covered elsewhere (see Chapter 1; Plate 1.3). Little is known about the majority of Quaternary time in this part of Britain; the evidence was removed by the glaciers and ice sheets of the last (Late Devensian) glaciation. Within the northern (Ouse) part of the Humber drainage catchment, traces of earlier Quaternary cycles are preserved only on the northern fringes of the Humber estuary, in the form of fluvial deposits of a late Middle Pleistocene palaeo-Foulness drainage system (Halkon, 1999, 2003; Schreve, 1999). Contrastingly, recent work in the Trent suggests that fluvial evidence in the southern Humber catchment, beyond the reach of Devensian glaciation, dates back over 500,000 years (White *et al.*, 2007; Bridgland *et al.*, in press a). In the Washlands, the last ice sheet would undoubtedly have advanced across a landscape bearing the scars of many previous Pleistocene glaciations, although each one would generally have removed evidence of the one before. Furthermore, the Pennine valleys result from polycyclic processes, with interglacial fluvial, lacustrine and terrestrial environments created between the various glaciations but leaving no surviving evidence of their former presence. The same fate awaits the Holocene evidence studied here when (or if?) the ice returns. The morphology of the sub-drift (rockhead) surface provides the sole clue about Washlands geomorphology during the last (Ipswichian) interglacial.

Borehole investigations within both the main river valleys of the project area have proved rockhead at considerable depths, revealing buried palaeo-valleys (Powell *et al.*, 1992; Cooper & Burgess, 1993; Frost, 1998). These buried valleys are infilled with mixtures of lacustrine, fluvial and glacial deposits of unknown age. There is an indication, beneath the overprint of subglacially eroded channels, that the buried valley of the pre-glacial River Swale flowed via the downstream end of the Wiske valley into the proto-Tees (Chapter 1; Plate 1.4). It is difficult to reconstruct this former, pre-glacial valley system, particularly towards the north of the area. The buried valley of the Ure extends north of Ripon in the same direction and roughly along the same axis as the present river but at elevations near present sea level (Powell *et al.*, 1988; Cooper & Burgess, 1993). A similar valley has also been detected beneath the Swale, joining the Ure channel to the south-east of the present confluence (Cooper, 1983). Rockhead contours also indicate a complex set of buried channels south of the present Ure, where there is a buried valley associated with a proto-Nidd system that was very different from the present-day river, the latter resulting from diversion along the ice margin at Knaresborough (Powell *et al.*, 1988). The lack of any evidence of a former Ure system further upstream may be of significance, since it has been proposed that the original Ure course extended east from around Leyburn towards Bedale and Leeming Bar. Here, as the Swale is approached, an enigmatic channel has been discovered beneath Snape Mires that appears to have flowed in the opposite direction to the present River Swale (Frost, 1998; Plate 1.4). This is probably a subglacial 'tunnel valley' feature, perhaps formed at a time during deglaciation when the ice front lay a few kilometres 'downstream' in the Vale of York. Alternative explanations are overdeepening by glacial erosion of soft Permian bedrock and collapse of subterranean gypsum karstic features (see Chapter 2.8.2).

The basal sediments in these buried valleys are sometimes of a fluvial, non-glacial character, although few detailed investigations have been completed and there are no specific age determinations. Given that they underlie tills of known Late Devensian age, they have been defined as Pre-Devensian (Cooper, 1983), although this should

perhaps be restated as pre-Late Devensian, allowing for possible deposition during the early parts of that stage. The Devensian ice completely covered and buried the pre-glacial Washlands landscape, so that after deglaciation there were significant changes to the drainage pattern, caused in part by subglacial erosion and in part by deposition, both subglacially and extra-glacially, by the ice and by meltwater.

At the maximum of the last (Late Devensian) glaciation, *c.* 26,000–19,000 BP (also termed the Dimlington Stadial, or the 'Last Glacial Maximum'(LGM)), the British ice sheet reached a maximum thickness in the Pennines of several hundred metres (Mitchell, 1991c, 2007; Aitkenhead *et al.*, 2002; Catt, 2007), although it would have thinned across the Washlands, where there is geomorphological evidence for an ice margin declining in elevation along the sides of the Vale of York towards the well-defined terminal moraines at York and Escrick (Kendall & Wroot, 1924; Penny, 1964; Frost, 1998; Chapter 1.4.3). Indeed, the upland of the North York Moors, between the research area and the North Sea, was never glaciated during the Devensian (cf. Kendall & Wroot, 1924; Gregory, 1962, 1965; Evans *et al.*, 2005).

The detailed story of the Washlands begins, therefore, with the evidence for the last glaciation and its demise.

5.2 Ice in the Washlands

Much of the landscape of the research area was covered, during the Late Devensian glaciation, with a veneer of till. Depositional landforms are also prevalent across much of the area, providing valuable records both of glacial limits and of deglaciation, although these have to be pieced together from careful scrutiny of the geomorphology, reinforced by sedimentological evidence from quarry sections and rare natural exposures.

5.2.1 The Last Ice Sheet

The Washlands lie at a critical position for understanding Late Devensian ice-sheet dynamics in northern England, being located where a major ice mass, flowing southwards down the Vale of York, met and coalesced with a glacier flowing east out of the Yorkshire Dales, predominantly from Wensleydale and its tributaries (Fig. 5.1). The glacial geomorphological patterns defined by the resultant landforms clearly demonstrate that the two ice masses can be interpreted as palaeo-ice streams (cf. Stokes & Clark, 2001; Clark & Stokes, 2004; Chapter 1.5). The Vale-of-York ice stream was itself composite; the main ice stream can be traced up-ice towards Stainmore, via the Vale of Mowbray and the middle Tees, to source areas in the Cumbrian Mountains and south-west Scotland (cf. Clark *et al.*, 2004a; Evans *et al.*, 2005). However, in the vicinity of Darlington, this stream coalesced with ice flowing southwards along the coast of north-east England, which also included a component sourced in the Lake District and

Age ¹⁴C BP	Stage	Nosterfield			Newby Wiske	Marfield	Sharow	Ripon North
		F45	SH1	Flasks 69				
Modern						Cyperaceae	Poaceae *Calluna* Cyperaceae	
500 --- --							• • • • • • •	
L. Medieval	Late							
1000 --- --	Holocene						*Corylus*	
E. Medieval						⊕ >	• • • • • • •	
1500 ---- ----								
Roman		Cyperaceae					Poaceae	
2000 --- --		*P. lanceolata*					Cyperaceae	
Iron Age		• • • • • • •	Cyperaceae				*P. lanceolata*	Poaceae
2500		*Alnus*	• • • • • • •				• • • • • • •	*Alnus*
---- ----- -----		*Corylus*	*Alnus*					*Corylus*
3000		• • • • • • •	*Corylus*				*Alnus*	
Bronze Age		*Pteridium*	Poaceae				*Corylus*	⊕
3500		Cyperaceae	• • • • • • •				*Quercus*	
		• • • • • • •						
4000		*Corylus*	*Alnus*					
---- ----- -----		*Pinus* ⊕	*Corylus*					
4500		*Betula*	*Betula*		⊕		• • • • • • •	
Neolithic			*Quercus*		*Alnus*			
5000	---- ----- ------		• • • • • • •		Cyperaceae			
5500			*Alnus*		• • • • • • •			
6000	Mid		*Quercus*		*Alnus*			
	Holocene	N	*Pinus*		*Quercus*			
6500		O	*Ulmus*		*Ulmus*			
Late			*Corylus*		*Tilia*			
7000		P						
Mesolithic	---- ----- -----	O	• • • • • • •		• • • • • • •			
7500		L	*Corylus-Pinus*		*Corylus*			
		L	*Quercus-Ulmus*		*Pinus*			
8000		E			• • • • • • •			
8500	Early	N			*Corylus*			
---- ----- -----			⊕ >	⊕	• • • • • • •			
9000	Holocene	N		*Corylus*	*Betula*			
Early		O		• • • • • • •				
9500					• • • • • • •			
Mesolithic				*Betula*	*Juniperus*	*Betula*		
10,000 -----	---- ----- -----	⊕	⊕ >	• • • • • • •	Cyperaceae	• • • • • • •		
	Loch			Cyperac.-Poac.	• • • • • • •	Poaceae		
10,500	Lomond			• • • • • • •		Cyperaceae		
	Stadial			Cyperaceae				
11,000	---- ----- -----			*Betula*		NO POLLEN		
Upper	Lateglacial			*Juniperus*				
11,500	(Windermere)					*Juniperus*		
Palaeolithic	Interstadial					*Betula*		
12,000	---- ----- -----							
12,500	'Older Dryas' Stadial							
Age ¹⁴C BP	Stage	F45	SH1	Flasks 69	Newby Wiske	Marfield	Sharow	Ripon North
		Nosterfield						

In the F45 column (Nosterfield), the vertical text "NO POLLEN" spans the central portion of the column.

Ripon South	Snape Mires					Langland's Farm	Thornton's Plantation	Stage	Age cal. BC / AD
	IL6	IL12	MH1	MH3	TG2				
Poaceae Cereal-type *P.lanceolata* *Calluna*								Late Holocene	1000 AD
									AD
									BC
									1000 BC
									2000 BC
Corylus ☺							*Alnus* *Corylus* *Betula*		3000 BC
					☺ >	*Alnus*			4000 BC
						Quercus Tilia Ulmus Alnus	*Corylus Alnus Betula Quercus Ulmus*	Mid Holocene	5000 BC
						Alnus Pinus Corylus			
									6000 BC
		Alnus				*Pinus Corylus*			
		Corylus	TUFA	TUFA		*Betula Corylus*	*Betula Corylus*	Early	7000 BC
Corylus			TUFA	*Corylus*	*Corylus*			Holocene	8000 BC
Betula		☺		MARL	☺	*Betula Cyperaceae*	*Betula Cyperaceae Poaceae*		9000 BC
		Betula ☺	*Betula* ☺	*Betula*					
			NO POLLEN	Cyperaceae				Loch Lomond Stadial	10,000 BC
		☺ >	Cyperaceae					Lateglacial (Windermere) Interstadial	11,000 BC
			Betula Juniperus	NOT STUDIED					
		☺ >	Cyperaceae Poaceae					'Older Dryas' Stadial	12,000 BC

Table 5.1. Correlation of new pollen data from the Swale–Ure Washlands project.

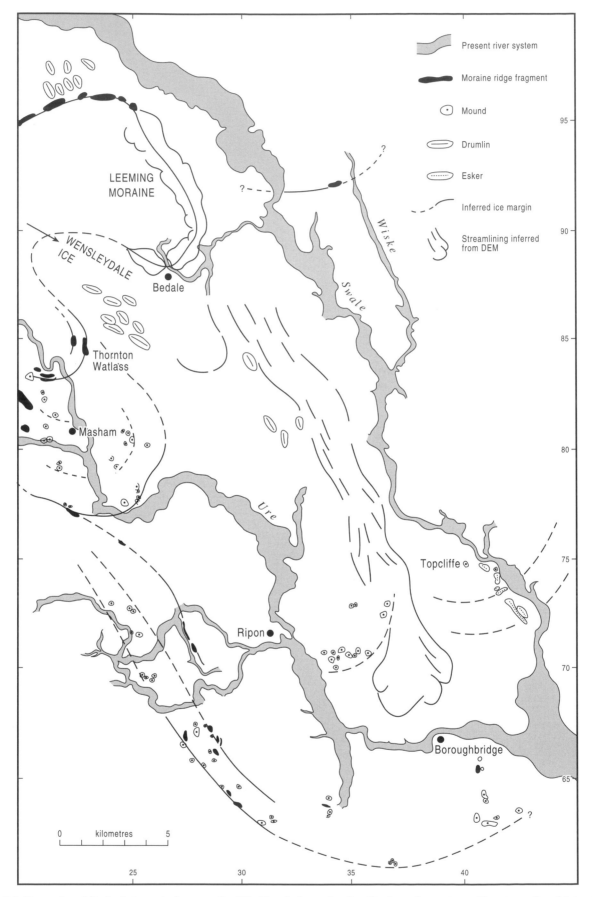

Fig. 5.1. Recessional limits interpreted across the Washlands from the distribution of moraines. The streamlined inter-lobate moraine is inferred from DEM of the area. Ice from Wensleydale is well differentiated from that in the Vale of York.

south-west Scotland, from where it had flowed eastwards through the Tyne Gap, meeting ice from the Cheviots and eastern Scotland (Evans *et al.*, 2005). Evidence for palaeo-ice streams from the Pennines can be found along the western limit of the Vale-of-York ice stream, where there was a complex interaction with eastward-flowing ice emanating from the dales, particularly the Wensleydale ice stream (Mitchell, 1994). All of this can be observed from the erratic composition of the different tills across the region (Fig. 1.3). Thus the Vale-of-York ice stream was a combination of ice from different sources; it incorporated ice from the western mountains (Lake District and Southern Uplands) that had flowed through Stainmore, where it joined ice from Teesdale in the northern Pennines and ice flowing southwards across County Durham from the Tyne Gap, Cheviots and Scotland, before finally meeting local ice from the Yorkshire Dales.

The delimitation of Late Devensian ice sheet margins within the Washlands has been based on field mapping of landforms and associated sediments, primarily till (Chapter 2.2). Understanding of the significance of these, however, requires an appreciation of their context within the wider area, particularly with respect to the maximum extent of glaciation within the Vale of York and West Yorkshire. To the south of the Washlands, the terminal moraines at Escrick and York were long regarded as defining the maximum extent of a large ice lobe that occupied the Vale of York at the LGM (see Chapter 1.4.3). These moraine ridges converge westwards towards the Pennines to form a composite lateral margin around Allerton Park, south of Boroughbridge, where the resultant topography is linked with the south-easterly diversion of meltwater channels, of the River Nidd at Knaresborough and the River Wharfe at Wetherby (Kendall & Wroot, 1924; Cooper & Burgess, 1993). This former ice limit can be extended into the Washlands, where it is marked by further large meltwater channels and moraine ridges, such as near Ripley between Ripon and Harrogate (Kendall & Wroot, 1924; Palmer, 1966, 1967; Cooper & Burgess, 1993; Chapter 2.2.2.1; Plate 2.1). It can then be traced north-westwards along the western flank of the Pennines towards Masham. If this marks the LGM limit, the implication would be that the high ground between Nidderdale and Wensleydale was not covered by ice. However, this is in contradiction to the established LGM drift limit as defined on the Soil Survey 1:625000 Map (cf. Catt, 1991a, b) and used for the BRITICE database (cf. Clark *et al.*, 2004a). Along the western margin of the Vale of York, the maximum drift limit of the Late Devensian ice sheet corresponds with the outer margin of the Escrick moraine, before turning sharply southwards at Knaresborough and then westwards just south of the Wharfe valley (Plate 1.2).

The established reconstruction includes, as part of the LGM ice margin, a conspicuous end moraine complex at Arthington, in Wharfedale (Penny, 1974). Conversely, it has also been proposed that this moraine marks the LGM limit of a separate Wharfedale outlet glacier, rather than

the main LGM ice sheet (Penny, 1964; Catt, 2007). This alternative interpretation appears to have been confirmed by recent investigations of glacial deposits down-valley from the moraine, which have demonstrated weathering and, indeed, temperate (interglacial) pedogenesis of the deposits, suggesting that they pre-date the last glaciation and that during the LGM the Wharfe glacier was not contiguous with the Vale-of-York ice (Barber, 2006). This reinterpretation may also explain the existence of highly weathered till in the Harrogate area, for which a pre-Devensian age has been suggested (Edwards, 1950; Cooper and Burgess, 1993; Cooper and Gibson, 2003).

In addition to the debate about details of the Pennine margin of the Vale-of-York ice sheet, there is compelling evidence that this ice extended further south, beyond the York–Escrick moraine system, towards Doncaster (ending near Wroot: Fig. 5.2). The proposal by Gaunt (1981) that there had been a surge of ice southwards across proglacial Lake Humber is now generally accepted, although open to further discussion and research (cf. Straw, 2002; Bateman *et al.*, 2001, 2008; Evans *et al.*, 2005; Murton *et al.*, 2009). Recent excavations in the Aire valley at Ferrybridge (SE 471243), south-west of York, have exposed till overlying a loess that was dated by OSL to 23,300 ± 1500 BP (Bateman *et al.*, 2008), thus placing the glacial event in the Late Devensian and confirming that the Vale-of-York ice lobe extended south of the Escrick moraine. The unpublished PhD research of Barber (2006) included work on a site at Moss Carr (SE 367263), to the east of Leeds, where weathered sands, silts and clays with organic remains were observed below a till in which glaciotectonic structures indicated an north-eastward ice flow direction. Barber interpreted the till as an ice marginal deposit of Late Devensian age. The consequence of both these additions to the story is to extend the overall width of the Vale-of-York ice lobe southwards and westwards of the well-defined moraine ridges at Escrick and York, which can no longer be regarded as the maximum extent of the Late Devensian ice sheet; instead they can be presumed to mark pronounced still-stands.

Within the Vale of Mowbray and the Vale of York, interaction between local Pennine ice and the more distantly sourced ice was dynamic, with temporal fluctuations in boundary positions between the two ice streams (Fig. 5.2). The reported presence of Shap Granite erratics (Fig. 1.3) as far west as Kirkby Malzeard (Raistrick, 1926) and observed at Easby, near Richmond, during field mapping indicates that, at some stage during the last glaciation, Vale of York ice dominated flow across all of the Washlands, abutting against the eastern flank of the Pennines. The rare granitic clasts recorded from the Nosterfield fan (Chapter 2.6.2; Table 2.2) may be a further reinforcement of this point. This north–south flow direction is confirmed by the drumlins at Brough Hall, to the west of Catterick village; within the main part of the Vale of York, the overall north–south topographic trend clearly reflects this dominant ice stream flow (Fig. 2.11).

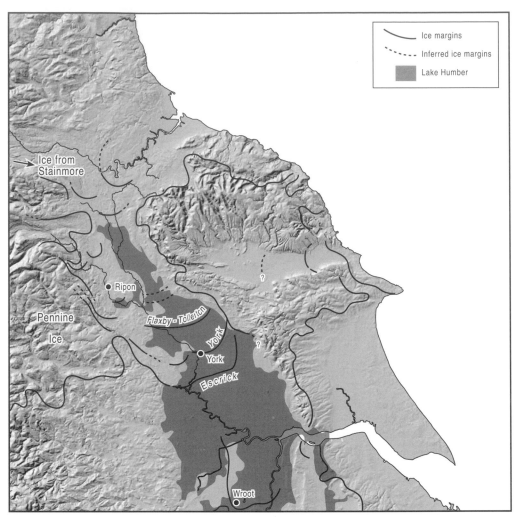

Fig. 5.2. Glacial geomorphology of the Washlands and surrounding region based on erratic content of different till units and proposed ice limits associated with different source areas. The base map is a hill-shaded relief image from the Land-Form PANORAMA™ digital terrain/elevation model © Crown Copyright Ordnance Survey. An EDINA Digimap/JISC supplied service.

However, the geomorphology of the Washlands also demonstrates that Pennine ice, particularly from Wensley-dale, had sufficient impetus to push outwards into the Vale of York. Evidence for this can be seen from north-west–south-east orientated drumlins around Thornton Watlass (Figs 2.10 & 5.1), which suggest that Pennine ice was able to enter the Vale of York and push the main flow eastwards to a zone of convergence along the Sherwood Sandstone escarpment (line of the A1 road). This is confirmed by the widespread distribution of a surface till with a Pennine clast provenance throughout the Washlands (Powell *et al.*, 1992; Cooper & Burgess, 1993), suggesting that this flow pattern occurred late in the glaciation.

The presence of eskers within the Vale of York, partic-ularly within the Swale catchment around Topcliffe (Fig. 2.23; Plate 2.1), reflects the compound origin of the main Vale-of-York palaeo-ice stream (Fig. 5.1). Studies from similar geomorphic situations, where individual ice lobes have become sutured to form one lobe, indicate that ice flow,

meltwater and sediment trajectories were directed towards the former lateral margins, now medial suture lines, forming 'inter-lobate glaciofluvial complexes' (Punkari, 1997a, b; Mäkinen, 2003). Such esker systems are often associated with ice margin retreat as the ice mass disintegrates into its constituent lobe structure. Again, this would have concentrated meltwater and sediment to the former margins, as represented in the medial (suture) location; it would also have influenced the pattern of deglaciation by controlling where the different ice streams 'unzipped' as the Vale-of-York ice retreated northwards during deglaciation. Thus the major esker system mapped by the BGS (Cooper & Burgess, 1993; Frost, 1998; Fig. 2.23) and reported by BRITICE (Clark *et al.*, 2004a) is more correctly a complex inter-lobate moraine system defining boundaries between Vale-of-York and Wensleydale ice. Further north within the Vale of York there may be a third component associated with northern County Durham ice (Figs 5.1 & 5.2).

5.2.2 Establishing a chronology for the glaciation

There are few available dates to constrain the last British ice sheet in northern England (Huddart & Glasser, 2002a; Evans *et al.*, 2005). This is particularly true within the Washlands, where attempts, as part of this project, to establish a chronostratigraphy by using OSL to date glacial outwash sequences (the Marfield gravels and the Nosterfield fan deposits: see Chapter 2) were unsuccessful (Appendix II). The nearest dated sequences are the glacial sediments exposed at Dimlington, on the Holderness coast (cf. Rose, 1985; Evans, 2002a; Catt, 2007; Chapter 1.5) and ^{14}C and OSL dates associated with Glacial Lake Humber (Gaunt, 1981; Bateman *et al.*, 2001, 2008; Chapter 1.5). These data constrain the period of maximum glaciation in the region and the timing of the ice-blockage of the Humber Gap to form a proglacial lake.

The glacial lithostratigraphy of the East Yorkshire coast is one of the best studied sequences associated with the Late Devensian glaciation (Rose, 1985; Huddart & Glasser, 2002a; Evans *et al.*, 2005; Catt, 2007). In Holderness, two tills have been defined associated with the main Late Devensian ice sheet in this area, distinguished on a number of different lithological parameters, including erratic content; the lower, more extensive Skipsea Till is characterized by erratics from eastern England, including Cheviot rocks, whereas the upper Withernsea Till has an erratic suite from the Lake District and south-west Scotland (Catt, 1991a, 1991b, 2007; Chapter 1.5). At Dimlington, two radiocarbon dates from stratified lacustrine organic silts preserved in lenses below these tills and above the pre-Devensian Basement Till (Evans *et al.*, 2005; Catt, 2007) give a ^{14}C calibrated age range of 21,475–22,140 cal. BP (cf. Bateman *et al.*, 2008), thus constraining the main Late Devensian ice advance along this coast to after that time (see Chapter 1.5 for further discussion). Recently published OSL dates from Ferrybridge, of 23,300 ± 1500 BP from loess below till and 20,500 ± 1200 BP from silts above the till, constrain the age of the ice advance within the Vale of York to between these dates (Bateman *et al.*, 2008). This suggests that the main ice advance down the Holderness coast was coincident with a more extensive advance in the Vale of York and Humberhead lowlands.

These dates also have important implications for the chronology of Glacial Lake Humber. The OSL dates constraining the age of the till exposed at Ferrybridge are both from sediments underlying Lake Humber beach deposits. In fact the lithostratigraphical sequence at Ferrybridge indicates that there was a lengthy period of colluvial deposition under periglacial conditions prior to the emplacement of gravels attributed to the lacustrine beach, since a third OSL date, obtained from sands within the beach unit, gave an age of 16,600 ± 1200 BP (Bateman *et al.*, 2008). The elevation of these gravels at *c.* 30 m suggests that they can be correlated with the 'Upper Littoral Sands and Gravels' of Edwards (1937) and related to the upper level of Glacial Lake Humber, which had been accepted

previously as dating from *c.* 25,000 BP, based on the bone found at Brantingham (Gaunt, 1974; see Chapter 1.5). The new date is thus much younger than expected, suggesting either a separate later development of the high-level lake or the existence of an ice dam across the Humber Gap for a longer period of time than hitherto realised.

Given the present uncertainties of radiocarbon calibration and the paucity of dates, these various age estimates are difficult to synthesize, although they suggest that the glacial advance in eastern England occurred earlier in the Dimlington Stadial than hitherto envisaged, perhaps related to a surge along the east coast (Sejrup *et al.*, 1994, 2005; Carr, 2004; Carr *et al.*, 2006).

In reconstructions of the last glaciation, the advance of the ice sheet along the Yorkshire coast can be regarded as contemporaneous with ice in the Vale of York reaching the York and Escrick moraines (e.g. Catt, 1991a, 2007; Evans *et al.*, 2005). There are, however, differences between the glacial sequences in the two areas. Unlike at Holderness, only a single till has been reported from the Vale of York (but see Chapter 2). This till, which is extensive across the Vale, has an erratic suite characterized by Lake District rocks, including Shap Granite, as well as a more local Pennine suite. In comparison, at the coast the extensive Skipsea till contains east-coast erratics, including material from the Cheviots (Evans, 2002a; Catt, 2007). This suggests that, at the time of their deposition, the coastal area was dominated by ice flowing from further north (the 'east-coast ice stream'), which had sufficient power to block western ice (the Stainmore/Vale-of-York ice stream) and divert it southwards at Darlington into the Vale of York (hence the western erratics). The presence of Withernsea Till, with Shap erratics, above the Skipsea Till in East Yorkshire indicates that at some stage the east-coast ice withdrew, allowing Stainmore ice to extend into and flow along the present coastal area. Shap erratics have been widely reported from offshore of the Tees estuary (Kendall & Wroot, 1924).

The situation is more complex within the Vale of Mowbray and the lower Tees, where multiple tills have long been reported (cf. Francis, 1970), which suggests that correlations between the coastal sequences and the Vale of York may be premature. Previous research has also reported a different till sequence from the Cleveland coast north of Flamborough Head, where a till with Lake District erratics (= Withernsea Till?) is overlain by another that is characterized by Cheviot erratics (Radge, 1940). This sequence is also reported from sites within the lower Tees, such as Rockcliffe Scar (NZ 313085), where four tills were reported in the 19th Century (Fox-Strangways *et al.*, 1886; cf. Francis, 1970). This site, which has not been studied in detail since then, has a lower till with Lake District erratics and an uppermost till with Cheviot erratics. Surface erratics of eastern provenance, including Scandinavia, have also been reported from Cleveland, extending into the upper Wiske catchment (Harmer, 1928; see Chapter 1, Fig. 1.3). This would suggest that the first ice movement through the lower Tees was the Stainmore ice stream, with a later southerly ice flow into the area, associated with the east-coast ice stream, that does not correlate with the established till sequence from Holderness (Catt, 2007). An alternative explanation invokes erosion of previously deposited till by the later east-coast ice stream, such that the upper Withernsea Till incorporates material deposited previously, thus inverting the erratic stratigraphy in Holderness, such that Shap erratics found on the surface in the Tees area and in Holderness would have been reworked into the later uppermost tills. This explanation, first proposed by Radge (1940) to explain the different erratics found in the upper till of the lower Tees, would negate the value of erratics as a means for distinguishing tills from different source areas and would make correlation across the region extremely difficult.

The observation, as part of this project, of two tills at the Scorton and Catterick quarries (Chapter 2.7.2) adds important information to the regional reconstruction. At Scorton, the sequence shows a basal grey-blue till overlain by thick outwash gravel and further overlain, towards the northern extremities of the workings in 2005–8, by a second upper red-brown till and further gravel. Erratics from the lower till suggest ice-source areas in the Lake District and southern Scotland, whereas in the upper till and gravels there are clasts of porphyry that indicate an origin from the direction of the Cheviots (see Chapter 2.7.2). A similar upper till was also observed in the present working quarry at Catterick village. Thus a till of north-eastern provenance has been observed well into the Vale of Mowbray, extending the limit of incursion by coastal ice further south than previously envisaged.

A general sequence of events to explain the till distribution between Holderness and the Vale of York thus involves the changing importance of different ice streams with time. From the geological evidence, in terms of number of tills and erratic content, it appears that the first advance of ice into Holderness deposited the Withernsea Till with Cheviot erratics (cf. Catt, 2007). This blocked the lower Tees and diverted the Stainmore ice stream into the Vale of York. As the coastal ice became less important, Stainmore–Tees ice was able to reach beyond the present coast, from where it flowed southwards along Holderness, depositing Skipsea Till with Lake District erratics (cf. Catt, 2007). This western-sourced ice then withdrew, possibly in relation to a shutdown of Stainmore as an ice conduit (Mitchell & Riley, 2006; Mitchell et al., 2008). Geomorphological evidence for the cessation of this palaeo-ice stream can be found in the Vale of Eden, to the west of Stainmore, where an earlier convergent flow pattern, clearly expressed in the drumlins towards the Stainmore pass, is replaced by a second, later ice-flow direction, determined from drumlin orientation northwards towards Carlisle (Letzer, 1978; Mitchell, 1994; Mitchell & Riley, 2006). This final flow direction reflected the increased dominance of the accumulation area in the western Pennines (Mitchell, 1994), with a westward extension of the ice divide towards the Lake District

contributing to flow down the Vale of Eden to the Solway Firth (Evans et al., 2005; Mitchell & Riley, 2006). Also the source area for the Wensleydale ice stream (Mitchell, 1994), the growth in influence of the western Pennine ice centre (at the expense of the Stainmore ice stream) was probably responsible for the readvance of ice to Marfield and the Leeming moraine, here termed the Wensleydale Readvance, which is thought to have been the last event associated with the glaciation of the Washlands (Chapter 2.2.1.1). The incursion of the east-coast ice stream into the Vale of Mowbray, as indicated by the upper till at Scorton and Catterick, is more difficult to place chronologically; dating is required to resolve this issue and establish a chronology but this will require more extensive regional research outside the Washlands in north-east England.

5.2.3 The pattern of deglaciation

Recession of the ice margin in the Vales of York and Mowbray is marked by various moraine ridges and hummock systems. The Flaxby–Tollerton moraine (Cooper & Burgess, 1993) crosses the Vale south of the project area and can be traced westwards from south of Boroughbridge (Fig. 5.2). Within the Swale catchment, mapping has revealed evidence for a further recessional limit, identified by moraine ridges at Ainderby Steeple, just to the west of Northallerton (Chapter 2.3.2.2). There is also geomorphological evidence suggestive of a number of recessional limits within the Washlands, particularly in the Ure valley (Fig. 5.1). Recessional ice margins, many originally noted by Raistrick (1926), are identified at Copt Hewick–Ripon, West Tanfield–Mickley, Aldburgh–Swinton (noted by Palmer, 1967, albeit with no details provided) and at Marfield, the last-mentioned associated with the Wensleydale Readvance.

Extensive spreads of meltwater gravels were formed at this time, invariably being left as the highest and best developed of the aggradational terraces in the various valleys. Ice-dammed lakes were also an important feature of the landscape of the Vale of York during the Late Devensian (see below), with deglaciation generating huge volumes of meltwater but also depriving some of the largest lakes of their ice barriers, leading to their drainage. During the Wensleydale Readvance, meltwater was an important influence on the recently deglaciated landscape of the Washlands, with progradation of sands and gravels into the lakes, such as that at Snape (see Chapter 2.8.2), from meltwater channel systems along the southern flank of the Wensleydale glacier (compare Figs 5.1 & 5.3).

As noted above in relation to the presence of eskers in the Vale of York, ice from different source areas 'unzipped' into individual flow segments, concentrating meltwater along the inter-lobate zone. It seems that the main Vale-of-York ice and Wensleydale ice began to divide just north of Boroughbridge, with the first individual stage of Wensleydale retreat being marked by the morainic mounds around Copt Hewick (see Chapter 2.2.1.1). DEM study has

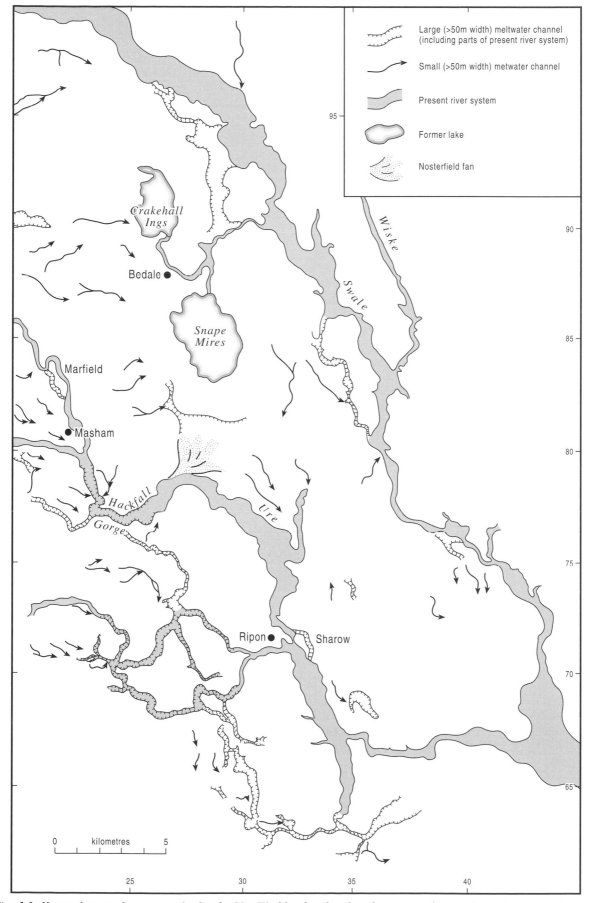

Fig. 5.3. *Key meltwater features in the Swale–Ure Washlands. Abandoned sections of river channel are also shown.*

indicated that the superficial deposits north of the Ure near Boroughbridge have a markedly lobate form (Fig. 5.1), identifying a major inter-lobate fan marking the initial separation of the two major ice streams.

A final stage in the deglaciation in the Washlands is marked by meltwater channels and moraines along the northern side of the former Ure valley near Catterick Garrison (Chapter 2.2.1.1), where they define the northern limit of a glacier flowing out of Wensleydale. This cuts across the north–south trending drumlins near Brough Hall, Catterick, indicating that the Vale-of-York ice had already retreated when Wensleydale ice readvanced to the Leeming Moraine. From Leeming, the southern limit of this ice lobe can be traced westwards towards Newton-le-Willows (Fig. 2.11), where it swings southwards towards the present Ure Valley, near Clifton Castle. Further south the moraine ridges at Marfield (Inner Hills), associated with the oscillations of a dynamic ice margin, suggest a subsidiary lobe related to the Wensleydale Readvance (Chapter 2.2.1.1; the Wensleydale ice lay to the west of the green-coloured ridges depicted on Plate 2.1).

As the ice retreated, the Pennine rivers were (re)established. Spectacular channels were cut by huge volumes of meltwater, such as at Hackfall, near Ripon, in this case issuing from the shrinking Wensleydale glacier. This same meltwater laid down the extensive fan gravels exploited by the quarries around Nosterfield (Chapter 2.6.2). By this time the river had already incised significantly into the glacial deposits, as represented at Marfield (Plate 5.1). The occurrence of large fossil ice wedge casts in the Nosterfield gravels indicates the presence of permafrost during fan deposition. The sedimentology and location of the Nosterfield fan reflect its formation during deglaciation, from outwash associated with a nearby limit of Wensleydale ice. The ice wedges were formed syngenetically, as the fan prograded under periglacial conditions. Although there are no dates to confirm this, the early basal radiocarbon dates from the Nosterfield Flasks 69 site, coupled with its stratigraphy and palaeoenvironmental data, indicate that the fan was formed well before the Loch Lomond Stadial (Chapter 3.2); indeed, the stadial is represented within the lower part of the basin infill at that site (Fig. 3.5). The pre- Loch Lomond Stadial radiocarbon date on the basal sediments from shaft F44 (Appendix I) supports an early data for fan formation. Associated with this is the more equivocal evidence from the margin of Snape Mires, where the presence of numerous small irregular ridges might represent former lithalsas, reflective of site-specific periglacial conditions (Chapter 2.8.2).

From similar ice wedge casts in gravels across north-western Europe, environmental reconstructions suggest formation of continuous permafrost across the exposed land surface as the ice sheets retreated. Palaeoclimatic reconstructions suggest a mean annual air temperature (MAAT) range of ≤ -8°C (cf. Huijzer & Vandenberghe, 1998; Vandenberghe *et al.*, 2004) and mean temperature of the coldest month of below -20 °C, together with a high annual temperature range and increased continentality (Vandenberghe *et al.*, 2004). Permafrost expansion continued through deglaciation until *c.* 19,000 years ago there is widespread evidence of degradation (thermokarst) well before the pronounced climatic warming of the Lateglacial period (Vandenberghe *et al.*, 2004). A similar sequence of conditions may well have prevailed in England but the paucity of dating constraint prevents detailed correlation. An important point to note, however, is that the early rivers were flowing across a periglacial landscape with extensive continuous permafrost, which would have had major hydrological implications for surface flow and channel pattern development. The presence of permafrost and tundra vegetation, coupled with low precipitation (with much of it as snow), would all have influenced runoff and the resultant channel pattern, giving rise to a diversity of river types (cf. Vandenberghe, 2001). For example, low flow in permafrost areas with well-developed tundra vegetation cover may have led to single-channel meandering fluvial regimes. Only in situations where there was a high sediment flux would braided channel patterns, typical of gravel-bed rivers, have developed (Vandenberghe, 1993, 2001, 2003; Kasse, 1998).

5.2.4 The 'Yorkshire Lake District'

Lowland areas just beyond the edges of ice sheets are invariably the locations of melt water lakes, repositories for the huge amounts of water released from melting ice during the spring and summer seasons. For much of the LGM, while the Washlands were submerged beneath the ice, a vast lake existed in the area now forming the lowermost reaches of the Ouse–Trent system: Lake Humber (Fig. 5.2). This lake is thought to have drained between 14,600 and 13,000 cal. BP (Metcalfe *et al.*, 2000). During deglaciation, as the ice-front retreated northwards and into the Pennines, there were periods of relative stability when the limit of glaciation lay in the Washlands, as indicated by the various moraine ridges discussed above (see also Chapter 2). At these times meltwater lakes formed, such as the notable one that occupied the Snape Mires area (Chapter 2.8.2; Fig. 5.3). Its relative longevity is indicated by the thickness (>18 m) of the glacio-lacustrine clay it left behind. After the ice disappeared and the glacial lake drained, numerous smaller, shallower water-bodies remained (Fig. 1.5), in which Lateglacial and early Holocene sediments, repositories for the palaeoenvironmental evidence documented in Chapter 3, have been preserved.

5.2.5 Glacial Sequence: summary

The sequence of glaciation can be summarized as follows:

- Stage 1: An early advance into the Vale of York, with the main flow maintained by ice entering eastern England from the Lake District and southern Scotland through the Stainmore Gap. This ice extended over the whole of the Washlands, confining Pennine ice within the dales.

- Stage 2: The main Vale-of-York ice stream became less dominant, allowing Wensleydale ice, sourced in the western Pennines, to expand into the Washlands and coalesce with the main Vale-of-York ice along the line of the present A1 road.

- Stage 3: General ice retreat from the Washlands and separation into two ice masses by 'unzipping' along former coalescent margins. This pattern is marked by a series of recessional ice limits across the Washlands, particularly of local ice as it retreated back into Wensleydale. The evidence from Marfield indicates dynamic fluctuations of the ice margin during retreat.

- Stage 4: Following withdrawal of the ice in the Vale of York, Wensleydale ice advanced to form the Leeming moraine and produced complex thrusting at Marfield (a local sequence of events for this section is described in chapter 2.6.1 but cannot be extended to a larger area). The cross-cutting of north–south drumlins by moraines and meltwater channels along the northern margin of this Wensleydale ice indicates that Vale-of-York ice was no longer present. This identifies a specific event termed the Wensleydale Readvance.

- Stage 5: There is also evidence of a readvance of the east-coast ice stream into the lower Tees, with the presence of an upper till at Scorton containing Cheviot erratics, extending as far south as Catterick to form the upper till at the quarry there. This may have occurred at the same time as the Wensleydale Readvance.

- Stage 6: Following these readvances, the ice sheet again retreated, forming a series of terminal moraines during its westward progression back into the Yorkshire Dales (uspstream of the study area).

In summary, the geomorphological evidence for the glaciation of the Washlands is more complex than previously envisaged, raising a number of issues that cannot be resolved from this small area. Intensive research over a wider region will necessary before this information can be fed into glaciological models (cf. Evans *et al.*, 2005; Clark *et al.*, 2006).

5.3 The early post-deglaciation (latest Devensian) rivers

During deglaciation the rivers of the Swale–Ure Washlands would have carried considerable volumes of water released by the melting ice and there would have been large peak floods during the spring snowmelt season. Charged with this meltwater, the rivers would have enjoyed high energy levels and therefore have been capable of transporting increased amounts of bed-load at a time when much

sediment was being dumped by the melting ice. Flowing in multiple (braided) channels, as is typical of sediment-charged rivers (e.g., Schumm & Kahn, 1972; Bridge, 1993), they would have carried mainly gravel and sand, which they deposited to form mobile bars separating the channels. In this dynamic state, the rivers would have been unstable, migrating frequently across the valley floor in response to flow variations and thus supporting only limited vegetation. 'Braided' rivers of this sort, characterized by large volumes of sediment and flowing in multiple, unstable channels, have modern-day analogues in glaciated landscapes, such as in Iceland and Greenland.

This period of enhanced flow during deglaciation is readily recognized in many northern British valleys, being represented by a relatively high-level 'glacial outwash' terrace, generally the highest member of the terrace sequence in the valley and often of much greater size and vertical separation than later terraces. This is true in the Wharfe (Howard *et al.*, 2000b), although in this case there are two such high-level terraces (see Fig. 1.7). Another example of an uppermost 'glacial outwash terrace' is seen in the River Tees near Darlington (Mills & Hull, 1976; Bridgland *et al.*, in press b; see below).

In the Ure, the Marfield and Nosterfield surfaces represent multiple 'glacial' gravel terraces (Plate 5.1), although whether either is the full equivalent with the 'outwash' terraces in other valleys is uncertain. In addition, field mapping in the Ure has revealed morphological features at high and intermediate levels that are interpreted as erosional terraces, cut by the meltwater-charged river during ice-retreat and revealing progressive incision into the recently-deglaciated landscape (see Chapter 2.4). These erosional terraces are well represented in the Ure system, such as at Masham (Plate 2.4B), North Stainley (Plate 2.4C) and Newby Hall (Plate 2.4D), as well as west of Ripon at Galphay Lane (Plate 2.4A), where they might represent an early Ure course, the Laver having perhaps formed in part of an abandoned section of the early post-glacial Ure valley (Chapter 2.4). Comparable features are less extensive in the Swale, but are well represented around Catterick, where they are higher than the 'outwash' terrace exploited by the gravel quarries (Chapter 2.6; Plate 2.4E).

Erosional terrace features of this sort have rarely been recognized in Britain. It is uncertain whether they are genuine 'strath' terraces, originating from a purely erosional fluvial regime, or whether they are veneered by thin water-laid sediments that have been missed by geological mapping. There might well be thin pebble/cobble lags on these terraces but these would be difficult to identify as such and to distinguish from a random scattering of clasts weathered from underlying glacial diamicton. The most convincing evidence in support of these features as genuine parts of the fluvial sequence is their disposition, adding higher elements to lower-level aggradational terrace sequences (see Chapter 2, Plate 2.3), sometimes also occurring at levels comparable with aggradational terraces elsewhere, and the fact that their surfaces are readily

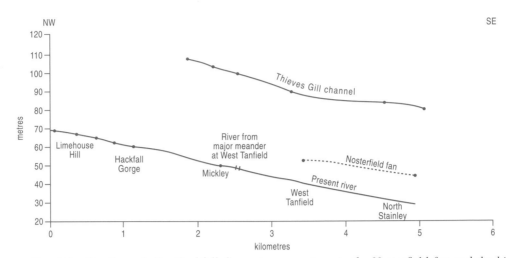

Fig. 5.4. Long profile of the Ure through the Hackfall Gorge in comparison to the Nosterfield fan and the high level early meltwater channel of Thieves Gill.

distinguished from unaltered glaciated terrain, which is characteristically undulating and dotted with depositional and meltwater features. Something has clearly flattened these areas and the only plausible agents would seem to be the meltwater-charged early deglacial rivers.

The formation of gravel-free erosional terraces during a period of deglaciation, as implied by the above interpretation, seems counter-intuitive; this was supposed to be a time of gravel-bed, outwash-charged, braided rivers, such as can be seen issuing from modern-day ice sheets. One possible explanation is that the profusion of fine-grained lacustrine and other glacial deposits mantling the recently deglaciated landscape might have led, locally, to fluvial bed-load lacking the familiar sand and gravel composition that is seen in most aggradational terrace sequences.

As erosional features, these terraces cannot be dated directly, but the timing of their formation is broadly constrained by their respective height above river. The highest such features, related to the Thieves Gill Channel (Fig. 5.4; Chapter 2.2.2), are higher above the river than the 'glacial terrace' deposits at Marfield, which date from late in the LGM. This should probably not be interpreted as an indication that the highest erosional terraces are older than the Marfield deposits; they could not have formed before the till, in which they are eroded, was emplaced by the Devensian ice and then revealed at the surface by glacial retreat. Their greater height in comparison with the Marfield 'glacial terrace' perhaps points to non-parallelism of downstream long profiles, as might be expected in a valley subjected to recent glaciation and the differential glacio-isostasy that would have occurred because of dissimilar ice thicknesses across the region.

Similar erosional terraces associated with deglaciation have been mapped on the recent BGS Leeds sheet (Cooper & Gibson, 2003), suggesting that they might be a previously overlooked geomorphological phenomenon of the Vale-

of-York catchment. One possible factor, peculiar to that catchment, that might relate to their formation is that, as deglaciation progressed, the newly reformed River Ouse–Trent system was rapidly incising into the soft sediments left by Lake Humber. This lacustrine basin, which for a period represented a separate base level, would have initially been a knick-point in the post-glacial Ouse–Trent system that would have been rapidly removed by incision. Rapid incision following removal of the knick-point might have manifested itself as repeated lowering of the valley floor in the Washlands, as represented by the erosional terraces of the Ure and Swale. An association with the drainage and incision of the Lake Humber basin would be in good agreement with the indication, from their position high within the landscape, that these features date from very early in the recorded sequence of the Washlands: soon after deglaciation. That would also concur with the earliest dates from the sedimentary archives, such as the Lateglacial deposits at Marfield (Chapter 3.4) and the Early Holocene terrace deposits at Ripon (Howard *et al.*, 2000a), which show that the river was already constrained within its present valley and flowing at < 15 m above its present level by those times. In addition, the constrained and incised channels of the two rivers near their confluence (and further downstream) also point to marked downcutting at around the Pleistocene–Holocene transition (Taylor *et al.*, 2000; Bridgland *et al.*, in press b; Chapter 2.4).

The highest erosional terraces are even higher above the fan gravels at Nosterfield than they are above the Marfield 'glacial terrace' (see above); the altitude of the Nosterfield fan relative to the Ure is difficult to determine with accuracy, since the modern valley floor sweeps past it in a south-eastwards direction, rapidly losing height, perhaps because this reach is just downstream of the Hackfall Gorge (Fig. 5.3), which marks a modern-day knick-point where the Magnesian Limestone escarpment is crossed. The river descends from *c.* 70 to 30 m O.D. in the region of this knick-point, over just 5 km downstream distance (Fig. 5.4), whereas the fan surface falls from *c.* 52 m O.D. near the escarpment to below 45 m O.D. in its distal areas. The fan is thus around 15 m above the modern Ure (Plate 5.1).

Despite the failure of OSL dating of their contained sand grains (see above), the age of the Nosterfield fan gravels is constrained by overlying organic sediments filling the various depressions in the Flasks, which are placed in the Lateglacial Interstadial by radiocarbon dating (Chapter 3.2.2; Appendix I). Syndepositional ice-wedge casts (Chapter 2.5.2) show that the fan was deposited subaerially under intensely cold conditions. The overlying Lateglacial Interstadial sediments show that this episode occurred during the latter part of the Dimlington Stadial; the fan could only have formed after this part of the lowland was deglaciated. It was clearly formed by sediment-charged water flowing out from the Hackfall Gorge. Whether ice was still present further upstream is less certain. There is little in the gravel content to suggest an immediate glacial source (Chapter 2.5.2), but it has been well noted above that the glaciation of Wensleydale was locally sourced, so the clast information merely confirms this point and does not preclude the presence of ice. The fan is much closer to modern river level than the high-level Thieves Gill Channel, which might suggest a significant separation in time, during which the valley downstream from the escarpment was incised.

5.4 Palaeoenvironments and Landscape Evolution

5.4.1 A false start to the current interglacial – the Lateglacial Interstadial

The Lateglacial period was characterized by major climatic fluctuations that occurred over a range of temporal scales (Atkinson *et al.*, 1987; Coope *et al.*, 1988; Lowe *et al.*, 1994; Huntley 1999; Björk *et al.*, 1998; Walker *et al.*, 2003), some of which were of the order of only a few centuries, but which led to considerable and often very rapid environmental changes. These fluctuations are clearly expressed in the changing vegetation of this transitional period, with rapidly responding, successional plant communities reflecting the pace of environmental change.

Ice retreat after *c.* 18,000 years ago (cf. Innes, 2002a) prompted a transition from barren polar desert to snow bed and sedge-tundra conditions as solifluction ceased, allowing the colonization of raw skeletal soils by Poaceae, Cyperaceae and *Salix herbacea*. This pioneer grass–sedge tundra flora was joined by open-ground taxa of taller stature, such as *Rumex*, *Artemisia* and *Thalictrum*, as conditions improved and soils became increasingly stable. Pollen records from the wider Swale–Ure region representative of this initial Lateglacial Stadial phase

(GS-2) are scarce and poor dating control for this period makes their recognition uncertain. None of the sites from the project has fossil-bearing sediments of this age. The early radiocarbon date of 16,713 ± 340 ^{14}C BP from the base of the kettle-hole at Kildale Hall (Keen *et al.*, 1984; Innes, 2002b), on the edge of the North York Moors *c.* 25 km to the north–east, is almost certainly too old because of hard water error; however, there are few other sites from which deglaciation can be dated. Somewhat further afield, pollen data from this period are seemingly represented in the eastern Vale of Pickering at Star Carr (Day, 1996) and in the southern Vale of York at Tadcaster (Bartley, 1962). In these cases the sediments are fine-grained silts and clays, often laminated, with a very low organic content because of the sparse nature of the vegetation cover and the short time since deglaciation. Although some *Betula* and *Pinus* are represented from the beginning of pollen deposition, this is probably because of long-distance transport, with any local birch growth attributable to *B. nana* (dwarf birch), which persists today under the specialist environmental conditions in upper Teesdale (Squires, 1978). The open, broken-ground flora of this early phase diversified as the period progressed, increases in herb taxa such as *Helianthemum* indicating a more closed, stable grassland type on soils becoming richer in nutrients and humic material. High *Helianthemum* frequencies, which are characteristic of this period (Pennington, 1977), are recorded from sites in the Yorkshire area (Blackburn, 1952; Hunt *et al.*, 1984). Plant succession and increasing climatic improvement after about 13,800 ^{14}C BP prompted the patchy spread of low shrubs like *Empetrum, Juniperus* and *Hippophaë* (sea buckthorn), but plant cover was still mainly grass and tall herb steppe. These early pollen assemblages were characterized by low taxa diversity. Shrub cover continued to thicken and in places tree-*Betula* seems to have been present before *c.* 13,000 [14]C (*c.* 15,000 cal.) BP, particularly in the south of the area and at sheltered locations (Innes, 2002a).

The abrupt rise in temperature recorded in the Greenland ice-core data at *c.* 13,000 ^{14}C BP (Lowe *et al.*, 1994) marks the start of the Lateglacial Interstadial (GI-1e), a warm phase of *c.* 2000 years duration (Fig. 1.2). Such was the rate and magnitude of this temperature rise that it could be regarded as marking the switch from a glacial to an interglacial climatic regime, were it not for the later, very severe, climatic reversion. It was, however, a major temperate interstadial. This sharp thermal rise is reflected clearly in lacustrine sites in the wider Swale–Ure region, with deposition changing from inorganic to slightly organic sediments, with a greatly increased micro- and macrofossil content. Although none of the project sites go back this far, all the dates for initial deposition of organic sediments in the east and north of the wider region, e.g. 13,045 ± 270 ^{14}C BP from The Bog, Roos (Beckett, 1981), and 13,042 ± 140 ^{14}C BP from Seamer Carrs (Jones, 1976a), are virtually identical and may be taken as representative of this important change throughout the area. The remarkable enhanced temperatures after 13,000 ^{14}C BP are demonstrated by dramatic changes in populations of insects at that time, these being a highly sensitive and highly mobile proxy that responds very quickly to environmental change (Lowe & Walker, 1997b). At some sites it seems that organic sedimentation and vegetational development was delayed, as at Routh Quarry in the Hull valley, where organic silts began to accumulate at 12,595 ± 80 BP (Gearey & Lillie, 2001). The oldest sediments identified in this project, the basal pollen zone at Mill House MH1 (MH1-a), is an analogue for the Routh Quarry data, as the period before *c.* 12,330 ^{14}C BP at Mill House 1 shows very open steppe-tundra environments unlike the steady succession to open woodland witnessed at the great majority of sites in the region. Local factors must have been operating at these two sites to delay environmental change until several centuries into the Interstadial. Perhaps the locations, in large lakes in the Snape Mires basin and the Humber lowlands, may have affected the taphonomy of pollen recruitment to the sites from distant vegetated areas.

More typically, the rise in temperature at the start of the Interstadial stimulated the expansion of a rich vegetation cover, although there would have been considerable time lags before community succession and soil maturation allowed vegetation to reach its full potential, with the development of closed canopy woodland. This was only achieved about 11,500 ^{14}C (*c.* 13,500 cal.) BP, fitting well with the *Betula* maximum at Mill House, by which time temperature had already fallen well below its 13,000 ^{14}C BP maximum (Walker *et al.*, 1994; Table 5.1). The initial interstadial vegetation was herbaceous steppe tundra and tall herb associations on developing soils, with taxa such as *Artemisia*, *Helianthemum*, *Rumex* and *Thalictrum*, as well as sedge and grassland, into which *Empetrum* and *Juniperus* spread quickly. *Juniperus* and *Betula* were present from the start of the phase and expanded rapidly, with copses of tree-*Betula* becoming established in many places, such as at Tadcaster (Bartley, 1962) and Dishforth Bog (Giles, 1992), in a succession to park-tundra. Several lowland sites show this early *Betula* expansion (Innes, 2002a). In many areas, however, *Juniperus* dominance may have continued and in several Lateglacial diagrams a phase of very high *Juniperus* pollen (both percentages and concentrations) up to about 12,500 ^{14}C (*c.* 14,500 cal.) BP is the distinctive feature, as in the Tees valley (Bellamy *et al.*, 1966), the Vale of Mowbray (Jones, 1976a) and the Vale of Pickering (Day, 1996), indicating abundant shrub juniper across much of the landscape. Thin organic deposits that lie below the main Lateglacial Interstadial organic sediments at several sites, such as at Skipsea Bail Mere in Holderness (Flenley, 1984), very probably date to around 13,000 ^{14}C (*c.* 15,000 cal.) BP and show the increase in rich herbaceous vegetation and then shrub and tree-birch pollen associated with this first Lateglacial temperature rise.

The development of increasingly dense *Juniperus* and *Betula* parkland was interrupted by a period of colder climate for a few centuries around 12,000 ^{14}C (*c.* 14,000 cal.) BP (Lowe *et al.*, 1994), episode GI-1d in the GRIP

event terminology for the Lateglacial (Björk *et al.*, 1998; Figs 1.2 & 5.5). Identified at Lateglacial sites in northern England, such as Blelham Bog in Cumbria (Pennington, 1975), this colder phase is distinct in several north-east England pollen diagrams (Innes, 2002a) as a reversal in the vegetation succession, with *Betula* and/or *Juniperus* showing a sharp temporary decline, to be replaced by grasses and herbaceous tundra type communities, before recovering to their former abundance with the return of temperate conditions after 12,000 ^{14}C BP. The dating and biological evidence from project profile Mill House MH1 (Chapter 3.8.3) suggest that zone MH1-c represents this widespread cold climate oscillation, when the rising *Betula* curve reverses and the *Juniperus* curve declines and these taxa are briefly replaced by enhanced Poaceae and Cyperaceae percentages and increases in open-ground weeds.

Although temperatures did not return to the thermal maximum achieved immediately after 13,000 ^{14}C BP, the return to a warmer climate after *c.* 12,000 ^{14}C BP initiated the maximum expansion and development of vegetation communities during the Lateglacial Interstadial across northern England (Innes, 2002a). The millennium following 12,000 ^{14}C BP can be broadly correlated with the main phase of the British Lateglacial (Windermere) Interstadial (cf. Allerød), equivalent to pollen zone II of the traditional British scheme (Godwin, 1975; Chapter 1; Figs 1.2 & 5.5). The expansion of tree-*Betula* woodland is the diagnostic vegetation change of this phase, at least in lowland areas such as the Swale–Ure Washlands, as time lags in ecosystem development and soil immaturity ceased to restrain plant successions. This spread of tree-*Betula* occurs at all the sequences in the region representative of this age and, amongst project sites, is seen at Nosterfield, in the Flasks 69 core (Chapter 3.2.3), at Marfield (Chapter 3.4) and in the MH1 core from the Snape Mires basin (Chapter 3.8.3). The degree to which closed *Betula* woodland became established varied across the region, depending on various environmental factors; in many places only open woodland developed, with spaces in the canopy within which shrub and lower stature communities persisted. In the study area something of a north–south gradient is apparent in the maximum *Betula* percentages achieved in the interstadial woodland maximum around 11,500 ^{14}C BP. Lowland sites in south and east Yorkshire show a full development of birch woods, although these were perhaps quite open, with *Betula* frequencies up to 80% of total land pollen at The Bog, Roos (Beckett, 1981), 70% at Bingley Bog (Keen *et al.*, 1988) and similar high figures at Tadcaster (Bartley, 1962) and Gransmoor (Walker *et al.*, 1993).

In the Tees lowlands, Blackburn (1952) noted that, although birch percentages pointed to locally dense stands of the tree, the persistence of *Helianthemum* and other arctic–alpine herbs throughout her pollen zone II (Allerød Interstadial) suggested open park-tundra rather than closed woodland. This agrees with data from nearby Kildale Hall (Jones, 1977a) and the findings of Bartley *et al.* (1976) in

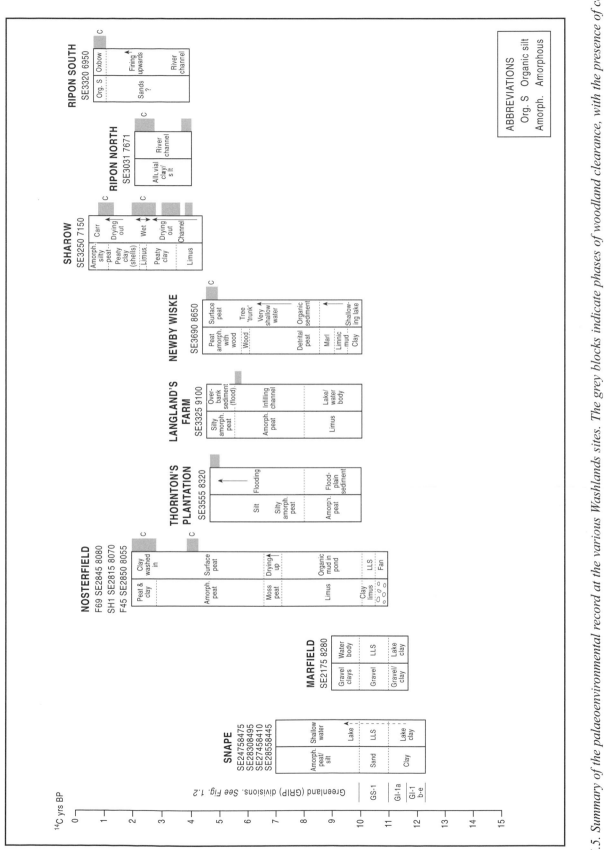

Fig. 5.5. *Summary of the palaeoenvironmental record at the various Washlands sites. The grey blocks indicate phases of woodland clearance, with the presence of cereal-type pollen, indicated by a 'c'.*

south Durham, where, at Thorpe Bulmer, the *Betula* peak is found to be much lower than at Yorkshire sites and indicates patchy park-tundra vegetation with extensive shrub and grassy areas. Thorpe Bulmer is the northernmost site in north-eastern England to show a distinct *Betula* maximum and may well have been close to the northern limit of birch-wood expansion during this period. Further north, in north Durham and Northumberland, *Juniperus* persists to the present day. In the late Interstadial, when *Betula* was dominant in North Yorkshire, *Juniperus* formed characteristic shrub–heath vegetation with *Empetrum* and grass–sedge associations, while *Betula* was very poorly represented (Innes, 2002a), even in the coastal lowlands, as at Bradford Kaims in north Northumberland (Bartley, 1966). Additional to this north–south gradient were the effects of local topographic and edaphic controls, which in places were critical, so that at Willow Garth, on the chalk upland of the Yorkshire Wolds (Bush, 1993), conditions remained open with a grass–sedge tundra environment that included some local *Juniperus* but with very little *Betula*. Similarly, in the limestone areas of the Yorkshire Pennines at Malham Tarn Moss (Pigott & Pigott, 1963), tree-*Betula* may not have been present at all and *Juniperus* and tundra herbs maintained a very open plant cover.

A low amplitude climatic oscillation that has been very widely recognized (Levesque *et al.*, 1993) occurred near the end of this Interstadial maximum expansion of woodland communities, corresponding with Greenland event GI-1b (Lowe *et al.*, 1999; Mayle *et al.*, 1999). Less distinct than the earlier cold oscillation, it still can be seen as reductions in *Betula* pollen percentages and their replacement by *Juniperus* and open-ground taxa, at east Yorkshire sites including Gransmoor (Walker *et al.*, 1993) and Star Carr (Day, 1996). Not previously recognized at inland Yorkshire pollen sites, the fall in *Betula* frequencies in zone MH1-e at Mill House, with increased grass and sedge pollen and the appearance of *Artemisia*, is interpreted as representing this colder episode. Within the present study, the final Interstadial woodland maximum has been recognized at the same three sites mentioned above, Mill House MH1, the Flasks 69 and Marfield. Some variation in the proportions of *Betula* and *Juniperus* may be seen between the profiles, with a greater element of *Juniperus* in the local woodland at Marfield. The full development of the vegetation during this period may be seen also in the wetland plant communities; at the three Swale–Ure project sites, and elsewhere in the region (Innes, 2002a), both the pollen and the other biological proxies show water bodies with extensive aquatic macrophyte populations and high levels of biological productivity.

In Lateglacial Interstadial sediments, pollen from several thermophilous forest trees, notably *Corylus* and *Alnus*, has been found at many sites throughout northern England, including the Yorkshire lowlands (e.g. Keen *et al.*, 1988). The localized presence of these trees in the Lateglacial, although unexpected, cannot be ruled out and is supported by reports of *Alnus* macrofossils from late in the Interstadial

at Willow Garth in east Yorkshire (Bush & Hall, 1987). A strong case against the presence of such thermophilous trees has been made by Tallantire (1992), however, and the recovery of pollen of *Corylus*, *Alnus* and other forest trees from the till beneath the Lateglacial sequence at Skipsea Withow Mere (Hunt *et al.*, 1984) suggests that reworking may potentially be responsible for such pollen records. The incorporation of till-derived mineral material into sediment profiles continued throughout the Lateglacial, as shown by the low organic content of many interstadial limnic deposits and the presence of reworked pre-Quaternary spores in the Lateglacial sediments at the project sites at Marfield and, especially, Snape Mires MH1. Long-distance transport is also a possibility, particularly in the case of *Pinus*. In this work these records are regarded as intrusive and are not considered in the interpretations of site records.

It remains to consider the possible influence of human populations on the environment during the Lateglacial Interstadial. The Upper Palaeolithic archaeological record in North Yorkshire is slight (Chapter 4), as it is for northern England as a whole (Laurie, 2003). There is enough, however, to show that the area was exploited by humans during this period. This is unsurprising, as the productive, mainly open vegetation of the Lateglacial, including widespread wetlands, would have supported considerable populations of large herbivores. The Lateglacial elk skeleton from interstadial sediments at Neasham Fen, in the Tees valley near Darlington (Blackburn, 1952), is an example of the game animals available for Palaeolithic hunters; there are several faunal records from this period to support the contention that the lowlands of the Swale–Ure area were a productive environment with substantial food resources. Evidence of actual hunting activity at this time is available from elsewhere in northern England (Hallam *et al.*, 1973). The presence of humans in the Pennine region before 12,000 ^{14}C BP is shown by cut marks on mountain hare bones from Derbyshire caves, AMS dates from which cluster between 12,000 and 12,500 ^{14}C BP (Housley, 1991). Artefact evidence of human presence becomes available after *c.* 12,000 ^{14}C BP, in the open woodland phase of the Lateglacial Interstadial that terminated at 11,000 ^{14}C BP due to the climatic reversal at the beginning of the Loch Lomond Stadial. Flint artefacts of this age have also been recorded at Skipsea Withow Mere (Gilbertson, 1984) and at Gransmoor (Sheldrick *et al.*, 1997), both in east Yorkshire, and at Victoria Cave, Settle, in the Yorkshire Pennines (Wymer, 1981). In the Vale of Pickering there are several sites with Upper Palaeolithic tools, such as at Flixton (Schadla-Hall, 1987), while less substantial evidence is available from the Yorkshire Dales and, indeed, in the project area (Laurie, 2003; see Chapter 4). People were clearly present in the area throughout the temperate Lateglacial Interstadial.

Considerable levels of microscopic charcoal are present within the interstadial sediments at the three sites in this study that represent this episode (Table 5.1) and also in earlier published data from this period (Innes, 2002a), as at Star Carr in the Vale of Pickering (Day, 1996). Fire must have had an influence on the Lateglacial vegetation, presumably delaying successions towards closed woodland and maintaining more open herb-rich vegetation that would have favoured large grazing animals. Any direct relationship between humans and fire cannot be proved, however, and should not be assumed. Natural fires may well have been common under the often fairly arid Lateglacial climatic regimes. Nevertheless, a human role in altering Lateglacial vegetation through deliberate or accidental initiation of fire remains a serious possibility.

The amelioration of climate, the maturation of soils and the development of woodland are all features of the initial stages of an interglacial (Birks, 1986) and the period from 13,000 to 11,000 ^{14}C BP has all the signs of just such a climatic transition having occurred. As had happened on previous occasions during the Devensian (Huddart & Glasser, 2002b), this episode of temperate climate and post-glacial environmental systems was terminated by a return to an intensely cold climate after c. 11,000 ^{14}C BP, sufficient to cause glaciers to reform in many uplands (cf. Gray & Coxon, 1991), including the Pennines (Mitchell, 1991d, 1996). The Lateglacial Interstadial can thus be viewed as a truncated rehearsal for the full interglacial conditions that were to become established in the Holocene.

5.4.2 Arctic conditions return – The Loch Lomond Stadial

The temperate-climate episode that had begun abruptly at around 13,000 ^{14}C BP proved to be temporary. In fact, gradual cooling began soon after this initial thermal maximum and, although several low-amplitude fluctuations occurred within the two thousand radiocarbon years of the Lateglacial Interstadial, this general cooling trend culminated in a period of harsh arctic climate after c. 11,000 ^{14}C BP. This change might have been brought about by the cooling of the North Atlantic Ocean, with less heat being brought by the Gulf Stream from the tropics to north-west Europe. Indeed, this might have been a negative-feedback response to deglaciation and major melting from the North American and Greenland ice sheets and the input of huge volumes of cold fresh water into the North Atlantic, lowering the salinity of the ocean and impeding the therom-haline circulation, the northward flow of warm currents and the system of heat transfer (Broeker et al., 1989; Moore, 2005; Broeker, 2006). Coleopteran (beetle), chironomid (non-biting midge) and ice-core records indicate a rapid switch to this cold event, as temperatures fell by several degrees centigrade (Coope et al., 1998; Lowe et al., 1994, 1995; Lowe & Walker, 1997b; Mayle et al., 1999). The cold phase was too short-lived for the regeneration of an ice cap over the Pennines, but the renewed cold and an increase in effective precipitation in the first part of the episode induced re-establishment of small glaciers in the highest parts of the Yorkshire uplands (Gray & Coxon, 1991; Mitchell, 1991d, 1996).

This very cold interval lasted from c. 11,000 to c. 10,000 ^{14}C BP, with the most severe conditions in the latter half (Lowe et al., 1994). Macrofossil remains of Dryas octopetala (mountain avens) characterize sediments of this cold phase in Scandinavia, where the early research on Lateglacial palaeoecology took place. Dryas pollen and macrofossils are much less common in the Loch Lomond Stadial of northern England and, indeed, were not recorded at any project sites, although this plant survives to the present day in uplands such as the Pennines and Snowdonia. Other herbaceous taxa are much more characteristic of this cold phase in northern England; many arctic–alpine plants flourished here during this period of glacial climate, being highly tolerant of cold and wind, and their pollen records are diagnostic of this tundra-type vegetation.

The warmth-loving plants that had established themselves during the temperate interstadial, developing Betula woodland even as temperatures were declining (see above), were driven south again by the arctic climate and replaced, first by dwarf shrub vegetation, such as Juniperus, Salix herbacea and Empetrum, and, finally, by steppe-tundra (as seen in the project pollen diagrams from Marfield, the Flasks 69 and Snape Mires MH1). The climate in this cold phase was also rather arid (Lowe et al., 1994) so that, as well as Poaceae and Cyperaceae, an enhanced Artemisia pollen curve (Tipping, 1985) is one of the most diagnostic features of this period (e.g., see the Marfield diagram, Fig. 3.10). Other typical herbs of open grassland or bare soils well represented in pollen diagrams include Thalictrum, Rumex, Plantago maritima and the Chenopodiaceae, Caryophyllaceae and Saxifragaceae families (see Snape Mires MH1, Fig. 3.22). Pollen diagrams from Tadcaster (Bartley, 1962) and Bingley Bog (Keen et al., 1988), in the south of the region, are typical in having very high frequencies of Artemisia at this time, plus a wide range of other open-ground arctic–alpine herbs at lesser values. Similar pollen stratigraphies occur to the north at Kildale Hall, in the Leven valley (Keen et al., 1984), Seamer Carrs, in the Vale of Mowbray (Jones, 1976a), and Gormire Lake on the western flank of the North York Moors (Blackham et al., 1981). There appears to be little significant regional variation in the Loch Lomond Stadial vegetation history across the region. The abundance of this suite of ruderal weeds in Loch Lomond times is confirmed by detailed macrofossil records from key sites in east Yorkshire, such as Skipsea Withow Mere (Hunt et al., 1984) and Willow Garth (Bush, 1993).

The extreme cold conditions that the Loch Lomond Stadial brought throughout northern England, with open, poorly vegetated ground and unstable frost-broken soils, is manifest, given the deposition of inorganic sediments in lakes formed in kettle holes and other basins. Erosion of soils from basin catchments makes such clastic layers virtually ubiquitous in limnic sequences, usually taking the form of silty clays with low pollen concentrations, unless older pollen, often Empetrum, has been reworked with the soil. Sometimes the sediment is a coarser-grained sand or even a gravel, such as at Marfield (Chapter 3.4), with no preserved microfossils. A clastic layer of this sort is typically sandwiched between the organic facies of the preceding Lateglacial Interstadial and the following Holocene.

Sedimentation within river systems such as the Swale and Ure usually constitutes sands and gravels, although some basal organic facies within palaeochannel fluvial sequences contain Loch Lomond Stadial fossil assemblages, as in the southern Vale of York (Dinnin, 1997a). The cold, arid and windy conditions of the Loch Lomond Stadial led to the aeolian erosion and redistribution of fluvioglacial sands, creating very extensive coversand formations in the southern Vale of York (Gaunt *et al.*, 1971). At Cawood, a peat sealed by coversand is dated to 10,469 ± 60 ^{14}C BP (Jones & Gaunt, 1976), peat within coversand near York is dated 10,700 ± 190 ^{14}C BP (Matthews, 1970) and a peaty soil sealed by aeolian sands at West Moor (Gaunt *et al.*, 1971) provides a maximum date for the start of wind transportation in the Vale of York of 11,100 ± 200 ^{14}C BP. In the Vale of Pickering, at Seamer Carr (Schadla-Hall, 1987), a blown sand layer showing signs of cryoturbation occurs above a peat containing Upper Palaeolithic flint artefacts and is sealed by early Holocene peat. Dates from the buried peat range between 10,200 and 11,300 ^{14}C BP, indicating a late Loch Lomond Stadial age for sand emplacement. These dates conform with an age of 10,413 ± 210 ^{14}C BP for organic muds at nearby Flixton, which yielded *Equus* bones, flint artefacts and a Loch Lomond Stadial pollen assemblage.

These coversand ages are in good agreement with dates constraining inwashed clastic units of Loch Lomond Stadial age in dated Lateglacial limnic sequences in Yorkshire. For example, at Routh Quarry, in the Hull valley (Lillie & Gearey, 2000), peat composed of the arctic moss *Homalothecium nitens* formed between 11,260 ± 75 ^{14}C BP and 10,740 ± 75 ^{14}C BP, the latter date being a maximum age for a Loch Lomond Stadial clay that rests upon the peat. Loch Lomond Stadial clays formed at The Bog, Roos (Beckett, 1981), between 11,220 ± 220 ^{14}C BP and 10,120 ± 180 ^{14}C BP, and after 10,700 ± 70 ^{14}C BP at Willow Garth in east Yorkshire (Bush, 1993). Dates for the termination of the Loch Lomond Stadial are similar throughout the region, at just before 10,000 ^{14}C BP; for example, 10,340 ± 200 ^{14}C BP at Din Moss, on the Scottish Border (Hibbert & Switsur, 1976), 10,150 ± 80 ^{14}C BP at Gransmoor in Holderness (Lowe *et al.*, 1999) and 10,350 ± 200 ^{14}C BP at Kildale Hall (Keen *et al.*, 1984). In general the timing of this last Lateglacial cold event seems closely comparable throughout north-east England, with ages of *c.* 11,000 ^{14}C BP to *c.* 10,000 ^{14}C BP. A feature of the Loch Lomond Stadial is the continued presence of high frequencies of microscopic charcoal (at those sites where micro-charcoal counts have been made), such as at Seamer Carr in the Vale of Pickering (Day, 1996). The aridity of the latter half of the Stadial especially (Lowe *et al.*, 1994), as suggested by high *Artemisia* frequencies, may have promoted natural

fires. It is presumed that climatic conditions were too severe to have encouraged human activity at the height of the Stadial, although occupation of cave sites may well have continued. Gale and Hunt (1985) have reported Palaeolithic flint artefacts in sediments with a Stadial pollen assemblage from Kirkhead Cave in Cumbria.

The new data from the Washlands presented in this volume generally agree well with the established regional picture. Unfortunately the deposits that represent the coldest phase of the Loch Lomond Stadial, at Marfield and at Mill House, Snape Mires (Chapter 3.4 and 3.8.3), do not preserve pollen, although at the latter site there is a pollen record for the earlier part of the Stadial. A low *Artemisia* presence is of interest here, although this marker taxon may have been more abundant during the colder, drier second half of the stadial. Certainly at Mill House, the macrofossil and insect evidence agrees in showing open grassland under cold conditions during this episode. Mollusca are also absent from the sediments from the most severe part of the stadial at these sites. This was also the case at Bingley Bog (Keen *et al.*, 1988), an exemplar for the Lateglacial record of this region (cf. Thomas, 1999), presumably due to extinction under the extremely severe climate. *Artemisia*, Cyperaceae and Poaceae dominate the stadial assemblages at the Flasks 69 (Chapter 3.2.3.4) and the final stages of the cold phase are represented at Newby Wiske (Chapter 3.3), where a tundra-type flora was being supplanted by *Juniperus* shrubs when pollen deposition commenced. The latter site also records the *Rumex* expansion that, continuing through *Empetrum* and *Juniperus* successions, heralded the end of the stadial period and the start of the transition into the *Betula* woodland of the early Holocene. It is interesting that high frequencies of micro-charcoal at Newby Wiske are confined to the Loch Lomond Stadial levels, and such evidence of fire is also present in analogous levels at the Flasks 69. Stadial environments were evidently conducive to regular fires in the steppe–tundra vegetation that existed, most likely caused by climatic aridity and lightning strike (Edwards *et al.*, 2000).

5.4.3 The climate warms – the early to mid-Holocene

As with the Lateglacial Interstadial, insect evidence (Coope, 1986; Coope *et al.*, 1998; Lowe & Walker, 1997b) indicates that the warming transition into the Holocene was abrupt, with very rapid displacement of Younger Dryas steppe–tundra communities by thermophilous species. This switch occurred a little before 10,000 radiocarbon years ago (Lowe *et al.*, 1994) and initiated the most recent, although presumably not the last, in the long series of temperate 'interglacial' interludes that have alleviated the generally cold global climates that have dominated most of the *c.* 2 million years of the Quaternary.

In the first few thousand years of the Holocene, conditions were generally warm and dry, causing falling groundwater levels and terrestrialization of small water bodies (Tipping, 1995a) and even a lengthy pause in sediment deposition at some sites (Walker, 2004). Summer temperatures were up to 3°C higher than those of today, although there were short-lived temperature fluctuations of the sort that had occurred in the Lateglacial. In particular, it has been established from Greenland ice core data that brief but very cold events occurred in the region of the North Atlantic at *c.* 9300 and 8200 BP, confirmed by proxy data analyses from lake sediments in northern England (Johnsen *et al.*, 2001; Marshall *et al.*, 2002). These might have been caused by surges in ice melting and the release of huge quantities of extremely cold meltwater into the Atlantic Ocean, perhaps after the sudden drainage of previously impounded glacial lakes in North America (Teller, 2003; Teller & Leverington, 2004). Such cold episodes must have interrupted the successions in thermophilous vegetation that began at the start of the Holocene, although in pollen diagrams it would be difficult to distinguish such climatically-driven effects from those related to human impacts (Edwards *et al.*, 2007). There are no indications of forest decline at times that could match these North Atlantic cold phases in any of the Washlands records. Despite the abruptness of the rise in temperature that took place just before 10,000 ^{14}C BP, plant responses were inevitably delayed by slow immigration rates for taller plants and by the slow development rates of soil profiles (Pennington, 1986).

The earliest Holocene vegetation was therefore species-rich grassland with low herbs like *Thalictrum*, within which taller thermophilous herbs became abundant in turn. *Rumex* species were characteristic of this pioneer phase, followed by associations with abundant *Filipendula*, the classic indicator of the warm, early-succession herbaceous phase of the infant interglacial. At Thorpe Bulmer (south-east Durham), for example, *Filipendula* was able to reach 20% of total land pollen before being shaded out by shrub taxa (Bartley *et al.*, 1976) and so must have been locally abundant. Virtually all pollen diagrams from northern England that cover this pioneer phase exhibit a peak in *Filipendula* to some degree, even those at altitude, such as Malham Tarn Moss in the Pennines (Pigott & Pigott, 1963). Occasionally, however, the taxon is hardly present, as at Bingley Bog (Keen *et al.*, 1988); there it was much more abundant in the Lateglacial Interstadial than the initial Holocene, as was also the case at Seamer Carrs (Jones, 1976a).

In the new Swale–Ure Washlands site records, low but significant pollen curves for *Filipendula* occur at Newby Wiske (Fig. 3.7), Marfield (Fig. 3.10), the Flasks 69 at Nosterfield (Fig. 3.5) and Ings Plantation IL12, Snape Mires (Fig. 3.20). Local factors would have controlled *Filipendula* abundance at particular sites and the lack of *Filipendula* macrofossils in the earliest Holocene sediments at these Washlands sites confirms that this plant was not of great local importance, unlike elsewhere in the wider region. Previously studied Washlands sites, such as Dishforth Bog (Giles, 1992), agree with this finding. It is possible that the

highest *Filipendula* values are augmented by the calcareous grassland species *F. vulgaris*, which could explain the record at Thorpe Bulmer, located in the limestone area of south-east Durham; more moderate values might be referable to *F. ulmaria*, a member of the lake-edge wetland suite of herbs. These initial Holocene wetland successions are an important part of environmental history, with this early phase of the interglacial typified by aquatic and marsh taxa in the early stages of hydroseral succession. At the same time, successions within algal communities are apparent, from *Pediastrum* to *Botryococcus* as at Marfield (Fig. 3.10), for example, reflecting changing water clarity and quality. Similarly, peaks in aquatic plants, like *Typha angustifolia* and *Typha latifolia* at the Flasks 69 (Fig. 3.5) and *Myriophyllum* species at Snape Mires IL6 (Fig. 3.19) and Langland's Farm (Fig. 3.28), underline the open-water nature of wetlands in this earliest Holocene phase. Macrofossil and mollusc records of this age from the Washlands sites confirm this situation.

Molluscan evidence from early Holocene sequences at Snape Mires is of considerable value. The occurrence of two 'Red Data Book' species amongst the aquatic assemblage from Ings Plantation (IL 12), namely *Myxas glutinosa* and *Pisidium pseudosphaerium*, is especially noteworthy (see Chapter 3.8.2.4; Plate 3.2c). For *P. pseudosphaerium* (found above 106 cm in the IL12 core), this is only its second record as a fossil from a British locality. The nearby Mill House tufa site has yielded large numbers of another mollusc species of note, *Vertigo genesii*, which is an arctic–alpine snail of very restricted occurrence in northern Britain (Plate 3.2b). It was, however, present in southern England during the Lateglacial (Preece & Bridgland, 1998, 1999) and its survival into the Holocene at Snape, together with the absence of early to mid-Holocene immigrants like *Discus*, implies that tufa deposition there was a short-lived, earliest Holocene phenomenon.

In the drier parts of the landscape, plant succession progressed quickly and shrub communities with *Empetrum*, *Juniperus* and *Salix* replaced the tall herb grassland flora of the initial warm phase (Innes, 2002d). *Populus* would also have been a significant part of this transitional shrub community, although its poorly preserved pollen is rarely recorded in regional pollen diagrams, and never in quantity. A peak in *Juniperus* pollen frequencies is an important phase in the early stages of Holocene vegetation history, but it varies in its timing (Tipping, 1987) and amplitude. A period of *Juniperus* abundance precedes a transition to wooded environments in much of the northern part of the area, like south-east Durham (Turner & Kershaw, 1973; Bartley *et al.,* 1976), but in more southerly lowland areas like the Vale of York and Holderness (Bartley, 1962; Beckett, 1981) the establishment of *Betula* woodland was rapid and forestalled major juniper expansion except where other environmental factors like soils and altitude delayed the expansion of birch. At Tadcaster (Bartley, 1962), for example, a very high peak of *Juniperus* occurs in the Lateglacial Interstadial record but it is hardly recorded at the start of the Holocene. At higher altitudes, *Juniperus* was extremely abundant in both time periods, particularly where also favoured by geology, as around Malham Tarn (Pigott & Pigott, 1963). At more intermediate altitudes, as at Ewe Crag Slack in the Cleveland Hills (Jones, 1978), *Empetrum* heath rather than juniper scrub seems to have preceded the *Betula* dominance of the early Holocene woodland. Within this Swale–Ure Washlands study, there are a number of examples of this shrub phase, although in no case is shrub pollen abundant; Newby Wiske (Fig. 3.7) is perhaps the most complete example. Only at Marfield, however, the furthest upstream in the Ure valley of the project sites, does a high *Juniperus* peak occur. Progression from herbaceous vegetation to *Betula* woodland, with only a low-scale shrub expansion, seems the norm; thus the vegetation history during this transitional phase in the Swale–Ure area seems to resemble that of the other sites in the Vale of Mowbray and the lower Tees, rather than that of the southern Vale of York.

Whatever the composition and abundance of the early Holocene shrub phase, the establishment of closed *Betula* woodland eventually occurred in the Washlands, as it did throughout the region except perhaps at very high altitudes. This marks the first stage in the development of mixed-species full-interglacial forest (Birks, 1989) that took place over the next three or four thousand years and would remain the established, relatively unbroken vegetation type across the region until the start of its degradation, under human impacts and then deteriorating climate, after *c.* 5000 ^{14}C BP. Between *c.* 9000 and 6000 ^{14}C BP, immigration of *Corylus, Pinus, Ulmus, Quercus, Alnus* and *Tilia* took place in succession, although even in such a small area as north Yorkshire there were significant variations in forest composition because of soil and topographical factors (Spikins, 2000). Nevertheless, a broadly representative age can be arrived at for the immigration and spread of each of the major forest trees in the first half of the Holocene; this has been used as a means of relative dating by defining regional pollen zones (Hibbert & Switsur, 1976; Innes, 2002d).

The boundaries of such regional pollen zones have been dated at several sites in northern England (Innes, 1999, 2002d). Notwithstanding the spatial variability, *Betula* forest was established throughout the area by a few centuries after 10,000 ^{14}C BP. At all of the relevant Swale–Ure sites, which now include all the Snape Mires sites (Chapter 3.8) as well as Newby Wiske and the Flasks 69, *Betula* entirely dominates early Holocene pollen spectra except where very local wetland vegetation is represented. Dense birch forest that shaded out almost all other land plants, or at least suppressed their flowering, covered the landscape. The *Betula* forest lasted for several centuries; the date for its beginning at the Flasks 69 (Chapter 3.2.3.4), 9990 ± 45 ^{14}C BP, may well be typical for the Washlands, as may be those of 9475 ± 40 ^{14}C BP at the Gallop, Snape Mires, and 9330 ± 40 ^{14}C BP at Ings Plantation IL12 (also in the Snape basin) for its end (Chapter 3.8). Immigration

by other taxa, primarily *Corylus* (Huntley, 1993; Tallantire, 2002), brought woodland diversification and the end of the birch-dominated forest. Its date at the Gallop might be slightly early in comparison with the regional average; it is clear that *Corylus* penetrated the birch woods and expanded to dominate the dryland vegetation in the centuries before 9000 ^{14}C BP (Innes, 2002d). The date of 9082 ± 90 ^{14}C BP at Neasham Fen, in the Tees valley (Bartley *et al.,* 1976), is one of the oldest in the lowlands of the region, whereas dates for hazel expansion as late as after 8670 ± 70 ^{14}C BP at Pow Hill, in the Pennines (Turner & Hodgson, 1981), may well characterize the surrounding uplands. In the Swale–Ure Washlands the *Corylus* rise is clearly marked in the profiles at Snape, but the full phase of *Corylus* dominance is best represented at Newby Wiske (Chapter 3.3). Conditions at that site were clearly extremely favourable for hazel, as its pollen is superabundant there and *Corylus* macrofossils are common; this is thus a good example of the ability of *Corylus* thickets to shade out other shrubs like *Juniperus* and *Salix* completely, as well as supplanting *Betula.*

The penetration and opening of the dense hazel woodland by taller species is the next element in forest history and is well represented at Newby Wiske, where *Ulmus* entered the hazel woods first, without greatly diminishing *Corylus* dominance, and then the expansion of *Pinus* and *Quercus* after 8650 ± 55 ^{14}C BP created more mixed woodland (Fig. 3.7). By way of comparison, broadly contemporaneous *Pinus* pollen abundance has also been recorded at Thornton Mire in Wensleydale, dated 8480 ± 80 ^{14}C BP (Honeyman, 1985). The *Corylus* dominance at Newby Wiske was probably not representative of the region in general, as other sites, such as at the three Snape profiles and Langland's Farm, record contemporaneous rises of *Pinus* and *Corylus,* suggesting that a more mixed forest was typical of the region after the *Betula* decline. An intermediate situation is recorded at the Flasks 69 (Fig. 3.5) and a wide spatial range in regional forest composition should perhaps be assumed. This has been shown to be the case in the adjacent Pennines in both the early and mid- Holocene (Turner & Hodgson, 1979, 1981) and will also have been the case in the lowlands, where base-rich soils would have favoured *Ulmus,* and later *Tilia,* while *Quercus* would have dominated in more acidic areas (Atherden, 1999). *Corylus* would have adopted an understory role in this diverse mixed deciduous forest and *Pinus,* after a phase of abundance (Bennett, 1984), would have retreated to areas of specialized conditions, like the sandstone crests of the North York Moors (Simmons *et al.,* 1993) or the limestone soils of east Durham (Bartley *et al.,* 1976), in response to competition from taxa like *Alnus.* In these favoured areas it persisted well into the mid-Holocene (Innes, 2008), but declined in most locations as the broadleaf trees advanced.

Although the decline of *Pinus* was delayed at altitude and in a few lowland areas, it was replaced by *Alnus* across most of its range at some stage during the mid-Holocene, with the *Pinus* fall and *Alnus* rise occurring together in most regional pollen diagrams. The history of *Pinus* in the Washlands is variable; although rising early with *Corylus* at Snape Mires and Langland's Farm, it failed to do so at other sites like Thornton's Plantation and Newby Wiske. As with most regional diagrams, peak values tend to be seen in the period immediately preceding the *Alnus* rise, illustrated well in the Washlands at Langland's Farm, where values of 40% of total land pollen were recorded (Fig. 3.28). At the Shakehole site at the Flasks, Nosterfield, *Pinus* remained highly significant until not long before 5000 ^{14}C BP, even though *Alnus* had been important for some time. Considerable regional variability seems to have existed, presumably due to local factors.

Alnus had been present at many sites throughout the early Holocene, as at Mordon Carr in the Durham lowlands (Bartley *et al.*, 1976), but its rise to abundance defines, in pollen diagrams, the start of the post-Boreal, wetter mid-Holocene climate period. A more oceanic climate prompted by the full separation of Britain from the continent during the previous millennium, and the stabilization of river regimes and floodplains after the completion of sea-level rise, would have greatly increased the wet habitats that favoured alder (Brown, 1988; Bennett, 1990). At most sites the *Alnus* populations were direct replacements of *Pinus*, although in places this change was delayed, as on the North York Moors, where the *Alnus* rise at West House Moss has been dated at 6650 ± 290 ^{14}C BP (Jones, 1977b). The date of *Alnus* expansion is thus strongly diachronous and must relate to local environmental influences (Chambers & Price, 1985; Chambers & Elliott, 1989). Altitude seems to have been one such influence; in lowland eutrophic fen–carr communities alder expansion was generally earlier than at higher elevations. Regional dates of 7640 ± 85 ^{14}C BP in the Vale of Pickering (Day, 1996), 7759 ± 67 ^{14}C BP at Mordon Carr, in lowland County Durham (Bartley *et al.*, 1976), and 7720 ± 50 ^{14}C BP at Askham Bog, in the Vale of York (Gearey & Lillie, 1999), reflect this early spread. In contrast, in the uplands, significantly later dates for the *Alnus* rise are recorded in the northern Pennines, for example 6120 ± 50 ^{14}C BP at Quick Moss, on the Tyne–Wear watershed (Rowell & Turner, 1985), and 6150 ± 160 ^{14}C BP at Red Sike Moss, upper Teesdale (Turner *et al.*, 1973). At Whirly Gill, on the elevated interfluve between Swaledale and Wensleydale some 488 m above O.D., Honeyman (1985) recorded a similarly late date of 6370 ± 70 ^{14}C BP. Around the region, age estimates for this important biostratigraphical feature are close to an average of *c.* 7000 ^{14}C BP; for example 6962 ± 90 ^{14}C BP at Neasham Fen in the Tees valley (Bartley *et al.*, 1976).

Further natural changes in the composition of the forest continued after the *Alnus* rise, however (Atherden, 1999; Innes, 1999, 2002d). The most significant was the expansion of *Tilia* (almost certainly *T. cordata*), the most thermophilous of the major British trees. Although present in low numbers from the early Holocene, *Tilia* expansion was delayed by its low rate of spread (Bennett, 1986). It

only became a major forest component in northern England after *c.* 7000 ^{14}C BP (Lang, 2003) and particularly in the several centuries before 5000 ^{14}C BP when, prevented by climatic and edaphic factors from further migration, it attained its northern distribution limit in the North Yorkshire and south Durham lowlands (Pigott & Huntley, 1978). In the Swale–Ure Washlands, at Newby Wiske, *Tilia* frequencies exceed those of *Ulmus* in this part of the record (Fig. 3.7), whereas at Langland's Farm (Fig. 3.28) they match *Quercus* during the same period. As *Tilia* does not produce as much pollen as the other major forest trees, these high frequencies must represent major *Tilia* populations in the Swale–Ure lowlands at this time, on the more base-rich, finer-textured clay soils (cf. Moore, 1977; Pigott & Huntley, 1980; Greig, 1982). Other more minor components of the forest also persisted in favourable habitats during the mid-Holocene; *Fraxinus* occurs rarely in the Washlands pollen record from this time and would have had to wait for later woodland disturbance to enable it to increase from its very low populations. It was more common at higher altitudes, particularly on favourable soils like the limestone at Malham Tarn Moss (Pigott & Pigott, 1959), where *Taxus* is also recorded, or where some limited disturbance had occurred, as on the North York Moors (Simmons *et al.*, 1993).

With the *Alnus* rise at *c.* 7000 ^{14}C BP, and then the expansion of *Tilia* to its highest values in the Holocene, the post-glacial deciduous forest was fully established and, except where broken by wetland or at the high altitudes, formed a continuous cover across the regional landscape that would last for the approximately 2000 years of the warm and wet mid-Holocene 'Atlantic' climatic period (Bennett, 1989). Macrofossil tree remains, which are crucial for establishing the mid-Holocene extent of regional tree cover, provide considerable evidence that the woodland, at least in a modified form, extended to very high altitudes indeed. Certainly the plateau summits of the North York Moors carried dense woodland, except at particular sites where human activity might have suppressed the growth of trees (Simmons *et al.*, 1993). There are no indications of a natural tree-line on that upland, on which stumps of very mature *Quercus*, *Pinus*, *Alnus* and *Betula* trees have been recorded from mid-Holocene peats on even the highest moors (Simmons & Innes, 1981, 1988), with radiocarbon dates ranging from *c.* 7000 to *c.* 5000 ^{14}C BP. There is no reason to suppose that trees had not colonized the high plateaux in the earlier Boreal episode, before peat had developed to provide a preservation medium for their remains.

The much higher Pennine uplands are also likely to have carried mixed woodland across summit plateaux (Birks, 1988), although at the highest elevations species-poor *Betula* woods may have dominated and there would have been locations where, due to exposure, cliffs, springs and other disturbed habitats, only open scrub woodland would have existed. Pollen diagrams from an altitude of almost 900 m, from peat containing sparse wood macrofossil remains on Cross Fell in the north Pennines, show mid-Holocene tree values and vegetational history very similar to those from much lower sites (Turner, 1984). Substantial macrofossil wood remains occur at the base of Pennine peats at virtually every altitude (Tallis & Switsur, 1983, Tallis, 1991; Turner & Hodgson, 1983; Laurie, 2004). Combined pollen and macrofossil evidence therefore indicates that, like in the North York Moors, there was no natural tree-line in the Pennines and, unless disturbed, the early and mid-Holocene catchments of the Washland rivers were entirely wooded. It can thus be assumed that tree cover was continuous, except where temporarily removed by rivers changing channel or by landslides. Many lowland wetlands would have supported carr-woodland, as at Newby Wiske, where wood remains comprising large trunks are common in the mid-Holocene peat.

It remains to be considered to what extent the vegetation patterns of the early and mid-Holocene, including the timing of the establishment of the various woodland trees and shrubs, was influenced by pre-agricultural human activity, in addition to natural factors of climate, soils and topography (Blackford *et al.*, 2006). The early and mid-Holocene period of forest formation and stability equates with the Mesolithic cultural period, as described in Chapter 4. The levels of population and technology of the Mesolithic hunter-gatherers were low and, although their material culture was well adapted for exploiting the resources of the post-glacial environment, it had very low impact upon the dense forest. There are finds of flint axes from this period (Chapter 4.3) but these were probably restricted to use around settlement sites, rather than in general felling of woodland. Nevertheless, in areas where Mesolithic sites are concentrated, suggesting long-term human activity, the occurrence of macro- and microscopic charcoal in sediment cores is persuasive evidence that widespread, and in places intensive, disturbance of woodland was associated with Mesolithic occupation (Jacobi *et al.*, 1976; Simmons, 1996). Attributing all fire during this long period to deliberate human activity is probably unwarranted (Tipping, 1996), as natural fires will have occurred as a result of lightning strikes, aided by episodes of drier climate (Tipping & Milburn, 2000), while accidental escape of domestic fire is also possible (Bennett *et al.*, 1990). It has been proposed, however, that the application of fire to the wider landscape by Mesolithic foragers could well have been routine, although perhaps targeted at preferred locations for maximum effectiveness, as a means of improving the resource yield of the forest (Mellars, 1976; Simmons & Innes, 1987). Pollen evidence has shown that, although perhaps spatially restricted, significant clearings were made by fire in the forest, causing grasses, herbs and shrubs to grow in profusion for several decades before closed woodland returned. Evidence of Mesolithic woodland disturbance was reviewed for the North York Moors by Innes and Simmons (1988) and for the wider north of England by Simmons and Innes (1985, 1987), who noted that most fire disturbances were located in the less densely wooded uplands, although a few significant examples occur in the lowlands around bodies of water (e.g. Taylor *et al.*, 1994b). Opened woodland, in its various successional stages of regeneration, would have been far more productive in both food plants and animals than closed-canopy, mature deciduous forest, and would have attracted grazing and browsing animals. Recently, some elements of this hypothesis, such as the increased herbivore presence on the land after burning and the interpretation of micro-charcoal data, have been tested and upheld (Innes & Simmons, 2000; Innes & Blackford, 2003b; Innes *et al.*, 2004).

The regional evidence can be summarized as showing maximum burning and/or pollen evidence of vegetation disturbance in areas where Mesolithic activity was greatest. Little charcoal or disturbance evidence is forthcoming from the lowlands to the east of the Pennines, except in the eastern Vale of Pickering. Important exceptions are at Hartlepool on the Durham coast (Waughman *et al.*, 2005) and at Seamer Carrs in the Vale of Mowbray (Jones, 1976a; Tooley *et al.*, 1982). Significantly, Mesolithic flints show that people were present at both locations. Charcoal, worked flints and evidence of woodland disturbance also occur together at Willow Garth, on the Yorkshire Wolds (Bush, 1988). It is, however, in the uplands of the North York Moors and Pennines where this juxtaposition of Mesolithic sites and fire can be seen most clearly. It must be remembered that this connection remains circumstantial, and causation cannot be proved. The lighter woods of the uplands, for example, probably drier and with more pyrophyte taxa like pine and hazel, might have been more conducive for both natural fire and Mesolithic occupation, with both being coincidental symptoms of the upland environment. However, at Star Carr, in the eastern Vale of Pickering, burning around the lake edges occurred in association with the early Mesolithic occupation, showing that there was a similar history of fire use in the lowlands, at least at important locations (Cloutman & Smith, 1988; Mellars & Dark, 1998; Cummins, 2000; Simmons *et al.*, in press). Furthermore, there is some evidence for a more direct link between people and fire: at East Bilsdale Moor, on the North York Moors, Simmons and Innes (1981, 1988) have shown that regional burning stopped around the time of the change from Mesolithic to Neolithic economies, allowing forest regrowth, which is suggestive of a cultural control.

In the wider region, Mesolithic flints are sometimes found in direct association with charcoal layers and vegetation change, as at Stump Cross (Walker, 1956) and Dunford Bridge (Radley *et al.*, 1974) in the Pennines; also at White Gill (Dimbleby, 1962) and Botany Bay (Simmons & Innes, 1988) in the North York Moors. The patterns of macro- and microscopic charcoal are such as to indicate repeated burning at particular sites and many small, localized, contained fires rather than a single wildfire, again suggesting human control (Simmons & Innes, 1996a; Innes & Simmons, 2000, 2001). With or without charcoal, the uplands adjacent to the Swale–Ure Washlands contain abundant pollen evidence for major disturbance impacts during the Mesolithic. North Gill is a type site for the many such events recorded on the North York Moors (Innes & Simmons, 1988, 1999) but the north and central Pennines contain comparable evidence (Simmons & Innes, 1987). Sites at Fountains Earth (Tinsley, 1975a), Valley Bog (Chambers, 1978), Pawlaw Mire (Sturludottir & Turner, 1985), Malham Tarn Moss (Pigott & Pigott, 1962) and Gate Gutter (Gear & Turner, 2001) are good examples, although the best is probably that of Soyland Moor (Williams, 1985).

Fire during Mesolithic times has been implicated in causing permanent environmental change, at least locally. Charcoal often lies beneath the base of blanket and basin peats at various altitudes in the region, for example at Mire Holes in Upper Teesdale (Squires, 1978) and at May Moss and Collier Gill on the North York Moors (Innes & Simmons, 1988). Burning may well have had a role in peat formation, with post-fire paludification after tree removal causing a switch to wetland conditions. Also, charcoal is often recorded at the level of major pollen zone changes, as though fire had changed forest composition and given new taxa the opportunity to become established. Charcoal often accompanies the rise of *Alnus* pollen, as at Seamer Carr in the Vale of Pickering (Cloutman & Smith, 1988), Malham Tarn Moss in the Pennines (Pigott & Pigott, 1963) or Burnfoothill Moss in the Solway lowlands (Tipping, 1995b). Fire may also have encouraged the early Holocene *Corylus* rise, as charcoal occurs in association with this pollen zone boundary at several sites, such as Flixton in the Vale of Pickering (Mellars & Dark, 1998). This is not always the case, however, and no charcoal is associated with the rise of hazel at the lowland Swale–Ure sites of Newby Wiske and the Flasks 69, although it is found at the Snape Mires sites. That the *Corylus* rise occurred earlier at Snape suggests that fire assisted its expansion, which was delayed where fire was absent.

In places, fire might have thus been an important trigger for *Corylus* expansion, but it would not have been a pre-requisite (Huntley, 1993). The long-term effects of fire in the uplands have been considered by Simmons and Innes (1985), who showed that repeated burning on the northern English hills led to degeneration of the woodland and the establishment of heath, bog and grassland over wide areas before the end of the Mesolithic. Mineral inwash in association with the charcoal layers suggests that soil erosion also resulted from forest fires, with Ewe Crag Slack and North Gill on the North York Moors representing good examples from the early and late Mesolithic respectively (Simmons *et al.*, 1975, 1993). No such consequences are envisaged for the lowlands except in very local situations, as the existing charcoal and pollen evidence indicate very little fire or forest opening at low altitude during the Mesolithic. The high micro-charcoal frequencies at Snape Mires are unusual in this respect and it may be that fire in the lowland was, at least locally, more common than received wisdom would suggest. Whether the Snape micro-

charcoal is natural or anthropogenic is uncertain, although the latter seems more likely.

5.4.4 The Lateglacial to early–mid-Holocene rivers

As with rivers throughout northern Britain (cf. Howard & Macklin, 1999; Howard *et al.*, 2000b; Smith & Boardman, 1994), the Ure and Swale have formed terraces since deglaciation, by a combination of erosion (downcutting) and aggradation of floodplain deposits, particularly sands and gravels. This process thus marks out successively lower valley-floor positions at intervals within a record of progressive fluvial incision into the deglaciated landscape (Plate 5.1). Although traditionally terrace formation has been ascribed to forcing by climatic and/or base-level factors (e.g. Törnqvist, 1998; Karner & Marra, 1998; Blum & Straffin, 2001), it has become increasingly clear that, both on longer and shorter timescales (i.e. full Quaternary fluvial sequences as well as Late Devensian–Holocene sequences), surface uplift is a key requirement (Kukla, 1975; Maddy, 1997; Bridgland, 2000; van den Berg & van Hoof, 2001; Bridgland & Westaway, 2007b; Bridgland *et al.*, in press b). This is especially the case with regard to early Holocene terraces, which have invariably been formed at a time of relative sea-level rise, rather than the falling base level that is supposed to enable fluvial incision. The required uplift might well be readily explained as a glacio-isostatic response to late Devensian deglaciation (cf. Bridgland, 1999; Bridgland & Austin, 1999). Support for this view comes from the absence of such terraces in the Trent system around Newark (Howard *et al.*, 1999a), which, although it shares its estuary with the Vale-of-York rivers and would therefore be expected to have experienced the same base-level influences, was not glaciated in the Devensian and therefore has not experienced isostatic rebound. Thus the Trent has mid–late Holocene sediments beneath its modern floodplain, as recorded at Langford Quarry, *c.* 15 km downstream of Newark (Howard *et al.*, 1999a; Howard, 2007a), in marked contrast with the Ure, in which sediments of comparable age occur in terrace deposits several metres above floodplain level (Plate 5.1).

The highest glaciofluvial gravels in the project area, as exemplified at Marfield (Chapter 2.3.1.1; Chapter 3.4), are up to 30 metres above the present Ure floodplain but, due to the considerable incision during deglaciation, glacial outwash-fed fan gravels also occur much lower in the terrace sequence, at Nosterfield (Plate 5.1). These fan gravels, deposited downstream of the Hackfall Gorge and studied in the Nosterfield Quarry (Chapter 2.6.2), represent the most extensive aggregate resource in the area. Downstream of Masham, glaciofluvial gravels can be found beneath the modern floodplain deposits, filling the old 'proto-Ure' (pre-glacial) channel mapped by the Geological Survey and noted by Howard *et al.* (2000a) at Ripon Racecourse. At that site those authors recorded the only datable example of Early Holocene fluvial deposits found thus far in either Washland river. In the Swale there is little in the way of terrace morphology; the glacial outwash gravels that have been extensively quarried are close to the valley bottom and have had Holocene gravels and alluvium emplaced above them locally (Chapter 2.7).

Lateglacial fluvial activity is recorded by channel erosion and other, indirect stratigraphical evidence. At Marfield a substantial channel, thought to have been occupied by the Ure and subsequently filled with Lateglacial and early Holocene organic sediments, forms one of the key project research sites (Chapter 3.4). The channel, its floor *c.* 18 m below the surface level of the Marfield 'glacial terrace' (Plate 5.1), was probably cut by Lateglacial Interstadial times. Indeed, there is basal gravel that possibly dates from the pre-interstadial colder episode. Further downstream, the evidence from Ripon Racecourse (Howard *et al.*, 2000a) shows that the river Ure had incised to within *c.* 10 m of its present level by the Lateglacial. The highest terrace here, Terrace No. 1 of Howard *et al.*, is within a couple of metres, relative to river level, of the Marfield channel deposits, suggesting broad equivalence (Plate 5.1), although the Lateglacial age of the terrace is inferred from the early Holocene evidence in Terrace 2. Another possible equivalent of this terrace was mapped during the present project at Norton Mills, near the Ripon North Quarry, and was exposed in a river bank section there, where it was studied (see Chapter 2.6.3; Figs 2.67–2.70). This terrace is *c.* 8.5 m above the Ure, slightly lower than the Howard *et al.* Terrace No 1 at Ripon Racecourse. Howard *et al.* (2000a) interpreted the fossiliferous sediments at their study site in Terrace 2 as earliest Holocene; the assemblages of plants and insects point to conditions similar to the present day, perhaps slightly cooler, with certain arctic–alpine species (e.g. the snail *Vertigo geyeri* (cf. Plate 3.2a) as well as pollen of *Armeria maritima* and Saxifragaceae) that had thrived during the Lateglacial lingering on. The Ripon South project site, its sediments dating from much later in the Holocene (Chapter 3.7), is located near to the Howard *et al.* (2000a) site but on the next lowest terrace, their Terrace No. 3. The surface of that terrace is little more than a metre lower in elevation, showing that very little further incision by the Ure took place here during several thousand years of the Holocene (Plate 5.1).

At the Ripon North project site, however, <10 km upstream, a terrace sequence aggraded to *c.* 5 m above river level, somewhat higher than Howard *et al.*'s Terrace No. 2 at the Racecourse, culminates in gravels containing *Theodoxus fluviatilis* (Plate 3.2f), a mid-Holocene immigrant into Britain (Holyoak, 1983; Chambers *et al.*, 1996), indicating deposition since the first appearance of that species, dated (in the Thames catchment) at around 6650 ^{14}C BP. The deposits here are therefore at least 3000 years younger than the seemingly lower Terrace 2 deposits at Ripon South. The covering finer-grained and organic sediments, which yielded palaeobotanical evidence and a radiocarbon date, show that fluvial accumulation at Ripon

North continued until < 2500 ^{14}C BP, although these could be overbank sediments added to a surface already above normal valley-floor level at times of high floods. At just 5 m above the Ure, the site would be regularly flooded at the present day. In connection with the apparent reversal of the terrace ages within a short distance, it should perhaps be emphasized that the lowest three terraces mapped by Howard *et al.* (2000a) around Ripon Racecourse are very close together in height, their separation owing much to the relative freshness of the recently formed channel-migration geomorphology (Fig. 2.57). The suggested age reversal raises questions about the validity of recognizing poorly separated terraces of this type as more than localized features in the landscape.

5.4.5 The beginning of agriculture – the early Neolithic *Ulmus* decline

While Mesolithic hunter-gatherers may have modified the forest in the Swale–Ure Washlands and adjacent areas through the use of fire, it has been the clearance of trees for agriculture, from the Neolithic period onwards, that has caused the transformation of the vegetation from almost entirely woodland in the mid-Holocene to the mainly open, grassland and cultivated landscape that exists today. This process of deforestation began slowly during the early Neolithic, however, and the earliest phases of human activity that included an agricultural component are very difficult to distinguish from those caused by foraging activity (Jones, 2000), which often included burning of vegetation and localized woodland opening, as the Mesolithic period drew to a close. Even within an area as small as Yorkshire, the timing of the transition from forager to farmer is difficult to discern. Radiocarbon dates for the very latest Mesolithic flint sites, such as March Hill Top and Dunford Bridge in the Pennines (Spikins, 1999, 2002; Switsur & Jacobi, 1975), range between 5100 and 5400 ^{14}C BP and so are comparable with the dates for some very early Neolithic monuments, such as the East Ayton Long Barrow in the Vale of Pickering, at 5040 ± 90 ^{14}C BP (Spratt, 1993), or 5380 ± 90 ^{14}C BP for the Whitwell Long Cairn in Derbyshire (Manby *et al.*, 2003b). A further archaeological sign of possible co-existence of Mesolithic and Neolithic cultures, in addition to the above-mentioned overlap in dated sites, is the common appearance of early Neolithic flint artefacts, such as leaf-shaped arrowheads, on otherwise typologically Late Mesolithic flint sites (Young, 1990; Spratt, 1993). Nevertheless there is no clear archaeological evidence for a cultural overlap.

Even more enigmatic is the palaeoecological evidence, which can be interpreted as showing a rather earlier introduction of agriculture than the Neolithic archaeological record might suggest, assuming that a Neolithic cultural identity is a pre-requisite for the introduction of agricultural techniques of animal husbandry and crop cultivation. Of major importance in this respect is the mid-Holocene decline in *Ulmus* pollen frequencies, which took place around 5000 ^{14}C BP throughout almost all of Britain and north-west Europe and is a clear benchmark horizon on pollen diagrams. This collapse in elm pollen frequencies must reflect a real diminution in elm populations and marks the first major event in the gradual decline from the post-glacial forest maximum. Dates of 5099 ± 50 ^{14}C BP at Gransmoor, east Yorkshire (Beckett, 1981), and 5080 ± 110 ^{14}C BP and 5010 ± 110 ^{14}C BP at White Moss and Eshton Tarn, west Yorkshire (Bartley *et al.*, 1990), are typical as mean ages for the decline of elm pollen, but in the lowlands the event often occurred rather earlier, in the first few centuries before 5000 ^{14}C BP. To the north of the Tees valley, there are earlier dates at Mordon Carr: 5305 ± 55 ^{14}C BP, at Neasham Fen: 5468 ± 80 ^{14}C BP and at Hartlepool: 5215 ± 80 ^{14}C BP (Bartley *et al.*, 1976; Innes *et al.*, 2005). Conversely, the *Ulmus* decline in the uplands often has later dates, within the few centuries after 5000 ^{14}C BP. For example, in the North York Moors it is dated 4767 ± 60 ^{14}C BP at North Gill and 4720 ± 90 ^{14}C BP at Fen Bogs (Simmons *et al.*, 1993), while at Valley Bog, in the North Pennines, Chambers (1978) obtained a date of 4794 ± 55 ^{14}C BP and at Soyland Moor in the central Pennines a date of 4865 ± 50 ^{14}C BP is recorded (Williams, 1985). There are also dates from three sites in the hills above Wensleydale: 4680 ± 50 ^{14}C BP from Fleet Moss, 4550 ± 50 ^{14}C BP at Thornton Mire and a little before 4790 ± 50 ^{14}C BP at Whirly Gill (Honeyman, 1985). Earlier dates seem to be related to better soils, often on limestone (Bartley *et al.*, 1976, 1990). The event was clearly diachronous across the region, with marked variation even over small distances (Turner *et al.*, 1993).

In many cases the *Ulmus* decline in the study area is accompanied by indications of forest opening, manifest in the pollen stratigraphy through reductions in tree pollen and increases in open-ground or agricultural indicator taxa, like *Plantago lanceolata* and cereal-type pollen, and sometimes with charcoal also present (as seen at Newby Wiske: Chapter 3.3). Such ecological evidence for forest opening suggests that early farming activity was in many cases responsible for an impact on the forest within which the cropping, damaging or destruction of elm trees was important. In particular, the presence of cereal-type pollen, assuming that this pollen type can be reliably attributed to cultivated grain (Tweddle *et al.*, 2005), indicates some form of agriculture as the agency of these phases of woodland disturbance, although the improvement of browsing conditions within the woodland and fodder for domesticated stock (Rasmussen, 1989) is likely to have been just as important a part of this 'forest farming' regime (Göransson, 1986; Moe & Rackham, 1992; Edwards, 1993; Innes *et al.*, 2006). The weight of evidence therefore suggests that the *Ulmus* decline is in some way a symptom of early farming techniques, and its radiocarbon dates place it firmly within the Neolithic cultural period.

Within the Washlands the pollen profile from Newby Wiske provides the clearest evidence for the *Ulmus* decline and early Neolithic agriculture. The start of the decline is dated there at 5241 ± 32 ^{14}C BP, which is a typical early date for a lowland site in this region. It is similar to that from Langland's Farm (Chapter 3.9.1), where the *Ulmus* decline occurred sometime after 5520 ± 50 ^{14}C BP. At Newby Wiske, prominent indications of clearance for agriculture begin with the falls in both *Ulmus* and *Tilia* pollen frequencies, as the cereal-type and *Plantago lanceolata* pollen curves rise and are sustained, along with a range of other weeds and micro-charcoal (Fig. 5.6). The first phase of the *Ulmus* fall, with high *P. lanceolata* and the fungal colonizer of damaged or moribund trees *Kretzschmaria deusta* (Innes *et al.*, 2006), lasted until 4921 ± 33 ^{14}C BP, after which some tree regeneration occurred, although agriculture continued and even expanded locally. That the first *Ulmus* decline agricultural impacts lasted about 300 radiocarbon years shows that the site was exploited agriculturally over several generations in the early Neolithic, with a considerable change in the vegetation and opening of the landscape.

Although Newby Wiske may be exceptional in that it lies in an area of particularly favourable fertile soils, such a lengthy *Ulmus* decline-related phase of agriculture followed by persistent farming and the maintenance of open areas is interesting, because the regional pollen evidence for early Neolithic impacts usually shows them to have been ephemeral or at least low-scale (Atherden, 1999). The *Ulmus* decline levels at Langland's Farm and in the Nosterfield Shakehole (Chapter 3.2.2) show only slight indications of agricultural activity. As noted in Chapter 4, there is little artefactual or monumental evidence for the early Neolithic in the Washlands to support the Newby Wiske pollen evidence for substantial agricultural activity, an imbalance that raises questions regarding the interpretation of both environmental and archaeological field data in terms of human occupation and land use in the earlier phases of prehistory. It may be that the Newby Wiske pollen site lies close to the location of the *Ulmus*-decline-related farming and thus retains a very clear signal, whereas most other pollen profiles from the region have been further from the source of the cultural pollen and so have received only a low-key record of local agricultural events.

Cereal pollen does not travel far from its source (Vuorela, 1973) and so for high levels of cereal-type pollen to have been recorded, the sample core must be from closely adjacent to the Neolithic farming or in an area with generally high cultivation levels. Honeyman (1985) identified cereal-type pollen at the *Ulmus* decline in the aforementioned sites above Wensleydale, upstream from the Washlands, their dates (4550 ± 50 ^{14}C BP at Thornton Mire, 4680 + 50 ^{14}C BP at Fleet Moss and before 4790 ± 50 ^{14}C BP at Whirly Gill) being typical both of the Wensleydale sites and the Yorkshire uplands in general. Sheltered locations of fertile limestone soils in the Dale could have encouraged early Neolithic cultivation in a way not common in the rest of the region around the Vales of York and Mowbray. Tinsley (1976) recorded very little evidence of early Neolithic agricultural activity at

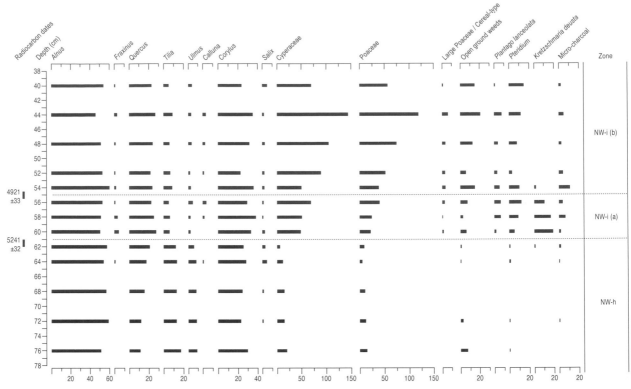

Fig. 5.6. Pollen diagram through the Ulmus *decline at Newby Wiske, calculated as percentages of total tree pollen. The first phase of the decline is labelled as zone NW-i(a) and marked by high frequencies of the fungal spore* Kretzschmaria deusta, *falls in elm and lime pollen, a rise in ash pollen and the rise of clearance and agricultural indicators.*

Fountains Earth, which is on the more exposed fells above Nidderdale, on the eastern flanks of the Pennines adjacent to the Washlands. It seems likely that in most places low-scale animal husbandry, as recorded by low levels of *Plantago lanceolata* pollen at and after the *Ulmus* decline, was typical of the low levels of early Neolithic influence on the vegetation across the region.

Other factors may well have been involved in the *Ulmus* decline, however, and clear evidence of farming in the form of cereal and other pollen types may not be present. Sturludottir and Turner (1985) have suggested that repetitive forest disturbance, especially using fire, may have caused the decline of elm at Pawlaw Mire and elsewhere in the Pennines through soil degeneration, a process leading to spread of blanket bog and moorland in the uplands (Simmons & Innes, 1985, 1987) and which could have been also driven by climatic deterioration at this time. Brown (1997b) has urged caution in attributing every creation of a woodland clearing in the Mesolithic or Neolithic to human agency and it has been demonstrated (Perry & Moore, 1987) that factors such as elm disease have, in modern times, produced a pollen signal very similar to that of the 5000 ^{14}C BP *Ulmus* decline, including the increase in weeds like *P. lanceolata*. Insect evidence from phases of forest clearance of *Ulmus*-decline date (Robinson, 2000; Clark & Edwards, 2004) has shown that the coloepteran vector of elm disease was present at *c.* 5000

[14]C BP and an explanation that includes both disease and human impacts is favoured by many investigators (Peglar, 1993; Peglar & Birks, 1993). A multi-causal origin is probably correct (Parker *et al.*, 2002), despite the undoubted diachroneity, with different factors of greater importance at different sites.

While any human impacts associated with the *Ulmus* decline must reflect Neolithic agriculture, there are several examples of disturbance phases in the previous millennium that could as well represent incipient Neolithic agriculture as the activities of the final Mesolithic occupants of the region, particularly those few records that include pollen grains of cereal-type (Innes *et al.*, 2003a). It is conceivable that the latest Mesolithic communities adopted elements of introduced Neolithic agricultural techniques, particularly if there was a protracted phase of transition between the two cultures, of which small-scale cereal cultivation might have been the most attractive addition to the forager's life. Some of these pre-*Ulmus*-decline cereal pollen and disturbance phases, while pre-dating the elm decline in their own peat profile, do not pre-date the regional elm decline (Edwards, 1988, 1989), because of the upland–lowland age dichotomy. For example, cereal-type pollen occurs within a well-defined clearance phase dated *c.* 5400 ^{14}C BP at North Gill, in the North York Moors (Simmons & Innes, 1996b), up to six hundred radiocarbon years before the elm decline at the same site, but synchronous with the elm decline (dated *c.* 5400 ¹⁴C BP) at sites in the nearby south Durham lowlands (Bartley *et al.*, 1976). A very early Neolithic agency for the North Gill phase seems likely, therefore, even though there is no Neolithic archaeological evidence from such an early date regionally. The same is likely to be true of the pre-*Ulmus*-decline cereal-type pollen, dated *c.* 5200 ¹⁴C BP, recognized at Gate Gutter on Stainmore by Gear and Turner (2001). Even though it occurs half a millennium before the elm decline in their profile, which has another typical late upland *Ulmus*-decline date at 4728 ± 52 ¹⁴C BP, it is well within the range of ages for the elm decline in the adjacent lowland areas.

There is pollen evidence for incipient agriculture in the region, however, that considerably pre-dates the earliest regional *Ulmus* decline. As the transition from a late Mesolithic to the earliest Neolithic material culture may be virtually impossible to observe in the archaeological record, such pollen data may be the only evidence available for the earliest agriculture (Williams, 1989). Williams (1985) has reported cereal-type pollen grains dated 5820 ± 95 ¹⁴C BP within clearance phases in duplicate peat cores at Soyland Moor in the Yorkshire Pennines. This is over half a millennium before the earliest regional elm decline and so very early indeed for cereal cultivation. Other sites in northern England have produced very similar evidence, with analogous early dates (Innes *et al.*, 2003a, b), and unless these cereal-type grains originate from wild grasses (cf. Tweddle *et al.*, 2005), a very early introduction of agriculture to the region seems possible.

5.4.6 The later Neolithic and the Bronze Age

As described in Chapter 4, it seems that the later Neolithic and early Bronze Age (3000–600 BC) was a time when the level of human settlement and activity in the area increased greatly. The evidence for this is that archaeological sites increase in number, size and function, while the palaeoenvironmental evidence for human impact shows a parallel increase in quantity and scale compared with the preceding periods. Whether this may be interpreted as resulting from an increase in population at this time, or merely a change in agricultural strategy, remains conjectural. The project site at Newby Wiske shows that, after the initial impact on the forest at the *Ulmus* decline, Neolithic activity continued and intensified, a clear indication of local agriculture being present (Chapter 3.3). This evidence continues to the truncation of the profile at *c.* 4315 ¹⁴C BP (Fig. 3.7).

Not only do the continuous curves for cereal-type pollen grains, *Plantago lanceolata*, *Taraxacum*-type and *Pteridium* indicate the establishment of a mixed farming system locally, but a general decline in trees and their replacement by grass pollen suggests a real change in the dryland vegetation, with the creation of clearings, presumably for fields, encouraging the maintenance of grassland and replacing the strategy of cultivating small plots and herding stock within an otherwise still dense woodland. The plant macrofossil remains from this later Neolithic (upper) part of the Newby Wiske sequence support this interpretation, as seeds from several weeds of open, disturbed ground occur. As weed seeds do not travel far, agricultural land and perhaps even Neolithic settlement must have been very close to the Newby Wiske site, most probably on the adjacent hill slopes. The attractiveness of the floodplain wetland edge for prehistoric economic and settlement activity is clear (cf. Brayshay & Dinnin, 1999).

It is unfortunate that the vegetation history at Newby Wiske does not continue beyond the 3rd Millennium BC, but later pollen stratigraphies are available at other Washlands study sites. Most significant are the pollen records from the two sites at Nosterfield that contain sediments of late Neolithic and early Bronze Age, as these lie close to the major triple-henge and associated archaeological landscape at Thornborough (see Chapter 4). The purpose and function of these monuments may remain open to debate but it is clear that this part of the Swale–Ure Washlands formed a very significant concentration of resources and activity in the late Neolithic and early Bronze Age (Harding, 1998, 2000a), which seems certain to have left a significant imprint upon the local landscape. The pollen data from the two Nosterfield sites, Shakehole-1 and F45 (Chapter 3.2), are equivocal in this regard.

The Shakehole-1 profile shows that the surrounding vegetation was largely-unbroken woodland, with oak and hazel on the drier calcareous soils and dense alder stands around the site itself on the marshier soils. Some indications of the creation of open areas is seen in the later Neolithic, with grassland weeds like *Plantago lanceolata* and *Taraxacum*-type occurring, but these clearings were very small and suggest very low-scale, temporary activity without any signs of arable cultivation or semi-permanent grassland. Natural processes could have created such ephemeral openings in the local shrub canopy, but the archaeological evidence suggests cultural activity around the site in this period (Harding, 1998; see Chapter 4) and so it is likely that human agency was involved. Brown (1997b) has drawn attention to the likelihood that clearings may have been created by people in the Neolithic (as in other periods) for a variety of reasons, and that an agricultural or economic purpose cannot be assumed. It is possible that small clearings may have served a ritual or social function of some sort, and openings created in the dense river floodplain woods may have had a particular significance (Brown, 2000) that had nothing to do with the production of food resources or domestic settlement. Such ideas, although bringing an important aspect of human behaviour into the discussion of vegetation change and landscape history, are largely untestable with palaeoenvironmental data. It is also possible that some of the apparent clearings within woods growing on and around mires and stream-valley wetlands were the result of the activities of beaver, which can have significant impacts in reducing tree cover around wetlands and changing their local hydrology (Wells *et al.*, 2000; Coles, 2001).

Alternatively, the low-intensity signal of vegetation change at the Shakehole-1 may simply be a function of the distance of tree clearance from the sampling site, rather than of the size of the clearing created, the filtering effects of tree canopies and undergrowth reducing the pollen source area of wetland sites within dense valley woodland (Brown, 1988, 1999; Waller, 1998). At Nosterfield F45, at around the same time (4000 ^{14}C BP), cereal-type pollen and a range of agricultural weeds (Fig. 3.2) suggest an economic use for the small clearing created at that location, where much lower alder percentages suggest a drier landscape and better transport of herbaceous pollen grains to the site. Despite their proximity in age and distance to the Thornborough monument complex, with the associated social focus and cultural activity that implies, there is no real need to invoke an explanation for forest opening other than that of small-scale agricultural activity by Neolithic subsistence farmers. Indeed, evidence for the cultivation of land before the building of monumental structures in the Neolithic is by no means unknown (Brown, 2000). For example, it has been demonstrated at Kilham Long Barrow in east Yorkshire, where the buried soil beneath the Neolithic monument contains environmental evidence of intensive clearance and cultivation (Manby, 1976).

Mid-Holocene floodplains, prior to the levelling of land surfaces by major alluviation in later prehistory (Buckland & Sadler, 1985; Lewin *et al.*, 2005), contained considerable topographic variability, with channels and basins contrasting with upstanding gravel bar ridges and mounds of glacial material (Dinnin & Brayshay, 1999). The use of higher and drier 'island' areas with dry soils and woodland type vegetation in preference to dense fen–carr dominated floodplain wetlands, which in any case would not be favourable for cultivation, seems a logical land-use strategy in lowland river valleys, whether for economic or other purposes (Robinson, 1992b; Brown, 2003). It may not be a coincidence that site F45 at Nosterfield, which contains much clearer evidence of cultivation, is significantly closer to the Thornborough henges than the Shakehole-1 site. The former may be recording substantial agricultural activity preceding, or associated with, the construction and use of the monuments, activity that does not register to any significant extent in the pollen record at the more distant and more densely vegetated Shakehole-1 location.

It could be suggested that a major social and ritual centre like Thornborough, located at the conjunction of an important north–south route through the region linked to the Swale and the Ure rivers, might also have been a centre of population or, at least at intervals, may have attracted large numbers of people to the area, and so may have required the considerable provision of food to sustain it. There is no evidence from the environmental data, however, for any large-scale food production in the Nosterfield area in the late Neolithic, even allowing for the low visibility of pollen evidence of cultivation in such environments, where the filtering and masking effects of the alder-carr vegetation make the detection of dryland vegetation changes

very difficult at any distance from their source (Waller, 1998; Binney *et al.*, 2005; Waller *et al.*, 2005). While some limited mixed farming went on in the Nosterfield area, the land remained well wooded. Even at F45, clearly a drier site than Shakehole-1 (since alder never reached abundance there), tree pollen frequencies attained 70% of total pollen at this time, indicating little open ground locally. The Thornborough henges, less than a kilometre to the south, may therefore have been constructed on higher land that had been previously cleared and intensively used, perhaps creating the distal evidence at F45, within an otherwise mostly wooded landscape. This would conform with evidence from other major lowland river valleys from which Neolithic environments have been reconstructed (cf. Keevill, 1992; Robinson, 1992b). It raises questions about the psychology of monument location during the Neolithic and the importance of trees and woodland to the landscape setting of tombs, henges and other structures (Cummings & Whittle, 2003). Many more pollen and other palaeobotanical data need to be collected, regarding the vegetation in the environs of Neolithic monuments during their construction and use, before those questions may be addressed.

In the wider region the evidence is similar. Sediment began accumulating at Sharow Mires at some stage in the later Neolithic, but there is no pollen evidence of local agriculture at that time (Chapter 3.8). To the north, however, at Mordon Carr in south-east Durham (Bartley *et al.*, 1976), there was major clearance at 4543 ± 70 ^{14}C BP, the evidence including high levels of cereal-type pollen, while Innes *et al.* (2005) have recorded evidence for similar large-scale clearance at nearby Hartlepool, where a charcoal layer has been radiocarbon dated to 4340 ± 70 ^{14}C BP. Major deforestation with cereal-type pollen also occurred in the mid-Neolithic at Skipsea Withow Mere, east Yorkshire, before soil erosion and colluviation, after 4500 ± 50 ^{14}C BP, buried the peat profile (Blackham & Flenley, 1984). In places Neolithic farming was intense enough to have had significant environmental impacts at the local scale in the lowlands, as shown by the long-term forest clearance with cereal-type pollen and soil erosion recorded at Gilderson Marr in east Yorkshire (Tweddle, 2001), but generally the evidence for forest clearance is poor in the lowlands throughout the region (Jones, 1976a; Lillie & Gearey, 1999; Dark, 2005). Regional sites at altitude show little sign of significant Neolithic farming; for example, the first clearance at Fountains Earth above Nidderdale (Tinsley, 1975a) was delayed until after 4000 ^{14}C BP, as it was around Stainmore (Gear & Turner, 2001).

Most sites in the Pennines record only sporadic and short-lived, low-intensity clearance, although greater impacts are recorded in some places with more fertile soil, such as Eshton Tarn in the Craven district of Yorkshire, where major clearance with cereals is dated to *c.* 4500 ^{14}C BP (Bartley *et al.*, 1990), and in the limestone areas of Wensleydale, where Honeyman (1985) reported significant clearance dated 4550 ± 50 ^{14}C BP. Later Neolithic woodland clearance on the North York Moors was also very low scale and sporadic (Simmons *et al.*, 1993); indeed, there is good macrofossil and pollen evidence for an expansion of tree cover in most of the uplands surrounding the Washlands during the Neolithic (Tallis & Switsur, 1983; Turner, 1991; Simmons *et al.*, 1993) together with a rise in the altitude of the tree line. The cessation in the uplands of the regular burning of the Mesolithic period, which had tended to suppress the height of the tree line, and its replacement by a Neolithic land management that did not use fire systematically, or by the withdrawal of human activity altogether from most of the upland, are possible reasons for this upward expansion of the tree line (Simmons & Innes, 1981, 1988). Alternatively, climate change might have been the major factor. Smith (2002) found evidence in the peat stratigraphy of lowland raised bogs in south Yorkshire that suggested a wetter climate in the mid- to late Neolithic, drier conditions in the mid- to late Bronze Age and then climatic deterioration towards the end of the Bronze Age.

Regionally, the cultural change to the Bronze Age after about 4000 ¹⁴C BP brought with it a much greater level of impact on the vegetation than previously, as forest clearance expanded spatially into the uplands and into more marginal wetland areas, as well as increasing in intensity (Simmons *et al.*, 1993; Atherden, 1999; Innes, 1999). A generally more congenial climate allowed this expansion into previously unfavourable areas. The Yorkshire Pennines provide good examples: at Rishworth, West Yorkshire, the first major clearance was at 4010 ± 100 ¹⁴C BP (Bartley, 1975); at Skell Moor, on the upland above Nidderdale, Tinsley (1975a, 1976) recorded intensive Bronze Age clearance dated to 3880 ± 100 ¹⁴C BP, whereas Honeyman (1985) recorded very substantial clearances dated between 3930 ± 50 ¹⁴C BP and 3600 ± 89 ¹⁴C BP at sites in Wensleydale. Further north, there is a date of 3620 ± 47 ¹⁴C BP for substantial forest clearance with limited cereal-type evidence from near Gate Gutter on Stainmore, in the Durham uplands (Gear & Turner, 2001). The North York Moors were also heavily affected in the early and mid-Bronze Age, with substantial deforestation for mixed farming with cereal-type pollen common (Simmons *et al.*, 1993). Few of these clearance phases are supported by radiocarbon dates, but by context they must be mid-Bronze Age, like the episode at Fen Bogs (Atherden, 1976a), dated to 3400 ± 90 ¹⁴C BP, and the later Bronze Age date of 3210 ± 90 ¹⁴C BP at Wheeldale Gill (Simmons & Cundill, 1974). Other regional upland sites, such as at Willow Garth on the Yorkshire Wolds, show similar increases in human impact on the forest at this time (Bush, 1993).

A comparable assault on the forest also occurred in the lowlands. On Hatfield Moors, in south Yorkshire, extensive clearances dated between 3715 ± 70 ¹⁴C BP and 3545 ± 70 ¹⁴C BP have been recorded (Tweddle, 2001; Smith, 2002), with burnt and axe-marked tree stumps indicating the type of activity that occurred. To the north, at Bishop Middleham in the Durham lowlands, successive episodes of tree clearance at 3660 ± 80 ¹⁴C BP and 3360 ± 80 ¹⁴C

BP, and 3544 ± 80 ¹⁴C BP at nearby Hutton Henry appear to have almost deforested the local fertile limestone soils (Bartley *et al.*, 1976). At Hartlepool Bay, several profiles have yielded evidence for intensive clearance, with cereal-type pollen (Waughman *et al.*, 2005); in two of these the clearance has been dated to 3892 ± 28 ¹⁴C BP and 3685 ± 75 ¹⁴C BP. One of the most noteworthy elements of the enhanced levels of forest clearance and agriculture in the mid-Bronze Age is the decline of *Tilia* pollen within clearance phases dated in the centuries around 3500 ¹⁴C BP, although the timing varies from site to site. The *Tilia* decline is the youngest regional-scale biostratigraphical marker in pollen diagrams (Innes, 1999) but its association with substantial forest clearance, and its diachroneity because of the local variability in clearance events, has meant that it cannot be used as more than a very broad chronological marker, one attributed to anthropogenic forest clearance for farming (Turner, 1962, 1965).

As Waller (1994) has pointed out, however, water-logging and the spread of peat in lowland wetlands may reduce the representation of *Tilia* in local diagrams, because of poor production and transmission of *Tilia* pollen and increases in effective sediment-basin size. This factor of wetland spread is clearly of relevance in later Holocene records from areas such as the Swale–Ure Washlands, particularly since it appears that *Tilia* might well have formed an important component of the forest at the wetland edge (Kirby & Gearey, 2001; Smith, 2002). Nevertheless, the human impact hypothesis remains the preferred explanation for the *Tilia* decline in the North Yorkshire lowlands. Dated examples in the north of the region include Hallowell Moss in County Durham, at 3645 ± 60 ¹⁴C BP (Donaldson & Turner, 1977), and the major clearance at Hutton Henry, dated 3544 ± 80 ¹⁴C BP (Bartley *et al.*, 1976). Other undated sites also include clear examples. At the kettle hole at Scamer Carrs, south of the Tees valley (Jones, 1976a), a sharp decline of *Tilia* is associated with a major increase in open ground indicators, many of which are weeds of cultivation and pasture. High levels of cereal-type pollen were also recognized. As the morphology of the kettle-hole basin precluded the kind of lateral spread of wetland that occurs in river valley bottoms, the *Tilia* decline here is almost certain to be the consequence of major agricultural expansion.

Before the present study there was no environmental evidence for Bronze Age activity within the Swale–Ure Washlands area to add to the archaeological evidence of an increased human presence described in Chapter 4, as published pollen records such as those of Bartley (1962), Keen *et al.* (1988) and Giles (1992) were truncated, with no later Holocene evidence surviving. Even where peat of the right age was present, factors of peat cutting or mixing made the pollen stratigraphy uncertain and difficult to interpret, as at Askham Bog in the Vale of York (Gearey & Lillie, 1999). The new data from the Nosterfield profiles are therefore a valuable addition to understanding the character of the regional lowland Bronze Age. In the

Shakehole-1 core, *Tilia* only becomes important after the *Ulmus* decline, late compared with the behaviour of *Tilia* regionally (Fig. 3.3). It declined sharply at some stage in the centuries before 3277 ± 75 ^{14}C BP, with increases in cereal-type pollen and other cultivation herbs, in a phase resembling that at Seamer Carrs. In the F45 core (Fig. 3.2) there is a major deforestation phase at a date that interpolates to the mid-Bronze Age, very possibly correlating with the Shakehole-1 episode, where a low *Tilia* curve disappears altogether and clearance indicators rise, especially *Pteridium*. Although this is less clear at Sharow Mires, there is intermittent clearance recorded between *c.* 4000 ^{14}C BP and 3371 ± 31 ^{14}C BP, after which already uncommon *Tilia* ceases to be recorded (Fig. 3.12). The new Washlands data agree with what little previous evidence exists in recording Bronze Age forest clearance for mixed agriculture at a variety of scales, incorporating long-term reduction and often removal of *Tilia* from the local woodland.

Almost all the pollen diagrams from North Yorkshire, lowland or upland, and from relevant adjacent areas such as County Durham, show evidence of forest clearance to one degree or another in the early and mid-Bronze Age. This great expansion in the distribution and intensity of the human impact upon the forest should perhaps not be surprising, as Bronze Age archaeological remains in North Yorkshire, lowland and upland, are abundant, greatly surpassing those of the preceding Neolithic. Increased populations and settlement should naturally have led to an increased need for food production and more intensive methods of land use. Previous examinations of the environmental evidence (Atherden, 1999; Simmons *et al.*, 1993) have stressed its mixed nature, with woodland opening for animal husbandry considered as important as for cereal cultivation. The relative importance of pastoral and arable farming in the Bronze Age economy remains conjectural, but it is clear that for the first time deforestation of large areas of land for agriculture occurred, rather than the previous piecemeal use of plots within the woodland. The recognition of land division boundaries of this age in the uplands (Spratt, 1981) supports the view of a more developed agricultural economy and higher population levels. Perhaps a decline in the importance of hunting and gathering in the Bronze Age, in comparison with the less sedentary Neolithic, can be surmised.

5.4.7 The later Bronze Age to the Roman Period

The later Bronze Age through to the transition into the Iron Age was a time of climatic and cultural change in northern England. The latter half of the 3rd Millenium BP (1st Millennium BC) saw the start of a gradual shift towards much cooler and wetter conditions (Barber *et al.*, 1993) that would have had implications for the distribution and type of land use conducted by late Bronze Age and early Iron Age communities, perhaps causing a withdrawal of human settlement and agriculture from those parts of the landscape that were economically more marginal. As well as the upland limits of cultivation, where the spread of blanket peat continued, these would have included the lowest parts of the valley bottoms and the wetlands they sustained. Although these wetland areas would still have been exploited for the wildlife and wood products they contained, and perhaps also for grazing of domestic stock, such hunting, foraging and browsing activities would not be apparent from pollen diagrams, in marked contrast to tree clearance for agriculture.

There is some evidence in the pollen data from the Washland sites for reduced human activity at this time. At Nosterfield F45, the mid-Bronze Age clearance is followed by an extended period from which there are no indications of disturbance; for example, micro-charcoal frequencies are very low indeed. All tree types show an increase, in particular the waterlogging-tolerant *Alnus* and *Salix* (Fig. 3.2), suggesting raised water tables and the spread of willow–alder carr and fen woodland across the local lowland. In practice, however, the effects of the gradual climatic downturn were not sufficiently severe to determine the activities of late Bronze Age groups, so that in places major cultivation still occurred. At Nosterfield (Shakehole-1), for example, an intense phase of cultivation with cereals took place at *c.* 3250 ^{14}C BP (the average age from two dates from the same level at the start of the phase), with *Quercus* and *Tilia* most affected by the clearance (see Chapter 3.2.2; Table 3.3). This suggests that clearance took place on higher, drier areas around the small depression, but the cultivation phase seems to have been short lived and the expansion of aquatic herbs and other wetland marsh taxa that followed the clearance must reflect rising water tables around the shakehole. Although supplemented by the hydrological effects of the clearance, a gradual increase in wetness was occurring at this site through the late Bronze Age, as at site F45. In the Sharow Mires record (Chapter 3.8), the same indications of gradually increasing water levels occur around the same time, with a marked increase in *Pediastrum* algae and aquatic herbs like *Typha angustifolia* and with only slight evidence of any disturbance of the local vegetation.

An acceleration of climatic deterioration, and therefore in the development of wetland habitats, can be discerned throughout the lowlands of the Washlands and the wider study area after about 3200 ^{14}C BP. That this had the consequence of deterring human activity and settlement in this lowland area is suggested by the very poor archaeological record for the latest Bronze Age and the early Iron Age, as discussed in Chapter 4. The period from about 3100 to 2500 ^{14}C BP appears to have been the time when the deterioration in climate increased in severity, with a particularly wet and cold phase near the end of that period. At Nosterfield SH1, a dramatic switch from wet woodland vegetation to a sedge-dominated marsh occurred after 2715 ± 45 ^{14}C BP and, while there are some indications of local agriculture, these are not sufficient to account for the sudden increased wetness. A change in climate may well have been responsible. A similar, although less pronounced change began somewhat before *c.* 2400 ^{14}C BP at nearby site F45 and at *c.* 2500 ^{14}C BP at Sharow Mires, while very wet conditions prevailed at Ripon North at about the same time (see Chapter 3.5). The lower sand and gravel deposits at Ripon South, which accumulated after the latest Neolithic (from a basal date in monolith 2M of 4011 ± 40 ^{14}C BP; a minimum age is given by the overlying Medieval channel-fill), may represent the fluvial signature of the same climatic deterioration event, causing a phase of coarse clastic deposition of a type that generally characterizes cold rather than interglacial episodes (Chapter 3.7). Although it is not tightly constrained in age, an association of this coarse gravel deposition with the wet climate and enhanced flooding regimes in the middle part of the 3rd Millennium BP is very possible.

This trend towards increased wetness, apparent in the Washlands, is visible in records of similar age throughout the region and beyond (Barber *et al.*, 1993). Around Hartlepool Bay, a major reduction in the archaeological evidence for human presence during this period coincides with an indication of accelerated peat formation and increased wetness (Waughman *et al.*, 2005). This agrees with the evidence from Neasham Fen in the Tees valley, on the northern fringes of the Washlands area, where, after *c.* 3300 ^{14}C BP, there is no evidence of human impact on the regenerated woodland until the mid-3rd Millennium BP (Bartley *et al.*, 1976). A similar succession of events has been described by Smith (2002) in the Humberhead levels of south Yorkshire, where extensive mid-Bronze Age agriculture ceased at around the Bronze Age to Iron Age transition, with no significant evidence of forest clearance until later in the 3rd Millennium BP. This cultural recession coincided in that area with environmental evidence of increased wetness, bog growth and carr woodland regeneration. The development of far wetter mire surfaces and the spread of peat across wet heathland has also been recorded from a little before 3000 ^{14}C BP (Boswijk & Whitehouse, 2002; Whitehouse, 2004), using plant-macrofossil and insect data.

In the centuries after 3000 ^{14}C BP, the mesotrophic wetland systems of the area rapidly changed to acid, ombrotrophic bogs. Although few deposits representing this period of cultural transition (late Bronze Age to Iron Age) are preserved in the Yorkshire lowlands, at St. George's Field, York (Lillie & Gearey, 1999), environmental evidence indicates mature undisturbed woodland and alluvial wetlands between 3240 ± 70 ^{14}C BP and 2760 ± 65 ^{14}C BP. The adjoining uplands, which are probably more sensitive to climate change, provide evidence in support of major climatic deterioration and a significant reduction in agricultural activity at this time. Analyses of pollen records and soil profiles on Bowes Moor, Stainmore, have revealed cessation of agriculture there from about 3000 ^{14}C BP with no sign of revival throughout the 3rd Millennium BP, with blanket peat spreading permanently across the land, at a location that had seen intensive mixed

agriculture extending well above 400 m O.D. during the mid-Bronze Age, between *c.* 3600 and *c.* 3200 ^{14}C BP (Gear & Turner, 2001; McHugh, 2001). Also in the Pennines, Honeyman (1985) recorded greatly reduced evidence of forest clearance at the time of the transition to the early Iron Age in Wensleydale.

Analogous evidence is available from the North York Moors, where the first half of the 3rd Millennium BP saw an interlude of woodland regeneration and blanket peat expansion between the intensive agricultural phases of the mid-Bronze Age and the later Iron Age (Atherden, 1976b, 1989; Simmons *et al.*, 1993; Oldfield *et al.*, 2003), with a shift to wet conditions at this time shown by detailed analyses of peat-bog surfaces at Harold's Bog on East Bilsdale Moor (Blackford & Chambers, 1999; Chambers & Blackford, 2001). Such changes in the macrofossil type and the degree of humification of bog surfaces are a very sensitive proxy for climate (Blackford, 2000), although local topographic and edaphic conditions on individual mires must be taken into account. Nevertheless, the weight of evidence, from peat stratigraphy in the Yorkshire region and beyond, for a severe switch to a wet, cold climate unfavourable for agriculture in the early 3rd Millennium BP is undeniable. Rowell and Turner (1985), who used peat humification as a proxy for accumulation rate and surface wetness, recorded a considerably wetter mire surface from 3130 ± 50 ^{14}C BP that lasted for several hundred years. Similarly, a clear recurrence surface (i.e. a layer of fresh peat recording rapid growth after a shift to wet conditions) has been dated to 2685 ± 50 ^{14}C BP at Featherbed Moss in the southern Pennines (Tallis & McGuire, 1972). This date is virtually identical to those of 2630 ± 60 ^{14}C BP for the 'wet shift' recorded by Blackford and Chambers (1991) at Harold's Bog and 2660 ± 50 ^{14}C BP for the major cold and wet phase recorded at Talkin Tarn in north-east Cumbria (Langdon *et al.*, 2004).

Similar dates for a major wet shift on ombrogenous mire surfaces in northern England (Barber *et al.*, 1994a, b; Mauquoy & Barber, 1999; Hughes *et al.*, 2000) make it certain that one of the most severe episodes of climatic deterioration in the entire Holocene occurred at about 2650 ^{14}C BP. The evidence from this project, at Nosterfield SH1, of a major increase in wetness soon after 2715 ± 45 ^{14}C BP must be a further indication of this apparently abrupt and very severe climatic deterioration. Van Geel *et al.* (1996) have considered this event in detail and concluded that its abruptness, severity and apparent synchroneity must have led to the disruption of agricultural systems, including withdrawal from more marginal areas, and changes in settlement patterns throughout north-west Europe and beyond. The regeneration of woodland, the spread of wetland and the near absence of forest clearance and agriculture, as indicated by the palaeoenvironmental and archaeological evidence from the Yorkshire region, can be interpreted as a consequence of this climate shift.

Some caution is required, as Tipping (2002) has noted that not all upland sites in northern Britain show clear signs of abandonment and there is difficulty in determining which sites were 'marginal' and therefore vulnerable to climate change (Young, 2000; Young & Simmonds, 1995). Also, a change to more appropriate and less palynologically visible land use may be misinterpreted in pollen diagrams as a cessation of activity. Dark (2006), who has reviewed the pollen evidence for land abandonment in Britain in this period, suggests that conversion from cultivation to pastoral systems and a less intensive use of the land may well be a more realistic interpretation. Increased wetness in uplands and lowland valley bottoms, where most pollen records are situated, may have caused their evacuation (van Geel *et al.*, 1996) in favour of better-drained locations that would not so easily be represented in the regional pollen archive. This could be of major significance in the Swale–Ure Washlands and their environs, for although the major climatic deterioration would have been felt everywhere, the human land-use and settlement response could have been very variable (Dark, 2006) as people adapted to changed conditions. In places where cultivation was still practised, an increase in its intensity might have been necessary unless there was a population collapse. There would almost certainly have been a major removal of farming and settlement from most of the valley bottoms in the Washlands, where the effects of the change to a very wet climatic regime would have been strongly felt, as has been demonstrated in other valley floors in western Europe (van Geel *et al.*, 1996, 1998).

The alluvial sediments preserved in the river valley floodplains of North Yorkshire confirm the environmental consequences of the climate change around 2650 ^{14}C BP, as the sequences of fluvially derived deposits reflect the past effects of climate on river discharge (Taylor & Macklin,1998; Merrett & Macklin, 1999; Howard *et al.*, 2000b; Taylor *et al.*, 2000), although the effects of anthropogenic land use (particularly agriculture) were also locally significant, increasing soil erosion and therefore sediment supply to the rivers (Macklin, 1999). Whether forced by climate or by anthropogenic factors, however, alluvial material, usually fine-grained, appears to have been delivered episodically to the sedimentary basins of the rivers from their catchments as pulses of sediment during flooding events.

The onset of significant alluviation and the deposition of substantial thicknesses of fine-grained fluvial sediment is thus linked to climatic and anthropogenic factors or, most probably, both. The dating of this phenomenon is invariably imprecise, because of missing evidence caused by erosion and the paucity of records that have been studied in detail (Macklin & Lewin, 2003; Macklin *et al.*, 2005). Nevertheless, virtually all relevant studies of Yorkshire rivers record a major episode of alluvial deposition coinciding with the *c.* 2650 ^{14}C BP climate event, from upper reaches, as in Wharfedale (Howard *et al.*, 2000b) to the Humber and Tees estuaries (Plater *et al.*, 2000; Rees *et al.*, 2000), as well as many stretches in between (Lewin *et al.*, 2005). An enhanced freshwater pulse

into the Humber estuary system at this time is probably also connected (Long *et al.*, 1998). The linkage of this regional episode of flooding and alluviation throughout the Ouse system to climate deterioration (Macklin *et al.*, 2000) seems secure, particularly with the greatly reduced levels of contemporaneous human impact. That the alluvial material deposited at this time is particularly coarse-grained emphasizes the severity of the flood regimes associated with this climate event. The elevated freshwater levels, the switch to marsh and bog vegetation and the deposition of clastic units within the Swale–Ure Washlands all agree well with this regional climatic deterioration.

In terms of environmental conditions and cultural response, the later Iron Age and Roman periods that followed during the last few centuries of the 3rd Millennium and the first few of the 2nd Millennium BP were profoundly different to the preceding wet phase of the early Iron Age. All of the climate studies referred to above agree that a dry and warm phase began about 2400 ^{14}C BP and lasted for several centuries. Without being overly deterministic, it is thus sensible to conclude that the major agricultural and settlement expansion that occurred in the late Iron Age and lasted through the Roman occupation was, if not driven, then at least encouraged by the much milder climate. Peat-based climate records from the North York Moors (Blackford & Chambers, 1991; Chiverrell & Atherden, 1999) are local archives for the wider Washlands area that confirm the more congenial climate that persisted until a further deterioration around 1400 ^{14}C BP.

The human populations of the area appear to have responded vigorously to the opportunity presented by climate amelioration after about 2400 ^{14}C BP, as seen in the great expansion in field systems and associated settlement across the central Yorkshire lowlands, including the Swale–Ure Washlands, and the adjacent uplands revealed by aerial photography and archaeological evidence (Spratt, 1993; Manby, 2003b; see Chapter 4). Later Iron Age agricultural expansion included greatly increased cereal production, deduced from pollen analysis but also from the common preservation of cereal grain on archaeological sites in the region (Van der Veen, 1992). The widespread discovery of beehive-shaped querns for grinding corn (they occur in 23 locations within the Washlands: Chapter 4.6.1) also suggests that when the area became the subject of Roman administration, in the later part of the 1st Century AD, a well-developed late Iron Age arable economy existed.

The drier climate greatly reduced the incidence of overbank flooding and alluviation (Macklin *et al.*, 2005), so that much of the lowland in the Ouse system became drier and more stable and thus available for intensive agricultural exploitation. The construction of large primary settlements like Stanwick, between the Swale and the Tees, and the industrial centres for iron smelting on the North York Moors and in south Yorkshire (Halkon, 2003; Halkon & Millett, 1999), illustrates the great social developments and organization taking place in the later Iron Age and the major increases in the agricultural resource base and population levels that permitted them. Although the mid-Bronze Age forest clearance had been considerable, at least in areas of favourable soil, the late Iron Age and Roman period was the time when the first really extensive deforestation occurred in the Yorkshire region, perhaps removing trees entirely from parts of the landscape (Atherden, 1999).

Within the project area there were hitherto few pollen diagrams that covered the late Iron Age and Roman period, but data from the present study provides evidence of agricultural expansion at that time. In the Nosterfield pollen diagrams (Figs 3.2 and 3.3), late Iron Age cereal-type pollen and accompanying weeds of cultivation suggest local mixed farming at around 2300 ^{14}C BP, but the sites in question are small wetlands that are dominated by local vegetation and so do not provide a clear picture of local farming intensity or character. Although still at a low scale of intensity, the cereal-type pollen record at Ripon North, which starts at 2325 ± 50 ^{14}C BP, indicates an environment with little woodland but with much local scrub and considerable evidence of grassland. It is very similar to the evidence from Ripon South, from what must be the same period, when the riverine lowlands in this area were probably still wet enough to discourage arable crops and favour animal husbandry.

The faunal evidence for well-developed stock rearing during this period (Hambleton, 1999) suggests that pastoral farming played a significant part in the agricultural economy. At Sharow Mires (Chapter 3.5) the record between 2450 ± 31 and 1494 ± 28 ^{14}C BP, which corresponds almost exactly with the late Iron Age and Roman periods, reveals a well-defined rise in cereal-type pollen and decline in oak pollen. Although masked by the high values of local wetland taxa, the Sharow Mires pollen diagram (Fig. 3.12) records a considerable expansion of cereal cultivation and woodland clearance during this cultural period and is thus in accord with the regional picture. Major and occasionally complete deforestation for farming is recorded throughout north-eastern England during the late Iron Age and Roman periods. Massive forest clearance took place on the North York Moors in Iron Age to Roman times, some records showing high cereal-type values, although others were apparently mainly for pasture (Simmons *et al.*, 1993). The best-dated examples are Fen Bogs, between 2280 ± 120 ^{14}C BP and 1530 ± 130 ^{14}C BP (Atherden, 1976a, b), and after 2190 ± 90 ^{14}C BP at Harwood Dale Bog (Atherden, 1989). Woodland removal and cereal cultivation increased greatly in the areas around the Roman Wall in the Tyne valley during the late Iron Age, as at Crag Lough (Dark, 2005).

Evidence from the Pennine upland is also clear; at Featherbed Moss, in the southern Pennines, evidence for very substantial clearance with some cereal-type pollen was dated by Tallis and Switsur (1973) to between 2251 ± 50 and 1400 ± 50 ^{14}C BP, while Tinsley (1975a, 1976) reported a major late Iron Age and Roman forest clearance with high cereal-type values dated after 2200 ± 80 ^{14}C BP above Nidderdale, overlooking the Swale–Ure Washlands.

Honeyman (1985) reported a major late Iron Age clearance phase in Wensleydale that continued and expanded into Roman times, and Smith (1986) recorded the first presence of cereal-type pollen during an intensified farming phase over the same periods at Gordale Beck in Craven. A significant expansion of heather, grasses and weeds of open ground occurred at Simy Folds, in upper Teesdale, around and after 2440 ± 80 ^{14}C BP, with significant levels of cereal-type pollen appearing after the initial clearance (Donaldson, in Coggins *et al.*, 1980). An earlier date of 2570 ± 80 ^{14}C BP for the start of a similar period, with elevated levels of heather, grasses and grassland weeds like *Plantago lanceolata*, occurs at Red Sike Moss, also in upper Teesdale (Turner *et al.*, 1973), although without cereal-type pollen. Gear and Huntley (2001) recorded a similar phase, dated 2198 ± 59 ^{14}C BP, when virtually all tree cover was removed from Bowes Moor, Stainmore, again with grassland and heathland expanding, but without pollen evidence of cereal agriculture. Iron Age (pre-Roman) clearance also occurred at Valley Bog in Teesdale, dated to 2215 ± 55 and 2175 ± 45 ^{14}C BP (Chambers, 1978), in this case with cereal-type pollen, so that arable activity had certainly spread into the uplands before the Roman administration began. The recording of such pollen evidence of cultivation in the Pennines will be dependent upon the agricultural potential of individual areas at that time and the distance of any cultivation from the pollen sampling site.

Regional deforestation for arable agriculture is also a feature of the south Yorkshire lowlands, creating a very open landscape indeed. Deforestation occurred around Thorne and Hatfield Moors after dated levels of 2085 ± 70, 2225 ± 70 and 2145 ± 65 ^{14}C BP (Dinnin, 1997a; Smith, 2002). On the Yorkshire Wolds at Willow Garth, Bush (1993) also recorded a major switch after 2120 ± 50 ^{14}C BP to arable cultivation with high cereal-type values, while at Askham Bog, near York, there was a sharp decline in oak and hazel and a rise in grass and cereal-type pollen after 2010 ± 90 ^{14}C BP (Kenward *et al.*, 1978; Gearey & Lillie, 1999). To the north of the Washlands, major forest clearance is seen to have begun in Weardale, at Bollihope Bog and Steward Shield Meadow, from 1730 ± 100 and 2060 ± 120 ^{14}C BP respectively (Roberts *et al.*, 1973) and at Quick Moss, further upstream (Rowell & Turner, 1985) from 2035 ± 50 ^{14}C BP. In the lowlands to the north of the study area, extensive deforestation took place in east Durham, with trees replaced by grassland almost completely at Hallowell Moss after 1956 ± 70 ^{14}C BP (Donaldson & Turner, 1977), while at Thorpe Bulmer and Hutton Henry (Bartley *et al.*, 1976) intensive deforestation occurred at 2064 ± 60 and 1842 ± 70 ^{14}C BP respectively, the former with high cereal-type values and a peak of *Cannabis*-type pollen at 1730 ± 120 ^{14}C BP. In areas of particularly fertile soils (cf. Turner, 1983), such as at Bishop Middleham on the Durham limestone (Bartley *et al.*, 1976), deforestation was completed during the Iron Age.

Although the first large-scale deforestation occurred

in most places in north-eastern England in the centuries before and after the arrival of the Romans, because of the age-range uncertainty inherent in radiocarbon dating it is very difficult, if not impossible, to distinguish whether the deforestation was caused by the Romans or by the local Iron Age communities (Dumayne & Barber, 1993). It would be logical to assume that the Romans' need for timber, security and extra cereal production to feed the military in this frontier zone of Britain would have led them to greatly increase forest clearance between York and Hadrian's Wall. The establishment of an extensive road system might also have contributed to this. The environmental evidence seems to show, however, that most areas experienced a high level of clearance in the late Iron Age, in the few centuries before the Romans appeared, and that this continued into and through the period of Roman control. This appears to be the case even in the area of the Wall itself, where Roman activity and impact might be expected to have been at a high level (Manning *et al.*, 1997; Tipping, 1997). North of the Wall the land was still widely forested through the pre-Roman Iron Age but became deforested during the Roman period, as at Fellend Moss, where clearance took place at 1948 ± 45 ^{14}C BP, and Fozy Moss, where massive and rapid clearance occurred from 1820 ± 45 ^{14}C BP (Dumayne & Barber, 1994). The standard error range that accompanies radiocarbon dates such as these still means, however, that the cultural context of these clearances remains uncertain.

It is likely that the Romans found a mixed land-use pattern in north-eastern England when they arrived, with much woodland remaining, but in many places a well-developed farming landscape had preceded them. This was the case even in the Pennines, where soil profiles beneath Roman earthworks (Tinsley & Smith, 1973) and Roman roads (Brayshay, 1999) record the landscapes in which those monuments were constructed. Nevertheless, the establishment of military bases and the civil settlements that developed around them, notably at Aldborough and Catterick, gave an impetus to deforestation, while the switch to a large-scale farming economy organized by the Romans is reflected in a cluster of high-status rural estates set on the eastern foothills of the Washlands (see Chapter 4). During the 2nd and 3rd Centuries AD, this rural area appears to have been one of the most prosperous in the north of England, with villas recorded at Middleham, Well, Langwith House, Snape and North Stainley (Chapter 4.7). The extensive forest clearance of the late pre-Roman Iron Age was clearly intensified further in Romano-British times (Turner, 1979), as much of the landscape was given over to food production. Expansion of farming activity seems to have occurred as high as Littondale in the Pennines during the 3rd Century (Maude, 1999), although the Washlands region shared a decline common to the rest of the province that seems to have set in well before the end of the Roman period. From the 3rd century onwards, settlement may have become less urban-based and more dispersed, a pattern more nearly that of the pre-Roman Iron Age. The

reason remains uncertain; it is perhaps environmentally deterministic to attribute the change to the start of the significant climatic deterioration that began towards the end of the Roman period (cf. Langdon *et al.*, 2004).

5.4.8 The Medieval and later periods

The archaeological evidence for the post-Roman period suggests that, following the collapse of the Roman administration, a significant local population continued to live in the Washlands, although adopting new economic structures and different lifestyles that were also archaeologically less 'visible'. Roman administration was replaced, in the Yorkshire region, with petty kingdoms such as those centred around Craven and Richmondshire (Chapter 4.8). Even the addition of immigrants from across the North Sea in the early Medieval period did not increase the pressure on the land, so the level of farming intensity probably returned to roughly that seen in pre-Roman (Iron Age) times. The regional palaeoenvironmental evidence for northern England (Fenton-Thomas, 1992; Dark, 2000; Huntley, 2000, 2002) largely concurs with the archaeological picture of a relaxation of human pressure on the landscape after the transition from the Roman occupation. There appears to have been a region-wide regeneration of woodland that implies a reduction in farming, certainly to the east of the Pennines (Higham, 1987). The climatic deterioration that occurred about 1400 ^{14}C BP (Blackford & Chambers, 1991; Chiverrell & Atherden, 1999, 2000; Langdon *et al.*, 2004) probably influenced this agricultural retreat, with arable areas either abandoned or converted to less intensive land-use regimes (Higham, 1987).

The removal of the Roman army and administration, and perhaps some of the Romanized population also, would have meant less need for intensive cereal production and so a much less organized and centralized farming system would have developed. A real reduction in agricultural activity seems to have occurred in the vicinity of Hadrian's Wall (Dark, 1996) and presumably also wherever there had been a concentration of Roman military and administrative personnel. At Fen Bogs, on the North York Moors (Atherden, 1976b, Chiverrell & Atherden, 1999), a radiocarbon date of 1530 $\pm$ 130 ^{14}C BP marks the change from the intensive and sustained clearance and farming of the Roman period to the regenerating woodland, scrub and heath of the post-Roman period. Similar dates for the same change have been obtained from the north of the region at Hallowell Moss (Donaldson & Turner, 1977) and Quick Moss (Rowell & Turner, 1985).

At Fortress Dike, above Upper Nidderdale, immediately to the west of the Washlands, cereal-type pollen disappears below a date of 1320 $\pm$ 80 ^{14}C BP, when tree regeneration started (Tinsley, 1975b, 1976), conforming to the regional pattern. The summit plateau of this upland, marginal to the Washlands, had been open grassland and farmland since the pre-Roman late Iron Age (Tinsley, 1976) and so the regeneration of woodland and heath returned it to conditions that had not been seen since the early Iron Age phase of cold, wet climate. A similar post-Roman period of land abandonment and reduced agricultural intensity in the upland has been recorded in Craven by Smith (1986). The climatic data for the last 2000 years derived from the peat-bog stratigraphies in the Pennine uplands (Tallis, 1995; Tallis & Livett, 1994) agrees well with the records of vegetational history, not only for this post-Roman period but for all of the last two millennia. On Thorne and Hatfield Moors, in south Yorkshire, Smith (2002) reported substantial post-Roman regeneration of woodland that persisted until after dates of 865 ± 60 ^{14}C BP and 910 ± 65 ^{14}C BP.

Although most of the region shows the same marked decline in the kind of intensive farming activity that requires the maintenance of non-wooded areas, and so is easily visible in pollen diagrams, open, farmed landscapes seem to have persisted in some localities, despite the climatic deterioration and the removal of the Romano-British agricultural system. These, unsurprisingly, include the areas of the best soils, such as the limestone districts of Durham to the north of the Tees valley; thus at Thorpe Bulmer (Bartley *et al.*, 1976) tree regeneration did not begin until 852 ± 60 ^{14}C BP. Perhaps less expected is the persistence of open vegetation with elements of farming until a similar date in Weardale (Roberts *et al.*, 1973), although much of the open vegetation in that case may have been on waste rather than exploited land. In the latter half of the 2nd Millennium BP there was some considerable variability in food production (Huntley, 1999), probably influenced by local factors, with developments such as the establishment of Viking York, and of urban centres generally, requiring beyond-subsistence farm productivity once again (Higham, 1986).

The establishment of ecclesiastical sites in the centuries after the Roman withdrawal at places such as Catterick, which remained such until AD 653, would have had economic implications, but it was the rise of Ripon as a religious centre thereafter that was particularly significant. This suggests that it was in the last two centuries before the Norman Conquest that most of the familiar settlement pattern of the Washlands was first established. The real influence of religious houses on the landscape would not be felt until the later Medieval period, however, when the creation of ranges and sheep husbandry would turn large areas into pastoral landscapes that otherwise would have been exploited for arable cultivation.

The environmental information gained from the Swale–Ure Washlands study provides an important addition to knowledge of the post-Roman period in the Yorkshire lowlands. The later pollen sequence from Sharow Mires, near Ripon, preserves an apparently continuous record of vegetation change from the start of a late Iron Age phase of arable cultivation, at 2450 ± 31 ^{14}C BP, until the present day (Chapter 3.8). The cereal-type curve at Sharow is not high but is continuous, and is accompanied by high values for grasses and the pasture weed *Plantago lanceolata,* until

it fades away after 1494 ± 28 ^{14}C BP (Fig. 3.12). There then followed a major expansion of trees, mainly alder and hazel but also oak and ash, and the great reduction of grass and weed pollen, including the virtual absence of cereal-type grains. This replacement of agricultural and other open-ground vegetation by scrub woodland fits well with the regional picture of agricultural reduction and withdrawal from many areas that were rendered difficult to farm by the negative climatic change and the removal of Roman administration after *c.* 1400 ^{14}C BP. This phase of agricultural decline and woodland regeneration ends in the Sharow Mires record at a point that is not directly dated but which, by interpolation between radiocarbon dates, must be *c.* 1000 ^{14}C BP. This is in close agreement with the proxy climate data derived from changes in peat bog surface wetness, which virtually all record a shift to a drier, warmer climate at this time (Chiverrell, 2001; Chiverrell & Menuge, 2003; Hughes *et al.*, 2000) that lasted for about three centuries, until *c.* 650 ^{14}C BP, constituting the 'Medieval Warm Period', although the degree to which temperatures increased remains debated (Bradley *et al.*, 2003). Cereal-type pollen frequencies are very high at Sharow in the sediments representing this phase, exceeding 10% of total land pollen, an extremely high level for this pollen type, which is produced in low numbers and is poorly transported. Cereal cultivation must have been going on very close to the Sharow wetland to have produced such levels, unless the mire was being used for some kind of processing that involved artificial transport of cereal crops to the site, for which there is no evidence.

The big reduction in tree and shrub pollen, and the presence of weeds of cultivation, like *Sinapis*-type and *Urtica*, together suggest major woodland clearance for cereal cultivation close to the site. Sharow Mires is another example of the extension of farming during these climatically favourable centuries of the Medieval Warm Period onto valley-bottom areas previously too wet for agriculture, encouraged also by the greatly reduced incidence of flooding in these river valleys during this period of stable dry climate (Lewin *et al.*, 2005; Macklin *et al.*, 2005). Substantiating evidence comes from the other Washlands site that includes Medieval data, Ripon South (Chapter 3.7). Here quiet-water alluvial deposition was established by 752 ± 25 ^{14}C BP, as seen in the upper channel fill of Section 1 (Plate 2.6), i.e. in the Medieval Warm Period. The pollen diagram (Fig. 3.17) shows an intense phase of cereal cultivation dated to 627 ± 27 ^{14}C BP, with extreme deforestation and cereal-type pollen values of over 50% of total land pollen, which must represent cereal fields adjacent to the site. Both Sharow Mires and Ripon South therefore have clear Medieval records of intensive cultivation under improved climatic conditions between about 1000 and 600 ^{14}C BP.

These data show that, while much information about Medieval agriculture in the 1st Millennium BP can be derived from documentary sources (Lamb, 1977), there is still a valuable role for pollen analysis; indeed, the conclusions from these two lines of evidence have tended to agree very well in North Yorkshire (Menuge, 1997). Thus the well-established massive expansion of farming, including intensive arable cultivation, in the centuries after about 1100 ^{14}C BP, is concordant with the evidence of a major expansion in local cereal growing from the Sharow Mires record. The strong but quite short-lived climatic amelioration of this Medieval Warm Period encouraged the taking in of hitherto marginal land, the use of previously waterlogged lowland alluvial soils and the extension of field systems in the uplands (Higham, 1987). In south Yorkshire, around the Humberhead levels (Smith, 2002), there was a great expansion of mixed farming, with development of an almost treeless landscape, after dates of 865 ± 60 and 910 ± 65 ^{14}C BP (Dinnin, 1997a). On the Yorkshire Wolds, at Willow Garth (Bush, 1993), high cereal-type values and arable indicators from 1170 ± 50 ^{14}C BP until modern times show the intensity of farming in the area. At Askham Bog, in the Vale of York (Kenward *et al.*, 1978), peak cereal-type and *Cannabis*-type pollen values occur before 470 ± 80 ^{14}C BP and so correlate with this phase of Medieval farming expansion. Even on the areas of heavier clay soils that had not seen major clearance previously, a marked expansion of farming activity occurred, as at Neasham Fen, in the Tees valley, after 1213 ± 60 ^{14}C BP (Bartley *et al.*, 1976).

Massive clearance is indicated at Fen Bogs, Goathland (North York Moors), for the period from 1060 ± 160 until 390 ± 100 ^{14}C BP, a situation paralleled at other sites in the North York Moors (Atherden, 1989, 1999; Chiverrell & Atherden, 1999, 2000). That this was a phenomenon common to the wider northern region is shown by evidence from many sites such as in the Tyne valley, at Fozy Moss, where Dumayne and Barber (1994) recorded evidence for sustained clearance for mixed farming after 925 ± 45 ^{14}C BP, and at Crag Lough where Dark (2005) recorded intensive cereal cultivation with other crops such as hemp (*Cannabis sativa*). On the upland above Nidderdale, Tinsley (1975b, 1976) has observed clearances for grassland pasture, but with some cereals, in phases after 1050 ± 80 ^{14}C BP and 480 ± 80 ^{14}C BP. Smith (1986) noted heavy woodland clearance on the upland limestone soils of west Yorkshire, where it commenced early, before 1190 ± 40 ^{14}C BP (Bartley *et al.*, 1990), and the evidence from Featherbed Moss in the southern Pennines (Tallis & Switsur, 1973) is again for substantial clearance, with pollen signals for cereal and pastoral indicator pollen high, indicating a very open Medieval landscape from 1023 ± 50 ^{14}C BP and continuing beyond 491 ± 50 ^{14}C BP. That Medieval woodland clearance was not always for agriculture is shown by the research of Wheeler (2008) in Bilsdale and the Seph valley, south-western North York Moors. Here clearance of oak woodland from the 13th Century to the early modern period resulted from industrial iron working, which required an abundant supply of fuel-wood. High charcoal frequencies and pollen evidence of the replacement of woodland by wet grassland point to almost complete local deforestation. Industrial activities will have caused similar impacts on the vegetation in the Pennine dales in this period (Hudson-Edwards *et al.*, 1997, 1999a).

In the Washlands, the Ripon South data show that a brief phase of cereal cultivation occurred there at 504 ± 26 ^{14}C BP (Chapter 3.7), but it is the record from Sharow Mires that continues into the late Medieval and post-Medieval periods, with the level of cereal-type pollen decreasing steadily after 605 ± 35 ^{14}C BP until it becomes very low indeed at about 482 ± 27 ^{14}C BP, after which it virtually ceases to be recorded (Chapter 3.5). This date for the end of significant cereal cultivation correlates well with the final part of the record at nearby Ripon South (Fig. 3.17). The withdrawal of arable farming from the Ure valley around Ripon, and presumably from other lowland river valleys of central Yorkshire, coincided with a further deterioration of climate after about 600 ^{14}C BP, which culminated in the 'Little Ice Age' cold and wet phase of the sixteenth to nineteenth centuries that is recognized in all regional climate signals from peat bog sediments (Tipping, 1995a; Chiverrell & Atherden, 1999; Chiverrell, 2001). Although perhaps not as pronounced as earlier climatic cold phases, the Little Ice Age was nevertheless sufficiently severe to drive farming activity, especially arable cultivation, out of marginal upland areas, sensitive to temperature and rainfall thresholds, and alluvial locations with heavy soils (Tipping, 1998). Around Sharow Mires the spread of wet grassland and heathland with heather and bracken displaced cultivation in the Little Ice Age and persisted virtually until the present day, when modern agrarian techniques, particularly intensive drainage, have permitted the cultivation of cereal crops once again.

The excellent Medieval records from Ripon South and Sharow in the Ure are exceptional. By way of comparison, in the Tyne, which has a well-researched Late Holocene fluvial archive (see below), periods of Medieval alluviation are recognized but there is no accompanying detailed palaeoenvironmental evidence; the dating of the alluviation is generally from organic material within clastic sediments or by methods other than radiocarbon (cf. Passmore & Macklin, 1994, 2000, 2001).

5.5 Human impact on the rivers: their later Holocene evolution

Although the Holocene is considered to be the latest in a series of interglacials, there are important differences between its record and those from the various Pleistocene temperate phases. These differences relate largely to the impact of human activities, which increased during the course of the Holocene, becoming of huge significance with the initiation of agriculture and culminating in the all-too familiar devastation related to recent pollution and habitat destruction. Documented from the numerous palynological records (see above), the effects of farming are believed to have impacted on rivers from the mid-Holocene onwards. An obvious and well-documented human impact is the onset of hillwash formation (Bell & Boardman, 1992), a direct result of agriculture and the consequent wide areas of bare ground, from which soil would have been eroded from even gently sloping fields into the river systems. The redistribution of this eroded soil is believed to be responsible for the deposition of thick Holocene alluvium in most British river valleys (e.g. Buckland & Sadler, 1985; Macklin *et al.*, 1992b; Tipping, 1992; Macklin, 1999; Chiverrell *et al.*, 2007a), a deposit for which there are few analogues in earlier interglacials.

Thus many bank sections of the middle and lower reaches of the Ure and Swale at the present day reveal yellow-brown alluvial sands and silts that form a thick blanket over earlier, peaty deposits and old land surfaces. This cap of sediment marks the onset of human-induced alluviation, related to agriculture. Some of the sites investigated in this study were chosen to clarify the timing and extent of late Holocene alluviation in this region. An increase in disturbed-ground plants in the diagram from Thornton's Plantation, Pickhill (Chapter 3.9.2), documents this change and its potential causal relationship with fine-grained fluvial sedimentation. The pollen record from this site, from before the onset of alluvial silt deposition, shows marshland vegetation dominated by local wetland herbs, grasses, sedges and birch. With the start of alluviation, the vegetation changed to local alder swamp–carr, which is typical of the wetter parts of floodplains at the present day. In addition, higher in the profile there is an increase in cereal-type pollen as well as ribwort plantain and dandelion family, changes indicating local pastoral and arable agriculture. The increased pollen of hazel and oak would have been blown in from drier land further away, after removal of local tree cover. It is likely that increased alluvial sedimentation here was a result of mid- and later Holocene farmers clearing the land and causing soil erosion, the soil being redeposited by the Swale as alluvium. Similarly, the mid-Holocene alluvial deposition at Langland's Farm seems to record the consequences of prehistoric agriculture, with silt deposition starting in the Neolithic (Chapter 3.9.1). The deposition of fine-grained sediment, perhaps flood-derived, early in the infilling of the upper channel at Ripon South (before the supposed oxbow became fully isolated from the river; Chapter 3.7) appears to coincide with intensive Medieval cultivation. These contrast with the earlier record of higher energy flooding events at this site, during periods of cold, wet climate, as represented by the underlying coarse-grained deposits, tentatively attributed to the late Bronze Age (see above). At these sites, and at several others where the stratigraphy was recorded but which were not chosen for full analysis, such coarse clastic fluvial sediments show that the Washlands rivers were capable, during the latter half of the Holocene, of depositing sand and gravel as well as finer-grained alluvium.

At Ripon South the terrace level is approximately 3 m

above the modern river. The floor of the abandoned channel at Sharow (Chapter 2.3.1.3) is at a similar level relative to the Ure (Plate 5.1), suggesting a broad equivalence in age with the Ripon South terrace, which is Terrace No. 3 of Howard *et al.* (2000a); however, by *c.* 5000 cal. BP, it would seem that the Sharow Channel had been abandoned by the main river, its final occupation being recorded by the basal gravel, *c.* 1.5 m below the dated horizon (Chapter 3.5). The base level of the Sharow Channel (*c.* 8 m below current river level; Plate 5.1) is not the lowest point, relative to the modern river, at which the Holocene Ure can be shown to have flowed in the Washlands. Borehole data from the Ripon Mineral assessment Report (Morigi and James, 1984), from two locations <5 km upstream of the divergence of the Sharow Channel from the existing Ure course, show gravel extending to >20 m below the modern river (unbottomed in both cases: boreholes 37 SW 103 & 37 SW 106; cf. Plate 5.1). Further upstream, boreholes reveal even thicker sequences, but these include glacial diamictons and so represent the glacigenic valley-fill that was seen in exposure at Ripon North Quarry (Chapter 2.6.3). Boreholes 103 and 106 revealed no diamictons and were described as including tufaceous cement in their lower parts, suggesting that they represent Holocene fluvial gravels. Thus there is a deeply incised buried valley beneath the modern Ure at Ripon, presumably one excavated since the Sharow Channel was abandoned, since that channel is significantly shallower. This key strand of evidence, available only because of the abandonment of this short stretch of valley, suggests that, in accommodation of glacio-isostatic rebound, the Ure had achieved an equilibrium valley floor level nearly 10 metres below that at present by *c.* 5000 cal. BP as represented by the Sharow Channel. Following this, and having been rerouted out of the Sharow Channel, it aggraded by *c.* 10 m to the levels represented by the later Holocene terraces, as well as incising to at least 20 m below modern river level (Plate 5.1). The closeness of the suggested age of the basal Sharow channel deposits and the date from low-level organic sediments (monolith 2M) within the Terrace 2 sequence at Ripon South (Chapter 3.7) suggests that this aggradation was rapid; it cannot be determined, however, whether it occurred before or after the deeper incision to >20 m below modern river level (although that incision clearly post-dated the abandonment of the Sharow Channel). It is possible that the Sharow Channel was abandoned during a major incision event, with incision continuing along the active channel; that would explain why only a thin gravel occurs at the base of the abandoned channel: little more than a lag.

The uppermost (channel-fill) sediments at Ripon South provided the only examples of large vertebrate fossils and incidental archaeological discoveries from the project. The fossils included domestic animals (sheep and cattle), while the most notable archaeological finds were a collection of characteristic shoes (Chapter 4.9.3; Fig. 4.22), the latter in particular serving to confirm the Late Holocene, Medieval age of these deposits. This is corroborated by the radiocarbon dating (Chapter 3.7; Appendix I). Given such a recent age, it is perhaps surprising that this is not the youngest of the terraces in the Ripon area; on the contrary, Howard *et al.* (2000a) mapped a later, lower terrace, No. 4 (Plate 5.1), although this is restricted to near-channel situations and is less extensive than the others (Fig. 2.57). There are no reports of exposures in Terrace No. 4, so no interpretation is possible beyond the post-Medieval age implied by the evidence from Terrace No. 3 in Ripon South Quarry. Its distinction as a lower terrace, albeit poorly separated from No. 3, indicates that the Ure has continued incising into its valley floor (at least until geologically recent times) as far downstream as Ripon. This recent incision, represented by the record of the shifting meandering channel at Ripon (Howard *et al.*, 2000a; Chapter 2.6.4), could perhaps be attributed to other climatic or anthropogenic factors, although it possible that further isostatic rebound, following the aggradation that has infilled the deeply incised channel, has had to be accommodated.

The sequence determined from the Ripon area has strong parallels in the Catterick reach of the Swale, documented in the work undertaken as part of the LOIS project (see Chapter 1.6.4; Macklin & Taylor, 1997; Macklin *et al.*, 2000; Taylor *et al.*, 2000). On the right bank of the Swale, in successive meander cores, Taylor and Macklin (1997) mapped up to eight terraces, many with flood channels across their valley-side edges (Figs 2.38 & 5.7b). As with the low-level terraces at Ripon, these have formed late in the Holocene as a result of meander migration. It is apparent from the dating evidence obtained by Taylor and Macklin (1997; Taylor *et al.*, 2000) that the meander deposits overlie older river gravels. It is clear that the Swale valley here is underlain by gravels formed at several different times, the earliest being the glacial outwash deposits exploited by the active quarries nearby (Lovell, 1982; Chapter 2.7; Fig. 2.38). It would also seem, from the published evidence, that the surface expression of meander-migration terraces results from a comparatively recent reworking of the uppermost part of much older deposits, as well as emplacement above them of channel and overbank sediments dating from the last few hundred years. By analogy, the record at Ripon South might well be similar, although the situation is less clear-cut and much of the geomorphological and stratigraphical evidence has been compromised by quarrying. Thus the mid-Holocene sandy facies at Ripon, although clearly inset into the Early Holocene sediments studied by Howard *et al* (2000a) *c.* 1 km to the north-west, might relate to a valley fill (filling the above-mentioned deeply incised channel) that has been reworked and incised much more recently, the mapped terraces and the Medieval channel-fill sediments (Fig. 2.57) recorded in the Brown and Potter Quarry representing part of that more recent activity. The tentative Medieval OSL age-estimate from the sandy facies in Section 3 at Ripon South provides limited further support for this suggestion.

Metal mining has had a further important impact on fluvial deposition in the Swale–Ure Washlands, traceable by the presence of contaminant minerals like lead and zinc (Macklin *et al.*, 1997; White, 1997; Coulthard & Macklin, 2003). The miners generally processed their materials in riverside settings, making use of the water for washing and grading and leaving mounds of spoil to be reworked by the rivers in subsequent floods. The artificially enhanced supply of sediment led to a phase of braiding by several of the Pennine streams while the activity was at its height (Macklin, 1986, 1997; Warburton *et al.*, 2002). Mining has been a major factor since about AD 1000 (Hudson-Edwards *et al.*, 1997, 1999a), continuing with greatly increasing rates of deposition into modern times, with most of the sediment retained in the Washland system (Chapter 1). No work on this particular aspect of the Swale–Ure record was undertaken as part of the present project.

5.6 The Swale and Ure records in a wider fluvial context

The fluvial archive from the Swale–Ure Washlands, documented here and summarized for the Ure in Plate 5.1, can be compared with records from other parts of Yorkshire Ouse system and from further afield. Not surprisingly, the nature of the Ure record has characteristics that place it between those of the lowland reaches of the Humber drainage and the upland Pennine rivers. Of the latter, the Wharfe is best documented (as noted in Chapter 1), thanks to the work of Howard *et al.* (2000b; Chapter 1.6.2; Fig. 1.7). Like the Ure (Plate 5.1) it has a terraced sequence, with four post-glacial terraces being recorded, the highest with a surface level some 20 m above the river and a minimum U-series age from calcite cement of >7000 years. This contrasts with the height of the early Holocene Ure terraces at Ripon, which are within 10 m of river level (Howard *et al.*, 2000a; Chapter 2.6.4; Plate 5.1). Higher level gravels are recognized within the Ure; these are glacial in origin, dating back to the late Devensian, which might indeed be the age of the highest Wharfe terrace, which Howard *et al.* considered likely to be 'Late Pleistocene'.

While the Upper Wharfe provides a well-studied comparative sequence from the upland headwaters of the Ouse system, valuable lowland analogues can be found further downstream in the Vale of York (Taylor *et al.*, 2000) and in the Trent and Idle valleys (Howard *et al.*, 1999b). The lower parts of all these systems are thought to have been inundated during the Dimlington Stadial by Glacial Lake Humber (Clark *et al.*, 2004a; Howard *et al.*, 1999b; Chapter 1.4.5). Only *c.* 10 km downstream from Ripon, at the confluence of the Ure and Swale (within the present project area, although downstream of all those sites investigated in detail), Taylor *et al.* (2000) reconstructed a valley cross-profile, based on borehole records constrained by ^{14}C dating, showing mid-Holocene sediments below river level, with only Pleistocene deposits preserved above the modern floodplain as terraces (see Chapter 2.4; Fig. 2.39). The river here occupies a valley floor confined on both sides by the aforementioned Pleistocene deposits, which are predominantly glacio-lacustrine sediments, and is underlain by sands and gravels proved in boreholes to be >12 m thick (Stanczyszyn, 1982). The mid-Holocene sediments recorded by Taylor *et al.* (2000) thus represent part of the infill, possibly representing much of the Holocene, of a deeply incised valley (Figs 2.39 & 5.7c). It has been suggested (Chapter 2.4) that this deep incision might have been a response to the drainage of Lake Humber following deglaciation of the Humber Gap. That would explain its prevalence in the lower parts of the Ouse system: Taylor *et al.* (2000) described a comparable sequence from the River Aire at Beal, *c.* 7 km downstream of Pontefract. The thick infill of the incised valley bottoms at sites like Myton-on-Swale and Beal can perhaps be attributed in part to the early Holocene sea-level rise (Long *et al.*, 1998; Shennan *et al.*, 2000). Comparison of the records from these lowland Ouse sites with those from the Ripon quarries (Howard *et al.*, 2000a; Chapters 2.6, 3.6 & 3.7) and from Catterick (Fig. 2.38) shows that the intra-Holocene valley incision recorded in the last two tapers rapidly downstream and has given way, in the Swale–Ure confluence area, to stacked sediment accumulation in a channel deeply incised at around the Pleistocene–Holocene boundary, this aggradation bringing the river up to a level only *c.* 2 m below the level of the fringing Pleistocene surface (Fig. 5.7c).

In the Idle valley south of Bawtry, the river flows upon, but is also inset into, a single gravel body attributed to the late Devensian (Smith *et al.*, 1973; Howard *et al.*, 1999b). Within its surface three separate terrace levels were recognized, interpreted by Smith *et al.* as erosional benches *c.* 12 m, 6–7 m and 3 m above the river (Fig. 5.7d). The lower facets are significantly closer to the valley floor than late Devensian gravels in the Ure; there is, however, a higher-level 'glacial gravel' terrace in the Idle valley (Fig. 5.7d). Howard *et al.* (1999b) recovered fossiliferous Lateglacial sediments from organic deposits overlying the late Devensian Idle gravel at Tiln, tentatively attributing them to the Windermere Interstadial, an interpretation supported by the occurrence of overlying sediments with characteristics of a colder climate, possibly representing the Loch Lomond Stadial. The implication of these data is that there are no equivalents in the Idle of the elevated Holocene aggradational terraces seen in the Swale–Ure Washlands, e.g. in the Ripon area. If the lowest terrace facets are Holocene erosional features they might, however, be broadly equivalent to the low-level aggradational terraces of the Ure (Plate 5.1).

In the Trent, deposits representing the last climate cycle are again to be found at low levels within the valley, forming what was formerly known as the Floodplain Terrace. In the latter half of the 20th Century, new Geological Survey mapping of the Middle Trent led to the reclassification of cold-climate deposits forming much of this terrace, attributable to the LGM, as the Holme Pierrepont Sand and Gravel (Brandon & Sumbler, 1988, 1991). This unit, up to 10 m thick, occurs beneath the modern valley-floor alluvium; it is overlain in places by a later gravel deposit, separately mappable, the Hemington Sand and Gravel, which locally forms a terrace *c.* 1 m above the Trent floodplain (Brandon & Cooper, 1997; Fig. 5.7e). This latter deposit is a rich source of archaeological remains, including fish-weirs, revetments, log boats, bridges and mill-dams, ranging in age from Neolithic to post-Medieval (Clay, 1992; Salisbury, 1992; Howard *et al.*, 1999b; Garton *et al.*, 2001; Cooper, 2003; Knight & Vyner, 2006), pointing to a Holocene age. Brown (1998) showed that the Hemington Sand and Gravel was formed by reworking of the Late Devensian Holme Pierrepont deposit as a result of high-magnitude discharges into the Middle Trent from headwaters in the Peak District (the Rivers Dove and Derwent) during intra-Holocene episodes of climatic deterioration. This deposit, therefore, is broadly comparable to the late Bronze Age–early Iron Age gravels of the Ure at Ripon, also attributed to the higher discharges associated with a climatic downturn. At Langford Quarry, 2 km south of Collingham, research since the mid-1990s has revealed evidence, particularly from dendrochronology from interbedded timber and environmentally diagnostic Coleoptera, suggesting significant sand and gravel deposition within the Neolithic and early Bronze Age (Howard *et al.*, 1999c; Howard, 2007a). The site has also produced (from the quarry conveyor belt) a Middle Bronze Age rapier, typologically datable to the 15th Century BC (Knight, 1997) and (from excavation) numerous animal and human bones (J. Rackham, in Howard, 2007a). The evidence from Langford Quarry supports earlier observations from further upstream, particularly around Colwick and Holme Pierrepont, suggesting high-energy fluvial deposition at this time (Salisbury *et al.*, 1984). Locally preserved above the Holme Pierrepont and Hemington sands and gravels are fossiliferous silts containing Lateglacial to early Holocene pollen assemblages, interpretations confirmed by radiocarbon dating (Coope & Jones, 1977; Greenwood *et al.*, 2003).

Between Newark and Gainsborough these low terrace deposits are increasingly covered by the Holocene alluvium of the Trent valley floor; as a result it is difficult to determine whether the Late Devensian Trent deposits continue to the Humber or extend along what is known to be the pre-Devensian course of the Trent, beneath the Witham valley alluvium, through the Lincoln Gap towards the Wash (White *et al.*, 2007; Bridgland *et al.*, in press, a). It seems likely, however, that the Holme Pierrepont deposits extend along both the Witham and modern Trent courses, suggesting that the diversion of the river took place during the deposition of this sedimentary unit. The example profile of the Trent illustrated in Figure 5.7 (part e) is from the Humber course c. 10 km downstream of the divergence from the erstwhile Witham route. According to Howard (2005), there was early Holocene incision in the Lower Trent and the Humber lowlands, associated with sea levels that were c. 17 m below present by 8000 years BP, after which marine transgression (peaking by 3000 years BP) led to the estuarine inundation of the Humber (cf. Metcalfe *et al.*, 2000). The possibility that this incision was a continued response to the drainage of Lake Humber should perhaps be considered (see above).

The Middle Trent differs slightly from the Idle in that the late Devensian gravels have little or no elevation above the floodplain, showing minimal incision by the Trent since the downcutting that preceded deposition of the Holme Pierrepont terrace deposits (Fig. 5.7e). There is thus progressively less post-deglaciation incision to be seen in successive records moving southward from the Ure, via the Idle, to the Trent. The contrast between the Ure sequence at (and upstream of) Ripon and that at the Ure–Swale confluence, in which evidence for intra-Holocene valley incision is entirely lacking, shows that the incision also tapers from upland to lowland (i.e. downstream). That these differing records are all to be found within a single drainage system would seemingly rule out base-level control as the causal factor in determining the degree of fluvial incision, particularly since upstream reaches show greater incision than downstream ones (incision brought about by declining sea level should cause upstream propagation of knick-points, potentially leading to greater numbers of terraces in downstream reaches rather than fewer, the latter being the situation in the post-Devensian Ouse). Furthermore, the relatively small geographical area involved means that climatic differences are unlikely to be responsible for the different incision patterns observed. The cause of this difference is instead likely to relate to the extent of the Devensian glaciation, which covered the Ouse catchment but was excluded from most of the Trent. It is in the areas covered with Devensian ice that the greatest incision is seen, raising the possibility that glacio-isostatic uplift, in response to deglaciation, has driven the incision. This suggestion is supported by records from other fluvial systems in areas glaciated during the Devensian, which also show terrace incision of varying degrees. For example, the Tyne has a well-developed terrace sequence (Aspinall *et al.*, 1986; Yorke, 2008). This and other examples will be explored briefly, to test the hypothesis that Holocene valley incision is a response to isostatic rebound following Late Devensian deglaciation.

Research on the Tyne has a lengthy pedigree, starting with late 19th Century observations of terraces by Lebour (1878, 1889, 1893). From the outset it was recognized that the early development of the river, as recorded by its terrace sequence, commenced with deglaciation and that the record was essentially one of incision into a glacial valley fill (Lebour, 1893; Woolacott, 1905), much as is seen in the Ure (Chapter 2; Plate 5.1). Since this pioneering work, attention give to the Tyne sequence was somewhat meagre prior to the geoarchaeologically driven research of the Macklin group (see Chapter1.6); there are, however, valuable summaries from the BGS and its predecessors (Mills & Holliday, 1998), including

their Mineral Assessment Reports, aimed at documenting aggregate resources (Giles, 1981; Lovell, 1981). Typically the BGS has mapped at least two Tyne terraces but only in certain reaches; for example, in the Hexham area separate 1st and 2nd terraces are recognized, respectively c. 5 m and c. 9 m above the river, with a mention of thin undifferentiated terrace remnants between the two (Lovell, 1981). In contrast, only undifferentiated terrace deposits are mapped in the Blaydon reach of the Tyne, further downstream (Giles, 1981). Macklin and Aspinall (1986) recognized a high-level glacial/Lateglacial terrace in the upper Tyne catchment, in the West Allen tributary, some 20 m above river level. There is a clear resemblance between this and the glacial terraces within the Ure system, such as at Nosterfield (Plate 5.1). Optimal preservation of a Tyne terrace staircase was reported from Lambley, where six terraces have been recognized (Passmore & Macklin, 2000). In a recent PhD project, Yorke (2008) has reassessed the record from the Tyne system. She identified four Tyne terraces, with glacial deposits preserved in terrace situations at higher levels. The highest terrace, T4, she considered likely to date from the Late Pleistocene, given its elevation c. 15 m above the river in the lower Tyne at Crawcrook. It would thus seem to be comparable with the high-level terrace in the West Allen, already likened above to the Nosterfield situation in the Ure (Plate 5.1). The higher-level glacial terraces in the Tyne would thus be analogous to the Marfield deposits, which sit c. 30 m above the Ure (Plate 5.1). The 3rd Tyne terrace is c. 10 m and the 2nd c. 8 m above the river. The latter is the terrace dated to 4940–4600 ^{14}C BP at Farnley Haughs by Passmore and Macklin (1994), with aggradation continuing to 1350–550 BC (based on palaeomagnetic dating). Yorke (2008) regards the lowest terrace as a late Holocene cut-and-fill feature, c. 4–5 m above the river and characterized by palaeochannels on its surface. She considers it equivalent to Passmore and Macklin's (2001) T4 at Lambley, dated by ^{14}C to AD 1160–1380 (1100–1300 according to Passmore & Macklin, 2000). This is entirely comparable with the low terrace at Ripon South quarry (T3 of Howard *et al.*, 2000a), again part of a cut-and-fill suite of closely spaced terraces, which yielded Medieval dates (see above). However, the Medieval sediments at Ripon occupy a channel overlying gravels dating from c. 4000 BP (Chapter 3.7), perhaps showing that incision to that level occurred considerably earlier than that between Tyne terraces T2 and T1, which was after 550 BC (see above).

North of the Tyne, BGS mapping shows that terraces are well developed in the valleys of the Till, Aln, Coquet, Font, Wansbeck, Pont and Blyth (Land *et al.*, 1974; Frost & Holliday, 1980; Lawrence & Jackson, 1986; Young *et al.*, 2002). Young *et al.* (2002) noted a consistency in the heights of these in the Morpeth district, with terraces recorded at 17 m, 10 m and 3 m above each of the Wansbeck, Pont, Font and Blyth. ALSF-funded work on the terrace sequence of the Tweed system, northern Northumberland, has provided new data from the northernmost extremity of England, of

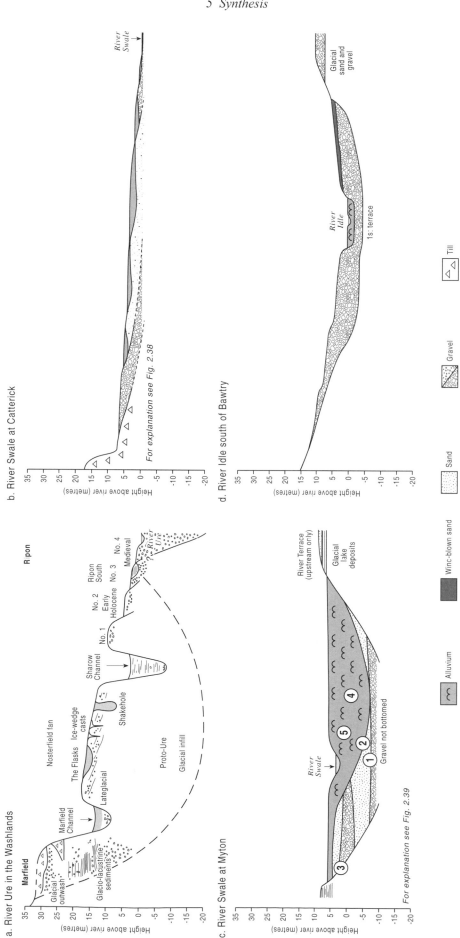

a. River Ure in the Washlands

b. River Swale at Catterick

c. River Swale at Myton

d. River Idle south of Bawtry

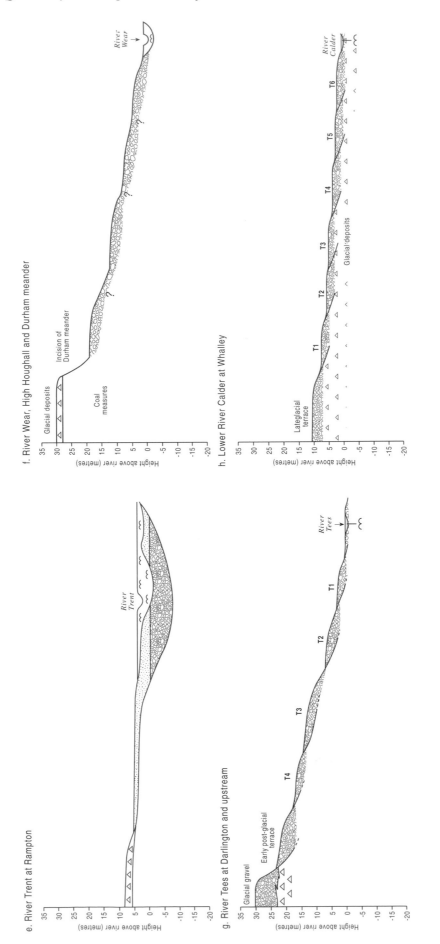

Fig. 5.7. Comparison of the terrace sequences in the Ure and Swale with various others discussed in the text. Sources (other than this project): b – data from Taylor and Macklin (1997) and Taylor et al. (2000); c – data from Taylor et al. (2000); d – data from Smith et al. (1973) and Howard et al. (1999b); e – data from Price (1975); f – data from Smith and Francis (1967); g – data from Mills and Hull (1976); h – data from Chiverrell et al. (2007b, fig. 89).

a comparable type to that described in this volume and similarly well constrained by radiocarbon dating (Passmore *et al.*, 2006; Bayliss *et al.*, 2008; Passmore & Waddington, 2009, in press). This builds on earlier work on the Tweed, in which Medieval alluvial fan deposits extending over a late Holocene terrace were investigated by multi-proxy analyses (Tipping & Halliday, 1994).

The Rivers Tees and Wear, falling between the Swale–Ure and the Tyne, are less well researched, but Geological Survey mapping (Smith & Francis, 1967; Mills & Hull, 1976; Smith, 1979; Gozzard & Price, 1982; Smith, 1994; Frost, 1998) and preliminary results of ALSF-funded work in the Tees (Mitchell *et al.*, in press) indicate that the modern rivers and their tributaries are incised significantly into the regional Late Devensian till-sheet, with some development of fluvial terraces in certain reaches (although these do not appear separately on published maps). For example, terraces are well developed in the Wear upstream of Durham at High Houghall, where four levels, described as "cut into sand and gravel", were recorded by Smith and Francis (1967, p. 252) at 3–4, *c.* 7, 10–12 and 16–19 m (Fig 5.7f) above the floodplain alluvium (the latter at *c.* 40 m O.D.). Terraces are less well preserved downstream of Durham, where the post-glacial incision by the Wear is instead readily apparent from the incised meanders of its lower valley, including the famous one that provides the classic defensive site of the ancient city. The narrow gorge reaches of the Lower Wear are developed where the post-glacial river has diverted from its pre-glacial course and incised into the Carboniferous (Coal Measures) bedrock (Beaumont, 1970). In the Tees valley, terraces are well developed between Barnard Castle and Darlington, where up to four, numbered upwards and respectively *c.* 3, 6–7, 10–14 and >15 m above the river, were described in the reach around and upstream of Piercebridge (Mills & Hull, 1976; Fig 5.7g). Further upstream supposedly older, early post-glacial terraces are preserved at up to 23 m above the floodplain, whereas coarse glacial gravels, up to 7.5 m thick and containing clasts from the Lake District, form a prominent south-bank terrace *c.* 30 m above the Tees at Stapleton, south-west of Darlington (Fig 5.7g). The last-mentioned deposits are perhaps equivalent to the meltwater gravels at Marfield, in the Ure, suggesting broadly similar amounts of incision into the glaciated landscape in the Tees lowlands as in the upstream part of the Swale–Ure Washlands (cf. Plate 5.1). The lowest terraces at Stapleton have yielded tree-trunks and mammalian remains (Mills & Hull, 1976), further reinforcing the similarity with the Ure (e.g. the sites at Ripon; see Chapter 3.6 & 3.7). Further downstream at Eryholme, where the Tees meanders southwards and makes its closest approach to the research area, impinging on the Northallerton Geological Survey map, three terraces were reported 3, 5 and 6 m above the river (Frost, 1998). The reported thicknesses of the gravels, up to 4.5 m, are comparable with those of the lowest Ure terraces.

Comparing more widely, an incised, terraced fluvial sequence developed on glaciated terrain to the west of the Pennines was documented in detail by Hooke *et al.* (1990) from the River Dane, in Cheshire. They noted three groups of terraces (high, middle and low), there being main terraces in each group as well as less-frequently represented subsidiary levels, all within a valley incised some 25 m through last glacial sediments into Triassic bedrock. In comparison with more recent studies they had little dating evidence from which to construct a detailed chronology. There are interesting parallels with the Swale–Ure data, however, notably the comparable incision into the glaciated landscape and the observation that the most recent floodplain development involved a combination of increased sinuosity and renewed incision.

Also on the western side of northern England, but considerably further north, one of the best developed post-deglaciation river terrace sequences is that recorded by Boardman (1994, 1997, 2002) in the Mosedale Beck, north-eastern Lake District (Chapter 1.6.2; Fig. 1.6). At least eight terraces occur in this system, the highest traceable as outwash from a small Loch Lomond Stadial glacier that occupied the Wolf Crags cirque, near the head of the Mosedale Beck valley. Some of the lower terraces have been dated in relation to overlying Holocene peat sequences (Anderson & Parker, 1997) and boulder spreads attributable to historical flash floods (Boardman, 1997). As a whole the sequence has been used for a comparative study of soil development on the different terraces (Smith & Boardman, 1994). These terraces are well preserved as landforms despite modest vertical separation, the highest terrace being only *c.* 7 m above the stream. Nonetheless this record shows impressive stream power so close to the valley head and again points to the important role of Lateglacial–Holocene incision in areas glaciated during the late Devensian. Its nearest parallel east of the Pennines would seem to be the South Tyne record from Lambley (Passmore & Macklin, 2000; see above).

Extensive ALSF-funded work on river terrace sequences and associated palaeoenvironments on the western side of the Pennines has been carried out more recently by a group led by Richard Chiverrell at Liverpool University (Chiverrell *et al.*, 2007b, 2008a, b). The most detailed report (Chiverrell *et al.*, 2007b) is copiously illustrated with river terrace mapping of the Ribble system, including the important south-bank Calder tributary, and well constrained by radiocarbon dating (cf. Bayliss *et al.*, 2008). It documents five Holocene terraces and one Lateglacial terrace in the lower reaches of the Ribble–Calder system, ranging up to *c.* 15 m above the modern valley floor (Fig. 5.7h). Again the pattern here confirms the formation of post-glacial terraces in an area glaciated during the Devensian, in marked contrast to the non-terraced Trent system (see above). That pattern, seemingly in support of glacio-isostasy as an important driver in fluvial incision, is further confirmed by earlier work from this team that documented terraces in the river systems draining to the Solway and Morecambe Bay (Chiverrell, 2006). Chiverrell *et al.* concluded, however, that anthropogenic factors were important in triggering terrace formation, particularly in the later Holocene, a view that is fully compatible with the notion that isostatic uplift was a key enabling factor. Buxton *et al.* (2000) had previously identified a late Holocene gravel terrace, which they attributed to the effects of later prehistoric land use and deforestation, beneath the Roman fort and settlement at Ribchester in the lower Ribble valley. Incision of valley floors, a requirement in terrace separation, has seldom been attributed directly to anthropogenic factors however, either in Britain or more widely; typically land-use factors have been seen to destabilize valley sides and alluvial fan surfaces (e.g. Harvey *et al.*, 1981; Litt, 1992; Werritty & McEwen, 1997; Tipping *et al.*, 1999; Higgitt *et al.*, 2001), leading to gulley incision in these locations and thus bringing about an increase in sediment supply to river valleys. For this reason, anthropogenic influences are normally linked with periods of enhanced aggradation on valley floors; i.e., the aggradational part of the river terrace formation cycle (Buckland & Sadler, 1985; van Andel *et al.*, 1990; Tipping, 1992; Brown, 1997a; Anderson *et al.*, 2000; Macklin *et al.*, 2000). As Warburton *et al.* (2002) concluded, a combination of 'anthropogenic conditioning' and 'climatic triggering' could explain much of the late Holocene fluvial record, including the recent incision at localities such as Catterick and Ripon (see above).

The recent ALSF-funded work should be viewed in the context of that preceding it on the wetter western side of the Pennines. For example, Harvey (1985) described several of the river systems of north-west England, in particular the Eden, Lune, Ribble, Mersey and their tributary valleys. As with the Ribble, terrace sequences are clearly marked in the Lune, Mersey and Eden, and are found as far south as the Dane and Weaver in Cheshire. All of these systems can be divided into an early higher-level set of terraces created by high-energy, fast-flowing rivers in Lateglacial or early post-glacial times, and a lower set that were created in the later Holocene, perhaps as a consequence of human activity and deforestation linked to major climatic events (Harvey, 1985; Chiverrell, 2006). Tipping (1995c) has recorded a very similar terrace record in the valley of the Kirtle Water in the Solway lowlands, with a high-level Late Devensian terrace and four late Holocene low-level terraces formed under the combined influence of climate and human agency. These examples agree well with the situation in the Swale–Ure Washlands, where, as already noted, Late Pleistocene and Lateglacial fluvial channels and terraces (including glacial outwash sediments) occur well above the River Ure, in contrast with late Holocene terrace deposits, which are just a few metres above the modern river (Plate 5.1; Fig. 5.7). Indeed, the position of the Lateglacial channel in the Ure (represented at Marfield: Chapter 3.4), 10–14 m above the valley floor, is comparable with that of the highest (?Lateglacial) terrace of the lower Calder, which is *c.* 10 m above the river (Chiverrell *et al.*, 2007b; Fig. 5.7h), and with the somewhat higher Lateglacial terrace of the Hodder, which, at 15 m above that river, is the highest recorded by Chiverrell *et al.* (2007b).

An interesting observation is the degree of conformity in the depth of incision by several of the east-coast rivers into the glaciated (Late Devensian) landscape: in some cases this is into a glacially-infilled earlier version of their valleys but, notably, other cases of incision into resistant bedrock are seen, such as the Wear at Durham. In the incised meander at Durham, the Wear flows *c.* 30 m below the glacial drift that caps the Coal Measures bedrock (Fig 5.7f). This is the same depth of incision as has been achieved by the Tees near Darlington (Fig 5.7g) and the Ure at Marfield (Plate 5.1). The Lower Tyne is similarly incised (e.g., indicated by the heights of the Tyne bridges), as is the Wear at Sunderland and the Blyth, the first significant river north of the Tyne).

In contrast, the Swale at Catterick, researched in detail by Taylor *et al.* (2000; cf. Taylor and Macklin, 1997), flows less than 20 m below the surrounding glaciated terrain, whereas further downstream, near its confluence with the Ure, both rivers flow only *c.* 2 m below the surrounding glacio-lacustrine beds (see above; Fig 5.7c). The explanation in the latter case is probably related to the deep incision, around the time of the Pleistocene–Holocene transition, that has affected the lower reaches of the rivers of the Ouse system and is perhaps a response to the drainage of Lake Humber (see above). The restricted incision, compared with the 30 m recorded in the Wear, Tees and Ure, shown by many other rivers in glaciated areas might be attributable to reduced stream power, coupled with resistant bedrock. This would explain the < 10 m of incision by the Mosedale Beck example (see above), a minor upland stream cutting through drift into Skiddaw Slate (Boardman, 1994, 2002). Resistant bedrock might also have constrained incision by the Swale at Catterick, where that river has only just left its upland bedrock-floored channel. These examples notwithstanding, there is nothing above to falsify the hypothesis that glacio-isostatic uplift following deglaciation has been a key factor in generating incision, and therefore river terraces, in regions glaciated during the Devensian, just as longer-timescale uplift has been invoked in recent years to explain Middle Pleistocene incision and terrace formation (Maddy, 1997; Bridgland, 2000; Maddy *et al.*, 2000; Bridgland & Westaway, 2007a, b). Important evidence in support of this argument is the absence of intra-Holocene incision in regions beyond the effects of the Late Devensian glaciation, as exemplified by the Trent (Fig 5.7e), with a transitional situation apparent from near the Devensian ice margin in the case of the Idle (Fig 5.7d). It might well be that the depth of incision, assuming it is a measure of the amount of uplift, can be related to former ice thickness, although that must remain a topic for the future (cf. Bridgland *et al.*, in press b).

5.6.1 Evidence for changes in fluvial regime and activity

Evidence from northern Britain for fluctuation of fluvial regime during the last climate cycle cannot compete with the excellent datasets from certain continental rivers, such as the Maas (Netherlands), Warta (Poland) and Tizsa (Hungary), in which shifting channels over very wide areas, coupled with minimal incision, have led to exemplary preservation of such records (Gábris & Nagy, 2005; Vandenberghe *et al.*, 1994; see Chapter 1.6). There have been relatively few Washlands exposures from which braiding or meandering regimes could be determined with confidence; indeed, the continental studies have relied largely on recognizing channel patterns rather than determining regimes from sedimentology. Thus the terraced nature of the Washlands record, particularly in the Ure, is a limiting factor, since by definition it implies destruction of pre-existing sedimentary archives during the incision phases between terraces; this is in marked contrast to the optimal continental records (above). Nonetheless, there are indications that the Ure and the Swale have occupied single thread meandering channels in the Washlands for much of the Holocene, replacing the sediment-charged outwash streams that marked the re-emergence of their valleys following deglaciation, which can be imagined to have been braided. The evidence of these early braided systems comes from the high-level gravels in the Ure at Marfield (Chapter 2.6.1), formed when ice was still present locally, and the fan at Nosterfield (Chapter 2.6.2), as well as the glacial gravels containing Lake District rocks that both border and underlie the Swale valley around Catterick (Chapter 2.3.2.2; Chapter 2.7.1). The suggestion of braiding comes from the occurrence of substantial sediment bodies dominated by coarse, sometimes cross-bedded gravels, with minimal evidence of finer-grained, lower energy or overbank material.

Two of the project sites coincide with abandoned palaeochannels of the Ure, which have potential relevance to the question of former sinuosity of the fluvial system. The older of the two is at Marfield, where an abandoned channel in close proximity to the quarry exploiting the high-level glacial deposits preserves Lateglacial and Early Holocene sediments (Chapter 2.6.1; Chapter 3.4). The base of this channel is 10 m above the modern river and > 20 m below the 'glacial' terrace (Plate 5.1). Unfortunately there are no radiocarbon dates, but the vegetational record clearly points to the earliest recovered sediments dating from the Lateglacial Interstadial. The channel thus dates either from the interstadial or from the latest main Devensian; it was certainly abandoned by the Ure by the interstadial, since the sedimentary infill is not that of an active river channel. It represents a parallel course to that of the modern Ure, between it and the higher-level terrace, and one of relatively low sinuosity (Fig. 3.9). Noteworthy, however, is that the modern Ure course, which cuts across the upstream end of the Marfield channel, is of markedly higher sinuosity (Figs 2.28 & 5.3). This sinuous course is incised by > 20 m into the landscape both upstream and downstream of the intersection with the channel, suggesting that it is preserved from an early phase of meandering, but there is no way of knowing whether that phase was soon after

the palaeochannel was abandoned or later, perhaps in the Early Holocene.

The second site in an abandoned Ure channel is that at Sharow Mires, on the north-eastern outskirts of Ripon (Figs 2.57, 3.11 & 5.3). This palaeochannel remains prominent in the landscape (Fig. 2.32) despite >11 m of Late Holocene infill (Chapter 3.5); it leaves the modern Ure course at Bell Banks and rejoins it, after *c.* 1.4 km, at Hewick Bridge (Fig. 2.57). Neither the modern river nor the palaeochannel are strongly sinuous, suggesting that the abandonment of this former Ure course was perhaps the result of avulsion rather than meander cut-off. Gravel at the base of the infill sequence, nearly 10 m below the level of the modern river, presumably records the last occupation by the Ure (see above); the overlying infill is of organic backwater or lacustrine sediments, the lower part dated by palynology and radiocarbon to the mid-Holocene (*c.* 5000 cal. BP). The evidence from Sharow thus fails to support a strongly meandering fluvial regime in the mid-Holocene. However, there is clear evidence of later meandering from the geomorphological mapping in the area just to the south, and downstream of the palaeochannel diversion, around Ripon Racecourse (Howard *et al.*, 2000a; Fig. 2.57); indeed, it was channel migration during this phase of late Holocene meandering that produced the lower terraces around Ripon (Plate 5.1). Whether the meandering here extended back over the entire Holocene, as might be supposed from the early Holocene dates obtained by Howard *et al.* from the 2nd highest of the four mapped terraces, is in fact uncertain. It is possible that the meandering channel of the Ure swept across this area later in the Holocene, reworking the upper part of a much earlier set of deposits. That is the scenario recorded quite clearly from the Swale at Catterick (Fig. 5.7b).

Much emphasis has been placed in recent years on the recognition of synchronous aggradational events in different river valleys, not just in northern Britain but also much further afield (Macklin *et al.*, 2000; Macklin & Lewin, 2003; Lewin *et al.*, 2005; Macklin *et al.*, 2005, 2006; Johnstone *et al.*, 2006). This has followed a debate in the literature on British post-glacial fluvial records over the relative roles of climate and anthropogenic factors as drivers of aggradation and terrace formation. One side of this debate has supposed climatic changes to be the key drivers, with other factors, particularly anthropogenic, 'blurring' the record (Macklin & Needham, 1992; Macklin & Lewin, 1993). More sceptical workers have pointed to examples in which clear non-synchrony was evident and questioned whether anthropogenic influences were not the major factor (Tipping, 1992; Tipping *et al.*, 1999). As with many controversies, it is probable that both factors have operated to a certain extent. As Tipping *et al.* noted, when aggradational events can be dated to a well-represented period, marked by similar records of deposition in several unrelated localities, then a climatic influence can be supposed: especially if a suitably-timed event can be identified in the climatic record.

The present project has not prioritized the collection of evidence for datable flood events, such as has been compiled by others in the Holocene fluvial community (Johnstone *et al.*, Macklin *et al.*, 2006; 2006; Chapter 1); the link with aggregate extraction sites has led to studies primarily at quarry workings, where the information has been dominantly on earlier deglacial (meltwater) deposits or phases of Holocene gravel aggradation, or on palaeoenvironmental evidence from above these. Nonetheless, an attempt was made to establish a date for the onset of alluviation in the Swale, an initiative that led to the analyses at the sites of Langland's Farm (Chapter 3.9.1) and Thornton's Plantation (Chapter 3.9.2). The evident increase in alluvial sedimentation at both these sites has been attributed to mid- and later Holocene clearance of the land and resultant soil erosion, feeding silt-sized material into the river. Of these only the Langland's Farm site is at all well dated; the record here would seem to point to enhanced flood deposition in the early Neolithic, at around 5000 cal. BP. Whether this could represent one or other of the two nearest Holocene flood events identified in the Johnstone *et al.* (2006) database, at 5540 and 4840 cal. BP, is uncertain.

The only other sites to record phases of significant fluvial activity are those at Ripon North and Ripon South. At Ripon North, a sequence of sands and silts, organic and perhaps fining upwards, was investigated and dated at its base and middle (Chapter 2.6.3; Chapter 3.6). It records sedimentation between *c.* 4300 and 2500 cal. BP and beyond, potentially encompassing at least four of the Johnstone *et al.* events, those at 4030, 3580, 2730 and 2560 (all recognized from glaciated catchments). At Ripon South, fluvial input into the lower part of the Medieval oxbow infill (see above, section 5.5) dates from 1000–800 cal. BP, although preservation within the accommodation space of the cut-off channel does not necessarily imply a significant phase of fluvial flood activity. The lower sand and gravel sequence at this site records a substantial fluvial aggradation phase from *c.* 4300–4200 cal. BP onwards (from the basal date in monolith sample 2M; Chapter 3.7), potentially similar in age to the sequence at Ripon North, although the dated sequence at the latter site is less coarse-grained.

5.6.2 Fluvial palaeoenvironmental records

As well as preserving a morphological record of river response to land readjustment following the retreat of glacial ice from northern England, the Swale–Ure Washland valleys also preserve a rich depositional legacy of alluvial sediment, including a wide variety of organic and fine-grained clastic units. As discussed above (section 5.4.6), such sediments represent an extremely complex and changing mosaic of wetland habitats and depositional environments, particularly for the early and mid-Holocene, when considerable topographic variability still existed within river valley floodplains: i.e., before the burial of

many channel features by greatly increased alluviation rates in the later Holocene. The palaeoecological data preserved in alluvial sediments, here and over the wider area, are invaluable for the reconstruction of landscape history and environmental conditions within the river valleys and their catchments, even allowing for some taphonomic uncertainties regarding the source areas of some of the microfossil assemblages, particularly pollen (Brown *et al.*, 2007b). Through the use of multidisciplinary research techniques (Dinnin & Brayshay, 1999; Smith *et al.*, 2001, 2005) such as those detailed in Chapter 3, the impacts of climate change, human activity and other environmental factors may be distinguished and understood. The results recorded in Chapter 3, and synthesized above (section 5.4), may be compared with evidence from analogous alluvial archives in northern England east of the Pennines, allowing an assessment of variability in river valley vegetation and environments across the region from the Trent in the south to the Tyne in the north.

Comparative palaeoenvironmental evidence is also available from the river systems that flow westward from the Pennines through eastern Cumbria and Lancashire, although data from these are less abundant than from the river systems of eastern England. A comparison between the two sides of the Pennines is of potential interest for a number of reasons, such as the potential cultural barrier presented by the upland and the well-known climatic differences. Alluvial deposits similar to those examined during the Swale–Ure project exist within most of these valleys, although as yet few major environmental studies have been completed on the peats and fine-grained clastic sediments that might yield such data. The potential for reconstruction of dated palaeoenvironmental archives in association with complex valley terrace sequences such as those recognized in the Ribble by Chiverrell *et al.* (2007b) is considerable. For example, one of the Ribble's largest tributaries, the Hodder, contains a peat-filled channel within its low terrace that has been dated palynologically to early post elm-decline (Neolithic) times (Harvey, 1985), providing a limiting age for terrace formation. Similarly, in the Carlingill area of the Howgill Fells, peat deposits interleave with and seal terrace features of the higher tributaries of the Lune (Cundill, 1976; Harvey & Chiverrell, 2004). Pollen and radiocarbon analyses of these organic layers have allowed precise timing and correlation of geomorphic events in this small upland catchment.

Larger scale lowland systems of north-west England are more directly comparable with the the Swale–Ure Washlands; these occur, for example, in the catchments and valleys of the Mersey and Eden. The extensive gravel terraces of the lower Mersey support major peat development that provides a full palaeoenvironmental record of vegetation change from the early Lateglacial to the present day (Shimwell, 1985; Hall *et al.*, 1995). Risley Moss, Carrington Moss, Holcroft Moss and Chat Moss constitute a string of raised bogs on the gravels of the Mersey valley, although fen and carr development was widespread in this alluvial system, with many of these never progressing to the raised-bog stage. There is evidence that in many river valleys alder-dominated fen–carr persisted unchanged for several hundred years or even longer (Wilkinson *et al*, 1999; Innes, 2001b). Despite some past attention (Birks, 1964, 1965a, 1965b; Hall *et al.*, 1995), there is potential for considerable further research on the Mersey terrace peatlands. Less work has been undertaken hitherto in the other large lowland valley system of north-west England, the Vale of Eden in Cumbria (Chiverrell, 2006). Generally the extensive research carried out on lowland river terrace formations in eastern England (Macklin *et al.*, 1992b, c; Taylor *et al.*, 2000) has not been matched to the west of the Pennines. Before the recent research in the Ribble by Chiverrell *et al.* (2007b) the only dated lowland fluvial archive was from the Irthing (Cotton *et al.*, 1999), a tributary of the Eden that runs west from the interfluve with the Tyne. Here three early Holocene terraces occur, followed by the creation of two further terraces in Bronze Age and late Medieval times. A full Holocene pollen record has been recovered from Midgeholme Moss (Wiltshire, 1997), near Birdoswald and adjacent to the Irthing, and a detailed mid- and late-Holocene pollen record is available from Butterburn Flow (Yeloff *et al.*, 2007) near the river's headwaters. A long pollen diagram covering the period from the early Holocene to the present is available from a sequence of alluvial sediments examined by Chinn and Innes (1995) at Wet Sleddale, in a tributary of the River Lowther in the south of the Eden catchment. Few similar records exist from such small valleys running into the Vale of Eden, primarily the work of Skinner and Brown (1999), who presented early and mid-Holocene data from Howgill Castle, a small valley mire in the Pennine foothills. In the upper Vale of Eden, although there are peat deposits in association with sands and gravels that form at least two terraces (Harvey, 1985), there have been few studies. Those at Kirkby Thore (Walker & Lambert, 1955) and Temple Sowerby (Skinner & Brown, 1999) have recorded only early Holocene sediments or peat profiles truncated by anthropogenic cutting. Although there is a need for further research in the Eden valley, those palaeoenvironmental data on climatic and human impact that have been recovered may be compared with several long proxy data archives from the north Cumbrian lowlands, where peat-bog sequences that cover the entire Holocene have been subjected to detailed study based on pollen, plant macrofossils and a range of other techniques of environmental reconstruction. The most significant of these are Bolton Fell Moss, Walton Moss and Butterburn Flow (Barber *et al.*, 1994b, 1998; Dumayne-Peaty & Barber, 1998; Hughes *et al.*, 2000; Yeloff *et al.*, 2007). The cycles of terrace formation and incision recorded in the fluvial archive sites of north-west England can thus be related to the composite effects of local anthropogenic deforestation, often most effectively within the last two millennia, and of regional climatic changes (Chiverrell, 2006).

Some direct comparisons may be made between the data

accrued in the Swale–Ure Washlands project and analogous projects in other English valley systems, particularly those in which an integrated set of environmental archaeology techniques have been applied to alluvial sediments. The pattern found in the Washlands alluvial sequences at Sharow and Ripon North is very similar to that recorded at Yoxall Bridge in the Staffordshire Trent valley (Smith *et al.*, 2001), where pollen, plant macrofossil and insect assemblages were studied. The Yoxall Bridge evidence is for alder-dominated valley wetlands occurring in Late Bronze Age times with standing water in reedbeds and fens within a cut-off meander channel. As with the Washlands and other Yorkshire data (Macklin *et al.*, 2000; Lewin *et al.*, 2005), the Late Bronze Age in the upper Trent was before the major onset of alluviation in the system (Knight & Howard, 1995), which is linked in both areas to the first major forest clearance in the mid- to later Iron Age. At Sharow, Ripon North and Yoxall Bridge, clearance in the valley bottoms, coupled with the first increase in evidence for cultivation, was delayed until the climatic improvement in the second half of the 3rd Millennium BP. Before that, all three sites show plant and insect evidence of wet, paludal valley floors with little alluviation, and with increasingly wet conditions during the early Iron Age climatic deterioration, indicated by deposition of wood and other debris, probably during flood events. A comparable story was obtained by Smith *et al.* (2005) in the Leicestershire Soar, again elucidated by the combination of insect and plant remains in alluvial sediments; this showed Late Bronze Age river valley vegetational and hydrological stability, followed by early Iron Age increased wetness and then later Iron Age clearance, alluviation and cultivation of valley bottoms. The Swale–Ure Washlands alluvial evidence appears to confirm the regional sequence of processes and events noted at sites such as documented here, where analogous integrated techniques have been employed.

There are records from lowland valleys throughout Britain of multi-channelled (anastomosing) river systems from the early Holocene, developed in response to a combination of low channel gradients, the abundance of fine-grained sediment and the stabilization of channel banks by vegetation growth (Rose *et al.*, 1980; Brown *et al.*, 1994; Howard, 2005). In the wider Humber system, the earliest record of post-glacial fluvial environments comes from organic deposits at Shardlow Quarry, in the Middle Trent, which have yielded a palynological record of woodland dominated by Scots pine and birch with high frequencies of fern spores and are radiocarbon dated to 9130 ± 70 BP (Brayshay, 1994). Other Trent sites, at Girton (Green, 1991; Howard 2007b) and Bole Ings, near Gainsborough (Dinnin, 1997b; Brayshay & Dinnin, 1999), have provided detailed palaeoenvironmental records based on pollen and Coleoptera from palaeochannel fills slightly later in the Holocene. At Bole Ings these records demonstrate the mostly dry nature of early Holocene floodplains, compared with the extensive mesotrophic wetlands of the later Holocene, as the landscape from *c*. 9000 to 7000 ^{14}C BP in the Middle Trent was characterized by a wooded floodplain with Scots pine on gravel islands and ridges, willow and poplar along the riverbank/wetland margins and deciduous hardwoods of oak, lime and elm on drier areas of the floodplain. The low recorded frequencies of plants associated with disturbed ground and grassland suggests that such open habitats were a minor component of the vegetation mosaic. High-energy river channels prone to shifting across valley floors, with fast-flowing water laying down coarse-grained sandy sediment, were characteristic of such early interglacial valleys. Channel movement would have been the main cause of vegetation disturbance at that time, when human impact was slight.

By mid-Holocene times (after *c*. 7000 BP), when alluvial records become available from most valleys, the river channels at Bole Ings and throughout the region became fixed, rates of flow diminished (perhaps due to the effects of sea-level rise and catchment hydrology on water tables; cf. Howard, 2005) and valleys supported denser wetland vegetation under impeded drainage. Fine-grained silts and clays, with organic deposition in places, became the characteristic sediment type, large quantities of such alluvium becoming stored on floodplains in the region. Low-energy deposition in association with marsh and fen–carr vegetation was characteristic of most river valleys at this stage and thereafter, as noted by Kirby and Gearey (2001) for the rivers of south Yorkshire, such as the Aire, Idle and Don. The alluvial record at Bole Ings and at Shibdon Pond in the Tyne valley (Passmore *et al*., 1992) commence around 7,000 BP, and record this change from early Holocene high-energy regimes and wooded floodplains to mid- and late Holocene depositional regimes, sediment-filled valleys and wetland vegetation.

From the mid-Holocene onwards, there are many more organic channel fills available for study, providing more accurate dating of sequences. This is particularly so after *c*. 3000 BP, probably because of increased wetness (Brayshay & Dinning, 1999) caused primarily by periodic and sometimes severe climatic deterioration (Brown *et al*., 2001; Macklin *et al*., 2005) as well as by increasingly significant human agricultural activity in catchments (Macklin *et al*., 2000; Taylor *et al*., 2000). Indeed, establishing the relative roles of climate and anthropogenic impact remains one of the principal remaining questions in Holocene geoarchaeology in north-west Europe (Macklin *et al*., 2006). Increased pollen and insect evidence for the spread of reedbeds, fen and fen–carr from the mid-Holocene suggests elevated water levels in valley floodplains. The Washlands alluvial records at Ripon North (Chapter 3.6) and Ripon South (Chapter 3.7) both begin after *c*. 4000 BP, reflecting this process. Holocene alluvial histories comparable with those from the Yorkshire Ouse basin rivers, recording climatic and human deforestation, have been reported from river valleys of differing sizes in areas to the north, such as the Coe Burn (Macklin *et al*., 1991) and the Tyne (Macklin *et al*., 1992b; Passmore *et al*., 1992;

Moores *et al*., 1999), from the eastern side of the Vale of York, in the Derwent system (Richards, 1981; Richards *et al*., 1987) and from the Foulness (Halkon & Innes, 2005), which flows south into the Humber estuary.

Later Holocene alluvial sediments are an invaluable palaeoenvironmental resource in this and comparable regions. They bury and preserve old land surfaces with their archaeological material and landscapes, while the sediments themselves contain a rich, long-term multi-proxy data record. Whereas other types of wetland site, such as peat bogs, often contain only truncated sequences, having been cut for fuel for example, alluvial deposits often preserve a record that continues until close to the present day. The Washland site at Ripon South (Chapter 3.7) is a good example of such a recent record, but others are relatively common, for instance in the Tyne (Rumsby & Macklin, 1994; Hudson-Edwards *et al*., 1997, 1999a, b; Merrett & Macklin, 1999), the Tees (Plater *et al*., 2000) and the Trent (Howard, 2005). They are clearly an important data source for future study of past landscape history, in this case from the surprisingly poorly represented recent past.

5.7 Conclusions

Since the last glaciation, the two main rivers of the Washlands – the Swale and the Ure – have flowed continuously across an evolving landscape. After emerging from beneath the ice they were characterized by high-energy, gravel-bed (and probably multi-channelled) glacial outwash streams. For a period following their emergence from the ice they probably formed part of a River Ouse system that flowed into Lake Humber, which had been formed by the glaciation and persisted into earliest Lateglacial times. When this lake eventually drained, the Ouse incised through the relatively soft sediments it had left behind and eliminated the locally raised base level that the lake had provided. A combination of this base-level lowering and glacio-isostatic rebound caused incision in the upper reaches of the Ouse system, of which the Swale and Ure are main arteries. This history of fluvial evolution is recorded in the various project sites and summarized in Plate 5.1.

Project sites have also provided a detailed history of 'biological' landscape evolution since deglaciation, particularly as recorded by palynology. An important achievement of the study has been the recovery of multiple cores from sites at Nosterfield and Snape Mires, which can thus be interpreted in three dimensions, so that spatial differences in features like the expansion of hazel or prehistoric human impacts can be assessed. The extension of the vegetation record in the northern Vale of York and Vale of Mowbray into the mid- and late Holocene, where previously it had been known mostly for the Lateglacial and early Holocene, is a valuable advance. In particular, the establishment of a post-Roman vegetation history in the central Yorkshire lowlands is important, as few palaeoenvironmental records exist for the last 2000 years, especially from alluvial sediment archives. The combined influences, in the last 5000 years, of human land use and changing climatic conditions, as shown by the pollen data, is a source of both interest and controversy, the resolving of which can perhaps inform future assessment of the archaeological patterns in the area.

In the modern era, many processes combine to destroy or bury the archaeology and palaeoenvironmental resources of the Washlands. Deep ploughing damages and flattens near-surface landforms and archaeological sites, whilst soils washed into the rivers are redeposited downstream in thick slugs of sediment, blanketing and burying such resources deep below the present surface. The extraction of minerals from the floodplains, principally sands and gravels, also causes the direct removal and destruction of archaeology, landforms and sediments. Other activities, such as urban expansion and road schemes, as well as flood defence construction, all threaten the fragile and important landscape and sediments of the Swale–Ure Washlands.

In many ways the work reported here has only scratched the surface of the landscape history of the Washlands. The sites that have been studied in detail show that there is a rich record here of environmental change and landscape evolution. No one single site has been found to cover the entire period since deglaciation, but in combination they represent a rich data resource that has shed considerable light on the latest Pleistocene–Holocene development of this area, midway between the Pennine uplands and the coast.

6 References

Abraham, D.A. (1981) *The sand and gravel resources of the country west of Boroughbridge, North Yorkshire. Description of 1:25,000 resources Sheet SE 36.* Institute of Geological Sciences Mineral Assessment Report 78.

Agar, R. (1954) Glacial and post-glacial geology of Middlesbrough and the Tees estuary. *Proceedings of the Yorkshire Geological Society,* 29, 237–253.

Aitkenhead, N., Barclay, W.J., Brandon, A., Chadwick, R.A., Chisholm, J.I., Cooper, A.H. & Johnson, E.W. (2002) *British Regional Geology: The Pennines and adjacent areas (4th edition).* British Geological Survey, Nottingham.

Allen, L.G. & Gibbard, P.L. (1993) Pleistocene evolution of the River Solent of southern England. *Quaternary Science Reviews,* 12, 503–528.

Allen, T., Hey, G. & Miles, D. (1997) A line of time: approaches to archaeology in the upper and middle Thames valley, England. *World Archaeology,* 29, 114–129.

Anderson, D.E. & Parker, A.G. (1997) A recent Holocene pollen sequence from the Mosedale Beck, Cumbria. In: *Geomorphology of the Lake District, a field guide* (ed. J. Boardman), pp. 11–22. British Geomorphological Research Group, Oxford.

Anderson, E., Harrison, S., Passmore, D.G. & Mighall, T.M. (2000) Holocene alluvial-fan development in the Macgillycuddy's Reeks, southwest Ireland. *Geological Society of America Bulletin,* 112, 1834–1849.

Andrews, J.E., Pedley, H.M. & Dennis, P.F. (1994) Stable isotope record of palaeoenvironmental change in a British Holocene tufa. *The Holocene,* 4, 349–355.

Angus, R.B. (1992) Insecta, Coleoptera, Hydrophilidae, Helophorinae. *Susswasserfauna von Mitteleuropa,* 20, 1–144.

Archaeological Services University of Durham (2005) *A1 Dishforth to Barton Improvement, North Yorkshire: Geophysical Surveys.* Archaeological Services University of Durham, ASUD Report, 1121.

Aspinall, R.J., Macklin, M.G. & Brewis, T. (1986) Metal mining and floodplain at Garrigill, and their influence on terrace and floodplain soil development. In: *Quaternary River Landforms and Sediments in the Northern Pennines* (eds M.G. Macklin & J. Rose), pp. 35–45. Quaternary Research Association/British Geomorphological Research Group, Newcastle upon Tyne.

Atherden, M. (1976a) Late Quaternary vegetational history of the North York Moors III. Fen Bogs. *Journal of Biogeography,* 3, 115–124.

Atherden, M. (1976b) The impact of late prehistoric cultures on the vegetation of the North York Moors. *Transactions of the Institute of British Geographers,* NS1, 284–300.

Atherden, M.A. (1989) Three pollen diagrams from the eastern North York Moors. *Naturalist,* 114, 55–63.

Atherden, M.A. (1999) The vegetational history of Yorkshire: a bog-trotter's guide to God's own country. *Naturalist,* 124, 137–156.

Atkinson, T.C., Briffa, K.R. & Coope, G.R. (1987) Seasonal temperatures in Britain during the past 22,000 years, reconstructed using beetle remains. *Nature,* 325, 587–592.

Bailey, R.N. (1980) *Viking Age Sculpture in Northern England.* Collins, London.

Balachowsky, A. (1949) Coleopteres, Scolytides. *Faune de France,* 50, 1–320.

Balfour-Browne, F. (1950) *British water beetles 2.* The Ray Society, London.

Ballantyne, C.K. (2002) Paraglacial geomorphology. *Quaternary Science Reviews,* 21, 1935–2017.

Ballantyne, C.K. & Harris C., eds (1994) *The Periglaciation of Great Britain.* Cambridge University Press, Cambridge.

Ballantyne, C.K., McCarroll D. & Stone J.O. (2007) Vertical dimensions of the Wicklow Mountains ice dome, eastern Ireland and implications for the extent of the last Irish ice sheet. *Quaternary Science Reviews,* 25, 2048–2058.

Barber, J. (2006) *Pleistocene glacial history of West Yorkshire.* PhD, University of Leeds.

Barber, K.E. (1993) Peatlands as scientific archives of past biodiversity. *Biodiversity and Conservation,* 2, 474–489.

Barber, K.E., Chambers, F.M., Dumayne, L., Haslam, C.J., Maddy, D. & Stoneman, R.E. (1994a) Climatic change and human impact in north Cumbria: peat stratgraphic and pollen evidence from Bolton Fell Moss and Walton Moss In: *The Quaternary of Cumbria: Field Guide* (eds J. Boardman & J. Walden), pp. 20–49. Quaternary Research Association, London.

Barber, K.E., Chambers, F.M., Maddy, D., Stoneman, R. & Brew, J.S. (1994b) A sensitive high-resolution record of late Holocene climate change from a raised bog in northern England. *The Holocene,* 4, 198–204.

Barber, K.E., Dumayne, L. & Stoneman, R. (1993) Climatic change and human impact during the late Holocene in northern Britain. In: *Climate Change and Human Impact on the Landscape: Studies in Palaeoecology and Environmental Archaeology* (ed. F.M. Chambers), pp. 225–236. Chapman & Hall, London.

Barber, K.E., Dumayne-Peaty, L., Hughes, P.D.M., Mauquoy, D. & Scaife, R. (1998) Replicability and variability of the recent macrofossil and proxy climate record from raised bogs: field stratigraphy and macrofossil data from Bolton Fell Moss and Walton Moss, Cumbria, England. *Journal of Quaternary Science,* 13, 515–528.

Barclay, A. & Bayliss, A. (2002) Cursus monuments and the radiocarbon problem. In: *Pathways and Ceremonies: The Cursus Monuments of Britain and Ireland* (eds A. Barclay & J. Harding), pp. 11–29. Neolithic Studies Group Seminar Papers, 4. Oxbow, Oxford.

Bartley, D.D. (1962) The stratigraphy and pollen analysis of lake deposits near Tadcaster, Yorkshire. *New Phytologist*, **61**, 277–287.

Bartley, D.D. (1966) Pollen analysis of some lake deposits near Bamburgh in Northumberland. *New Phytologist*, **65**, 141–156.

Bartley, D.D. (1975) Pollen analytical evidence for prehistoric forest clearance in the upland area west of Rishworth, West Yorkshire. *New Phytologist*, **74**, 375–381.

Bartley, D.D., Chambers, C. & Hart-Jones, B. (1976) The vegetational history of parts of south and east Durham. *New Phytologist*, **77**, 437–488.

Bartley, D.D., Jones, I.P. & Smith, R.T. (1990) Studies in the Flandrian vegetational history of the Craven District of Yorkshire: the lowlands. *Journal of Ecology*, **78**, 611–632.

Barton, N. & Roberts, A. (2004) The Mesolithic period in England: current perspectives and new research. In: *Mesolithic Scotland and its Neighbours* (ed. A. Saville), pp. 339–358. Society of Antiquaries of Scotland, Edinburgh.

Bateman, M.D. & Buckland, P.C. (2001) Non glacial and post glacial history. In: *The Quaternary of East Yorkshire and North Lincolnshire: Field Guide* (eds M.D. Bateman, P.C. Buckland, C.D. Frederick, & N.J. Whitehouse), pp. 13–24. Quaternary Research Association, London.

Bateman, M.D., Buckland, P.C., Frederick, C.D. & Whitehouse, N.J., eds (2001) *The Quaternary of East Yorkshire and North Lincolnshire: Field Guide*. Quaternary Research Association, London.

Bateman, M.D., Murton, J.B. & Crowe, W. (2000) Late Devensian and Holocene depositional environments associated with the coversands around Caistor, north Lincolnshire. *Boreas*, **16**, 1–16.

Bateman, M.D., Murton, J.B., Chase, B., Frederick, C.D. & Gaunt, G.D. (2008) The Late-Devensian pro-glacial Lake Humber: new evidence from littoral deposits at Ferrybridge, Yorkshire, England. *Boreas*, **37**, 195–210.

Bayliss, A., Cook, G., Bronk Ramsey, C., van der Plicht, J. & McCormac, G. (2008) *Radiocarbon dates from samples funded by English Heritage under the Aggregates Levy Sustainability Fund 2004–2007*. English Heritage, Swindon.

Beaumont, P. (1968) *A History of glacial research in northern England from 1860 to the present day*. Department of Geography, University of Durham. Occasional Paper Series No. 9.

Beckett, S.C. (1981) Pollen diagrams from Holderness. *Journal of Biogeography*, **8**, 177–198.

Beebee, T.J.C. & Griffiths, R.A. (2000) *Amphibians and Reptiles, a Natural History of the British Herpetofauna*, London.

Beijerinck, W. (1947) *Zadenatlas der nederlandsche flora. Ten behoeve van de botanie, palaeontologie, bodumkultuur en warenkennis*, Veenman & Zonen, Wageningen.

Bell, M. & Boardman, J., eds (1992) *Past and Present Soil Erosion: Archaeological and Geographical Perspectives*. Oxbow Books, Oxford.

Bell, M. & Neumann, H. (1997) Prehistoric intertidal archaeology and environments in the Severn estuary, Wales. *World Archaeology*, **29**, 95–113.

Bell, M. & Walker, M.J.C. (2005) *Late Quaternary Environmental Change: Physical and Human Perspectives*. Pearson/Prentice Hall., Harlow.

Bellamy, D.J., Bradshaw, M.E., Millington, M.R. & Simmons, I.G. (1966) Two Quaternary deposits in the lower Tees basin. *New Phytologist*, **65**, 429–442.

Benfield, A.C. (1983) *The geology of the country around Dalton, north Yorkshire with particular reference to the sand and gravel resources; description of 1:25,000 sheet SE 47*. Institute of Geological Sciences.

Benn, D. & Evans, D.J.A. (1998) *Glaciers and Glaciation*. Edward Arnold, London.

Bennett, K.D. (1984) The post-glacial history of *Pinus sylvestris* in the British Isles. *Quaternary Science Reviews*, **3**, 133–155.

Bennett, K.D. (1986) The rate of spread and population increase of forest trees during the postglacial. *Philosophical Transactions of the Royal Society of London*, **B314**, 523–531.

Bennett, K.D. (1989) A provisional map of forest types for the British Isles 5000 years ago. *Journal of Quaternary Science*, **4**, 141–144.

Bennett, K.D. (1990) Postglacial history of alder (*Alnus glutinosa* (L) Gaertn.) in the British Isles. *Journal of Quaternary Science*, **5**, 123–133.

Bennett, K.D., Simonson A.B. & Peglar S.M. (1990) Fire and man in postglacial woodlands of eastern England. *Journal of Archaeological Science*, **17**, 635–642.

Bennett, K.D., Whittington, G. & Edwards, K.J. (1994) Recent plant nomenclatural changes and pollen morphology in the British Isles. *Quaternary Newsletter*, **73**, 1–6.

Berendsen, H.J.A. (1993) Holocene fluvial geomorphology of the floodplain of the rivers Rhine and Meuse in the Netherlands. In: *Geomorphology and Geoecology, Fluvial Geomorphology, Zeitschrift fur Geomorphologie, Supplementband* (eds I. Douglas & J. Hagedorn), pp. 97–107. E. Schweizerbart Science Publishers, Stuttgart.

Berg, B.E. & Bastow, M. (1992) *Peat from the Rushwood Estate, Nosterfield, North Yorkshire (SE 277805)*. West Yorkshire Archaeological Service. Unpublished Report.

Berglund, B.E. & Ralska-Jasiewiczowa, M. (1986) Pollen analysis and pollen diagrams. In: *Handbook of Holocene Palaeoecology and Palaeohydrology* (ed. B.E. Berglund), pp. 453–473. Wiley, New York.

Best, R.H. (1956) Westward pro-glacial drainage in Cleveland. *Proceedings of the Yorkshire Geological Society*, **30**, 301–319.

Bettis, E.A. (1995) *Archaeological geology of the Archaic Period in North America*. Special Papers (Geological Society of America, 297).

Bettis, E.A. & Mandel, R.D. (2002) The effects of temporal and spatial patterns of Holocene erosion and alluviation on the archaeological record of the central and eastern Great Plains, USA. *Geoarchaeology*, **17**, 141–154.

Binney, H.A., Waller, M.P., Bunting, M.J. & Armitage, R.A. (2005) The interpretation of fen carr pollen diagrams: the representation of the dryland vegetation. *Review of Palaeobotany and Palynology*, **134**, 197–218.

Birks, H.H. (2003) The importance of plant macrofossils in the reconstruction of Late-glacial vegetation and climate: examples from Scotland, western Norway and Minnesota, USA. *Quaternary Science Reviews*, **22**, 453–473.

Birks, H.J.B. (1964) Chat Moss, Lancashire. *Memoirs and Proceedings of the Manchester Literary and Philosophical Society*, **106**, 1–24.

Birks, H.J.B. (1965a) Late-glacial deposits at Bagmere, Cheshire and Chat Moss, Lancashire. *New Phytologist*, **64**, 270–275.

Birks, H.J.B. (1965b) Pollen analytical investigations at Holcroft Moss, Lancashire and Lindow Moss, Cheshire. *Journal of Ecology*, **53**, 299–314.

Birks, H.J.B. (1986) Late Quaternary biotic changes in terrestrial and lacustrine environments, with particular reference to north-west Europe. In: *Handbook of Holocene Palaeoecology and Palaeohydrology* (ed. B. Berglund), pp. 3–65. Wiley, Chichester.

Birks, H.J.B. (1988) Long-term ecological change in the British uplands. In: *Ecological Change in the Uplands* (eds M.B. Usher & D.B.A. Thompson), pp. 37–56. Blackwell, Oxford.

Birks, H.J.B. (1989) Holocene isochron maps and patterns of tree-spreading in the British Isles. *Journal of Biogeography*, **16**, 503–540.

Birks, H.J.B. & Birks, H.H. (1980) *Quaternary Palaeoecology.* Edward Arnold, London.

Björk, S., Walker, M.J.C., Cwynar, L.C., Johnsen, S., Knudsen, K.L., Lowe, J.J., Wohlfarth, B. & INTIMATE members. (1998) An event stratigraphy for the Last Termination in the North Atlantic region based on the Greenland ice core record: a proposal from the INTIMATE group. *Journal of Quaternary Science*, **13**, 283–292.

Black, S., Howard, A.J. & Macklin, M.G. (1998) U-Series dating of cemented river gravels and tufa deposits in Upper Wharfedale, between Kettlewell and Grassington. In: *The Quaternary of the Eastern Yorkshire Dales. Field Guide.* (eds A.J. Howard & M.G. Macklin), pp. 31–44. Quaternary Research Association, London.

Blackburn, K. (1938) Linton Mires, Wharfedale. Glacial and Post Glacial history. Part II. Biological. *University of Durham Philosophical Society Proceedings*, **10**, 24–37.

Blackburn, K. (1952) The dating of a deposit containing an elk skeleton found at Neasham, near Darlington, County Durham. *New Phytologist*, **51**, 364–377.

Blackford, J.J. (2000) Palaeoclimate records from peat bogs. *Trends in Ecology and Evolution,* **15**, 193–198.

Blackford, J.J. & Chambers, F.M. (1991) Proxy records of climate from blanket mires: evidence for a dark age (1400 BP) climatic deterioration in the British Isles. *The Holocene*, **1**, 63–67.

Blackford, J.J. & Chambers, F.M. (1999) Harold's Bog, East Bilsdale Moor. In: *The Quaternary of North-East England. Field Guide* (eds D.R. Bridgland, B.P. Horton, & J.B. Innes), pp. 91–98. Quaternary Research Association, London.

Blackford, J.J., Innes, J.B., Kelly, A.E. & Jones, S.L. (2006) Recent research from the peatlands of the North York Moors: human impact and climatic change. In: *Wetland Archaeology and Environments: Regional Issues, Global Perspectives* (eds M. Lillie & S. Ellis), pp. 229–241. Oxbow Books, Oxford.

Blackham, A., Davies, C. & Flenley, J. (1981) Evidence for late Devensian landslipping and late Flandrian forest regeneration at Gormire Lake, North Yorkshire In: *The Quaternary in Britain* (eds J. Neale & J. Flenley), pp. 184–194. Pergamon Press, London.

Blackham, A. & Flenley, J.R. (1984) A pollen analytical study of the Flandrian vegetational history at Skipsea Withow. In: *Late Quaternary Environments and Man in Holderness.* (ed. G.G. Gilbertson), pp. 159–164. British Archaeological Reports, British Series 134, Oxford.

Blum, M.D. & Straffin, E.C. (2001) Fluvial responses to external forcing: examples from the Massif Central, France, the Texas Coastal Plain (USA), the Sahara of Tunisia, and the lower Mississippi valley (USA). . In: *River Basin Sediment Systems: Archives of Environmental Change* (eds D. Maddy, M.G. Macklin, & J. Woodward), pp. 195–228. Balkema, Rotterdam.

Boardman, J., ed. (1981) *Field Guide to Eastern Cumbria.* Quaternary Research Association, London.

Boardman, J. (1994) Mosedale. In: *Cumbria: Field Guide* (eds J. Boardman & J. Walden), pp. 165–172. Quaternary Research Association, Oxford.

Boardman, J. (1997) *Geomorphology of the Lake District: a field guide.* British Geomorphological Research Group, Oxford.

Boardman, J. (2002) Thornsgill and Mosedale. In: *Quaternary of Northern England*, Geological Conservation Review Vol 25 (eds D. Huddart & N.F. Glasser), pp. 46–51. Joint Nature Conservation Committee, Peterborough.

Boreham, S., White, T.S., Bridgland, D.R., Howard, A.J. & White, M.J. (in press) The Quaternary history of the Wash fluvial network. *Proceedings of the Geologists' Association*, **121**.

Bos, J.A.A., Dickson, J.H., Coope, G.R. & Jardine, W.G. (2004) Flora, fauna and climate of Scotland during the Weichselian Middle Pleniglacial – palynological, macrofossil and coleopteran investigations. *Palaeogeography, Palaeoclimatology, Palaeoecology*, **204**, 65–100.

Boswijk, G. & Whitehouse, N.J. (2002) *Pinus* and *Prostomis*: a dendrochronological and palaeoentomological study of a mid-Holocene woodland in eastern England. *The Holocene*, **12**, 585–596.

Boulton, G.S. & Hagdorn, M. (2006) Glaciology of the British Isles ice sheet during the last glacial cycle. *Quaternary Science Reviews*, **25**, 3359–3390.

Boulton, G.S., Jones, A.S., Clayton, K.M. & Kenning, M.J. (1977) A British ice sheet model and patterns of glacial erosion and deposition in Britain In: *British Quaternary Studies: Recent Advances* (ed. F.W. Shotton), pp. 231–246. Clarendon Press, Oxford.

Boulton, G.S., Smith, G.D., Jones, A.S. & Newsome, J. (1985) Glacial geology and glaciology of the last mid-latitude ice sheets. *Journal of the Geological Society of London*, **142**, 447–474.

Bowen, D.Q., ed. (1999) *A Revised Correlation of Quaternary Deposits in the British Isles.* Geological Society Special Report 23, Bath.

Bowen, D.Q. & Gibbard, P.L. (2007) The Quaternary is here to stay. *Journal of Quaternary Science*, **22**, 3–8.

Bowen, D.Q., Phillips, F.M., McCabe, A.M., Knutz, P.C. & Sykes, G.A. (2002) New data for the Last Glacial Maximum in Great Britain and Ireland. *Quaternary Science Reviews*, **21**, 89–101.

Bradley, R. & Edmonds, M. (1993) *Interpreting the axe trade.* Cambridge University Press, Cambridge.

Bradley, R.S., Hughes, M.K. & Diaz, H.F. (2003) Climate in Medieval time. *Science*, **302**, 404–405.

Brandon, A. & Cooper, A.H. (1997) *Geology of the Etwall area: 1:10,000 sheet SK 23SE* (WA/97/03). British Geological Survey.

Brandon, A. & Sumbler, M.G. (1988) An Ipswichian fluvial deposit at Fulbeck, Lincolnshire and the chronology of the Trent terraces. *Journal of Quaternary Science*, **3**, 127–133.

Brandon, A. & Sumbler, M.G. (1991) The Balderton Sand and Gravel: pre-Ipswichian cold stage fluvial deposits near Lincoln, England. *Journal of Quaternary Science*, **6**, 117–138.

Brayshay, B. (1994) *Palynological assessment of sediment sample SLS/02/0011 from Shardlow, Derbyshire.* University of Sheffield.

Brayshay, B. (1999) Some palaeoenvironmental evidence for marginality in the upper Mersey Basin. In: *Living on the Edge of*

Empire: Models, Methodology and Marginality. (ed. M. Nevell), pp. 82–89. Archaeology North-West 3, Manchester.

Brayshay, B.A. & Dinnin, M. (1999) Integrated palaeoecological evidence for biodiversity at the floodplain–forest margin. *Journal of Biogeography,* **26,** 115–131.

Brears, P.C.D. (1971) *The English Country Pottery: Its History and Techniques.* David and Charles, Newton Abott.

Brickstock, R.J., Cardwell, P.A., Busby, P.A., Cool, H.E.M., Huntley, J.P., Evans, J., Makey, P., Ronan, D. & Wilson, P.R. (2007) Catterick metal detection project 1997–1999, with an appendix on 1,003 evaluation excavations south of Bainess (Site 506) and within the suburb of Cataractonium, north of the River Swale (Site 511). *Yorkshire Archaeological Journal,* **79,** 65–154.

Bridge, J.S. (1993) The interaction between channel geometry, water flow, sediment transport and deposition in braided rivers. In: *Braided Rivers.* (eds J.L Best & C.S. Bristow), pp. 13–71. Geological Society of London, Special Publication 75.

Bridge, J.S. (2003) *Rivers and Floodplains.* Blackwell, Oxford.

Bridgland, D.R., ed. (1986a) *Clast Lithological Analysis. Technical Guide 3.* Quaternary Research Association, Cambridge.

Bridgland, D.R. (1986b) The rudaceous components of the East Essex gravel; their characteristics and provenance. *Quaternary Studies,* **2,** 34–44.

Bridgland, D.R. (1988) The Pleistocene fluvial stratigraphy and palaeogeography of Essex. *Proceedings of the Geologists' Association,* **99,** 291–314.

Bridgland, D.R., ed. (1994) *Quaternary of the Thames.* Geological Conservation Review Vol. 7. Chapman & Hall, London.

Bridgland, D.R. (1998) The Pleistocene history and early human occupation of the River Thames valley. In: *Stone Age Archaeology, Essays in Honour of John Wymer* (eds N. Ashton, F. Healy, & P. Pettit), pp. 29–37. Oxbow, Oxford.

Bridgland, D.R. (1999) The Pleistocene of north-east England. In: *The Quaternary of North-east England. Field Guide* (eds D.R. Bridgland, B.P. Horton, & J.B. Innes), pp. 1–9. Quaternary Research Association, London.

Bridgland, D.R. (2000) River terrace systems in north-west Europe: an archive of environmental change, uplift and early human occupation. *Quaternary Science Reviews,* **19,** 1293–1303.

Bridgland, D.R. (2003) The evolution of the River Medway, S.E. England, in the context of Quaternary palaeoclimate and the Palaeolithic occupation of N.W. Europe. *Proceedings of the Geologists' Association,* **114,** 23–48.

Bridgland, D.R., Allen, P., Blackford, J.J., Parfitt, S. & Preece, R.C. (1995) New work on the Aveley Silts and Sands – A13 Road Improvement. In: *The Quaternary of the Lower Reaches of the Thames. Field Guide* (eds D.R. Bridgland, P. Allen, & B.A. Haggart), pp. 201–216. Quaternary Research Association, Durham.

Bridgland, D.R. & Austin, W.E.N. (1999) Shippersea Bay to Hawthorn Hive. In: *The Quaternary of North-East England. Field Guide* (eds D.R. Bridgland, B.P. Horton, & J.B. Innes), pp. 51–56. Quaternary Research Association, London.

Bridgland, D.R. & Westaway, R. (2007a) Climatically controlled river terrace staircases: a worldwide Quaternary phenomenon. *Geomorphology,* **98,** 285–315.

Bridgland, D.R. & Westaway, R. (2007b) Preservation patterns of Late Cenozoic fluvial deposits and their implications: results from **IGCP**449. *Quaternary International,* **189,** 5–38.

Bridgland, D.R., White, T.S., Howard, A.J. & White, M.J. (in press a) *The Quaternary of the Trent.* Oxbow, Oxford

Bridgland, D.R., Westaway, R., Howard, A.J., Innes, J.B., Long, A.J., Mitchell, W.A., White, M.J., White, T.S. (in press b) The role of glacio-isostasy in the formation of post-glacial river terraces in relation to the MIS 2 ice limit: evidence from northern England. *Proceedings of the Geologists' Association.*

Britnell, R. (2003) Boroughs, markets and fairs. In: *Historical Atlas of North Yorkshire.* (ed. R.A. Butlin), pp. 104–105. Smith Settle, Otley.

Broeker, W.S. (2006) Was the Younger Dryas triggered by a flood? *Science,* **312,** 1146–1148.

Broeker, W.S., Kennett, J.P., Flower, B.P., Teller, J.T., Trumbore, S., Bonani, G. & Wolfli, W. (1989) The routing of meltwater from the Laurentide Ice Sheet during the Younger Dryas cold episode. *Nature,* **341,** 318–321.

Bromehead, C.E.N. (1912) On diversions of the Bourne near Chertsey. *Summary of progress of the Geological Survey of Great Britain [for 1911],* 74–77.

Bronk Ramsey, C. (1995) Radiocarbon Calibration and Analysis of Stratigraphy: The OxCal Program. *Radiocarbon,* **37,** 425–430.

Bronk Ramsey, C. (1998) Probability and dating. *Radiocarbon,* **40,** 461–474.

Brothwell, D.R. & Pollard, A.M., eds (2001) *Handbook of Archaeological Sciences.* Wiley, Chichester.

Brown, A.G. (1988) The palaeoecology of *Alnus* (alder) and the postglacial history of floodplain vegetation: pollen percentage and influx data from the West Midlands. *New Phytologist,* **110,** 425–436.

Brown, A.G. (1997a) *Alluvial Geoarchaeology: Floodplain Archaeology and Environmental Change.* Cambridge University Press.

Brown, A.G. (1997b) Clearances and clearings: deforestation in Mesolithic/Neolithic Britain. *Oxford Journal of Archaeology,* **16,** 133–146.

Brown, A.G. (1998) Fluvial evidence of the Medieval Warm Period and the Late Medieval Climatic Deterioration in Europe. In: *Palaeohydrology and Environmental Change.* (eds G. Benito, V.R. Baker, & K.J. Gregory), pp. 43–52. Wiley, Chichester.

Brown, A.G. (1999) Characterising prehistoric lowland environments using local pollen assemblages. *Quaternary Proceedings,* **7,** 585–594.

Brown, A.G. (2000) Floodplain vegetation history: clearings as ritual spaces. In: *Plants in Neolithic Britain and Beyond* (ed. A. Fairbairn), pp. 49–62. Oxbow Books, Oxford.

Brown, A.G. (2002) Floodplain landscapes and archaeology: fluvial events and human agency. *Journal of Wetland Archaeology,* **2,** 89–104.

Brown, A.G. (2003) Divisions of floodplain space and sites on riverine 'islands': functional, ritual, social or liminal places. *Journal of Wetland Archaeology,* **3,** 3–15.

Brown, A.G., Carpenter, R.G. & Walling, D.E. (2007b) Monitoring fluvial pollen transport, its relationship to catchment vegetation and implications for palaeoenvironmental studies. *Review of Palaeobotany and Palynology,* **147,** 60–76.

Brown, A.G., Cooper, L., Salisbury, C.R. & Smith, D.N. (2001) Late Holocene channel changes in the middle Trent: channel response to a thousand year flood record. *Geomorphology,* **39,** 69–82.

Brown, A.G. & Keough, M. (1992) Palaeochannels, palaeolandsurfaces and three dimensional reconstruction of floodplain environmental change. In: *Lowland floodplain rivers:*

geomorphological perspectives (eds P.A. Carling & G.E. Petts), pp. 185–202. Wiley, Chichester.

Brown, A.G., Keough, M. & Rice, R.J. (1994) Floodplain evolution in the East Midlands, United Kingdom: the Lateglacial and Flandrian alluvial record from the Soar and Nene valleys. *Philosophical Transactions of the Royal Society of London,* **A348,** 261–293.

Brown, E.J., Rose, J., Coope, G.R. & Lowe, J.J. (2007a) An MIS 3 age organic deposit from Balglass Burn, central Scotland: palaeoenvironmental significance and implications for the timing of the onset of the LGM ice sheet in the vicinity of the British Isles. *Journal of Quaternary Science,* **22,** 295–308.

Buckland, P.C. & Sadler, J. (1985) The nature of late Flandrian alluviation in the Humberhead levels. *East Midland Geographer,* **8,** 239–251.

Burbank, D.W. & Anderson, R.S. (2001) *Tectonic Geomorphology.* Blackwell, Oxford.

Burgess, C. (1995) A Bronze Age rapier from Catterick Bridge. *Yorkshire Archaeological Journal,* **67,** 1–6.

Burl, A. (1991) The Devil's Arrows, Boroughbridge, North Yorkshire. *Yorkshire Archaeological Journal,* **63,** 1–24.

Burroughs, M., ed. (2001) *Villas of the Brigantes and the Parisi: Criteria for Site Location.* Certificate in Continuing Education in Celtic Studies, University of Manchester.

Burton, J. (2003) Religious Houses. In: *Historical Atlas of North Yorkshire* (ed. R.A. Butlin), pp. 90–95. Smith Settle, Otley.

Bush, M.B. (1988) Early Mesolithic disturbance: a force on the landscape. *Journal of Archaeological Science,* **15,** 453–462.

Bush, M.B. (1993) An 11400 year palaeoecological history of a British chalk grassland. *Journal of Vegetation Science,* **4,** 47–66.

Bush, M.B. & Hall, A.R. (1987) Early Flandrian *Alnus:* immigration or expansion. *Journal of Biogeography,* **14,** 479–481.

Butlin, R.A. (2003) Agriculture. In: *Historical Atlas of North Yorkshire* (ed. R.A. Butlin), pp. 143–162. Smith Settle, Otley.

Butlin, R.A. & Roberts, N. (1995) *Ecological relations in historical times: human impact and adaptation.* Biogeography and Historical Geography Research Groups. Oxford, Blackwell.

Buxton, K., Howard-Davis, C., Innes, J.B. & McHugh, M. (2000) Pre-Roman deposition and environment. In: *Bremetenacum. Excavations at Roman Ribchester 1980, 1989–1990.* (eds K. Buxton & C. Howard-Davis), pp. 15–24. Lancaster University Archaeology Unit, Lancaster.

Cameron, A.G. (1878) Notes on some peat at Kildale and West Hartlepool. *Geological Magazine,* **5,** 351.

Campbell, S. & Bowen, D.Q. (1989) *Quaternary of Wales.* Geological Conservation Review Vol. 2. Nature Conservancy Council, Peterborough.

Cardwell, P. (1995) Excavation of the hospital of St Giles by Brompton Bridge, North Yorkshire. *Archaeological Journal,* **152,** 109–245

Cardwell, P. & Speed, G. (1996) Prehistoric occupation at St Giles, by Brompton Bridge, North Yorkshire. *Durham Archaeological Journal,* **12,** 27–40.

Carr, S.J. (1999) The micromorphology of the Last Glacial Maximum sediments in the southern North Sea. *Catena,* **35,** 123–148.

Carr, S.J. (2004) The North Sea Basin. In: *Quaternary Glaciations – Extent and Chronology: Part 1: Europe.* (eds J. Ehlers & P.L. Gibbard), pp. 261–270. Elsevier, Amsterdam.

Carr, S.J., Holmes, R., Van der Meer, J.J.M. & Rose, J. (2006) The Last Glacial Maximum in the North Sea Basin: micromorphological evidence of extensive glaciation. *Journal of Quaternary Science,* **21,** 131–153.

Catt, J.A. (1991a) Late Devensian glacial deposits and glaciations in eastern Europe and the adjoining offshore region. In: *Glacial Deposits in Great Britain and Ireland.* (eds J. Ehlers, P.L. Gibbard, & J. Rose), pp. 61–68. Balkema, Rotterdam.

Catt, J.A. (1991b) The Quaternary history and glacial deposits of East Yorkshire. In: *Glacial Deposits in Great Britain and Ireland,* (eds J. Ehlers, P.L. Gibbard, & J. Rose), pp. 185–191. Balkema, Rotterdam.

Catt, J.A. (2007) The Pleistocene glaciations of Eastern Yorkshire: a review. *Proceedings of the Yorkshire Geological Society,* **56,** 177–207.

Chambers, C. (1978) A radiocarbon dated pollen diagram from Valley Bog, on the Moor House Nature Reserve. *New Phytologist,* **80,** 273–280.

Chambers, F.M. & Blackford, J.J. (2001) Mid- and late-Holocene climatic changes: a test of periodicity and solar forcing in proxy-climate data from blanket bogs. *Journal of Quaternary Science,* **16,** 329–338.

Chambers, F.M. & Elliott, L. (1989) Spread and expansion of *Alnus* Mill. in the British Isles: timing, agencies and possible vectors. *Journal of Biogeography,* **16,** 541–550.

Chambers, F.M., Mighall, T. & Keen, D.H. (1996) A Holocene pollen and molluscan record from Enfield Lock, Middlesex, U.K. *Proceedings of the Geologists' Association,* **107,** 1–17.

Chambers, F.M. & Price, S.-M. (1985) Palaeoecology of *Alnus* (Alder): early post–glacial rise in a valley mire, north-west Wales. *New Phytologist,* **101,** 333–344.

Chapman, M. R., Shackleton, N.J. & Duplessy, J.C. (2000) Sea surface temperature variability during the last glacial-interglacial cycle: assessing the magnitude and pattern of climate change in the North Atlantic. *Palaeogeography, Palaeoclimatology, Palaeoecology,* **157,** 1–25.

Charlesworth, J.K. (1957) *The Quaternary Era.* Arnold, London.

Chinn, S.J. & Innes, J.B. (1995) Pollen analysis from Wet Sleddale. *Transactions of the Cumberland and Westmorland Antiquarian and Archaeological Society,* **95,** 19–22.

Chiverrell, R.C. (2001) A proxy record of late Holocene climate change from May Moss, northeast England. *Journal of Quaternary Science,* **16,** 9–29.

Chiverrell, R.C. (2006) Past and future perspectives upon landscape instablity in Cumbria. *Regional Environmental Change,* **6,** 101–114.

Chiverrell, R.C. & Atherden, M.A. (1999) Climate change and human impact – evidence from peat stratigraphy at sites in the eastern North York Moors. In: *The Quaternary of Northeast England. Field Guide* (eds D.R. Bridgland, B. Horton, & J.B. Innes), pp. 113–130. Quaternary Research Association, London.

Chiverrell, R.C. & Atherden, M.A. (2000) Post Iron Age vegetation history and climate change on the North York Moors: a preliminary report. In: *People as agents of environmental change.* (eds R.A. Nicholson & T.P. O'Connor), pp. 45–59. Oxbow Books, Oxford.

Chiverrell, R.C. & Menuge, N.J. (2003) Climate change. In: *Historical Atlas of North Yorkshire.* (ed. R.A. Butlin), pp. 22–24. Smith Settle, Otley.

Chiverrell, R.C., Harvey, A.M. & Foster, G.C. (2007a) Hillslope gullying in the Solway Firth–Morecambe Bay region,

Great Britain: responses to human impact and/or climatic deterioration. *Geomorphology*, **84**, 317–343.

Chiverrell, R.C., Thomas, G.S.P., Foster, G.C., Lang, A., Marshall, P., Hamilton, D. & Huckerby, E. (2007b) The Landscape: a heritage resource. In: *Aggregate extraction in the lower Ribble valley* (eds J. Quartermaine & R.C. Chiverrell), pp. 95–132 (plus 52 figures). Available online, University of Liverpool: http://www.liv.ac.uk/geography/research/ribble/Project_Report.htm

Chiverrell, R.C., Thomas, G.S.P. & Foster, G.C. (2008) Sediment–landform assemblages and digital elevation data: testing an improved methodology for the assessment of sand and gravel aggregate resources in north-western Britain. *Engineering Geology*, **99**, 40–50.

Chiverrell, R.C., Foster, G.C., Thomas, G.S.P., Marshall, P. & Hamilton, D. (2009) Robust chronologies for landform development. *Earth Surface Processes and Landforms*, **34**, 319–328.

Clark, C.D., Evans, D.J.A., Khatwa, A., Bradwell, T., Jordan, C.J., Marsh, S.H., Mitchell, W.A. & Bateman, M.D. (2004a) Map and GIS database of glacial landforms and features related to the last British Ice Sheet. *Boreas*, **33**, 359–375.

Clark, C.D., Gibbard, P.L. & Rose, J. (2004b) Pleistocene glacial limits in England, Scotland and Wales. In: *Quaternary Glaciations – Extent and Chronology: Part 1: Europe.* (eds J. Ehlers & P.L. Gibbard), pp. 47–82. Elsevier, Amsterdam.

Clark, C.D., Greenwood, S. & Evans, D.J.A. (2006) Palaeo-glaciology of the last British–Irish ice sheet: challenges and some recent developments. In: *Glacier Science and Environmental Change* (ed. P.G. Knight), pp. 248–264. Blackwell, Oxford.

Clark, C.D. & Stokes, C. (2004) Palaeo-ice stream Landsystem. In: *Glacial Landsystems.* (ed. D.J.A. Evans), pp. 204–227. Arnold, London.

Clark, S.H.E. & Edwards, K.J. (2004) Elm bark beetle in Holocene peat deposits and the northwest European elm decline. *Journal of Quaternary Science*, **19**, 525–528.

Clarke, M.L., Milodowski, A.E., Bouch, J.E., Leng, M.J. & Northmore, K.J. (2007) New OSL dating of UK loess: indications of two phases of Late Glacial dust accretion in SE England and climate implications. *Journal of Quaternary Science*, **22**, 361–371.

Clay, P. (1992) A Norman mill dam at Hemington Fields, Castle Donnington, Leicestershire. In: *Alluvial Archaeology in Britain.* (eds S. Needham & M.G. Macklin), pp. 163–168. Oxbow, Oxford.

Cloutman, E.W. & Smith, A.G. (1988) Palaeoenvironments in the Vale of Pickering. Part 3: environmental history at Star Carr. *Proceedings of the Prehistoric Society*, **54**, 37–58.

Coggins, D., Fairless, K.J. & Batey, C.E. (1980) Simy Folds: an Early Medieval settlement site in Upper Teesdale. *Medieval Archaeology*, **27**, 1–26.

Coles, B. (2001) The impact of beaver activity on stream channels: some implications for past landscapes and human activity. *Journal of Wetland Archaeology*, **1**, 55–82.

Coles, B. & Colville, B. (1980) A glacial relict mollusc. *Nature*, **286**, 761.

Conneller, C. & Schadla-Hall, T. (2003) Beyond Star Carr: The Vale of Pickering in the 10th Millennium BP. *Proceedings of the Prehistoric Society*, **69**, 85–105.

Coope, G.R. (1977a) Quaternary Coleoptera as aids in the interpretation of environmental history. In: *British Quaternary Studies: recent advances.* (ed. F.W. Shotton), pp. 55–68. Clarendon Press, Oxford.

Coope, G.R. (1977b) Fossil coleopteran assemblages as sensitive indicators of climatic changes during the Devensian (Last) cold stage. *Philosophical Transactions of the Royal Society of London*, **B280**, 313–340.

Coope, G.R. (1986) Coleoptera analysis. In: *Handbook of Holocene Palaeoecology and Palaeohydrology* (ed. B.E. Berglund), pp. 703–713. Wiley, Chichester.

Coope, G.R. & Brophy, J.A. (1972) Late Glacial environmental changes indicated by a coleopteran succession from North Wales. *Boreas*, **1**, 97–142.

Coope, G.R. & Jones, P.F. (1977) Boulton Moor SK 382317. In: *The English Midlands. Guidebook for Excursion A2, X INQUA Congress 1977* (ed. F.W. Shotton), pp. 25–26. GeoAbstracts, Norwich.

Coope, G.R., Lemdahl, G., Lowe, J.J. & Walkling, A. (1998) Temperature gradients in northwestern Europe during the last glacial–interglacial transition (14–9 ^{14}C kyr BP) interpreted from coleopteran assemblages. *Journal of Quaternary Science*, **13**, 419–434.

Cooper, A.H. (1983) *The geology of the country north and east of Ripon, north Yorkshire with particular reference to the sand and gravel resources; description of 1:25, 000 Sheet SE 37.* Institute of Geological Sciences.

Cooper, A.H. (1986) Subsidence and foundering of strata caused by the dissolution of Permian gypsum in the Ripon and Bedale area, north Yorkshire. In: *The English Zechstein and related topics.* (eds G.M. Harwood & D.B. Smith), pp. 127–139. Geological Society of London.

Cooper, A.H. (1989) Airborne multispectral scanning of subsidence caused by Permian gypsum dissolution at Ripon, North Yorkshire *Quarterly Journal of Engineering Geology*, **22**, 219–229.

Cooper, A.H. (1995) *Subsidence hazards due to the dissolution of Permian gypsum in England; investigation and remediation.* Paper presented at the Karst Geohazards – Engineering and Environmental Problems in Karst Terrane, Proceedings of the Fifth Multi-disciplinary conference on sinkholes and the environmental impact of karst, Gatlinburg, Tennessee.

Cooper, A.H. (1998) Subsidence hazards caused by the dissolution of Permian gypsum in England: geology, investigation and remediation. In: *Geohazards in Engineering Geology* (eds J.G. Maund & M. Eddleston), pp. 265–275. Geological Society, Bath.

Cooper, A.H. (2006) *Gypsum Dissolution Geohazards at Ripon, North Yorkshire, UK. Field Trip Guide Ripon.* Geological Society, London.

Cooper, A.H. & Burgess, I.C. (1993) *Geology of the country around Harrogate (Sheet 62).* Her Majesty's Stationery Office.

Cooper, A.H. & Gibson, A. (2003) *Geology of the Leeds district – brief description of the geological map. Sheet explanation of the British Geological Survey. 1:50,000 Sheet 70 Leeds (England and Wales).*

Cooper, L.P. (2003) Hemington Quarry, Castle Donington, Leicestershire, UK: a decade beneath the alluvium in the confluence zone. In: *Alluvial Archaeology in Europe* (eds A.J. Howard, M.G. Macklin & D.G. Passmore), pp. 27–41. Balkema.

Cotton, J.A., Heritage, G.L., Large, A.G.L. & Passmore, D.G. (1999) Biotic response to Late Holocene floodplain evolution in the River Irthing catchment, Cumbria In:

Floodplains: Interdisciplinary Approaches (eds S.B. Marriott & J. Alexander), pp. 163–178. Geological Society, London Special Publication 163.

Coulthard, T.J. & Macklin, M.G. (2003) Modelling long-term contamination in river systems from historical metal mining. *Geology*, **31**, 451–454.

Coulthard, T.J., Lewin, J. & Macklin, M.G. (2005) Modelling differential catchment response to environmental change. *Geomorphology*, **69**, 222–241.

Cowling, E.T. & Stickland, H.J. (1947) Two Mesolithic riverside sites in Yorkshire. *Yorkshire Archaeological Journal*, **36**, 445–462.

Crawford, G.M. (1980) *Bronze Age Burial Mounds in Cleveland*. Cleveland County Council, Middlesbrough.

Cummings, V. & Whittle, A. (2003) Tombs with a view: landscape, monuments and trees. *Antiquity*, **77**, 255–266.

Cummins, G. (2000) FIRE! Accidental or strategic use of fire in the early Mesolithic of the eastern Vale of Pickering. In: *Mesolithic Lifeways* (ed. R. Young), pp. 75–84. Leicester University, Leicester Archaeology Monographs 7, Leicester.

Cundill, P.R. (1976) Late Flandrian vegetation and soils in Carlingill valley, Howgill Fells. *Transactions of the Institute of British Geographers*, **NS1**, 301–309.

Currant, A. & Jacobi, R.M. (2001) A formal mammalian biostratigraphy for the Late Pleistocene of Britain. *Quaternary Science Reviews*, **20**, 1707–1716.

Dalton, A.C. (1941) Lake Humber as interpreted by the glaciation of England and Wales. *North Western Naturalist*, **16**, 256–265.

Dandurand, J.L., Gout, R., Hoefs, J., Menschel, G., Schott, J. & Usdowski, E. (1982) Kinetically controlled variations of major components and carbon and oxygen isotopes in a calcite-precipitating spring. *Chemical Geology*, **36**, 299–315.

Daniell, C. (2003) Communications. In: *Historical Atlas of North Yorkshire* (ed. R.A. Butlin), pp. 101–104. Smith Settle, Otley.

Daniels, R. (1988) Excavated rural medieval buildings in the Tees lowlands. *Durham Archaeological Journal* **4**, 37–44.

Daniels, R. (2002) Medieval boroughs of northern England. In: *Past, Present and Future: The Archaeology of Northern England* (eds C. Brooks, R. Daniels, & A. Harding), pp. 185–197. Architectural and Archaeological Society of Durham and Northumberland Research Report 5, Durham.

Dark, P. (1996) Palaeoecological evidence for landscape continuity and change in Britain ca AD 400–800. In: *External Contacts and the Economy of Late Roman and Post-Roman Britain* (ed. K.R. Dark), pp. 23–51. Boydell, Woodbridge.

Dark, P. (2000) *The Environment of Britain in the First Millennium AD*. Duckworth, London.

Dark, P. (2005) Mid- to late-Holocene vegetational and land-use change in the Hadrian's Wall region: a radiocarbon-dated pollen sequence from Crag Lough, Northumberland, England. *Journal of Archaeological Science*, **32**, 601–618.

Dark, P. (2006) Climate deterioration and land-use change in the first millennium BC: perspectives from the British palynological record. *Journal of Archaeological Science*, **33**, 1381–1395.

Darvill, T. & Fulton, A.K. (1998) *MARS: the Monuments at Risk Survey in England, 1995*. Bournemouth University and English Heritage.

Day, P. (1996a) Devensian Late-glacial and early Flandrian environmental history of the Vale of Pickering. *Journal of Quaternary Science*, **11**, 9–24.

Day, P. (1996b) Dogs, deer and diet at Star Carr: a reconsideration of C-isotope evidence from early Mesolithic dog remains from the Vale of Pickering, Yorkshire, England. *Journal of Archaeological Science*, **23**, 783–787.

Day, P. & Mellars, P.A. (1994) 'Absolute' dating of Mesolithic human activity at Star Carr, Yorkshire: new palaeoecological studies and identification of the 9600 BP 'plateau'. *Proceedings of the Prehistoric Society*, **60**, 417–422.

Dennis, I.A., Macklin, M.G., Coulthard, T.J. & Brewer, P.A. (2003) The impact of the October/November 2000 floods on contaminant metal dispersal in the River Swale, North Yorkshire. *Hydrological Processes*, **17**, 1641–1657.

Dennison, E. (1993) *A1 Dishforth to North of Leeming Improvements: Archaeological Desk-Top Survey: Volume 1: Factual Report*. prepared for The Department of Transport.

Dennison, E. (2006) *A684 Bedale, Aiskew and Leeming Bar Bypass Scheme*. Report for North Yorkshire County Council.

Dewey, H. & Bromehead, C.E.N. (1915) *The geology of the country around Windsor and Chertsey*. Memoir of the Geological Survey.

Dewey, H. & Bromehead, C.E.N. (1921) *The geology of south London*. Memoir of the Geological Survey.

Dewey, H., Bromehead, C.E.N., Chatwin, C.P. & Dines, H.G. (1924) *The geology of the country around Dartford*. Memoir of the Geological Survey.

Dickson, J.A.D. (1966) Carbonate identification and genesis as revealed by staining. *Journal of Sedimentary Petrology*, **36**, 491–505.

Dimbleby, G.W. (1962) *The Development of British Heathlands and their Soils*. Oxford Forestry Memoir 23, Oxford.

Dinnin, M. (1997a) Introduction to the palaeoenvironmental survey. In: *Wetland Heritage of the Humberhead Levels* (eds R. Van de Noort & S. Ellis), pp. 31–45. University of Hull.

Dinnin, M. (1997b) Holocene beetle assemblages from the Lower Trent floodplain at Bole Ings, Nottinghamshire, UK. In: *Studies in Quaternary Entomology* (eds A.C. Ashworth, P.C. Buckland, & J.P. Sadler), pp. 83–104. Quaternary Proceedings, Quaternary Research Association, London.

Dinnin, M. & Brayshay, B.A. (1999) The contribution of a multiproxy approach in reconstructing floodplain development. In: *Floodplains: Interdisciplinary Approaches* (eds S.B. Marriott & A. Alexander), pp. 179–195. Geological Society of London Special Publication 163.

Donaldson, A.M. & Turner, J. (1977) A pollen diagram from Hallowell Moss, near Durham City, UK. *Journal of Biogeography*, **4**, 25–33.

Dumayne, L. & Barber, K.E. (1993) Invader or native? – vegetation clearance in northern Britain during Romano-British time. *Vegetation History and Archaeobotany*, **2**, 29–36.

Dumayne, L. & Barber, K.E. (1994) The impact of the Romans on the environment of northern England: pollen data from three sites close to Hadrian's Wall. *The Holocene*, **4**, 165–173.

Dumayne-Peaty, L. & Barber, K.E. (1998) Late Holocene vegetational history, human impact and pollen representativity variations in northern Cumbria, UK. *Journal of Quaternary Science*, **13**, 147–164.

Dury, G.H. (1955) Bed-width and wavelength in meandering valleys, *Nature*, **176**, 31–32.

Dury, G.H. (1958) Tests of a General Theory of Misfit Streams. *Transactions and Papers (Institute of British Geographers)*, **25**, 105–118

Edwards, K.J. (1988) The hunter-gatherer/agricultural transition and the pollen record in the British Isles. In: *The Cultural*

Landscape – Past, Present and Future. (eds H.H. Birks, H.J.B. Birks, P.E. Kaland, & D. Moe), pp. 255–266. Cambridge University Press.

Edwards, K.J. (1989) The cereal pollen record and early agriculture. In: *The Beginnings of Agriculture.* (eds A. Milles, D. Williams, & N. Gardner), pp. 113–135. British Archaeological Reports, International Series 496, Oxford.

Edwards, K.J. (1993) Models of forest farming for north-west Europe. In: *Climate Change and Human Impact on the Landscape* (ed. F.M. Chambers), pp. 134–155. Chapman & Hall, London.

Edwards, K.J. (1999) Palynology and people: observations on the British record. *Quaternary Proceedings*, **7**, 531–544.

Edwards, K.J. & Whittington, G. (2001) Lake sediments, erosion and landscape change during the Holocene in Britain and Ireland. *Catena*, **42**, 143–173.

Edwards, K.J., Whittington, G. & Tipping, R.M. (2000) The incidence of microscopic charcoal in Lateglacial deposits. *Palaeogeography, Palaeoclimatology, Palaeoecology*, **164**, 247–262.

Edwards, K.J., Langdon, P.G. & Sugden, H. (2007) Separating climatic and possible human impacts in the early Holocene: biotic response around the time of the 8200 cal. yr BP event. *Journal of Quaternary Science*, **22**, 77–84.

Edwards, M.A., Trotter, F.M. & Wray, D.A. (1954) *The Pennines and Adjacent areas.* (3rd ed.). HMSO, 3rd edition.

Edwards, W. (1937) A Pleistocene strand line in the Vale of York. *Proceedings of the Yorkshire Geological Society*, **23**, 103–118.

Edwards, W. (1938) The glacial geology (in the geology of the country around Harrogate). *Proceedings of the Geologists' Association*, **49**, 333–343.

Edwards, W., Mitchell, G.H. & Whitehead, T.H. (1950) Geology of the district north and east of Leeds. HMSO, London.

Elgee, F. (1908) The glaciation of North Cleveland. *Proceedings of the Yorkshire Geological Society*, **16**, 372–382.

Elias, S.A. (2006) Quaternary beetle research: the state of the art. *Quaternary Science Reviews*, **25**, 1731–1737.

Ellis, N.V., Bowen, D.Q., Campbell, S., Knill, J.L., McKirdy, A.P., Prosser, C.D., Vincent, M.A. & Wilson, R.C.L. (1996) *An Introduction to the Geological Conservation Review* (vol. 1). Joint Nature Conservation Committee, Peterborough.

Evans, D.J.A. (2002a) Dimlington (TA 390 220). In: *Quaternary of Northern England.* Geological Conservation Review Vol. 25 (eds D. Huddart & N.F. Glasser), pp. 139–144. Joint Nature Conservation Committee, Peterborough.

Evans, D.J.A. (2002b) Gransmoor. In: *Quaternary of Northern England.* Geological Conservation Review Vol. 25 (eds D. Huddart & N.F. Glasser), pp. 257–264. Joint Nature Conservation Committee, Peterborough.

Evans, D.J.A. (2004) *Glacial Landsystems.* Arnold, London.

Evans, D.J.A., Thomson, S.A. & Clark, C.D. (2001) Introduction to the Late Quaternary of East Yorkshire and North Lincolnshire. In: *The Quaternary of East Yorkshire and North Lincolnshire. Field Guide* (eds M.D. Bateman, P.C. Buckland, C.D. Frederick, & N.J. Whitehouse), pp. 1–12. Quaternary Research Association, London.

Evans, D.J.A. & O'Cofaigh, C. (2003) Depositional evidence for marginal oscillations of the Irish Sea ice stream in southeast Ireland during the last glaciation. *Boreas*, **32**, 76–101.

Evans, D.J.A., Clark, C.D. & Mitchell, W.A. (2005) The last British Ice Sheet: a review of the evidence utilised in the compilation of the Glacial Map of Britain. *Earth Science Reviews*, **70**, 253–312.

Evans, J. (1872) *The ancient stone implements, weapons, and ornaments of Great Britain.* Longmans, Green, Reader and Dyer, London.

Evans, J.G. (1972) *Land Snails in Archaeology.* Seminar Press, London.

Evans, J.G. (1991) River valley bottoms and archaeology in the Holocene. In: *The Wetland Revolution in Prehistory* (ed. B. Coles), pp. 47–53. Prehistoric Society, WARP Occasional Paper 6.

Everest, J.D., Bradwell, T., Fogwill, C.J. & Kubik, P.W. (2006) Cosmogenic ¹⁰Be age constraints for the Wester Ross readvance moraine: more insights into British Ice Sheet behaviour. *Geografiska Annaler*, **88A**, 9–17.

Everest, J.D. & Kubik, P.W. (2006) The deglaciation of eastern Scotland: cosmogenic ¹⁰Be evidence for a Lateglacial still-stand. *Journal of Quaternary Science*, **21**, 95–104.

Eyles, N., McCabe, A.M. & Bowen, D.Q. (1994) The stratigraphic and sedimentological significance of late Devensian ice sheet surging in Holderness. *Quaternary Science Reviews*, **13**, 727–759.

Falinski, J.B. (1978) Uprooted trees, their distribution and influence in the primeval forest biotope. *Vegetatio*, **38**, 175–183.

Faulkner, N. (2003) The debate about the end of Roman Britain: a review of evidence and methods,. *Archaeological Journal*, **159**, 59–76.

Fenton-Thomas, C. (1992) Pollen analysis as an aid to the reconstruction of patterns of land-use and settlement in the Tyne–Tees region during the first millennia BC and AD. *Durham Archaeological Journal*, **8**, 51–62.

Fleming, A. (1996) Early roads to the Swaledale lead mines. *Yorkshire Archaeological Journal*, **68**, 89–100.

Fleming, A. (1998) *Swaledale: Valley of the Wild River.* Edinburgh University Press, Edinburgh.

Flenley, J.R. (1984) Towards a vegetational history of the meres of Holderness. In: *Late Quaternary Environments and Man in Holderness* (ed. D.D. Gilbertson), pp. 165–175. British Archaeological Reports, British Series 134, Oxford.

Ford, T. & Pedley, H.M. (1996) A review of tufa and travertine deposits of the World. *Earth Science Reviews*, **41**, 117–175.

Foulds, S.A. & Macklin, M.G. (2006) Holocene land-use changes and its impact on river basin dynamics in Great Britain and Ireland. *Progress in Physical Geography*, **30**, 589–604.

Fox-Strangways, C. (1873) *The geology of the country north and east of Harrogate.* Memoir of the Geological Survey.

Fox-Strangways, C., Cameron, A.G. & Barrow, G. (1886) *The geology of the country around Northallerton and Thirsk.* Memoir of the Geological Survey.

Francis, E.A. (1970) Quaternary. In: *The Geology of Durham County. Transactions of the Natural History of Northumberland, Durham and Newcastle upon Tyne,* (eds G.A.L. Johnson & G. Hickling), **41**, 134–152.

Frederick, C.D., Buckland, P.C., Bateman, M.D. & Owens, B. (2001) South Ferriby Cliff (SE 998225) and Eastside Farm (SD 946208). In: *The Quaternary of East Yorkshire and North Lincolnshire. Field Guide* (eds M.D. Bateman, P.C. Buckland, C.D. Frederick, & N.J. Whitehouse), pp. 103–112. Quaternary Research Association, London.

Frost, D.V. (1998) *Geology of the country around Northallerton.* Memoir of the Geological Survey.

Frost, D.V. & Holliday, D.W. (1980) *Geology of the country around Bellingham.* Memoir of the Geological Survey.

Gábris, Gy. & Nagy, B. (2005) Climate and tectonically controlled river style changes on the Sajó-Hernád alluvial fan (Hungary). In: *Alluvial Fans: Geomorphology, Sedimentology, Dynamics* (eds A.M. Harvey, A.E. Mather & M. Stokes), Geological Society of London Special Publication 251, 61–67.

Gale, R. & Cutler, D. (2000) *Plants in Archaeology.* Royal Botanic Gardens, Kew, London.

Gale, S.J. & Hunt, C.O. (1985) The stratigraphy of Kirkhead cave, an upper Palaeolithic site in northern England. *Proceedings of the Prehistoric Society*, **51**, 283–304.

Gao, C., Boreham, S., Preece, R.C., Gibbard, P.L. & Briant, R.M. (2007) Fluvial response to rapid climate change during the Devensian (Weichselian) Lateglacial in the River Great Ouse, southern England, UK. *Sedimentary Geology*, **202**, 193–210.

Garton, D., Elliott, L. & Salisbury, C.R. (2001) Aston-upon-Trent, Argosy Washolme (SK431291). *Derbyshire Archaeological Journal*, **121**, 196–200.

Gaunt, G.D. (1970) A temporary section across the Escrick moraine at Wheldrake, East Yorkshire. *Journal of Earth Sciences, Leeds*, **8**, 163–170.

Gaunt, G.D. (1974) A radiocarbon date relating to Lake Humber. *Proceedings of the Yorkshire Geological Society*, **40**, 195–197.

Gaunt, G.D. (1976) The Devensian maximum limit in the Vale of York. *Proceedings of the Yorkshire Geological Society*, **40**, 631–637.

Gaunt, G.D. (1981) Quaternary history of the southern part of the Vale of York. In: *The Quaternary of Britain* (eds J. Neale & J. Flenley), pp. 82–97. Pergamon, Oxford.

Gaunt, G.D. (1994) *Geology of the country around Goole, Doncaster and the Isle of Axholme.* Memoir of the Geological Survey.

Gaunt, G.D., Jarvis, R.A. & Matthews, B. (1971) The late Weichselian sequence in the Vale of York. *Proceedings of the Yorkshire Geological Society*, **38**, 281–284.

Gaunt, G.D., Buckland, P.C. & Bateman, M.D. (2006) The geological background to the development and demise of a wetland – the Quaternary history of the Humberhead levels. *Bulletin of the Yorkshire Naturalists' Union*, **45**, 7–48.

Gayner, J.S. & Melmore, S. (1936a) The Pleistocene geology of the area between the Tees and the Trent. *Quarterly Journal of the Geological Society of London*, **92**, 362–364.

Gayner, J.S. & Melmore, S. (1936b) Lateglacial lacustrine conditions in the Vale of York and Tees basin. *North Western Naturalist*, **11**, 228.

Gear, A. & Turner, J. (2001) Palynological evidence for changing patterns of land use. In: *Stainmore: the Archaeology of a North Pennine Pass* (ed. B.E. Vyner), pp. 24–34. Tees Archaeology Monograph Series 1, Hartlepool.

Gearey, B. & Lillie, M. (1999) Aspects of Holocene vegetational changes in the Vale of York: palaeoenvironmental investigation at Askham Bog. In: *Wetland Heritage of the Vale of York: an archaeological survey* (eds R. Van de Noort & S. Ellis), pp. 109–122. University of Hull.

Gearey, B. & Lillie, M. (2001) Routh Quarry TA 087437 and TA 097435. In: *The Quaternary of East Yorkshire and North Lincolnshire: Field Guide* (eds M.D. Bateman, P.C. Buckland, C.D. Frederick, & N.J. Whitehouse), pp. 69–72. Quaternary Research Association, London.

Gibbard, P.L., Smith, A.G., Zalasiewicz, J.A., Barry, T.L., Cantrill, D., Coe, A.L., Cope, J.C.W., Gale, A.S., Gregory, F.J., Powell, J.H., Rawson, P.R., Stone, P. & Waters, C.N. (2005) What status for the Quaternary? *Boreas*, **34**, 1–12.

Gibbard, P.L. & van Kolfschoten, T. (2005) The Pleistocene and Holocene Epochs. In: *A Geological Time Scale 2004* (eds F. Gradstein, J. Ogg, & A. Smith), pp. 441–452. Cambridge University Press.

Gibbard, P.L. & West, R.G. (2000) Quaternary chronostratigraphy: the nomenclature of terrestrial sequences. *Boreas*, **29**, 329–336.

Gilbertson, D.D., ed. (1984) *Environments and Man in Holderness.* British Archaeological Reports, British Series 134, Oxford.

Giles, J.R.A. (1981) *The sand and gravel resources of the country around Blaydon, Tyne and Wear. Description of 1:25000 sheet NZ06,16.* Institute of Geological Sciences Mineral Assessment Report 74.

Giles, J.R.A. (1982) *The sand and gravel resources of the country around Bedale, North Yorkshire. Description of 1:25000 sheet SE28.* Institute of Geological Sciences Mineral Assessment Report 119.

Giles, J.R.A. (1992) Late Devensian and early Flandrian environments at Dishforth Bog, north Yorkshire. *Proceedings of the Yorkshire Geological Society*, **49**, 1–10.

Girling, M.A. (1985) An old forest beetle fauna from a Neolithic and Bronze Age peat deposit at Stileway. *Somerset Levels Papers*, **11**, 80–83.

Glasser, N., Etienne, J.L., Hambrey, M.J., Davies, J.R., Waters, R.A. & Wilby, P.R. (2004) Glacial meltwater erosion and sedimentation as evidence for multiple glaciations in west Wales. *Boreas*, **33**, 224–237.

Gledhill, T. (2003) Medieval woodland. In: *Historical Atlas of North Yorkshire* (ed. J.A. Butlin), pp. 75–78. Smith Settle, Otley.

Godwin, H. (1975) *History of the British Flora.* (2nd ed.). Cambridge University Press.

Godwin, H. & Willis, E.H. (1959) Cambridge University natural radiocarbon measurements. I. *American Journal of Science Radiocarbon Supplement* **1**, 63–75.

Gonzalez, S. & Huddart, D. (2002) Star Carr (TA 028810) Potential GCR site. In: *Quaternary of Northern England*, Geological Conservation Review Vol. 25 (eds D. Huddart & N.F. Glasser), pp. 443–455. Joint Nature Conservation Review Committee, Peterborough.

Goodchild, J.G. (1875) The glacial phenomena of the Eden valley. *Quarterly Journal of the Geological Society of London*, **31**, 363–380.

Göransson, H. (1982) The utilization of the forests in north-west europe during early and middle Neolithic. *PACT*, **7**, 207–221.

Göransson, H. (1986) Man and the forests of Nemoral broad-leafed trees during the Stone Age. *Striae*, **24**, 143–152.

Goudie, A.S., Viles, H.A. & Pentecost, A. (1993) The late–Holocene tufa decline in Europe. *The Holocene*, **3**, 181–186.

Gozzard, J.R. & Price, D. (1982) *The sand and gravel resources of the country east and south-east of Darlington, Durham. Description of 1:25,000 resource sheet NZ 31 and 30.* Institute of Geological Sciences Mineral Assessment Report 111.

Gray, J.M. & Coxon, P. (1991) The Loch Lomond Stadial glaciation in Britain and Ireland. In: *Glacial Deposits in*

Britain and Ireland (eds J.Ehlers, P.L. Gibbard & J. Rose), pp. 89–105. Balkema, Rotterdam.

Grayson, D.K. (2001) The archaeological record of human impacts on animal populations. *Journal of World Prehistory*, **15**, 1–69.

Green, C.P. & McGregor, D.F.M. (1978) Pleistocene gravel trains of the River Thames. *Proceedings of the Geologists Association*, **89**, 143–156.

Green, F. (1991) *Girton Gravel Pit SK 825670*. Unpublished report, Trent and Peak Archaeological Trust. University of Nottingham.

Greenwood, M.T., Agnew, M.D. & Wood, P.J. (2003) The use of caddisfly fauna (Insecta: Trichoptera) to characterise the Late-glacial River Trent, England. *Journal of Quaternary Science*, **18**, 645–661.

Greenwood, S.L., Clark, C.D. & Hughes, A.L.C. (2007) Formalising an inversion methodology for reconstructing ice-sheet retreat patterns from meltwater channels: applications to the British ice sheet. *Journal of Quaternary Science*, **22**, 637–645.

Gregory, K. (1962) The deglaciation of eastern Eskdale *Proceedings of the Yorkshire Geological Society*, **33**, 363–380.

Gregory, K. (1965) Proglacial Lake Eskdale after sixty years. *Transactions of the Institute of British Geographers*, **36**, 149–162.

Gregory, K.J., ed. (1997) *Fluvial Geomorphology of Great Britain*. Geological Conservation Review, Vol. 13. Joint Nature Conservation Committee, Peterborough.

Greig, D.C., ed. (1971) *British Regional Geology: The South of Scotland (3rd edition)*. British Geological Survey, Edinburgh.

Greig, J.R.A. (1982) Past and present limewoods of Europe. In: *Archaeological Aspects of Woodland Ecology* (eds M. Bell & S. Limbrey), pp. 23–55. British Archaeological Reports, International Series 146, Oxford.

Greig, J.R.A. (1996) Great Britain–England. In: *Palaeoecological Events During the Last 15000 years: Regional Syntheses of Palaeoecological Studies of Lakes and Mires in Europe* (eds B.E. Berglund, H.J.B. Birks, M. Ralska-Jasiewiczowa, & H.E. Wright), pp. 15–76. John Wiley, Chichester.

Griffiths, H.I. & Pedley, H.M. (1995) Did changes in late Last Glacial and early Holocene atmospheric CO_2 concentrations control rates of tufa precipitation? *The Holocene*, **5**, 238–242.

Grimm, E.C., ed. (1991) *Tilia version 2.0b4 and TiliaGraph 2.0b5. Programme for the analysis and display of microfossil data*. Illinois State Museum, Springfield, Illinois.

Gurney, S.D. (2000) Relict cryogenic mounds in the UK as evidence of climate change. In: *Linking Climate Change to Land Surface Change* (eds S.J. McLaren & D.R. Kniveton), pp. 209–229. Kluwer, Dordrecht.

Gwilt, A. & Heslop, D. (1995) Iron Age and Roman querns from the Tees valley. In: *Moorland Monuments, Studies in the Archaeology of North-East Yorkshire in Honour of Raymond Hayes and Don Spratt* (ed. B.E. Vyner), pp. 38–45. Council for British Archaeology, Research Report, 101, London.

Hale, D. & Platell, A. (2007) A grandstand view. *Current Archaeology*, **209**, 43–47.

Halkon, P. (1999) The early landscape of the Foulness valley, East Yorkshire. In: *The Quaternary of North-East England. Field Guide*. (eds D.R. Bridgland, B.P. Horton, & J.B. Innes), pp. 173–175. Quaternary Research Association, London.

Halkon, P. (2003) Researching an ancient landscape: the Foulness valley, East Yorkshire. In: *The Archaeology of Yorkshire. An Assessment at the Beginning of the 21st Century* (eds T.G. Manby, S. Moorhouse, & P. Ottaway), pp. 261–274. Yorkshire Archaeological Society Occasional Paper 3, Leeds.

Halkon, P. & Millett, M. (1999) *Rural Settlement and industry: Studies in the Iron Age and Roman Archaeology of lowland East Yorkshire*. Yorkshire Archaeological Report 4. Yorkshire Archaeological Society Roman Antiquities Section and East Riding Archaeological Society, Leeds.

Halkon, P. & Innes, J.B. (2005) Prehistoric settlement and economy in a changing environmental landscape: an East Yorkshire (UK) case study. *European Journal of Archaeology*, **8**, 225–259.

Hall, A.M., Peacock, J.D. & Connell, E.R. (2003) New data for the Last Glacial Maximum in Great Britain and Ireland: a Scottish perspective on the paper by Bowen et al. (2002). *Quaternary Science Reviews*, **22**, 1551–1554.

Hall, D., Wells, C.E. & Huckerby, E. (1995) *The Wetlands of Greater Manchester*. Lancaster University Archaeological Unit.

Hall, R.A. (2003) Yorkshire AD 700–1066. In: *The Archaeology of Yorkshire. An assessment at the beginning of the 21st century* (eds T.G. Manby, S. Moorhouse, & P. Ottoway), pp. 171–180. Yorkshire Archaeological Society Occasional Paper 3, Leeds.

Hall, R.A. & Whyman, N. (1996) Settlement and monasticism at Ripon, from the 7th to the 11th centuries AD. *Medieval Archaeology*, **40**, 62–150.

Hallam, J.S., Edwards, B.J.N., Barnes, B. & Stuart, A.J. (1973) The remains of a Late Glacial elk associated with barbed points from High Furlong, near Blackpool, Lancashire. *Proceedings of the Prehistoric Society*, **39**, 100–128.

Hambleton, E. (1999) *Animal Husbandry Regimes in Iron Age Britain*. British Archaeological Reports, British Series 282, Oxford.

Hansen, M. (1987) The Hydrophiloidea (Coleoptera) of Fennoscandia and Denmark. In: *Fauna Entomologica Scandinavica*, 18, pp. 254. E J Brill, Leiden.

Harding, A.F. & Lee, G.L. (1987) Henge monuments and related sites of Great Britain: air photo evidence and catalogue. British Archaeological Reports, British Series 175, Oxford.

Harding, J. (1997) Interpreting the Neolithic: the monuments of North Yorkshire. *Oxford Journal of Archaeology*, **16**, 279–295.

Harding, J. (1998) Recent fieldwork at the Neolithic monument complex of Thornborough, North Yorkshire. *Northern Archaeology*, **15/16**, 27–38.

Harding, J. (2000a) Late Neolithic ceremonial centres, ritual and pilgrimage: the monument complex of Thornborough, North Yorkshire. In: *Neolithic Orkney in its European context* (ed. A. Ritchie), pp. 31–46. McDonald Institute for Archaeological Research, Cambridge.

Harding, J. (2000b) Henge monuments and landscape features in northern England: monumentality and nature. In: *Neolithic Orkney in its European context* (ed. A. Ritchie), pp. 267–275. McDonald Institute for Archaeological Research, Cambridge.

Harding J. (2000c) From coast to vale, moor to dale: patterns in later prehistory. In: *Northern Pasts: Interpretations of the Later Prehistory of Northern England and Southern Scotland* (eds. J. Harding & R. Johnstone), pp.1–14. British Archaeological Reports, British Series 302, Oxford.

Harding, J. (2003) *Henge Monuments of the British Isles*. Tempus, Stroud.

Harding, J. & Barclay, A. (1999) An introduction to the cursus monuments of Neolithic Britain and Ireland. In: *Pathways and Ceremonies: The Cursus Monuments of Britain and Ireland* (eds A. Barclay & J. Harding), pp. 1–8. Neolithic Studies Group Seminar Papers, 4, Oxbow Books, Oxford.

Harding, J. & Johnson, B. (2003a) *'Fieldwalking at the Thornborough monument complex, North Yorkshire*. http://thornborough.ncl.ac.uk/reports/pubs_reports_fieldwalking

Harding, J. & Johnson, B. (2003b) *The Mesolithic, Neolithic and Bronze Age Archaeology of the Ure–Swale Catchment*. Draft Report, The University of Newcastle.

Harding, P., Bridgland, D.R., Madgett, P.A. & Rose, J. (1991) Recent investigations of Pleistocene sediments near Maidenhead, Berkshire, and their archaeological content. *Proceedings of the Geologists' Association*, **102**, 25–53.

Harmer, F.W. (1928) The distribution of erratics and drift. *Proceedings of the Yorkshire Geological Society*, **21**, 79–150.

Harrison, K. (1935) The glaciation of the eastern side of the Vale of York. *Proceedings of the Yorkshire Geological Society*, **23**, 54–59.

Hartley, B.R. & Fitts, L. (1988) *The Brigantes*. Alan Sutton, Gloucester.

Harvey, A.M. (1985) The river systems of north-west England. In: *The Geomorphology of North-west England* (ed. R.H. Johnson), pp. 122–142. Manchester University Press.

Harvey, A.M. (2001) Coupling between hillslopes and channel in upland fluvial systems in the Howgill Fells, northwestern England: temporal implications. *Catena*, **42**, 225–250.

Harvey, A.M. (2002) Effective timescales of coupling in fluvial systems. *Geomorphology*, **44**, 175–201.

Harvey, A.M. & Chiverrell, R.C. (2004) Carlingill, Howgill Fells. In: *The Quaternary of the Isle of Man and North West England. Field Guide* (eds R.C. Chiverrell, A.J. Plater, & G.S.P. Thomas), pp. 177–193. Quaternary Research Association, London.

Harvey, A.M., Oldfield, F., Baron, A.F. & Perason, G.W. (1981) Dating of Post-glacial landforms in the central Howgills. *Earth Surface Processes and Landforms*, **6**, 401–412.

Heslop, D.H. (1983) Excavations in Yarm. eds. Cleveland County Archaeology Section. In: *Recent Excavations in Cleveland*, pp. 37–43. Cleveland County Council, Middlesbrough.

Heslop, D.H. (1984) Initial excavations at Ingleby Barwick, Cleveland. *Durham Archaeological Journal*, **1**, 23–34.

Heslop, D.H. (1987) *The Excavation of the Iron Age Settlement at Thorpe Thewles, Cleveland, 1980–1982*. Council for British Archaeology, Research Report 65, London.

Hey, R.W. (1965) Highly quartzose pebble gravels in the London Basin. *Proceedings of the Geologists' Association*, **76**, 403–420.

Hibbert, F.A. & Switsur, V.R. (1976) Radiocarbon dating of Flandrian pollen zones in Wales and northern England. *New Phytologist*, **77**, 793–807.

Hickin, N.E. (1963) *The Insect Factor in Wood Decay*. Hutchinson, London.

Hiemstra, J.F., Evans, D.J.A., Scourse, J.D., McCarroll, D., Furze, M.F.A. & Rhodes, E. (2006) New evidence for a grounded Irish Sea glaciation of the Isles of Scilly, UK. *Quaternary Science Reviews*, **25**, 299–309.

Higgitt, D.L., Warburton, J. & Evans, M.G. (2001) Sediment transfer in upland environments. In: *Geomorphological Processes and Landscape Change: Britain in the last 1000 years* (eds D.L Higgitt & E.M. Lee), pp. 190–214, RGS-IBG Book Series, Blackwell, Oxford.

Higham, N. (1986) *The Northern Counties to AD 1000*, Longman, London.

Higham, N. (1987) Landscape and land use in northern England: a survey of agricultural potential, c.500 BC – AD 1000. *Landscape History*, **9**, 35–44.

Hill, W. (1911) Flint and chert. *Proceedings of the Geologists' Association*, **22**, 61–95.

Holland, D.G. (1972) *A key to the larvae, pupae and adults of the British Species of Elminthidae* (vol. 26). Freshwater Biological Association, Ambleside.

Holmen, M. (1987) The aquatic Adephaga (Coleoptera) of Fennoscandia and Denmark. I. Gyrinidae, Haliplidae, Hygrobiidae and Noteridae. *Fauna Entomologica Scandinavica*, **20**, 1–168.

Holyoak, D.T. (1983) The colonization of Berkshire, England, by land and freshwater Mollusca since the Late Devensian *Journal of Biogeography*, **10**, 483–498.

Honeyman, A. (1985) *Studies in the Holocene vegetational history of Wensleydale*, PhD thesis, University of Leeds.

Hooke, J.M., Harvey, A.M., Miller, S.Y. & Redmond, C.E. (1990) The chronology and stratigraphy of the alluvial terraces of the River Dane valley, Cheshire, NW England. *Earth Surface Processes and Landforms*, **15**, 717–737.

Hosfield, R.T. & Chambers, J.C. (2005) Pleistocene geochronologies for fluvial sedimentary sequences: an archaeologist's perspective. *Journal of Quaternary Science*, **20**, 285–296.

Housley, R.A. (1991) AMS dates from the Lateglacial and early post-glacial in north-west Europe: a review. In: *The Late Glacial in North-West Europe: Human Adaptation and Environmental Change at the end of the Pleistocene* (eds N. Barton, A.J. Roberts, & D.A. Roe), pp. 25–39. CBA Research Report 77, Council for British Archaeology, London.

Howard, A.J. (2005) The contribution of geoarchaeology to understanding the environmental history and archaeological resource of the Trent valley, UK. *Geoarchaeology*, **20**, 93–107.

Howard, A.J. (2007a) Langford Quarry (SK 8200 6020). In: *The Quaternary of the Trent & Adjoining Regions. Field Guide* (eds T.S. White, D.R. Bridgland, A.J. Howard, & M.J. White). Quaternary Research Association, London.

Howard, A.J. (2007b) Girton Quarry (SK 8270 6970). In: *The Quaternary of the Trent & Adjoining Regions. Field Guide* (eds T.S. White, D.R. Bridgland, A.J. Howard, & M.J. White). Quaternary Research Association, London.

Howard, A.J., Smith, D.N., Garton, D., Hillam, J. & Pearce, M. (1999a) Middle to Late Holocene environments in the Middle to Lower Trent valley. In: *Fluvial Processes and Environmental Change* (eds A.G. Brown & T.M. Quine), pp. 165–178. Wiley, Chichester.

Howard, A.J., Bateman, M.D., Garton, D., Green, F.M.L., Wagner, P. & Priest, V. (1999b) Evidence of Late Devensian and early Flandrian processes and environments in the Idle Valley at Tiln, North Nottinghamshire. *Proceedings of the Yorkshire Geological Society*, **52**, 383–393.

Howard, A.J., Hunt, C.O., Rushworth, G., Smith, D. & Smith, W. (1999c) *Girton Quarry Northern Extension*. Unpublished report, Trent & Peak Archaeological Unit, University of Nottingham.

Howard, A.J., Keen, D.H., Mighall, T.M., Field, M.H., Coope, G.R., Griffiths, H.I. & Macklin, M.G. (2000a) Early Holocene environments of the River Ure near Ripon, North Yorkshire, UK. *Proceedings of the Yorkshire Geological Society*, **53**, 31–42.

Howard, A.J. & Macklin, M.G., eds (1998) *The Quaternary of the Eastern Yorkshire Dales. Field Guide*. Quaternary Research Association, London.

Howard, A.J. & Macklin, M.G. (1999) A generic geomorphological approach to archaeological interpretation and prospection in British river valleys: a guide for archaeologists investigating Holocene landscapes. *Antiquity*, **73**, 527–541.

Howard, A.J. & Macklin, M.G. (2003) The Rivers of North Yorkshire. In: *Historical Atlas of North Yorkshire* (ed. R.A. Butlin), pp. 14–17. Smith Settle, Otley.

Howard, A.J., Macklin M,.G., Black, S. & Hudson-Edwards, K. (2000b) Holocene river development and environmental change in upper Wharfedale, Yorkshire Dales, England. *Journal of Quaternary Science*, **15**, 239–252.

Howard, A.J., Macklin, M.G. & Passmore, D.G. (2003) *Alluvial Archaeology in Europe*. Balkema, Rotterdam.

Howard, A.J., Whyman, M., Challis, K. & McManus, K. (2008) Recent Work on the Geomorphological and Archaeological Landscape of the Vale of York Funded by the Aggregates Levy Sustainability Fund. In: *Yorkshire Landscapes Past and Present*. (eds M. Atherden & T. Milsom), pp. 69–76. PLACE Research Centre, York.

Howarth, J.H. (1908) The ice-borne boulders of Yorkshire. *The Naturalist*, March 97–99, April 143–146, May 175–180, June 219–224, July 245–252.

Hubberten, H.W., Andreev, A., Astakhov, V.I., Demidov, I., Dowdeswell, J.A., Henrikson, M., Hjort, C., Homark-Nielsen, M., Jakobsson, M., Kuzima, S., Larsen, E., Lunkka, J.P., Lysa, A., Mangerud, J., Moller, P., Saarnisto, M., Schirrmeister, L., Sher, A.V., Siegert, C., Siegert, M.J. & Svendsen, J.I. (2004) The periglacial climate and environment in northern Eurasia during the Last Glaciation. *Quaternary Science Reviews*, **23**, 1333–1357.

Huddart, D. (2002) Norber Erratics (SD 765 700). In: *Quaternary of Northern England*. Geological Conservation Review Vol. 25 (eds D. Huddart & N.F. Glasser), pp. 200–203. Joint Nature Conservation Committee, Peterborough.

Huddart, D. & Glasser, N.F. (2002a) The Devensian glacial record In: *Quaternary of Northern England*, Geological Conservation Review Vol. 25. (eds D. Huddart & N.F. Glasser), pp. 87–131. Joint Nature Conservation Committee, Peterborough.

Huddart, D. & Glasser, N.F., eds (2002b) *Quaternary of Northern England*. Geological Conservation Review Vol. 25, Joint Nature Conservation Committee, Peterborough.

Hudson, R.G.S., Versey, H.C., Edwards, W. & Rastrick, A. (1938) The geology of the country around Harrogate. *Proceedings of the Geologists' Association*, **49**, 333–343.

Hudson-Edwards, K., Macklin, M. & Taylor, M.P. (1997) Historical metal mining inputs to Tees river sediment. *Science of the Total Environment*, **194–5**, 437–445.

Hudson-Edwards, K., Macklin, M.G.F., R & Passmore, D.G. (1999a) Medieval lead pollution in the River Ouse at York, England. *Journal of Archaeological Science*, **26**, 809–819.

Hudson-Edwards, K., Macklin, M.G. & Taylor, M.P. (1999b) 2000 years of sediment borne heavy metal storage in the Yorkshire Ouse, NE England, UK. *Hydrological Processes*, **13**, 1087–1102.

Hughes, P.D.M., Mauquoy, D., Barber, K.E. & Langdon, P.E. (2000) Mire development pathways and palaeoclimatic records from a full Holocene peat archive at Walton Moss, Cumbria. *The Holocene*, **10**, 465–479.

Huijzer, B. & Vandenberge, J. (1998) Climate reconstruction of the Weichselian Pleniglacial in northwestern and central Europe. *Journal of Quaternary Science*, **13**, 391–417.

Hunt, C.O., Hall, A.R. & Gilbertson, D.D. (1984) The palaeobotany of the Late Devensian sequence at Skipsea Withow Mere. In: *Late Quaternary Environments and Man in Holderness* (ed. D.D. Gilbertson), pp. 81–108. British Archaeological Reports, British Series 134, Oxford.

Huntley, B. (1993) Rapid early-Holocene migration and high abundance of Hazel (*Corylus avellana* L.): alternative hypotheses. In: *Climate Change and Human Impact on the Landscape* (ed. F.M. Chambers), pp. 205–215. Chapman and Hall, London.

Huntley, B. (1999) The influence of a changing climate. In: *The Historical Biology of the Mersey Basin* (ed. E. Greenwood), pp. 3–11. Liverpool University Press, Liverpool.

Huntley, J.P. (1999) Saxon–Norse economy in northern Britain: food for thought. *Durham Archaeological Journal*, **14/15**, 77–81.

Huntley, J.P. (2000) Late Roman transition in the North: the palynological evidence. In: *The Late Roman Transition in the North* (eds T. Wilmott & P. Wilson), pp. 67–71. British Archaeological Reports, British Series 299, Oxford.

Huntley, J.P. (2002) Environmental archaeology: Mesolithic to Roman period. In: *Past, Present and Future. The Archaeology of Northern England.* (eds C. Brooks, R. Daniels, & A. Harding), pp. 79–93. Architectural and Archaeological Society of Durham and Northumberland, Research Report 5, Durham.

Huntley, J.P. & Stallibrass, S. (1995) Plant and vertebrate remains from archaeological sites in northern England: data reviews and future directions. *Architectural and Archaeological Society of Durham and Northumberland Research Report*, **4**, 7–18.

Hutton, R. (1994) *The Rise and Fall of Merry England: the ritual year 1400–1700*. Oxford University Press.

Imbrie, J. (1984) The orbital theory of Pleistocene climate: support from a revised chronology of the marine ^{18}O record. In: *Milankovitch and Climate: understanding the response of astronomical forcing* (ed. A.L. Berger), pp. 269–305. Reidel, Dordrecht.

Imbrie, J. & Imbrie, K.P. (1979) *Ice Ages:solving the mystery*. MacMillan, London.

Innes, J.B. (1992) *Soil pollen analyses from the Medieval settlement at Elton, Stockton, Cleveland*. Report for Cleveland Archaeology Unit, Hartlepool.

Innes, J.B. (1999) Regional vegetational history. In: *The Quaternary of North-east England. Field Guide* (eds D.R. Bridgland, B. Horton, & J.B. Innes), pp. 21–34. Quaternary Research Association, London.

Innes, J.B. (2001a) The results of pollen analyses from Ravock Moor. In: *Stainmore: the Archaeology of a North Pennine Pass* (ed. B.E. Vyner), pp. 41–47. Tees Archaeology Monograph Series 1: Tees Archaeology, Hartlepool.

Innes, J.B. (2001b) Pollen analyses. In: *Romano-British, Medieval and Prehistoric Settlement in Lowland North-West England: Excavations on the Line of the A5300 Link Road in Tarbock and Halewood, Merseyside.* (eds R.W. Cowell & R.A.

Philpott), pp. 19–23. National Museums and Galleries on Merseyside, Liverpool.

Innes, J.B. (2002a) The Late-glacial record of northern England: introduction. In: *Quaternary of Northern England*, Geological Conservation Review Vol. 25 (eds D. Huddart & N.F. Glasser), pp. 211–220. Joint Nature Conservation Committee, Peterborough.

Innes, J.B. (2002b) Kildale Hall (NZ 609 097). In: *Quaternary of Northern England*, Geological Conservation Review Vol. 25 (eds D. Huddart & N.F. Glasser), pp. 251–257. Joint Nature Conservation Committee, Peterborough.

Innes, J.B. (2002c) Tadcaster (SE 499 430). In: *Quaternary of Northern England*, Geological Conservation Review Vol. 25 (eds D. Huddart & N.F. Glasser), pp. 251–257. Joint Nature Conservation Committee, Peterborough.

Innes, J.B. (2002d) The Holocene record of northern England: introduction. In: *Quaternary of Northern England*, Geological Conservation Review Vol. 25 (eds D. Huddart & N.F. Glasser). Joint Nature Conservation Committee, Peterborough.

Innes, J.B. (2005) Fungal spore assemblages. In: *Die Jungsteinzeitliche Seeufersiedlung Arbon Bleiche 3. Umwelt und Wirtschaft.* (eds S. Jacomet, U. Leuzinger & J. Schibler), pp. 348–350. Archäologie im Thurgau 12. Amt für Archäologie, Frauenfeld.

Innes, J.B. (2008) Tree remains from a buried mid-Holocene palaeoforest in upland north-east Yorkshire. *Quaternary Newsletter*, **115**, 40–43.

Innes, J.B. & Simmons, I.G. (1988) Disturbance and diversity: floristic changes associated with pre-elm decline woodland recession in north east Yorkshire. In: *Archaeology and the Flora of the British Isles* (ed. M. Jones), pp. 7–20. Oxford University Committee for Archaeology Monograph 14, Oxford.

Innes, J.B. & Simmons, I.G. (1999) North Gill. In: *The Quaternary of North-East England. Field Guide* (eds D.R. Bridgland, B.P. Horton, & J.B. Innes), pp. 99–112. Quaternary Reseach Association, London.

Innes, J.B. & Simmons, I.G. (2000) Mid Holocene charcoal stratigraphy, fire history and palaeoecology at North Gill, North York Moors, UK. *Palaeogeography, Palaeoclimatology, Palaeoecology*, **164**, 151–161.

Innes, J.B. & Simmons, I.G. (2001) Fire and prehistoric moorland history in the North York Moors upland. In: *Moorland Research Review 1995–2000* (eds R. Charles, S. Wightman, & M. Hammond), pp. 114–117. North York Moors National Park Authority, Helmsley.

Innes, J.B. & Blackford, J.J. (2003a) Yorkshire's palaeo-environmental resource. In: *The Archaeology of Yorkshire, An Assessment at the Beginning of the 21st Century.* (eds T.G. Manby, S. Moorhouse, & P. Ottaway), pp. 25–30. Yorkshire Archaeological Society Occasional Paper 3, Leeds.

Innes, J.B. & Blackford, J.J. (2003b) The ecology of Late Mesolithic woodland disturbance: model testing with fungal spore assemblage data. *Journal of Archaeological Science*, **30**, 185–194.

Innes, J.B., Blackford, J.J. & Rowley-Conwy, P.A. (2003a) The start of the Mesolithic–Neolithic transition in north-west Europe – the palynological contribution. *Antiquity Project Gallery*, **77**, (297). http://antiquity.ac.uk/projGall/blackford/blackford.html

Innes, J.B., Blackford, J.J. & Davey, P.J. (2003b) Dating the introduction of cereal cultivation to the British Isles: early

palaeoecological evidence from the Isle of Man. *Journal of Quaternary Science*, **18**, 603–613.

Innes, J.B., Blackford, J.J. & Simmons, I.G. (2004) Testing the integrity of fine spatial resolution palaeoecological records: micro-charcoal data from near-duplicate peat profiles from the North York Moors, UK. *Palaeogeography, Palaeoclimatology, Palaeoecology*, **214**, 295–307.

Innes, J.B., Donaldson, M. & Tooley, M.J. (2005) The palaeo-environmental evidence. In: *Archaeology and Environment of Submerged Landscapes in Hartlepool Bay, England.* (ed. M. Waughman), pp. 78–120. Tees Archaeology Monograph Series 2, Hartlepool.

Innes, J.B., Blackford, J.J. & Chambers, F.M. (2006) *Kretzschmaria deusta* and the North-West European mid-Holocene *Ulmus* decline at Moel y Gerddi, North Wales, UK. *Palynology*, **30**, 121–132.

Jackson, A.F., Murray, T., Macklin, M.G. & Taylor, M.P. (1998) Internal morphology and extent of palaeochannels, Catterick, using ground penetrating radar. In: *The Quaternary of the Eastern Yorkshire Dales. Field Guide* (eds A.J. Howard & M.G. Macklin), pp. 54–66. Quaternary Research Association, London.

Jacobi, R.M. (1991) The Creswellian, Creswell and Cheddar. In: *The Late Glacial in North-West Europe: Human Adaptation and Environmental Change at the End of the Pleistocene* (eds N. Barton, A.J. Roberts, & D.A. Roe), pp. 128–140. Council for British Archaeology Research Report 77, London.

Jacobi, R.M., Tallis, J.H. & Mellars, P.A. (1976) The southern Pennine Mesolithic and the ecological record. *Journal of Archaeological Science*, **3**, 307–320.

Jannson, K.N. & Glasser, N.F. (2005) Palaeoglaciology of the Welsh sector of the British–Irish Ice Sheet. *Journal of the Geological Society of London*, **162**, 25–37.

Jessop, L. (1986) Dung Beetles and Chafers. In: *Handbooks for the Identification of British Insects*, pp. 1–53. Royal Entomological Society of London.

Jing, Z., Rapp, G. & Gao, T. (1997) Geoarchaeological aids in the investigation of early Shang civilisation on the floodplain of the lower Yellow River, China. *World Archaeology*, **29**, 36–50.

Johnsen, S.J., Dahl-Jensen, D., Gundestrup, N., Steffensen, J.P., Clausen, H.B., Miller, H., Masson-Delmotte, V., Sveinbjornsdottir, A.E. & White, J. (2001) Oxygen isotope and palaeotemperature records from six Greenland ice-core stations: Camp Century, Dye-3, GRIP, GISP2, Renland, and NorthGRIP. *Journal of Quaternary Science*, **16**, 299–307.

Johnson, G.A.L. (1970) Geology. In: *Durham County and City with Teesside* (ed. J.C. Dewdney), pp. 3–25. British Association, Durham.

Johnson, P.G. (1969) *The glacial influence of the relief of part of the western side of the Vale of York*, PhD thesis, University of Leeds.

Johnson, P.G. (1974) Evidence for abandoned river courses in the west of the Vale of York. *Proceedings of the Yorkshire Geological Society*, **40**, 223–232.

Johnstone, E., Macklin, M.G. & Lewin, J. (2006) The development and application of a database of radiocarbon-dated Holocene fluvial deposits in Great Britain. *Catena*, **66**, 14–23.

Joly, C., Barille, L., Barreau, M., Mancheron, A. & Visset, L. (2007) Grain and annulus diameter as criteria for distinguishing pollen grains of cereal from wild grasses. *Review of Palaeobotany and Palynology*, **146**, 221–233.

Jones, A. (1994) *Healam Bridge, North Yorkshire: An Archaeological Evaluation*. University of Birmingham Field Archaeology Unit, Report 306.

Jones, A.P., Tucker, M.E. & Hart, J.K., eds (1999a) *The Description and Analysis of Quaternary Stratigraphic Field Sections. Technical Guide 7*. Quaternary Research Association, London.

Jones, A.P., Tucker, M.E. & Hart, J.K (1999b) Guidelines and recommendations. In: *The Description and Analysis of Quaternary Stratigraphic Field Sections. Technical Guide 7*. (eds A.P. Jones, M.E. Tucker & J.K. Hart), pp. 27–76. Quaternary Research Association, London.

Jones, G. (2000) Evaluating the importance of cultivation and collection in Neolithic Britain. In: *Plants in Neolithic Britain and Beyond* (ed. A. Fairbairn), pp. 79–84. Oxbow Books, Oxford.

Jones, M.K. (1991) Food consumption – plants. In: *Roman Britain: Recent Trends*, pp. 21–27. J.R. Collis Publications, Sheffield.

Jones, R.L. (1976a) Late Quaternary vegetational history of the North York Moors IV: Seamer Carrs. *Journal of Biogeography*, **3**, 397–406.

Jones, R.L. (1976b) The activities of Mesolithic man: further palaeobotanical evidence from north-east Yorkshire. In: *Geoarchaeology: Earth Science and the Past* (eds D.A. Davidson & M.L. Shackley), pp. 355–367. Duckworth, London.

Jones, R.L. (1977a) Late Devensian deposits from Kildale, north-east Yorkshire. *Proceedings of the Yorkshire Geological Society*, **41**, 185–188.

Jones, R.L. (1977b) Late Quaternary vegetational history of the North York Moors V. The Cleveland Dales. *Journal of Biogeography*, **4**, 353–362.

Jones, R.L. (1978) Late Quaternary vegetational history of the North York Moors VI. The Cleveland Moors. *Journal of Biogeography*, **5**, 81–92.

Jones, R.L. & Gaunt, G.D. (1976) A dated Late Devensian organic deposit at Cawood, near Selby. *Naturalist*, **101**, 121–123.

Jones, R.L. & Keen, D.H. (1993) *Pleistocene Environments in the British Isles*. Chapman and Hall, London.

Jones, R.L., Keen, D.H. & Robinson, J.E. (2000) Devensian Lateglacial and early Holocene floral and faunal records from NE Northumberland. *Proceedings of the Yorkshire Geological Society*, **53**, 97–110.

Jones, R.T., Marshall, J.D., Crowley, S.F., Bedford, A., Richardson, N., Bloemendal, J. & Oldfield, F. (2002) A high resolution, multi-proxy Late-glacial record of climate change and intrasystem responses in north-west England. *Journal of Quaternary Science*, **17**, 329–340.

Joyce, A.A. & Mueller, R.G. (1997) Prehispanic human ecology of the Rio Verde drainage basin, Mexico. *World Archaeology* **29**, 75–94.

Kageyama, M., Laine, A., Abe-Ouchi, A., Braconnet, P., Cortijo, E., Crucifix, M., De Vernal, A., Guiot, J., Hewitt, C.D., Kitoh, A., Kucera, M., Marti, O., Ohgaito, R., Otto-Bliesner, B., Peltier, W., Rosell-Mele, A., Vettoretti, G., Weber, S.L., Yu, Y. & members (2006) Late Glacial Maximum temperatures over the North Atlantic, Europe and western Siberia: a comparison between PMIP models, MARGO sea-surface temperatures and pollen-based reconstructions. *Quaternary Science Reviews*, **25**, 2082–2102.

Karner, D.B. & Marra, F. (1998) Correlation of fluviodeltaic aggradational sections with glacial climate history: a revision of the Pleistocene stratigraphy of Rome. *Geological Society of America Bulletin*, **110**, 748–758.

Kasse, C. (1998) Depositional model for cold-climate tundra rivers. In: *Palaeohydrology and Environmental Change* (eds G. Benito, V.R. Baker & K.J. Gregory), pp. 83–97. Wiley, Chichester.

Katz, N.J., Katz, S.V. & Kipiani, M.G. (1965) *Atlas and keys of fruits and seeds occurring in the Quaternary deposits of the USSR*. Nauka, Moscow.

Keen, D.H. (1989) The molluscan fauna of a Flandrian tufa at Lower Beck, Malham, North Yorkshire. *Journal of Conchology*, **33**, 173 179.

Keen, D.H. (2001) Towards a late Middle Pleistocene non-marine molluscan biostratigraphy for the British Isles. *Quaternary Science Reviews*, **20**, 1657–1665.

Keen, D.H., Jones, R.L. & Robinson, J.E. (1984) A Late Devensian and early Flandrian fauna and flora from Kildale. north-east Yorkshire. *Proceedings of the Yorkshire Geological Society*, **44**, 385–397.

Keen, D.H., Jones, R.L., Evans, R.A. & Robinson, J.E. (1988) Faunal and floral assemblages from Bingley Bog, West Yorkshire and their significance for Late Devensian and early Flandrian environmental changes. *Proceedings of the Yorkshire Geological Society*, **47**, 125–138.

Keevill, G.D. (1992) Life on the edge: archaeology and alluvium at Redlands Farm, Stanwick, Northants. In: *Alluvial Archaeology in Britain* (eds S. Needham & M.G. Macklin), pp. 177–183. Oxbow Books, Oxford.

Kendall, P.F. (1902) A system of glacier-lakes in the Cleveland Hills. *Quarterly Journal of the Geological Society*, **58**, 471–571.

Kendall, P.F. (1903) The glacier lakes of Cleveland. *Proceedings of the Yorkshire Geological Society*, **15**, 1–40.

Kendall, P.F. & Howarth, J.H. (1902) The Yorkshire Boulder Committee and its Fifteenth Year's work, 1900–1 *Naturalist*, July 1902, 211–216.

Kendall, P.F. & Wroot, H.E. (1924) *Geology of Yorkshire*. Scholar Press, Menton.

Kenward, H., Williams, D., Spencer, P., Greig, J.R., Rackham, J.D. & Brinklow, D. (1978) The environment of Anglo–Scandinavian York. In: *Viking Age York and the North* (ed. R.A. Hall), pp. 58–73, London.

Kerney, M.P. (1999) *Atlas of the Land and Freshwater Molluscs of Great Britain and Ireland*. Harley Books, Colchester.

Kerney, M.P. & Cameron, R.A.D. (1979) *A Field Guide to the Land Snails of Great Britain and Ireland*. Collins, London.

Kerney, M.P., Cameron, R.A.D. & Jungbluth, J.H. (1983) *Die Landschnecken Nord- und Mitteleuropas*. Paul Parey, Hamburg & Berlin.

Killeen, I.J. (2005) Studies of the round-mouthed whorl snail *Vertigo genesii* (Gastropoda: Vertiginidae) in northern England: observations on population dynamics and life history. *Journal of Conchology*, **38**, 701–710.

Killeen, I.J., Aldridge, D.C. & Oliver, P.G. (2004) *Freshwater Bivalves of the British Isles*. Field Studies Council, Shrewsbury.

King, C.A.M. (1976) *The Geomorphology of the British Isles: Northern England*. Methuen, London.

Kirby, J.R. (2001) Regional Late-Quaternary marine and perimarine records. In: *The Quaternary of East Yorkshire and North Lincolnshire: Field Guide* (eds M.D. Bateman, P.C.

Buckland, C.D. Frederick, & N.J. Whitehouse), pp. 25–34. Quaternary Research Association, London.

Kirby, J.R. & Gearey, B.R. (2001) Pattern and process of Holocene vegetation and wetland development in the Humber lowlands. In: *Wetlands in the Landscape; Archaeology, Conservation, Heritage* (ed. M.A. Atherden), pp. 41–67. PLACE Research Centre, York.

Kleman, J. & Glasser, N.F. (2007) The subglacial thermal organisation (STO) of ice sheets. *Quaternary Science Reviews*, **26**, 585–597.

Knight, D. (1997) A Bronze Age rapier from Langford, Nottinghamshire. *Transactions of the Thoroton Society of Nottinghamshire*, **101**, 59–61.

Knight D. & Howard A.J. (1995) *Archaeology and alluvium in the Trent Valley. An archaeological assessment of the floodplain and gravel terraces.* 2nd impression. Trent and Peak Archaeological Trust, Nottingham.

Knight, D. & Vyner, B. (2006) *Making Archaeology Matter: Quarrying and Archaeology in the Trent Valley.* York Archaeological Trust.

Knight, J. (2004) Pleistocene glaciations in Ireland. In: *Quaternary Glaciations – Extent and Chronology: Part 1: Europe.* (eds J. Ehlers & P.L. Gibbard), pp. 182–191. Elsevier, Amsterdam.

Knight, J. (2005) The Irish Sea Basin. In: *The Glaciations of Wales and Adjacent Areas* (eds C.A. Lewis & A.E. Richards), pp. 177–188. Logaston Press, Herefordshire.

Knight, J., Coxon, P., McCabe, A.M. & McCarron, S.G. (2004) Pleistocene glaciations in Ireland. In: *Quaternary Glaciations – Extent and Chronology* (eds J. Ehlers & P.L. Gibbard), pp. 183–191. Elsevier, Amsterdam.

Knutz, P.C., Austin, W.E.N. & Jones, E.J.W. (2001) Millennial-scale depositional cycles related to British Ice Sheet variability and North Atlantic paleocirculation since 45 kyr BP., Barra Fan, UK margin. *Paleoceanography*, **16**, 53–64.

Koch, K.C. (1989) *Die Käfer Mitteleuropas, Ökologie*, **1**. Goecke & Evers, Krefeld.

Koch, K.C. (1992) *Die Käfer Mitteleuropas, Ökologie*, **3**. Goecke & Evers, Krefeld.

Kukla, G.J. (1975) Loess stratigraphy of central Europe. In: *After the Australopithecines* (eds K.W. Butzer & G.L. Isaac), pp. 99–188. Mouton, The Hague.

Land, D.H., Calver, M.A. & Harrison, R.K. (1974) *Geology of the Tynemouth District.* Memoir of the Geological Survey.

Lamb, H.H. (1977) The Late Quaternary history of the climate of the British Isles. In: *British Quaternary Studies: Recent Advances.* (ed. F.W. Shotton), pp. 283–298. Clarendon, Oxford.

Lambeck, K., Yokoyama, Y. & Purcell, T. (1991) Into and out of the last glacial maximum: sea level change during Oxygen Isotope Stages 3 and 2. *Quaternary Science Reviews*, **21**, 343–360.

Lane, S.N. (2003) More floods, less rain? Changing hydrology in a Yorkshire context. In: *Global Warming in a Yorkshire Context* (ed. M.A. Atherden), pp. 35–70. PLACE Research Centre, York.

Lang, G. (2003) Immigration and expansion of *Tilia* in Europe since the last Glacial. In: *Aspects of Palynology and Palaeoecology* (ed. S. Tonkov), pp. 21–41. PENSOFT, Sofia.

Lang, J. (2001) *Corpus of Anglo-Saxon Stone Sculpture: VI. Northern Yorkshire.* Oxford University Press.

Langdon, P.G., Barber, K.E. & Lomas-Clarke (previously Morriss),

S.H. (2004) Reconstructing climate and environmental change in northern England through chironomid and pollen analyses: evidence from Talkin Tarn, Cumbria. *Journal of Palaeolimnology*, **32**, 197–213.

Laurie, T.C. (2003) Researching the prehistory of Wensleydale, Swaledale and Teesdale. In: *The Archaeology of Yorkshire: An Assessment at the Beginning of the 21st Century* (eds T.G. Manby, S. Moorhouse, & P. Ottaway), pp. 223–253. Yorkshire Archaeological Society Occasional Paper 3, Leeds.

Laurie, T.C. (2004) Springs, woods and transhumance: reconstructing a Pennine landscape. *Landscapes*, **5**, 73–102.

Lawrence D.J.D. & Jackson I. (1986) *Geology of the Ponteland-Morpeth district: 1:10000 sheets NZ17NE and NZ18NE, SE parts of 1:50000 sheets 9 (Rothbury) and 14 (Morpeth).* Her Majesty's Stationery Office London.

Lebour, G.A.L. (1878) *Outlines of the Geology of Northumberland.* Lambert & Co., Newcastle upon Tyne.

Lebour, G.A.L. (1889) Recent and sub-Recent deposits. In: *Handbook of Geology and Natural History* (ed. G.A.L. Lebour). Lambert & Co., Newcastle upon Tyne.

Lebour, G.A.L. (1893) On certain surface features of the glacial deposits of the Tyne valley. *Transactions of the Natural History of Northumberland, Durham and Newcastle upon Tyne*, **9**, 191–195.

Legge, A.J. & Rowley-Conwy, P.A. (1988) *Star Carr Revisited.* Birkbeck College, University of London.

Leopold, L.B. & Wolman, M.G. (1960) River meanders. *Geological Society of America Bulletin*, **71**, 769–793.

Letzer, J.M. (1978) *The glacial geomorphology of the region bounded by Shap Fells, Stainmore and the Howgill Fells in eastern Cumbria.* MPhil thesis, University of London.

Levesque, A.J., Mayle, F.E., Walker, I.R. & Cwynar, L.C. (1993) The amphi-Atlantic oscillation: a proposed Late-Glacial climatic event. *Quaternary Science Reviews*, **12**, 629–643.

Lewin, J. (1992) Alluvial sedimentation style and archaeological sites: the Lower Vyrnwy, Wales. In: *Alluvial Archaeology in Britain.* (eds S. Needham & M.G. Macklin), pp. 103–109. Oxbow Monograph 27, Oxford.

Lewin, J. & Macklin, M.G. (2003) Preservation potential for Late Quaternary river alluvium. *Journal of Quaternary Science*, **18**, 106–115.

Lewin, J., Macklin, M.G. & Johnstone, E. (2005) Interpreting alluvial archives: sedimentological factors in the British Holocene fluvial record. *Quaternary Science Reviews*, **24**, 1873–1889.

Lewis, H.C. (1887) The terminal moraine of the great glaciers of England. *Nature*, **36**, 573.

Lewis, H.C. (1894) *Glacial Geology of Great Britain and Ireland.* Longman, Green and Co., London.

Lewis, S.G. & Maddy, D. (1999) Description and analysis of Quaternary fluvial sediments: a case study from the upper River Thames, UK. In: *The Description and Analysis of Quaternary Stratigraphic Field Sections. Technical Guide 7* (eds A.P. Jones, M.E. Tucker, & J.K. Hart), pp. 111–136. Quaternary Research Association, London.

Lillie, M. (2001) Holocene human-landscape interactions. In: *The Quaternary of East Yorkshire and North Lincolnshire. Field Guide* (eds M.D. Bateman, P.C. Buckland, C.D. Frederick, & N.J. Whitehouse), pp. 47–51. Quaternary Research Association, London.

Lillie, M. & Gearey, B. (1999) Introduction to the palaeoenvironmental survey. In: *Wetland Heritage of the Vale of*

York. (eds R. van de Noort & S. Ellis), pp. 21–33. University of Hull.

Lillie, M. & Gearey, B. (2000) Palaeoenvironmental survey of the Hull valley and research at Routh Quarry. In: *Wetland Heritage of the Hull Valley* (eds R. Van de Noort & S. Ellis), pp. 31–82. University of Hull.

Lindroth, C.H. (1974) Coleoptera, Carabidae. In: *Handbooks for the Identification of British Insects, Vol. 5*, pp. 1–141. Royal Entomological Society of London.

Lindroth, C.H. (1985) The Carabidae (Coleoptera) of Fennoscandia and Denmark. *Fauna Entomologica Scandinavica*, **15**, 1–225.

Lindroth, C.H. (1986) The Carabidae (Coleoptera) of Fennoscandia and Denmark. *Fauna Entomologica Scandinavica*, **15**, 233–297.

Lindroth, C.H. (1992) *Ground Beetles (Carabidae) of Fennoscandia. A Zoogeographical study, Parts 1, 2 and 3 (English Translation of 1945 German text).* Intercept, Andover.

Litt, T. (1992) Investigations on the extent of the early Neolithic settlement in the Elbe-Saale region and on its influence on the natural environment. In: *Evaluation of land surfaces cleared from forests by prehistoric man in Early Neolithic times and the time of migrating Germanic tribes.* (ed. B. Frenzel), pp. 83–91. Gustav Fischer Verlag, Stuttgart.

Long, A.J., Innes, J.B., Kirby, J.R., Lloyd, J.M., Rutherford, M.M., Shennan, I. & Tooley, M.J. (1998) Holocene sea-level change and coastal evolution in the Humber Estuary, eastern England: an assessment of rapid coastal change. *The Holocene*, **8**, 229–247.

Long, A.J., Innes, J.B., Shennan, I. & Tooley, M.J. (1999) Coastal stratigraphy: a case study from Johns River, Washington. In: *The Description and Analysis of Quaternary Stratigraphic Field Sections. Technical Guide 7* (eds A.P. Jones, M.E. Tucker, & J.K. Hart), pp. 267–286. Quaternary Research Association, London.

Long, A.J., Bridgland, D.R., Innes, J.B., Mitchell, W.A., Rutherford, M. & Vyner, B. (2004) *The Swale-Ure Washlands: Landscape History and Human Impacts.* Department of Geography, Durham University.

Long, D. & Tipping, R. (1998) Nosterfield, North Yorkshire: Report on the Sediment Stratigraphies of Three Shafts (F44, F45 & F46). Department of Environmental Science, University of Stirling.

Longfield, S.A. & Macklin, M.G. (1999) The influence of recent environmental change on flooding and sediment fluxes in the Yorkshire Ouse basin, north-east England. *Hydrological Processes*, **13**, 1051–1066.

Lord, T.C., O'Connor, T.P., Siebrandt, D.C. & Jacobi, R.M. (2007) People and large carnivores as biostratinomic agents in Lateglacial cave assemblages *Journal of Quaternary Science*, **22**, 681–694.

Lovell, J.H. (1981) *The sand and gravel resources of the country around Hexham, Northumberland. Description of 1:25,000 resource sheet NY 86 and 96.* Institute of Geological Sciences Mineral Assessment Report 65.

Lovell, J.H. (1982) *The sand and gravel resources of the country around Catterick, North Yorkshire. Description of 1:25,000 resource Sheet SE 29.* Institute of Geological Sciences Mineral Assessment Report 120.

Loveluck, C. (2003) The archaeology of post-Roman Yorkshire, AD 400 to 700: overview and future directions for research. In: *The Archaeology of Yorkshire: An Assessment at the Beginning of the 21st Century* (ed. T.G. Manby, S. Moorhouse, & P. Ottoway), pp. 151–170. Yorkshire Archaeological Society Occasional paper 3, Leeds.

Lowe, J.J. (2001) Quaternary geochronological frameworks. In: *Handbook of Archaeological Sciences* (eds D.R. Brothwell & A.M. Pollard), pp. 9–21. Wiley, Chichester.

Lowe, J.J. & Walker, M.J.C. (1997a) *Reconstructing Quaternary Environments.* Addison Wesley Longman, London.

Lowe, J.J. & Walker, M.J.C. (1997b) Temperature variation in NW Europe during the last glacial/interglacial transition (14–9 ^{14}C ka BP) based upon the analysis of coleopteran assemblages – the contribution of Professor G. R. Coope. *Quaternary Proceedings*, **5**, 165–175.

Lowe, J.J. & Walker, M.J.C. (2000) Radiocarbon dating the last glacial–interglacial transition (^{14}C ka BP) in terrestrial and marine records: the need for new quality assurance protocols. *Radiocarbon*, **42**, 53–68.

Lowe, J.J., Ammann, B., Birks, H.H., Björck, S., Coope, G.R., Cwynar, L., de Beaulieu, J-L., Mott R.J., Peteet D.M. & Walker M.J.C. (1994) Climatic changes in areas adjacent to the North Atlantic during the last glacial-interglacial transition (14–9 ka BP): a contribution to IGCP-253. *Journal of Quaternary Science,* **9**, 185–198.

Lowe, J.J., Coope, R.G., Lemdahl, G. & Walker, M.J.C. (1995) The Younger Dryas climate signal in land records from NW Europe. In: *The Younger Dryas* (eds S.R. Troelstra, J.E. van Hinte, & G.M. Ganssen), pp. 3–25. Koninklijke Nederlandse Akademie van Wetenschappen, Amsterdam & Oxford.

Lowe, J.J., Birks, H.H., Brooks, S.J., Coope, G.R., Harkness, D.D., Mayle, F.E., Sheldrick, C., Turney, C.S.M. & Walker, M.J.C. (1999) The chronology of palaeoenvironmental change during the Last Glacial–Holocene transition: towards an event stratigraphy for the British Isles. *Journal of the Geological Society of London*, **156**, 397–410.

Lucht, W.H. (1987) *Die Kafer Mitteleuropas: Katalog.* Goecke and Evers, Krefeld.

McCabe, A.M. & Clark, P.U. (2003) Deglacial chronology from County Donegal, Ireland: implications for deglaciation of the British–Irish ice sheet. *Journal of the Geological Society of London*, **156**, 411–423.

McCabe, A.M., Clark, P.U. & Clark, J. (2005) AMS ^{14}C dating of deglacial events in the Irish Sea Basin and other sectors of the British–Irish ice sheet. *Quaternary Science Reviews*, **24**, 1673–1690.

McCabe, A.M., Clark, O.U. & Clark, J. (2007a) Radiocarbon constraints on the history of the western Irish ice sheet prior to the Last Glacial Maximum. *Geology*, **35**, 147–150.

McCabe, A.M., Clark, P.U., Smith, D.E. & Dunlop, P. (2007b) A revised model for the last deglaciation of eastern Scotland. *Journal of the Geological Society of London*, **164**, 313–316.

McCarroll, D., Scourse, J.D. & Johns, C. (2006) Shipman Head Down. In: *The Isles of Scilly. Field Guide* (ed. J.D. Scourse), pp. 147–148. Quaternary Research Association, London.

McCarthy, M.R. & Brooks, C.M. (1988) *Medieval Pottery in Britain AD 900–1600.* Leicester University Press.

McCave, I.N. (1969) Correlation of marine and nonmarine strata with example from the Devonian of New York State. *American Association of Petroleum Geologists Bulletin*, **53**, 155–162.

McHugh, M. (2001) Soils, vegetation and land-use change on Bowes Moor. In: *Stainmore: the Archaeology of a North Pennine Pass* (ed. B.E. Vyner), pp. 35–41. Tees Archaeology Monograph Series 1, Hartlepool.

Macklin, M.G. (1986) Channel floodplain metamorphosis in the River Nent, Cumberland. In: *Quaternary River Landforms and Sediments in the Northern Pennines. Field Guide* (eds M.G. Macklin & J. Rose), pp. 13– 19, Quaternary Research Association/British Geomorphological Research Group, Newcastle upon Tyne.

Macklin, M.G. (1997) Black Burn, Cumbria (NY 685415). In: *Fluvial Geomorphology of Great Britain* (ed. K.J. Gregory), pp. 205–209, Geological Conservation Review Series 13, Chapman & Hall, London.

Macklin, M.G. (1999) Holocene river environments in Prehistoric Britain: human interaction and impact. In: *Holocene Environments of Prehistoric Britain.* (eds K.J. Edwards & J. Sadler), pp. 521–530. Wiley, Chichester.

Macklin, M.G. & Aspinall, R.J. (1986) Historic floodplain sedimentation in the River West Allan, Northumberland: a case study of channel change in an upland gravel-bed river in the northern Pennines. In: *Quaternary River Landforms and Sediments in the Northern Pennines. Field Guide* (eds M.G. Macklin & J. Rose), pp. 7–17. Quaternary Research Association/British Geomorphological Research Group, Newcastle upon Tyne.

Macklin, M.G. & Needham, S. (1992) Studies in British alluvial archaeology: potential and prospect. In: *Alluvial Archaeology in Britain* (eds S. Needham & M.G. Macklin), pp. 9–23. Oxbow Monograph, 27, Oxford.

Macklin, M.G. & Lewin, J. (1993) Holocene alluviation in Britain. *Zeitschrift für Geomorphologie Supplement Band*, **88**, 109–122.

Macklin, M.G. & Lewin, J. (2003) River sediments, great floods and centennial-scale Holocene climate change. *Journal of Quaternary Science*, **18**, 101–105.

Macklin, M.G., Passmore, D.G., Stevenson, A.C., Cowley, D.C., Edwards, D.N. & O'Brien, C.F. (1991) Holocene alluviation and land-use change on Callaly Moor, Northumberland, England. *Journal of Quaternary Science*, **6**, 225–232.

Macklin, M.G., Passmore, D.G., Cowley, D.C., Stevenson, A.C. & O'Brien, C.F. (1992c) Geoarchaeological enhancement of river valley archaeology in North East England. In: *Geoprospection in the archaeological landscape* (ed. P. Spoerry), pp. 43–58. Oxford Monograph 18, Oxford.

Macklin, M.G., Passmore, D.G. & Rumsby, B.T. (1992b) Climate and cultural signals in Holocene alluvial sequences: the Tyne basin, Northern England. In: *Alluvial Archaeology in Britain* (eds S. Needham & M.G. Macklin), pp. 123–139. Oxford Monograph 27, Oxford.

Macklin, M.G., Rumsby, B.T. & Heap, T. (1992a) Flood alluviation and entrenchment: Holocene valley floor development and transformation in the British uplands *Geological Society of America Bulletin*, **104**, 631–643.

Macklin, M.G., Hudson-Edwards, K. & Dawson, E.J. (1997) The significance of pollution from historic mining in the Pennine orefields on river sediment contaminant fluxes to the North Sea. *Science of the Total Environment*, **194–195**, 391–397.

Macklin, M.G., Taylor, M.P., Hudson-Edwards, K. & Howard, A.J. (2000) Holocene environmental change in the Yorkshire Ouse Basin and its influence on river dynamics and sediment fluxes to the coastal zone. In: *Holocene Land–Ocean Interaction and Environmental Change around the North Sea* (eds I. Shennan & J. Andrews), pp. 87–96. Geological Society of London Special Publication 166.

Macklin, M.G., Johnstone, E. & Lewin, J. (2005) Pervasive and long-term forcing of Holocene river instability and flooding in Great Britain by centennial-scale climate change. *The Holocene*, **15**, 937–943.

Macklin, M.G., Benito, G., Gregory, K.J., Johnstone, E., Lewin, J., Michczynska, D.J., Soja, R., Starkel, L. & Thorndycraft, V.R. (2006) Past hydrological events in the Holocene fluvial record of Europe. *Catena*, **66**, 145–154.

MacLeod, D. (2002) Cropmarks in the A1 corridor between Catterick and Brompton-on-Swale. In: *Cataractonium: Roman Catterick and its Hinterland* (ed. P.R. Wilson), pp. 36–45. Council for British Archaeology Research Report 128, London.

McMillan, A.A. & Powell, J.H. (1999) *BGS Rock Classification Scheme, Volume 4 : Classification of artificial (man-made) ground and natural superficial deposits – applications to geological maps and datasets in the UK* (RR 99–04). British Geological Survey.

McMillan, A.A., Hamblin, R.J.O. & Merritt, J.W. (2005) *An overview of the lithostratigraphic framework for the Quaternary and Neogene deposits of Great Britain (onshore)* (RR/04/04). British Geological Survey.

Macklin, M.G. (1997) Northern England. In: *Fluvial Geomorphology of Great Britain* (ed. K.J. Gregory). Joint Nature Conservation Committee, Peterborough.

Maddy, D. (1997) Uplift driven valley incision and river terrace formation in southern England. *Journal of Quaternary Science*, **12**, 539–435.

Maddy, D., Keen, D.H., Bridgland, D.R. & Green, C.P. (1991) A revised model for the Pleistocene development of the River Avon, Warwickshire. *Proceedings of the Geologists' Association*, **148**, 473–484.

Maddy, D., Green, C.P., Lewis, S.G. & Bowen, D.Q. (1995) Pleistocene Geology of the Lower Severn Valley. *Quaternary Science Reviews*, **14**, 209–222.

Maddy, D., Bridgland, D.R. & Green, C.P. (2000) Crustal uplift in southern England: evidence from the river terrace records. *Geomorphology*, **33**, 167–181.

Majerus, M.E.N. (1994) *Ladybirds*. Harper Collins, London.

Mäkinen, J. (2003) Time-transgressive deposits of repeated depositional sequences within interlobate glaciofluvial (esker) sediments in Köyliö, SW Finland. *Sedimentology*, **50**, 327–360.

Manby, T.G. (1976) The excavation of the Kilham Long Barrow, East Riding of Yorkshire. *Proceedings of the Prehistoric Society*, **42**, 111–159.

Manby, T.G. (1980) Bronze Age settlement in eastern Yorkshire. In: *The British Later Bronze Age* (ed. J. Barrett & R. Bradley), pp. 307–370. British Archaeological Reports, British Series 83, Oxford.

Manby, T.G. (2003a) The Late Upper Palaeolithic and Mesolithic in Yorkshire. In: *The Archaeology of Yorkshire: an Assessment at the Beginning of the 21st Century* (eds T.G. Manby, S. Moorhouse, & P. Ottaway), pp. 31–33. Yorkshire Archaeological Society Occasional paper 3, Leeds.

Manby, T.G. (2003b) The Iron Age of central and Pennine Yorkshire. In: *The Archaeology of Yorkshire: An Assessment at the Beginning of the 21st Century* (eds T.G. Manby, S. Moorhouse, & P. Ottaway), pp. 121–124. Yorkshire Archaeological Society Occasional Paper 3, Leeds.

Manby, T.G. (2006) *Scorton: North Yorkshire Prehistoric Pottery.* Report for Northern Archaeological Associates.

Manby, T.G., Moorhouse, S. & Ottaway, P. eds (2003a) *The*

Archaeology of Yorkshire: An Assessment at the Beginning of the 21st Century. Yorkshire Archaeological Society Occasional Paper 3, Leeds.

Manby, T.G., King, A. & Vyner, B. (2003b) The Neolithic and Bronze Ages: a time of early agriculture. In: *The Archaeology of Yorkshire: An Assessment at the Beginning of the 21st Century* (eds T.G. Manby, S. Moorhouse, & P. Ottaway), pp. 35–116. Yorkshire Archaeological Society Occasional Paper 3, Leeds.

Manning, A., Tipping, R. & Birley, R. (1997) Roman impact on the environment at Hadrian's Wall: precisely dated pollen analyses from Vindolanda, northern England. *The Holocene*, **7**, 175–186.

Margary, I.D. (1967) *Roman Roads in Britain*. John Baker, London.

Marshall, J.D., Jones, R.T., Crowley, S.F., Oldfield, F., Nash, S. & Bedford, A. (2002) A high resolution Lateglacial isotopic record from Hawes Water, Northwest England. *Palaeogeography, Palaeoclimatology, Palaeoecology*, **185**, 25–40.

Martin-Consuegra, E., Chisvert, N., Caceres, L. & Ubera, J.L. (1998) Archaeological, palynological and geological contibutions to landscape reconstruction in the alluvial plain of the Guadalquivir River at San Bernardo, Sevilla, Spain. *Journal of Archaeological Science*, **25**, 521–532.

Matthews, B. (1970) Age and origin of aeolian sand in the Vale of York. *Nature*, **227**, 1234–1236.

Maude, K. (1999) The very edge. Reappraising Romano-British settlement in the Central Pennines: the Littondale experience. In: *Living on the Edge of Empire: Models, Methodology and Marginality.* (ed. M. Nevell), pp. 42–46. Archaeology North-West 3, Manchester.

Mauquoy, D. & Barber, K.E. (1999) A replicated 3,000 yr proxy-climate record from Coom Rigg Moss and Felecia Moss, the Border Mires, northern England. *Journal of Quaternary Science*, **14**, 263–275.

Mayle, F.E., Bell, M., Birks, H.H., Brooks, S.J., Coope, G.R., Lowe, J.J., Sheldrick, C., Shijie, L., Turney, C.S.M. & Walker, M.J.C. (1999) Climate variations in Britain during the last Glacial–Holocene transition (15.0 – 11.5 cal ka BP): comparison with the GRIP ice-core record. *Journal of the Geological Society, London*, **156**, 411–423.

Mellars, P.A. (1976) Fire ecology, animal populations and man: a study of some ecological relationships in prehistory. *Proceedings of the Prehistoric Society*, **42**, 15–45.

Mellars, P.A. & Dark, P. (1998) *Star Carr in Context*. McDonald Institute for Archaeological Research, Cambridge.

Melmore, S. (1932) The buried valleys of Holderness and the Vale of York. *Naturalist*, 357–362.

Melmore, S. (1935) *Glacial geology of Holderness and the Vale of York*. The Author, Acomb.

Melmore, S. (1940) The river terraces of the Ouse and Derwent. *Proceedings of the Yorkshire Geological Society*, **24**, 245–251.

Melmore, S. & Harrison, K. (1934) The western limit of the final glaciation in the Vale of York. *Proceedings of the Yorkshire Geological Society*, **22**, 246–253.

Menuge, N., J (1997) *Climate Change on the North York Moors*. Occasional Paper No. 1, PLACE Research Centre, York.

Menzies, I.S. & Cox, M.L. (1996) Notes on the natural history, distribution and identification of British reed beetles. *British Journal of Entomology and Natural History*, **9**, 137–162.

Merrett, S.P. & Macklin, M.G. (1999) Historic river response to extreme flooding in the Yorkshire Dales, northern England In: *Fluvial Processes and Environmental Change* (eds A.G. Brown & T.M. Quine), pp. 521–532. Wiley, Chichester.

Merritt, J.W., Auton, C.A., Connell, E.R., Hall, A.M. & Peacock, J.D. (2003) *Cainozoic Geology and Landscape Evolution of North-East Scotland*. Memoir of the British Geological Survey, Sheets 66E, 67, 76E, 77, 86E, 87W, 87E, 95, 96W, 96E, and 97 (Scotland). Edinburgh.

Metcalfe, S.E., Ellis, S., Horton, B.P., Innes, J.B., McArthur, J., Mitlehner, A., Parkes, A., Pethick, J.S., Rees, J., Ridgway, J., Rutherford, M.M., Shennan, I. & Tooley, M.J. (2000) The Holocene evolution of the Humber Estuary: reconstructing change in a dynamic environment. In: *Holocene Land–Ocean Interaction and Environmental Change around the North Sea* (eds I. Shennan & J. Andrews), pp. 97–118. Geological Society of London Special Publication 166, London.

Miall, A.D. (1977) A review of the braided stream depositional environment. *Earth Science Reviews*, **13**, 1–62.

Miall, A.D. (1978) Lithofacies types and vertical profile models in braided rivers: a summary. In: *Fluvial Sedimentology* (ed. A.D. Miall), Canadian Society of Petroleum Geologists, Memoir 5, 605–625.

Miall, A.D. (1985) Architectural-element analysis: a new method of facies analysis applied to fluvial deposits. *Earth Science Reviews*, **22**, 261–308.

Millett, M. (1992) *The Romanisation of Britain*. Cambridge University Press.

Mills, D.A.C. & Holliday, D.W. (1998) *Geology of the district around Newcastle upon Tyne, Gateshead and Consett*. Memoir of the Geological Survey.

Mills, D.A.C. & Hull, J.H. (1976) *Geology of the district around Barnard Castle*. Memoir of the Geological Survey.

Mitchell, G.F., Penny, L.F., Shotton, F.W. & West, R.G. (1973) *A correlation of Quaternary deposits of the British Isles*. Geological Society of London Special Report 4. Scottish Academic Press, Edinburgh.

Mitchell, W.A. (1991a) *Western Pennines. Field Guide*. Quaternary Research Association, London.

Mitchell, W.A. (1991b) Geomorphological mapping: an introduction In: *Western Pennines. Field Guide* (ed. W.A. Mitchell), pp. 19–23. Quaternary Research Association, London.

Mitchell, W.A. (1991c) Dimlington Stadial Ice Sheet in the Western Pennines. In: *Western Pennines. Field Guide* (ed. W.A. Mitchell), pp. 25–42. Quaternary Research Association, London.

Mitchell, W.A. (1991d) Loch Lomond Stadial landforms and palaeoglaciological reconstruction. In: *Western Pennines. Field Guide* (ed. W.A. Mitchell), pp. 43–53. Quaternary Research Association, London.

Mitchell, W.A. (1994) Drumlins in ice sheet reconstructions with reference to the western Pennines, northern England. *Sedimentary Geology*, **91**, 313–331.

Mitchell, W.A. (1996) Significance of snowblow in the generation of Loch Lomond Stadial (Younger Dryas) glaciers in the western Pennines, northern England. *Journal of Quaternary Science*, **11**, 233–248.

Mitchell, W.A. (2007) Reconstructions of the Late Devensian (Dimlington Stadial) British–Irish Ice Sheet: the role of the upper Tees drumlin field, north Pennines, England. *Proceedings of the Yorkshire Geological Society*, **56**, 221–234.

Mitchell, W.A. & Riley, J.M. (2006) Drumlin map of the western

Pennines and southern Vale of Eden, Northern England. *Journal of Maps*, v.2006, 10–16.

Mitchell, W.A., Innes, J.B., Bridgland, D.R., Long, A.J., Rutherford, M.M. & Warwick, S. (2008) Landscape evolution of the Swale-Ure Washlands. In: *Yorkshire Landscapes Past and Present*. (eds M. Atherden & T. Milsom), pp. 77–87. PLACE Research Centre, York.

Mitchell, W.A., Bridgland, D.R. & Innes, J.B. (in press) Late Quaternary evolution of the Tees–Swale interfluve east of the Pennines: the role of glaciation in the development of river systems in northern England. *Proceedings of the Geologists' Association*.

Mix, A.C., Bard, E. & Schneider, R. (2001) Environmental processes of the ice age: land, oceans and glaciers (EPILOG). *Quaternary Science Reviews*, **20**, 627–657.

Moe, D. & Rackham, O. (1992) Pollarding and a possible explanation of the Neolithic elmfall. *Vegetation History and Archaeobotany*, **1**, 63–68.

Moloney, C., Holbrey, R., Wheelhouse, P. & Roberts, I. (2003) *Catterick Racecourse, North Yorkshire: The Re-use and Adaptation of a Monument from Prehistoric to Anglian Times*. Archaeological Services WYAS Occasional Series, 4, Leeds.

Moore, J.A. (1986) *Charophytes of Great Britain and Ireland*. Botanical Society of the British Isles Handbook 5, London.

Moore, J.W. (1954) Excavations at Flixton, site 2. In: *Excavations at Star Carr* (ed. J.G.D. Clark), pp. 192–194. Cambridge University Press.

Moore, P.D. (1977) Ancient distribution of lime trees in Britain. *Nature*, **268**, 13–14.

Moore, P.D., Webb, J.A. & Collinson, M.E. (1991) *Pollen Analysis*. Blackwell, Oxford.

Moore T.C. (2005) The Younger Dryas: from whence the fresh water. *Palaeooceanography*, **20**, PA4021, doi:10.1029/2005PA001170.

Moores, A.J., Passmore, D.G. & Stevenson, A.C. (1999) High resolution palaeochannel records of Holocene valley floor environments in the North Tyne Basin, northern England. In: *Fluvial Processes and Environmental Change* (eds A.G. Brown & T.A. Quine), pp. 283–310. Wiley, Chichester.

Moorhouse, S. (2003) Medieval Yorkshire: a rural landscape for the future. In: *The Archaeology of Yorkshire: An Assessment at the Beginning of the 21st Century*, (ed. T.G. Manby, S. Moorhouse & P. Ottaway), pp. 181–214. Yorkshire Archaeological Society Occasional paper 3, Leeds.

Morigi, A.N. & James, J.W.C. (1984) *The sand and gravel resources of the area northeast of Ripon, North Yorkshire; description of 1:25,000 resource sheet SE 37 and part of SE 47*. Institute of Geological Sciences Mineral Assessment Report 143.

Murton, D.K., Pawley, S.M. & Murton, J.B. (in press) Glacio-lacustrine sediments in the Vale of York and the Late Devensian Glacial history of Eastern England. *Proceedings of the Geologists' Association*.

Needham, S. & Macklin, M.G., eds (1992) *Alluvial Archaeology in Britain*. Oxbow Monograph 27, Oxford.

Nilsson, A.N. & Holmen, M. (1995) The aquatic Adephaga (Coleoptera) of Fennoscandia and Denmark: II. Dytiscidae. *Fauna Entomologica Scandinavica*, **32**, 1–92.

Norris, A., Bartley, D.D. & Gaunt, G.D. (1971) An account of the deposit of shell marl at Burton Salmon, west Yorkshire. *Naturalist*, **917**, 57–63.

Northern Archaeological Associates (2002) *Hollow Banks Quarry, Scorton, North Yorkshire: An Archaeological Post-Excavation Assessment*.

Northern Archaeological Associates (2006) *A1 Dishforth to Barton, Archaeological Evaluation Trenching in Non-Scheduled Areas: Post-Excavation Assessment Report for A1D2B Joint Venture*.

O'Cofaigh, C. & Evans, D.J.A. (2001) Sedimentary evidence for bed conditions associated with a grounded Irish Sea glacier, southern Ireland. *Journal of Quaternary Science*, **16**, 435–454.

O'Cofaigh, C. & Evans, D.J.A. (2007) Radiocarbon constraints on the age of the maximum advance of the British-Irish Ice Sheet in the Celtic Sea. *Quaternary Science Reviews*, **26**, 1197–1203.

Okland, J. (1990) *Lakes and Snails: Environment and Gastropoda in 1500 Norwegian lakes, ponds and rivers*. Universal Book Services, Oegstgeest.

Oldfield, F., Wake, R., Boyle, J., Jones, R., Nolan, S., Gibbs, Z., Appleby, P., Fisher, E. & Wolff, G. (2003) The late-Holocene history of Gormire Lake (NE England) and its catchment: a multiproxy reconstruction of past human impact. *The Holocene*, **13**, 677–690.

Oldroyd, D. (2002) *Earth, Water, Ice and Fire: Two Hundred Years of Geological Research in the English Lake District* (vol. 25). The Geological Society, London.

Osborne, P.J. (1974) *Airaphilus elongatus* (Gyll.) Col.Cucujiidae present in Britain in Roman times. *Entomologists Monthly Magazine*, **109**, 236.

Ottoway, P. (2003) The archaeology of the Roman period in the Yorkshire region: a rapid resource assessment. In: *The Archaeology of Yorkshire: An Assessment at the Beginning of the 21st Century* (eds T.G. Manby, S. Moorhouse, & P. Ottoway), pp. 125–149. Yorkshire Archaeological Society, Occasional paper 3, Leeds.

Oxford Archaeology North L.U.A.U. (1995) *A1 Dishforth to North of Leeming (Yorkshire Museum) North Yorkshire. Unpublished evaluation interim report*.

Palmer, J. (1966) Landforms, drainage and settlement in the Vale of York. In: *Geography as Human Ecology* (eds S.R. Eyres & G.R.J. Jones), pp. 91–121. Edward Arnold, London.

Palmer, J. (1967) Landforms. In: *Leeds and its Region* (eds M.W. Beresford & G.R.J. Jones), pp. 16–29. Arnold, Leeds.

Parker, A.G., Goudie A.S., Anderson D.E., Robinson J.E. & Bonsall C. (2002) A review of the mid-Holocene elm decline in the British Isles. *Progress in Physical Geography*, **26**, 1–45.

Parker-Pearson, M. & Sydes, R.E. (1997) The Iron Age enclosures and prehistoric landscape of Sutton Common, South Yorkshire. *Proceedings of the Prehistoric Society*, **63**, 221–259.

Passmore, D.G. & Macklin, M.G. (1994) Provenance of fine-grained alluvium and late Holocene land-use change in the Tyne basin, northern England. *Geomorphology*, **9**, 127–142.

Passmore, D.G. & Macklin, M.G. (1997) Geoarchaeology of the Tyne Basin: Holocene river valley environments and the archaeological record. In: *Landscape archaeology in Tynedale* (ed. C. Tolan-Smith), pp. 11–27. University of Newcastle-upon-Tyne: Tyne Solway Ancient and Historic Landscape Research Programme Monograph 1.

Passmore, D.G. & Macklin, M.G. (2000) Late Holocene channel and floodplain development in a wandering gravel-bed river: the river South Tyne at Lambley, northern England. *Earth Surface Processes and Landforms*, **25**, 1237–1256.

Passmore, D.G. & Macklin M.G. (2001) Late Holocene alluvial sediment budgets in an upland gravel bed river: the River South Tyne, northern England. In: *River Basin Sediment Systems: Archives of Environmental Change* (eds D. Maddy, M.G. Macklin, & J. Woodward), pp. 423–444. Balkema, Rotterdam.

Passmore, D.G. & Waddington, C. (2009) *Managing archaeological landscapes. Till-Tweed Studies, North-East England Volume 1.* Oxbow Books, Oxford.

Passmore, D.G. & Waddington, C. (in press) *Archaeology and Environment in North Northumberland. Till-Tweed Studies, North-East England Volume 2.* Oxbow Books, Oxford.

Passmore, D.G., Macklin, M.G., Stevenson, A.C., O'Brien, C.F. & Davies, B.A.S. (1992) A Holocene alluvial sequence in the lower Tyne valley, northern Britain: a record of river response to environmental change. *The Holocene*, **2**, 138–147.

Passmore, D.G., Waddington, C. & van der Schriek, T. (2006) Enhancing the evaluation and management of river valley archaeology: geoarchaeology in the Till-Tweed catchment, northern England. *Archaeological Prospection*, **13**, 269–281.

Peck, V.L., Hall, J.R., Zahn, R., Grousset, F., Hemmings, S.R. & Scourse, J.D. (2007) The relationship of Heinrich events and their European precursors over the past 60 ka BP: a multiproxy ice-rafted debris provenance study in the North East Atlantic. *Quaternary Science Reviews*, **26**, 862–875.

Pedley, H.M. (1987) The Flandrian (Quaternary) Caerwys tufa, North Wales: an ancient barrage tufa deposit. *Proceedings of the Yorkshire Geological Society*, **46**, 141–152.

Pedley, H.M. (1990) Classification and environmental models of cool freshwater tufas. *Sedimentary Geology*, **68**, 143–154.

Pedley, H.M. (1992) Freshwater (phytoherm) reefs: the role of biofilms and their bearing on marine reef cementation. *Sedimentary Geology*, **79**, 45–60.

Pedley, H.M. (1993) Sedimentology of the Late Quaternary tufas in the Wye and Lathkill valleys, North Derbyshire. *Proceedings of the Yorkshire Geological Society*, **49**, 197–206.

Pedley, H.M. (1994) Prokaryote-microphyte biofilms and tufas: a sedimentological perspective. *Kaupia, Darmstädter Beiträge zur Naturgeschichte* **4**, 45–60.

Pedley, H.M. & Hill, I. (2002) The recognition of barrage and paludal tufa systems by GPR: case studies in the geometry and correlation of hidden Quaternary freshwater carbonate facies. In: *Ground Penetrating Radar in Sediments* (eds C.S. Bristow & H.M. Jol), pp. 207–223. Geological Society Special Publication 211, London.

Peel, R.F. & Palmer, J. (1955) The physiography of the Vale of York. *Geography*, **40**, 215–227.

Peglar, S.M. (1993) The mid-Holocene *Ulmus* decline at Diss Mere, Norfolk, UK: a year-by-year pollen stratigraphy from annual laminations. *The Holocene*, **3**, 1–13.

Peglar, S.M. & Birks, H.J.B. (1993) The mid-Holocene *Ulmus* fall at Diss Mere, south-east England – disease and human impact. *Vegetation History and Archaeobotany*, **2**, 61–68.

Pell Frischmann, P. (1999) *A1 Dishforth to North of Leeming Improvements, North Yorkshire: Cultural Heritage.* Stage 3 Assessment Report for The Department of Transport.

Penkman, K.E.H. (2005) *Amino acid geochronology: a closed system approach to test and refine the UK model.* Unpublished PhD. Thesis, University of Newcastle-upon-Tyne.

Penkman, K.E.H., Preece, R.C., Keen, D.H., Maddy, D., Schreve, D.C. & Collins, M.J. (2007) Testing the aminostratigraphy of fluvial archives: the evidence from intra-crystalline proteins within freshwater shells. *Quaternary Science Reviews*, **26**, 2958–2969.

Penkman, K.E.H., Kaufman, D.S., Maddy, D.M. & Collins, M.J. (2008a) Closed-system behaviour of the intra-crystalline fraction of amino acids in mollusc shells. *Quaternary Geochronology*, **3**, 2–25.

Penkman, K.E.H., Preece, R.C., Keen, D.H. & Collins, M.J. (2008b) *British aggregates: An improved chronology using amino acid racemization and degradation of intra-crystalline amino acids (IcPD).* English Heritage Research Department Report.

Penkman, K.E.H., Preece, R.C., Keen, D.H. & Collins, M.J. (in press) Amino acid geochronology of the type Cromerian of West Runton, Norfolk, UK. *Quaternary International*

Pennington, W. (1975) A chronostratigraphic comparison of Late-Weichselian and Late-Devensian subdivisions, illustrated by two radiocarbon-dated profiles from western Britain. *Boreas*, **4**, 157–171.

Pennington, W. (1977) The Late Devensian flora and vegetation of Britain. *Philosophical Transactions of the Royal Society of London*, **B280**, 247–270.

Pennington, W. (1986) Lags in adjustment of vegetation to climate caused by the pace of soil development: evidence from Britain. *Vegetatio*, **67**, 105–118.

Penny, L.F. (1964) A review of the last glaciation in Great Britain. *Proceedings of the Yorkshire Geological Society*, **34**, 387–411.

Penny, L.F. (1974) Quaternary. In: *Geology and mineral resources of Yorkshire* (D.H. Rayner & J.E. Hemingway, eds), pp. 254–264, Yorkshire Geological Society, Leeds.

Penny, L.F., Coope G.R. & Catt J.A. (1969) Age and insect fauna of the Dimlington Silts, east Yorkshire. *Nature*, **224**, 65–67.

Pentecost, A. (1993) British travertines: a review. *Proceedings of the Geologists' Association*, **104**, 23–49.

Pentecost, A. (1995) The Quaternary travertine deposits of Europe and Asia Minor. *Quaternary Science Reviews*, **14**, 1005–1028.

Pentecost, A. (1998) The significance of calcite (travertine) formation by algae in a moss dominated travertine from Matlock Bath, Derbyshire. *Archiv für Hydrobiologie* **143**, 487–509.

Pentecost, A. & Lord, A. (1988) Post glacial tufas and travertines from the Craven District of Yorkshire. *Cave Science*, **15**, 141–152.

Perry, I. & Moore, P.D. (1987) Dutch elm disease as an analogue of Neolithic elm decline. *Nature*, **326**, 72–73.

Phillips, J.A. (1829) *Illustrations of the geology of Yorkshire, Part I, The Yorkshire Coast.* privately printed.

Pigott, C.D. & Huntley, J.P. (1978) Factors controlling the distribution of *Tilia cordata* at the northern limits of its geographical range I. Distribution in north-west England. *New Phytologist*, **81**, 429–441.

Pigott, C.D. & Huntley, J.P. (1980) Factors controlling the distribution of *Tilia cordata* at the northern limits of its geographical range II. History in north-west England. *New Phytologist*, **84**, 145–164.

Pigott, C.D. & Pigott, M.E. (1963) Late Glacial and Postglacial deposits at Malham, Yorkshire. *New Phytologist*, **62**, 317–334.

Pigott, M.E. & Pigott, C.D. (1959) Stratigraphy and pollen analysis of Malham Tarn and Tarn Moss. *Field Studies*, **1**, 84–107.

Pissart, A. (2002) Palsas, lithalsas and remnants of these periglacial mounds. *Progress in Physical Geography*, **26**, 605–621.

Pissart, A. (2003) The remnants of Younger Dryas lithalsas in the Haute Fagnes Plateau in Belgium and elsewhere in the world. *Geomorphology*, **52**, 5–38.

Plater, A.J., Ridgway, J., Rayner, B., Shennan, I., Horton, B.P., Hayworth, E.Y., Wright, M.R., Rutherford, M.M. & Wintle, A.G. (2000) Sediment provenance and flux in the Tees estuary: the record from the Late Devensian to the present. In: *Holocene Land–Ocean Interaction and Environmental Change around the North Sea* (eds I. Shennan & J. Andrews), pp. 171–195. Geological Society of London. Special Publication 166, London.

Pounder, E.J. (1979) *Alluvial fans and river terraces: a study of their morphology and development in selected parts of the Swale and Usk valleys*. MPhil thesis, Birkbeck College, University of London.

Powell, J.H., Cooper, A.H. & Benfield, A.C. (1992) *Geology of the country around Thirsk*. Memoir of the Geological Survey.

Preece, R.C. (1978) The biostratigraphy of Flandrian tufas in southern Britain. Unpublished Ph.D. Thesis, University of London.

Preece, R.C. (1980) The biostratigraphy and dating of the tufa deposit at the Mesolithic site at Blashenwell, Dorset, England. *Journal of Archaeological Science*, **7**, 345–363.

Preece, R.C. & Robinson, J.E. (1982) Mollusc, ostracod and plant remains from early postglacial deposits near Staines. *The London Naturalist*, **61**, 145–157.

Preece, R.C. & Turner, C. (1990) The tufas at Caerwys and Ddol. In: *North Wales. Field Guide*. (eds K. Addison, M.J. Edge & R. Watkins), pp.162–166. Quaternary Research Association, Coventry.

Preece, R.C. & Bridgland, D.R. (1998) *Late Quaternary Environmental Change and Prehistory: Excavations at Holywell Coombe, South east England*. Chapman & Hall, London.

Preece, R.C. & Bridgland, D.R. (1999) Holywell Coombe, Folkestone, UK: a 13,000 year history of an English Chalkland valley. *Quaternary Science Reviews*, **18**, 1075–1125.

Preston, C.D. (1995) *Pondweeds of Great Britain and Ireland*. Botanical Society of the British Isles Handbook 8, London.

Preston, C.D., Pearman, D.A. & Dines, T.D. (2002) *New Atlas of the British and Irish Flora*. Oxford University Press.

Prestwich, J. (1860) On the occurrence of flint-implements associated with the remains of animals of extinct species in beds of a late geological period, in France at Amiens and Abbeville, and in England at Hoxne. *Philosophical Transactions of the Royal Society of London*, **150**, 272–317.

Price, D. (1975) *The sand and gravel resources of the country around Newton-on-Trent, Lincolnshire. Description of 1:25,000 resource sheet SK87*. Institute of Geological Sciences Mineral Assessment Report 15.

Pryor, F.M.M., French, C.A.I. & Taylor, M. (1986) Flag Fen, Fengate, Peterborough I: discovery, reconnaissance and initial excavations. *Proceedings of the Prehistoric Society,* **52**, 1–24.

Punkari, M. (1997a) Subglacial processes of the Scandinavian Ice Sheet in Fennoscandia inferred from flow-parallel features and lithostratigraphy. *Sedimentary Geology*, **111**, 263–283.

Punkari, M. (1997b) Glacial and fluvioglacial deposits in the interlobate areas of the Scandinavian ice sheet. *Quaternary Science Reviews*, **16**, 741–753.

Radge, G.W. (1940) The glaciation of north Cleveland. *Proceedings of the Yorkshire Geological Society*, **24**, 180–204.

Radley, J. (1974) The Prehistory of the Vale of York. *Yorkshire Archaeological Journal*, **46**, 10–22.

Radley, J., Tallis, J.H. & Switsur, V.R. (1974) The excavation of three 'narrow-blade' Mesolithic sites in the southern Pennines, England. *Proceedings of the Prehistoric Society*, **40**, 1–19.

Rahtz, P. (1989) *Little Ouseburn Barrow 1958*. York University Archaeological Publications, 7.

Raistrick, A. (1926) The glaciation of Wensleydale, Swaledale and the adjoining parts of the Pennines. *Proceedings of the Yorkshire Geological Society*, **20**, 366–410.

Raistrick, A. (1927) Periodicity of glacial retreat in West Yorkshire. *Proceedings of the Yorkshire Geological Society*, **21**, 24–29.

Raistrick, A. (1931a) The pre-glacial Swale. *Naturalist*, 233–237.

Raistrick, A. (1931b) The glaciation of Northumberland and Durham. *Proceedings of the Yorkshire Geological Society*, **22**, 199–214.

Raistrick, A. (1931c) The glaciation of Wharfedale, Yorkshire. *Proceedings of the Yorkshire Geological Society*, **22**, 9–30.

Raistrick, A. (1932) The correlation of retreat stages across the Pennines. *Proceedings of the Yorkshire Geological Society*, **22**, 199–214.

Raistrick, A. (1933) The glacial and post-glacial periods of Yorkshire. *Proceedings of the Geologists' Association*, **44**, 263–269.

Rasmussen, P. (1989) Leaf foddering of livestock in the Neolithic: archaeobotanic evidence from Weier, Switzerland *Journal of Danish Archaeology*, **8**, 51–71.

RCHME [Royal Commission on the Historical Monuments of England] (1997) *Cropmarks in the Catterick Area, North Yorkshire: Air Photographic Analysis*.

Rees, J.G., Ridgway, J., Ellis, S., Knox, O.B., Newsham, R.W. & Parkes, A. (2000) Holocene sediment storage in the Humber estuary. In: *Holocene Land–Ocean Interaction and Environmental Change around the North Sea* (eds I. Shennan & J. Andrews), pp. 119–143. Geological Society of London, Special Publication 166, London.

Reimer, P.J., Baillie, M.G.L., Bard, E., Bayliss, A., Beck, J.W., Bertrand, C., Blackwell, P.G., Buck, C.E., Burr, G., Cutler, K.B., Damon, P.E., Edwards, R.L., Fairbanks, R.G., Friedrich, M., Guilderson, T.P., Hughen, K.A., Kromer, B., McCormac, F.G., Manning, S., Bronk Ramsey, C., Reimer, R.W., Remmele, S., Southon, J.R., Stuiver, M., Talamo, S., Taylor, F.W., van der Plicht, J. & Weyhenmeyer, C.E. (2004) INTCAL04 Terrestrial radiocarbon age calibration 0–26 CAL KYR BP. *Radiocarbon*, **46**, 1029–1058.

Richards, K.S. (1981) Evidence of Flandrian valley alluviation in Staindale, North York Moors. *Earth Surface Processes and Landforms*, **6**, 183–186.

Richards, K.S., Peters, N.R., Robertson-Rintoul, M.S.E. & Switsur, V.R. (1987) Recent valley sediments in the North York Moors: evidence and interpretation. In: *International Geomorphology Part 1* (ed. V. Gardiner), pp. 869–883. Wiley, Chichester.

Roberts, B.K., Turner, J. & Ward, P.F. (1973) Recent forest history and land-use in Weardale, northern England. In: *Quaternary Plant Ecology* (eds H.J.B. Birks & R.G. West), pp. 207–221. Blackwell, Oxford.

Roberts, I. (2005) *Ferrybridge Henge: The Ritual landscape.*

Yorkshire Archaeology, 10. Archaeological Services WYAS, Leeds.

Robinson, M.A. (1978) A comparison between the effects of man on the environment of the first gravel terrace and floodplain of the Upper Thames valley during the Iron Age and Roman period. In: *The Effects of Man on the Landscape: the Lowland Zone* (eds S. Limbrey & J.G. Evans), pp. 35–43. Council for British Archaeology Research Report 21, London.

Robinson, M.A. (1992a) Environmental archaeology of the river gravels: past achievements and future directions. In: *Developing Landscapes of Lowland Britain.* (eds M. Fulford & E. Nichols), pp. 47–62. Occasional Paper 14, Society of Antiquaries of London.

Robinson, M.A. (1992b) Environment, archaeology and alluvium on the river gravels of the south Midlands. In: *Alluvial Archaeology in Britain* (eds S. Needham & M.G. Macklin), pp. 197–208. Oxbow Books, Oxford.

Robinson, M.A. (1993) The scientific evidence. In: *The Prehistoric Landscape and Iron Age Enclosed Settlement at Mingies Ditch, Hardwick-with-Yelford, Oxon.* (eds T.G. Allan & M.A. Robinson), pp. 101–141. Thames Valley Landscapes 2, Oxford Archaeology Unit.

Robinson, M.A. (2000) Coleopteran evidence for the elm decline, Neolithic activity in woodland, clearance and the use of the landscape. In: *Plants in Neolithic Britain and Beyond* (ed. A. Fairbairn), pp. 27–36. Oxbow Books, Oxford.

Robinson, M.A. & Lambrick, G.H. (1984) Holocene alluviation and hydrology in the Upper Thames basin. *Nature*, **308**, 809–814.

Roe, D.A. (1981) *The Lower and Middle Palaeolithic Periods in Britain.* Routledge and Kegan Paul, London.

Rose, J. (1980) Landform development around Kisdon, upper Swaledale, Yorkshire. *Proceedings of the Yorkshire Geological Society*, **43**, 201–219.

Rose, J. (1985) The Dimlington Stadial/Dimlington Chronozone: a proposal for naming the main glacial episode of the Late Devensian in Britain. *Boreas*, **14**, 225–230.

Rose, J. (1994) Major river systems of central and southern Britain during the Early and Middle Pleistocene. *Terra Nova*, **6**, 435–443.

Rose, J. (2006) Quaternary geology and geomorphology of the area around Kisdon, upper Swaledale. In: *Yorkshire Rocks and Landscape: A Field Guide.* 3rd edition. (eds C. Scrutton & J. Powell), pp. 42–50. Yorkshire Geological Society, Leeds.

Rose, J. & Letzer, J.M. (1977) Superimposed drumlins. *Journal of Glaciology*, **18**, 471–480.

Rose, J., Turner, C., Coope, G.R. & Bryan, M.D. (1980) Channel changes in a lowland river catchment over the last 13,000 years. In: *Timescales in Geomorphology* (eds R.A. Cullingford, D.A. Davidson, & J. Lewin), pp. 159–176. Wiley, Chichester.

Rowe, P. (2006) *Nosterfield 2005: Intervention 11: The Flasks – Flint Report.* Report for Field Archaeological Specialists.

Rowell, T.K. & Turner, J. (1985) Litho-, humic- and pollen stratigraphy at Quick Moss, Northumberland. *Journal of Ecology*, **73**, 11–25.

Rowley-Conwy, P.A. (1998) Faunal remains and antler artefacts. In: *Star Carr in Context* (eds P.A. Mellars & P. Dark), pp. 99–107. McDonald Institute Monographs, Cambridge.

Rumsby, B.T. (2001) Valley floor and floodplain processes. In: *Geomorphological processes and landscape change: Britain in the last 1000 years* (eds D.L. Higgitt & M. Lee), pp. 90–115. Blackwell, Oxford.

Rumsby, B.T. & Macklin M.G. (1994) Channel and floodplain response to recent abrupt climate change: the Tyne basin, northern England. *Earth Surface Processes and Landforms*, **19**, 499–515.

Salisbury, C.R. (1992) The archaeological evidence for palaeochannels in the Trent Valley. In: *Alluvial Archaeology in Britain* (eds S. Needham & M.G. Macklin), pp. 155–162. Oxbow Monograph 27, Oxford.

Salisbury, C.R., Whitley, P.J., Litton, C.D. & Fox, J.L. (1984) Flandrian courses of the River Trent at Colwick, Nottingham. *Mercian Geologist*, **9**, 189–207.

Scaife, R.G. & Burrin, P.J. (1992) Archaeological inferences from alluvial sediments: some findings from southern England. In: *Alluvial Archaeology in Britain* (eds S. Needham & M.G. Macklin), pp. 75–91. Oxbow Monograph 27, Oxford.

Schadla-Hall, T. (1987) Recent investigations of the early Mesolithic landscape in the Vale of Pickering. In: *Mesolithic Northwest Europe: Recent Trends* (eds M. Zvelebil & H. Blankholm), pp. 46–54. Department of Archaeology, University of Sheffield.

Schadla-Hall, T. (1989) The Vale of Pickering in the early Mesolithic in context. In: *The Mesolithic in Europe* (ed. C. Bonsall), pp. 218–224. John Donald, Edinburgh.

Schreve, D.C. (1999) Bielsbeck Farm, East Yorkshire (SE861378). In: *The Quaternary of North-East England. Field Guide* (eds D.R. Bridgland, B.P. Horton, & J.B. Innes), pp. 176–179. Quaternary Research Association, London.

Schreve, D.C., Bridgland, D.R., Allen, P., Blackford, J.J., Gleed-Owen, C.P., Griffiths, H.I., Keen, D.H. & White, M.J. (2002) Sedimentology, palaeontology and archaeology of late Middle Pleistocene River Thames terrace deposits at Purfleet, Essex, UK. *Quaternary Science Reviews*, **21**, 1423–1464.

Schumm, S. & Kahn, H. (1972) Experimental study of channel patterns. *Bulletin of the Geological Society of America*, **83**, 1755–1770.

Scourse, J.D., Hall, J.R., McCave, I.N., Young, J.R. & Sugdon, C. (2000) The origin of Heinrich layers: evidence from H2 for European precursor events. *Earth and Planetary Science Letters*, **182**, 187–195.

Sedgewick, C.M. (1998) Historic metal contamination at Reeth, upper Swaledale. In: *The Quaternary of the Eastern Yorkshire Dales. Field Guide* (eds A.J. Howard & M.G. Macklin), pp. 67–75. Quaternary Research Association, London.

Sedgwick, A. (1825) On the origin of alluvial and diluvial formations. *Annals of Philosophy*, **xi**, 231–247.

Sejrup, H.-P., Haflidson, H., Aarseth, I., King, E., Forsberg, C.F., Long, D. & Rokoengen, K. (1994) Late Weichselian glaciation history of the northern North Sea. *Boreas*, **23**, 1–23.

Sejrup, H.-P., Larsen, E., Landvik, J., King, E.L., Haflidason, H. & Nesje, A. (2000) Quaternary glaciation in southern Fennoscandia: evidence from southwestern Norway and the northern North Sea region. *Quaternary Science Reviews*, **19**, 667–685.

Sejrup, H.-P., Hjelstuen, B.O., Dahlgren, K.I.T., Haflidason, H., Kuijpers, A., Nygard, A., Praeg, D., Stoker, M.S. & Vorren, T.O. (2005) Pleistocene glacial history of the NW European continental margin. *Marine and Petroleum Geology*, **22**, 1111–1129.

Shackleton, N.J. (2006) Formal Quaternary stratigraphy – what do we expect and need? *Quaternary Science Reviews*, **25**, 3458–3462.

Sheldrick, C., Lowe, J.J. & Reynier, M.J. (1997) Palaeolithic barbed point from Gransmoor, East Yorkshire. *Proceedings of the Prehistoric Society*, **63**, 359–370.

Shennan, I. & Andrews, J. (2000) An introduction to Holocene land-ocean interaction and environmental change around the western North Sea. In: *Holocene Land-Ocean Interactions and Environmental Change around the North Sea* (eds I. Shennan & J. Andrews), pp. 1–7. Geological Society of London Special Publication 166.

Shennan, I., Bradley, S., Milne, G., Brooks, A., Bassett, S. & Hamilton, S. (2006) Relative sea-level changes, glacial isostatic modelling and ice sheet reconstructions from the British Isles since the Last Glacial Maximum. *Journal of Quaternary Science*, **21**, 585–599.

Shennan, I., Lambeck, K., Horton, B.P., Innes, J.B., Lloyd, J.M., McArthur, J.J. & Rutherford, M.M. (2000) Holocene isostasy and relative sea-level changes on the east coast of England. In: *Holocene Land-Ocean Interaction and Environmental Change around the North Sea* (eds I. Shennan & J. Andrews), pp. 275–298. Geological Society of London Special Publication 166.

Sheppard, T. (1902) The Yorkshire Boulder Committee and its work – a retrospective. *The Naturalist*, July 1902, 217–222.

Sherlock, S.J. & Welch, M.G. (1992) *An Anglo-Saxon Cemetery at Norton, Cleveland*. Council for British Archaeology Research Report 82, London.

Sherlock, S.J. & Simmons, M. (2008) A seventh-century royal cemetery at Street House, north-east Yorkshire, England. *Antiquity*, **82**, http://www.antiquity.ac.uk/ProjGall/sherlock/index.html

Shimwell, D.W. (1985) The distribution and origins of the lowland mosslands. In: *The Geomorphology of North-west England* (ed. R.H. Johnson), pp. 299–312. Manchester University Press.

Simmons, I.G. (1995) The history of the early human environment. In: *Moorland Monuments* (ed. B.E. Vyner), pp. 5–15. Council for British Archaeology Research Report 101, York.

Simmons, I.G. (1996) *The Environmental Impact of Later Mesolithic Cultures*. Edinburgh University Press.

Simmons, I.G. & Cundill, P.R. (1974) Late Quaternary vegetational history of the North York Moors I. Pollen analyses of blanket peats. *Journal of Biogeography*, **1**, 159–169.

Simmons, I.G. & Innes, J.B. (1981) Tree remains in a North York Moors peat profile. *Nature*, **294**, 76–78.

Simmons, I.G. & Innes, J.B. (1985) Late Mesolithic land-use and its environmental impacts in the English uplands. *Biogeographical Monographs*, **2**, 7–17.

Simmons, I.G. & Innes, J.B. (1987) Mid-Holocene adaptations and later Mesolithic forest disturbance in northern England. *Journal of Archaeological Science*, **14**, 385–403.

Simmons, I.G. & Innes, J.B. (1988) Late Quaternary vegetational history of the North York Moors X. Investigations on East Bilsdale Moor. *Journal of Biogeography*, **15**, 299–324.

Simmons, I.G. & Innes, J.B. (1996a) Prehistoric charcoal in peat profiles at North Gill, North Yorkshire Moors, England. *Journal of Archaeological Science*, **23**, 193–197.

Simmons, I.G. & Innes, J.B. (1996b) The ecology of an episode of prehistoric cereal cultivation on the North York Moors. *Journal of Archaeological Science*, **23**, 613–618.

Simmons, I.G., Atherden, M.A., Cundill, P.R. & Jones, R.L. (1975) Inorganic layers in soligenous mires of the North York Moors. *Journal of Biogeography*, **2**, 49–56.

Simmons, I.G., Atherden, M.A., Cloutman, E.W., Cundill, P.R.,

Innes, J.B. & Jones, R.L. (1993) Prehistoric Environments. In: *Prehistoric and Roman Archaeology of Northeast Yorkshire* (ed. D.A. Spratt), pp. 15–50. Council for British Archaeology Research Report 87, London.

Simmons, I.G., Innes, J.B. & Cummins, G.E. (in press) Palaeo-ecology. In: *The Early Mesolithic in the Vale of Pickering*. McDonald Institute Monographs, Cambridge.

Sissons, J.B. (1958) Subglacial erosion in southern Northumberland. *Scottish Geographical Magazine*, **74**, 163–174.

Sissons, J.B. (1960a) Some aspects of glacial drainage channels in Britain, Part 1. *Scottish Geographical Magazine*, **76**, 131–146.

Sissons, J.B. (1960b) Some aspects of glacial drainage channels in Britain, Part 2. *Scottish Geographical Magazine*, **77**, 15–36.

Sissons, J.B. (1974) A Lateglacial ice cap in the central Grampians, Scotland. *Transactions of the Institute of British Geographers*, **62**, 95–114.

Sissons, J.B. (1976) *The Geomorphology of the British Isles: Scotland*. Methuen, London.

Sissons, J.B. (1980) The Loch Lomond Advance in the Lake District, northern England. *Transactions of the Royal Society of Edinburgh (Earth Sciences)*, **71**, 13–27.

Skinner, C. & Brown, A.G. (1999) Mid-Holocene vegetation diversity in eastern Cumbria. *Journal of Biogeography*, **26**, 45–54.

Smith, A. (1979) *The sand and gravel resources of the country west of Darlington, County Durham. Description of 1:25,000 resource sheet NZ 11 and 21*. Institute of Geological Sciences Mineral Assessment Report 40.

Smith, A.G. & Pilcher, J.R. (1973) Radiocarbon dates and vegetational history of the British Isles. *New Phytologist*, **72**, 903–914.

Smith, B.M. (2002) *A Palaeoecological Study of Raised Mires in the Humberhead Levels*. British Archaeological Reports, British Series 336, Oxford.

Smith, D.B. (1994) *Geology of the country around Sunderland*. Memoir of the Geological Survey.

Smith, D.B. & Francis, E.A. (1967) *Geology of the country between Durham and West Hartlepool*. Memoir of the Geological Survey.

Smith, D.N. (2000) Disappearance of elmid riffle beetles from lowland river systems – the impact of alluviation. In: *People as an Agent of Environmental Change*. (eds T. O'Connor & R. Nicholson), pp. 75–80. Oxbow Books, Oxford.

Smith, D.N. & Howard, A.J. (2004) Identifying changing fluvial conditions in low gradient alluvial archaeological landscapes: Can Coleoptera provide insights into changing discharge rates and floodplain evolution? *Journal of Archaeological Science*, **31**, 109–120.

Smith, D.N. & Whitehouse, N.J. (2005a) Beetle faunas, woodland history and the palaeoenvironment. *Landscape Archaeology and Ecology*, **5**, 82–85.

Smith, D.N. & Whitehouse, N.J. (2005b) Not seeing the woods for the trees: a palaeoentomological perspective on woodland decline. In: *The Fertile Ground*. (eds M. Brinkley, W. Smith & D.N. Smith), pp. 136–161. Oxbow Books, Oxford.

Smith, D.N., Osborne, P. & Barratt, J. (2000) Beetles and evidence of past environments at Goldcliff. In: *Prehistoric Intertidal Archaeology in the Welsh Severn Estuary*. (eds M. Bell, A. Caseldine & H. Neumann), pp. 245–260. Council for British Archaeology Research Report 120, London.

Smith, D.N., Roseff, R. & Butler, S. (2001) The sediments,

pollen, plant macrofossils and insects from a Bronze Age channel fill at Yoxall Bridge, Staffordshire. *Environmental Archaeology*, **6**, 1–12.

Smith, D.N., Roseff, R., Bevan, L., Butler, A.G., Hughes, S.G. & Monckton, A. (2005) Archaeological and environmental investigations of a Late Glacial and Holocene river valley sequence on the River Soar, at Croft, Leicestershire. *The Holocene*, **15**, 353–377.

Smith, E.G., Rhys, G.H. & Goossons, R.F. (1973) The geology of the country around East Retford, Worksop and Gainsborough (explanation of sheet 101). Memoir of the Geological Survey.

Smith, M.J. & Clark, C.D. (2005) Methods for the visualisation of digital elevation models for landform mapping. *Earth Surface Processes and Landforms*, **30**, 885–900.

Smith, M.J., Rose, J. & Booth, S. (2006) Geomorphological mapping of glacial landforms from remotely sensed data: an evaluation of the principal data sources and an assessment of their quality. *Geomorphology*, **76**, 148–165.

Smith, M.J.B. (1994) *The Excavated Bronze Age Barrows of North East Yorkshire*. Architectural and Archaeological Society of Durham and Northumberland, Research Report, 3.

Smith, R.F. & Boardman, J. (1994) Soils in Mosedale. In: *Cumbria Field Guide*, pp. 173–177. Quaternary Research Association, London.

Smith, R.T. (1986) Aspects of the soil and vegetation history of the Craven District of Yorkshire. In: *Archaeology in the Pennines*. (eds T.G. Manby & P. Turnbull), pp. 3–28. British Archaeological Reports, British Series 158, Oxford.

Sparks, B.W. (1961) The ecological interpretation of Quaternary non-marine Mollusca. *Proceedings of the Linnean Society of London*, **172**, 71–80.

Spikins, P.A. (1999) *Mesolithic Northern England: environment, population and settlement*. British Archaeological Reports, British Series 283, Oxford.

Spikins, P.A. (2000) GIS models of past vegetation: an example from northern England, 10,000–5000 BP. *Journal of Archaeological Science*, **27**, 219–234.

Spikins, P.A. (2002) *Prehistoric People of the Pennines*. West Yorkshire Archaeology Service, Leeds.

Spratt, D.A. (1978) Prehistoric field and land boundary systems in the North York Moors. In: *Early Land Allotment in the British Isles: a Survey of Recent Work*. (eds H.C. Bowen & P.J. Fowler). British Archaeological Reports, British Series 48, Oxford.

Spratt, D.A. (1981) Prehistoric boundaries on the North Yorkshire Moors. In: *Prehistoric Communities in Northern England* (ed. G.W. Barker), pp. 87–103. Department of Prehistory and Archaeology, University of Sheffield.

Spratt, D.A. (1989) *Linear Earthworks of the Tabular Hills, Northeast Yorkshire*. Sheffield University Department of Archaeology and Prehistory.

Spratt, D.A. (1993) *Prehistoric and Roman Archaeology of North-East Yorkshire*. Council for British Archaeology Research Report 87, London.

Spratt, D.A. & Simmons, I.G. (1976) Prehistoric activity and environment on the North York Moors. *Journal of Archaeological Science*, **3**, 193–210.

Squires, R.H. (1978) Conservation in upper Teesdale: contributions from the palaeoecological record. *Transactions of the Institute of British Geographers*, **NS3**, 129–150.

Stace, C. (1997) *New Flora of the British Isles*. (2nd ed.). Cambridge University Press.

Stallibrass, S. (2005) The faunal evidence. In: *Archaeology and Environment of Submerged Landscapes in Hartlepool Bay, England*. (ed. M. Waughman), pp. 74–77. Tees Archaeology Monograph Series 2, Hartlepool.

Stanczyszyn, R. (1982) *The sand and gravel resources of the country around Tholthorpe, North Yorkshire; description of 1:25,000 resource sheet SE 46*. Institute of Geological Sciences. Mineral Assessment Report 88.

Still, L. & Vyner, B.E. (1986) Air photographic evidence for later prehistoric settlement in the lower Tees valley. *Durham Archaeological Journal*, **2**, 11–23.

Still, L., Vyner, B.E. & Bewley, R. (1989) A decade of air survey in Cleveland and the Tees valley hinterland and a strategy for air survey in County Durham. *Durham Archaeological Journal*, **5**, 1–10.

Stockmarr, J. (1971) Tablets with spores used in absolute pollen analysis. *Pollen et Spores*, **13**, 615–621.

Stokes, C.R. & Clark, C.D. (1999) Geomorphological criteria for identifying Pleistocene ice streams. *Annals of Glaciology*, **28**, 67–74.

Stokes, C.R. & Clark, C.D. (2001) Palaeo-ice streams. *Quaternary Science Reviews*, **20**, 1437–1457.

Stone, J.O. & Ballantyne, C.K. (2006) Dimensions and deglacial chronology of the Outer Hebrides ice cap, northwest Scotland: implications of cosmic ray exposure dating. *Journal of Quaternary Science*, **21**, 75–84.

Straw, A. (2002) The Late Devensian limit in the Humberhead area – a reappraisal. *Quaternary Newsletter*, **97**, 1–10.

Straw, A. & Clayton, K.M. (1979) *Geomorphology of the British Isles: Eastern and Central England*. Methuen, London.

Strong, G.E. & Giles, J.R.A. (1983) *The sand and gravel resources of the country around West Tanfield, North Yorkshire; description of 1:25,000 resource sheet SE 27*. Institute of Geological Sciences Mineral Assessment Report 135.

Stuart, A.J. (1999) Late Pleistocene megafaunal extinctions. In: *Extinctions in Near Time: causes, contexts and consequences* (ed. R.D.E. MacPhee), pp. 257–270. Kluwer Academic Press, New York.

Sturludottir, S.A. & Turner, J. (1985) The elm decline at Pawlaw Mire: an anthropogenic interpretation. *New Phytologist*, **99**, 323–329.

Switsur, V.R. & Jacobi, R.M. (1975) Radiocarbon dates for the Pennine Mesolithic. *Nature*, **256**, 32–34.

Symoens, J.J., Duvigneaud, P. & Vanden Berghen, C. (1951) Apercu sur la vegetation des tufs calcaires de la Belgique. *Bulletin Societé Royale de Belgique*, **83**, 329–352.

Tallantire, P.A. (1992) The alder [*Alnus glutinosa* (L.) Gaertn.] problem in the British Isles: a third approach to its palaeo-history. *New Phytologist*, **122**, 717–731.

Tallantire, P.A. (2002) The early Holocene spread of hazel (*Corylus avellana* L.) in Europe, north and west of the Alps: an ecological hypothesis. *The Holocene*, **12**, 81–96.

Tallis, J.H. (1991) Forest and moorland in the south Pennine uplands in the mid-Flandrian period. III. The spread of moorland – local, regional and national. *Journal of Ecology*, **79**, 401–415.

Tallis, J.H. (1995) Climate and erosion signals in British blanket peats: the significance of *Racomitrium lanuginosum* remains. *Journal of Ecology*, **83**, 1021–1030.

Tallis, J.H. & McGuire, J. (1972) Central Rossendale: the evolution of an upland vegetation I. The clearance of woodland. *Journal of Ecology*, **60**, 721–737.

Tallis, J.H. & Switsur, V.R. (1973) Studies on southern Pennine peats. VI. A radiocarbon-dated pollen diagram from Featherbed Moss, Derbyshire. *Journal of Ecology*, **61**, 743–751.

Tallis, J.H. & Switsur, V.R. (1983) Forest and moorland in the south Pennine uplands in the mid-Flandrian period. II. The hillslope forests. *Journal of Ecology*, **71**, 585–600.

Tallis, J.H. & Livett, E.A. (1994) Pool-and-hummock patterning in a southern Pennine blanket mire I. Stratigraphic profiles for the last 2800 years. *Journal of Ecology*, **82**, 775–788.

Tavener, P. (1996) Evidence of Neolithic activity near Marton-le-Moor, North Yorkshire. In: *Neolithic Studies in No-Man's Land* (ed. P. Frodsham), pp. 183–187. Northern Archaeology 13/14.

Taylor, D.M., Griffiths, H.I., Pedley, H.M. & Prince, I. (1994a) Radiocarbon dated Holocene pollen and ostracod sequences from barrage tufa-dammed fluvial systems in the White Peak, Derbyshire, UK. *The Holocene*, **4**, 356–364.

Taylor, D.M., Pedley, H.M., Davies, P. & Wright, M.W. (1998) Pollen and mollusc records for environmental change in central Spain during the mid- and late Holocene. *The Holocene*, **21**, 463–478.

Taylor, J.J., Innes, J.B. & Jones, M.D.H. (1994b) Archaeological site location by the integration of geophysical and palynological techniques in an environmental survey role. In: *Whither Environmental Archaeology?* (eds R.M. Luff & P.A. Rowley-Conwy), pp. 13–23. Oxbow Monograph 38, Oxford.

Taylor, M.P. & Macklin, M.G. (1997) Holocene alluvial sedimentation and valley floor development: the River Swale, Catterick, North Yorkshire. *Proceedings of the Yorkshire Geological Society*, **51**, 317–327.

Taylor, M.P. & Macklin, M.G. (1998) Holocene alluvial sedimentation of the River Swale at Catterick, North Yorkshire. In: *The Quaternary of the Eastern Yorkshire Dales. Field Guide* (eds A.J. Howard & M.G. Macklin), pp. 83–87. Quaternary Research Association, London.

Taylor, M.P., Macklin, M.G. & Hudson-Edwards, K. (2000) River sedimentation and fluvial response to Holocene environmental change in the Yorkshire Ouse Basin, northern England. *The Holocene*, **10**, 201–212.

Teasdale, D. & Hughes, D. (1999) The glacial history of North-East England. In: *The Quaternary of North-east England. Field Guide* (eds D.R. Bridgland, B.P. Horton, & J.B. Innes), pp. 10–17. Quaternary Research Association, London.

Teller, J.T. (2003) Controls, history, outbursts and impact of large late-Quaternary proglacial lakes in North America. In: *The Quaternary Period in the United States, INQUA Anniversary volume* (eds A. Gillespie, S. Porter, & B. Atwater), pp. 45–61. Elsevier, Amsterdam.

Teller, J.T. & Leverington, D.W. (2004) Glacial Lake Agassiz: a 5000-year history of change and its relationship to the $\delta^{18}O$ record of Greenland. *Geological Society of America Bulletin*, **116**, 729–742.

Thomas, G.S.P. (1999) Northern England. In: *A Revised Correlation of Quaternary Deposits in the British Isles* (ed. D.Q. Bowen), pp. 91–98. Geological Society of London Special Report 23.

Thomas, G.S.P., Chiverrell, R.C. & Huddart, D. (2004) Ice-marginal depositional responses to readvance episodes in the Late Devensian deglaciation of the Isle of Man. *Quaternary Science Reviews*, **23**, 85–106.

Thomas, N. (1955) The Thornborough Circles, near Ripon, North Riding. *Yorkshire Archaeological Journal*, **38**, 425–445.

Thompson, A., Hine, P.D., Greig, J.R. & Peach, D.W. (1996)

Assessment of subsidence arising from gypsum solution: Summary Report. Department of the Environment. Symonds Group Ltd, East Grinstead.

Thorne, C.R. & Lewin, J. (1979) Bank processes, bed material movement and planform development in a meandering river. In: *Adjustments of the Fluvial System* (eds D. Rhodes & G. Williams), pp. 117–137. Kendall/Hunt, Dubuque, Iowa.

Tilley, C. (1994) *A Phenomenology of Landscape.* Berg, Oxford.

Tinsley, H.M. (1975a) The former woodland of the Nidderdale Moors and the role of early man in its decline. *Journal of Ecology*, **63**, 1–26.

Tinsley, H.M. (1975b) The vegetation of upper Nidderdale: man's impact in the post-Romano-British period. In: *Environment, Man and Economic Change* (eds A.D.M. Phillips & B.J. Turton), pp. 146–163. Longman's, London.

Tinsley, H.M. (1976) Cultural influences on Pennine vegetation with particular reference to north Yorkshire. *Transactions of the Institute of British Geographers*, **NS1**, 310–322.

Tinsley, H.M. & Smith, R.T. (1973) Ecological investigations at a Romano-British earthwork in the Yorkshire Pennines. *Yorkshire Archaeological Journal*, **46**, 23–33.

Tipping, R. (1985) Loch Lomond Stadial *Artemisia* pollen assemblages and Loch Lomond Readvance regional firn-line altitudes. *Quaternary Newsletter*, **46**, 1–11.

Tipping, R.M. (1987) The prospects for establishing synchroneity in the early postglacial pollen peak of *Juniperus* in the British Isles. *Boreas*, **16**, 155–164.

Tipping, R.M. (1992) The determination of cause in the generation of major prehistoric valley fills in the Cheviot Hills, Anglo-Scottish Border. In: *Alluvial Archaeology in Britain* (eds S. Needham & M.G. Macklin), pp. 111–121. Oxbow Monograph 27, Oxford.

Tipping, R. (1994) Fluvial chronology and valley floor evolution of the upper Bowmont valley, Borders Region, Scotland. *Earth Surface Processes and Landforms*, **19**, 641–657.

Tipping, R. (1995a) Holocene evolution of a lowland Scottish landscape: Kirkpatrick Fleming, Part I: peat and pollen-stratigraphic evidence for raised moss development and climate change. *The Holocene*, **5**, 69–81.

Tipping, R. (1995b) Holocene evolution of a lowland Scottish landscape: Kirkpatrick Fleming, Part II: regional vegetation and land use changes. *The Holocene*, **5**, 833–896.

Tipping, R. (1995c) Holocene evolution of a lowland Scottish landscape: Kirkpatrick Fleming, Part III: fluvial history. *The Holocene*, **5**, 184–195.

Tipping, R.M. (1996) Microscopic charcoal records, inferred human activity and climate change in the Mesolithic of northernmost Scotland. In: *The Early Prehistory of Scotland* (eds T. Pollard & A. Morrison), pp. 39–61. Edinburgh University Press, Edinburgh.

Tipping, R.M. (1997) Pollen analysis and the impact of Rome on native agriculture around Hadrian's Wall. In: *Reconstructing Iron Age Societies* (eds A. Gwilt & C. Haselgrove), pp. 239–247. Oxbow Monograph 71, Oxford.

Tipping, R.M. (1998) Cereal cultivation on the Anglo-Scottish Border during the 'Little Ice Age'. In: *Life on the Edge: Human Settlement & Marginality* (eds C.M. Mills & G. Coles), pp. 9–12. Oxbow Books, Oxford.

Tipping, R.M. (2000) Nosterfield, North Yorkshire. Report on the completion of C14 dating for sediments from F44, F45, F36 and FIND 14: recommendations and proposals for further work. Department of Environmental Science, University of Stirling. Mike Griffiths & Associates.

Tipping, R.M. (2002) Climatic variability and 'marginal' settlement in upland British landscapes: a re-evaluation. *Landscapes*, **3**, 10–28.

Tipping, R. & Halliday, S.P. (1994) The age of alluvial fan deposition at a site in the Southern Uplands of Scotland. *Earth Surface Processes and Landforms*, **19**, 333–348.

Tipping, R.M. & Milburn, P. (2000) Mid-Holocene charcoal fall in southern Scotland – temporal and spatial variability. *Palaeogeography, Palaeoclimatology, Palaeoecology*, **164**, 177–193.

Tipping, R.M., Milburn, P. & Halliday, S.P. (1999) Fluvial processes, land use and climate change 2000 years ago in Upper Annanadale, southern Scotland. In: *Fluvial Processes and Environmental Change* (eds A.G. Brown & T.M. Quine), pp. 311–327. Wiley, Chichester.

Tolley, H. (1962) *The determination and mapping of landforms in the Vale of York*. MA thesis, University of Leeds.

Tooley, M.J. (1981) Methods of reconstruction. In: *The Environment in British Prehistory* (eds I.G. Simmons & M.J. Tooley), pp. 1–48. Duckworth, London.

Tooley, M.J., Rackham, D.J. & Simmons, I.G. (1982) A red deer (*Cervus elaphus* L.) skeleton from Seamer Carrs, Cleveland, England: provenance of the skeleton and palaeoecology of the site. *Journal of Archaeological Science*, **6**, 365–376.

Topping, P. (1992) Excavation of the Cursus at Scorton, North Yorkshire, 1978. *Yorkshire Archaeological Journal*, **54**, 7–21.

Törnquist, T.E. (1998) Longitudinal profile evolution of the Rhine–Meuse system during the last deglaciation: interplay of climate change and glacio-eustasy. *Terra Nova*, **10**, 11–15.

Tottenham, C.E. (1954) Coleoptera: Staphylinidae, Piestinae to Euasthetinae. *Handbooks for the Identification of British Insects*. **4 (8a)**, 1–79. Royal Entomological Society, London.

Troels-Smith, J. (1955) Karakterisaring af Løse Jordater (Characterisation of Unconsolidated Sediments). *Danmarks geologiske Undersøgelse*, **IV.3**, 1–73.

Trotter, S.E. & Hollingworth, S.E. (1932) The glacial sequence in northern England. *Geological Magazine*, **69**, 374–380.

Turner, J. (1962) The *Tilia* decline: an anthropogenic interpretation. *New Phytologist*, **61**, 328–341.

Turner, J. (1965) A contribution to the history of forest clearance. *Proceedings of the Royal Society of London*, **B161**, 343–352.

Turner, J. (1979) The environment of northeast England during Roman times as shown by pollen analysis. *Journal of Archaeological Science,* **6**, 285–290.

Turner, J. (1983) Some pollen evidence for the environment of northern Britain 1000 BC to AD 1000. In: *Settlement in Northern Britain 1000 BC to AD 1000.* (eds J.C. Chapman & H.C. Mytum), pp. 3–27. British Archaeological Reports, British Series 118, Oxford.

Turner, J. (1984) Pollen diagrams from Cross Fell and their implications for former tree-lines. In: *Lake Sediments and Environmental History* (eds E.Y. Haworth & J.W.G. Lund), pp. 317–357. Leicester University Press.

Turner, J. (1991) Studies in the vegetational history of the Northern Pennines IV. Variations in the composition of the late Flandrian forests and comparisons with those of the early and mid-Flandrian. *New Phytologist*, **117**, 165–174.

Turner, J. & Kershaw, A.P. (1973) A Late- and Post-glacial pollen diagram from Cranberry Bog, near Beamish, County Durham. *New Phytologist*, **72**, 915–928.

Turner, J. & Hodgson, J. (1979) Studies in the vegetational history of the northern Pennines I. Variations in the composition of the early Flandrian forests. *Journal of Ecology*, **67**, 629–646.

Turner, J. & Hodgson, J. (1981) Studies in the vegetational history of the northern Pennines II. An atypical pollen diagram from Pow Hill, County Durham. *Journal of Ecology*, **69**, 171–188.

Turner, J., Hewetson, V.P., Hibbert, F.A., Lowry, K.H. & Chambers, C. (1973) The history of the vegetation and flora of Widdybank Fell and the Cow Green reservoir basin, Upper Teesdale. *Philosophical Transactions of the Royal Society of London*, **B265**, 327–340.

Turner, J., Simmons, I.G. & Innes, J.B. (1993) Spatial diversity in the mid-Flandrian vegetation history of North Gill, North Yorkshire. *New Phytologist*, **123**, 599–647.

Tweddle, J.C. (2001) Regional Vegetational History. In: *The Quaternary of East Yorkshire and North Lincolnshire. Field Guide* (eds M.D. Bateman, P.C. Buckland, C.D. Frederick, & N.J. Whitehouse), pp. 35–46. Quaternary Research Association, London.

Tweddle, J.C., Edwards, K.J. & Fieller, N.R.J. (2005) Multivariate statistical and other approaches for the separation of cereal from wild Poaceae pollen using a large Holocene dataset. *Vegetation History and Archaeobotany*, **14**, 15–30.

van Andel, T., Zangger, E. & Demitrack, A. (1990) Land use and soil erosion in prehistoric and historical Greece. *Journal of Field Archaeology*, **17**, 379–396.

Van de Noort, R. & Ellis, S., eds (1999) *Wetland Heritage of the Vale of York*. Humber Wetland Project, University of Hull.

van den Berg, M.W. & van Hoof, T. (2001) The Maas terrace sequence at Maastricht, SE Netherlands: evidence for 200 m of late Neogene and Quaternary surface uplift. In: *River Basin Sediment Systems: Archives of Environmental Change.* (eds D. Maddy, M.G. Macklin, & J.C. Woodward), pp. 45–86. Balkema, Abingdon.

van der Plicht, J. & Hogg, A. (2006) A note on reporting radiocarbon. *Quaternary Geochronology,* **1**, 237–240.

van der Veen, M. (1992) *Crop Husbandry Regimes. An Archaeobotanical Study of Farming in Northern England 1000 BC – AD 500.* Sheffield Archaeological Monographs 3. Department of Archaeology and Prehistory, University of Sheffield.

van Geel, B. & Renssen, H. (1998) Abrupt climate change around 2,650 BP in North-West Europe: evidence for climatic teleconnections and a tentative explanation. In: *Water, Environment and Society in Times of Climatic Change.* (eds A.S. Issar & N. Brown), pp. 21–41. Kluwer, Dordrecht.

van Geel, B., Buurman, J. & Waterbolk, H.T. (1996) Archaeological and palaeoecological indications of an abrupt climate change in The Netherlands, and evidence for climatological teleconnections around 2650 BP. *Journal of Quaternary Science*, **11**, 451–460.

van Geel, B., Raspopov, O.M., van der Plicht, J. & Renssen, H. (1998) Solar forcing of abrupt climate change around 850 calendar years BC. In: *Natural Catastrophes During Bronze Age Civilisations* (eds B.J. Peiser, T. Palmer, & M.E. Bailey), pp. 162–168. British Archaeological Reports, International Series 728, Oxford.

Vandenberghe, J. (1993) Changing fluvial processes under changing periglacial conditions. *Zeitschrift für Geomorphologie*, Supplement Band **88**, 17–28.

Vandenberghe, J. (2001) A typology of Pleistocene cold-based rivers. *Quaternary International*, **79**, 111–121.

Vandenberghe, J. (2003) Climate forcing of fluvial system development: an evolution of ideas. *Quaternary Science Reviews*, **22**, 2053–2060.

Vandenberghe, J. (2007) The fluvial cycle at cold-warm-cold transitions in lowland regions: a refinement of theory. *Geomorphology*, **98**, 275–284.

Vandenberghe, J. & Woo, M.-K. (2002) Modern and ancient periglacial river types. *Progress in Physical Geography*, **26**, 479–506.

Vandenberghe, J., Kasse, C., Bohnke, S. & Kozarski, S. (1994) Climate-related river activity at the Weichselian-Holocene transition: a comparative study of the Warta and Maas rivers. *Terra Nova*, **6**, 476–485.

Vandenberghe, J., Lowe, J.J., Coope, G.R., Litt, T. & Zöller, L. (2004) Climatic and environmental variability in the Mid-Latitude Europe sector during the last interglacial–glacial cycle. In: *Past Climate Variability through Europe and Africa*. (eds R. Battarbee, F. Gasse & C. Stickley), pp. 393–416. PEPIII Conference Proceedings, Kluwer, Dordrecht.

Veitch, W.Y. (1899) Prehistoric Middlesborough. *Proceedings of the Cleveland Naturalists' Field Club*, for 1986–1898, 5–12.

Veitet, W.U. (1881) On the geology of the district around Middlesbrough. *Proceedings of the Yorkshire Geological Society*, **7**, 284.

von den Driesch, A. (1976) *A Guide to the Measurement of Animal Bones from Archaeological Sites*. Peabody Museum of Archaeology and Ethnology, Harvard University, Cambridge, Massachusetts.

Vuorela, I. (1973) Relative pollen rain around cultivated fields. *Acta Botanica Fennica*, **102**, 3–27.

Vyner, B.E., ed. (1990) *Medieval Rural Settlement in the North-East of England*. Archaeological and Architectural Society of Durham and Northumberland, Research Report, 2.

Vyner, B. (1995) The brides of place: cross-ridge boundaries reviewed. In: *Moorland Monuments* (ed. B.E. Vyner), pp. 16–30. Council for British Archaeology, Research Report 101, York.

Vyner, B.E. (1998) *Pottery from excavations at Nosterfield*. Report for Mike Griffiths Associates.

Vyner, B.E. (1999) *Nosterfield, North Yorkshire, 1999: Assessment of Finds from Fieldwork and Excavation*. Report for Mike Griffiths Associates.

Vyner, B.E. (2000) Lost horizons: the location of activity in the later Neolithic and early Bronze Age in north-east England. In: *Northern Pasts: Interpretations of the Later Prehistory of Northern England and Southern Scotland* (eds. J. Harding & R. Johnstone), pp. 101–110. British Archaeological Reports, British Series 302, Oxford.

Vyner, B.E. (2001a) *Stainmore: The Archaeology of a North Pennine Pass*. Tees Archaeology Monograph Series, 1.

Vyner, B.E. (2001b) *Report on the Iron Age and Roman period pottery assemblage excavated from Scorton, North Yorkshire*. Report for Field Archaeology Specialists.

Vyner, B.E. (2003a) The Upper Palaeolithic and the Earlier Mesolithic. In: *Historical Atlas of North Yorkshire* (ed. R.A. Butlin), pp. 30–34. Smith Settle, Otley.

Vyner, B.E. (2003b) Pottery. In: *Catterick Racecourse, North Yorkshire: The Re-use and Adaptation of a Monument from Prehistoric to Anglian Times* (eds C. Moloney, R. Holbrey, P.

Wheelhouse, & I. Roberts). Archaeological Services WYAS Occasional Series 4, Leeds.

Vyner, B. (2007) A great north route in Neolithic and Bronze Age Yorkshire: the evidence of landscapes and monuments. *Landscapes*, **8**, 68–84.

Vyner, B.E. (forthcoming) Cleveland Ways: early routes in the lower Tees valley and the North Yorkshire Moors. *Durham Archaeological Journal*.

Wainright, G.J. & Longworth, I.H. (1969) The excavation of a group of round barrows on Ampleforth Moor, Yorkshire. *Yorkshire Archaeological Journal*, **42**, 283–294.

Walker, D. (1955) Lateglacial deposits at Lunds, Yorkshire. *New Phytologist*, **54**, 343–349.

Walker, D. (1956) A site at Stump Cross, Grassington, Yorkshire, and the age of the Pennine microlithic industry. *Proceedings of the Prehistoric Society*, **22**, 23–28.

Walker, D. & Lambert, C.A. (1955) Boreal deposits at Kirkby Thore, Westmorland. *New Phytologist*, **54**, 209–214.

Walker, M.J.C. (2004) A lateglacial pollen record from Hallsenna Moor, near Seascale, Cumbria. NW England, with evidence for arid conditions during the Loch Lomond (Younger Dryas) Stadial and early Holocene. *Proceedings of the Yorkshire Geological Society*, **55**, 33–42.

Walker, M.J.C. (2005) *Quaternary Dating Methods*. Wiley, Chichester.

Walker, M.J.C., Coope, G.R. & Lowe, J.J. (1993) The Devensian (Weichselian) late-glacial palaeoenvironmental record from Gransmoor, East Yorkshire, England. *Quaternary Science Reviews*, **12**, 659–680.

Walker, M.J.C., Bohncke, S.J.P., Coope, G.R., O'Connell, M., Usinger, H. & Verbruggen, C. (1994) The Devensian/Weichselian Late Glacial in northwest Europe (Ireland, Britain, north Belgium, the Netherlands, northwest Germany. *Journal of Quaternary Science*, **9**, 109–118.

Walker, M.J.C., Bryant,C., Coope, G.R., Harkness, D.D., Lowe, J.J. & Scott, E.M. (2001) Towards a radiocarbon chronology of the Late-Glacial: sample selection strategies. *Radiocarbon*, **43**, 1007–1021.

Walker, M.J.C., Coope, G.R., Sheldrick, C., Turney, C.S.M., Lowe, J.J., Blockley, S.P.E. & Harkness, D.D. (2003) Devensian late-glacial environmental changes in Britain: a multi-proxy environmental record from Llanilid, South Wales, UK. *Quaternary Science Reviews*, **22**, 475–520.

Waller, M.P. (1994) Paludification and pollen representation: the influence of wetland size on *Tilia* representation in pollen diagrams. *The Holocene*, **4**, 430–434.

Waller, M.P. (1998) An investigation into the palynological properties of fen peat through multiple pollen profiles from south-eastern England. *Journal of Archaeological Science*, **25**, 631–642.

Waller, M.P., Binney, H.A., Bunting, M.J. & Armitage, R.A. (2005) The interpretation of fen carr pollen diagrams: pollen-vegetation relationships within the fen carr. *Review of Palaeobotany and Palynology*, **133**, 179–202.

Waltham, A.C., Simms, M.J., Farrant, A.R. & Goldie, H.S., eds (1997) *Karst and Caves of Great Britain*. Chapman and Hall, London.

Warburton, J., Danks, M. & Wishart, D. (2002) Stability of an upland gravel-bed stream, Swinhope Burn, Northern England. *Catena*, **49**, 309–329.

Watson, E.V. (1995) *British Mosses and Liverworts*. (3 ed.). Cambridge University Press.

Waughman, M., ed. (2005) *Archaeology and Environment of Submerged Landscapes in Hartlepool Bay, England.* Tees Archaeology Monograph 2, Hartlepool.

Wells, A.J. (1955) The glaciation in the Teesdale–Swaledale Watershed. *Proceedings of the University of Durham Philosophical Society,* **12,** 82–93.

Wells, A.K., Gossling, F., Kirkaldy, J. & Oakley, K.P. (1947) Studies of pebbles from the Lower Cretaceous rocks (Weald Research Committee, Report, No. 37). *Proceedings of the Geologists' Association,* **58,** 194–258.

Wells, C.E., Hodgkinson, D. & Huckerby, E. (2000) Evidence for the possible role of beaver (*Castor fiber*) in the prehistoric ontogenesis of a mire in northwest England, UK. *The Holocene,* **10,** 503–508.

Werritty, A. & McEwan, L.J. (1997) Eas na Broige Debris Cone, Highland (NN 192598). In: *Fluvial Geomorphology of Great Britain* (ed. K.J. Gregory), pp. 95–97, Geological Conservation Review Series 13, Chapman & Hall, London.

West, R.G. (1970) Pollen zones in the Pleistocene of Great Britain and their correlation. *New Phytologist,* **69,** 1179–1183.

Wheeler, J. (2008) The environmental impacts of iron-working on the woodlands of Rievaulx and Bilsdale, North York Moors, UK, c.1132–1647. In: *Yorkshire Landscapes Past and Present.* (eds M. Atherden & T. Milsom), pp. 61–67. PLACE Research Centre, York.

White, R. (1997) *Yorkshire Dales: Landscapes Through Time.* Great Northern Books, Ilkley.

White, T.S., Bridgland, D.R., Howard, A.J. & White, M.J. (2007) *The Quaternary of the Trent Valley & Adjoining Regions. Field Guide.* Quaternary Research Association, London.

Whitehouse, N.J. (2004) Mire ontogeny, environmental and climatic change inferred from fossil beetle successions from Hatfield Moors, eastern England. *The Holocene,* **14,** 79–93.

Whitehouse, N.J. (2006) The Holocene British and Irish ancient forest fossil beetle fauna: implications for forest history, biodiversity and faunal colonisation. *Quaternary Science Reviews,* **25,** 1755–1789.

Wilkinson, D.M., Clare, T. & Corkish, J. (1999) The history of carr woodland at Birks Wood, northern Lake District. *Naturalist,* **124,** 157–162.

Williams, C.T. (1985) *Mesolithic Exploitation Patterns in the Central Pennines. A Palynological study of Soyland Moor.* British Archaeological Reports, British Series 139, Oxford.

Williams, E. (1989) Dating the introduction of food production into Britain and Ireland. *Antiquity,* **63,** 510–521.

Willing, M.J. (1985) The Biostratigraphy of Flandrian tufa deposits in the Cotswold and Mendip districts. Unpublished Ph.D. Thesis, University of Sussex.

Wilson, A.A. (1957) *Geology between Masham and Great Whernside.* unpublished PhD thesis, University of Durham.

Wilson, L.J., Austin, W.E.N. & Jansen, E. (2002) The last British Ice Sheet: growth, maximum extent and deglaciation. *Polar Research,* **21,** 243–250.

Wilson, P.R., ed. (2002) *Cataractonium: Roman Catterick and its Hinterland.* Council for British Archaeology Research Report 128.

Wilson, P.R., Cardwell, P., Cramp, R.J., Evans, J., Taylor-Wilson, R., Thompson, A. & Wacher, J.S. (1996) Early Anglian Catterick and Catraeth. *Medieval Archaeology,* **40,** 1–61.

Wiltshire, P.E.J. (1997) The pre-Roman environment. In: *Birdoswald: Excavations of a Roman Fort on Hadrian's Wall and its Successor Settlements: 1987–1992.* (ed. C.T. Wilmott), pp. 25–40. English Heritage Archaeological Report 14, London.

Wood, E.S. (1971) The excavation of a Bronze Age barrow: Greenhowe, North Deighton, Yorkshire. *Yorkshire Archaeological Journal,* **43,** 2–32.

Woolacott, D. (1905) The superficial deposits and pre-glacial valleys of the Northumberland and Durham coalfield. *Quarterly Journal of the Geological Society of London,* **61,** 64–96.

Wymer, J.J. (1968) *Lower Palaeolithic Archaeology in Britain, as represented by the Thames Valley.* John Baker, London.

Wymer, J.J. (1977) *Gazeteer of Mesolithic Sites in England and Wales.* CBA Research Report 20, GeoAbstracts and the Council for British Archaeology, Norwich.

Wymer, J.J. (1981) The Palaeolithic. In: *The Environment in British Prehistory* (eds I.G. Simmons & M.J. Tooley), pp. 49–81. Duckworth, London.

Wymer, J.J. (1999) *The Lower Palaeolithic occupation of Britain.* Wessex Archaeology and English Heritage, Salisbury.

Yeloff, D., van Geel, B., Broekens, P., Bakker, J. & Mauquoy, D. (2007) Mid- to late-Holocene vegetation and land-use history the Hadrian's Wall region of northern England: the record from Butterburn Flow. *The Holocene,* **17,** 527–538.

Yorke, L. (2008) *Late Quaternary valley fill sediments in the River Tyne valley: Understanding Late Devensian glaciation and early postglacial response in northern England.* PhD thesis, University of Hull.

Young, B., Lawrence, D.J.D. & Woodhall, D.G. (2002) *Geology of the Morpeth district: a brief description of the geological map sheet 14 (Morpeth).* Her Majesty's Stationery Office London.

Young, R. (1990) Mixed lithic scatters and the Mesolithic–Neolithic transition in north-east England: a speculation. In: *Breaking the Stony Silence* (ed. I. Brooks & P. Philips), pp. 161–185. British Archaeological Reports, British Series 213, Oxford.

Young, R. (2000) Continuity and change: marginality and later prehistoric settlement in the northern uplands. In: *Northern Pasts: Interpretations of the Later Prehistory of Northern England and Southern Scotland* (ed. J. Harding & R. Johnstone), pp. 71–80. British Archaeological Reports, British Series 302, Oxford.

Young, R. (2006) *The flint assemblage in Marne Barracks, Catterick, Yorkshire: post-excavation and analysis.* On behalf of Gallifordtry Construction Ltd for Debut Management Services and Defence Estates.

Young, R. & Simmonds, T. (1995) Marginality and the nature of later prehistoric upland settlement in the north of England. *Landscape History,* **17,** 5–16.

7 Index

Colour Plates

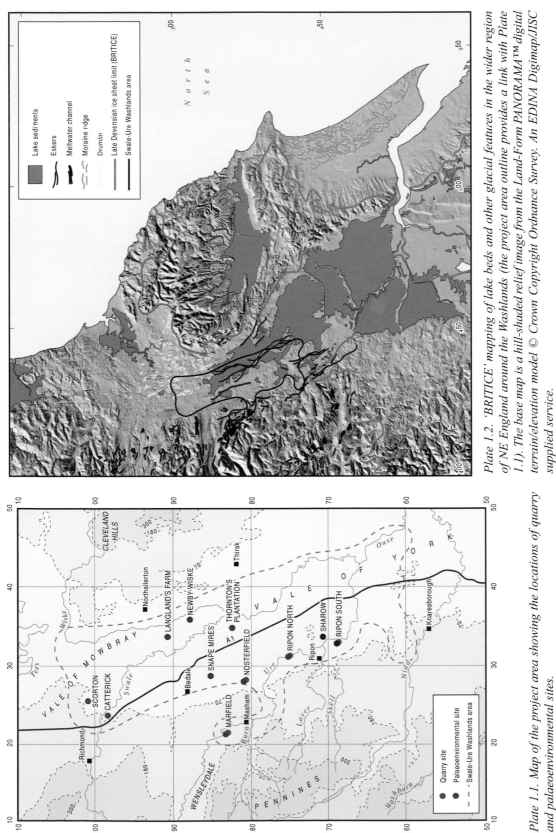

Plate 1.2. 'BRITICE' mapping of lake beds and other glacial features in the wider region of NE England around the Washlands (the project area outline provides a link with Plate 1.1). The base map is a hill-shaded relief image from the Land-Form PANORAMA™ digital terrain/elevation model © Crown Copyright Ordnance Survey. An EDINA Digimap/JISC supplied service.

Plate 1.1. Map of the project area showing the locations of quarry and palaeoenvironmental sites.

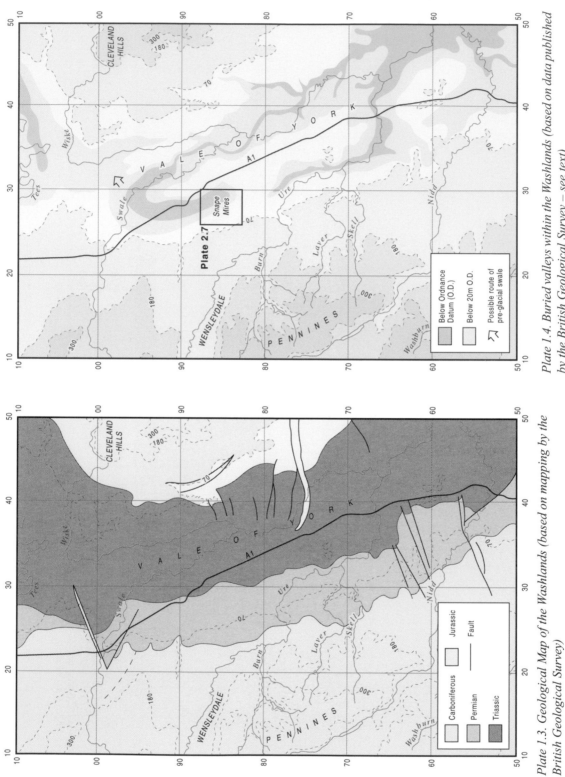

Plate 1.4. Buried valleys within the Washlands (based on data published by the British Geological Survey – see text)

Plate 1.3. Geological Map of the Washlands (based on mapping by the British Geological Survey)

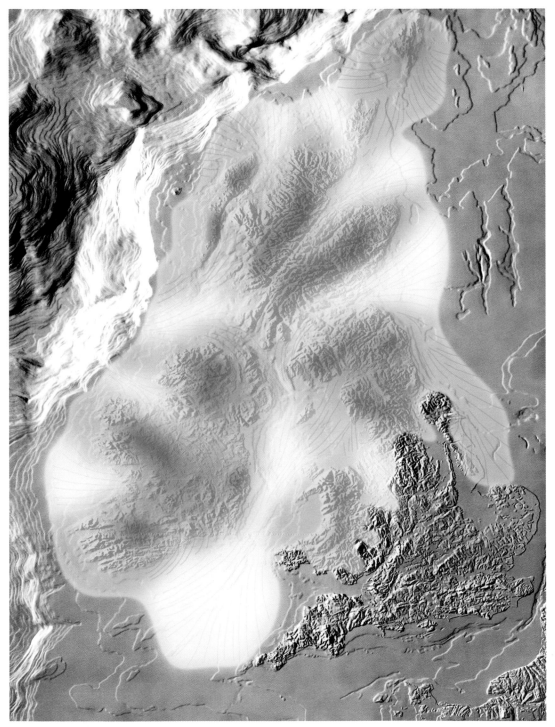

Plate 1.5. Reconstruction of the last Glacial British–Irish Ice Sheet, using information from Lambeck et al. (1991), Bowen et al. (2002) and Sejrup et al. (2005). Background DEM from MOUNTAIN HIGH MAPS®

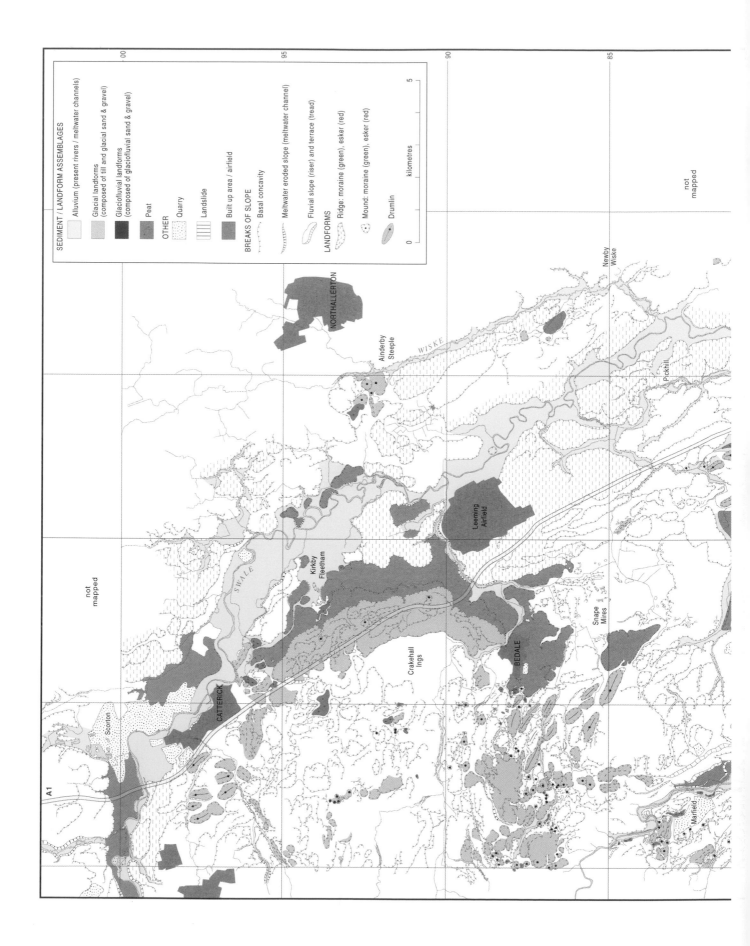

SEDIMENT / LANDFORM ASSEMBLAGES

Alluvium (present rivers / meltwater channels)

Glacial landforms
(composed of till and glacial sand & gravel)

Glaciofluvial landforms
(composed of glaciofluvial sand & gravel)

Peat

OTHER

Quarry

Landslide

Built up area / airfield

BREAKS OF SLOPE

Basal concavity

Meltwater eroded slope (meltwater channel)

Fluvial slope (riser) and terrace (tread)

LANDFORMS

Ridge: moraine (green), esker (red)

Mound: moraine (green), esker (red)

Drumlin

kilometres

0   5

A1

Scorton

not
mapped

CATTERICK

S W A L E

Kirkby
Fleetham

Crakehall
Ings

BEDALE

Snape
Mires

Leeming
Airfield

NORTHALLERTON

Ainderby
Steeple

W I S K E

Newby
Wiske

Pickhill

not
mapped

Masham

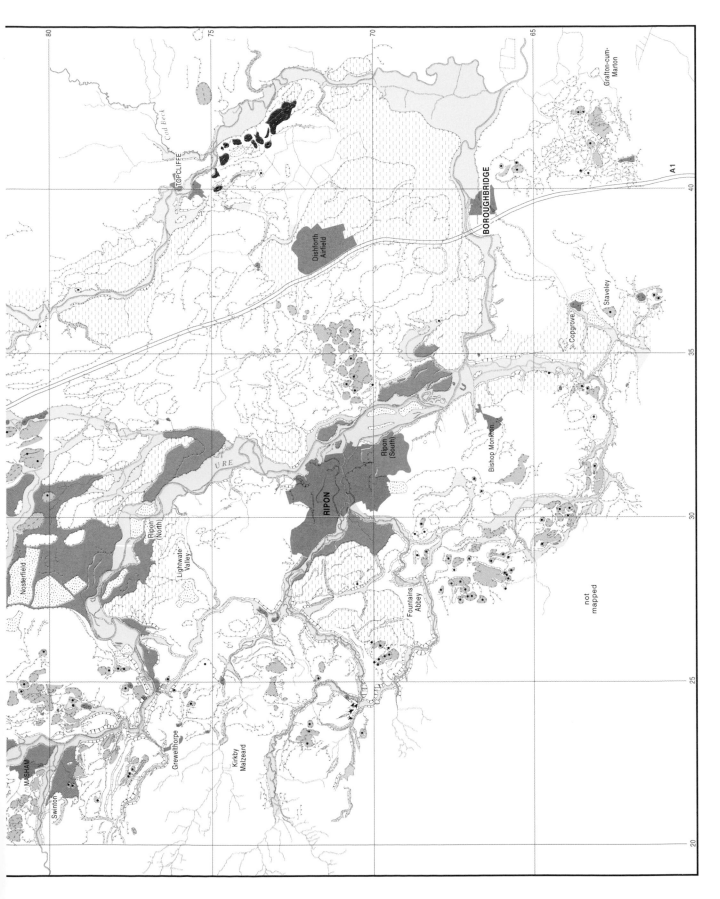

Plate 2.1. Geomorphological Map of the Swale-Ure Washlands. An electronic version of this map is to be found in the CD in the back pocket of this book. Original mapping was completed at a scale of 1:25,000. The Ordnance Survey grid is used.

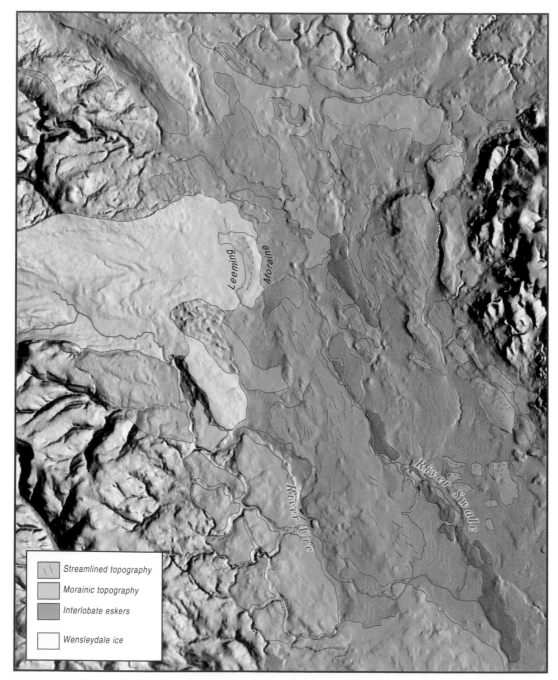

Plate 2.2. NEXTMap© DEM of the Washlands and the surrounding area, annotated to show glacial features. For copyright reasons this is presented as a layer on the lower resolution (50 m) OS Panorama™ DEM.

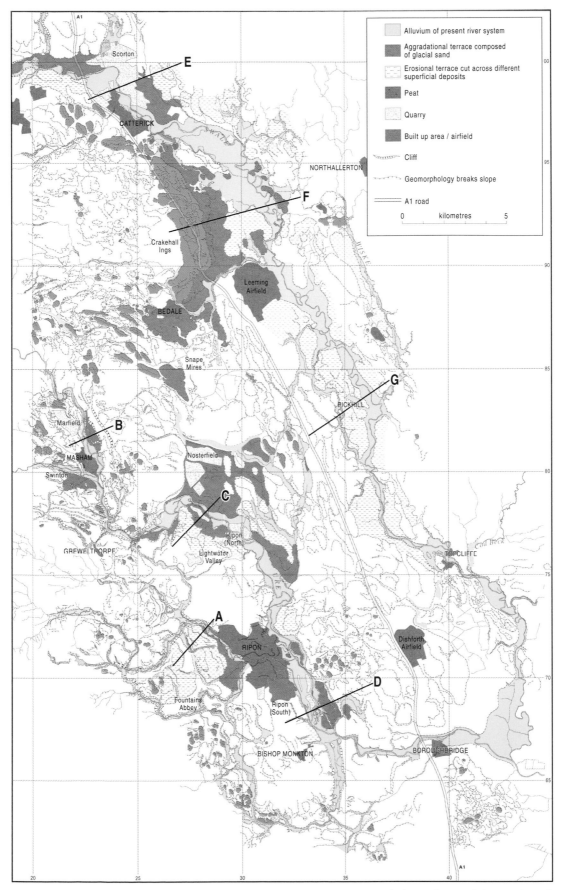

Plate 2.3. River terraces within the Swale-Ure Washlands based on the geomorphological map (Plate 2.1) and published superficial geological maps (British Geological Survey). An electronic version of the geomorphological map is to be found in the CD in the back pocket of this book. Original field mapping was completed at a scale of 1:25,000. Ordnance Survey grid.

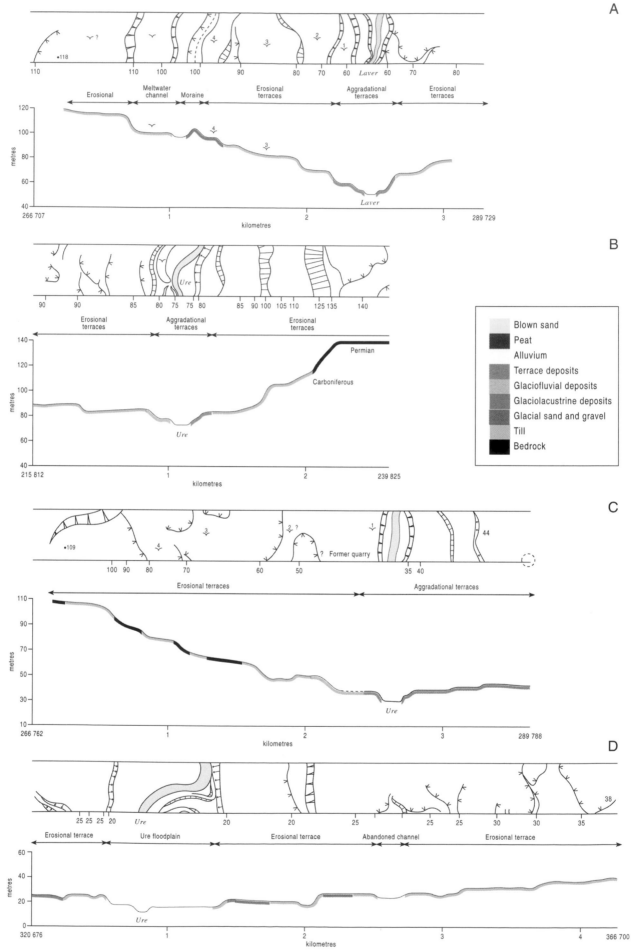

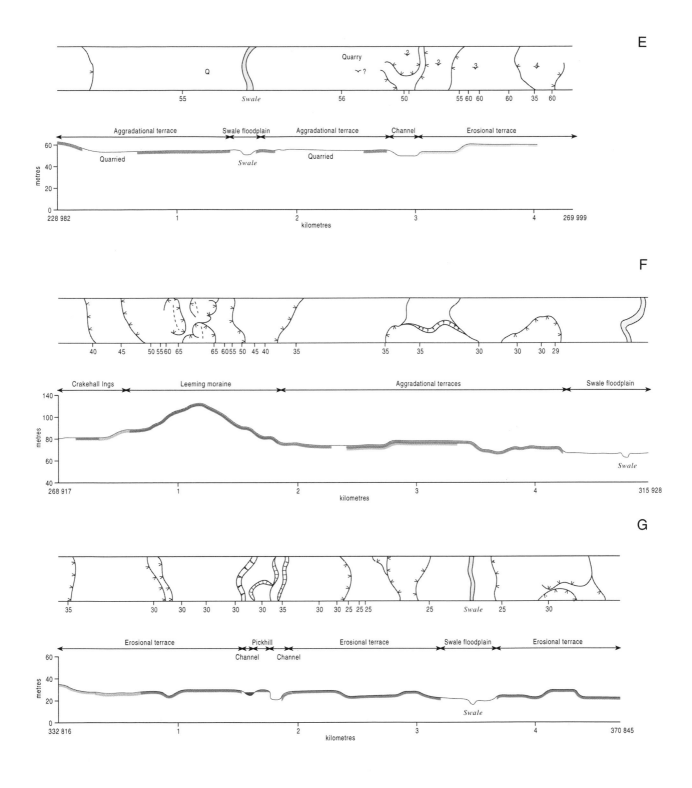

Plate 2.4. Cross sections showing terrace sequences in different reaches of the Swale and Ure systems: A – across the Laver valley; B – across the Ure between Masham and Gebdykes quarry; C – across the Ure at North Stainley; D – across the Ure at Newby Hall; E – across the Swale at Catterick; F – across the Swale from Crakehall Ings and across the Leeming moraine towards Scruton; G – across the Swale valley at Pickhill.

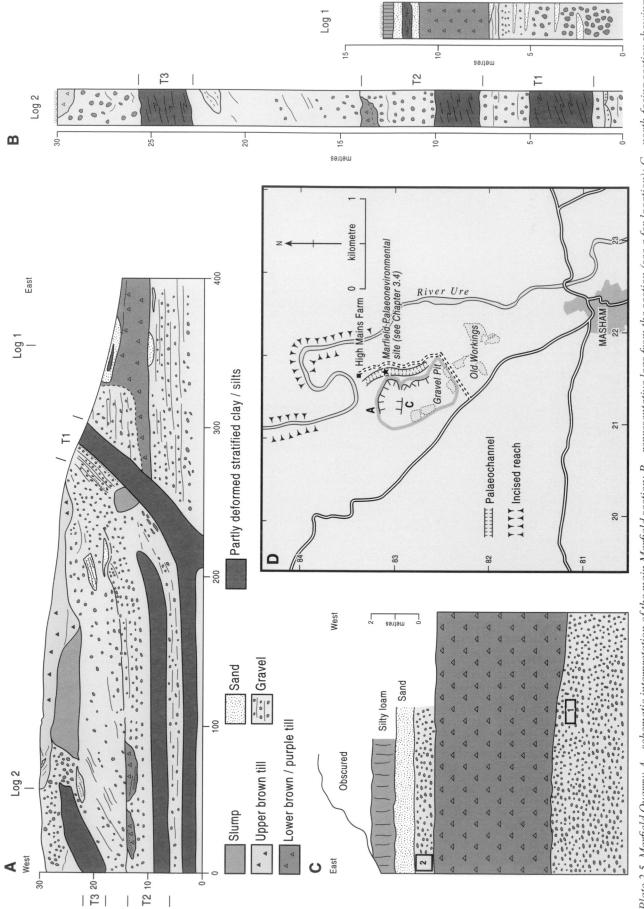

Plate 2.5. Marfield Quarry: A – schematic interpretation of the main Marfield section; B – representative logs from the section (see a for location); C – north-facing section showing gravels and interbedded till with locations of samples taken for clast lithological analysis (marked by boxes); D – map of the quarry, showing the location of parts A & C, as well as the relation to the High Mains palaeochannel (see Chapter 3.4) and the incised course of the modern River Ure.

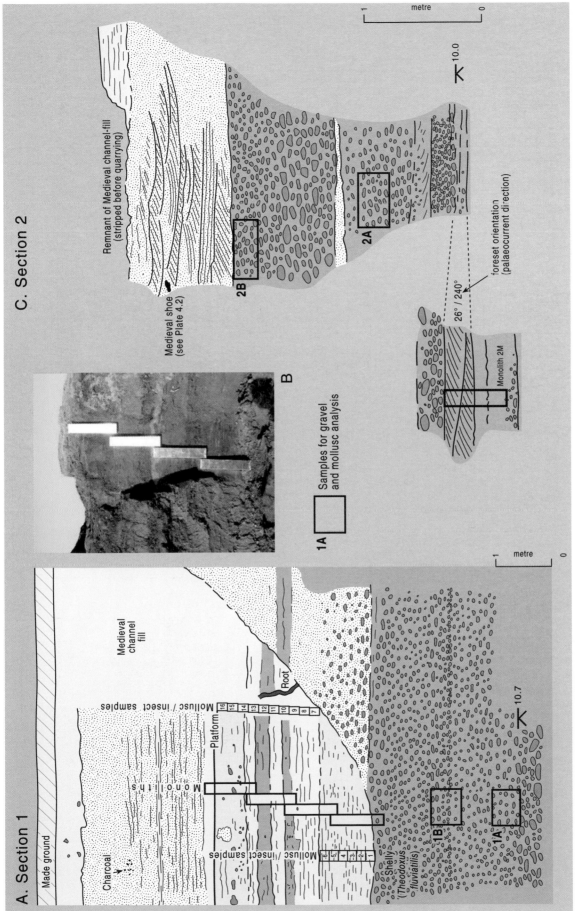

Plate 2.6. Ripon South Quarry: A – Section 1, showing the Medieval organic channel-fill cut into the mid-Holocene sands and gravels. The locations of bulk samples for clast and molluscan analysis are indicated, as is the column sampling for molluscs and beetles and the four monolith sample tins in situ. C – Section 2, on the eastern side of the quarry (see Fig. 2.57), showing the locations of bulk samples for clast and molluscan analysis. Also shown is the outlying monolith sample 2M, from which the basal organic sediment and radiocarbon date were obtained (see also Fig. 2.58).

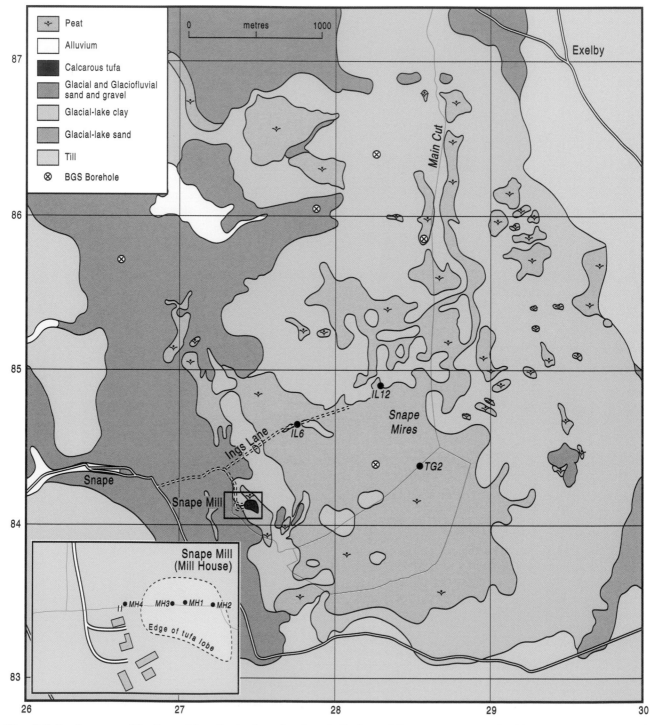

Plate 2.7. Geology map of the Snape Mires Basin (based on British Geological Survey mapping with additions and modifications), showing the location of the main palaeoenvironmental sample localities (Chapter 3.8). For Mill House an inset is provided to show the positions of the various sampled points (see Plate 2.8).

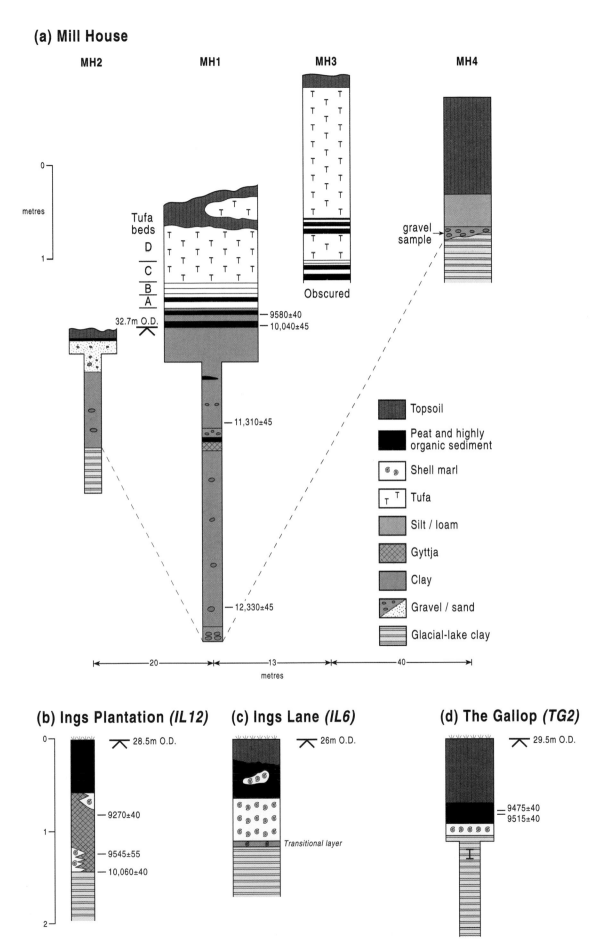

Plate 2.8. Snape Mires: recorded sedimentary sequences (for locations see Plate 2.7)

Plate 3.1. (left) Coring for palaeoenvironmental samples: a – extracting from the peat-filled shakehole, Nosterfield SH1; b –Lateglacial sediment in Russian corer, Marfield channel; c – Holocene marl and peat core transferred to plastic guttering, Newby Wiske

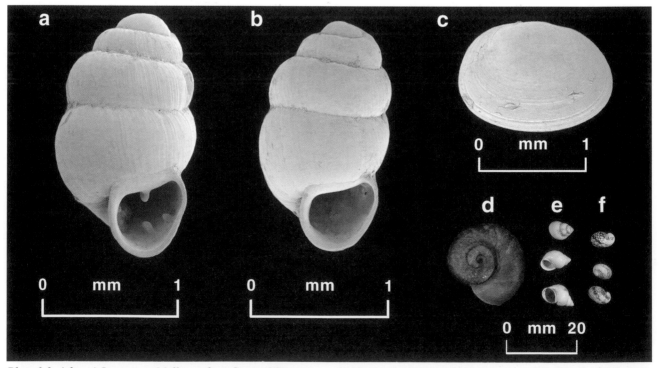

Plate 3.2. (above) Important Mollusca from Snape Mires: a–c – Scanning electron microscope images (Cambridge University Zoology Department): a – Vertigo geyeri; b – Vertigo genesii; c – Pisidium pseudosphaerium; d–f – gastropods from River Ure sediments at Ripon: d – Planorbarius corneus; e – Bithynia tentaculata; f – Theodoxus fluviatilis.

Plate 3.3. (right) Views, at various zoom ratings, of the MH1 stream section, Snape Mires, showing the basal tufa overlying the organic sequence, with two conspicuous organic peaty layers near the top of the latter (in c these are being sampled by monolith).

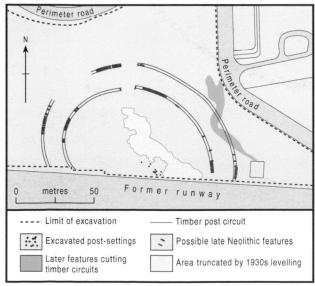

Plate 4.1. Plan of a later Neolithic timber enclosure at Marne Barracks, Catterick, radiocarbon dated to 2580–2480 cal BC (late Neolithic/early Bronze Age). Drawing courtesy of Archaeological Services Durham University on behalf of the MoD, © Defence Estates.

Plate 4.2. The first Medieval shoe to be found in the Ripon South quarry, with artist's impression of its original form.

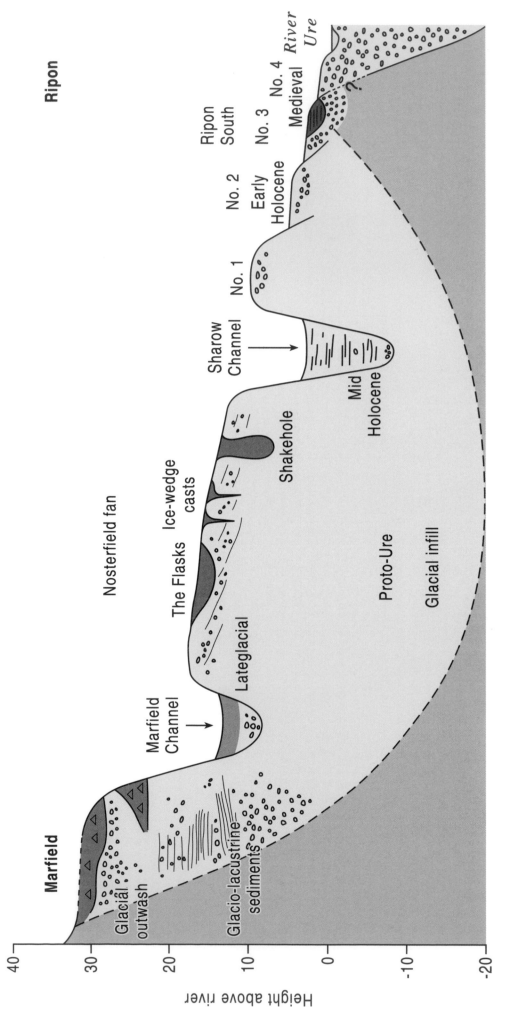

Plate 5.1. Schematic cross section through the Late Quaternary sedimentary record in the Ure valley